Research Methods in Management

Research Methods in Management

Edited by

MARION FRENZ, KLAUS NIELSEN AND GEOFF WALTERS

SAGE

Los Angeles | London | New Delhi
Singapore | Washington DC

SAGE Publications Ltd
1 Oliver's Yard
55 City Road
London EC1Y 1SP

SAGE Publications Inc.
2455 Teller Road
Thousand Oaks, California 91320

SAGE Publications India Pvt Ltd
B 1/I 1 Mohan Cooperative Industrial Area
Mathura Road
New Delhi 110 044

SAGE Publications Asia-Pacific Pte Ltd
33 Pekin Street #02-01
Far East Square
Singapore 048763

Library of Congress Control Number: 2009927116

British Library Cataloguing in Publication data

A catalogue record for this book is available from the British Library

ISBN 978-1-84920-369-2 (pbk)

Typeset by C&M Digitals (P) Ltd, Chennai, India
Printed in Great Britain by CPI Antony Rowe, Chippenham, Wiltshire
Printed on paper from sustainable resources

FSC
Mixed Sources
Product group from well-managed forests and other controlled sources
Cert no. SGS-COC-2953
www.fsc.org
© 1996 Forest Stewardship Council

Contents

Research Methods in Management I

MARION FRENZ, KLAUS NIELSEN
and GEOFF WALTERS

1.0 Introduction

Welcome to the main textbook accompanying the Research Methods in Management module taught at Birkbeck's Management Department. This textbook is customized by Sage Publications to fit the unique purpose of our taught module. It is a compilation of individual chapters, or parts, taken from different teaching books, or articles taken from academic journals, which, taken together, cover the entire range of topics relevant to the module.

This introductory chapter has two aims: to provide an introduction to Research Methods in Management; and to guide you through the individual chapters in this book. It is structured in the following way. First, we start by summarising the aims and main parts of Research Methods in Management. Second, specific elements of the module are discussed in more detail and with explicit reference to the specific chapters presented in this text. This part follows the sequence of lectures. The first section is a general introduction to research design followed by an introduction to qualitative methods. The next two sections are about two of the most widely used methods in management research, case studies and surveys. Then follows an introduction to the quantitative methods and finally there is a section on the philosophy of science.

1.1 Research Methods in Management

Research Methods in Management is core to all postgraduate degree programmes taught in the Department of Management. It is your *academic tool kit* which helps you to assess the quality of academic research, and, thus, bears relevance to all of your academic activities. The aims of the module are twofold: to provide you with the necessary knowledge and understanding to critically appraise published work in the area of management, and to provide you with the necessary skills to design and carry out your own research.

Research starts by defining a specific research question or a research problem. This involves theoretical/conceptual considerations concerned with the formulation of the relevant questions or development of specific hypotheses. Some research is concerned with uncovering causal relationships between two or more factors, for example, the impact lengths of revision time may have on exam performance. Other research attempts to uncover the meaning attached by individuals or groups to various social events and relationships, for example, students' perception of studying and learning.

Addressing research questions involves collecting and analysing evidence. The role of research design is generally to ensure that we collect appropriate evidence in an appropriate fashion and analyse the evidence in an appropriate way. It is crucial that the research is conducted in a rigorous way and that the findings are relevant. Sometimes rigour and relevance can be achieved simultaneously if the research is organized in a proper way. In other cases there may be a trade-off between rigour and relevance. These are issues covered in detail in the lectures.

When the purpose is to uncover causal relationships the role of research design is to ensure that the evidence used to analyse a relationship can sustain a causal claim and to assess the extent to which a causal relationship uncovered by the empirical evidence is applicable to a wider population, for example, all firms, all individuals. When the purpose is to uncover the meaning of social events and relationships the role of research design is to ensure that the evidence supports sensible interpretations of the phenomena in question.

The relevant research design is dependent on the research question. Some questions require a specific form of enquiry whereas other questions require another research design. However, the choice of research design is also dependent on the philosophical and theoretical assumptions of the student and the researcher. Some of the most important issues in this respect are touched on in Lecture 1, 9 and 10 whereas the lectures in-between introduce qualitative and quantitative methods in general and go into detail with some of the most relevant methods used in management studies.

1.2 Specific topics

1.2.1 Introduction to research design

Lecture 1 starts with an introduction to research design. This is based on two texts: De Vaus (2001) (chapters 1-3) and Creswell (2009) (chapter 1). The point of departure in De Vaus (2001) is the distinction between different types of research questions: what is going on; and why it is going on. Much research is about identifying causes of a specific phenomenon, for example, the effect of firm level innovation on profitability. The research design most suitable to address a specific research question is dependent on several factors, including the prior knowledge about the phenomenon in question, the level of abstraction, and the complexity of causal linkages. Creswell (2009) sees research design as plans for a study, and the design process is seen to include three important interlinked elements: philosophical assumptions, strategies of inquiry and specific research methods. In the text, different philosophical worldviews, different strategies of inquiry and different research methods are outlined. Three different types of research design (qualitative, quantitative and mixed methods) are identified and the linkages between these elements are explored.

A proper understanding of design issues discussed in these texts will underpin your further reading and understanding of the remaining materials of the course – starting with qualitative designs.

1.2.2 Qualitative methods

In addition to the general introduction, Lecture 1 also includes a brief introduction to qualitative research based on Myers (2009) (chapter 2). Myers outlines the main differences between qualitative and quantitative research, discusses what types of research questions can be answered by means of qualitative methods, and briefly introduces some of the most important quality issues related to qualitative research.

Lecture 2 further introduces qualitative methods by means of two texts: Lee and Lings (2008) (chapters 9 and 10) and Creswell (2009) (chapters 3, 7 and 9). Qualitative research is based on meanings expressed through words and other non-numerical symbols. The evidence consists of non-standardised data requiring classification into categories. Qualitative methods are especially useful when the purpose of research is explorative, when rich or thick description of a phenomenon is required, and when focus is on the interpretation of phenomena by individuals and groups. They may also be used to uncover cause-effect relationships. Interviewing is a popular technique for collection of qualitative data. Other techniques include observation, focus groups and documentary sources. Chapter 9 in Lee and Lings (2008) outlines the range of different qualitative data sources and collection methods. Qualitative analysis can be described as a process of extracting and presenting the key ideas, themes and concepts present, and often hidden, in the rich collected data. Coding of data and data reduction are crucial elements in qualitative data analysis, which is what chapter 10 in Lee and Lings (2008) is about. Creswell (2009) provides supplementary knowledge about qualitative data collection and analysis. This text also discusses the important role of theory in qualitative research. Often, the purpose of qualitative research is theory development rather than theory testing, and, often, qualitative researchers use a theoretical lens or perspective in their research. Both texts discuss how to ensure high quality in qualitative research.

1.2.3 Case studies

The case study is one of the most popular approaches within social science research. This is the topic of Lecture 3. A case study can be defined as a research strategy with the objective to understand the dynamics within a contemporary case setting, particularly where the researcher has little or no control. Within management studies the case study can be used to better understand an individual organisation, a group of organisations, or a particular industry. A case study can draw on both qualitative and quantitative data and utilise different types of data collection method. For this reason case study research can result in rich and detailed evidence from a range of sources, allowing for methodological triangulation in order to improve the internal validity of the research findings. However case study research cannot be used to make statistical generalizations where the results are used to make inferences about the broader population. Nevertheless where case study research is grounded in a theoretical context the results can be related back to theory and used to make analytical generalizations.

These issues are explored in further detail within the lecture on case studies in week three. The objectives of the lecture are to introduce the case study as a research strategy; to understand the different types of case study and the different objectives that researchers might have for choosing this particular research approach; to consider the advantages and disadvantages of the case study strategy; and to consider the practicalities of undertaking case study research by introducing the key stages that researchers should be aware of. The case study readings in this collection to accompany the lecture intend to provide a broad introduction to case study research. Chapter 7 in Myers (2009) provides an introduction to case study research. It is useful in providing an overview of the objectives of case study research, and the different approaches to case study research, in addition to potential advantages and disadvantages. Myers (2009) identifies that case study research is not an easy option, particularly for inexperienced researchers. To overcome this there is a need for a thorough case study design from the outset. The second reading by Yin (2009) taken from the fourth edition of his seminal text on case study research, addresses this point. It focuses on components of case study design, considers different types of case study, and the need to address validity and reliability in order to maximise the quality of case study research. The final reading by Silver, Randolph and Seibert (2006) differs from the first two in that it provides an example of empirical case study research into two different types of organization and how they sought to achieve greater empowerment within each organization.

1.2.4 Survey design

Surveys are quantitative information about items (for example 2,000 UK households) in a population (all UK households). Lecture 4 introduces survey design. As with all research theory plays an important role when designing surveys and this is explained in chapters 5 and 6 in Lee and Lings (2008). Survey design requires that we move from the abstract level of theory to the specific level of what can be observed and measured empirically in the real world. The quality of research is constrained by the quality of data that feeds into it. Data collection for surveys often takes the form of questionnaires and chapters 7 and 11 in Lee and Lings (2008) discusses how questionnaire items (the questions in a questionnaire) are developed and assessed. A key aim of survey method is to generalise from a sample (a sub-set of the population) onto a wider population, and this puts certain demands on the properties of samples. How to select a sample suitable for statistical generalisation is discussed in chapter 11.

1.2.5 Analysing quantitative data

The main text is Field (2009). Once data has been compiled in the form of a survey, statistical software packages are used to analyse the data. The software most commonly used is SPSS. Secondary statistical data is analysed in the same way. Chapter 3 in Field (2009) provides an overview of the SPSS environment; how to enter or import data; how to organize data and outputs. We use computer laboratory sessions to practise SPSS throughout this part of the course.

Lecture 5 is concerned with the following topics: presenting data; computing descriptive statistics, i.e. summarizing variables through measures of central location and measures of dispersion; and testing common assumptions in statistics, with an emphasis on issues around normal distribution. In relation to this lecture, Field (2009) in chapter 5 focuses on exploring assumptions in statistical methods. Lectures 6 and 7 explore the relationships between two or more variables, for example the relationship between advertising budgets and record sales. The relevant statistics are coupled with inferential statistics. It is the element of inference that contributes much to the popularity of statistical methods in social science research. Inferential statistics assess the probability that a relationship found in a sample holds in the wider population the sample is drawn from. The course covers the most popular techniques, ranging from the Chi-square test discussed in chapter 14 in Burns and Burns (2008) to multiple linear regression techniques covered in chapter 7 in Field (2009).

6.6.6 Philosophy of science

Enlightenment challenged theology as the hitherto only legitimate path to knowledge through the propagation of a methodology (nowadays called positivism) used by natural science. This methodology was then (without further question) also employed by social sciences. Eventually, the question "What are scientists really doing and what should they do when they conduct research?" was asked. Attempts to answer this question are what we call "the philosophy of science". It is important to have a proper understanding of the different philosophical assumptions hidden beneath management research in order to appreciate the strengths and weaknesses of each, in order to appreciate how different philosophical assumptions influence the criteria we use to judge research quality, and in order to be able to locate one's own philosophical position.

Lecture 8 introduces a set of basic concepts in the philosophy of science and discusses the rationale behind different research strategies. Crotty (1998) defines crucial concepts such as ontology, epistemology, theoretical perspective, methodology and methods/research techniques. He outlines how methods, methodologies and theoretical perspectives are derived from epistemological assumptions, i.e. assumptions about the best ways of inquiring into the nature of the world and establishing 'truth". Crotty contributes to the clarification of issues which are perceived as confusing by many. According to him, it is not qualitative versus quantitative research that constitutes the great divide in social science. It is rather the distinction between an objectivist and constructivist epistemology, i.e. whether it is perceived as possible to uncover an objective "truth", or whether all knowledge is socially constructed. Originally, all social science was positivist/objectivist, assuming that the social life is patterned in a cause-effect form, that knowledge is arrived at thorough the use of the senses and the application of reason, that there is a clear distinction facts/values, and that natural and social sciences share a common logic and methodology of enquiry. Chapters 3 and 4 in Smith (1998) outline in some detail the main characteristics of positivism, its philosophical foundation and major traditions. The text explores the central debates on deduction versus induction. It outlines Popper's critique of inductivism and his falsificationist alternative. It also identifies various strands of idealism as well as phenomenology and constructivism which all have epistemological assumptions that diverge radically from positivism. Human behaviour is unpredictable and is therefore seen as rule-governed rather than law-like. The role of consciousness and meaning is stressed as well as the unavoidable interaction between the researcher and the subject matter.

Scientific progress was once seen as a continuous process where new knowledge is added to existing knowledge in an incremental way. This view has been challenged and substituted by the concepts of paradigm and paradigm shifts pioneered by Thomas Kuhn. Lecture 9 is about paradigms and similar discontinuous views of knowledge development. Paradigms are shared theoretical structures and methodological approaches about which there is high degree of consensus among a group of researchers. The truth of a scientific statement is only relevant to those who share the belief system upon which such "truths" are based. Following Kuhn, scientific development is characterized by paradigm shifts and is accordingly far from continuous. Chapter 5 in Smith (1998) presents the ideas behind the paradigm concept, the criticism of the concept and the alternative positions developed by Lakatos and Feyerabend.

The discussion of paradigms is often explicitly related to natural science and it is controversial to what extent it fits social sciences and management. Two journal articles by Pfeffer (1993) and Clarke and Clegg (2000), which are not included in this book, discuss the existence of paradigms in organization science and management, respectively.

1.3 Conclusion

We hope that this book will provide all postgraduate management students at Birkbeck with the methodological tool kit that makes it possible for them to conduct research of a high standard, as well as equip them with the knowledge and critical perspectives needed to critically assess research findings in books and journals as well as their own research.

Good luck with the book.

1 The Context of Design

DAVID DeVAUS

Before examining types of research designs it is important to be clear about the role and purpose of research design. We need to understand what research design is and what it is not. We need to know where design fits into the whole research process from framing a question to finally analysing and reporting data. This is the purpose of this chapter.

Description and explanation

Social researchers ask two fundamental types of research questions:

1 *What* is going on (descriptive research)?
2 *Why* is it going on (explanatory research)?

Descriptive research

Although some people dismiss descriptive research as 'mere description', good description is fundamental to the research enterprise and it has added immeasurably to our knowledge of the shape and nature of our society. Descriptive research encompasses much government sponsored research including the population census, the collection of a wide range of social indicators and economic information such as household expenditure patterns, time use studies, employment and crime statistics and the like.

Descriptions can be concrete or abstract. A relatively concrete description might describe the ethnic mix of a community, the changing age profile of a population or the gender mix of a workplace. Alternatively the description might ask more abstract questions such as 'Is the level of social inequality increasing or declining?', 'How secular is society?' or 'How much poverty is there in this community?'

Accurate descriptions of the level of unemployment or poverty have historically played a key role in social policy reforms (Marsh, 1982). By demonstrating the existence of social problems, competent description can challenge accepted assumptions about the way things are and can provoke action.

Good description provokes the 'why' questions of explanatory research. If we detect greater social polarization over the last 20 years (i.e. the rich are getting richer and the poor are getting poorer) we are forced to ask 'Why is this happening?' But before asking 'why?' we must be sure about the fact and dimensions of the phenomenon of increasing polarization. It is all very well to develop elaborate theories as to why society might be more polarized now than in the recent past, but if the basic premise is wrong (i.e. society is not becoming more polarized) then attempts to explain a non-existent phenomenon are silly.

Of course description can degenerate to mindless fact gathering or what C.W. Mills (1959) called 'abstracted empiricism'. There are plenty of examples of unfocused surveys and case studies that report trivial information and fail to provoke any 'why' questions or provide any basis for generalization. However, this is a function of inconsequential descriptions rather than an indictment of descriptive research itself.

Explanatory research

Explanatory research focuses on *why* questions. For example, it is one thing to describe the crime rate in a country, to examine trends over time or to compare the rates in different countries. It is quite a different thing to develop explanations about why the crime rate is as high as it is, why some types of crime are increasing or why the rate is higher in some countries than in others.

The way in which researchers develop research designs is fundamentally affected by whether the research question is descriptive or explanatory. It affects what information is collected. For example, if we want to explain why some people are more likely to be apprehended and convicted of crimes we need to have hunches about why this is so. We may have many possibly incompatible hunches and will need to collect information that enables us to see which hunches work best empirically.

Answering the 'why' questions involves developing *causal* explanations. Causal explanations argue that phenomenon *Y* (e.g. income level) is affected by factor *X* (e.g. gender). Some causal explanations will be simple while others will be more complex. For example, we might argue that there is a *direct* effect of gender on income (i.e. simple gender discrimination) (Figure 1.1a). We might argue for a causal chain, such as that gender affects choice of field of training which in turn affects

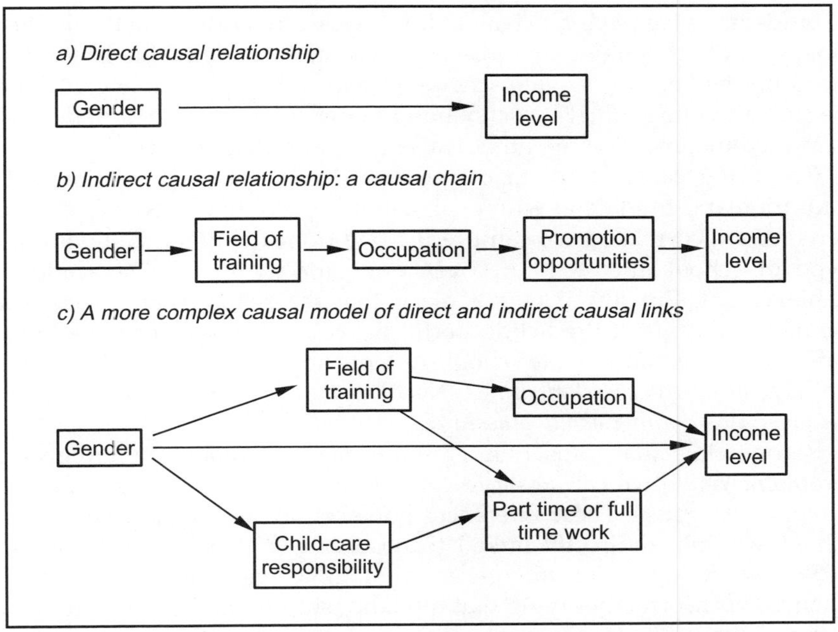

Figure 1.1 *Three types of causal relationships*

occupational options, which are linked to opportunities for promotion, which in turn affect income level (Figure 1.1b). Or we could posit a more complex model involving a number of interrelated causal chains (Figure 1.1c).

Prediction, correlation and causation

People often confuse correlation with causation. Simply because one event follows another, or two factors co-vary, does not mean that one causes the other. The link between two events may be coincidental rather than causal.

There is a correlation between the number of fire engines at a fire and the amount of damage caused by the fire (the more fire engines the more damage). Is it therefore reasonable to conclude that the number of fire engines causes the amount of damage? Clearly the number of fire engines and the amount of damage will *both* be due to some third factor – such as the seriousness of the fire.

Similarly, as the divorce rate changed over the twentieth century the crime rate increased a few years later. But this does not mean that divorce causes crime. Rather than divorce causing crime, divorce and crime rates might both be due to *other* social processes such as secularization, greater individualism or poverty.

Students at fee paying private schools typically perform better in their final year of schooling than those at government funded schools. But this need not be because private schools *produce* better performance. It may be that attending a private school and better final-year performance are *both* the outcome of some other cause (see later discussion).

Confusing causation with correlation also confuses prediction with causation and prediction with explanation. Where two events or characteristics are correlated we can predict one from the other. Knowing the type of school attended improves our capacity to predict academic achievement. But this does not mean that the school type affects academic achievement. Predicting performance on the basis of school type does not tell us *why* private school students do better. *Good prediction does not depend on causal relationships. Nor does the ability to predict accurately demonstrate anything about causality.*

Recognizing that causation is more than correlation highlights a problem. While we can observe correlation *we cannot observe cause.* We have to *infer* cause. These inferences however are 'necessarily fallible . . . [they] are only indirectly linked to observables' (Cook and Campbell, 1979: 10). Because our inferences are fallible we must minimize the chances of incorrectly saying that a relationship is causal when in fact it is not. *One of the fundamental purposes of research design in explanatory research is to avoid invalid inferences.*

Deterministic and probabilistic concepts of causation

There are two ways of thinking about causes: deterministically and probabilistically. The smoker who denies that tobacco causes cancer because he smokes heavily but has not contracted cancer illustrates deterministic causation. Probabilistic causation is illustrated by health authorities who point to the increased chances of cancer among smokers.

Deterministic causation is where variable X is said to cause Y if, and only if, X *invariably* produces Y. That is, when X is present then Y will 'necessarily, inevitably and infallibly' occur (Cook and Campbell, 1979: 14). This approach seeks to establish causal *laws* such as: whenever water is heated to 100 °C it always boils.

In reality laws are never this simple. They will always specify particular *conditions* under which that law operates. Indeed a great deal of scientific investigation involves specifying the conditions under which particular laws operate. Thus, we might say that *at sea level* heating *pure* water to 100 °C will always cause water to boil.

Alternatively, the law might be stated in the form of 'other things being equal' then X will always produce Y. A deterministic version of the relationship between race and income level would say that other things being equal (age, education, personality, experience etc.) then a white person will [always] earn a higher income than a black person. That is, race (X) causes income level (Y).

Stated like this the notion of deterministic causation in the social sciences sounds odd. It is hard to conceive of a characteristic or event that will invariably result in a given outcome even if a fairly tight set of conditions is specified. The *complexity* of human social behaviour and the *subjective, meaningful and voluntaristic* components of human behaviour mean that it will never be possible to arrive at causal statements of the type 'If *X*, and *A* and *B*, then *Y* will always follow.'

Most causal thinking in the social sciences is *probabilistic* rather than *deterministic* (Suppes, 1970). That is, we work at the level that a given factor increases (or decreases) the probability of a particular outcome, for example: being female increases the probability of working part time; race affects the probability of having a high status job.

We can improve probabilistic explanations by specifying conditions under which *X* is less likely and more likely to affect *Y*. But we will never achieve complete or deterministic explanations. Human behaviour is both *willed* and *caused*: there is a double-sided character to human social behaviour. People *construct* their social world and there are creative aspects to human action but this freedom and agency will always be constrained by the structures within which people live. Because behaviour is not simply determined we cannot achieve deterministic explanations. However, because behaviour is constrained we can achieve probabilistic explanations. We can say that a given factor will increase the likelihood of a given outcome but there will never be certainty about outcomes.

Despite the probabilistic nature of causal statements in the social sciences, much popular, ideological and political discourse translates these into deterministic statements. Findings about the causal effects of class, gender or ethnicity, for example, are often read as if these factors invariably and completely produce particular outcomes. One could be forgiven for thinking that social science has demonstrated that gender completely and invariably determines position in society, roles in families, values and ways of relating to other people.

Theory testing and theory construction

Attempts to answer the 'why' questions in social science are theories. These theories vary in their *complexity* (how many variables and links), *abstraction* and *scope*. To understand the role of theory in empirical research it is useful to distinguish between two different styles of research: theory testing and theory building (Figure 1.2).

Theory building

Theory building is a process in which research begins with observations and uses *inductive* reasoning to derive a theory from these observations.

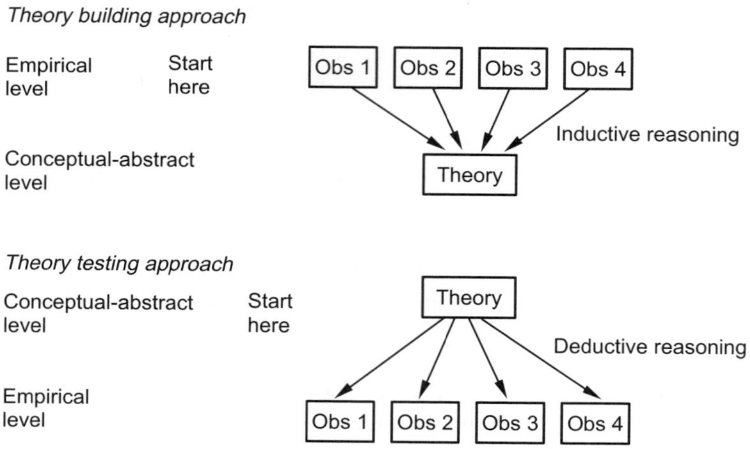

Figure 1.2 *Theory building and theory testing approaches to research*

These theories attempt to make sense of observations. Because the theory is produced *after* observations are made it is often called *post factum* theory (Merton, 1968) or *ex post facto* theorizing.

This form of theory building entails asking whether the observation is *a particular case of a more general factor*, or how the observation *fits into a pattern or a story*. For example, Durkheim observed that the suicide rate was higher among Protestants than Catholics. But is religious affiliation a particular case of something more general? Of what more general phenomenon might it be an indicator? Are there other observations that shed light on this? He also observed that men were more suicidal than women, urban dwellers more than rural dwellers and the socially mobile more than the socially stable. He argued that the common factor behind all these observations was that those groups who were most suicidal were also less well socially integrated and experienced greater ambiguity about how to behave and what is right and wrong. He theorized that one of the explanations for suicidal behaviour was a sense of normlessness – a disconnectedness of individuals from their social world. Of course, there may have been other ways of accounting for these observations but at least Durkheim's explanation was consistent with the facts.

Theory testing

In contrast, a theory testing approach *begins* with a theory and uses theory to guide which observations to make: it moves from the general to the particular. The observations should provide a test of the worth of the theory. Using *deductive* reasoning to derive a set of propositions from the theory does this. We need to develop these propositions so that

		Parents divorced?	
		No	Yes
Parental conflict	Low	(a)	(b)
	High	(c)	(d)

Figure 1.3 *The relationship between divorce and parental conflict*

if the theory is true then certain things should follow in the real world. We then assess whether these predictions are correct. If they are correct the theory is supported. If they do not hold up then the theory needs to be either rejected or modified.

For example, we may wish to test the theory that it is not divorce itself that affects the wellbeing of children but the level of conflict between parents. To test this idea we can make predictions about the wellbeing of children under different family conditions. For the simple theory that it is parental conflict rather than divorce that affects a child's wellbeing there are four basic 'conditions' (see Figure 1.3). For each 'condition' the theory would make different predictions about the level of children's wellbeing that we can examine.

If the theory that it is parental conflict rather than parental divorce is correct the following propositions should be supported:

- *Proposition 1: children in situations (a) and (b) would be equally well off* That is, where parental conflict is low, children with divorced parents will do just as well as those whose parents are married.
- *Proposition 2: children in situations (c) and (d) should be equally poorly off* That is, children in conflictual couple families will do just as badly as children in post-divorce families where parents sustain high conflict.
- *Proposition 3: children in situation (c) will do worse than those in situation (a)* That is, those with married parents in high conflict will do worse than those who have married parents who are not in conflict.
- *Proposition 4: children in situation (d) will do worse than those in situation (b)* That is, those with divorced parents in high conflict will do worse than those who have divorced parents who are not in conflict.
- *Proposition 5: children in situation (b) will do better than those in situation (c)* That is, children with divorced parents who are not in conflict will do better than those with married parents who are in conflict.
- *Proposition 6: children in situation (a) will do better than those in situation (d)* That is, children with married parents who are not in conflict will do better than those with divorced parents who are in conflict.

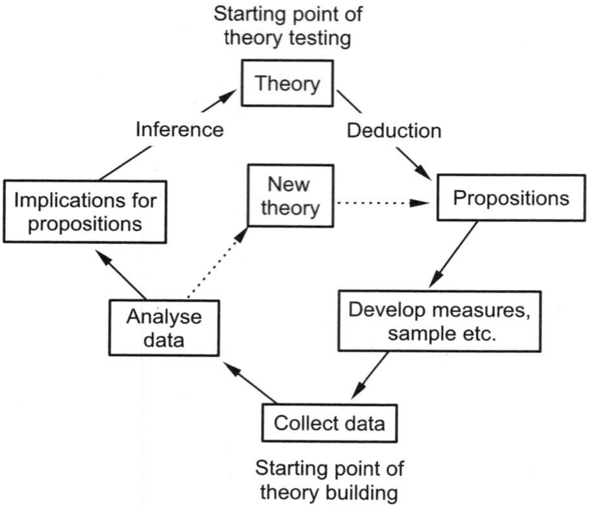

Figure 1.4 *The logic of the research process*

No single proposition would provide a compelling test of the original theory. Indeed, taken on its own proposition 3, for example, would reveal nothing about the impact of divorce. However, taken as a package, the *set* of propositions provides a stronger test of the theory than any single proposition.

Although theory testing and theory building are often presented as alternative modes of research they should be part of one ongoing process (Figure 1.4). Typically, theory building will produce a plausible account or explanation of a set of observations. However, such explanations are frequently just one of a number of possible explanations that fit the data. While plausible they are not necessarily compelling. They require systematic testing where data are collected to specifically evaluate how well the explanation holds when subjected to a range of crucial tests.

What is research design?

How is the term 'research design' to be used in this book? An analogy might help. When constructing a building there is no point ordering materials or setting critical dates for completion of project stages until we know what sort of building is being constructed. The first decision is whether we need a high rise office building, a factory for manufacturing machinery, a school, a residential home or an apartment block. Until this is done we cannot sketch a plan, obtain permits, work out a work schedule or order materials.

Similarly, social research needs a design or a structure before data collection or analysis can commence. A research design is *not* just a work plan. A work plan details what has to be done to complete the project but the work plan will flow from the project's research design. *The function of a research design is to ensure that the evidence obtained enables us to answer the initial question as unambiguously as possible.* Obtaining relevant evidence entails specifying the type of evidence needed to answer the research question, to test a theory, to evaluate a programme or to accurately describe some phenomenon. In other words, when designing research we need to ask: given this research question (or theory), what type of evidence is needed to answer the question (or test the theory) *in a convincing way*?

Research design 'deals with a *logical* problem and not a *logistical* problem' (Yin, 1989: 29). Before a builder or architect can develop a work plan or order materials they must first establish the type of building required, its uses and the needs of the occupants. The work plan flows from this. Similarly, in social research the issues of sampling, method of data collection (e.g. questionnaire, observation, document analysis), design of questions are all subsidiary to the matter of 'What evidence do I need to collect?'

Too often researchers design questionnaires or begin interviewing far too early – before thinking through what information they require to answer their research questions. Without attending to these research design matters at the beginning, the conclusions drawn will normally be weak and unconvincing and fail to answer the research question.

Design versus method

Research design is different from the method by which data are collected. Many research methods texts confuse research designs with methods. It is not uncommon to see research design treated as a mode of data collection rather than as a logical structure of the inquiry. But there is nothing intrinsic about any research design that requires a particular method of data collection. Although cross-sectional surveys are frequently equated with questionnaires and case studies are often equated with participant observation (e.g. Whyte's *Street Corner Society*, 1943), data for any design can be collected with any data collection method (Figure 1.5). How the data are collected is irrelevant to the *logic* of the design.

Failing to distinguish between design and method leads to poor evaluation of designs. Equating cross-sectional designs with questionnaires, or case studies with participant observation, means that the designs are often evaluated against the strengths and weaknesses of the method rather than their ability to draw relatively unambiguous conclusions or to select between rival plausible hypotheses.

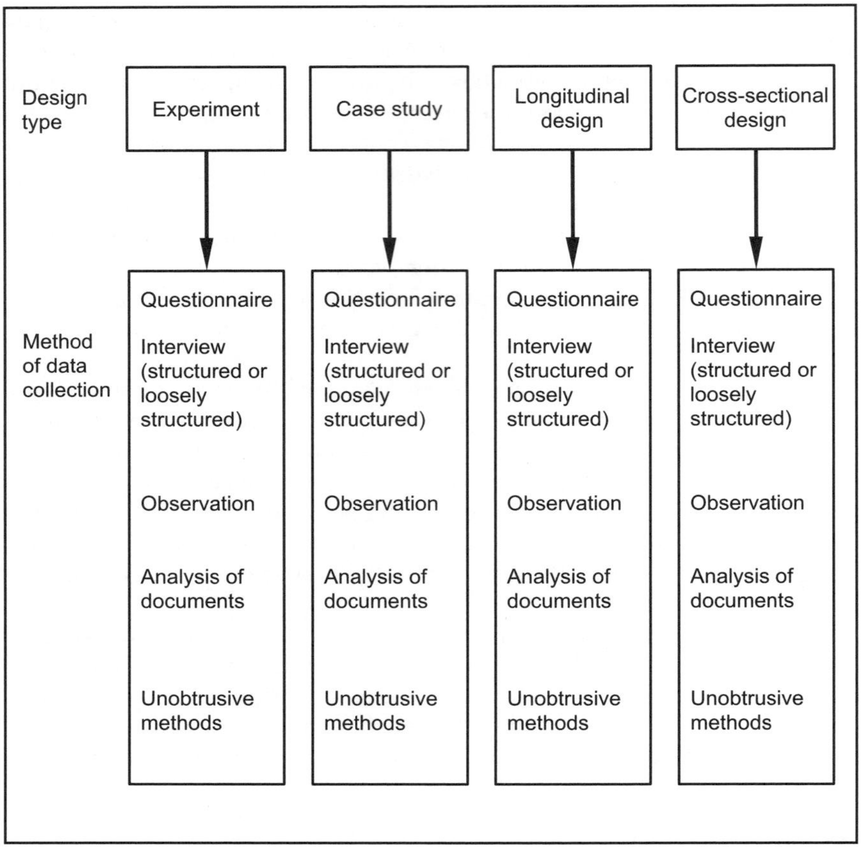

Figure 1.5 *Relationship between research design and particular data collection methods*

Quantitative and qualitative research

Similarly, designs are often equated with qualitative and quantitative research methods. Social surveys and experiments are frequently viewed as prime examples of quantitative research and are evaluated against the strengths and weaknesses of statistical, quantitative research methods and analysis. Case studies, on the other hand, are often seen as prime examples of qualitative research – which adopts an interpretive approach to data, studies 'things' within their context and considers the subjective meanings that people bring to their situation.

It is erroneous to equate a particular research design with either quantitative or qualitative methods. Yin (1993), a respected authority on case study design, has stressed the irrelevance of the quantitative/qualitative distinction for case studies. He points out that:

> a point of confusion . . . has been the unfortunate linking between the case study method and certain types of data collection – for example those focusing on qualitative methods, ethnography, or participant observation. People have thought that the case study method required them to embrace these data collection methods . . . On the contrary, the method does not imply any particular form of data collection – which can be qualitative or quantitative. (1993: 32)

Similarly, Marsh (1982) argues that quantitative surveys can provide information and explanations that are 'adequate at the level of meaning'. While recognizing that survey research has not always been good at tapping the subjective dimension of behaviour, she argues that:

> Making sense of social action . . . is . . . hard and surveys have not traditionally been very good at it. The earliest survey researchers started a tradition . . . of bringing the meaning from outside, either by making use of the researcher's stock of plausible explanations . . . or by bringing it from subsidiary in-depth interviews sprinkling quotes . . . liberally on the raw correlations derived from the survey. Survey research became much more exciting . . . when it began including meaningful dimensions in the study design. [This has been done in] two ways, firstly [by] asking the actor either for her reasons directly, or to supply information about the central values in her life around which we may assume she is orienting her life. [This] involves collecting a sufficiently complete picture of the context in which an actor finds herself that a team of outsiders may read off the meaningful dimensions. (1982: 123–4)

Adopting a sceptical approach to explanations

The need for research design stems from a sceptical approach to research and a view that scientific knowledge must always be provisional. The purpose of research design is to reduce the ambiguity of much research evidence.

We can always find some evidence consistent with almost any theory. However, we should be sceptical of the evidence, and rather than seeking evidence that is *consistent* with our theory we should seek evidence that provides a *compelling* test of the theory.

There are two related strategies for doing this: eliminating rival explanations of the evidence and deliberately seeking evidence that could *disprove* the theory.

Plausible rival hypotheses

A fundamental strategy of social research involves evaluating 'plausible rival hypotheses'. We need to examine and evaluate alternative ways of explaining a particular phenomenon. This applies regardless of whether the data are quantitative or qualitative; regardless of the particular research design (experimental, cross-sectional, longitudinal or case

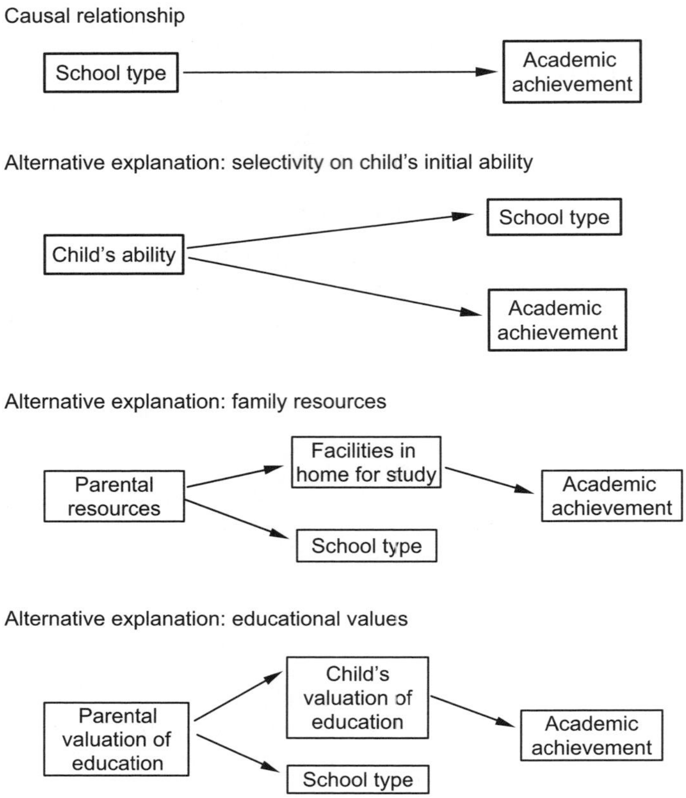

Figure 1.6 *Causal and non-causal explanations of the relationship between school type and academic achievement*

study); and regardless of the method of data collection (e.g. observation, questionnaire). Our mindset needs to anticipate alternative ways of interpreting findings and to regard any interpretation of these findings as provisional – subject to further testing.

The idea of evaluating plausible rival hypotheses can be illustrated using the example of the correlation between type of school attended and academic achievement. Many parents accept the causal proposition that attendance at fee paying private schools improves a child's academic performance (Figure 1.6). Schools themselves promote the same notion by prominently advertising their pass rates and comparing them with those of other schools or with national averages. By implication they propose a causal connection: 'Send your child to our school and they will pass (or get grades to gain entry into prestigious institutions, courses).' The data they provide are consistent with their proposition that these schools produce better results.

But these data are not compelling. There are at least three other ways of accounting for this correlation without accepting the causal link between school type and achievement (Figure 1.6). There is the *selectivity* explanation: the more able students may be sent to fee paying private schools in the first place. There is the *family resources* explanation: parents who can afford to send their children to fee paying private schools can also afford other help (e.g. books, private tutoring, quiet study space, computers). It is this help rather than the type of school that produces the better performance of private school students. Finally, there is the family *values* explanation: parents who value education most are prepared to send their children to fee paying private schools and it is this family emphasis on education, not the schools themselves, that produces the better academic performance. All these explanations are equally consistent with the observation that private school students do better than government school students. Without collecting further evidence we cannot choose between these explanations and therefore must remain open minded about which one makes most empirical sense.

There might also be methodological explanations for the finding that private school students perform better academically. These methodological issues might undermine any argument that a causal connection exists. Are the results due to questionable ways of measuring achievement? From what range and number of schools were the data obtained? On how many cases are the conclusions based? Could the pattern simply be a function of chance? These are all possible alternative explanations for the finding that private school students perform better.

Good research design will anticipate competing explanations *before* collecting data so that relevant information for evaluating the relative merits of these competing explanations is obtained. In this example of schools and academic achievement, thinking about alternative plausible hypotheses beforehand would lead us to find out about the parents' financial resources, the study resources available in the home, the parents' and child's attitudes about education and the child's academic abilities before entering the school.

The fallacy of affirming the consequent Although evidence may be consistent with an initial proposition it might be equally consistent with a range of alternative propositions. Too often people do not even think of the alternative hypotheses and simply conclude that since the evidence is consistent with their theory then the theory is true. This form of reasoning commits the logical *fallacy of affirming the consequent*. This form of reasoning has the following logical structure:

- If A is true then B should follow.
- We observe B.
- Therefore A is true.

If we apply this logic to the type of school and achievement proposition, the logical structure of the school type and achievement argument becomes clearer.

Initial proposition:

- Private schools produce better students than do government schools.

The test:

- *If A then B* If private schools produce better students (A) then their students should get better final marks than those from government funded schools (B).
- *B is true* Private school students do achieve better final marks than government school students (observe B).
- *Therefore A is true* Therefore private schools do produce better students (A is true).

But as I have already argued, the better performance of private school students might also reflect the effect of other factors. The problem here is that any number of explanations may be correct and the evidence does not help rule out many of these. For the social scientist this level of indeterminacy is quite unsatisfactory. In effect we are only in a position to say:

- If A [or C, or D, or E, or F, or . . .] then B.
- We observe B.
- Therefore A [or C, or D, or E, or F, or . . .] is true.

Although explanation (A) is still in the running because it is consistent with the observations, we cannot say that it is the most plausible explanation. We need to test our proposition more thoroughly by evaluating the worth of the alternative propositions.

Falsification: looking for evidence to disprove the theory

As well as evaluating and eliminating alternative explanations we should rigorously evaluate our own theories. Rather than asking 'What evidence would constitute support for the theory?', ask 'What evidence would convince me that the theory is *wrong*?' It is not difficult to find evidence consistent with a theory. It is much tougher for a theory to survive the test of people trying to disprove it.

Unfortunately some theories are closed systems in which any evidence can be interpreted as support for the theory. Such theories are said to be non-falsifiable. Many religions or belief systems can become closed systems whereby all evidence can be accommodated by the theory and nothing will change the mind of the true believer. Exchange theory (Homans, 1961; Blau, 1964) is largely non-falsifiable. It assumes that we always maximize our gains and avoid costs. But we can see almost anything as a gain. Great sacrifices to care for a disabled relative can be interpreted as a gain (satisfaction of helping) rather than a loss (income, time for self etc.). We need to frame our propositions and define our terms in such a way that they are capable of being disproven.

The provisional nature of support for theories

Even where the theory is corroborated and has survived attempts to disprove it, the theory remains provisional:

> falsificationism stresses the ambiguity of confirmation . . . corroboration gives only the comfort that the theory has been tested and survived the test, that even after the most impressive corroborations of predictions it has only achieved the status of 'not yet disconfirmed'. This . . . is far from the status of 'being true'. (Cook and Campbell, 1979: 20)

There always may be an unthought-of explanation. We cannot anticipate or evaluate every possible explanation. The more alternative explanations that have been eliminated and the more we have tried to disprove our theory, the more confidence we will have in it, but we should avoid thinking that it is *proven*.

However we can *disprove* a theory. The logic of this is:

- If theory A is true then B should follow.
- B does *not* follow.
- Therefore A is not true.

So long as B is a valid test of A the absence of B should make us reject or revise the theory. In reality, we would not reject a theory simply because a single fact or observation does not fit. Before rejecting a plausible theory we would require multiple disconfirmations using different measures, different samples and different methods of data collection and analysis.

In summary, we should adopt a sceptical approach to explanations. We should anticipate rival interpretations and collect data to enable the winnowing out of the weaker explanations and the identification of which alternative theories make most empirical sense. We also need to ask what data would challenge the explanation and collect data to evaluate the theory from this more demanding perspective.

Summary

This chapter has outlined the purpose of research design in both descriptive and explanatory research. In explanatory research the purpose is to develop and evaluate causal theories. The probabilistic nature of causation in social sciences, as opposed to deterministic causation, was discussed.

Research design is not related to any particular method of collecting data or any particular type of data. Any research design can, in principle, use any type of data collection method and can use either quantitative or qualitative data. Research design refers to the *structure* of an enquiry: it is a logical matter rather than a logistical one.

It has been argued that the central role of research design is to minimize the chance of drawing incorrect causal inferences from data. Design is a logical task undertaken to ensure that the evidence collected enables us to answer questions or to test theories as unambiguously as possible. When designing research it is essential that we identify the type of evidence required to answer the research question in a convincing way. This means that we must not simply collect evidence that is consistent with a particular theory or explanation. Research needs to be structured in such a way that the evidence also bears on alternative rival explanations and enables us to identify which of the competing explanations is most compelling empirically. It also means that we must not simply look for evidence that supports our favourite theory: we should also look for evidence that has the potential to disprove our preferred explanations.

2 Tools for Research Design

DAVID DeVAUS

To achieve a reasonable research design we need to attend to a number of matters before we arrive at the final design. The first section of this chapter outlines these preliminary steps that precede design. It then expands on the idea of alternative rival hypotheses that was introduced in Chapter 1. The second section introduces a number of concepts that are fundamental to designing good research – internal validity, external validity and measurement error.

Before design

In the same way that an architect needs to know the purpose of the building before designing it (is it an office building, a factory or a home?) social researchers must be clear about their research question before developing a research design.

Focusing and clarifying the research question

The first question to ask is, 'What question am I trying to answer?' Specifying a question is more than identifying a topic. It's not enough to say, 'I'm interested in getting some answers about family breakdown.' What answers to what questions? Do you want to know the extent of family breakdown? Who is most vulnerable to family breakdown? Changing rates of breakdown? Over what period? Where? Or are you really looking at the causes of breakdown? The effects of family breakdown? All the effects or just particular ones?

Focusing descriptive research questions

To narrow the focus of descriptive research we need to specify the scope of what is to be described. The following guidelines, using family breakdown as an example, help narrow down a descriptive research topic into a researchable question.

1 What is the *scope of the core concepts*? What is to be included in the concept *family breakdown*? Do we mean divorce? What about

separation? Are we referring only to the breakdown in marital relationships? Do we mean the *total* breakdown or simply poor relationships? What about relationships between parents and children or between children? Until we specify what we mean by our core concepts it is going to be impossible to begin the description.

2 What is the *time frame* for the description? Is our interest in change over time or just about *contemporary* levels of family breakdown? If it is about change, over what period?

3 What is the *geographical* location for the description? Is the interest in family breakdown in a particular community, in different regions or the whole nation? Is it comparative, looking at breakdown in different types of countries (e.g. highly industrialized versus rapidly industrializing versus impoverished countries)?

4 How *general* is the description to be? Do you want to be able to describe patterns for specific subgroups (e.g. among those who married as teenagers, among those who are in *de facto* relationships, second marriages etc.)?

5 What *aspect* of the topic are you interested in? Is the interest in rates of breakdown? The experience? Laws? Attitudes and beliefs?

6 How *abstract* is your interest? Is your interest in family breakdown or in family breakdown as a reflection of something more abstract (e.g. social fragmentation, social conflict, individualism, the role of the state in the private lives of citizens)?

7 What is the *unit of analysis*? The unit of analysis is the 'thing' about which we collect information and from which we draw conclusions. Often this is a person (e.g divorced person) but it may be 'things' such as organizations (divorce courts), a family as a whole, events (e.g. divorces), periods (divorce in different years), places (communities, countries).

The questions we can answer will depend on the unit of analysis. We could compare divorced individuals with non-divorced individuals (individual as the unit of analysis). We could study a series of divorces and examine what the process of becoming divorced was (event as unit of analysis). We might use year as the unit of analysis and track changes in divorce rates since 1945. Using countries we might examine the different divorce rates in different types of countries with a view to comparing the patterns in different types of countries. Alternatively families might be the units of analysis and we may want to look at the characteristics of divorcing families (e.g. size, family income, family type, nature of relationships in family) compared with those of non-divorcing families.

Thinking beyond individuals as units of analysis broadens the range of research questions we ask and broadens the range and sources of data available. For example, if years were the unit of analysis we would obtain statistics from the relevant national collection agencies regarding divorce for each year. We would also collect other information about each year (e.g. unemployment level, inflation rate, changes to laws) that was relevant to the hypotheses.

Focusing explanatory research questions

In framing explanatory questions we need to further specify our focus. Explanatory research explores causes and/or consequences of a phenomenon, so the research question must be clear about the style of explanatory research and identify which causes or consequences it will investigate.

Before outlining some different types of explanatory research it is useful to introduce some terms.

- *Dependent variable* This is the variable that is treated as the *effect* in the causal model: it is dependent on the influence of some other factor. The dependent variable is also referred to as the outcome variable and in causal diagrams it is conventionally designated as the Y variable.
- *Independent variable* This is the variable that is the presumed *cause*. It is also called the predictor variable, the experimental variable or the explanatory variable and is designated in causal diagrams as the X variable (as in education (X) $\rightarrow$ income level (Y)).
- *Intervening variables* These variables come between the independent variable and the dependent variable in a causal chain. They are the *means* by which cause X produces effect Y. Intervening variables are represented in causal diagrams by the symbol Z, as illustrated in Figure 2.1.
- *Extraneous variables* Two variables can be correlated without being causally related. The correlation may be due to the two factors being outcomes of a third variable (see Chapter 1). This third variable is called an extraneous variable and is also symbolized as Z in causal diagrams, and the form of this relationship is illustrated in Figure 2.2.

Searching for causes or effects This is the least focused type of explanatory research. It involves identifying the core phenomenon (e.g. changes in divorce rate since World War II) and then searching for causes or consequences of this. Searching for causes would involve identifying possible causal factors (e.g. changing values, decline in religion, changing population mix, economic changes, legal reforms, changes in welfare support for lone parents). We would then design research to evaluate which of these causes helps explain changes in divorce rates. This form of research question is illustrated in Figure 2.3.

Alternatively we might focus on the consequences rather than causes of changes in divorce rate (Figure 2.4).

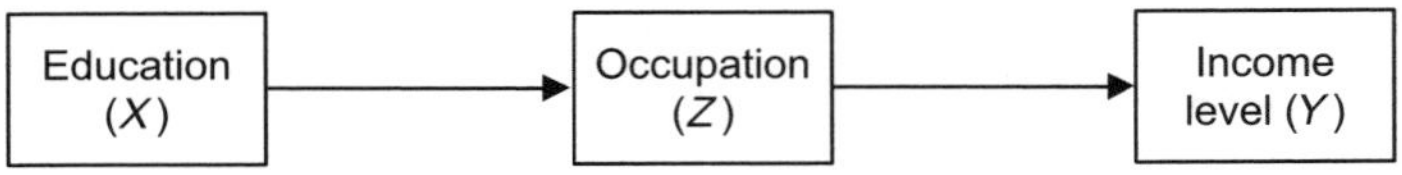

Figure 2.1 *An intervening variable*

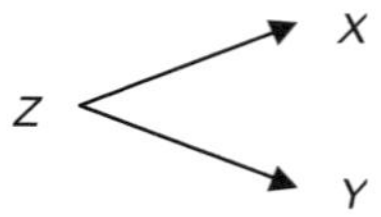

Figure 2.2 *An extraneous variable*

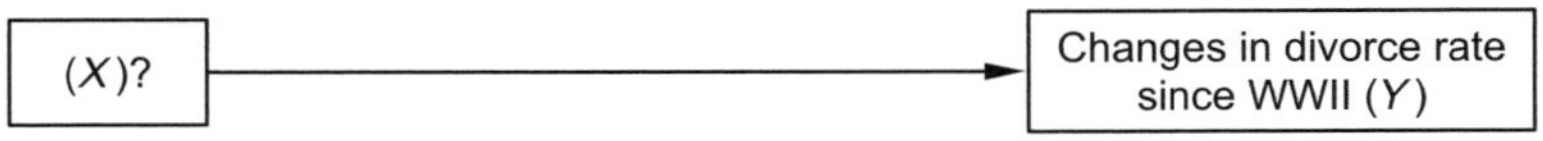

Figure 2.3 *Searching for causes*

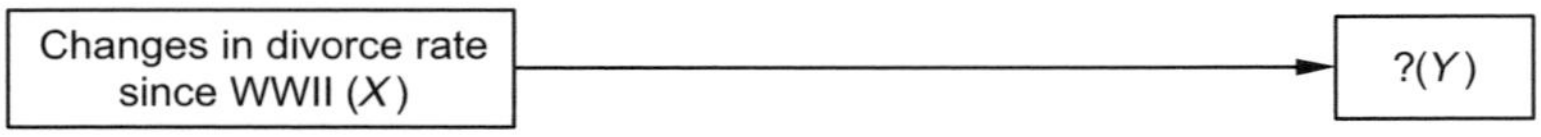

Figure 2.4 *Searching for effects*

Exploring a simple causal proposition A more focused research question will specify a *particular* causal proposition to evaluate (Figure 2.5). It might propose an impact of a particular factor or examine a specific consequence. For example, we might propose that changes in government benefits to lone parents have led to an increase in divorce rates since World War II.

More complex causal models Such propositions are simplistic in that they do not spell out the mechanisms by which the two factors might be related. We might develop more complex models that spell out some of the mechanisms in the causal chain. This fuller model then becomes the focus of the research and provides the framework within which the research design will be framed (Figure 2.6).

When clarifying a research question it is helpful to draw diagrams like those in Figures 2.1–2.5. It is also helpful to ask four key questions:

1 What am I trying to explain (i.e. what is the dependent variable)?
2 What are the possible causes (what are the independent variables)?
3 Which causes will I explore?

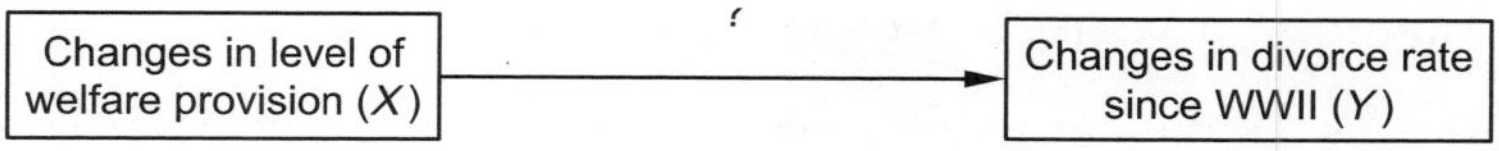

Figure 2.5 *A specific causal proposition*

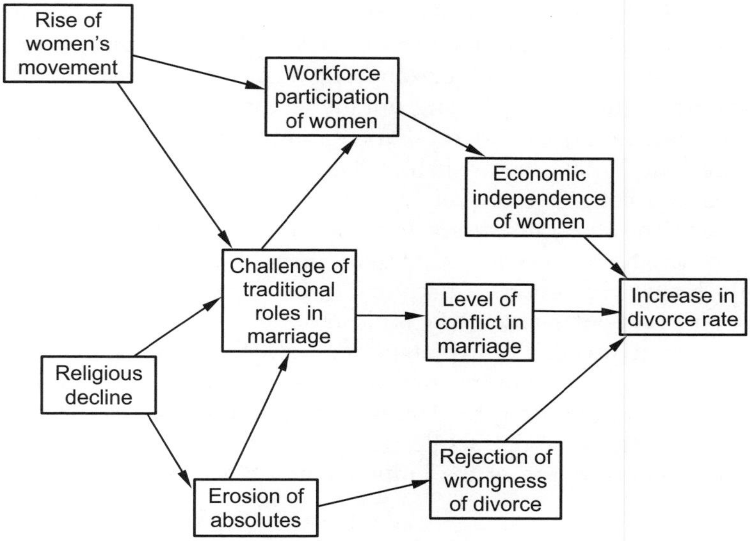

Figure 2.6 *A more complex causal model for increases in divorce*

4 What possible mechanisms connect the presumed causes to the presumed effects (what are the intervening variables)?

Another way of framing research questions is to formulate different ways of understanding a phenomenon and then compare which of these competing approaches best fits the facts. For example, we might compare three different ways of understanding changes in divorce rates: an economic approach, a social values approach and a legislative approach. The economic approach might argue that changes in divorce rates stem from economic factors such as the level of affluence, access of women to work and levels of welfare support for lone parents. The social values explanation might seek to explain the increased divorce rate in terms of increasing levels of individualism and greater social acceptance of divorce. A legislative approach might focus on the impact of legislative changes such as no-fault divorce or new rules regarding property division.

Idiographic and nomothetic explanations

The above examples focus on particular causes and consequences and attempt to provide only a *partial* explanation of changes in divorce rates. These explanations are called *nomothetic* explanations – partial explanations of a class of cases rather than a 'full' explanation of a particular case. They involve an examination of relatively few causal factors and a larger number of cases. In contrast, *idiographic* explanations focus on particular cases and develop as complete an explanation of each case as possible. They involve examining as many factors as possible that contribute to the case including unique factors.

A nomothetic explanation of divorce might focus on the importance of a single contributing factor such as the intergenerational transmission of divorce. Are couples more likely to divorce if one of their parents have divorced? The study might involve comparing people who had divorced with those who had not to see if the divorcees were more likely to have a family history of divorce. In contrast, an idiographic approach might focus on a particular divorced couple and build a full explanation of why *this* couple divorced. The explanation would consider the family history of the couple and examine this along with many other contributing factors. The idiographic explanation would provide us with a good understanding of the *case* while the nomothetic explanation would provide an understanding of the influence of a *factor*.

Identifying plausible rival hypotheses

In Chapter 1 I stressed the importance of identifying plausible rival ways of accounting for the phenomenon being studied. Obviously it makes sense to anticipate these alternatives before carrying out the research. But how do we identify these alternative explanations? There are two main types of rival hypotheses and these suggest ways of anticipating alternative explanations.

Theoretical and substantive rivals

There is no magical way of producing a set of alternative substantive or theoretical explanations. In the end the researcher must formulate them. The more familiar the researcher is with the particular substantive topic and with social science models and theories, the more likely they are to anticipate different ways of interpreting a given set of results. The following provide sources of alternative explanations.

The theoretical literature Broad approaches in a discipline can present different ways of viewing any question. Suppose, for example, that we wanted to understand why some people seem to have happier marriages than other people do. An explanation could concentrate on the *personal attributes* of the couple – their personality, their values and beliefs and their interpersonal skills. It could focus on *economic* factors and interpret marital happiness in terms of the costs and benefits to each partner. Alternatively, the explanation could adopt a *life course perspective* that interprets differences in marital happiness according to where the couple is in the life course (e.g. newly married, before children, young children, adolescent children, empty nest, later life). A feminist approach might try to explain marital happiness in terms of gender roles, division of labour and power within the relationship. A demographer might focus on the birth cohorts (e.g. depression marriages, postwar marriages, 1990s marriages etc.). Other researchers might seek to explain marital happiness in structural terms such as the couple's level of social disadvantage. Social network theorists might concentrate on the extent to which a couple is integrated into the wider family and community and is able to receive support from these networks.

This list is not exhaustive. The point is that different approaches (e.g. psychological, life course, exchange, structural, feminist) will have a particular 'angle' which alerts us to different ways of looking at an issue. When thinking about a problem, ask yourself questions such as 'How might a feminist account for this?', 'How might a Freudian psychologist explain this?', 'How would an exchange theorist account for this?', 'What might a conflict theorist say?'

Other researchers Previous research on the topic can be a rich source of competing explanations. Read the literature in journals and search electronic databases. Review articles and introductory overviews can be extremely helpful.

Practitioners, key informants, policy makers, advocates 'Insiders' with practical knowledge of a field can be invaluable. In a study on divorce, marriage counsellors, married couples, divorced people and advocacy groups can provide valuable insights. Literature such as novels and plays can also provide keen ideas that can be tested systematically (e.g. Tolstoy's novel *Anna Karenina* provides one way of interpreting marital unhappiness).

Own experience, hunches, and intuitions Do not ignore your own experience, your own intuitions and hunches. In the end all explanations start with hunches that spring from individuals who have ideas and observe things around them. Use these insights, experiences and observations and test them systematically.

There is no right way of developing ideas. Do not limit yourself to formal social science research or to research on the very specific topic you are working on. Use diverse sources of ideas. Brainstorm with a group and debate the topic. Think laterally: if your topic is marriage breakdown, look beyond the marriage and divorce literature.

Technical/methodological rivals

If findings are likely to be due to poor measurement (see below) then any theoretical interpretation of these results will be unconvincing. Throughout this book I will identify many technical and methodological factors that can undermine the conclusions we draw from our research. Good research design will minimize the threat from these sources.

I will not at this point go into these methodological issues in detail. However, it will be helpful to highlight the types of methodological rivals that will be examined. These are outlined in Goldenberg (1992).

1 *Demand characteristics of the situation.*
2 *Transient personal characteristics* such as the respondent's mood, attention span, health etc.
3 *Situational factors* such as anonymity, people present when data were being collected, gender, age and class of investigator and respondent.
4 *Sampling of items* Are the concepts well measured?
5 *Nature of the sample* Can we generalize from the sample?
6 *Lack of clarity of the instrument* Are the questions clear and unambiguous?
7 *Format of data collection* Are the results an artifact of the data collection method? Would different patterns be found if a different method was used (e.g. observation rather than questionnaire)?
8 *Variation in the administration of the instrument* in studies tracking change over time.
9 *Processing/analysis errors.*

Operationalization

Most social science research involves making observations that we presume tap concepts. If we were conducting a study on the effect of marital breakdown on the wellbeing of children we would need first to work out what is meant by marriage breakdown, wellbeing and children. This involves defining these concepts, which in turn requires developing a *nominal definition* and an *operational definition* of each concept.

Concepts are, by their nature, not directly observable. We cannot see social class, marital happiness, intelligence etc. To use concepts in research we need to translate concepts into something observable – something we can measure. This involves defining and clarifying abstract concepts and developing indicators of them. This process of clarifying abstract concepts and translating them into specific, observable measures is called operationalization and involves *descending the ladder of abstraction*.

Clarifying concepts

Before developing indicators of concepts we must first clarify the concepts. This involves developing both nominal and operational definitions of the concept.

Nominal definitions Concepts do not have a fixed or correct meaning. Marriage breakdown could be defined in terms of the law (such as whether the decree nisi has been granted), the quality of the relationship or practical arrangements (living apart). Similarly, we need to define children. Is a child defined by a blood relationship, a legal relationship (includes adopted), a social relationship (*de facto* parents), chronological age, level of dependency or some other criterion? By deciding on the type of definition we provide a *nominal definition*: it specifies the meaning of the concept but remains abstract.

Different definitions produce different findings. Consequently, defining concepts is a crucial stage of research. It needs to be done deliberately and to be systematically and carefully justified. There are three steps in developing and narrowing down a nominal definition.

First, *obtain a range of definitions*. Look at review articles, discipline dictionaries (e.g. a dictionary of sociology), encyclopaedias (e.g. an encyclopaedia of social sciences) and journal articles. Look for both explicit and implicit definitions.

Second, *decide on a definition*. From your list either select one definition or create a better definition from the common elements of several definitions. Explain and justify your approach.

Third, *delineate the dimensions of the concept*. Many concepts have a number of dimensions and it is helpful to spell these out as they can help to further refine your definition. This can be illustrated using the concept of the *child's wellbeing*. We can think of a number of dimensions of wellbeing: emotional, psychological, physical, educational, financial, social, environmental, legal etc. If we are arguing that marriage breakdown affects a child's wellbeing, what sort of wellbeing are we talking about? All of these? Just one or two? Having delineated various dimensions you will need to decide which are of interest in the present study. You may examine all aspects or limit yourself to one or two.

A concept may have *subdimensions*. Suppose we focused on *social* wellbeing. This broad concept could incorporate subdimensions such as the level of safety in the neighbourhood, the nature of the child's relationships and her experiences of social discrimination. The subdimension of 'relationships with others' could be further divided into relationships with particular people such as mother, father, peers, siblings and grandparents. Having settled on the particular relationships with which we are going to deal, we would need to identify what *aspects* of the relationships to measure and decide how to measure them (see below). In Figure 2.7 relationships are measured according to the level of

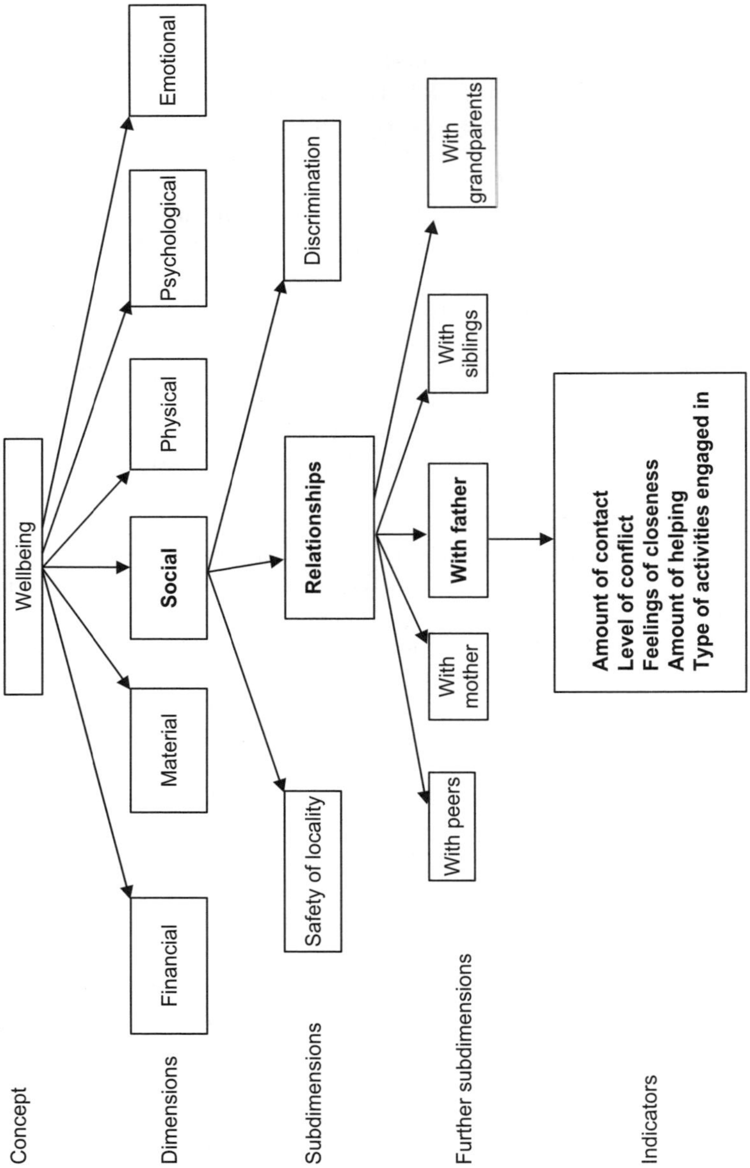

Figure 2.7 *Dimensionalizing the concept of child's wellbeing*

contact, conflict, closeness, helping and type of shared activities. These measures or indicators would then provide the core around which to frame specific questions or to focus an observational study.

In this example I have focused on one dimension at each level but I could have been exhaustive and developed measures for each conceivable dimension and subdimension. The decision of whether to adopt a focused or an exhaustive approach will depend on what you are interested in. The advantage of adopting a systematic approach as outlined in Figure 2.7 is that it helps focus and refine the research question and forces you to make deliberate decisions about how to measure a concept.

Operational definitions Having defined the concepts you will develop an *operational definition* – the observations to measure the concept. What *indicators* of marriage breakdown will you use? We might operationally define marriage breakdown according to the quality of the relationship. Using this definition we might measure breakdown according to level of conflict, type of communication, signs of lack of affection and level of cooperation or lack of cooperation.

How well such indicators tap the concept as defined will have a critical bearing on the value of the conclusions drawn from the study. If the indicators tap something other than what we claim they do then our conclusions can be easily challenged. For example, if our measures of marital breakdown simply tap social class differences in marital style rather than breakdown then our conclusions about marital breakdown will be suspect.

Once the operational definition of the concept has been developed we come to the final stage of operationalization. This entails the precise way in which the indicators will be measured. This might involve developing questions for a questionnaire or identifying what and how observations will be made. Articulating the mechanics of these strategies is beyond the scope of this book.

Concepts for research design

Two concepts, internal and external validity, are fundamental to developing research designs. Ideally research designs should be both internally and externally valid.

Internal validity

We need to be confident that the research design can sustain the causal conclusions that we claim for it. The capacity of a research design to do this reflects its internal validity.

Imagine a research project that compares the emotional adjustment of children from divorced families and intact families. It finds that children from divorced families are less well adjusted than children from intact families. Can we conclude that divorce caused emotional maladjustment? Not on the basis of these results. The design does not enable us to eliminate alternative explanations. The poorer adjustment of children with divorced parents might be due to adjustment differences that predated parental divorce.

A different research study may deal with this problem by tracking children before parents divorce and for some years afterwards. It may find that these children do show a significant decline in emotional adjustment after their parents' divorce. Does the research design show that divorce is producing this decline in adjustment? No. The decline in adjustment may simply reflect a general decline in emotional adjustment as children get older. The same decline may be evident among children from intact families.

Yet another study might try to overcome this problem by tracking changes in adjustment of children before and after their parents divorce and changes among children from intact families as well. If children from intact families show less deterioration in adjustment than children from divorcing families, this must surely demonstrate the effect of divorce. No. We would need to be sure that the two groups of children were comparable in other relevant respects (e.g. age). The different rates of change in adjustment could be because those from divorcing families were younger on average. Maybe younger children show greater changes in adjustment over a particular period than older children. It may be age differences rather than having divorced parents that account for the adjustment changes of the two groups of children.

Internal validity is the extent to which the structure of a research design enables us to draw unambiguous conclusions from our results. The way in which the study is set up (e.g. tracking changes over time, making comparisons between comparable groups) can eliminate alternative explanations for our findings. The more the structure of a study eliminates these alternative interpretations, the stronger the internal validity of the study. A central task of research design is to structure the study so that the ambiguities in the above examples are minimized. It is impossible to eliminate all ambiguities in social research but we can certainly reduce them.

External validity

External validity refers to the extent to which results from a study can be generalized beyond the particular study. A study may have good internal validity but its value is limited if the findings only apply to the people in that particular investigation. The critical question is whether the results are likely to apply more widely. The most common threat to our capacity to generalize more widely from a research study is the use of unrepresentative samples. This, and other threats to external validity, will be discussed more fully in Chapters 5, 8, 11 and 14.

Measurement error

A further threat to the conclusions that can be drawn from any study is measurement error. This occurs when we use flawed indicators to tap concepts (see Chapter 1).

Types of measurement error

Indicators must meet two fundamental criteria. They must be both valid and reliable. A valid indicator in this context means that the indicator measures the concept we say it does. For example an IQ test is used to measure intelligence. If it really measures intelligence the test would be valid. If the IQ test measured something else instead, such as education level or cultural background, then it would be an invalid measure of intelligence.

Reliability means that the indicator *consistently* comes up with the same measurement. For example, if people consistently obtain the same IQ score on repeated IQ tests, then the test would be reliable. If their results fluctuate wildly depending on when they take the test, then it would be unreliable.

Validity The earlier discussion of internal validity related to the validity of the *research design*. It addressed the question: is the research design delivering the conclusions that we claim it delivers? In addition we need to examine the validity of the *measures* used in any piece of research.

The validity of a measure depends both on the use to which it is put and on the sample for which it is used. For example, the validity of using frequency of arguments between partners to measure marital happiness turns on what we mean by marital happiness. The validity of this measure may vary for different cultural groups and for the same cultural group in different historical periods. Measures of children's emotional adjustment will vary according to their age and their cultural group.

There are three basic ways of assessing validity. *Criterion validity* is best suited to situations where there are well-established measures of a concept that need adapting, shortening or updating. It involves comparing the way people rate on the new measure with how they rate on well-established measures of the concept. If ratings on the new measure match those of an established measure we can be confident of its validity.

Criterion validity has two limitations. First, it requires that the established benchmark is valid. If the benchmark is invalid then it is of little value in assessing the new measure. Second, there are no established measures for many social science concepts.

Sometimes criterion groups can be used to assess criterion validity. Instead of comparing a measure against an existing benchmark measure, the new measure can be trialled. For example, a new measure of marital happiness could be trialled on couples who seek marital counselling. We would expect that this group of couples would normally obtain low scores on a valid measure of marital happiness. If these couples actually obtain high scores on the marital happiness measure we would probably want to question whether the measure was really tapping marital happiness.

Content validity evaluates how well the measures tap the different aspects of the concept as we have defined it. A test of arithmetic skills that only tested subtraction skills would clearly not be a valid measure of arithmetic skills. Similarly a measure of marital happiness that only asked about the frequency of arguments between partners would probably lack content validity unless we had defined marital happiness simply as the absence of arguments. Measures of marital happiness could also include the nature of the arguments, leisure activities shared by partners, communication, methods of resolving conflict, the quality of the sexual relationship etc.

Given disagreement about the 'content' of many social science concepts it can be difficult to develop measures that have agreed validity. Even if we can agree on the concept and measure it using a whole battery of questions, we then face the problem of the *relative importance* of the various components of the measure. For example, should measures of the frequency of arguments be as important as the nature of the arguments, the method of conflict resolution, the style of communication or statements about level of subjective marital satisfaction?

Construct validity relies on seeing how well the results we obtain when using the measure fit with theoretical expectations. To validate a measure of marital happiness we might anticipate, on the basis of theory, that happiness will vary in predictable ways according to stage in the life cycle. If the results of a study provide confirmation, this could reflect the validity of our measure of marital happiness. However, this approach to assessing validity relies on the correctness of our expectations. If our theory is not supported this could be for one of two reasons: the measure of marital happiness could be wrong or the theory against which the measure is being benchmarked may be wrong.

There is no ideal way of assessing validity. If a measure passes all three tests it is more likely to be valid but we cannot be certain. In the final analysis we will need to *argue* for the validity of our measures.

Reliability A reliable measure is one that gives the same 'reading' when used on repeated occasions. For example, *assuming there was no actual change*, a reliable measure of marital happiness should yield the same 'reading' if it is used on different occasions. A thermometer that measured body temperature as 97.4 °F one minute and 105 °F the next would be useless. Which measurement is right? Does the change reflect real change or just measurement 'noise'?

Unreliability can stem from many sources. Poor question wording may cause a respondent to understand the question differently on different occasions. Different interviewers can elicit different answers from a person: the match of age, gender, class and ethnicity of an interviewer and interviewee can influence responses. Asking questions about which people have no opinion, have insufficient information or require too precise an answer can lead to unreliable data. The answers to some questions can be affected by mood and by the particular context in which they are asked.

Measures need to be both valid and reliable. Although these two concepts are related they are not the same. A measure can be reliable without being valid. That is, a measure can be consistently wrong. For example, people consistently underestimate their level of alcohol consumption in questionnaire surveys. Alcohol consumption measures are reliable but do not accurately tell us about the true level of alcohol consumed.

Measures will never be perfectly reliable and perfectly valid. These are not all or nothing concepts and the goal is to maximize the reliability and validity. If these aspects of measurement are weak then the results of the study that uses them might plausibly be attributed to poor measurement rather than telling us anything about social reality.

Forms of measurement error

Error can take different forms and the consequences of error will vary depending on its form. These forms of error are *random, constant* and *correlated*.

Random error is that which has no systematic form. It means that in some cases a measurement for a variable might be too low while in others it is too high. The measurement of someone's weight might display random error. Sometimes people underestimate their weight while others may overestimate it, but if these errors are random there will be the same number of over- and underestimates and the size of the overestimates will be the same on average as the underestimates. When the average (mean) is calculated for the whole group it will be accurate because the overestimates and the underestimates cancel each other out. Furthermore, these mis-estimates are not correlated with any other characteristic (e.g. gender, age) but are truly random. Because random error does not distort means and is uncorrelated with other factors, it is less serious than other forms of error.

Constant error occurs where there is the same error for every case. For example, if everyone underreported their weight by 5 kilograms we would have constant error. Such error is uncorrelated with other characteristics. Although purely constant error will be rare there will be variables for which there will typically be a component of constant error (e.g. overstatements of frequency of sexual intercourse and understatements about the amount of alcohol consumed). Because such error is constant it does not cancel out but has an effect on sample estimates. Thus the average weight of the sample would be an underestimate to the extent of the constant error.

Correlated error takes place when the amount and direction of error vary systematically according to other characteristics of respondents. For example, if women tend to overestimate their weight while men underestimate theirs then this error would be correlated with gender. If the format or language in a questionnaire is difficult then mistakes in answering questions may well be correlated with education. This would produce results that make it appear that people with different levels of education behave or think differently while in fact it is only their capacity to understand the question that differs.

A crucial goal of the design and administration of survey instruments is the minimization of the various forms of measurement error. Achieving this entails paying careful attention to question wording, indicator quality, interviewer and observer training, and to ways of identifying social desirability responses and other forms of deliberate misrepresentation by respondents. In many cases it is difficult to identify the extent to which such errors actually occur. However, this does not reduce the need to do all that one can to minimize their likelihood and to have built-in checks to identify some sources of error. Such checks include looking for inconsistencies in answers, using multiple questions rather than single questions to tap concepts, identifying social desirability response sets, making inter-interviewer checks and careful fieldwork supervision.

Summary

This chapter has emphasized the importance of clarifying research questions and concepts before developing a research design. Lack of clarity regarding the research question and the central research concepts will severely compromise any research design. Guidelines were provided to help focus both descriptive and explanatory research questions and to clarify the concepts they employ.

It is also unwise to develop a research design unless alternative ways of understanding the matter at the heart of the research question have been identified. Since one of the purposes of research design is to help identify which of a range of alternative explanations work best it is desirable that these alternative explanations be identified before the research design is developed. The design can then be structured in such a way that relevant data are collected to enable us to choose between these alternatives. Guidelines were provided to assist in identifying these alternative explanations.

Finally, three core concepts that are at the heart of good design were discussed. These were the concepts of internal validity, external validity and measurement error. Later chapters will evaluate the various designs using these concepts.

3

Causation and the Logic of Research Design

DAVID DeVAUS

Establishing causal relationships is at the heart of explanatory research design. However, it is not a simple matter to establish that one event causes another (Blalock, 1964; Hage and Meeker, 1988). The main reason why it is difficult to establish causal relationships is because we cannot actually *observe* one phenomenon producing change in another. Even though one event might always follow another we do not know that this is because one event causes the other. Causal relationships must therefore be inferred rather than observed. *The purpose of research design in explanatory research is to improve the quality of our causal inferences.*

Inferring causal relationships

Criteria for inferring cause

In Chapter 1 I distinguished between probabilistic and deterministic concepts of causation. Probabilistic approaches to causation are those that argue that a given factor increases (or decreases) the probability of a particular outcome. For example we may argue that there is a causal relationship between gender and working part time – that gender affects the probability of working part time.

In order to infer that a probabilistic causal relationship exists between two variables, two basic criteria must be met. First, there must be co-variation of causal and outcome variables (e.g. between gender and being a full time or part time worker); and second, the assertion that one variable affects the other must make sense.

Co-variation

If two factors are causally related they must *at least* be correlated: they must co-vary. If *X* causes *Y* then people who differ from one another on *X* should tend to differ from one another on *Y*. For example, if we were to argue that working in the private sector rather than the public sector makes people more achievement oriented at work we would, *at the very*

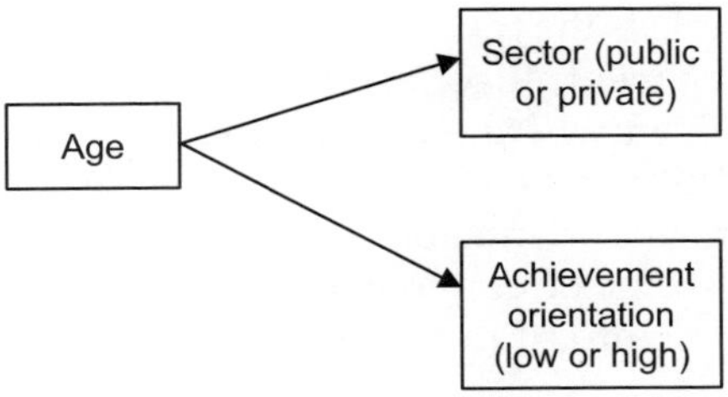

Figure 3.1 *A spurious relationship*

least, need to demonstrate that private sector workers had a higher achievement orientation than public sector workers. If two factors did not co-vary – that is public and private sector workers had identical levels of work achievement – then we would be hard pressed to argue that they are causally related.[1]

However, while co-variation is a precondition it is not enough for us to assert that the variables are causally related. Correlations can also reflect non-causal relationships. When two variables or events are correlated but not causally related the relationship between the two variables is said to be spurious (see Chapter 1). For example, the correlation between sector of employment and employment orientation might be due entirely to a third variable such as age (Figure 3.1). Younger people might be more likely than older people to work in the private sector and younger people might also have a higher achievement orientation than older people. These two patterns will mean that sector and achievement orientation are correlated (more young people in the private sector, so therefore the private sector is associated with achievement orientation). However the link between sector and achievement orientation is coincidental rather than causal.

It must make sense

Any assertion that co-variation reflects a causal relationship must be plausible. It must make sense at three levels.

Time order If two variables are correlated the cause must come *before* the effect. Causal reasoning has no time for the assertion that a future event can have a present effect (teleological explanation). Our causal proposition must be such that the causal variable occurs before the presumed effect. The time gap between cause and effect can be minutes or may be years (e.g. the effect of education on income can take many years to show itself).

Even though two variables might be causally related it can sometimes be difficult to work out which variable comes first and therefore to establish which variable is the cause and which is the effect. For example, does sector of employment affect achievement orientation or is it the other way around? Even where we assert that one variable comes first the causal relationship may be two-way. That is, sector of employment may affect achievement orientation which in turn influences future decisions about the sector of employment in which one works. Causal relationships can be reciprocal (two-way) rather than one-way.

Dependent variable must be capable of change If we say that a correlation between two variables is because one is causing the other, we must make sure that the dependent variable (the effect) is *capable* of being changed. If it cannot be changed then a causal account of the relationship makes no sense. For example, any causal relationship between sex and income could only be in the direction of sex affecting income. The opposite proposition (income→sex) makes no sense.

Theoretical plausibility The causal assertion must make sense. We should be able to tell a story of how *X* affects *Y* if we wish to infer a causal relationship between *X* and *Y*. Even if we cannot empirically demonstrate *how X* affects *Y* we need to provide a plausible account of the connection (plausible in terms of other research, current theory etc.). For example, to support the assertion that sector of employment affects achievement orientation we might argue that the private sector fosters the development of an achievement orientation by strategies such as paying performance bonuses, developing a culture of higher expectations, providing better resources and creating less job security. When backed up by this type of reasoning, any correlation between employment sector and achievement orientation can be plausibly interpreted in causal terms.

Types of causal patterns

Direct and indirect causal relationships

Causal relationships can be either *direct* or *indirect*. A direct relationship is one where we assert that the cause affects the outcome directly rather than via other variables. An indirect causal relationship is one where the cause has its effect by operating via its influence on another variable that, in turn, produces the effect. The variable through which the two variables are related is called the *intervening* variable: it comes in time and in a causal sequence between the initial cause and the effect. For example, we might argue that the way the private sector produces higher achievement orientation is by making employees fear for their jobs (the intervening variable) (Figure 3.2).

Indirect causal relationships may be simple (as in Figure 3.2) or consist of an extended causal chain or a number of different causal paths (Figure 3.3).

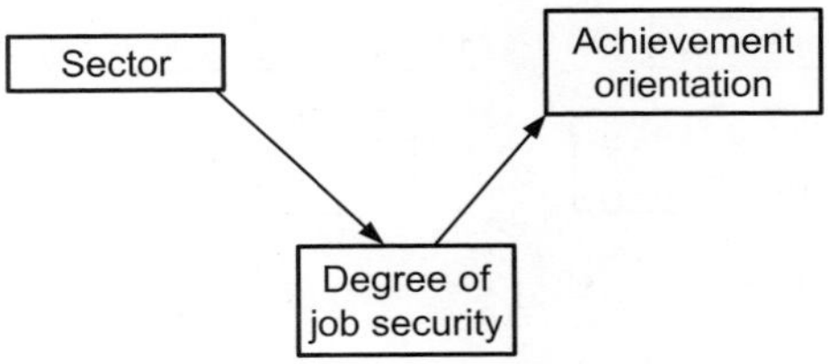

Figure 3.2 *An indirect causal relationship*

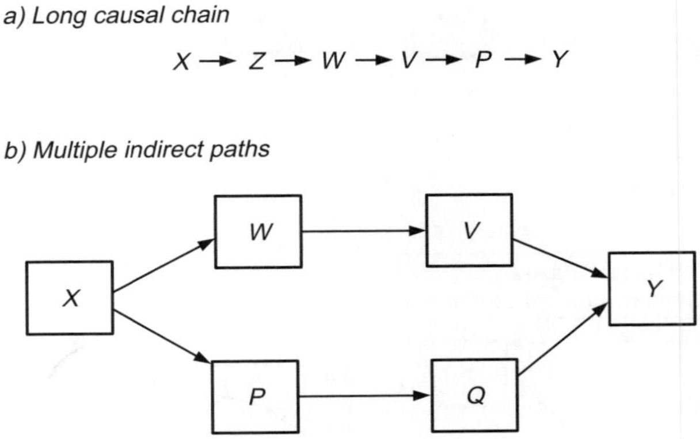

Figure 3.3 *More complex indirect causal relationships*

Types of relationships in a three-variable model

Any relationship between two variables will consist of two components – a causal component and a non-causal (spurious) component. The causal component can consist of a direct component, an indirect component or both.

It follows then that any relationship between two variables can be interpreted as:

- a direct causal relationship
- an indirect causal relationship
- a spurious relationship
- any combination of these.

Figure 3.4 illustrates the possibilities where we have three variables which, for the purpose of the example, I will call *X*, *Y* and *Z*. The relationship between *X* and *Y* could be any of the following:

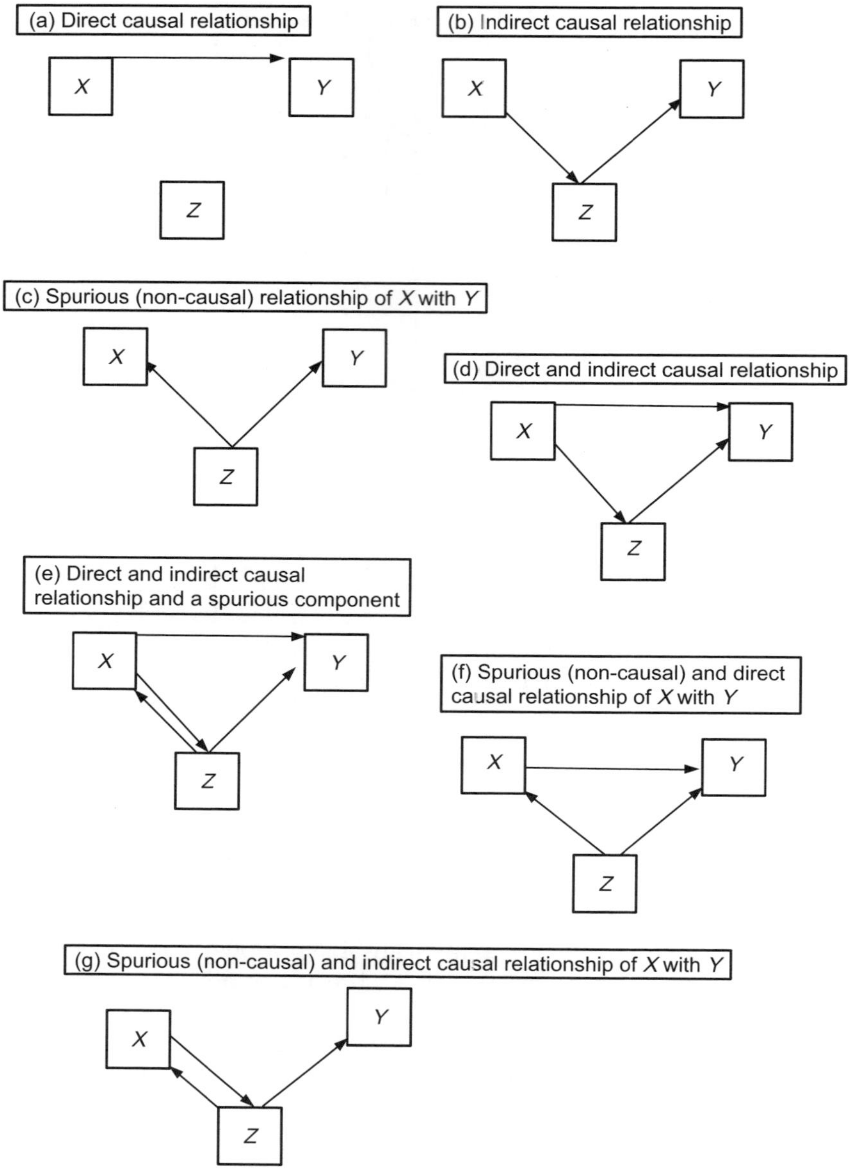

Figure 3.4 *Types of relationships between three variables*

(a) *Direct causal* Y follows X in time, Y is capable of being changed, and it is plausible that X could produce changes in Y. In the absence of finding any other variable that is responsible for this relationship we may continue to argue that the observed correlation is direct and is causal (Figure 3.4a).

(b) *Indirect causal* Y follows X in time, Y is capable of being changed, and it is plausible that X could produce changes in Y. However, in this case we are spelling out the mechanism by which X affects Y. We may think of Z as a single mechanism or a whole lot of intervening variables (Figure 3.4b).

(c) *Spurious* X and Y are not causally related to one another. Even though Y might follow X in time and be capable of being changed, both X and Y are joint effects of some third variable Z. X and Y co-vary purely because Z has a simultaneous effect on both X and Y (Figure 3.4c).

(d) *Both direct and indirect* The effect of X may be partly via its effect on an intervening variable and partly direct (Figure 3.4d).

(e) *Direct and indirect causal and spurious* The relationship between X and Y could consist of three components: a direct causal part ($X \rightarrow Y$), an indirect causal part ($X \rightarrow Z \rightarrow Y$) and a spurious part ($X \leftarrow Z \rightarrow Y$) (Figure 3.4e).

(f) *Direct causal relationship combined with a spurious component* (Figure 3.4f).

(g) *Indirect causal relationship combined with a spurious component* (Figure 3.4g).

This set of possibilities results from situations in which we have only three variables. The more variables we take into account, the more complex matters become.

When we collect and analyse data it can be helpful to draw diagrams to spell out the ways in which we propose variables are interrelated. We need to specify:

1 whether relationships are presumed to be causal or spurious
2 whether causal relationships are expected to be direct or indirect
3 the mechanisms (intervening variables) underlying any indirect causal relationships.

Resolving these matters allows us to articulate our research question and the most plausible line of explanation.

Providing a frame of reference

The logic of making comparisons is fundamental to testing causal models. Consequently a central element in designing an explanatory

Proposition Divorce leads to emotional problems in young children. [divorce → emotional problems of children] *Observation* We find that many children with divorced parents have emotional problems.
Proposition Private schools produce high academic performance among their students. [private schools → high performance] *Observation* There are many instances of students from private schools achieving highly.
Proposition Youth unemployment is responsible for youth suicide. [unemployment → high suicide rate] *Observation* 50% of young people who commit suicide are unemployed.

Figure 3.5 *Propositions and observations without a comparative frame of reference*

research study is providing a comparative frame of reference. Different research designs go about the task of providing comparisons in different ways.

Comparing groups

By making comparisons we provide a frame of reference within which to try to make sense of particular findings. The importance of this can be seen in the illustrations in Figure 3.5. In these examples the observation in each case hardly provides convincing support of the proposition. One reason for this is that there is no frame of reference within which to make sense of the observations. There are no groups with which to compare and contrast the observations. It is only by making *comparisons* that our observations take on much meaning and we are able to eliminate alternative explanations.

The proposition that *divorce leads to emotional problems in young children* would encourage us to expect to find emotional problems among children whose parents are divorced. But finding such evidence will not get us very far. To go further down the path of explanation we must make comparisons. Are emotional problems greater than, the same as or less than those among children from intact families? Do the observations among children of divorced parents simply reflect that which we would find among *any* group of children?

Proposition Divorce leads to emotional problems in young children. *Restated proposition* Children whose parents have divorced are more likely to display emotional problems *than are children whose parents have not divorced.* [parental marital status → level of emotional problems]
Proposition Private schools produce high academic performance among their students. *Restated proposition* Private schools will have higher levels of academic performance among their students *than will government schools.* [school type → level of academic performance]
Proposition Youth unemployment is responsible for youth suicide. *Restated proposition* Unemployed youth are more likely to commit suicide *than employed youth.* [employment status → suicide rate]

Figure 3.6 *Using propositions with an explicit comparative frame of reference*

It will be recalled that when we say that two variables are related it means that *variation* or difference on one variable is linked to differences on the other variable. In this instance we have two variables: (1) parents' marital status (married versus divorced) and (2) child's emotional adjustment (low versus high). If our research design included only divorced parents we could say nothing about the impact of divorce on children. Even if 100 per cent of the children from divorced parents had a low level of emotional adjustment we could draw no conclusions about the impact of parental divorce on children's emotional adjustment. We would need to compare the adjustment of the children with divorced parents with the adjustment of children from intact families. The *difference* in adjustment levels in the two groups will provide strong evidence regarding the alleged effect of divorce on children's emotional adjustment.

The propositions in Figure 3.5 only mention one particular group (children of divorced parents; private school students; suicidal youth). It can be helpful to restate the propositions to highlight the implicit comparisons. Figure 3.6 restates these propositions using explicit comparisons.

Multiple comparison groups

The independent variables above (parents' marital status, school type, youth employment status) have all been treated as two-category variables (dichotomies). However, we are not restricted to comparisons of just two groups. Multiple comparison groups are possible and will arise from at least two circumstances.

Independent variables with more than two categories Where independent variables have more than two categories we can compare more groups and provide stronger and subtler tests of theories. For example, in examining the effect of divorce on children we could simply classify marriages into divorced or intact, or we could classify them as single (never married), intact, separated, widowed, divorced (repartnered) and divorced (not repartnered). If we took the latter approach we could make multiple comparisons. In doing so we can get a clearer picture of what is going on. If we find that it is the children of divorced parents who have repartnered who have the most problems we achieve a more focused understanding of the impact of parental marital status on children. We have learned that it is not divorce *per se* but the arrangements that follow divorce that are critical. Had we simply compared divorced and intact marriages we might never have identified this.

Combined effects of different independent variables It is possible that it is only when people have a particular *combination* of characteristics that an effect is produced. For example, it may be the *joint* effects of gender and age rather than each independently that is linked to suicide. We may hypothesize that when a person is both male and young, the likelihood of suicide is at its highest. If, for the purpose of this example, we think of age as a dichotomous variable (15–35 = young; 35+ = old), then we can think in terms of four groups based on the combination of these two independent variables. These are illustrated in Figure 3.7.

Comparing time points

A finding that children from divorced families are less well adjusted emotionally than those from intact families *presumes* that divorce is responsible for this difference. The problem with a simple comparison between groups (divorced and intact) is that it does not tell us whether divorce has actually produced any *change* in the emotional adjustment of children. Any conclusions would be much more convincing if we could track the emotional adjustment of children both before and after divorce to see if there was any change in the emotional adjustment of children following divorce.

By tracking children over time we could see if there was a change in emotional adjustment of the children and evaluate whether this was attributable to their parents' divorce.

MULTIPLE PRE-TESTS AND POST-TESTS

In the above example the measurement of emotional adjustment at the beginning of the study is often referred to as the 'pre-test' and the

	Male	Female
Young	Group 1: young males	Group 2: young females
Old	Group 3: old males	Group 4: old females

Figure 3.7 *Multiple comparison groups created by combining two independent variables*

remeasurement at the end is called the 'post-test'. Between the pre-test and the post-test certain critical events occur – in this case parental divorce (or non-divorce as the case may be). These events serve as the independent variables in the study – i.e. the presumed causal variable behind the observed change. In some designs these intervening events are called the intervention or the treatment (see Chapter 4).

We can collect data about more than two time points rather than being restricted to simple 'before' and 'after' data collections. We might have repeated measurements over an extended period to track 'ups' and 'downs' and to track *trends* before and after any critical event. Multiple 'pre-tests' and multiple post-tests can help distinguish between short term and long term trends. They also help identify the effect of the 'intervention' or independent variable. For example, a simple measure of emotional adjustment before and after divorce might show a decline in adjustment. But what if there was strong evidence of the decline having commenced well before the divorce? Only multiple measures before divorce would show that a trend had already begun. Similarly, a simple post-test might show that adjustment is lower after divorce but multiple post-tests might show poor adjustment immediately after divorce but a steady improvement over time (see Chapter 6).

Making meaningful comparisons

Ideally the groups we are comparing should be the same in all relevant respects except in regard to the independent variable. For example, if we want to test the idea that non-government schools produce students that achieve better academically than government schools we would need to be confident that both types of schools contained comparable students. We would need this so that we could be confident that the only relevant difference between the two sets of students is in the type of school attended. If the students differed in additional ways, how would we know which of the differences was responsible for any differences in academic achievement?

Comparisons of children from divorced and intact families are complicated by the fact that typically children of divorced parents are older than children from intact families. Any differences between the level of emotional adjustment of the two sets of children could be due to age differences rather than the marital status of their parents.

The same problem can arise when looking at the same group or category of people over time. Ideally with comparisons over time the only differences between the pre-test and the post-test should be the event we are proposing as the cause of any change. However, many events can occur which can account for the change and these may confuse our comparisons and our attribution of what lies behind the change in the outcome variable (see Chapter 4 for further discussion).

Since comparisons are central to good research design we must ensure that they are meaningful. The more we can remove unintended and unknown differences between groups, the more we reduce the risk of mistaking spurious relationships for causal relationships – that is, the more we eliminate alternative plausible explanations.

There are four main strategies for maximizing the comparability of groups.

Matching

When recruiting the groups we can deliberately match them on relevant characteristics. Thus when comparing students attending government schools on the one hand and fee paying private schools on the other hand we should ensure that the two sets of students are similar in terms of intelligence, aspirations, parental resources, education values, family history, gender and age. By comparing like with like we should be able to isolate the effect of the type of school on academic achievement.

The problem in comparing like with like is to establish the identity of all the variables on which we need to match the groups. We can match for the characteristics that we know might contaminate our results but there may be other factors that we have not thought of.

Ex post facto matching Ideally groups should be matched at the beginning of the study before critical events (e.g. divorce, attending the school). Another approach referred to by Spector (1981: 48) as a 'patchwork procedure' involves creating matched groups from a whole pool of study participants *after* all the data have been collected. For example, we might have a large number of students from government and fee paying private schools. From this pool we could extract a group of government school students and a group of fee paying private school students who are comparable in terms of intelligence, aspirations, parental resources, values about the importance of education, family history, gender, and age. We could then compare these groups and see if there were differences in their level of academic achievement.

There are many problems with this approach. The obvious one is that we must have the relevant information on which to match. Since this will always be limited, the groups are likely to remain unmatched on important but unknown factors. Another problem is that many cases from both groups simply will not have matches from the other group and will have to be discarded. If we match on more than a small number of factors we will often end up with only a very small number of people in the study since the number of cases from both groups that match can be quite small.[2]

Randomization

A simpler and more effective way of making groups comparable is to randomly allocate people to different groups at the beginning of a study. By randomly assigning individuals to each group any differences between groups should be random rather than systematic. So long as groups are large enough, random assignment should automatically produce groups with comparable profiles on both known and unknown factors. From a statistical perspective, random assignment of people to groups will make the groups identical for all intents and purposes and provides what Davis calls 'The all purpose spuriosity insurance of randomization' (1985: 35). We control for an infinite number of plausible rival hypotheses *without specifying what any of them are* (Campbell, 1989).

This is the approach taken in drug trials. Individuals are randomly assigned to one of several groups and each group is then given a different drug. Since the groups should have virtually identical profiles to begin with, any differences in outcomes between the groups should be due to the different treatments administered to each group. However, this approach is often not applicable in social research because practical and ethical considerations preclude us assigning people to groups and then doing something to one group to see what effect it has (see Chapter 5). Advantages and drawbacks of this approach to social research are discussed in Chapters 4 and 5.

Matched block designs

While randomization minimizes the chances of initial differences between groups there is still the chance that there will be differences between the groups – especially in smaller groups. Where we want to be certain that the groups are comparable on a particular characteristic we can take an additional step to guarantee that the groups are comparable at least on specific variables. This is achieved with what is called the randomized block design – a combination of both randomization and matching.

Suppose we wanted to evaluate the effect on academic performance of three methods of delivering university courses: (1) face-to-face delivery of lectures and tutorials, (2) correspondence using written materials and (3) electronically using the internet and e-mail. Further, suppose that we could assign individuals to one of these three modes. Random allocation would be the obvious way. But suppose we want to be absolutely certain that the students in each of the three modes are of comparable academic ability.

To achieve this we would do the following:

1 Obtain a measure of academic ability at the pre-test.
2 Rank all the students from highest to lowest ability.
3 Select the three students with the highest ability (because we have three learning modes). This group of three students is block 1.
4 Randomly allocate each of the three students to a group (one to face-to-face; one to written correspondence; and one to electronic learning).
5 Select the next three most able students (block 2) and repeat the random allocation to groups.
6 Repeat this until all students have been allocated to one of the three groups.

Statistical controls

An alternative way of making groups comparable is to do so at the data analysis stage after data have been collected. It involves multivariate analysis that, in one respect, matches groups on specified variables (see Chapter 12 for a discussion of the logic of some of these techniques).

Although the procedures of multivariate analysis can be very complex, the essential logic is simple. Suppose we want to compare the emotional adjustment of children from divorced and intact families but we believe that any comparison would be confounded by the fact that, on average, children whose parents divorce are older than those from intact families. Any greater maladjustment among children whose parents have divorced could occur because they are older, as older children display greater maladjustment.

Multivariate analysis removes any effects that might be due to age by comparing like with like – by selecting, say, preschoolers and comparing those from divorced and intact families to see if, despite similarity of age, the children show different levels of adjustment. The same comparisons could be repeated among say 5–8 year olds, 9–12 year olds, 13–15 year olds and so on.

The obvious shortcomings of this approach are similar to that of matching. We can remove the influence of variables that we have thought of and on which we have data but we cannot remove the effects of unknown variables, or those for which we have no data. Since we can never know what factors we have missed there is always the danger that factors we have not thought of may be contributing to group differences.

Interventions and independent variables

Throughout this chapter I have used the terms 'intervention', 'treatment', 'independent variable' and 'groups' more or less interchangeably. Research designs vary in terms of the type of independent variable employed and in the number of independent variables built into the study.

TYPES OF INDEPENDENT VARIABLES

When thinking in causal terms ($X \rightarrow Y$) X is the independent variable. When we conduct the research and do the analysis we compare the outcomes (Y) for different groups. The groups are defined according to which category of the independent variable they belong to. In some studies the investigator introducing an *active intervention* defines the independent variable (e.g. allocate different people to one of three modes of course delivery – face-to-face, correspondence or electronic). In other situations the independent variable is defined by a *naturally occurring 'intervention'* (e.g. a person retires or remains employed). In other situations the independent variable is determined by the relatively *fixed attributes* of participants (e.g. sex, education, race etc.) rather than by interventions of any sort.

NUMBER OF INTERVENTIONS

Research designs can also differ in terms of the number of interventions that are made. Where the independent variable involves either an active or a passive intervention we can examine the effect of single versus repeated interventions. We can see whether a single intervention has a different impact than the cumulative impact of repeated interventions. For example, we might be evaluating the impact of teachers giving students negative feedback on their work. Initial criticism of the work may boost a student's effort and performance but repeated negative feedback may lower performance as the student loses confidence. A multiple intervention design helps refine our understanding of the way in which interventions affect participants and enables us to rule out alternative ways of interpreting results.

Dimensions of a research design

The above discussion has identified six core elements of a research design. The particular mix of the elements in any study will yield different designs.

These six main elements in producing a research design are:

1 *The number of groups in the design* Designs will vary from those with no comparisons (e.g. single case design of case study) to those with many different comparison groups.
2 *The number of 'pre-test' measurement phases* Designs vary from those with no 'pre-test' (e.g. cross-sectional designs and some experimental designs) to those with a series of 'pre-tests' which establish pre-existing trends before an event.
3 *The number of 'post-test' measurement phases* All designs require at least one 'post-test' – the measurement of an outcome variable. In some designs (e.g. cross-sectional) there will be one 'post-test', while other designs can have many post-tests to help distinguish between short and long term outcomes.
4 *The method of allocation of cases to groups* In multiple group designs groups can be made comparable by allocating people to different groups by random allocation, 'pre-test' matching, *post hoc* matching or block matching or by using statistical controls in the analysis phase.
5 *The nature of the intervention* Studies that rely on existing variation (cross-sectional designs and those with 'fixed' independent variables) have no interventions. Other designs rely on interventions between a pre-test and a post-test. These 'interventions' may be either active or natural.[3]
6 *The number of interventions* Designs with an intervention can have either a single intervention or multiple interventions. Multiple interventions can be used to identify the effect of cumulative 'treatments'.

A range of research designs

The combination of the possibilities created by these six elements of a research design yields a large number of possible designs. A useful summary discussion of many of these designs is provided by Spector (1981). To impose some order on this range of possibilities it is helpful to think in terms of four broad types of design. For each design type, decisions taken by the investigator will produce variations within the type. These four types provide the structure for the rest of the book. The four broad types of design are experimental, longitudinal, cross-sectional and case study. I will examine each of these in turn.

Experimental design

The classic version of the experimental design has the following elements:

1 One pre-intervention (pre-test) measure on the outcome variable.
2 Two groups: one group that is exposed to the intervention (the experimental group) and one group that is not exposed to the intervention (the control group).

Method of allocation to groups	Pre-test	Intervention (X)	Post-test
Random (experimental group)	Measure on outcome variable (Y)	'Treatment'	Measure on outcome variable (Y)
Random (control group)	Measure on outcome variable (Y)	No 'treatment'	Measure on outcome variable (Y)

Figure 3.8 *Classic experimental design*

3 Random allocation to the groups before the pre-test.
4 One intervention (test/treatment).
5 One post-intervention (post-test) measure on the outcome variable.

This design is illustrated in Figure 3.8.

The analysis of any effect of the intervention focuses on changes in the experimental group before and after the intervention and a comparison with the rate of change in the control group. If the change is greater in the experimental group than in the control group the researcher will attribute this to the impact of the independent variable (the treatment).

Longitudinal design

The basic form of this design involves:

1 One group.
2 One pre-'intervention' measurement on the outcome variable.
3 One 'intervention' where everyone receives the 'treatment'.
4 One post-'intervention' measurement on the outcome variable.

In effect, this design is similar to the experimental design except that there is no control group and typically only one 'experimental' group. The design is illustrated in Figure 3.9.

The analysis in this design compares the pre-intervention measures with the post-intervention measures. Change in these scores can reflect the influence of X on Y. However, the absence of a randomized control

Method of allocation to groups	Pre-test	Intervention (X)	Post-test
Random (one group)	Measure on outcome variable (Y)	'Treatment'	Measure on outcome variable (Y)

Figure 3.9 *Simple longitudinal design*

group makes it difficult to know whether the intervention or some other factor produces any change.

Cross-sectional design

The basic elements of the cross-sectional design are as follows:

1 Instead of interventions the cross-sectional design relies on existing variations in the independent variable(s) in the sample.
2 At least one independent variable with at least two categories is present.
3 Data are collected at one point of time.
4 There is no random allocation to 'groups'.

This design mirrors the post-intervention phase of the classic experimental design but without any random allocation to 'groups' being made. The data for this design are collected at one point of time and are analysed by examining the extent to which variation in the outcome variable is linked with group differences. That is, to what extent do those in different categories of the independent variable differ in relation to the outcome variable? Causal relationships are established by utilizing statistical controls rather than by random allocation of people to groups.

This design is illustrated in Figure 3.10. In this case the 'intervention' is simply being in a different category of the independent variable.

Case studies

Case study designs rely less on comparing cases than on exhaustive analysis of individual cases and then on comparing cases. A distinguishing characteristic of case studies is that contextual information is collected about a case so that we have a context within which to understand causal processes.

Method of allocation to groups	Pre-test	Intervention (X)	Post-test
Non-random	None	'Treatment'	Measure on outcome variable (Y)
Non-random	None	No 'treatment'	Measure on outcome variable (Y)

Figure 3.10 *Simple cross-sectional design*

Case study designs might consist of a single case study (e.g. a community study, a study of an organization) or a series of case studies with perhaps each case testing a theory from a different angle. It is useful to think of a case study in a similar way to an experiment. We do not finally reject or accept a theory on the basis of a single experiment; we try to replicate an experiment and conduct it under a variety of conditions. Similarly, a case study project that entails a single case study is analogous to a single experiment. If similar results are found in repeated case studies, or predictable differences in results are found for particular cases in the study, then we develop greater confidence in the findings of the cases in the same way that we gain confidence in experimental results that are found in repeated experiments.

Summary

This chapter has examined ways of structuring research designs to help draw convincing causal inferences from the research. Since causes cannot be observed they must be inferred from observations. However, incorrect inferences can easily be made. The chapter has considered ways of structuring research to improve the quality of these inferences. A range of ways of interpreting correlations between variables was outlined and criteria required for inferring that a correlation reflects a causal connection were provided.

The chapter emphasized the importance of making meaningful comparisons between groups as a core element of drawing causal inferences.

One of the tasks of research design is to structure the research so that meaningful comparisons of outcomes between groups can be made.

Finally, the chapter outlined six core elements of research designs: number of groups, number of pre-tests, number of post-tests, nature of allocation to groups, type of interventions and number of interventions. Research designs vary in the way these elements are dealt with. Four main types of research design – experimental, longitudinal, cross-sectional and case study – were then briefly described. These broad categories of design provide the framework for the remainder of this book.

Notes

1 There can be exceptions to this where a suppressor variable may be operating to mask a causal relationship. See Rosenberg (1968: Chapter 4).

2 We shall see later that this problem of loss of cases can be overcome with certain forms of multivariate analysis.

3 A naturally occurring intervention is an event that takes place between pre-test and post-test without the investigator initiating any intervention. An example might be a study of families over time in which some families experience parental divorce. Divorce is the 'natural intervention'.

4 The Selection of a Research Design

JOHN W. CRESWELL

Research designs are plans and the procedures for research that span the decisions from broad assumptions to detailed methods of data collection and analysis. This plan involves several decisions, and they need not be taken in the order in which they make sense to me and the order of their presentation here. The overall decision involves which design should be used to study a topic. Informing this decision should be the worldview assumptions the researcher brings to the study; procedures of inquiry (called strategies); and specific methods of data collection, analysis, and interpretation. The selection of a research design is also based on the nature of the research problem or issue being addressed, the researchers' personal experiences, and the audiences for the study.

THE THREE TYPES OF DESIGNS

In this book, three types of designs are advanced: qualitative, quantitative, and mixed methods. Unquestionably, the three approaches are not as discrete as they first appear. Qualitative and quantitative approaches should not be viewed as polar opposites or dichotomies; instead, they represent different ends on a continuum (Newman & Benz, 1998). A study *tends* to be more qualitative than quantitative or vice versa. Mixed methods research resides in the middle of this continuum because it incorporates elements of both qualitative and quantitative approaches.

Often the distinction between qualitative and quantitative research is framed in terms of using words (qualitative) rather than numbers (quantitative), or using closed-ended questions (quantitative hypotheses) rather than open-ended questions (qualitative interview questions). A more complete way to view the gradations of differences between them is in the basic philosophical assumptions researchers bring to the study, the types of research strategies used overall in the research (e.g., quantitative experiments or qualitative case studies), and the specific methods employed in conducting these strategies (e.g., collecting data quantitatively on instruments versus collecting qualitative data through observing a setting). Moreover, there is a historical evolution to both approaches, with the quantitative approaches dominating the forms of research in the social sciences from the late 19th century up until the mid-20th century. During the latter half of the 20th century, interest in qualitative research increased and along with it, the development of mixed methods research (see Creswell, 2008, for more of this history). With this background, it should prove helpful to view definitions of these three key terms as used in this book:

- **Qualitative research** is a means for exploring and understanding the meaning individuals or groups ascribe to a social or human problem. The process of research involves emerging questions and procedures, data typically collected in the participant's setting, data analysis inductively building from particulars to general themes, and the researcher making interpretations of the meaning of the data. The final written report has a flexible structure. Those who engage in this form of inquiry support a way of looking at research that honors an inductive style, a focus on individual meaning, and the importance of rendering the complexity of a situation (adapted from Creswell, 2007).

- **Quantitative research** is a means for testing objective theories by examining the relationship among variables. These variables, in turn, can be measured, typically on instruments, so that numbered data can be analyzed using statistical procedures. The final written report has a set structure consisting of introduction, literature and theory, methods, results, and discussion (Creswell, 2008). Like qualitative researchers, those who engage in this form of inquiry have assumptions about testing theories deductively, building in protections against bias, controlling for alternative explanations, and being able to generalize and replicate the findings.

- **Mixed methods research** is an approach to inquiry that combines or associates both qualitative and quantitative forms. It involves philosophical assumptions, the use of qualitative and quantitative approaches, and the mixing of both approaches in a study. Thus, it is more than simply collecting and analyzing both kinds of data; it also involves the use of both approaches in tandem so that the overall strength of a study is greater than either qualitative or quantitative research (Creswell & Plano Clark, 2007).

These definitions have considerable information in each one of them. Throughout this book, I discuss the parts of the definitions so that their meanings become clear to you.

THREE COMPONENTS INVOLVED IN A DESIGN

Two important components in each definition are that the approach to research involves philosophical assumptions as well as distinct methods or procedures. **Research design**, which I refer to as the *plan or proposal to conduct research*, involves the intersection of philosophy, strategies of inquiry, and specific methods. A framework that I use to explain the interaction of these three components is seen in Figure 1.1. To reiterate, in planning a study, researchers need to think through the philosophical worldview assumptions that they bring to the study, the strategy of inquiry that is related to this worldview, and the specific methods or procedures of research that translate the approach into practice.

Philosophical Worldviews

Although philosophical ideas remain largely hidden in research (Slife & Williams, 1995), they still influence the practice of research and need to be identified. I suggest that individuals preparing a research proposal or plan make explicit the larger philosophical ideas they espouse. This information will help explain why they chose qualitative, quantitative, or mixed methods

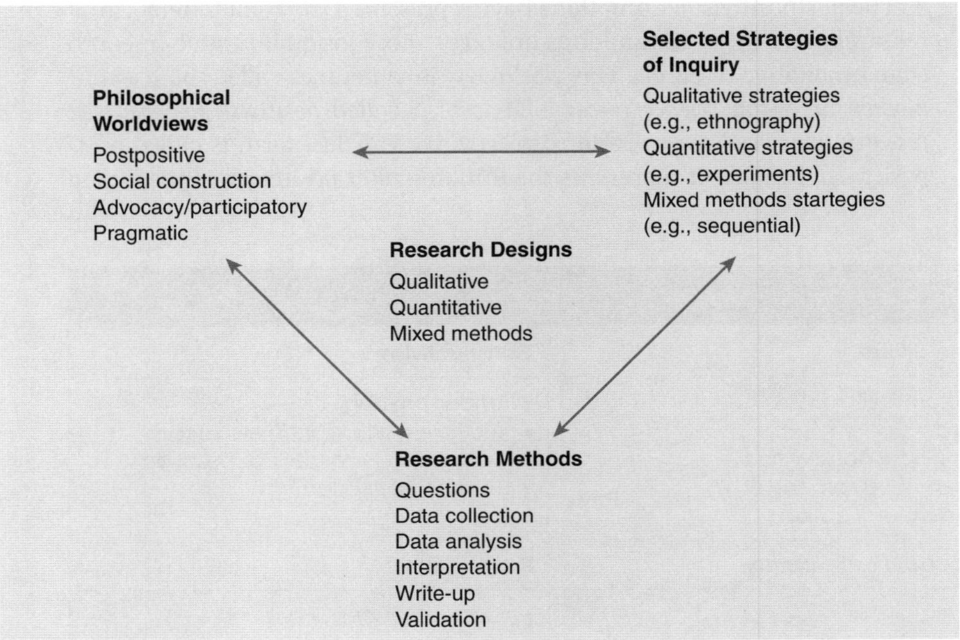

Figure 1.1 A Framework for Design—The Interconnection of Worldviews, Strategies of Inquiry, and Research Methods

approaches for their research. In writing about worldviews, a proposal might include a section that addresses the following:

- The philosophical worldview proposed in the study
- A definition of basic considerations of that worldview
- How the worldview shaped their approach to research

I have chosen to use the term **worldview** as meaning "a basic set of beliefs that guide action" (Guba, 1990, p. 17). Others have called them *paradigms* (Lincoln & Guba, 2000; Mertens, 1998); *epistemologies* and *ontologies* (Crotty, 1998), or *broadly conceived research methodologies* (Neuman, 2000). I see worldviews as a general orientation about the world and the nature of research that a researcher holds. These worldviews are shaped by the discipline area of the student, the beliefs of advisers and faculty in a student's area, and past research experiences. The types of beliefs held by individual researchers will often lead to embracing a qualitative, quantitative, or mixed methods approach in their research. Four different worldviews are discussed: postpositivism, constructivism, advocacy/participatory, and pragmatism. The major elements of each position are presented in Table 1.1.

The Postpositivist Worldview

The postpositivist assumptions have represented the traditional form of research, and these assumptions hold true more for quantitative research than qualitative research. This worldview is sometimes called the *scientific method* or doing *science research*. It is also called *positivist/postpositivist research, empirical science,* and *postpostivism*. This last term is called postpositivism because it represents the thinking after positivism, challenging

Table 1.1 Four Worldviews

Postpositivism	**Constructivism**
• Determination • Reductionism • Empirical observation and measurement • Theory verification	• Understanding • Multiple participant meanings • Social and historical construction • Theory generation
Advocacy/Participatory	**Pragmatism**
• Political • Empowerment Issue-oriented • Collaborative • Change-oriented	• Consequences of actions • Problem-centered • Pluralistic • Real-world practice oriented

the traditional notion of the absolute truth of knowledge (Phillips & Burbules, 2000) and recognizing that we cannot be "positive" about our claims of knowledge when studying the behavior and actions of humans. The postpositivist tradition comes from 19th-century writers, such as Comte, Mill, Durkheim, Newton, and Locke (Smith, 1983), and it has been most recently articulated by writers such as Phillips and Burbules (2000).

Postpositivists hold a deterministic philosophy in which causes probably determine effects or outcomes. Thus, the problems studied by postpositivists reflect the need to identify and assess the causes that influence outcomes, such as found in experiments. It is also reductionistic in that the intent is to reduce the ideas into a small, discrete set of ideas to test, such as the variables that comprise hypotheses and research questions. The knowledge that develops through a postpositivist lens is based on careful observation and measurement of the objective reality that exists "out there" in the world. Thus, developing numeric measures of observations and studying the behavior of individuals becomes paramount for a postpositivist. Finally, there are laws or theories that govern the world, and these need to be tested or verified and refined so that we can understand the world. Thus, in the scientific method, the accepted approach to research by postpostivists, an individual begins with a theory, collects data that either supports or refutes the theory, and then makes necessary revisions before additional tests are made.

In reading Phillips and Burbules (2000), you can gain a sense of the key assumptions of this position, such as,

1. Knowledge is conjectural (and antifoundational)—absolute truth can never be found. Thus, evidence established in research is always imperfect and fallible. It is for this reason that researchers state that they do not prove a hypothesis; instead, they indicate a failure to reject the hypothesis.

2. Research is the process of making claims and then refining or abandoning some of them for other claims more strongly warranted. Most quantitative research, for example, starts with the test of a theory.

3. Data, evidence, and rational considerations shape knowledge. In practice, the researcher collects information on instruments based on measures completed by the participants or by observations recorded by the researcher.

4. Research seeks to develop relevant, true statements, ones that can serve to explain the situation of concern or that describe the causal relationships of interest. In quantitative studies, researchers advance the relationship among variables and pose this in terms of questions or hypotheses.

5. Being objective is an essential aspect of competent inquiry; researchers must examine methods and conclusions for bias. For example, standard of validity and reliability are important in quantitative research.

The Social Constructivist Worldview

Others hold a different worldview. Social constructivism (often combined with interpretivism; see Mertens, 1998) is such a perspective, and it is typically seen as an approach to qualitative research. The ideas came from Mannheim and from works such as Berger and Luekmann's (1967) *The Social Construction of Reality* and Lincoln and Guba's (1985) *Naturalistic Inquiry*. More recent writers who have summarized this position are Lincoln and Guba (2000), Schwandt (2007), Neuman (2000), and Crotty (1998), among others. **Social constructivists** hold assumptions that individuals seek understanding of the world in which they live and work. Individuals develop subjective meanings of their experiences—meanings directed toward certain objects or things. These meanings are varied and multiple, leading the researcher to look for the complexity of views rather than narrowing meanings into a few categories or ideas. The goal of the research is to rely as much as possible on the participants' views of the situation being studied. The questions become broad and general so that the participants can construct the meaning of a situation, typically forged in discussions or interactions with other persons. The more open-ended the questioning, the better, as the researcher listens carefully to what people say or do in their life settings. Often these subjective meanings are negotiated socially and historically. They are not simply imprinted on individuals but are formed through interaction with others (hence social constructivism) and through historical and cultural norms that operate in individuals' lives. Thus, constructivist researchers often address the processes of interaction among individuals. They also focus on the specific contexts in which people live and work, in order to understand the historical and cultural settings of the participants. Researchers recognize that their own backgrounds shape their interpretation, and they position themselves in the research to acknowledge how their interpretation flows from their personal, cultural, and historical experiences. The researcher's intent is to make sense of (or interpret) the meanings others have about the world. Rather than starting with a theory (as in postpostivism), inquirers generate or inductively develop a theory or pattern of meaning.

For example, in discussing constructivism, Crotty (1998) identified several assumptions:

1. Meanings are constructed by human beings as they engage with the world they are interpreting. Qualitative researchers tend to use open-ended questions so that the participants can share their views.

2. Humans engage with their world and make sense of it based on their historical and social perspectives—we are all born into a world of meaning bestowed upon us by our culture. Thus, qualitative researchers seek to understand the context or setting of the participants through visiting this context and gathering information personally. They also interpret what

they find, an interpretation shaped by the researcher's own experiences and background.

3. The basic generation of meaning is always social, arising in and out of interaction with a human community. The process of qualitative research is largely inductive, with the inquirer generating meaning from the data collected in the field.

The Advocacy and Participatory Worldview

Another group of researchers holds to the philosophical assumptions of the advocacy/participatory approach. This position arose during the 1980s and 1990s from individuals who felt that the postpostivist assumptions imposed structural laws and theories that did not fit marginalized individuals in our society or issues of social justice that needed to be addressed. This worldview is typically seen with qualitative research, but it can be a foundation for quantitative research as well. Historically, some of the advocacy/participatory (or emancipatory) writers have drawn on the works of Marx, Adorno, Marcuse, Habermas, and Freire (Neuman, 2000). Fay (1987), Heron and Reason (1997), and Kemmis and Wilkinson (1998) are more recent writers to read for this perspective. In the main, these inquirers felt that the constructivist stance did not go far enough in advocating for an action agenda to help marginalized peoples. An **advocacy/participatory worldview** holds that research inquiry needs to be intertwined with politics and a political agenda. Thus, the research contains an action agenda for reform that may change the lives of the participants, the institutions in which individuals work or live, and the researcher's life. Moreover, specific issues need to be addressed that speak to important social issues of the day, issues such as empowerment, inequality, oppression, domination, suppression, and alienation. The researcher often begins with one of these issues as the focal point of the study. This research also assumes that the inquirer will proceed collaboratively so as to not further marginalize the participants as a result of the inquiry. In this sense, the participants may help design questions, collect data, analyze information, or reap the rewards of the research. Advocacy research provides a voice for these participants, raising their consciousness or advancing an agenda for change to improve their lives. It becomes a united voice for reform and change.

This philosophical worldview focuses on the needs of groups and individuals in our society that may be marginalized or disenfranchised. Therefore, theoretical perspectives may be integrated with the philosophical assumptions that construct a picture of the issues being examined, the people to be studied, and the changes that are needed, such as feminist perspectives, racialized discourses, critical theory, queer theory, and disability theory—theoretical lens to be discussed more in Chapter 3.

Although these are diverse groups and my explanations here are generalizations, it is helpful to view the summary by Kemmis and Wilkinson (1998) of key features of the advocacy or participatory forms of inquiry:

1. Participatory action is recursive or dialectical and focused on bringing about change in practices. Thus, at the end of advocacy/participatory studies, researchers advance an action agenda for change.

2. This form of inquiry is focused on helping individuals free themselves from constraints found in the media, in language, in work procedures, and in the relationships of power in educational settings. Advocacy/participatory studies often begin with an important issue or stance about the problems in society, such as the need for empowerment.

3. It is emancipatory in that it helps unshackle people from the constraints of irrational and unjust structures that limit self-development and self-determination. The advocacy/participatory studies aim to create a political debate and discussion so that change will occur.

4. It is practical and collaborative because it is inquiry completed *with* others rather than *on* or *to* others. In this spirit, advocacy/participatory authors engage the participants as active collaborators in their inquiries.

The Pragmatic Worldview

Another position about worldviews comes from the pragmatists. Pragmatism derives from the work of Peirce, James, Mead, and Dewey (Cherryholmes, 1992). Recent writers include Rorty (1990), Murphy (1990), Patton (1990), and Cherryholmes (1992). There are many forms of this philosophy, but for many, **pragmatism** as a worldview arises out of actions, situations, and consequences rather than antecedent conditions (as in postpositivism). There is a concern with applications—what works—and solutions to problems (Patton, 1990). Instead of focusing on methods, researchers emphasize the research problem and use all approaches available to understand the problem (see Rossman & Wilson, 1985). As a philosophical underpinning for mixed methods studies, Tashakkori and Teddlie (1998), Morgan (2007), and Patton (1990) convey its importance for focusing attention on the research problem in social science research and then using pluralistic approaches to derive knowledge about the problem. Using Cherryholmes (1992), Morgan (2007), and my own views, pragmatism provides a philosophical basis for research:

- Pragmatism is not committed to any one system of philosophy and reality. This applies to mixed methods research in that inquirers draw liberally from both quantitative and qualitative assumptions when they engage in their research.

- Individual researchers have a freedom of choice. In this way, researchers are free to choose the methods, techniques, and procedures of research that best meet their needs and purposes.

- Pragmatists do not see the world as an absolute unity. In a similar way, mixed methods researchers look to many approaches for collecting and analyzing data rather than subscribing to only one way (e.g., quantitative or qualitative).

- Truth is what works at the time. It is not based in a duality between reality independent of the mind or within the mind. Thus, in mixed methods research, investigators use both quantitative and qualitative data because they work to provide the best understanding of a research problem.

- The pragmatist researchers look to the *what* and *how* to research, based on the intended consequences—where they want to go with it. Mixed methods researchers need to establish a purpose for their mixing, a rationale for the reasons why quantitative and qualitative data need to be mixed in the first place.

- Pragmatists agree that research always occurs in social, historical, political, and other contexts. In this way, mixed methods studies may include a postmodern turn, a theoretical lens that is reflective of social justice and political aims.

- Pragmatists have believed in an external world independent of the mind as well as that lodged in the mind. But they believe that we need to stop asking questions about reality and the laws of nature (Cherryholmes, 1992). "They would simply like to change the subject" (Rorty, 1983, p. xiv).

- Thus, for the mixed methods researcher, pragmatism opens the door to multiple methods, different worldviews, and different assumptions, as well as different forms of data collection and analysis.

Strategies of Inquiry

The researcher not only selects a qualitative, quantitative, or mixed methods study to conduct, the inquirer also decides on a type of study within these three choices. **Strategies of inquiry** are types of qualitative, quantitative, and mixed methods designs or models that provide specific direction for procedures in a research design. Others have called them *approaches to inquiry* (Creswell, 2007) or *research methodologies* (Mertens, 1998). The strategies available to the researcher have grown over the years as computer technology has pushed forward our data analysis and ability to analyze complex models and as individuals have articulated new procedures for conducting social science research. Select types will be emphasized in Chapters 8, 9, and 10, strategies frequently used in the social sciences. Here I introduce those that are discussed later and that are cited in examples throughout the book. An overview of these strategies is shown in Table 1.2.

Table 1.2 Alternative Strategies of Inquiry

Quantitative	Qualitative	Mixed Methods
• Experimental designs • Non-experimental designs, such as surveys	• Narrative research • Phenomenology • Ethnographies • Grounded theory studies • Case study	• Sequential • Concurrent • Transformative

Quantitative Strategies

During the late 19th and throughout the 20th century, strategies of inquiry associated with quantitative research were those that invoked the postpositivist worldview. These include true experiments and the less rigorous experiments called *quasi-experiments* and *correlational studies* (Campbell & Stanley, 1963) and specific single-subject experiments (Cooper, Heron, & Heward, 1987; Neuman & McCormick, 1995). More recently, quantitative strategies have involved complex experiments with many variables and treatments (e.g., factorial designs and repeated measure designs). They have also included elaborate structural equation models that incorporate causal paths and the identification of the collective strength of multiple variables. In this book, I focus on two strategies of inquiry: surveys and experiments.

Can do 'Qualitative Surveys' too. Open-ended questions.

● **Survey research** provides a quantitative or numeric description of trends, attitudes, or opinions of a population by studying a sample of that population. It includes cross-sectional and longitudinal studies using questionnaires or structured interviews for data collection, with the intent of generalizing from a sample to a population (Babbie, 1990).

● **Experimental research** seeks to determine if a specific treatment influences an outcome. This impact is assessed by providing a specific treatment to one group and withholding it from another and then determining how both groups scored on an outcome. Experiments include true experiments, with the random assignment of subjects to treatment conditions, and quasi-experiments that use nonrandomized designs (Keppel, 1991). Included within quasi-experiments are single-subject designs.

Qualitative Strategies

In qualitative research, the numbers and types of approaches have also become more clearly visible during the 1990s and into the 21st century. Books have summarized the various types (such as the 19 strategies identified by Wolcott, 2001), and complete procedures are now available on specific qualitative inquiry approaches. For example, Clandinin and Connelly (2000) constructed a picture of what narrative researchers do.

Moustakas (1994) discussed the philosophical tenets and the procedures of the phenomenological method, and Strauss and Corbin (1990, 1998) identified the procedures of grounded theory. Wolcott (1999) summarized ethnographic procedures, and Stake (1995) suggested processes involved in case study research. In this book, illustrations are drawn from the following strategies, recognizing that approaches such as participatory action research (Kemmis & Wilkinson, 1998), discourse analysis (Cheek, 2004), and others not mentioned (see Creswell, 2007b) are also viable ways to conduct qualitative studies:

- **Ethnography** is a strategy of inquiry in which the researcher studies an intact cultural group in a natural setting over a prolonged period of time by collecting, primarily, observational and interview data (Creswell, 2007b). The research process is flexible and typically evolves contextually in response to the lived realities encountered in the field setting (LeCompte & Schensul, 1999).

- **Grounded theory** is a strategy of inquiry in which the researcher derives a general, abstract theory of a process, action, or interaction grounded in the views of participants. This process involves using multiple stages of data collection and the refinement and interrelationship of categories of information (Charmaz, 2006; Strauss and Corbin, 1990, 1998). Two primary characteristics of this design are the constant comparison of data with emerging categories and theoretical sampling of different groups to maximize the similarities and the differences of information.

Induction & Deduction.

- **Case studies** are a strategy of inquiry in which the researcher explores in depth a program, event, activity, process, or one or more individuals. Cases are bounded by time and activity, and researchers collect detailed information using a variety of data collection procedures over a sustained period of time (Stake, 1995).

- **Phenomenological research** is a strategy of inquiry in which the researcher identifies the essence of human experiences about a phenomenon as described by participants. Understanding the lived experiences marks phenomenology as a philosophy as well as a method, and the procedure involves studying a small number of subjects through extensive and prolonged engagement to develop patterns and relationships of meaning (Moustakas, 1994). In this process, the researcher brackets or sets aside his or her own experiences in order to understand those of the participants in the study (Nieswiadomy, 1993).

- **Narrative research** is a strategy of inquiry in which the researcher studies the lives of individuals and asks one or more individuals to provide stories about their lives. This information is then often retold or restoried by the researcher into a narrative chronology. In the end, the narrative combines views from the participant's life with those of the researcher's life in a collaborative narrative (Clandinin & Connelly, 2000).

Mixed Methods Strategies

Mixed methods strategies are less well known than either the quantitative or qualitative approaches. The concept of mixing different methods originated in 1959 when Campbell and Fisk used multimethods to study validity of psychological traits. They encouraged others to employ their multimethod matrix to examine multiple approaches to data collection. This prompted others to mix methods, and soon approaches associated with field methods, such as observations and interviews (qualitative data), were combined with traditional surveys (quantitative data; Sieber, 1973). Recognizing that all methods have limitations, researchers felt that biases inherent in any single method could neutralize or cancel the biases of other methods. Triangulating data sources—a means for seeking convergence across qualitative and quantitative methods—was born (Jick, 1979). By the early 1990s, the idea of mixing moved from seeking convergence to actually integrating or connecting the quantitative and qualitative data. For example, the results from one method can help identify participants to study or questions to ask for the other method (Tashakkori & Teddlie, 1998). Alternatively, the qualitative and quantitative data can be merged into one large database or the results used side by side to reinforce each other (e.g., qualitative quotes support statistical results; Creswell & Plano Clark, 2007). Or the methods can serve a larger, transformative purpose to advocate for marginalized groups, such as women, ethnic/racial minorities, members of gay and lesbian communities, people with disabilities, and those who are poor (Mertens, 2003).

These reasons for mixing methods have led writers from around the world to develop procedures for mixed methods strategies of inquiry, and these take the numerous terms found in the literature, such as *multimethod, convergence, integrated,* and *combined* (Creswell & Plano Clark, 2007), and shape procedures for research (Tashakkori & Teddlie, 2003).

In particular, three general strategies and several variations within them are illustrated in this book:

- **Sequential mixed methods** procedures are those in which the researcher seeks to elaborate on or expand on the findings of one method with another method. This may involve beginning with a qualitative interview for exploratory purposes and following up with a quantitative, survey method with a large sample so that the researcher can generalize results to a population. Alternatively, the study may begin with a quantitative method in which a theory or concept is tested, followed by a qualitative method involving detailed exploration with a few cases or individuals.

- **Concurrent mixed methods** procedures are those in which the researcher converges or merges quantitative and qualitative data in order to provide a comprehensive analysis of the research problem. In this design, the investigator collects both forms of data at the same time and then integrates the information in the interpretation of the overall results. Also, in this design, the researcher may embed one smaller form of data within another larger data collection in order to analyze different types of questions (the qualitative addresses the process while the quantitative, the outcomes).

- **Transformative mixed methods** procedures are those in which the researcher uses a theoretical lens (see Chapter 3) as an overarching perspective within a design that contains both quantitative and qualitative data. This lens provides a framework for topics of interest, methods for collecting data, and outcomes or changes anticipated by the study. Within this lens could be a data collection method that involves a sequential or a concurrent approach.

Research Methods

The third major element in the framework is the specific **research methods** that involve the forms of data collection, analysis, and interpretation that researchers propose for their studies. As shown in Table 1.3, it is useful to consider the full range of possibilities of data collection and to organize these methods, for example, by their degree of predetermined nature, their use of closed-ended versus open-ended questioning, and their focus on numeric versus nonnumeric data analysis. These methods will be developed further in Chapters 8 through 10.

Researchers collect data on an instrument or test (e.g., a set of questions about attitudes toward self-esteem) or gather information on a behavioral checklist (e.g., observation of a worker engaged in a complex skill). On the other end of the continuum, collecting data might involve visiting a research site and observing the behavior of individuals without predetermined questions or conducting an interview in which the individual is allowed to talk openly about a topic, largely without the use of specific

Table 1.3 Quantitative, Mixed, and Qualitative Methods

Quantitative Methods →	Mixed Methods	← Qualitative Methods
• Pre-determined • Instrument based questions • Performance data, attitude data, observational data, and census data • Statistical analysis • Statistical interpretation	• Both pre-determined and emerging methods • Both open- and closed-ended questions • Multiple forms of data drawing on all possibilities • Statistical and text analysis • Across databases interpretation	• Emerging methods • Open-ended questions • Interview data, observation data, document data, and audio-visual data • Text and image analysis • Themes, patterns interpretation

questions. The choice of methods turns on whether the intent is to specify the type of information to be collected in advance of the study or allow it to emerge from participants in the project. Also, the type of data analyzed may be numeric information gathered on scales of instruments or text information recording and reporting the voice of the participants. Researchers make interpretations of the statistical results, or they interpret the themes or patterns that emerge from the data. In some forms of research, both quantitative and qualitative data are collected, analyzed, and interpreted. Instrument data may be augmented with open-ended observations, or census data may be followed by in-depth exploratory interviews. In this case of mixing methods, the researcher makes inferences across both the quantitative and qualitative databases.

RESEARCH DESIGNS AS WORLDVIEWS, STRATEGIES, AND METHODS

The worldviews, the strategies, and the methods all contribute to a research design that *tends* to be quantitative, qualitative, or mixed. Table 1.4 creates distinctions that may be useful in choosing an approach. This table also includes practices of all three approaches that are emphasized in remaining chapters of this book.

Typical scenarios of research can illustrate how these three elements combine into a research design.

- *Quantitative* approach—Postpositivist worldview, experimental strategy of inquiry, and pre- and post-test measures of attitudes

In this scenario, the researcher tests a theory by specifying narrow hypotheses and the collection of data to support or refute the hypotheses. An experimental design is used in which attitudes are assessed both before and after an experimental treatment. The data are collected on an instrument that measures attitudes, and the information is analyzed using statistical procedures and hypothesis testing.

- *Qualitative* approach—Constructivist worldview, ethnographic design, and observation of behavior

In this situation, the researcher seeks to establish the meaning of a phenomenon from the views of participants. This means identifying a culture-sharing group and studying how it develops shared patterns of behavior over time (i.e., ethnography). One of the key elements of collecting data in this way is to observe participants' behaviors by engaging in their activities.

- *Qualitative* approach—Participatory worldview, narrative design, and open-ended interviewing

For this study, the inquirer seeks to examine an issue related to oppression of individuals. To study this, stories are collected of individual oppression

Table 1.4 Qualitative, Quantitative, and Mixed Methods Approaches

Tend to or Typically . . .	Qualitative Approaches	Quantitative Approaches	Mixed Methods Approaches
• Use these philosophical assumptions	• Constructivist/ advocacy/ participatory knowledge claims	• Post-positivist knowledge claims	• Pragmatic knowledge claims
• Employ these strategies of inquiry	• Phenomenology, grounded theory, ethnography, case study, and narrative	• Surveys and experiments	• Sequential, concurrent, and transformative
• Employ these methods	• Open-ended questions, emerging approaches, text or image data	• Closed-ended questions, predetermined approaches, numeric data	• Both open- and closed-ended questions, both emerging and predetermined approaches, and both quantitative and qualitative data and analysis
• Use these practices of research as the researcher	• Positions him- or herself • Collects participant meanings • Focuses on a single concept or phenomenon • Brings personal values into the study • Studies the context or setting of participants • Validates the accuracy of findings • Makes interpretations of the data • Creates an agenda for change or reform • Collaborates with the participants	• Tests or verifies theories or explanations • Identifies variables to study • Relates variables in questions or hypotheses • Uses standards of validity and reliability • Observes and measures information numerically • Uses unbiased approaches • Employs statistical procedures	• Collects both quantitative and qualitative data • Develops a rationale for mixing • Integrates the data at different stages of inquiry • Presents visual pictures of the procedures in the study • Employs the practices of both qualitative and quantitative research

using a narrative approach. Individuals are interviewed at some length to determine how they have personally experienced oppression.

- *Mixed methods* approach—Pragmatic worldview, collection of both quantitative and qualitative data sequentially

The researcher bases the inquiry on the assumption that collecting diverse types of data best provides an understanding of a research problem. The study begins with a broad survey in order to generalize results to a population and then, in a second phase, focuses on qualitative, open-ended interviews to collect detailed views from participants.

CRITERIA FOR SELECTING A RESEARCH DESIGN

Given the possibility of qualitative, quantitative, or mixed methods approaches, what factors affect a choice of one approach over another for the design of a proposal? Added to worldview, strategy, and methods would be the research problem, the personal experiences of the researcher, and the audience(s) for whom the report will be written.

The Research Problem

A research problem, more thoroughly discussed in Chapter 5, is an issue or concern that needs to be addressed (e.g., the issue of racial discrimination). Certain types of social research problems call for specific approaches. For example, if the problem calls for (a) the identification of factors that influence an outcome, (b) the utility of an intervention, or (c) understanding the best predictors of outcomes, then a quantitative approach is best. It is also the best approach to use to test a theory or explanation.

On the other hand, if a concept or phenomenon needs to be understood because little research has been done on it, then it merits a qualitative approach. Qualitative research is exploratory and is useful when the researcher does not know the important variables to examine. This type of approach may be needed because the topic is new, the topic has never been addressed with a certain sample or group of people, and existing theories do not apply with the particular sample or group under study (Morse, 1991).

A mixed methods design is useful when either the quantitative or qualitative approach by itself is inadequate to best understand a research problem or the strengths of both quantitative and qualitative research can provide the best understanding. For example, a researcher may want to both generalize the findings to a population as well as develop a detailed view of the meaning of a phenomenon or concept for individuals. In this research, the inquirer first explores generally to learn what variables to study and then studies those variables with a large sample of individuals.

Alternatively, researchers may first survey a large number of individuals and then follow up with a few participants to obtain their specific language and voices about the topic. In these situations, collecting both closed-ended quantitative data and open-ended qualitative data proves advantageous.

Personal Experiences

Researchers' own personal training and experiences also influence their choice of approach. An individual trained in technical, scientific writing, statistics, and computer statistical programs and familiar with quantitative journals in the library would most likely choose the quantitative design. On the other hand, individuals who enjoy writing in a literary way or conducting personal interviews or making up-close observations may gravitate to the qualitative approach. The mixed methods researcher is an individual familiar with both quantitative and qualitative research. This person also has the time and resources to collect both quantitative and qualitative data and has outlets for mixed methods studies, which tend to be large in scope.

Since quantitative studies are the traditional mode of research, carefully worked out procedures and rules exist for them. Researchers may be more comfortable with the highly systematic procedures of quantitative research. Also, for some individuals, it can be uncomfortable to challenge accepted approaches among some faculty by using qualitative and advocacy/participatory approaches to inquiry. On the other hand, qualitative approaches allow room to be innovative and to work more within researcher-designed frameworks. They allow more creative, literary-style writing, a form that individuals may like to use. For advocacy/participatory writers, there is undoubtedly a strong stimulus to pursue topics that are of personal interest—issues that relate to marginalized people and an interest in creating a better society for them and everyone.

For the mixed methods researcher, the project will take extra time because of the need to collect and analyze both quantitative and qualitative data. It fits a person who enjoys both the structure of quantitative research and the flexibility of qualitative inquiry.

Audience

Finally, researchers write for audiences that will accept their research. These audiences may be journal editors, journal readers, graduate committees, conference attendees, or colleagues in the field. Students should consider the approaches typically supported and used by their advisers. The experiences of these audiences with quantitative, qualitative, or mixed methods studies can shape the decision made about this choice.

SUMMARY

In planning a research project, researchers need to identify whether they will employ a qualitative, quantitative, or mixed methods design. This design is based on bringing together a worldview or assumptions about research, the specific strategies of inquiry, and research methods. Decisions about choice of a design are further influenced by the research problem or issue being studied, the personal experiences of the researcher, and the audience for whom the researcher writes.

WRITING EXERCISES

Writing Exercises

1. Identify a research question in a journal article and discuss what design would be best to study the question and why.

2. Take a topic that you would like to study, and using the four combinations of worldviews, strategies of inquiry, and research methods in Figure 1.1, discuss a project that brings together a worldview, strategies, and methods. Identify whether this would be quantitative, qualitative, or mixed methods research.

3. What distinguishes a quantitative study from a qualitative study? Mention three characteristics.

ADDITIONAL READINGS

Cherryholmes, C. H. (1992, August-September). Notes on pragmatism and scientific realism. *Educational Researcher, 14*, 13–17.

Cleo Cherryholmes discusses pragmatism as a contrasting perspective from scientific realism. The strength of this article lies in the numerous citations of writers about pragmatism and a clarification of one version of pragmatism. Cherryholmes's version points out that pragmatism is driven by anticipated consequences, reluctance to tell a true story, and the embrace of the idea that there is an external world independent of our minds. Also included in this article are numerous references to historical and recent writers about pragmatism as a philosophical position.

Crotty, M. (1998). *The foundations of social research: Meaning and perspective in the research process.* Thousand Oaks, CA: Sage.

Michael Crotty offers a useful framework for tying together the many epistemological issues, theoretical perspectives, methodology, and methods of social research. He interrelates the four components of the research process and shows in a table a representative sampling of topics of each component. He then goes on to discuss nine different theoretical orientations in social research, such as postmodernism, feminism, critical inquiry, interpretivism, constructionism, and positivism.

Kemmis, S., & Wilkinson, M. (1998). Participatory action research and the study of practice. In B. Atweh, S. Kemmis, & P. Weeks (Eds.), *Action research in practice: Partnerships for social justice in education* (pp. 21–36). New York: Routledge.

Stephen Kemmis and Mervyn Wilkinson provide an excellent overview of participatory research. In particular, they note the six major features of this inquiry approach and then discuss how action research is practiced at the individual level, the social level, or both levels.

Guba, E. G., & Lincoln, Y. S. (2005). Paradigmatic controversies, contradictions, and emerging confluences. In N. K. Denzin & Y. S. Lincoln, *The Sage handbook of qualitative research* (3rd ed., pp. 191–215). Thousand Oaks, CA: Sage

Yvonna Lincoln and Egon Guba have provided the basic beliefs of five alternative inquiry paradigms in social science research: positivism, postpositivism, critical theory, constructivism, and participatory. These extend the earlier analysis provided in the first and second editions of the *Handbook*. Each is presented in terms of ontology (i.e., nature of reality), epistemology (i.e., how we know what we know), and methodology (i.e., the process of research). The participatory paradigm adds another alternative paradigm to those originally advanced in the first edition. After briefly presenting these five approaches, they contrast them in terms of seven issues, such as the nature of knowledge, how knowledge accumulates, and goodness or quality criteria.

Neuman, W. L. (2000). *Social research methods: Qualitative and quantitative approaches.* Boston: Allyn & Bacon.

Lawrence Neuman provides a comprehensive research method text as an introduction to social science research. Especially helpful in understanding the alternative meaning of methodology is Chapter 4, titled, "The Meanings of Methodology," in which he contrasts three methodologies—positivist social science, interpretive social science, and critical social science—in terms of eight questions (e.g., What constitutes an explanation or theory of social reality? What does good evidence or factual information look like?).

Phillips, D. C., & Burbules, N. C. (2000). *Postpositivism and educational research.* Lanham, MD: Rowman & Littlefield.

D. C. Phillips and Nicholas Burbules summarize the major ideas of postpostivist thinking. Through two chapters, "What is Postpositivism?" and "Philosophical Commitments of Postpositivist Researchers," the authors advance major ideas about postpositivism, especially those that differentiate it from positivism. These include knowing that human knowledge is conjectural rather than unchallengeable and that our warrants for knowledge can be withdrawn in light of further investigations.

5 Overview of Qualitative Research

MICHAEL D. MYERS

Objectives

By the end of this chapter, you will be able to:

- Understand the purpose of qualitative research
- Appreciate the benefits of qualitative research
- Recognize what counts as research and what does not
- Distinguish between quantitative and qualitative research
- Decide whether or not to use triangulation
- See how qualitative research can contribute to the rigour and relevance of research

WHY DO QUALITATIVE RESEARCH?

Qualitative research methods are designed to help researchers understand people and what they say and do. They are designed to help researchers understand the social and cultural contexts within which people live.

One of the key benefits of qualitative research is that it allows a researcher to see and understand the *context* within which decisions and actions take place. It is often the case that human decisions and actions can only be understood in context – it is the context that helps to 'explain' why someone acted as they did. And this context (or multiple contexts) is best understood by talking to people.

Qualitative researchers contend that it is virtually impossible to understand why someone did something or why something happened in an organization without talking to people about it. Imagine if the police tried to solve a serious crime without being able to talk to the suspects or witnesses. If the police were restricted to using only quantitative data, almost no crimes would be solved. Imagine if lawyers and judges were not allowed to question or cross-examine witnesses in court. The validity and reliability of any court decision would be thrown into serious doubt. So, likewise, qualitative researchers argue that if you want to understand people's motivations, their reasons, their actions, and the context for their beliefs and actions in an in-depth way, qualitative research is best. Kaplan and Maxwell (1994) say that the goal of understanding a phenomenon from the point of view of the participants and its particular social and institutional context is largely lost when textual data are quantified.

One of the primary motivations for doing qualitative research, as opposed to quantitative research, comes from the observation that, if there is one thing which distinguishes humans from the natural world, it is their ability to talk. It is only by talking to people, or reading what they have written, that we can find out what they are thinking, and understanding their thoughts goes a long way towards explaining their actions.

TYPES OF QUESTIONS USING QUALITATIVE RESEARCH

The questions that a qualitative researcher might typically ask are what, why, how, and when questions:

- **What** is happening here?
- **Why** is it happening?
- **How** has it come to happen this way?
- **When** did it happen?

WHAT IS RESEARCH?

In a university setting, research is defined as an *original investigation* undertaken in order to contribute to knowledge and understanding in a particular field. Research is a creative activity leading to the production of *new* knowledge. The knowledge produced is new in the sense that the facts, the interpretation of those facts, or the theories used to explain them might not have been used in a particular way before in that specific discipline.

Research typically involves enquiry of an empirical or conceptual nature and is conducted by people with specialist knowledge about the subject matter, theories, and methods in a specific field. Research may involve contributing to the intellectual infrastructure of a subject or discipline (e.g. by publishing a dictionary). In some fields, such as engineering, computer science, or information systems, research can also include the experimental design of new artefacts. Engineers often try to develop new or substantially improved materials, devices, products, or processes.

Of course, as more research is published, the subject matter, theories, and methods used in a particular field may change over time. For this reason, scholars in many disciplines will write a literature review of previous relevant research to show that they understand and are up-to-date with the latest thinking.

But how do we know that the research results are new? How do we know that the findings are original? How do we know that the research was conducted in a rigorous manner?

The only way to tell if the research findings are both sound and original is if those findings are open to scrutiny and formal evaluation by experts in a particular field. That is, the findings must be evaluated by those who are experienced and 'qualified' to do so. If these experts, in evaluating the research, find that the results are sound, and that the findings are new *to them*, then we can say that the research project represents an original contribution to knowledge.

This way of evaluating the quality of research in science is called the peer review system. The peer review system exists in all scientific disciplines and is in effect a system of quality assurance. Of course, the peer review system is a social system, and as such it has its drawbacks, but it does ensure that only research of a certain standard is published. I discuss the peer review system and the publication process in more detail in Part VI.

It should be clear from the above discussion that some activities do not count as research in a university setting (Tertiary Education Commission, 2005). Some of these activities are as follows:

- The preparation of teaching materials. Teaching materials are excluded since they are not normally formally evaluated by experts in the field as a whole. For example, case study books written for teaching purposes are written primarily for students, not researchers. As Yin describes, 'For teaching purposes, a case study need not contain a complete or accurate rendition of actual events; rather, its purpose is to establish a framework for discussion and debate among students'(2003: 2). The distinction between producing case studies for teaching and research is discussed more fully in Chapter 7.
- The provision of advice or opinion, e.g. consulting work.
- Feasibility studies (where the output is a recommendation to a client).
- Routine data collection (where there is no attempt to contribute to new knowledge in the field as a whole).
- Routine information systems development (where the output is a new or improved product for a client, not the experimental design of a new product or service).
- Any other routine professional practice.

QUANTITATIVE AND QUALITATIVE RESEARCH COMPARED

There are many different ways to classify and characterize different types of research. However, one of the most common distinctions is between qualitative and quantitative research methods (Table 2.1).

Table 2.1 Examples of qualitative and quantitative research

Qualitative research **A focus on text**	**Quantitative research** **A focus on numbers**
Action research	Surveys
Case study research	Laboratory experiments
Ethnography	Simulation
Grounded theory	Mathematical modelling
Semiotics	Structured equation modelling
Discourse analysis	Statistical analysis
Hermeneutics	Econometrics
Narrative and metaphor	

Quantitative research methods were originally developed in the natural sciences to study natural phenomena. Examples of quantitative methods now well accepted in the social sciences include survey methods, laboratory experiments, formal methods (e.g. econometrics), and numerical methods such as mathematical modelling. All quantitative researchers emphasize numbers more than anything else. That is, the numbers 'come to represent values and levels of theoretical constructs and concepts and the interpretation of the numbers is viewed as strong scientific evidence of how a phenomenon works' (Straub, Gefen, & Boudreau, 2004). Most quantitative researchers use statistical tools and packages to analyse their data.

Qualitative research methods were developed in the social sciences to enable researchers to study social and cultural phenomena. Examples of qualitative methods are action research, case study research, and grounded theory. Qualitative data sources include observation and participant observation (fieldwork), interviews and questionnaires, documents and texts, and the researcher's impressions and reactions. Qualitative data are mostly a record of what people have said. For example, interviews (the most common technique for collecting qualitative data) record what one of your informants said about a particular topic; field notes record what the researcher experienced or thought about a particular topic or event; and documents record what the author of the document wrote at the time. In all cases, these qualitative data can help us to understand people, their motivations and actions, and the broader context within which they work and live.

In the 1980s most business disciplines favoured quantitative research. In the 1990s, however, there was an increased interest in qualitative research in almost every business discipline. The quality of this research improved over time such that many articles using qualitative research have now been published in the top peer-reviewed journals of virtually every business discipline.

My view is that both quantitative and qualitative research approaches are useful and needed in researching business organizations. Both kinds of research are important, and both kinds of research can be rigorous. Most of the resources and readings cited in this book have been peer reviewed by leading experts and published in the top journals in the various business disciplines. However, there are advantages and disadvantages in each approach.

Generally speaking, quantitative research is best if you want to have a large sample size and you want to generalize to a large population. In this case the objective is to study a particular topic across many people or many organizations. You want to find out trends or patterns that apply in many different situations. Various statistical techniques can be used to analyse your data.

A major disadvantage of quantitative research is that, as a general rule, many of the social and cultural aspects of organizations are lost or are treated in a superficial manner. The 'context' is usually treated as 'noise' or as something that gets in the way. The quantitative researcher trades context for the ability to generalize across a population.

Qualitative research is best if you want to study a particular subject in depth (e.g. in one or a few organizations). It is good for exploratory research, when the particular topic is new and there is not much previously published research on that topic. It is also ideal for studying the social, cultural, and political aspects of people and organizations.

A major disadvantage of qualitative research, however, is that it is often difficult to generalize to a larger population. You can generalize from qualitative research, but not by using sampling logic. For instance, if you conduct three in-depth case studies of three organizations, a sample size of three does not count for much in statistical terms. Three cases are no better than one. Therefore it is normally impossible for qualitative researchers to make generalizations from a sample to a population.

However, you can generalize from qualitative research to theory, and you can generalize from just one case study or one ethnography (Klein & Myers, 1999; Lee & Baskerville, 2003; Yin, 2003). How you can use qualitative research to make generalizations and how the contributions and quality of qualitative research studies can be evaluated is discussed in each of the chapters in Part III.

Although the qualitative/quantitative distinction in research methods is by far the most common, there are other distinctions which can be made. Research methods have variously been classified as objective versus subjective (Burrell & Morgan, 1979), as being concerned with the discovery of general laws (nomothetic) versus being concerned with the uniqueness of each particular situation (idiographic), as aimed at prediction and control versus aimed at explanation and understanding, as taking an outsider (etic) versus taking an insider (emic) perspective, and so on. Considerable controversy continues to surround the use of these terms (Myers & Avison, 2002). However, a discussion of these distinctions is beyond the scope of this book. For a fuller discussion see Luthans and Davis (1982) and Morey and Luthans (1984). See also Chapter 3 which discusses the various philosophical perspectives that can inform research.

TRIANGULATION

Triangulation is the idea that you should do more than just one thing in a study. That is, you should use more than one research method, use two or more techniques to gather data, or combine qualitative and quantitative research methods in the one study. Triangulation is an excellent idea if you want to look at the same topic from different angles. It allows you to gain a 'fuller' picture of what is happening. It allows you to triangulate data from interviews with data from documents, or data from two different research methods (e.g. a qualitative case study with quantitative data from a survey).

TRIANGULATING CASE STUDY DATA

Doing marketing research, Fournier (1998) conducted three in-depth case studies looking at the relationships consumers form with brands. She triangulated data within her case studies.

She used multiple stories from the same person, interviews conducted with the same persons at multiple points in time, and information from other data sources such as grocery lists, shelf contents, stories of other household members, and so forth. In addition, researchers who had multiple encounters with informants in previous stages were employed. Thus interpretations were triangulated across researchers and authors as well.

It is relatively common for qualitative researchers to triangulate data within a study using just one research method. For example, a researcher conducting a case study of one organization might triangulate interview data with data from published or unpublished documents; or an ethnographer might triangulate data from interviews with data from observation. Many qualitative research methods require the triangulation of data in some way or other.

Much less common, however, and much more difficult, is when researchers try to combine two or more research methods in the one study. The idea is to triangulate data and findings on the same topic, but to use different methods. Triangulation is especially challenging if the research methods are substantially different in their underlying philosophy or approach, e.g. when researchers try to combine qualitative and quantitative research methods.

TRIANGULATING QUALITATIVE AND QUANTITATIVE DATA

An excellent example of triangulating data obtained from the use of qualitative and quantitative research methods is Markus' (1994a) study of how and why managers use email. Her study questioned the assumptions of media richness theory (that 'richness is better') and demonstrated how a 'lean' medium such as email could be used for complex communication.

To answer her research question, 'how and why do managers use email?', Markus used two research methods. First, she used a quantitative method, a statistically analysed survey. The survey was sent to a large sample of managers. Second, she used a qualitative method called analytic induction. The data were purely textual – mostly she used email messages that were sent by managers. She also obtained data from interviews.

Using both quantitative and qualitative research methods meant that Markus had quantitative data (e.g. frequency of email use) and qualitative data (transcripts of email message exchanges). Her findings and conclusions are rigorous and convincing.

I believe it can be difficult for most people to do this kind of triangulation well. This is because you need to be well trained and become an expert in multiple research methods, not just one. Also, each method has its own underlying perspective and involves the use of certain techniques. It can take months, if not years, for someone to become proficient in the use of just one particular method, e.g. ethnography. However, if you have the inclination, enthusiasm, and time, this is certainly a worthwhile and viable option. It is something that can be done (Mingers, 2001).

A slightly easier way to achieve the triangulation of research methods is for a single study to include multiple researchers. In this case, each researcher brings to the table his or her own method of expertise and experience. Having multiple researchers and multiple perspectives on any research topic can be positive. A key requirement for the project to be successful, however, is for the researchers concerned to respect each other's expertise and method. There must be mutual respect for any real dialogue to take place. In such cases, the research findings can be truly outstanding.

RESEARCH IN BUSINESS AND MANAGEMENT

All research in business and management focuses on a topic that is of relevance to one or more of the business and management disciplines. This disciplinary area is actually very broad and depending upon your background and institution may include the following: accounting and finance; commercial law; economics; human resource management; logistics and supply chain management; organizational behaviour and organizational development; information systems; management strategy and international business; marketing; and operations management. Of course, these business and management disciplines often build on research from other disciplines, such as statistics, psychology, or sociology. The list of potentially relevant disciplines is very large.

A key feature of a qualitative or quantitative study, as opposed to a purely conceptual study, is that it is an empirical investigation, i.e. it relies on empirical data from the natural or social world. The empirical investigation seeks to contribute to the body of knowledge in a particular field. A simple model of the process of empirical research in business and management is represented in Figure 2.1.

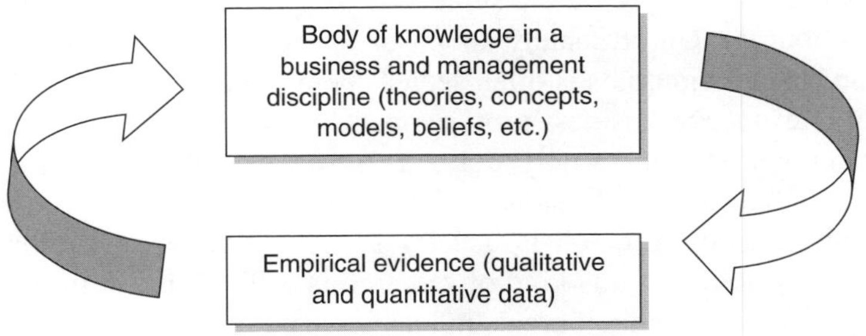

Figure 2.1 A model of research in business and management

As can be seen in the figure, a researcher finds a topic or a research problem that is relevant to the body of knowledge in a particular discipline. Normally the research questions are derived from the research literature, but they could come from current business practice or your own intuitive hunches (Marshall & Rossman, 1989). In order to answer the questions raised by the problem, the researcher subsequently uses a research method to find some empirical evidence. These findings are hopefully significant enough such that they are published and hence add to the body of knowledge. A new researcher then comes along and starts the process once more.

RIGOUR AND RELEVANCE IN RESEARCH

A perennial issue for researchers in business and management is the apparent trade-off between rigour and relevance (Table 2.2). It has become a common complaint over the past decade that research in business schools has become more rigorous at the expense of relevance.

Table 2.2 Rigour and relevance

Rigorous research	Relevant research
'Scientific research'	Relevant to business practitioners
Emphasis on meeting scientific standards such as validity and reliability	Emphasis on being immediately relevant to practice
Subject to academic peer review	Published in consulting reports or industry magazines
Published in academic journals	
Theoretical contribution	Practical contribution

Rigorous research is usually defined as research that meets the standards of 'scientific' research; it is research that has been conducted according to the scientific model of research, subject to peer review, and published in an academic journal. Unfortunately, much of the research that is published in academic business journals is often seen as being too theoretical and of little practical relevance to business professionals.

Relevant research is usually defined as research that is of immediate relevance to business professionals. The research results can be used right away. This kind of research is usually seen as more akin to consulting. Unfortunately, much of this kind of research is difficult if not impossible to get published in academic journals in business and management. The lack of a theoretical contribution almost guarantees rejection.

In my own field of information systems, the issue of rigour versus relevance seems to be discussed at almost every conference. Most academics tend to agree with the notion that research in information systems and business schools more generally should be more relevant to business professionals. In practice, however, they are faced with the need to gain tenure and promotion. In order to gain tenure, most business schools in research universities require faculty members to have a record of publication in reputable academic journals. This job requirement means that most faculty members end up postponing indefinitely their desire (if they have one) to conduct 'relevant' research.

As an example of this debate in the management literature more generally, Bennis and O'Toole (2005) argue that business schools focus far too much on what they call 'scientific' research. Writing in the *Harvard Business Review*, they claim that business management is not a scientific discipline, but a profession. They lament the fact that business schools have followed a scientific model of research rather than a professional model (as found, for example, in medicine and law). They say that graduating business students are ill equipped to wrangle with the complex, unquantifiable issues that are the reality of business. As most decisions in business are made on the basis of messy and incomplete data, they are particularly critical of statistical and quantitative research which they believe can blind rather than illuminate (Bennis & O'Toole, 2005).

I must admit that I do not entirely agree with Bennis and O'Toole's argument. In my view, the focus on research in business schools has transformed them from having a mostly vocational focus to being proper scholarly institutions. Faculty members have become scholars rather than consultants. Also, while most academic research may not be immediately relevant to business professionals, it may become relevant over the longer term. In fact, I would argue that one of the failings of contemporary management is the predilection to seek 'silver bullets', i.e. quick fixes, or magic solutions to more deep-seated problems. Few silver bullets turn out to be of any long-lasting value.

However, I do agree with them that research in business and management could be much more relevant than it is right now, and that it should be able to deal with 'complex, unquantifiable issues that are the reality of business'. And this is where the value of qualitative research lies.

It is my view that qualitative research is perhaps the best way for research in business and management to become both rigorous and relevant at the same time. It allows scholarship and practice to come together. Qualitative researchers study real situations, not artificial ones (as, for example, in a laboratory experiment). To do a good qualitative study, qualitative researchers need to engage actively with people in real organizations. An in-depth field study, in particular, needs to look at the complexity of organizations including the 'complex, unquantifiable issues' that are the reality of business. A case study researcher or an ethnographer may well study the social, cultural, and political aspects of a company.

Hence, if you are trying to decide whether to do qualitative or quantitative research in a business discipline, the choice should not be made on the basis of whether one approach is more rigorous than the other. This would have been a valid question in the 1980s and early 1990s, but it is no longer a valid question today. Rather, the choice should be more on the topic, on the research question you want to ask, on the basis of your own interest and experience, and how relevant you want to be to practice. It is also important to consider the expertise of your supervisor or faculty members in your institution. If you want to use qualitative research but there is no one with the qualifications, interest, or experience to supervise you at your university, then it is probably best to choose a different topic and method, or change university.

Exercises

1. Conduct a brief literature search using Google Scholar or some other bibliographic database and see if you can find both qualitative and quantitative articles in your chosen field. What kinds of topics appear?
2. Looking at some of the articles you found in more detail, can you describe the research problem and the research questions? Can you describe the research method(s) that the author(s) used? Did any of them use triangulation?
3. Looking at these same articles, would you describe some of them as more rigorous or relevant than the others? Why?

Further Reading

Books

There are two books which I recommend for anyone wanting to do qualitative research at PhD level; both these books are required or recommended texts in many doctoral-level courses in business.

First, *The Sage Handbook for Qualitative Research* (Denzin & Lincoln, 2005) provides a collection of readings with authors selected from many disciplines. It examines the various paradigms for doing qualitative work, the strategies developed for studying people in their natural setting, and a variety of techniques for collecting, analysing, interpreting, and reporting findings.

Second, *Qualitative Data Analysis: An Expanded Sourcebook* (2nd edn) (Miles & Huberman, 1994) is also very useful.

A third book that is an excellent primer for novice researchers is *Doing Qualitative Research* (Silverman, 2005).

Websites on the Internet

There are quite a few useful websites on qualitative research:

- The ISWorld Section on Qualitative Research is at http://www.qual.auckland.ac.nz/
- The Qualitative Report is an online journal dedicated to qualitative research and critical enquiry at http://www.nova.edu/ssss/QR/index.html
- Sage Publications is arguably the leading publisher of qualitative methodology texts at http://www.sagepublications.com
- Narrative Psychology is an excellent resource on narrative and related areas at http://narrativepsych.com
- The Association for Qualitative Research has useful information at http://www.latrobe.edu.au/www/aqr/
- QualPage includes calls for papers, conferences, discussion forums, and publishers at http://www.qualitativeresearch.uga.edu/QuaiPage
- The International Journal of Social Research Methodology is a new cross-disciplinary journal designed to foster discussion and debate in social research methodology at http://tandf.co.uk/journals
- Forum: Qualitative Social Research is a bilingual (English/German) online journal for qualitative research edited by Katja Mruck. The main aim of the forum is to promote discussion and cooperation between qualitative researchers from different nations and social science disciplines at http://qualitative-research.net/fqs/fqs-eng.htm
- Evaluation and Social Research Methods has links to books, manuals, and articles on how to do evaluation and social research at http://gsociology.icaap.org/methods

6 The Use of Theory

JOHN W. CRESWELL

1. Scholarly productivity is the desired behavior or activity.
2. Locus of control is the generalized expectancy that rewards are or are not dependent upon specific behaviors.
3. Reinforcements are the rewards from scholarly work and the value attached to these rewards.
4. The educational institution is the psychological situation which furnishes many of the rewards for scholarly productivity.

With these specific variables, the formula for behavior which was developed by Rotter (1975) would be adapted to read: The potential for scholarly behavior to occur within an educational institution is a function of the expectancy that this activity will lead to specific rewards and of the value that the faculty member places on these rewards. In addition, the interaction of interpersonal trust with locus of control must be considered in relation to the expectancy of attaining rewards through behaviors as recommended in subsequent statements by Rotter (1967). Finally, certain characteristics, such as educational preparation, chronological age, post-doctoral fellowships, tenure, or full-time versus part-time employment may be associated with the scholarly productivity of nurse faculty in a manner similar to that seen within other disciplines. *(Author applied the concepts to her study.)*

The following statement represents the underlying logic for designing and conducting this study. If faculty believe that: (a) their efforts and actions in producing scholarly works will lead to rewards (locus of control), (b) others can be relied upon to follow through on their promises (interpersonal trust), (c) the rewards for scholarly activity are worthwhile (reward values), and (d) the rewards are available within their discipline or institution (institutional setting), then they will attain high levels of scholarly productivity (pp. 12–16). *(Author concluded with the if-then logic to relate the independent variables to the dependent variables.)*

QUALITATIVE THEORY USE

Variation in Theory Use in Qualitative Research

Qualitative inquirers use theory in their studies in several ways. First, much like in quantitative research, it is used as a broad explanation for behavior and attitudes, and it may be complete with variables, constructs, and hypotheses. For example, ethnographers employ cultural themes or "aspects of culture" (Wolcott, 1999, p. 113) to study in their qualitative projects, such as social control, language, stability and change, or social organization, such as kinship or families (see Wolcott's 1999 discussion about texts that address cultural topics in anthropology). Themes in this context provide a ready-made series of hypotheses to be tested from the literature. Although researchers might not refer to them as theories, they provide broad explanations that anthropologists use to study the culture-sharing behavior and attitudes of people. This approach is popular in qualitative health science research in which investigators begin with a theoretical model, such as the adoption of health practices or a quality of life theoretical orientation.

Second, researchers increasingly use a **theoretical lens** or **perspective in qualitative research,** which provides an overall orienting lens for the study of questions of gender, class, and race (or other issues of marginalized groups). This lens becomes an advocacy perspective that shapes the types of questions asked, informs how data are collected and analyzed, and provides a call for action or change. Qualitative research of the 1980s underwent a transformation to broaden its scope of inquiry to include these theoretical lenses. They guide the researchers as to what issues are important to examine (e.g., marginalization, empowerment) and the people that need to be studied (e.g., women, homeless, minority groups). They also indicate how the researcher positions himself or herself in the qualitative study (e.g., up front or biased from personal, cultural, and historical contexts) and how the final written accounts need to be written (e.g., without further marginalizing individuals, by collaborating with participants). In critical ethnography studies, researchers begin with a theory that informs their studies. This causal theory might be one of emancipation or repression (Thomas, 1993).

Some of these qualitative theoretical perspectives available to the researcher are as follows (Creswell, 2007):

- *Feminist perspectives* view as problematic women's diverse situations and the institutions that frame those situations. Research topics may include policy issues related to realizing social justice for women in specific contexts or knowledge about oppressive situations for women (Olesen, 2000).

- *Racialized discourses* raise important questions about the control and production of knowledge, particularly about people and communities of color (Ladson-Billings, 2000).

- *Critical theory* perspectives are concerned with empowering human beings to transcend the constraints placed on them by race, class, and gender (Fay, 1987).

- *Queer theory*—a term used in this literature—focuses on individuals calling themselves lesbians, gays, bisexuals, or transgendered people. The research using this approach does not objectify individuals, is concerned with cultural and political means, and conveys the voices and experiences of individuals who have been suppressed (Gamson, 2000).

- *Disability inquiry* addresses the meaning of inclusion in schools and encompasses administrators, teachers, and parents who have children with disabilities (Mertens, 1998).

Rossman and Rallis (1998) capture the sense of theory as critical and postmodern perspectives in qualitative inquiry:

> As the 20th century draws to a close, traditional social science has come under increasing scrutiny and attack as those espousing critical and postmodern perspectives challenge objectivist assumptions and traditional norms for the conduct of research. Central to this attack are four interrelated notions: (a) Research fundamentally involves issues of power; (b) the research report is not transparent but rather it is authored by a raced, gendered, classed, and politically oriented individual; (c) race, class, and gender are crucial for understanding experience; and (d) historic, traditional research has silenced members of oppressed and marginalized groups. (p. 66)

Third, distinct from this theoretical orientation are qualitative studies in which theory (or some other broad explanation) becomes the *end point*. It is an inductive process of building from the data to broad themes to a generalized model or theory (see Punch, 2005). The logic of this inductive approach is shown in Figure 3.5.

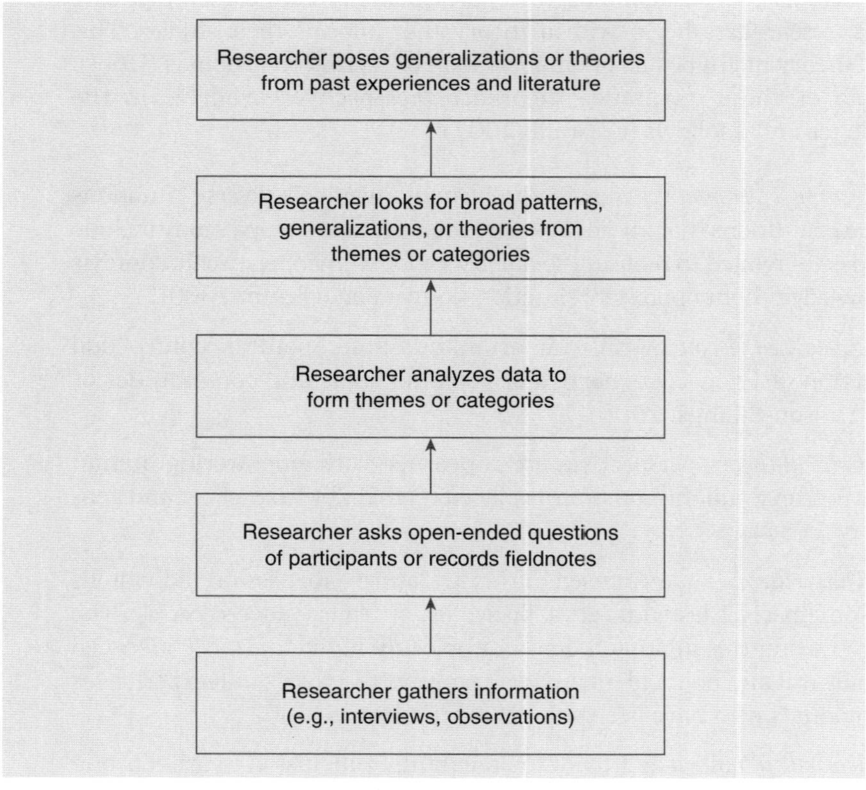

Figure 3.5 The Inductive Logic of Research in a Qualitative Study

The researcher begins by gathering detailed information from participants and then forms this information into categories or themes. These themes are developed into broad patterns, theories, or generalizations that are then compared with personal experiences or with existing literature on the topic.

The development of themes and categories into patterns, theories, or generalizations suggests varied end points for qualitative studies. For example, in case study research, Stake (1995) refers to an assertion as a *propositional generalization*—the researcher's summary of interpretations and claims—to which is added the researcher's own personal experiences, called "naturalistic generalizations" (p. 86). As another example, grounded theory provides a different end point. Inquirers hope to discover a theory that is grounded in information from participants (Strauss & Corbin, 1998). Lincoln and Guba (1985) refer to "pattern theories" as explanations that develop during naturalistic or qualitative research. Rather than the deductive form found in quantitative studies, these pattern theories or generalizations represent interconnected thoughts or parts linked to a whole.

Neuman (2000) provides additional information about pattern theories:

> Pattern theory does not emphasize logical deductive reasoning. Like causal theory, it contains an interconnected set of concepts and relationships, but it does not require causal statements. Instead, pattern theory uses metaphor or analogies so that relationship "makes sense." Pattern theories are systems of ideas that inform. The concepts and relations within them form a mutually reinforcing, closed system. They specify a sequence of phases or link parts to a whole. (p. 38)

Fourth and finally, some qualitative studies *do not employ any explicit theory.* However, the case can be made that no qualitative study begins from pure observation and that prior conceptual structure composed of theory and method provides the starting point for all observations (Schwandt, 1993). Still, one sees qualitative studies that contain no *explicit* theoretical orientation, such as in phenomenology, in which inquirers attempt to build the essence of experience from participants (e.g., see Riemen, 1986). In these studies, the inquirer constructs a rich, detailed description of a central phenomenon.

My **research tips** on theory use in a qualitative proposal are as follows:

- Decide if theory is to be used in the qualitative proposal.
- If it is used, then identify how the theory will be used in the study, such as an up-front explanation, as an end point, or as an advocacy lens.
- Locate the theory in the proposal in a manner consistent with its use.

Locating the Theory in Qualitative Research

How theory is used affects its placement in a qualitative study. In those studies with a cultural theme or a theoretical lens, the theory occurs in the opening passages of the study. Consistent with the emerging design of qualitative inquiry, the theory may appear at the beginning and be modified or adjusted based on participant views. Even in the most theory-oriented qualitative design, such as critical ethnography, Lather (1986) qualifies the use of theory:

> Building empirically grounded theory requires a reciprocal relationship between data and theory. Data must be allowed to generate propositions in a dialectical manner that permits use of *a priori* theoretical frameworks, but which keeps a particular framework from becoming the container into which the data must be poured. (p. 267)

Example 3.2 *A Theory Early in a Qualitative Study*

Murguia, Padilla, and Pavel (1991) studied the integration of 24 Hispanic and Native American students into the social system of a college campus. They were curious about how ethnicity influenced social integration, and they began by relating the participants' experiences to a theoretical model, the Tinto model of social integration. They felt that the model had been "incompletely conceptualized and, as a consequence, only imprecisely understood and measured" (p. 433).

Thus, the model was not being tested, as one would find in a quantitative project, but modified. At the end of the study, the authors refined Tinto's model and advanced their modification that described how ethnicity functions. In contrast to this approach, in qualitative studies with an end point of a theory (e.g., a grounded theory), a pattern, or a generalization, the theory emerges at the end of the study. This theory might be presented as a logic diagram, a visual representation of relationships among concepts.

Example 3.3 *A Theory at the End of a Qualitative Study*

Using a national database of 33 interviews with academic department chairpersons, we (Creswell & Brown, 1992) developed a grounded theory interrelating variables (or categories) of chair influence on scholarly performance of faculty. The theory section came into the article as the last section,

(Continued)

(Continued)

where we presented a visual model of the theory developed inductively from categories of information supplied by interviewees. In addition, we also advanced directional hypotheses that logically followed from the model. Moreover, in the section on the model and the hypotheses, we compared the results from participants with results from other studies and the theoretical speculations in the literature. For example, we stated,

> This proposition and its sub-propositions represent unusual, even contrary evidence, to our expectations. Contrary to proposition 2.1, we expected that the career stages would be similar not in type of issue but in the range of issues. Instead we found that the issues for post-tenure faculty covered almost all the possible problems on the list. Why were the tenured faculty's needs more extensive than non-tenured faculty? The research productivity literature suggests that one's research performance does not decline with the award of tenure (Holley 1977). Perhaps diffuse career goals of post-tenure faculty expand the possibilities for "types" of issues. In any case, this sub-proposition focuses attention on the understudied career group that Furniss (1981) reminds us needs to be examined in more detail.
>
> (Creswell & Brown, 1992, p. 58)

As this example shows, we developed a visual model that interrelated variables, derived this model inductively from informant comments, and placed the model at the end of the study, where the central propositions in it could be contrasted with the existing theories and literature.

7 Research Questions and Hypotheses

JOHN W. CRESWELL

Investigators place signposts to carry the reader through a plan for a study. The first signpost is the purpose statement, which establishes the central direction for the study. From the broad, general purpose statement, the researcher narrows the focus to specific questions to be answered or predictions based on hypotheses to be tested. This chapter begins by advancing several principles in designing and scripts for writing qualitative research questions; quantitative research questions, objectives, and hypotheses; and mixed methods research questions.

QUALITATIVE RESEARCH QUESTIONS

In a qualitative study, inquirers state research questions, not objectives (i.e., specific goals for the research) or hypotheses (i.e., predictions that involve variables and statistical tests). These research questions assume two forms: a central question and associated subquestions.

The **central question** is a broad question that asks for an exploration of the central phenomenon or concept in a study. The inquirer poses this question, consistent with the emerging methodology of qualitative research, as a general issue so as to not limit the inquiry. To arrive at this question, *ask*, "What is the broadest question that I can ask in the study?" Beginning researchers trained in *quantitative* research might struggle with this approach because they are accustomed to the reverse approach: identifying specific, narrow questions or hypotheses based on a few variables. In qualitative research, the intent is to explore the complex set of factors surrounding the central phenomenon and present the varied perspectives or meanings that participants hold. The following are guidelines for writing broad, qualitative research questions:

- *Ask one or two central questions followed by no more than five to seven subquestions.* Several subquestions follow each general central question; the subquestions narrow the focus of the study but leave open the questioning. This approach is well within the limits set by Miles and Huberman (1994), who recommended that researchers write no more than a dozen qualitative research questions in all (central and subquestions). The subquestions, in turn, can become specific questions used during interviews (or in observing or when looking at documents). In developing an interview protocol or guide, the researcher might ask an ice breaker question at the beginning, for example, followed by five or so subquestions in the study (see Chapter 9). The interview would then end with an additional wrap-up or summary question or ask, as I did in one of my qualitative case studies, "Who should I turn to, to learn more about this topic?" (Asmussen & Creswell, 1995).

● *Relate the central question to the specific qualitative strategy of inquiry.* For example, the specificity of the questions in ethnography at this stage of the design differs from that in other qualitative strategies. In ethnographic research, Spradley (1980) advanced a taxonomy of ethnographic questions that included a mini-tour of the culture-sharing group, their experiences, use of native language, contrasts with other cultural groups, and questions to verify the accuracy of the data. In critical ethnography, the research questions may build on a body of existing literature. These questions become working guidelines rather than truths to be proven (Thomas, 1993, p. 35). Alternatively, in phenomenology, the questions might be broadly stated without specific reference to the existing literature or a typology of questions. Moustakas (1994) talks about asking what the participants experienced and the contexts or situations in which they experienced it. A phenomenological example is, "What is it like for a mother to live with a teenage child who is dying of cancer?" (Nieswiadomy, 1993, p. 151). In grounded theory, the questions may be directed toward generating a theory of some process, such as the exploration of a process as to how caregivers and patients interact in a hospital setting. In a qualitative case study, the questions may address a description of the case and the themes that emerge from studying it.

● *Begin the research questions with the words* what *or* how *to convey an open and emerging design.* The word *why* often implies that the researcher is trying to explain why something occurs, and this suggests to me a cause-and-effect type of thinking that I associate with *quantitative* research instead of the more open and emerging stance of qualitative research.

● Focus on a single phenomenon or concept. As a study develops over time, factors will emerge that may influence this single phenomenon, but begin a study with a single focus to explore in great detail.

● Use exploratory verbs that convey the language of emerging design. These verbs tell the reader that the study will

- Discover (e.g., grounded theory)
- Seek to understand (e.g., ethnography)

- Explore a process (e.g., case study)
- Describe the experiences (e.g., phenomenology)
- Report the stories (e.g., narrative research)

● Use these more exploratory verbs that are nondirectional rather than directional words that suggest *quantitative* research, such as "affect," "influence," "impact," "determine," "cause," and "relate."

● Expect the research questions to evolve and change during the study in a manner consistent with the assumptions of an emerging design. Often in *qualitative* studies, the questions are under continual review and reformulation (as in a grounded theory study). This approach may be problematic for individuals accustomed to *quantitative* designs, in which the research questions remain fixed throughout the study.

● *Use open-ended questions* without reference to the literature or theory unless otherwise indicated by a qualitative strategy of inquiry.

● *Specify the participants and the research site* for the study, if the information has not yet been given.

Here is a script for a qualitative central question:

__________ (How or what) is the __________ ("story for" for narrative research; "meaning of" the phenomenon for phenomenology; "theory that explains the process of" for grounded theory; "culture-sharing pattern" for ethnography; "issue" in the "case" for case study) of __________ (central phenomenon) for __________ (participants) at __________ (research site).

The following are examples of qualitative research questions drawn from several types of strategies.

Example 7.1 *A Qualitative Central Question From an Ethnography*

Finders (1996) used ethnographic procedures to document the reading of teen magazines by middle-class European American seventh-grade girls. By examining the reading of teen zines (magazines), the researcher explored how the girls perceive and construct their social roles and relationships as they enter junior high school. She asked one guiding central question in her study:

> How do early adolescent females read literature that falls outside the realm of fiction?
>
> (Finders, 1996, p. 72)

Finders's (1996) central question begins with *how*; it uses an open-ended verb, *read*; it focuses on a single concept, the literature or teen magazines; and it mentions the participants, adolescent females, as the culture-sharing group. Notice how the author crafted a concise, single question that needed to be answered in the study. It is a broad question stated to permit participants to share diverse perspectives about reading the literature.

Example 7.2 *Qualitative Central Questions From a Case Study*

Padula and Miller (1999) conducted a multiple case study that described the experiences of women who went back to school, after a time away, in a psychology doctoral program at a major Midwestern research university. The intent was to document the women's experiences, providing a gendered and feminist perspective for women in the literature. The authors asked three central questions that guided the inquiry:

> (a) How do women in a psychology doctoral program describe their decision to return to school? (b) How do women in a psychology doctoral program describe their reentry experiences? And (c) How does returning to graduate school change these women's lives?
>
> (Padula & Miller, 1999, p. 328)

These three central questions all begin with the word *how*; they include open-ended verbs, such as "describe," and they focus on three aspects of the doctoral experience—returning to school, reentering, and changing. They also mention the participants as women in a doctoral program at a Midwestern research university.

8 Qualitative Procedures

JOHN W. CRESWELL

Qualitative procedures demonstrate a different approach to scholarly inquiry than methods of quantitative research. Qualitative inquiry employs different philosophical assumptions; strategies of inquiry; and methods of data collection, analysis, and interpretation. Although the processes are similar, qualitative procedures rely on text and image data, have unique steps in data analysis, and draw on diverse strategies of inquiry.

In fact, the strategies of inquiry chosen in a qualitative project have a dramatic influence on the procedures, which, even within strategies, are anything but uniform. Looking over the landscape of qualitative procedures shows diverse perspectives ranging from social justice thinking (Denzin & Lincoln, 2005), to ideological perspectives (Lather, 1991), to philosophical stances (Schwandt, 2000), to systematic procedural guidelines (Creswell, 2007; Corbin & Strauss, 2007). All perspectives vie for center stage in this unfolding model of inquiry called qualitative research.

This chapter attempts to combine many perspectives, provide general procedures, and use examples liberally to illustrate variations in strategies. This discussion draws on thoughts provided by several authors writing about qualitative proposal design (e.g., see Berg, 2001; Marshall & Rossman, 2006; Maxwell, 2005; Rossman & Rallis, 1998). The topics in a proposal section on procedures are characteristics of qualitative research, the research strategy, the role of the researcher, steps in data collection and analysis, strategies for validity, the accuracy of findings, and narrative structure. Table 9.1 shows a checklist of questions for designing qualitative procedures.

THE CHARACTERISTICS OF QUALITATIVE RESEARCH

For many years, proposal writers had to discuss the characteristics of qualitative research and convince faculty and audiences as to their legitimacy. Now these discussions are less frequently found in the literature and there is some consensus as to what constitutes qualitative inquiry. Thus, my suggestions about this section of a proposal are as follows:

Table 9.1 A Checklist of Questions for Designing a Qualitative Procedure

________	Are the basic characteristics of qualitative studies mentioned?
________	Is the specific type of qualitative strategy of inquiry to be used in the study mentioned? Is the history of, a definition of, and applications for the strategy mentioned?
________	Does the reader gain an understanding of the researcher's role in the study (past historical, social, cultural experiences, personal connections to sites and people, steps in gaining entry, and sensitive ethical issues)?
________	Is the purposeful sampling strategy for sites and individuals identified?
________	Are the specific forms of data collection mentioned and a rationale given for their use?
________	Are the procedures for recording information during the data collection procedure mentioned (such as protocols)?
________	Are the data analysis steps identified?
________	Is there evidence that the researcher has organized the data for analysis?
________	Has the researcher reviewed the data generally to obtain a sense of the information?
________	Has coding been used with the data?
________	Have the codes been developed to form a description or to identify themes?
________	Are the themes interrelated to show a higher level of analysis and abstraction?
________	Are the ways that the data will be represented mentioned—such as in tables, graphs, and figures?
________	Have the bases for interpreting the analysis been specified (personal experiences, the literature, questions, action agenda)?
________	Has the researcher mentioned the outcome of the study (developed a theory, provided a complex picture of themes)?
________	Have multiple strategies been cited for validating the findings?

- Review the needs of potential audiences for the proposal. Decide whether audience members are knowledgeable enough about the characteristics of qualitative research that this section is not necessary.
- If there is some question about their knowledge, present the basic characteristics of qualitative research in the proposal and possibly discuss a

recent qualitative research journal article (or study) to use as an example to illustrate the characteristics.

- Several lists of characteristics might be used (e.g., Bogdan & Biklen, 1992; Eisner, 1991; Hatch, 2002; LeCompte & Schensul, 1999; Marshall & Rossman, 2006), but I will rely on a composite analysis of several of these writers that I incorporated into my book on qualitative inquiry (Creswell, 2007). My list captures both traditional perspectives and the newer advocacy, participatory, and self-reflexive perspectives of qualitative inquiry. Here are the characteristics of qualitative research, presented in no specific order of importance:
  - Natural setting—Qualitative researchers tend to collect data in the field at the site where participants experience the issue or problem under study. They do not bring individuals into a lab (a contrived situation), nor do they typically send out instruments for individuals to complete. This up close information gathered by actually talking directly to people and seeing them behave and act within their context is a major characteristic of qualitative research. In the natural setting, the researchers have face-to-face interaction over time.
  - Researcher as key instrument—Qualitative researchers collect data themselves through examining documents, observing behavior, or interviewing participants. They may use a protocol—an instrument for collecting data—but the researchers are the ones who actually gather the information. They do not tend to use or rely on questionnaires or instruments developed by other researchers.
  - Multiple sources of data—Qualitative researchers typically gather multiple forms of data, such as interviews, observations, and documents, rather than rely on a single data source. Then the researchers review all of the data, make sense of it, and organize it into categories or themes that cut across all of the data sources.
  - Inductive data analysis—Qualitative researchers build their patterns, categories, and themes from the bottom up, by organizing the data into increasingly more abstract units of information. This inductive process illustrates working back and forth between the themes and the database until the researchers have established a comprehensive set of themes. It may also involve collaborating with the participants interactively, so that participants have a chance to shape the themes or abstractions that emerge from the process.
  - Participants' meanings—In the entire qualitative research process, the researcher keeps a focus on learning the meaning that the participants hold about the problem or issue, not the meaning that the researchers bring to the research or writers express in the literature.
  - Emergent design—The research process for qualitative researchers is emergent. This means that the initial plan for research cannot be

tightly prescribed, and all phases of the process may change or shift after the researcher enters the field and begins to collect data. For example, the questions may change, the forms of data collection may shift, and the individuals studied and the sites visited may be modified. The key idea behind qualitative research is to learn about the problem or issue from participants and to address the research to obtain that information.

- Theoretical lens—Qualitative researchers often use lens to view their studies, such as the concept of culture, central to ethnography, or gendered, racial, or class differences from the theoretical orientations discussed in Chapter 3. Sometimes the study may be organized around identifying the social, political, or historical context of the problem under study.
- Interpretive—Qualitative research is a form of interpretive inquiry in which researchers make an interpretation of what they see, hear, and understand. Their interpretations cannot be separated from their own backgrounds, history, contexts, and prior understandings. After a research report is issued, the readers make an interpretation as well as the participants, offering yet other interpretations of the study. With the readers, the participants, and the researchers all making interpretations, it is apparent how multiple views of the problem can emerge.
- Holistic account—Qualitative researchers try to develop a complex picture of the problem or issue under study. This involves reporting multiple perspectives, identifying the many factors involved in a situation, and generally sketching the larger picture that emerges. A visual model of many facets of a process or a central phenomenon aid in establishing this holistic picture (see, for example, Creswell & Brown, 1992).

STRATEGIES OF INQUIRY

Beyond these general characteristics are more specific strategies of inquiry. These strategies focus on data collection, analysis, and writing, but they originate out of disciplines and flow throughout the process of research (e.g., types of problems, ethical issues of importance; Creswell, 2007b). Many strategies exist, such as the 28 approaches identified by Tesch (1990), the 19 types in Wolcott's (2001) tree, and the 5 approaches to qualitative inquiry by Creswell (2007). As discussed in Chapter 1, I recommend that qualitative researchers choose from among the possibilities, such as narrative, phenomenology, ethnography, case study, and grounded theory. I selected these five because they are popular across the social and health sciences today. Others exist that have been addressed adequately in qualitative books, such as participatory action research (Kemmis & Wilkinson, 1998) or discourse analysis (Cheek, 2004). For the five approaches, researchers might study individuals (narrative, phenomenology); explore processes, activities, and events (case study, grounded theory); or learn about broad culture-sharing behavior of individuals or groups (ethnography).

In writing a procedure for a qualitative proposal, consider the following **research tips:**

- Identify the specific approach to inquiry that you will be using.
- Provide some background information about the strategy, such as its discipline origin, the applications of it, and a brief definition of it (see Chapter 1 for the five strategies of inquiry).
- Discuss why it is an appropriate strategy to use in the proposed study.
- Identify how the use of the strategy will shape the types of questions asked (see Morse, 1994, for questions that relate to strategies), the form of data collection, the steps of data analysis, and the final narrative.

THE RESEARCHER'S ROLE

As mentioned in the list of characteristics, qualitative research is interpretative research, with the inquirer typically involved in a sustained and intensive experience with participants. This introduces a range of strategic, ethical, and personal issues into the qualitative research process (Locke et al., 2007). With these concerns in mind, inquirers explicitly identify reflexively their biases, values, and personal background, such as gender, history, culture, and socioeconomic status, that may shape their interpretations formed during a study. In addition, gaining entry to a research site and the ethical issues that might arise are also elements of the researcher's role.

- Include statements about past experiences that provide background data through which the audience can better understand the topic, the setting, or the participants and the researcher's interpretation of the phenomenon.
- Comment on connections between the researcher and the participants and on the research sites. "Backyard" research (Glesne & Peshkin, 1992) involves studying the researcher's own organization, or friends, or immediate work setting. This often leads to compromises in the researcher's ability to disclose information and raises difficult power issues. Although data collection may be convenient and easy, the problems of reporting data that are biased, incomplete, or compromised are legion. If studying the backyard is necessary, employ multiple strategies of validity (as discussed later) to create reader confidence in the accuracy of the findings.
- Indicate steps taken to obtain permission from the Institutional Review Board (see Chapter 4) to protect the rights of human participants. Attach, as an appendix, the approval letter from the IRB and discuss the process involved in securing permission.

● Discuss steps taken to gain entry to the setting and to secure permission to study the participants or situation (Marshall & Rossman, 2006). It is important to gain access to research or archival sites by seeking the approval of **gatekeepers**, individuals at the research site that provide access to the site and allow or permit the research to be done. A brief proposal might need to be developed and submitted for review by gatekeepers. Bogdan and Biklen (1992) advance topics that could be addressed in such a proposal:

- Why was the site chosen for study?
- What activities will occur at the site during the research study?
- Will the study be disruptive?
- How will the results be reported?
- What will the gatekeeper gain from the study?

● Comment about sensitive ethical issues that may arise (see Chapter 3, and Berg, 2001). For each issue raised, discuss how the research study will address it. For example, when studying a sensitive topic, it is necessary to mask names of people, places, and activities. In this situation, the process for masking information requires discussion in the proposal.

DATA COLLECTION PROCEDURES

Comments about the role of the researcher set the stage for discussion of issues involved in collecting data. The data collection steps include setting the boundaries for the study, collecting information through unstructured or semistructured observations and interviews, documents, and visual materials, as well as establishing the protocol for recording information.

● Identify the *purposefully selected* sites or individuals for the proposed study. The idea behind qualitative research is to **purposefully select** participants or sites (or documents or visual material) that will best help the researcher understand the problem and the research question. This does not necessarily suggest random sampling or selection of a large number of participants and sites, as typically found in *quantitative* research. A discussion about participants and site might include four aspects identified by Miles and Huberman (1994): the *setting* (where the research will take place), the *actors* (who will be observed or interviewed), the *events* (what the actors will be observed or interviewed doing), and the *process* (the evolving nature of events undertaken by the actors within the setting).

● Indicate the type or types of data to be collected. In many qualitative studies, inquirers collect multiple forms of data and spend a considerable time in the natural setting gathering information. The collection procedures in qualitative research involve four basic types, as shown in Table 9.2.

Table 9.2 Qualitative Data Collection Types, Options, Advantages, and Limitations

Data Collection Types	Options Within Types	Advantages of the Type	Limitations of the Type
Observations	• Complete participant—researcher conceals role • Observer as participant—role of researcher is known • Participant as observer—observation role secondary to participant role • Complete observer—researcher observes without participating	• Researcher has a first-hand experience with participant. • Researcher can record information as it occurs. • Unusual aspects can be noticed during observation. • Useful in exploring topics that may be uncomfortable for participants to discuss.	• Researcher may be seen as intrusive. • Private information may be observed that researcher cannot report. • Researcher may not have good attending and observing skills. • Certain participants (e.g., children) may present special problems in gaining rapport.
Interviews	• Face-to-face—one-on-one, in-person interview • Telephone—researcher interviews by phone • Focus group—researcher interviews participants in a group • E-mail internet interview	• Useful when participants cannot be directly observed. • Participants can provide historical information. • Allows researcher control over the line of questioning.	• Provides indirect information filtered through the views of interviewees. • Provides information in a designated place rather than the natural field setting. • Researcher's presence may bias responses. • Not all people are equally articulate and perceptive.

(Continued)

Table 9.2 (Continued)

Data Collection Types	Options Within Types	Advantages of the Type	Limitations of the Type
Documents	• Public documents, such as minutes of meetings, or newspapers • Private documents, such as journals, diaries, or letters	• Enables a researcher to obtain the language and words of participants. • Can be accessed at a time convenient to researcher—an unobtrusive source of information. • Represents data which are thoughtful in that participants have given attention to compiling them. • As written evidence, it saves a researcher the time and expense of transcribing.	• Not all people are equally articulate and perceptive. • May be protected information unavailable to public or private access. • Requires the researcher to search out the information in hard-to-find places. • Requires transcribing or optically scanning for computer entry. • Materials may be incomplete. • The documents may not be authentic or accurate.
Audio-Visual Materials	• Photographs • Videotapes • Art objects • Computer software • Film	• May be an unobtrusive method of collecting data. • Provides an opportunity for participants to directly share their reality. • It is creative in that it captures attention visually.	• May be difficult to interpret. • May not be accessible publicly or privately. • The presence of an observer (e.g., photographer) may be disruptive and affect responses.

NOTE: This table includes material taken from Merriam (1998), Bogdan & Biklen (1992), and Creswell (2007).

- **Qualitative observations** are those in which the researcher takes field notes on the behavior and activities of individuals at the research site. In these field notes, the researcher records, in an unstructured or semistructured way (using some prior questions that the inquirer wants to know), activities at the research site. Qualitative observers may also engage in roles varying from a non-participant to a complete participant.
- In **qualitative interviews**, the researcher conducts face-to-face interviews with participants, interviews participants by telephone, or engages in focus group interviews, with six to eight interviewees in each group. These interviews involve unstructured and generally open-ended questions that are few in number and intended to elicit views and opinions from the participants.
- During the process of research, the investigator may collect **qualitative documents**. These may be public documents (e.g., newspapers, minutes of meetings, official reports) or private documents (e.g., personal journals and diaries, letters, e-mails).
- A final category of qualitative data consists of **qualitative audio and visual materials**. This data may take the form of photographs, art objects, videotapes, or any forms of sound.

● In a discussion about data collection forms, be specific about the types and include arguments concerning the strengths and weaknesses of each type, as discussed in Table 9.2.

● Include data collection types that go beyond typical observations and interviews. These unusual forms create reader interest in a proposal and can capture useful information that observations and interviews may miss. For example, examine the compendium of types of data in Table 9.3 that can be used, to stretch the imagination about possibilities, such as gathering sounds or tastes, or using cherished items to elicit comments during an interview.

DATA RECORDING PROCEDURES

Before entering the field, qualitative researchers plan their approach to data recording. The proposal should identify what data the researcher will record and the procedures for recording data.

● Use a *protocol* for recording observational data. Researchers often engage in multiple observations during the course of a qualitative study and use an **observational protocol** for recording information while observing. This may be a single page with a dividing line down the middle to separate *descriptive notes* (portraits of the participants, a reconstruction of dialogue, a description of the physical setting, accounts of particular

Table 9.3 A List of Qualitative Data Collection Approaches
Observations
• Gather field notes by conducting an observation as a participant. • Gather field notes by conducting an observation as an observer. • Gather field notes by spending more time as a participant than as an observer. • Gather field notes by spending more time as an observer than as a participant. • Gather field notes first by observing as an outsider and then moving into the setting and observing as an insider.
Interviews
• Conduct an unstructured, open-ended interview and take interview notes. • Conduct an unstructured, open-ended interview, audiotape the interview, and transcribe it. • Conduct a semistructured interview, audiotape the interview, and transcribe the interview. • Conduct a focus group interview, audiotape the interview, and transcribe it. • Conduct different types of interviews: email, face-to-face, focus group, online focus group, telephone interviews
Documents
• Keep a journal during the research study. • Have a participant keep a journal or diary during the research study. • Collect personal letters from participants. • Analyze public documents (e.g., official memos, minutes, records, archival material). • Examine autobiographies and biographies. • Have participants take photographs or videotapes (i.e., photo elicitation). • Chart audits • Medical records
Audio-visual Materials
• Examine physical trace evidence (e.g., footprints in the snow). • Videotape or film a social situation or an individual or group. • Examine photographs or videotapes. • Collect sounds (e.g., musical sounds, a child's laughter, car horns honking). • Collect e-mail messages. • Collect cell phone text messages. • Examine possessions or ritual objects. • Collect sounds, smells, tastes, or any stimuli of the senses.

SOURCE: Adapted from Creswell (2007).

events, or activities) from *reflective notes* (the researcher's personal thoughts, such as "speculation, feelings, problems, ideas, hunches, impressions, and prejudices" Bogdan & Biklen, 1992, p. 121). Also written on this form might be *demographic information* about the time, place, and date of the field setting where the observation takes place.

- Use an **interview protocol** for asking questions and recording answers during a qualitative interview. This protocol includes the following components:
  - A heading (date, place, interviewer, interviewee)
  - Instructions for the interviewer to follow so that standard procedures are used from one interview to another
  - The questions (typically an ice-breaker question at the beginning followed by 4–5 questions that are often the subquestions in a qualitative research plan, followed by some concluding statement or a question, such as, "Who should I visit with to learn more about my questions?"
  - Probes for the 4–5 questions, to follow up and ask individuals to explain their ideas in more detail or to elaborate on what they have said
  - Space between the questions to record responses
  - A final thank-you statement to acknowledge the time the interviewee spent during the interview (see Creswell, 2007)

- Researchers record information from interviews by making handwritten notes, by audiotaping, or by videotaping. Even if an interview is taped, I recommend that researchers take notes, in the event that recording equipment fails. If audiotaping is used, researchers need to plan in advance for the transcription of the tape.

- The recording of documents and visual materials can be based on the researcher's structure for taking notes. Typically, notes reflect information about the document or other material as well as key ideas in the documents. It is helpful to note whether the information represents primary material (i.e., information directly from the people or situation under study) or secondary material (i.e., secondhand accounts of the people or situation written by others). It is also helpful to comment on the reliability and value of the data source.

DATA ANALYSIS AND INTERPRETATION

Discussion of the plan for analyzing the data might have several components. The process of data analysis involves making sense out of text and image data. It involves preparing the data for analysis, conducting different analyses, moving deeper and deeper into understanding the data (some qualitative researchers like to think of this as peeling back the layers of an onion), representing the data, and making an interpretation of the larger meaning of the data. Several generic processes might be stated in the proposal that convey a sense of the overall activities of qualitative data analysis, such as the following drawn from my own thoughts (Creswell, 2007) and those of Rossman and Rallis (1998):

- It is an ongoing process involving continual reflection about the data, asking analytic questions, and writing memos throughout the study. I say that qualitative data analysis is conducted concurrently with gathering data, making interpretations, and writing reports. While interviews are going on, for example, the researcher may be analyzing an interview collected earlier, writing memos that may ultimately be included as a narrative in the final report, and organizing the structure of the final report.

- Data analysis involves collecting open-ended data, based on asking general questions and developing an analysis from the information supplied by participants.

- Often we see qualitative data analysis reported in journal articles and books that is a generic form of analysis. In this approach, the researcher collects qualitative data, analyzes it for themes or perspectives, and reports 4–5 themes. I consider this approach to be basic qualitative analysis; today many qualitative researchers go beyond this generic analysis to add a procedure within one of the qualitative strategies of inquiry. For example, *grounded theory* has systematic steps (Corbin & Strauss, 2007; Strauss & Corbin, 1990, 1998). These involve generating categories of information (open coding), selecting one of the categories and positioning it within a theoretical model (axial coding), and then explicating a story from the interconnection of these categories (selective coding). *Case study* and *ethnographic research* involve a detailed description of the setting or individuals, followed by analysis of the data for themes or issues (see Stake, 1995; Wolcott, 1994). *Phenomenological research* uses the analysis of significant statements, the generation of meaning units, and the development of what Moustakas (1994) calls an essence description. *Narrative research* employs restorying the participants' stories using structural devices, such as plot, setting, activities, climax, and denouement (Clandinin & Connelly, 2000). As these examples illustrate, the processes as well as the terms differ from one analytic strategy to another.

- Despite these analytic differences depending on the type of strategy used, qualitative inquirers often use a general procedure and convey in the proposal the steps in data analysis. An ideal situation is to blend the general steps with the specific research strategy steps. An overview of the data analysis process is seen in Figure 9.1. As a **research tip,** I urge researchers to look at qualitative data analysis as following steps from the specific to the general and as involving multiple levels of analysis.

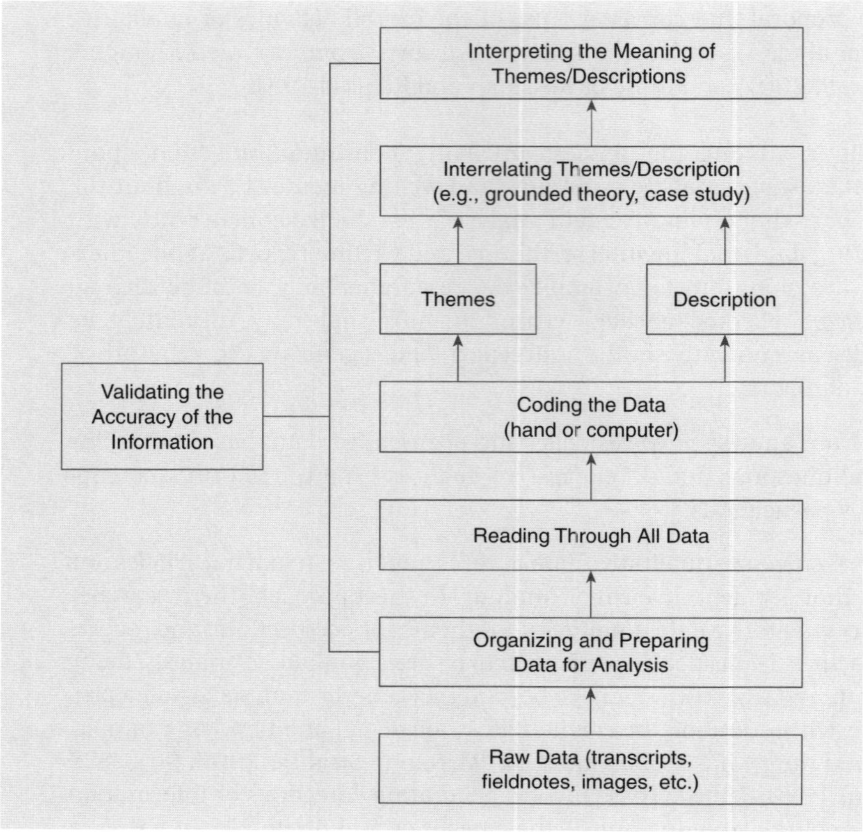

Figure 9.1 Data Analysis in Qualitative Research

This figure suggests a linear, hierarchical approach building from the bottom to the top, but I see it as more interactive in practice; the various stages are interrelated and not always visited in the order presented. These levels are emphasized in the following steps:

Step 1. *Organize and prepare* the data for analysis. This involves transcribing interviews, optically scanning material, typing up field notes, or sorting and arranging the data into different types depending on the sources of information.

Step 2. Read through all the data. A first step is to obtain a *general sense* of the information and to reflect on its overall meaning. What general ideas are participants saying? What is the tone of the ideas? What is the impression of the overall depth, credibility, and use of the information? Sometimes qualitative researchers write notes in margins or start recording general thoughts about the data at this stage.

Step 3. Begin detailed analysis with a coding process. **Coding** is the process of organizing the material into chunks or segments of text before bringing meaning to information (Rossman & Rallis, 1998, p. 171). It involves taking text data or pictures gathered during data collection, segmenting sentences (or paragraphs) or images into categories, and labeling those categories with a term, often a term based in the actual language of the participant (called an *in vivo* term).

Before proceeding to Step 4, consider some remarks that will provide detailed guidance for the coding process. Tesch (1990, pp. 142–145) provides a useful analysis of the process in eight steps:

1. Get a sense of the whole. Read all the transcriptions carefully. Perhaps jot down some ideas as they come to mind.
2. Pick one document (i.e., one interview)—the most interesting one, the shortest, the one on the top of the pile. Go through it, asking yourself, "What is this about?" Do not think about the substance of the information but its underlying meaning. Write thoughts in the margin.
3. When you have completed this task for several participants, make a list of all topics. Cluster together similar topics. Form these topics into columns, perhaps arrayed as major topics, unique topics, and leftovers.
4. Now take this list and go back to your data. Abbreviate the topics as codes and write the codes next to the appropriate segments of the text. Try this preliminary organizing scheme to see if new categories and codes emerge.
5. Find the most descriptive wording for your topics and turn them into categories. Look for ways of reducing your total list of categories by grouping topics that relate to each other. Perhaps draw lines between your categories to show interrelationships.
6. Make a final decision on the abbreviation for each category and alphabetize these codes.
7. Assemble the data material belonging to each category in one place and perform a preliminary analysis.
8. If necessary, recode your existing data.

These eight steps engage a researcher in a systematic process of analyzing textual data. Variations exist in this process. As a **research tip,** I encourage qualitative researchers to analyze their data for material that can address the following:

- Codes on topics that readers would expect to find, based on the past literature and common sense

- Codes that are surprising and that were not anticipated at the beginning of the study
- Codes that are unusual, and that are, in and of themselves, of conceptual interest to readers (e.g., in Asmussen and Creswell, 1995, we identified *retriggering* as one of the codes/themes in the analysis that suggested a new dimension for us to a gunman incident on campus and that seemed to connect with experiences of others on campus)
- Codes that address a larger theoretical perspective in the research

As an alternative conceptualization, consider the list by Bogdan and Biklen (1992, pp. 166–172) of the types of codes that they look for in a qualitative database:

- Setting and context codes
- Perspectives held by subjects
- Subjects' ways of thinking about people and objects
- Process codes
- Activity codes
- Strategy codes
- Relationship and social structure codes
- Preassigned coding schemes

One further issue about coding is whether the researcher should (a) develop codes *only* on the basis of the emerging information collected from participants, (b) use predetermined codes and then fit the data to them, or (c) use some combination of predetermined and emerging codes. The traditional approach in the social sciences is to allow the codes to emerge during the data analysis. In the health sciences, a popular approach is to use predetermined codes based on the theory being examined. In this case, the researchers might develop a **qualitative codebook**, a table or record that contains a list of predetermined codes that researchers use for coding the data. This codebook might be composed with the names of codes in one column, a definition of codes in another column, and then specific instances (e.g., line numbers) in which the code was found in the transcripts. Having such a codebook is invaluable when multiple researchers are coding the data from different transcripts. This codebook can evolve and change during a study based on close analysis of the data, even when the researcher is not starting from an emerging code perspective. For researchers who have a distinct theory they want to test in their projects, I would recommend that a preliminary codebook be developed for coding the data and permit the codebook to develop and change based on the information learned during the data analysis. The use of a codebook is especially helpful for fields in which *quantitative* research dominates and a more systematic approach to *qualitative* research is needed.

Returning to the general coding process, some researchers have found it useful to hand code qualitative transcripts or information, sometimes using color code schemes and to cut and paste text segments onto note cards. This is a laborious and time-consuming approach. Others tend to use qualitative computer software programs to help code, organize, and sort information that will be useful in writing the qualitative study. Several excellent computer software programs are available, and they have similar features: good tutorials and demonstration CDs, ability to incorporate both text and image (e.g., photographs) data, the feature of storing and organizing data, the search capacity of locating all text associated with specific codes, interrelated codes for making queries of the relationship among codes, and the import and export of qualitative data to *quantitative* programs, such as spreadsheets or data analysis programs.

The basic idea behind these programs is that using the computer is an efficient means for storing and locating qualitative data. Although the researcher still needs to go through each line of text (as in transcriptions) and assign codes, this process may be faster and more efficient than hand coding. Also, in large databases, the researcher can quickly locate all passages (or text segments) coded the same and determine whether participants are responding to a code idea in similar or different ways. Beyond this, the computer program can facilitate comparing different codes (e.g., How do males and females—the first code of gender—differ in terms of their attitudes to smoking—a second code) These are just a few features of the software programs that make them a logical choice for qualitative data analysis over hand coding. As with any software program, qualitative software programs require time and skill to learn and employ effectively, although books for learning the programs are widely available (e.g., Weitzman & Miles, 1995).

Most of the programs are available only on the PC platform. The computer software programs that my staff and I use in my research office are these:

- MAXqda (http://www.maxqda.com/). This is an excellent PC-based program from Germany that helps researchers systematically evaluate and interpret qualitative texts. It has all of the features mentioned earlier.

- Atlas.ti (http://www.atlasti.com). This is another PC-based program from Germany that enables a researcher to organize text, graphic, audio, and visual data files, along with coding, memos and findings, into a project.

- QSR NVivo (http://www.qsrinternational.com/) This program, from Australia, features the popular software program N6 (or Nud.ist) and NVivo concept mapping in combination. It is available only for Windows PC.

- HyperRESEARCH (http://www.researchware.com/). This is a program available for either the MAC or PC. It is an easy-to-use qualitative software package enabling users to code, retrieve, build theories, and conduct analyses of the data.

Step 4. Use the coding process to generate a description of the setting or people as well as categories or themes for analysis. *Description* involves a detailed rendering of information about people, places, or events in a setting. Researchers can generate codes for this description. This analysis is useful in designing detailed descriptions for case studies, ethnographies, and narrative research projects. Then use the coding to generate a small number of *themes* or categories, perhaps five to seven categories for a research study. These themes are the ones that appear as major findings in qualitative studies and are often used to create headings in the findings sections of studies. They should display multiple perspectives from individuals and be supported by diverse quotations and specific evidence.

Beyond identifying the themes during the coding process, qualitative researchers can do much with themes to build additional layers of complex analysis. For example, researchers interconnect themes into a story line (as in narratives) or develop them into a theoretical model (as in grounded theory). Themes are analyzed for each individual case and across different cases (as in case studies) or shaped into a general description (as in phenomenology). Sophisticated qualitative studies go beyond description and theme identification and into complex theme connections.

Step 5. Advance how the description and themes will be *represented* in the qualitative narrative. The most popular approach is to use a narrative passage to convey the findings of the analysis. This might be a discussion that mentions a chronology of events, the detailed discussion of several themes (complete with subthemes, specific illustrations, multiple perspectives from individuals, and quotations) or a discussion with interconnecting themes. Many qualitative researchers also use visuals, figures, or tables as adjuncts to the discussions. They present a process model (as in grounded theory), advance a drawing of the specific research site (as in ethnography), or convey descriptive information about each participant in a table (as in case studies and ethnographies).

Step 6. A final step in data analysis involves making an **interpretation** or meaning of the data. Asking, "What were the lessons learned?" captures the essence of this idea (Lincoln & Guba, 1985). These *lessons* could be the researcher's personal interpretation, couched in the understanding that the inquirer brings to the study from her or his own culture, history, and experiences. It could also be a meaning derived from a comparison of the findings with information gleaned from the *literature* or *theories.* In this way, authors suggest that the findings confirm past information or diverge from it. It can also suggest *new questions* that need to be asked—questions raised by the data and analysis that the inquirer had not foreseen earlier in the study. One way ethnographers can end a study, says Wolcott (1994), is to ask further questions. The questioning approach is also used in advocacy and participatory approaches to qualitative research. Moreover, when qualitative researchers use a theoretical lens, they can form interpretations that call for action agendas for reform and change. Thus, interpretation in qualitative research can take many forms, be adapted for different types of designs, and be flexible to convey personal, research-based, and action meanings.

RELIABILITY, VALIDITY, AND GENERALIZABILITY

Although validation of findings occurs throughout the steps in the process of research (as shown in Figure 9.1), this discussion focuses on it to enable a researcher to write a passage into a proposal on the procedures for validating the findings that will be undertaken in a study. Proposal developers need to convey the steps they will take in their studies to check for the accuracy and credibility of their findings.

Validity does not carry the same connotations in qualitative research as it does in quantitative research, nor is it a companion of reliability (examining stability or consistency of responses) or generalizability (the external validity of applying results to new settings, people, or samples; both are discussed in Chapter 8). **Qualitative validity** means that the researcher checks for the accuracy of the findings by employing certain procedures, while **qualitative reliability** indicates that the researcher's approach is consistent across different researchers and different projects (Gibbs, 2007).

How do qualitative researchers check to determine if their approaches are consistent or reliable? Yin (2003) suggests that qualitative researchers need to document the procedures of their case studies and to document as many of the steps of the procedures as possible. He also recommends setting up a detailed case study protocol and database. Gibbs (2007) suggests several **reliability procedures:**

- Check transcripts to make sure that they do not contain obvious mistakes made during transcription.

- Make sure that there is not a drift in the definition of codes, a shift in the meaning of the codes during the process of coding. This can be accomplished by constantly comparing data with the codes and by writing memos about the codes and their definitions (see the discussion on a qualitative codebook).

- For team research, coordinate the communication among the coders by regular documented meetings and by sharing the analysis.

- Cross-check codes developed by different researchers by comparing results that are independently derived.

Proposal writers need to include several of these procedures as evidence that they will have consistent results in their proposed study. I recommend that several procedures be mentioned in a proposal and that single researchers find another person who can cross-check their codes, for what I call **intercoder agreement** (or cross-checking). Such an agreement might be based on whether two or more coders agree on codes used for the same passages in the text (it is not that they code the same passage of text, but whether another coder would code it with the same or a similar code). Statistical procedures or reliability subprograms in qualitative computer software packages can then be used to determine the level of consistency of coding. Miles and Huberman (1994) recommend that the consistency of the coding be in agreement at least 80% of the time for good qualitative reliability.

Validity, on the other hand, is one of the strengths of qualitative research, and it is based on determining whether the findings are accurate from the standpoint of the researcher, the participant, or the readers of an account (Creswell & Miller, 2000). Terms abound in the qualitative literature that speak to this idea, such as *trustworthiness*, *authenticity*, and *credibility* (Creswell & Miller, 2000), and it is a much-discussed topic (Lincoln & Guba, 2000).

A procedural perspective that I recommend for research proposals is to identify and discuss one or more strategies available to check the accuracy of the findings. The researcher actively incorporates **validity strategies** into their proposal. I recommend the use of multiple strategies, and these should enhance the researcher's ability to assess the accuracy of findings as well as convince readers of that accuracy. There are eight primary strategies, organized from those most frequently used and easy to implement to those occasionally used and more difficult to implement:

- *Triangulate* different data sources of information by examining evidence from the sources and using it to build a coherent justification for themes. If themes are established based on converging several sources of data or perspectives from participants, then this process can be claimed as adding to the validity of the study.

- Use *member checking* to determine the accuracy of the qualitative findings through taking the final report or specific descriptions or themes back to participants and determining whether these participants feel that they are accurate. This does not mean taking back the raw transcripts to check for accuracy; instead, the researcher takes back parts of the polished product, such as the themes, the case analysis, the grounded theory, the cultural description, and so forth. This procedure can involve conducting a follow-up interview with participants in the study and providing an opportunity for them to comment on the findings.

- Use *rich, thick description* to convey the findings. This description may transport readers to the setting and give the discussion an element of shared experiences. When qualitative researchers provide detailed descriptions of the setting, for example, or provide many perspectives about a theme, the results become more realistic and richer. This procedure can add to the validity of the findings.

- Clarify the *bias* the researcher brings to the study. This self-reflection creates an open and honest narrative that will resonate well with readers. Reflectivity has been mentioned as a core characteristic of qualitative research. Good qualitative research contains comments by the researchers about how their interpretation of the findings is shaped by their background, such as their gender, culture, history, and socioeconomic origin.

- Also present *negative* or *discrepant information* that runs counter to the themes. Because real life is composed of different perspectives that do not always coalesce, discussing contrary information adds to the credibility of an account. A researcher can accomplish this in discussing evidence about a theme. Most evidence will build a case for the theme; researchers can also present information that contradicts the general perspective of the theme. By presenting this contradictory evidence, the account becomes more realistic and hence valid.

- Spend *prolonged time* in the field. In this way, the researcher develops an in-depth understanding of the phenomenon under study and can convey detail about the site and the people that lends credibility to the narrative account. The more experience that a researcher has with participants in their actual setting, the more accurate or valid will be the findings.

- Use *peer debriefing* to enhance the accuracy of the account. This process involves locating a person (a peer debriefer) who reviews and asks questions about the qualitative study so that the account will resonate with people other than the researcher. This strategy—involving an interpretation beyond the researcher and invested in another person—adds validity to an account.

- Use an *external auditor* to review the entire project. As distinct from a peer debriefer, this auditor is not familiar with the researcher or the project and can provide an objective assessment of the project throughout the process of research or at the conclusion of the study. The role is similar to that of a fiscal auditor, and specific questions exist that auditors might ask (Lincoln & Guba, 1985). The procedure of having an independent investigator look over many aspects of the project (e.g., accuracy of transcription, the relationship between the research questions and the data, the level of data analysis from the raw data through interpretation) enhances the overall validity of a qualitative study.

Qualitative generalization is a term that is used in a limited way in qualitative research, since the intent of this form of inquiry is not to generalize findings to individuals, sites, or places outside of those under study (see Gibbs, 2007, for his cautionary note about qualitative generalizability). In fact, the value of qualitative research lies in the particular description and themes developed *in context* of a specific site. *Particularity* rather than *generalizability* (Greene & Caracelli, 1997) is the hallmark of qualitative research. However, there are a few discussions in the qualitative literature about generalizability, especially as applied to case study research in which the inquirer studies several cases. Yin (2003), for example, feels that qualitative case study results can be generalized to some *broader theory.* The generalization occurs when qualitative researchers study additional cases and generalize findings to the new cases. It is the same as the *replication logic* used in experimental research. However, to repeat a case study's findings in a new case setting requires good documentation of qualitative procedures, such as a protocol for documenting the problem in detail and the development of a thorough case study database (Yin, 2003).

THE QUALITATIVE WRITE-UP

A plan for a qualitative procedure should end with some comments about the narrative that emerges from the data analysis. Numerous varieties of narratives exist, and examples from scholarly journals illustrate models. In a plan for a study, consider advancing several points about the narrative.

The basic procedure in reporting the results of a qualitative study are to develop descriptions and themes from the data (see Figure 9.1), to present these descriptions and themes that convey multiple perspectives from participants and detailed descriptions of the setting or individuals. Using a qualitative strategy of inquiry, these results may also provide a chronological narrative of an individual's life (narrative research), a detailed description of their experiences (phenomenology), a theory generated from the data (grounded theory), a detailed portrait of a culture-sharing group (ethnography), or an in-depth analysis of one or more cases (case study).

Given these different strategies, the findings and interpretation sections of a plan for a study might discuss how the sections will be presented: as objective accounts, fieldwork experiences (Van Maanen, 1988), a chronology, a process model, an extended story, an analysis by cases or across cases, or a detailed descriptive portrait (Creswell, 2007).

At the specific level, some **writing strategies** might be as follows:

- Use quotes and vary their length from short to long embedded passages.
- Script conversation and report the conversation in different languages to reflect cultural sensitivity.

- Present text information in tabular form (e.g., matrices, comparison tables of different codes).
- Use the wording from participants to form codes and theme labels.
- Intertwine quotations with (the author's) interpretations.
- Use indents or other special formatting of the manuscript to call attention to quotations from participants.
- Use the first person "I" or collective "we" in the narrative form.
- Use metaphors and analogies (see, for example, Richardson, 1990, who discusses some of these forms).
- Use the narrative approach typically used within a qualitative strategy of inquiry (e.g., description in case studies and ethnographies, a detailed story in narrative research).
- Describe how the narrative outcome will be compared with theories and the general literature on the topic. In many qualitative articles, researchers discuss the literature at the end of the study (see the discussion in Chapter 2).

Example 9.1 *Qualitative Procedures*

The following is an example of a qualitative procedure written as part of a doctoral proposal (Miller, 1992). Miller's project was an ethnographic study of first-year experiences of the president of a 4-year college. As I present this discussion, I refer back to the sections addressed in this chapter and highlight them in boldfaced type. Also, I have maintained Miller's use of the term *informant,* although today, the more appropriate term, *participant,* should be used.

The Qualitative Research Paradigm

The qualitative research paradigm has its roots in cultural anthropology and American sociology (Kirk & Miller, 1986). It has only recently been adopted by educational researchers (Borg & Gall, 1989). The intent of qualitative research is to understand a particular social situation, event, role, group, or interaction (Locke, Spirduso, & Silverman, 1987). It is largely an investigative process where the researcher gradually makes sense of a social phenomenon by contrasting, comparing, replicating, cataloguing and classifying the object of study (Miles & Huberman, 1984). Marshall and Rossman (1989) suggest that this entails immersion in the everyday life of the setting chosen for the study; the researcher enters the informants' world and through ongoing interaction, seeks the informants' perspectives and meanings. *(Qualitative assumptions are mentioned.)*

Scholars contend that qualitative research can be distinguished from quantitative methodology by numerous unique characteristics that are inherent in the design. The following is a synthesis of commonly articulated assumptions regarding characteristics presented by various researchers.

1. Qualitative research occurs in natural settings, where human behavior and events occur.

2. Qualitative research is based on assumptions that are very different from quantitative designs. Theory or hypotheses are not established a priori.

3. The researcher is the primary instrument in data collection rather than some inanimate mechanism (Eisner, 1991; Frankel & Wallen, 1990; Lincoln & Guba, 1985; Merriam, 1988).

4. The data that emerge from a qualitative study are descriptive. That is, data are reported in words (primarily the participant's words) or pictures, rather than in numbers (Fraenkel & Wallen, 1990; Locke et al., 1987; Marshall & Rossman, 1989; Merriam, 1988).

5. The focus of qualitative research is on participants' perceptions and experiences, and the way they make sense of their lives (Fraenkel & Wallen, 1990; Locke et al., 1987; Merriam, 1988). The attempt is therefore to understand not one, but multiple realities (Lincoln & Guba, 1985).

6. Qualitative research focuses on the process that is occurring as well as the product or outcome. Researchers are particularly interested in understanding how things occur (Fraenkel & Wallen, 1990; Merriam, 1988).

7. Idiographic interpretation is utilized. In other words, attention is paid to particulars; and data is interpreted in regard to the particulars of a case rather than generalizations.

8. Qualitative research is an emergent design in its negotiated outcomes. Meanings and interpretations are negotiated with human data sources because it is the subjects' realities that the researcher attempts to reconstruct (Lincoln & Guba, 1985; Merriam, 1988).

9. This research tradition relies on the utilization of tacit knowledge (intuitive and felt knowledge) because often the nuances of the multiple realities can be appreciated most in this way (Lincoln & Guba, 1985). Therefore, data are not quantifiable in the traditional sense of the word.

(Continued)

(Continued)

10. Objectivity and truthfulness are critical to both research traditions. However, the criteria for judging a qualitative study differ from quantitative research. First and foremost, the researcher seeks believability, based on coherence, insight and instrumental utility (Eisner, 1991) and trustworthiness (Lincoln & Guba, 1985) through a process of verification rather than through traditional validity and reliability measures. *(Qualitative characteristics are mentioned.)*

The Ethnographic Research Design

This study will utilize the ethnographic research tradition. This design emerged from the field of anthropology, primarily from the contributions of Bronislaw Malinowski, Robert Park and Franz Boas (Jacob, 1987; Kirk & Miller, 1986). The intent of ethnographic research is to obtain a holistic picture of the subject of study with emphasis on portraying the everyday experiences of individuals by observing and interviewing them and relevant others (Fraenkel & Wallen, 1990). The ethnographic study includes in-depth interviewing and continual and ongoing participant observation of a situation (Jacob, 1987) and in attempting to capture the whole picture reveals how people describe and structure their world (Fraenkel & Wallen, 1990). *(The author used the ethnographic approach.)*

The Researcher's Role

Particularly in qualitative research, the role of the researcher as the primary data collection instrument necessitates the identification of personal values, assumptions and biases at the outset of the study. The investigator's contribution to the research setting can be useful and positive rather than detrimental (Locke et al., 1987). My perceptions of higher education and the college presidency have been shaped by my personal experiences. From August 1980 to May 1990 I served as a college administrator on private campuses of 600 to 5,000. Most recently (1987–1990), I served as the Dean for Student Life at a small college in the Midwest. As a member of the President's cabinet, I was involved with all top level administrative cabinet activities and decisions and worked closely with the faculty, cabinet officers, president and board of trustees. In addition to reporting to the president, I worked with him through his first year in office. I believe this understanding of the context and role enhances my awareness, knowledge and sensitivity to many of the challenges, decisions and issues encountered as a first year president and will assist me in working with the informant in this study. I bring knowledge of both the structure of higher education and of the role the college presidency. Particular attention will be paid to the role of the new president in initiating change, relationship building, decision making, and providing leadership and vision.

Due to previous experiences working closely with a new college president, I bring certain biases to this study. Although every effort will be made to ensure objectivity, these biases may shape the way I view and understand the data I collect and the way I interpret my experiences. I commence this study with the perspective that the college presidency is a diverse and often difficult position. Though expectations are immense, I question how much power the president has to initiate change and provide leadership and vision. I view the first year as critical; filled with adjustments, frustrations, unanticipated surprises and challenges. *(Author reflected on her role in the study.)*

Bounding the Study

Setting

This study will be conducted on the campus of a state college in the Midwest. The college is situated in a rural Midwestern community. The institution's 1,700 students nearly triple the town's population of 1,000 when classes are in session. The institution awards associate, bachelor and master's degrees in 51 majors.

Actors

The informant in this study is the new President of a state college in the Midwest. The primary informant in this study is the President. However, I will be observing him in the context of administrative cabinet meetings. The president's cabinet includes three Vice Presidents (Academic Affairs, Administration, Student Affairs) and two Deans (Graduate Studies and Continuing Education).

Events

Using ethnographic research methodology, the focus of this study will be the everyday experiences and events of the new college president, and the perceptions and meaning attached to those experiences as expressed by the informant. This includes the assimilation of surprising events or information, and making sense of critical events and issues that arise.

Processes

Particular attention will be paid to the role of the new president in initiating change, relationship building, decision making, and providing leadership and vision. *(Author mentioned data collection boundaries.)*

Ethical Considerations

Most authors who discuss qualitative research design address the importance of ethical considerations (Locke et al., 1982; Marshall & Rossman, 1989; Merriam, 1988; Spradley, 1980). First and foremost, the researcher has

(Continued)

(Continued)

an obligation to respect the rights, needs, values, and desires of the informant(s). To an extent, ethnographic research is always obtrusive. Participant observation invades the life of the informant (Spradley, 1980) and sensitive information is frequently revealed. This is of particular concern in this study where the informant's position and institution are highly visible. The following safeguards will be employed to protect the informant's rights: 1) the research objectives will be articulated verbally and in writing so that they are clearly understood by the informant (including a description of how data will be used), 2) written permission to proceed with the study as articulated will be received from the informant, 3) a research exemption form will be filed with the Institutional Review Board (Appendixes B1 and B2), 4) the informant will be informed of all data collection devices and activities, 5) verbatim transcriptions and written interpretations and reports will be made available to the informant, 6) the informant's rights, interests and wishes will be considered first when choices are made regarding reporting the data, and 7) the final decision regarding informant anonymity will rest with the informant. *(Author addressed ethical issues and IRB review.)*

Data Collection Strategies

Data will be collected from February through May, 1992. This will include a minimum of bi-monthly, 45 minute recorded interviews with the informant (initial interview questions, Appendix C), bimonthly two hour observations of administrative cabinet meetings, bi-monthly two hour observations of daily activities and bi-monthly analysis of the president's calendar and documents (meeting minutes, memos, publications). In addition, the informant has agreed to record impressions of his experiences, thoughts and feelings in a taped diary (guidelines for recorded reflection, Appendix D). Two follow-up interviews will be scheduled for the end of May 1992 (See Appendix E for proposed timeline and activity schedule). *(The author proposed to use face-to-face interviews, participate as observer, and obtain private documents.)*

To assist in the data collection phase I will utilize a field log, providing a detailed account of ways I plan to spend my time when I am on-site, and in the transcription and analysis phase (also comparing this record to how time is actually spent). I intend to record details related to my observations in a field notebook and keep a field diary to chronicle my own thinking, feeling, experiences and perceptions throughout the research process. *(The author recorded descriptive and reflective information.)*

Data Analysis Procedures

Merriam (1988) and Marshall and Rossman (1989) contend that data collection and data analysis must be a simultaneous process in qualitative research. Schatzman and Strauss (1973) claim that qualitative data analysis primarily entails classifying things, persons, and events and the properties which characterize them. Typically throughout the data analysis process ethnographers index or code their data using as many categories as possible (Jacob, 1987). They seek to identify and describe patterns and themes from the perspective of the participant(s), then attempt to understand and explain these patterns and themes (Agar, 1980). During data analysis the data will be organized categorically and chronologically, reviewed repeatedly, and continually coded. A list of major ideas that surface will be chronicled (as suggested by Merriam, 1988). Taped interviews and the participant's taped diary will be transcribed verbatim. Field notes and diary entries will be regularly reviewed. *(Author described steps in data analysis.)*

In addition, the data analysis process will be aided by the use of a qualitative data analysis computer program called HyperQual. Raymond Padilla (Arizona State University) designed HyperQual in 1987 for use with the Macintosh computer. HyperQual utilizes HyperCard software and facilitates the recording and analysis of textual and graphic data. Special stacks are designated to hold and organize data. Using HyperQual the researcher can directly "enter field data, including interview data, observations, researcher's memos, and illustrations...(and) tag (or code) all or part of the source data so that chunks of data can be pulled out and then be reassembled in a new and illuminating configuration" (Padilla, 1989, pp. 69–70). Meaningful data chunks can be identified, retrieved, isolated, grouped and regrouped for analysis. Categories or code names can be entered initially or at a later date. Codes can be added, changed or deleted with HyperQual editor and text can be searched for key categories, themes, words or phrases. *(Author mentions the proposed use of computer software for data analysis.)*

Verification

In ensuring internal validity, the following strategies will be employed:

1. Triangulation of data—Data will be collected through multiple sources to include interviews, observations and document analysis;

2. Member checking—The informant will serve as a check throughout the analysis process. An ongoing dialogue regarding my interpretations of the informant's reality and meanings will ensure the truth value of the data;

3. Long terms and repeated observations at the research site—Regular and repeated observations of similar phenomena and settings will occur on-site over a four month period of time;

(Continued)

(Continued)

4. Peer examination—a doctoral student and graduate assistant in the Educational Psychology Department will serve as a peer examiner;

5. Participatory modes of research—The informant will be involved in most phases of this study, from the design of the project to checking interpretations and conclusions; and

6. Clarification of researcher bias—At the outset of this study researcher bias will be articulated in writing in the dissertation proposal under the heading, "The Researcher's Role."

The primary strategy utilized in this project to ensure external validity will be the provision of rich, thick, detailed descriptions so that anyone interested in transferability will have a solid framework for comparison (Merriam, 1988). Three techniques to ensure reliability will be employed in this study. First, the researcher will provide a detailed account of the focus of the study, the researcher's role, the informant's position and basis for selection, and the context from which data will be gathered (LeCompte & Goetz, 1984). Second, triangulation or multiple methods of data collection and analysis will be used, which strengthens reliability as well as internal validity (Merriam, 1988). Finally, data collection and analysis strategies will be reported in detail in order to provide a clear and accurate picture of the methods used in this study. All phases of this project will be subject to scrutiny by an external auditor who is experienced in qualitative research methods. *(Author identified strategies of validity to be used in the study.)*

Reporting the Findings

Lofland (1974) suggests that although data collection and analysis strategies are similar across qualitative methods, the way the findings are reported is diverse. Miles and Huberman (1984) address the importance of creating a data display and suggest that narrative text has been the most frequent form of display for qualitative data. This is a naturalistic study. Therefore, the results will be presented in descriptive, narrative form rather than as a scientific report. Thick description will be the vehicle for communicating a holistic picture of the experiences of a new college president. The final project will be a construction of the informant's experiences and the meanings he attaches to them. This will allow readers to vicariously experience the challenges he encounters and provide a lens through which readers can view the subject's world. *(Outcomes of the study were mentioned.)*

SUMMARY

This chapter explored the steps that go into developing and writing a qualitative procedure. Recognizing the variation that exists in qualitative studies, the chapter advances a general guideline for procedures. This guideline includes a discussion about the general characteristics of qualitative research if audiences are not familiar with this approach to research. These characteristics are that the research takes place in the natural setting, relies on the researcher as the instrument for data collection, employs multiple methods of data collection, is inductive, is based on participants' meanings, is emergent, often involves the use of a theoretical lens, is interpretive, and is holistic. The guideline recommends mentioning a strategy of inquiry, such as the study of individuals (narrative, phenomenology), the exploration of processes, activities and events (case study, grounded theory), or the examination of broad culture-sharing behavior of individuals or groups (ethnography). The choice of strategy needs to be presented and defended. Further, the proposal needs to address the role of the researcher: past experiences, personal connections to the site, steps to gain entry, and sensitive ethical issues. Discussion of data collection should include the purposeful sampling approach and the forms of data to be collected (i.e., observations, interviews, documents, audiovisual materials). It is useful to also indicate the types of data recording protocols that will be used. Data analysis is an ongoing process during research. It involves analyzing participant information, and researchers typically employ general analysis steps as well as those steps found within a specific strategy of inquiry. More general steps include organizing and preparing the data, an initial reading through the information, coding the data, developing from the codes a description and thematic analysis, using computer programs, representing the findings in tables, graphs, and figures, and interpreting the findings. These interpretations involve stating lessons learned, comparing the findings with past literature and theory, raising questions, and/or advancing an agenda for reform. The proposal should also contain a section on the expected outcomes for the study. Finally, an additional important step in planning a proposal is to mention the strategies that will be used to validate the accuracy of the findings, demonstrate the reliability of procedures, and discuss the role of generalizability.

WRITING EXERCISES

Writing Exercises

1. Write a plan for the procedure to be used in your qualitative study. After writing the plan, use Table 9.1 as a checklist to determine the comprehensiveness of your plan.

2. Develop a table that lists, in a column on the left, the steps you plan to take to analyze your data. In a column on the right, indicate the steps as they apply directly to your project, the research strategy you plan to use, and data that you have collected.

ADDITIONAL READINGS

Marshall, C., & Rossman, G. B. (2006). *Designing qualitative research* (4th ed.). Thousand Oaks, CA: Sage.

Catherine Marshall and Gretchen Rossman introduce the procedures for designing a qualitative study and a qualitative proposal. The topics covered are comprehensive. They include building a conceptual framework around a study; the logic and assumptions of the overall design and methods; methods of data collection and procedures for managing, recording, and analyzing qualitative data; and the resources needed for a study, such as time, personnel, and funding. This is a comprehensive and insightful text from which both beginners and more experienced qualitative researchers can learn.

Flick, U. (Ed.). (2007). *The Sage Qualitative Research Kit.* London: Sage.

This is an eight-volume kit edited by Uwe Flick that is authored by different world-class qualitative researchers and was created to collectively address the core issues that arise when researchers actually do qualitative research. It addresses how to plan and design a qualitative study, the collection and production of qualitative data, the analysis of qualitative data (e.g., visual data, discourse analysis), and the issues of quality in qualitative research. Overall, it presents a recent, up-to-date window into the field of qualitative research.

Creswell, J. W. (2007). *Qualitative inquiry and research design: Choosing among five approaches* (2nd ed.). Thousand Oaks, CA: Sage.

Sometimes those who write about qualitative research take a philosophical stance toward the topic and readers are left without an understanding of the procedures and practices actually used in designing and conducting a qualitative study. My book takes five approaches to qualitative inquiry—narrative research, phenomenology, grounded theory, ethnography, and case study—and discusses how the procedures for conducting these forms of inquiry are both similar and different. In the end, readers can more easily choose which of the five would best suit their research problems as well as their personal styles of research.

9 Collecting Qualitative Data

NICK LEE and IAN LINGS

SUPERVISOR'S VIEW: PROFESSOR EVERT GUMMESSON

There remains a lot to be done in developing our skills of collecting higher quality qualitative data. Quantitative researchers have the same quality problem but they live under the illusion that numbers are precise and objective. It's a snug life in the best of all worlds. 'No worries', to quote Crocodile Dundee.

Qualitative researchers live messier lives. One disturbing observation is that our ability to collect – or rather generate data, because data are primarily socially constructed – does not seem to improve. Case studies today are not built on higher data quality than 20 years ago. Where is the progress? The techniques that are presented in handbooks are the same, except that the Internet has opened up new opportunities.

However, business reality (my field of research) is risky, ambiguous, fuzzy, chaotic and unpredictable. I have advocated that we should start with the basic issue, that of access, and then do our best to get close to the phenomenon we are chasing. Although we can't do without it, the research ritual is not the real thing; it's the validity and relevance of results that count. Advice from books and classes is a great starting point, but to match professional explorers – Columbus, Sherlock Holmes, Einstein, investigative journalists like Mike Wallace of '60 Minutes', or businesspeople breaking new ground like Richard Branson – researchers have to: (a) practice; (b) use all senses, intuition, experience, wisdom, insights, judgement, creativity and audacity; and (c) be systematic and reflective, swing between involvement and detachment and between being law-and-order bureaucrats and free-wheeling entrepreneurs.

Research techniques have no life of their own – they only come alive through the researcher's persona.

VIEW FROM THE TRENCHES: JENNIFER WALKER

Start early and expect setbacks! My advice to anyone embarking on qualitative research is never to underestimate the difficulty and time-consuming nature of this form of data collection. As soon as you know what your methodology is, get going! It will take you longer than you think! I remember realising the enormity of the task that lay before me as I watched with jealousy my quantitative data-collecting friends receiving their questionnaires within hours of whipping up a quick group email. Qualitative research usually relies on a relatively small number of people giving up a significant amount of time, often for little or no reward. To convince anyone to participate is a challenge in itself, but it can be done!

I conducted three focus groups for my M.Sc. dissertation, and struggled to get committed people who could attend the sessions all at the same time. I found that if someone sounded slightly non-committal, then they almost always eventually dropped out. It's practically impossible to coerce people into giving up their time, so only add a participant to your list if they sound genuinely interested in attending. I was tempted on occasions to put off my focus group sessions for certain potential participants who I thought would be excellent respondents, but who had limited spare time. This isn't a good idea as it can just lead to deadlines being pushed back and other respondents losing interest. It can sometimes be frustrating and demoralising, but if you always assume that there will be a few no-shows, you can compensate for it. It is useful to have some back-up participants ready to step in if necessary as a depleted focus group can limit the flow of conversation and reduce the strength of your results.

All-in-all though, if you're determined and organised, collecting qualitative data can give you a real sense of achievement and can provide fantastically interesting results for analysis.

Qualitative research is an interesting area (do you notice I keep saying that about everything?). I remember a few years ago when I was still a bright young (and good-looking) lecturer asking a class whether they felt that they preferred qualitative to quantitative research. When a vote was called for, at least 70 per cent of the class voted that yes they did indeed prefer doing qualitative to quantitative work. Intrigued, I picked on one of the students as to a reason why: 'Because you can like, blag it can't you?' was the answer. Of course, this student was referring to the idea that you could simply make qualitative results up, rather than be forced to use objective formulae and procedures as in quantitative approaches. That moment permanently shaped my own personal approach to qualitative work, and teaching it. No, not towards 'blagging it', but towards demonstrating how qualitative work can be just as rigorous as many think quantitative work is – from whatever philosophical perspective one comes from.

In fact, depending on how experienced a researcher you are, you may have already come across the manifestations of the 'qualitative-quantitative divide' in your career. In fact, the various disagreements touched on in Chapter 3 are in some ways related to this. As I have already mentioned, arguments between researchers who are committed to qualitative and/or quantitative methodologies have been heated and destructive throughout the last 50 years in various social science fields. However, if you remember back to Chapter 3, I suggested that these arguments should not be conducted at the methodological level, but are instead mainly concerned with alternative ways of looking at the world. Once you become clear about your philosophical standpoint, methodological decisions are (or should be) in fact mainly technical – i.e. which type of data can answer your research question most effectively? It is from this perspective that the following chapter (and in fact the next six chapters) should be read.

More specifically, I hope that as a researcher you will decide on the appropriate methodology for each part of your research project in light of your needs, not dependent on any prejudices of yourself or your colleagues/supervisor. As a result, this chapter is mainly concerned with the practicalities of qualitative data collection. Nevertheless, where different philosophical standpoints would suggest contrasting or alternative techniques, I spend time noting these, and their implications for doing good research. However, one thing you should be immediately aware of is that – despite the 'blagging' image – doing good qualitative research is just as (if not more) difficult than doing good quantitative work. Even though there are no complex formulae or numbers, there are many other difficult ideas to come to terms with.

My ultimate aim here is to provide an overview of qualitative data collection which can be used by all researchers, not just those who are committed interpretivists. At the same time, I want to show how good qualitative work can be useful even in the most hard-core scientific research projects. Anyway, at the end of this chapter I really hope you have come to terms with these key ideas:

- What 'rigour' is in qualitative research.
- The importance of sampling to the quality of your research.
- The range of different qualitative data sources and collection methods.
- How important decisions on transcribing and recording your data are.

Why is it Important to Know This Stuff?

This chapter will be read by two types of people, those who are thinking about taking a qualitative approach to their project, and a few interested readers who wish to gain a basic understanding of qualitative data collection, but have little intention of ever actually doing it. I think this is a sad situation. As I have said and will repeatedly stress, methodology decisions should not be based on prior prejudices, but on what is the best way of getting data and analysing it *for the issue in question.* There are so many researchers who consider themselves as 'quantitative' or 'qualitative', without a real understanding of either why or what the 'other' methodology actually entails. Inaccuracy and dogma are rife in social science!

The enlightened researcher (which will be everyone who reads this book cover to cover, I hope) can make the appropriate methodological decision in light of their research question – which will of course also depend on their philosophical standpoint. Therefore, a good researcher will have at the very least a basic grounding in both quantitative and qualitative data collection and analysis issues. Fundamentally, we are dealing with the same issues as in many of the later chapters – i.e. how do we actually obtain data from the real world? This is shown in Figure 9.1, which by now I imagine is looking kind of familiar.

A repeated theme of mine is the idea of critical self-evaluation. Understanding about different research methods will allow you to see exactly where your own position is, and why you are holding it. This allows you to clearly defend yourself when you are challenged. If an examiner (or reviewer) asks you 'why did (or didn't) you use a qualitative approach)' you will need a good answer. The material in this chapter is a good start on how to answer a question like that.

On a pragmatic level, the material in this chapter should be useful to everyone. Firstly, of course, it provides an introduction to how to get out into the field and collect data. It also distils a number of unfortunate mistakes and other experiences I have had out there myself – hopefully you won't repeat them after reading it! But, even if you never get out into the wide world and collect qualitative data, you will almost certainly need to evaluate other projects (e.g. articles) which have done so – without a grounding in the area you may not be able to do so effectively. Even worse, you may never read any qualitative research, and miss out on a rich and fascinating section of your own theoretical literature. And of course, if all you want to do is criticise qualitative research, well you are going to need to know about it somewhat aren't you?

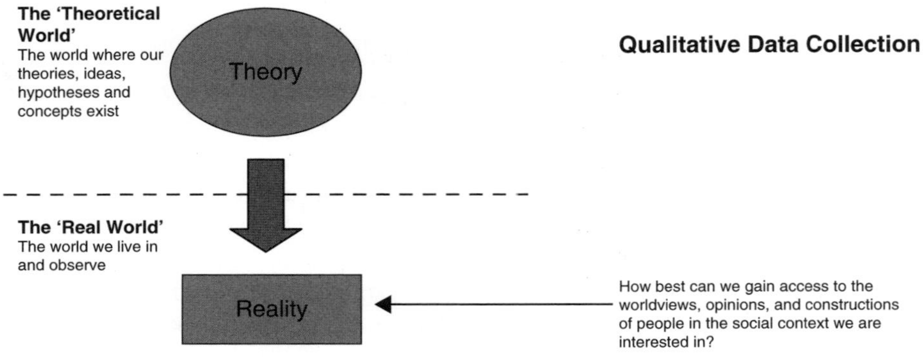

Figure 9.1 The place of qualitative data collection

Rigour in qualitative research

The concept of 'rigour' is not one which most quantitatively oriented researchers would associate with qualitative research. Normally, such researchers assume qualitative work to be 'soft', 'subjective', and maybe a little bit 'flaky'. Certainly, the subjectivity of qualitative work can be one of its prime strengths, in particular when we consider the contextually situated nature of qualitative work (see Chapter 3 for some more information on context and subjectivity). In fact, some philosophical perspectives actually 'play up' to this soft and subjective image, inherently disagreeing with the very idea that research itself can ever be objective (again, have a look at Chapter 3 if this isn't that clear to you). However, for the beginning researcher, I feel that it isn't really necessary to get into these debates. In fact, many researchers who use or want to use qualitative work are not fundamentally committed to an interpretivist philosophical framework. For those researchers, the idea of rigour is a key one. That said, if one wishes to evaluate rigour, surely one needs to have some criteria to do so? Of course, as usual, this has been the source of some debate.

Rigour is a slippery notion. It can be taken in a broad sense to refer to the 'quality' of your research methods – are they consistent with good practice in your particular context? Or in an even more general sense, is there *any* kind of coherent strategy behind your research efforts at all? In qualitative research there are many different ways of approaching the idea of rigour. Perhaps a good place to start are concepts of reliability and validity. You should remember these two ideas from the couple of chapters about measurement, and how they can be used to help judge the quality of your measurement (and thus your research). However, in a qualitative context we don't really 'measure' things in the same way as in a quantitative one. So are reliability and validity still relevant? Well, as is the case with most things in this book, there are different ways to approach the issue.

Some qualitative methodologists have tried to transfer notions of reliability and validity directly to qualitative research (without the measurement connotations of course). Judging by the references that appear in assignments, one book which is quite popular with my students is by Mason (1996), which clearly appropriates validity from quantitative research, describing it as essentially being about answering the question of whether you are actually observing or measuring what you say you are. Or in other words, is what you 'say' is happening in your research actually happening? Or are you in fact deluded (say by your inherent biases). We'll look at this in a lot more detail in the next chapter about analysis. Others have looked at *external* and *internal* concepts of validity and reliability (e.g. LeCompte *et al.*, 1993). External reliability essentially refers to whether your study can be replicated by another researcher, which is a complicated idea in qualitative research, being as it depends so heavily on the context and the researcher. Internal reliability is not really relevant to single-researcher studies, as it refers to whether different researchers agree about the same piece of data. Internal validity is quite similar to the approach to validity mentioned above, and concerns whether your theoretical ideas match up to the data. External validity is similar to notions of 'generalisability' which you have no doubt heard of before. Here we are talking about whether your findings can be applied to other social contexts apart from the one you have studied. In qualitative terms this can be a difficult question as the logic behind qualitative work is quite different from the statistical logic behind quantitative generalisation. Of course, the approaches to validity and reliability mentioned above are not the only way of looking at the concept of rigour in qualitative research. Alternative View 9.1 covers some different ways of exploring the issues.

Alternative View 9.1: Alternative Approaches to the Rigour Issue

Not all qualitative researchers have been happy to simply appropriate ideas of reliability and validity from traditional quantitative research. Instead, authors such as Guba and Lincoln (e.g. 1994) suggest using **trustworthiness** as a criterion for evaluating qualitative research. In turn, trustworthiness consists of four main components. Firstly, *credibility* refers to whether your findings bear any relationship to the data you drew them from. *Transferability* is about whether you can justifiably transfer your findings to any other contexts. *Dependability* is similar to reliability in that it's about how well you can assure people of your findings and the way you got to them from the raw social context. Finally, *confirmability* refers to whether you can show people that you acted appropriately in your research, in terms of not being influenced by biases (either from your own personal values, or theoretical background).

There are even more extreme approaches to rigour, which in fact seem to reject the very concept itself. For example, Lather (1993) draws from postmodern theory to create something she calls 'ironic validity', which appears to consider traditional concepts of validity mere rhetorical devices.

The interpretive philosophical standpoint of course considers reality to be a social construction between actors (e.g. the researcher and the subject), so how can we ever assess the 'accuracy' of our representations in relation to some objective standard? Thus, it seems that some authors have replaced a concern for such standards with notions of whether a research project provides any 'benefit' to its constituency. That said, Seale (2004) strongly criticises such approaches to evaluating the rigour of qualitative research, which 'substitute moral values and political positions as guarantors of standards', calling them 'frighteningly weak' (p. 409). Instead, he argues for – rather than objective criteria – a recognition of 'the value of careful scholarship, commitment to rigorous argument, attending to the links between claims and evidence, consideration of all viewpoints before taking a stance, [and] asking and answering important rather than trivial research questions' (pp. 409–410). These ideas would appear to be a useful guide to research practice for most scholars

Of course, it can be seen that these ideas of how to approach the question of rigour are inextricably bound up with how you view the world, the existence of an objective truth, and the possibility of a researcher ever uncovering it. If one believes one is trying to uncover the essential 'truth' of a social situation by doing research, then of course, traditional notions of 'validity' are appropriate when evaluating the quality of your representation of that reality. However, if one believes that there is no such thing as a truth (remember Chapter 3?) then it seems somewhat futile to attempt to see how close our research has come to uncovering it. Instead, researchers from this (non-realist) perspective tend to reject the concepts of reliability and validity, and focus on the characteristics of the representation, almost as an end in itself (see Alternative View 9.1).

Personally, I tend to take something of a middle ground here. As you are no doubt aware by now, I do believe that there is an external reality which I am investigating, but also recognise that in a qualitative context this reality may be represented in different ways. It is the researcher's job to convince their audience that their own representation is somehow valuable, and in my opinion this means it should somehow bear some credible relation to the data and situation which I drew it from. In other words, is my interpretation of that social situation **justifiable**? It is the process of convincing the audience of that justifiability which I believe is the key task of the researcher. I flatly reject the Feyerabendian[1] notion that any conclusion is useful if it somehow provides benefit, whether or not it is based on any kind of justifiable interpretation of data. Conclusions should always be in some way justified in relation to the data and the way it was collected and analysed or interpreted, whether this be quantitative or qualitative. In a qualitative context one can take many approaches to this justification process, as hopefully, I have already shown. However, as you move through this and the next chapter, you'll come across related ideas of validity and reliability very regularly. In fact, whatever approach you take, an appreciation for the various concepts of validity and reliability should permeate all of your qualitative research, from design to analysis to the write-up. Hopefully, the tools in these chapters will help you come to terms with assessing the rigour of your qualitative work, since without assuring the reader of the rigour of your findings, how can a reader be sure of the value of those findings to them?

Qualitative sampling

Sampling is an issue which often causes students and researchers some confusion within a qualitative context. More specifically, most of us are brought up on the logic of statistical sampling (see Chapter 11 for this), and then when we learn about qualitative sampling we have considerable trouble fitting it into that model. At worst, we assume that either (a) we should try to achieve the ideal of 'probability sampling' for qualitative research, or (b) all qualitative sampling is 'convenience'. Neither of these assumptions is particularly helpful, and lead to some considerable misperceptions about qualitative work.

The key issue to consider is that qualitative sampling actually relies on a completely different logic to quantitative sampling. In fact, it can be argued that one isn't actually collecting data at all, but instead *generating* it in conjunction with your participants. Alternative View 9.2 discusses this idea. In terms of 'ideals', while the quantitative approach is based around the ideal of a random selection of a (usually large) sample of cases from a given population, to my mind good qualitative work is based around the ideal of a 'purposive' selection of a small number of cases from the population – which is about as far away from 'random' sampling as you can get. There are many ways of exploring why this is the case, but I want to try to get away from philosophical arguments and make this point relevant to all researchers. The simple practical reasons we can't rely on the standard statistical logic of sampling in qualitative research are due to its reliance on small samples, and the necessity to generate rich information about your research questions (if we aren't doing the latter, then why use qualitative research at all?) Therefore, we need a sampling

---

[1] I think I just made that word up, but if you don't know what I mean, go back to Chapter 2 and look at Alternative View 2.2 to brush up on your philosophy.

method that helps us select cases that are likely to be able to provide us with this rich information.

Alternative View 9.2: Data Collection or Data *Generation*?

There are two alternative ways of looking at data – which you can probably work out for yourself from close reading of Chapters 2 and 3. However, now is probably a good time to revisit them in the context of practicalities. First of all, the traditional positivistic/realist approach would consider data to simply 'exist' in the world, waiting for you to collect it. In this framework, the method you use to collect it should be the appropriate one of course, but the researcher themselves should have no influence on the research subjects or the data. Moreover, many research theorists who take a more interpretive approach to research would consider this unrealistic, particularly in the case of qualitative research. Instead, a researcher could consider that they *generate* the data in conjunction with the participants or data sources. In other words, the very interaction of the researcher with the respondent, context, data source, and situation act together with the researcher's own perceptions to co-create the actual corpus of data. Furthermore, the researcher is usually at least implicitly analysing the data at the same time. In this framework, data does not exist independent of the research itself. This subjective and interactionist framework is repeatedly referred to in other chapters of this book, and many of the further readings given at the end of this chapter develop it more fully.

Without a knowledge of the qualitative sampling logic, researchers can make the mistake of assuming their qualitative sampling must be 'convenience', as most general research texts discuss this method (in their chapters on 'sampling'), and convenience sampling looks quite similar to what one may have to do in a qualitative project. Unfortunately, this leads to the misperception that qualitative methods are not based on a rigorous sampling methodology, which then impacts on perceptions of the validity of qualitative work – and especially the external validity. In fact, good qualitative work should have a systematic and well-defined sampling plan, which allows the researcher to define exactly why each case is selected, rather than simply grabbing the first few people on the street, your flatmates, or whoever responds first to your request for participants.[2]

Along these lines, a good base to build from in learning about qualitative sampling is the idea of **purposive sampling**. Purposive sampling is exactly what it sounds like, sampling with a *purpose*. Most of the time the purpose here is to sample cases or people who are *relevant*

[2] Indeed, these last three would be classic 'convenience' samples.

to your research questions. This could of course mean pretty much whatever you want it to mean, but I like to think of it as looking for the cases which are likely to provide information regarding your key research objectives and theoretical questions. Of course, you'll note that you should therefore have some kind of idea regarding your theory before you go out into the field. I think this is a good idea, but you should be aware that some researchers do not agree (see Alternative View 9.3). Also, you should not forget that cases which are relevant to your research are not restricted to those which you think will support your theory; *deviant cases* are ones which you think have characteristics which mean they may contradict your theory. A very strong test of the theory is therefore whether it holds in such deviant cases.

Alternative View 9.3: To Theorise or not to Theorise?

There is a school of thought among qualitative researchers which advocates beginning a qualitative project with no appreciation of existing theory. This kind of thinking probably comes from the grounded theory perspective of Glaser and Strauss (1967). They argued in their seminal book that the researcher should be *tabula rasa*, a blank slate, before going into the field. Those of you with good memories should recall this phrase from Chapter 2, as it was used by John Locke in his argument for pure Empiricism (and thus I find the use of it somewhat ironic in this context). The argument against prior theorising seems to be based on the idea that an awareness of previous theory might bias your ability to let the data truly speak to you, and your interpretation will be contaminated by your pre-existing mental models.

Of course, it is a little naive to imagine that a researcher is ever able to completely cut himself or herself off from theory about their subject for all kinds of practical reasons. I mean, it's not as if researchers start off on research projects without first being interested in them, and looking around for information. Most of us get our ideas from reading theory anyway! In fact, the use of prior theory appears to have caused something of a bust-up between Glaser and Strauss in later years. Strauss' subsequent work (e.g. Strauss and Corbin, 1998) actually advocates some appreciation of prior literature before going into the field, while Glaser (1992) remains committed to the idea of letting theory 'emerge' from data with no prior knowledge.

Whether or not you go along with the possibility that one can ever be completely *tabula rasa*, this argument has an important upshot. Basically, as a researcher you should be very careful as to how you let your appreciation of existing theory influence your research, and be sure that you are not being overly biased.

Purposive sampling has considerable overlap with **theoretical sampling**, which is a specific term introduced by Glaser and Strauss (1967) in their work on *grounded theory*.

Grounded theory is a complicated and specific qualitative method, but concepts from it have found their way into many qualitative research methods, including the ones I like to use. Theoretical sampling is, I think, a very good structure to base your qualitative sampling strategy on. You can think of it as beginning with purposive sampling as above (although there is disagreement on how much theory you should have before you go into the field for the first time, see Alternative View 9.3), but then continuing as an iterative process, by letting the theories and findings which emerge from your data influence the next round of sampling. In other words, the theory controls the data collection. IDE 9.1 provides an example of how theoretical sampling could work in the context of a practical research project.

IDE 9.1: Theoretical Sampling

When I conducted my own Ph.D. research, I began with a qualitative study of sales force members. My preliminary reading of the relevant literature had suggested that it was going to be important to tap both sides of the manager–employee dyad. So this was my first theoretical criteria. Furthermore, early theoretical ideas had emerged regarding the likely influence of other characteristics, such as gender, job experience, and industry type. Selecting cases which varied on these characteristics was also an important criteria for my sample.

An important component of theoretical sampling is to look for 'deviant cases'. Such cases are ones which seem likely to provide information that might contradict your theory, and you are usually better able to select such cases the more time you have spent on the project. For example, after a few interviews, it became clear that certain industries (e.g. photocopiers) seemed to be populated by highly aggressive managers, some of whom commented that other industries were less so. As a result, I moved on to select some cases from the health care industry, as this was one which had been specifically mentioned by respondents as being 'softer'. If I could still uncover similar behavioural styles in industries such as machine tools or photocopiers, I could be more certain of my theory.

Another key way I worked was to use 'snowballing' methods. More specifically, I asked each respondent at the end of the interview to suggest managers (or salespeople) they knew who would (a) be interested in participating, and (b) provide either similar or contradictory information. Combining this with the theoretical criteria, I was able to develop a very comprehensive sampling strategy. Furthermore, using an iterative and continuous process of transcribing and analysis (i.e. not waiting until the end to start) I was able to judge the point when I began to reach 'theoretical saturation', and therefore stop collecting data.

One thing theoretical sampling has much to say on is sample size, a concept that is often used as a stick to beat qualitative work with. Specifically, as already mentioned, qualitative work tends to use small samples, which goes against the traditional statistical logic of large, random samples. Theoretical sampling takes the actual size of the sample to be less than relevant. Instead, since theoretical sampling is an iterative process, you should continue sampling until you reach what is called *theoretical saturation*. Although this concept can be difficult to grasp, you can think of theoretical saturation for a particular idea or concept as being reached when no new information about that concept comes to light in repeated cases, you are very clear about what that concept actually is and how it varies, and that the relationships between it and other concepts are well defined (Strauss and Corbin, 1998). Of course, this means that one does not select a sample size prior to research design, but that it develops somewhat organically as the research proceeds.

That said, as a rule of thumb, it is unlikely that you will gain enough information on a reasonably complex theory from fewer than 20 interviews, and the more complex your theory is, the more interviews will be needed. This complexity can be concerned with how many sub-groups you need to sample (men and women, different social classes, many different industrial groups, etc.), or the number of theoretical concepts in your study, or many other things. One useful way of describing this to yourself, to aid in selecting your final sample size, is detailed in Figure 9.2, with reference to a study of sales manager problem resolution I conducted for my Ph.D. dissertation.

However, although it is easy to do, you shouldn't fall into the trap of automatically thinking that 'people' are the only sampling units. In fact in qualitative research many other units may be relevant. For example, in research on customer complaints, the appropriate sampling unit may be an incident of poor service – and each single person may have multiple instances of this. In organisational psychology the relevant unit may be managerial

Position	**Industry Type**					
	Capital Equipment		**Office Products**		**Health Care**	
	Gender					
	M	*F*	*M*	*F*	*M*	*F*
Sales Manager						
Salesperson						

Figure 9.2 A sample matrix

punishment interactions, again an individual manager may have many of these to draw from. In relationship research the best unit may be failed relationships, and I can imagine that most people have a string of such sampling units! In situations like this your sample may consist of 20 *people*, but many more relevant units, and you should think in terms of this when you do your sampling. For example, no matter how many actual people you sample, you can never reach theoretical saturation unless you sample enough variety in the appropriate unit.

Of course, there are times when convenience sampling is all we can do. However, it is vital we are aware of what kind of respondents we need, and where to find them. One way of doing this is to use snowball sampling. In such situations, you can use one informant to suggest others who may have useful information on your research topic. Or you can use personal contacts to help you find the right people or cases to sample. Again though, you are looking for people who have the right kind of information for your study, not just anyone. For example, for the type of study suggested in Figure 9.2 there was no point in asking my fellow-student flatmates for interviews as they would have virtually no information of relevance. However, I could have asked them for some contacts of people they knew in business who would have been useful.

The key point to take away here is that sampling is an extremely important part of qualitative research, and should be treated as such. In my opinion, the entire usefulness (call it validity if you want) of your study rests on the appropriate selection of sampling units. If you can not justify to the reader why your sample is appropriate, why should they place any worth in your findings? Of course, once you decide on your sampling method, you then need to decide on how you will actually access your data, which is what the next sections deal with.

Interviewing

Interviewing is probably the most popular technique in academic qualitative research. It's also a very useful base to build from in looking at other qualitative techniques, so you should take the material in this section as relevant to other qualitative data collection methods as well. Interviewing is useful because it's very flexible, both in terms of content and time, and can be tailored to suit your research questions, respondents, and your own lifestyle much more effectively than many other qualitative methods. However, you should not get *qualitative* interviewing confused with the structured interviewing you might do in quantitative research – where you may get a respondent to fill in a structured questionnaire face-to-face or over the telephone. A good way to make this distinction is to think of qualitative interviews as **in-depth interviews**, which also gives a nice flavour of their roots in depth psychology and psychoanalysis. In-depth interviews are of course far less structured than quantitative interviews, and to a greater or lesser extent are driven by the interviewee, not the interviewer. Furthermore, in-depth interviews commonly go off-track to pursue interesting angles and examples, and this freewheeling, flexible approach is usually encouraged by the interviewer to some extent. The key difference however is that in an in-depth interview we are looking for *rich, in-depth* answers which tap deeply into the respondents own experiences, feelings, and opinions.

That said, in-depth interviews can be split into two main types, the **unstructured** and the **semi-structured**. While these are essentially two ends of a continuum (and thus rarely used in their purest form) they provide a useful contrast. In a totally unstructured interview, the interviewer will at the most use a few brief topics (sometimes just one) to prompt the interviewee, who is then allowed to respond however they want. Probing by the interviewer is only done to follow up points of interest, or to keep things going along smoothly. Conversely, the semi-structured interview is guided by a more detailed *topic guide* which will contain some fairly specific questions to ask, and likely ways of probing, examples to ask for and so on. There remains a lot of flexibility to follow up individual points, but in general the same questions will be asked of each interviewee.

Unstructured interviews are usually used when the researcher feels that even a basic structure will 'impose' a particular worldview on interviewees, and prejudice access to their internal views, feelings and experiences. You should make the link here back to Chapter 3, and be thinking that this kind of opinion is likely to be held most strongly by the committed phenomenologist. My own feelings are that using unstructured interviews can make it very difficult in pragmatic terms to generate useful data, since there is no guarantee that the respondent will talk about anything relevant! However, the philosophical point is well-made, and unstructured interviews can be very useful in the right circumstances. Semi-structured interviews, on the other, hand are particularly useful if you already have a clear theoretical appreciation of your topic (e.g. from a literature review), which allows you to structure a good topic guide. Also, in multi-person data collection teams, or multiple-site (or case) investigations some structure is needed to make sure all the interviews are comparable. Nevertheless, the choice of structure is dependent both on philosophical and practical considerations. The more committed to a social constructivist, non-realist viewpoint, the lesser degree of structure you are likely to desire, although you should balance this against practical considerations.

I referred above to something called a topic guide, which can also be called an interview guide. It's your key document, and a good one will ensure that your interviews go well. It is essentially a memory prompt, and schedule for your interview. Of course, it will contain different degrees of detail depending on how structured you wish to make your interview, but I will discuss here a guide for a typical semi-structured interview. You need to think very carefully about how you will get the information you want – how will you ask questions to access the internal worldviews and experiences of your respondents, which will enable you to answer your research questions? Without a guide, your interview can quickly descend into either (a) chaos, when the interviewee goes off on completely irrelevant tangents (such as relating stories of their last birthday party, which has happened to me), or (b) awkward silence when you have no idea what to say next. Some parts of an example interview guide are provided in Figure 9.3, from my own doctoral research. You should in particular try to order your topics in some consistent way, which will help the flow of the interview. For example, start with broad topics followed by more detailed probing. Furthermore, if there are particular questions you tend to forget, or sound awkward asking, write these down to help you out. Also, if you have trouble linking sections of the interview together, write down some link phrases to help.

Of course, the key part to your interview is the actual questions you ask. They are the way that you access the internal world of your respondents, so they had better be good. While

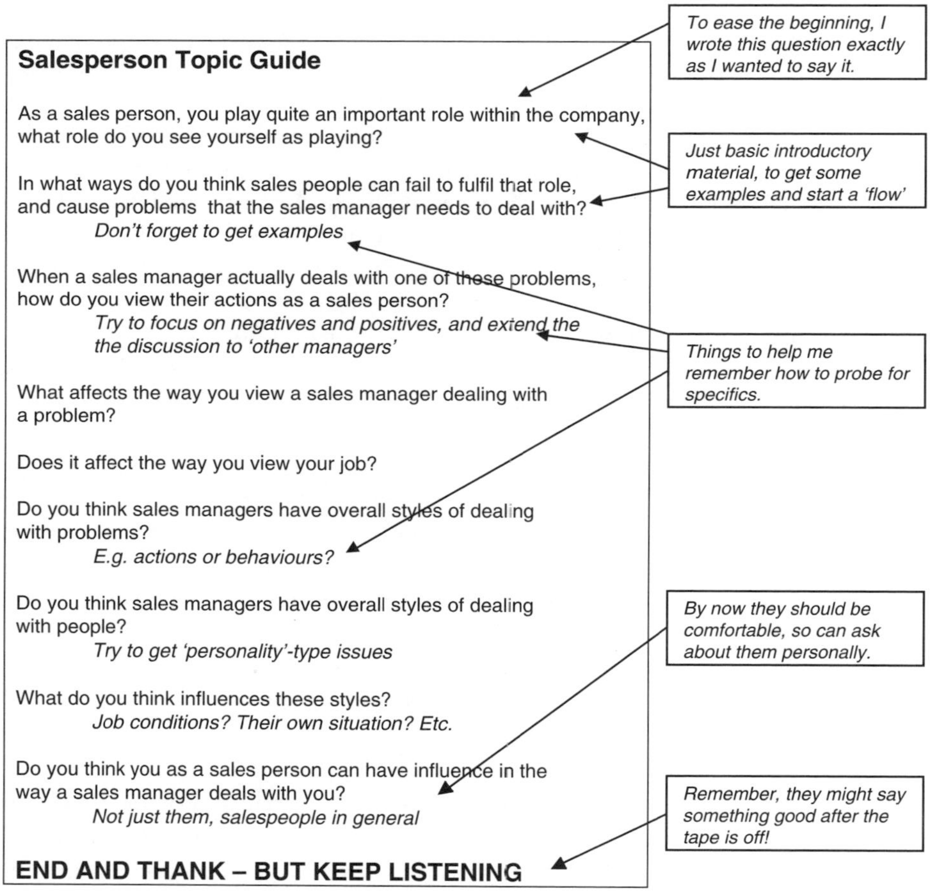

Figure 9.3 Example brief topic guide

good interviewing is a skill (simply watch a variety of TV talk shows for an illustration of how skill is important), there are a number of key different types of questions which you can learn which should help you develop into a great interviewer. There are also some questions you need to avoid at all costs. IDE 9.2 shows the different types of questions you should know about.

Finally, there are some practicalities (which are also relevant to other types of qualitative data collection) which should stand you in good stead. Most of these are based on my own experience (i.e. mistakes) so trust me, they are important. First, make sure you are prepared, that you know the topic, as well as the interviewee's own situational context, to help you understand the interview better. Prepare by *practising* interviewing, perhaps interviewing your friends, getting videoed and watching yourself (painful, I know), to find out where you tend to go wrong or right. You would be stunned just how helpful this is. If possible make sure the setting is quiet and private. I have interviewed people in restaurants, canteens, and all kinds of noisy places; it's not ideal let me tell you.

IDE 9.2: Different Types of Questions

Questioning techniques are vital to qualitative interviewing, you need to understand how to use questions to get the rich data you want. The worst type of question in a qualitative interview is one that results in a closed 'yes' or 'no' answer – you might as well get them to tick a box! Here are some more useful types of questions:

Introductory	*'Can you tell me about...?'*
Follow-up	*Use active listening, repeating,reflections*
Probing	*'Can you expand on...?'*
Specifying	*What, 'why, when, how much of...?'*
Structuring	*'Can we move to...?'*
Interpreting	*'Does that mean...?'*

For some more sensitive topics, you need to be a little more creative. For example, when I was doing research on sales manager problem resolution, I came to realise (eventually), that people were often more comfortable talking about 'other' people than themselves or their employees. I used some of the following techniques to gain information in that context:

Hypothetical	*'Suppose your manager was to sack me, what would that be like?'*

Devil's Advocate	*'Some say problem employees bring it on themselves, what do you say?'*
Ideal Position	*'How would an ideal manager deal with this problem?'*
Interpretive	*'Would you say that dealing with problem employees is more difficult than you expected?'*

Also, make sure you have your equipment completely sorted, and you know how it works! I'll be talking more about tape recording later on. Finally, make sure you get to the location nice and early, so you are not late, panicky and sweaty, which is never a good look, and tends to get things off to a bad start.

During the interview, I usually begin by getting a basic record of key data on each respondent, such as demographics and the like, which is really useful later on when you may wish to make comparisons across different groups, or get a feel for the context of the interview. When questioning, try not to get over-excited and lead the respondent down paths you particularly want them to go; let them get there themselves. Conversely, you must be interested in the respondent and what they have to say; at all costs try not to look bored! When you have finished the interview, it's also often useful to switch off the tape recorder, or use some other obvious 'close' (like 'thanks' or the like), and just keep chatting a little while. You will find that many fascinating points come up here, so keep your ears open. After the interview, as soon as possible make a few basic notes on what happened, and the key points were, as well as your own first thoughts on the information. This summary can be really useful later on when you analyse, and just to get clear in your head lessons for the next interview.

Focus groups

Focus groups are a form of qualitative data collection which involves the simultaneous participation of a number (usually around five to eight) of respondents, along with a moderator or facilitator. They have been common for many years in commercial market research, but only recently have they made inroads into academic social and organisational research. Even in academic marketing research their use is relatively infrequent. Focus groups should not be thought of as simply a way of saving resources by getting more respondents at the same time (i.e. 'simultaneous individual interviews'), but as a specific method in their own right. By definition, a focus group is *focused* on a particular topic, and should be used because the researcher wishes to explore the way that topic is discussed or constructed *by the group*, not as a set of individuals. As a result, group dynamics and processes are of key importance to a researcher who wishes to use focus groups. This means that a moderator should spend some time learning about group dynamics (hopefully with some practice before the first group). In particular, watch for participants who either (a) try to take over the group, or (b) avoid expressing any opinions at all. Such participants need to managed carefully.

Focus groups are especially useful for topics which are of common public concern to the group you wish to study, such as advertising, consumption, politics, or health. Within an organisational research context, focus groups are useful to explore many kinds of issues, such as change management, organisational policies, and the like. They can also be useful in a highly exploratory context when you wish to gain a basic grounding in a social setting, or particular topic, since they allow the researcher to observe how social actors interact, use language, and provide a wide range of viewpoints. Focus groups also mean the moderator has less power to direct the group than in an individual interview, which allows participants more scope to bring issues of importance to them out. As well as this, the group setting provides more scope for participants to be challenged and have their views argued with. While this can be a challenge for the moderator, it has the advantage of providing a more genuine picture of how issues are discussed and thought about in the social world. Thus, a well-run focus group can give more opportunity to study how the social world is constructed by participants – as we do not experience the world in isolation, but construct it together with other actors.

Nevertheless, focus groups are not always the appropriate choice. First of all, for the inexperienced researcher it can be a major challenge to moderate a focus group. This can be exacerbated by the type of respondents you wish to use. For example, you should be very careful about the make-up of your focus group in terms of the mix of demographics and their relation to your research topic. Sometimes you may wish to bring opposing viewpoints together for a specific purpose, but in many cases this can cause major problems to the moderator. In such situations, professional moderators may be required. For example, for one particular study, I and a colleague wished to examine young children's opinions and attitudes to Fair Trade products (see Nicholls and Lee, 2006). As children are notoriously difficult to control in group situations, we used a trained moderator to collect the data. Furthermore, some types of people are very difficult to organise into a focus group, often simply because of scheduling problems. Table 9.1 provides a very basic comparison of the kinds of topics and respondents which are most ideally suited to either individual or focus group interviews. However, this table is not a set of 'rules', just a set of things to consider when selecting your method. Any topic or respondent can be appropriate to any method, depending on specific contextual considerations.

When designing a focus group study, it is of course necessary to consider the number of groups needed, and how many participants should be in each group. In terms of the number of groups, there is no set figure that automatically means the research is 'done'. I think that the **theoretical saturation** concept introduced above is a useful guide to this decision. However, it does depend on exactly how complex your study is, and in particular how much it depends on respondent differences such as gender, age, and other demographics.

Table 9.1 Focus groups and interviews

Focus groups ideally suited to:	**Interviews ideally suited to:**
Research Objectives	
• Orient yourself to a field or language • Explore a range of attitudes, opinions • Observe consensus, etc. • Add context to quant work	• Explore the world of the individual in depth • Do case studies with repeated interviews over time • Test an instrument or questionnaire
Types of topic	
• Issues of public interest or common concern, e.g. politics, media, new tech. • Issues of an unfamiliar or hypothetical nature	• Detailed individual experiences, choices, or personal biography • Issues of sensitivity which may provoke anxiety, embarrassment, etc.
Types of respondent	
• Must not be from different backgrounds, which may inhibit discussion or cause problems	• Difficult to recruit • Elite or high status • Business people (usually) • Children under 7

In such situations you may wish to stratify your sample to include as many different features are represented. In terms of the number of participants per group, this decision depends on both practical and theoretical considerations. Firstly, without a reasonable number (I think five) of participants, a focus group will not exhibit enough social interaction, making it a bit pointless. However, beyond a certain point (I think about eight to ten) the interaction is just too complex, factions develop, some people become dominant, and things can easily get out of hand. Some say that smaller groups should be used in situations where topics are complex and involving, and larger groups when topics are less involving and you want a wide range of opinions (e.g. Morgan, 1998a). My own feeling is that a group size of six to eight is pretty good for almost all purposes. However, make sure to take into account the possibility that some participants may not show up on the day – this is surprisingly common, as Jennifer related at the very start of this chapter.

At the beginning of the focus group, make sure to introduce yourself, and give a basic appreciation for the topic. As well as this, get agreement on the some basic 'ground rules' such as only one person talking at a time, confidentiality, impartiality, and that all opinions are welcome and the necessity for disagreement (while acceptable) must only be constructive and not personal. While questioning techniques can be similar to individual interviews, focus groups often require a bit more structuring to get the group interaction going effectively.

In particular, you should not expect too much out of the group at the start, and instead focus on 'ice-breaking' activities (hopefully of general relevance to your topic) to get everyone comfortable interacting and participating. It is also important to remember to take advantage of the social situation of a focus group, and build in activities and questioning techniques which are designed to involve all participants and encourage them to interact among themselves. One common mistake made by inexperienced moderators is simply to ask questions of everyone one-by-one, without encouraging any interaction. It is of course essential to have a topic guide, and also to remember to continue to probe for more specific examples from your respondents, as sometimes focus groups can rely on 'shared knowledge' which the moderator or analyst does not have access to. At the end of the session, make sure to end things on a positive note, thank everybody, and explain what will happen to the information you have just gained.

Observation

Perhaps the other major method of qualitative data collection is observation. While the interviewing techniques described above come mainly from a depth-psychology background, observational techniques are mainly drawn from anthropological research, where it was common for researchers to actually enter and participate in a culture they wished to study. While there are some general concepts of observation which can be applied to most situation, beginning researchers need to realise that almost every social situation is different, and in most cases they will need to rely as much on improvisation or even luck as much as knowledge gleaned from textbooks. Also, going into a social setting to observe it – especially covertly – can be an intimidating, scary, and even dangerous experience (imagine being exposed as a social researcher studying football-hooligan or drug-dealing culture). And the emotional difficulties don't stop once you are finished, many observational researchers have to grapple with feelings of betrayal while writing up and publishing their work, after having spent so much time in that social situation. I've even known some researchers to 'go native', and disappear into the culture they were studying! So observational research is not for the faint-hearted, but it can offer incredible insights.

The first issue to deal with is gaining access to the situation you wish to study, which is not an easy task. In 'closed' settings (e.g. schools, firms or other formally organised situations like cults, etc.) you will usually need boundless determination to get the chance to enter the organisation for research purposes. Useful avenues can be friends, contacts within the setting, or academic supporters who may have some influence. Of course, you will almost always need the support of gatekeepers such as leaders or managers. To get this you generally need to be willing to negotiate exactly what you want (in terms of time and access) and often need to offer something in return (like a report). But be careful that in your enthusiasm to gain access, you don't end up in a situation where you are effectively paralysed (low access, lack of ability to publish your work, or becoming a cheap consultant for the firm). Gaining actual *physical* access to 'public' situations (e.g. communities, gangs, clubs) can be easier, but in almost every social situation even if you can gain physical access, you will need some way 'in' to the social side of that situation. In such cases finding a respected member of the situation who will take you 'under their wing' is really useful, as is having contacts inside the group. However, in situations where neither of these is available, it can sometimes come down to simply 'hanging around' the setting until you gain some kind of interaction with the actors. Of course, you will almost always have to make sure you look like you might 'fit in' with that group, so try not to dress in a suit and tie if you want to study an illegal motorbike gang, unless they are called 'The Devil's Accountants' perhaps.

Of course, the access problem can be eased a little if you become a 'covert' observer, and enter that situation without telling anyone you are a researcher. Although this does not ease the task of getting 'social' access always, it can help gaining access to the physical situation. But such techniques are fraught with difficulties and ethical concerns. Is it right to gain information from people without their knowing you are 'studying' them? What happens if you get found out? Can you even bring yourself to write up the research without feeling as if you have betrayed the people who have likely become your friends? Covert access can have major benefits though, allowing you to access parts of the context never available to overt researchers (especially in situations where a public 'front' is presented). However, it can actually make it very difficult to do your job. For example, it is not really acceptable to pull out a notebook while you are having what everyone else thinks is a normal conversation!

But just getting into the context is not the end of it. You still need to somehow gain the trust of those people within the organisation or setting. Many will think you are some kind of official 'inspector' at first, and your actions in the early part of your research (particularly if you see inappropriate activities) will determine the trust you gain. A simple way of getting a picture of this is to watch virtually any movie about undercover cops, or when a 'new guy' joins some army unit or police force (even better if it is a 'geek', a 'woman' or some other 'different' person). Focus on allaying people suspicions, playing up your knowledge and expertise, demonstrating your trustworthiness, and looking for any tests that participants might give you. Also, within the observation, you will also likely want to interview people, and similar issues concerning sampling as those already discussed will then come into play. That said, you will need to take into account the social context, your own 'overtness' and other specific issues when you are conducting interviews within an observational study.

Documentary sources of data

There are a vast amounts of other types of data that qualitative researchers can collect. In particular, while the previous discussion focuses on generating data from 'real' situations and face-to-face interactions, qualitative research can just as well utilise pre-existing data such as documents, or other textual data. One fast-growing source of data for qualitative analysis is of course the Internet. The Internet provides a vast resource of textual data for qualitative research. Much of this data can be treated similarly to any other document (as I will introduce below). However, the Internet is not just a document repository, it is also a hub for genuine social interaction. More specifically, there are thousands of 'virtual communities' on the Internet, where interested participants share experiences and information. These communities can be an amazingly rich source of data for the qualitative researcher. In fact, they can allow you quite easily to track the history of a particular topic, as well as the social network which underlies a given community, because all messages are usually kept online. Of course, if one wishes to research within an online community, it is good practice to ask permission from the moderator, as well as the participants where possible. The observation and analysis of interaction on the Internet is currently a very recent development, but it is likely that with the increasing use of the Internet in contemporary society, it will become more and more important to the qualitative researcher.

There are many other types of documents and textual data existing that the qualitative researcher can access. The government produces many official documents, such as policies, enquiry reports, White Papers and the like. These can prove to be of great importance to many qualitative research projects in social science. As well as official documents, private sources also produce masses of documentary data rich in meaning and insight. For example, companies produce annual reports, mission statements, product literature, catalogues, press releases and advertisements – to name but a few. Organisations also tend to produce a lot of 'private' material such as minutes of meetings, internal policy documents, memos and the like. Social and organisational researchers often find that this kind of material (when it is accessible) is a goldmine of information. And of course, in today's world no mention of documentary data would be complete without mentioning the mass media. Newspapers, television, magazines, and many other media sources can provide substantial information to the qualitative researcher. In fact, my first ever piece of published research was a qualitative analysis of how the word 'ruthless' was used in mass-media descriptions of managers (Lee and Cadogan, 1998[3]).

Individuals also create masses of documentary data and other information throughout their lives that can be used in qualitative analysis. For example, historical and political researchers commonly use personal letters and diaries as sources of data in their research, although social and organisational researchers have not utilised these as often. That said, it is more common for social researchers to actually collect data by asking potential respondents to write a diary, or letters, for the specific purposes of the research. For example, consumption and purchase diaries are a reasonably common way for consumer researchers to collect data. E-mails can

[3]This paper was published at a conference, so it will be hard to get hold of. Not to worry, you aren't missing much!

also be a useful source of information, where they are recorded. Narratives and life stories (e.g. autobiographies) can also be useful sources of data, whether they are generated expressly for the research or collected by a researcher.

However, when we are collecting data not generated specifically for the purposes of our research project, we need to spend some time evaluating how useful that data can be. There are many different criteria which could be used, but Scott (1990) provides a rigorous yet simple set of very useful things to think about. First, you should question the *authenticity* of the data. Is the data 'real'? Are you absolutely sure of who wrote it, or where it came from? *Credibility* is also an issue, and you must be sure that the information is free from bias or error, or at the very least be aware of the likely biases in that information. Scott also suggests that you must have an awareness of how *representative* your data is – is it typical, or if not how idiosyncratic is it? Finally, you must also assess how *meaningful* the information is, or in other words can you actually understand it. While these are difficult criteria to pass with flying colours, or even to evaluate in many pieces of data, it is very important that you spend time considering them when you are working with documentary data. In fact, you can consider this as an extension to the rigour discussion right at the beginning of this chapter.

Recording your data

Of course, gaining access to a social situation, or individual, or group, is not the final piece in the data collection puzzle. Once this is done, you need to have some way of recording your data. Probably the key decision is whether you take notes, or use some kind of electronic device such as a tape recorder, video recorder, or in today's high-tech world, some kind of digital recording device (I've even seen some people recording my lectures on an Ipod – or maybe they were listening to music!). Where at all possible, in interview or focus group contexts (observation will be discussed later) I recommend using a recording device. However, not all researchers recommend this, and some feel that it can unnecessarily restrict the information you actually retain for analysis (see Gummesson 2000, for example). That said, to my mind at least, not worrying about writing notes frees your mind to concentrate on the progress of the interview, enhancing your ability to build rapport, and react to interesting information. Also, I have found that sometimes respondents can see you writing down some things and start second-guessing what they are going to say next, either trying to avoid saying controversial things, or keep saying what is clearly the 'right' thing. Furthermore, in a focus group I always advise where possible to video record the group. This is because it can get very hard to tell who is speaking at any point in time using only audio recordings, especially if multiple people speak simultaneously. Of course, transcribing a video tape can get messy, with all the fast forwarding and rewinding, but with the increasing use of digital video this is less of a problem. When using some kind of audio tape recorder, I always make sure to use two things: (a) full-size 90 minute tapes, and (b) an external microphone.

Smaller 'dictaphone'-style tapes are dependent on having a transcribing machine (and they can get very expensive), and longer than 90 minute tapes have very thin tape that breaks easily with all the use they get in transcribing. That said, if your tape does break, don't panic, because with a bit of ingenuity you can actually stick it back together with thin tape. Just make sure to copy it as soon as you possibly can afterwards! Also, when you set up in an interview or focus group, make sure you test the equipment first with the respondent. There's nothing worse than running a 90 minute interview, getting back and finding that the microphone was in the wrong place and all you can hear is your own voice!

Sometimes you will have to take notes. This is particularly relevant for observational research. Even if you were able to tape a whole day, imagine transcribing it! Field notes are the method of choice in recording observational research. One key rule I have always lived by (after learning the hard way) is *never assume you will remember something*, no matter how important it may be. The human mind forgets quickly, and massively. A useful strategy, inspired by Bryman (2004), is to take notes in three ways. First are what I call **mental notes**. As soon as something happens which you need to record, make a mental note of it. This simple act can help a lot. Then, as soon as practical, make a **brief note** in your notebook. It's normally best to do this discreetly, rather than in front of everybody – this can make people feel very self-conscious (which is why I recommend the mental notes above). Then, at the end of the day spend some time writing up **full field notes** of the day with as much detail as possible, including context, time, date and the like. Again, never assume you will remember the details later on. If in doubt, write it down. Remember that these notes are in fact the raw material for your analysis, so if you don't have any data, you don't have a project.

Transcribing interview and focus group recordings is a thorny issue for many researchers. One decision which needs to be made is *who* will do the transcribing. Unfortunately, transcribing is in many cases both time consuming and boring. Thus, researchers often like to employ professional transcribers. I do not recommend this myself, which tends to make me unpopular with my students. Transcribing interviews yourself has so many advantages that I think where possible it should be the method of choice. Firstly it gets you intimately connected with your data, and allows your mind to begin thinking about the issues immediately. Secondly, your presence at the interview should minimise mistakes and misunderstandings in the transcription. Also, I strongly advocate transcribing interviews as soon as possible, not waiting until the end of the research programme. Since you can guarantee over four hours transcribing for each hour of interview, spreading this out is beneficial. It also allows you to take into account any issues which arise in an interview prior to the next one. The other major question in transcribing is *what* to transcribe. My own personal feeling is to transcribe everything, even things you think right now are irrelevant. This is because you never know at the beginning of a project exactly what will be the outcome at the end. Missing out swathes of data runs the risk of prejudicing what you come out with, which in my opinion kind of misses the point of a qualitative approach. Related to this is the question of whether you should transcribe just words, or other utterances, gestures, and the like. Of course, if you are using a specific analysis method like discourse analysis (see Chapter 10), you will probably utilise a more detailed transcription scheme, but I tend to focus on the words and the pauses and utterances ('um', 'ah', and the like) primarily.

Summary

Understanding how to collect qualitative data is a vital part of becoming a well-rounded researcher. Even more so, it is important to break down the prejudices which exist in many field of social science, that qualitative data can be 'easy' to collect, or even reliant on random chance and being in the right place at the right time. A qualitative data collection programme can be as detailed and rigorous as any quantitative study. Indeed, unless you have philosophical disagreements with the very concept of rigour and truth in research, qualitative research should always be done with concern for these concepts. As has already (and will be repeatedly) said in this book, without high-quality data, none of your conclusions are trustworthy, and assuring readers of this is one of your most important tasks as a researcher.

Key points to take from this chapter:

- Rigour in qualitative research is associated with the 'quality' of your research methods.
- Validity is an important concept in qualitative research; however, there have been various different approaches to it from different researchers.
- Thinking about whether the claims you make from your findings are **justifiable** is a good way of thinking about concepts of validity and reliability.
- Sampling is a key part of your research design, and will have major impacts on your conclusions.
- There are various ways a qualitative researcher can collect data: 'in person', such as interviews, focus groups, and observation.
- There are also vast amounts of documentary evidence available to the qualitative researcher, some of which are relatively untapped by social scientists.
- Recording and transcribing your data are also a very important parts of the process, and should not be treated as an 'afterthought'.

Further reading

There are many general sources on qualitative methods for social and organisational researchers. However, original ideas can also be found in literature dedicated to management research. A selection of both of these sources would include:

- *Qualitative Methods in Management Research* by Evert Gummesson: The concepts in this book were touched upon in the previous chapter when I wrote about 'action research'. This book (and much of Professor Gummesson's other work) is an original and useful contribution to qualitative methods from a specifically 'management research' viewpoint, which stands apart from the more 'traditional' sociological sources given below.

- *Doing Qualitative Research* by David Silverman: An excellent introduction to the field, and Silverman has a great perspective on qualitative research. This book has been a pretty big influence on my own thinking about qualitative methods.
- *An Introduction to Qualitative Research* by Uwe Flick: A more 'theoretical' book than Silverman's, but includes some excellent information about the philosophical background and development of qualitative research.
- *Basics of Qualitative Research: Techniques and Procedures for Developing Grounded Theory* by Anselm Strauss and Juliet Corbin. Grounded theory has also been a big influence in many ways on my qualitative research techniques (although I would never say my work was 'true' grounded theory), and I think all budding researchers should explore it. Strauss' perspective is to my mind more pragmatic and useful than Glaser's, and I like this book a lot.
- *Qualitative Research Practice* edited by Clive Seale, Giampetro Gobo, Jaber F. Gubrium and David Silverman. This is a big book with many different chapters by different authors. I have found it a very useful resource of perspectives and techniques about qualitative research. If you can't afford it yourself, try to get your library to get it so you can look at it.

EXERCISES

1. What makes qualitative research 'qualitative'?
2. Does your answer to question 1 mean that all numeric measures are fundamentally incompatible with qualitative research?
3. Which philosophical perspective (see Chapters 2 and 3) do you think could be best considered as the base for qualitative research methods? Why is this?
4. If you have previously been considering a quantitative research project, think about how your project could be addressed using qualitative research:
    a. Would qualitative work add anything to your existing methodology?
    b. Could your existing methodology be replaced by a totally qualitative approach?
    c. Is your topic fundamentally inappropriate to qualitative research, and if so, why do you think this is?
5. Do you think the Logical Positivists would be keen on qualitative methods? Why or why not?
    a. Another angle – is qualitative research compatible with empiricist philosophy?
6. Hey, it's pretty much halfway through now – why don't you give yourself a pat on the back and take the night off – go out to a club and do some dancing.

10 Qualitative Data Analysis

NICK LEE and IAN LINGS

SUPERVISOR'S VIEW: PROFESSOR CHRIS HACKLEY

Dr Nick Lee's chapter on qualitative research is powerfully well-informed and exceptionally well-written. Reading it with enthusiasm, it stimulated two recurring thoughts. The first was 'Where are the citations to my publications which Lee promised?[1]' I read thousands of words a week, all with a finely honed sense of literary appreciation, yet no word in the incomparable lexicon of Western literature gives me the satisfaction of 'Hackley' followed by 2005, 1998 or whatever. I'm not soliciting undeserved praise, you understand. Someone could write: 'There have been many outstanding studies in this field, with the deplorable exception of Hackley (200X), quite the most inept, scurrilous and fraudulent piece of "work" ever published', and I'd still feel the same glow of existential affirmation. The second thing which kept occurring to me as I read this chapter was 'Should we be talking about *qualitative* research or *interpretive* research?' What I mean is this: research needs data sets (empirical research anyway). Qualitative or quantitative, and usually both in some degree. What separates research paradigms, if you will, is whether the findings are presented as facts or interpretations. My own Ph.D. was based on my version of discourse analysis, and I offered a number of 'interpretive repertoires' induced from my interview data. To my great relief, my examiner didn't ask me to thoroughly explain this inductive process. He didn't ask questions like 'why those interpretive repertoires, and not others?' He didn't ask because he knew the answer. I was explaining my interpretation of these data sets, not claiming to have discovered some new facts. As you'd expect, I had to offer some philosophical arguments as justification. As is made clear in this very chapter, using, and most importantly, justifying qualitative data findings can be far more difficult than it looks. But my examiner understood the interpretive research approach well so he was receptive to those kinds of arguments. And in case you were wondering, the story of my Ph.D. research was published as Hackley (2000). There, got one in.

[1] Note from Nick: They're actually in Chapter 3!

VIEW FROM THE TRENCHES: DR JANE MATTHIESEN

'You *don't* want me to do a questionnaire?!' That was my first reaction when my supervisor first proposed using *only* qualitative methods in my Ph.D. After shock came fear. First of all, I didn't know anything about qualitative methodology, apart from the very superficial stuff they teach in most research degrees, and had no idea *how* to do qualitative work. Secondly, I came from a strongly positivistic quantitative discipline (psychology) and was very aware that most people in my field didn't think much of qualitative work, so I also had no idea why I would *want* to do qualitative work. I was in denial. This quickly turned into anger and frustration. Why would my supervisor want me to use this methodology if he knows it would undermine the quality of my work? Is he trying to sabotage me? The next stage was bargaining. I agreed to do some qualitative work but only if I could 'validate' it using quantitative methods. We had a deal: I'd do 100 interviews and 1,000 questionnaires. I started interviewing people and loved the work. It was exciting to deal with real people instead of pieces of paper, being able to push and probe rather than just taking everything at face value. Seeing when people were unsure, deceitful, sad or angry. It was a fantastic experience. Then came depression – I had to analyse all these beautiful rich words and turn them into useful data (and in my mind, that still meant numbers). The qualitative analysis was extremely difficult and time-consuming, the frequency counts painful. It was undoubtedly much more intense than any quantitative analysis I would have been able to concoct, but the beautiful thing was that, in the end, I had meaning and not just numbers. And all of a sudden I understood why my supervisor had told me that qualitative work was 'enough'. The interviews offered plenty of data to fill two Ph.D.s. That was the moment of insight and the moment I stopped grieving for quantitative methods!

Qualitative data analysis tends to suffer from a rather unfortunate image problem, as you can see from Jane's story above. This problem causes those who have never tried to do 'proper' qualitative analysis to assume it is *ad hoc,* lacking in rigour, and biased (remember 'blagging it'?) This problem also causes the ill-informed beginning researcher to gravitate towards qualitative approaches because they think they are 'easier'. Sometimes this leads to poor research. A vicious circle then ensues which perpetuates the negative image of qualitative analysis. More often it leads to the researcher 'drowning' in masses of data, with absolutely no idea what to do with it, and a rather sheepish realisation that indeed, qualitative research was not as easy as it looked.

It should come as no surprise to you then when I say that for many people qualitative research has the unhealthy image of being 'easy'. This is caused by a few things. Firstly is the fact that many social scientists remain dogmatically wedded to the traditional quantitative model of scientific research, and mistrust qualitative research in general. But hopefully the fact that you are reading Chapter 10 (well done by the way) of this book should mean that you are not entirely one of those. More pressing a concern to my mind is the general lack of information about qualitative analysis available. I look up to the shelves of my study and see literally over 50 books about quantitative analysis, I then look to the left and see but a solitary volume entitled *Qualitative Data Analysis*. While this is not to say information is not available from other sources,[2] the point remains valid. For many researchers, particularly in the past, qualitative analysis was like a 'black box' – some data went in, and some findings came out. There was no real concern as to how the researcher arrived at those findings.

The aim of this chapter is to provide a solid platform for you to conduct rigorous qualitative analysis, which will allow the various constituencies of your work to have confidence in your findings. Of course, this chapter is by no means the final word on analysis, but it should provide a good jumping-off point for you to go forward into the sometimes rather deep waters of qualitative analysis. Again, like the previous chapter, I aim to avoid where possible philosophical discussion, as I feel those decisions need to be made independently, prior to methodological ones. But of course where philosophy is unavoidable it will without fail raise its head! Thus, this chapter should be read in a pragmatic manner, not an ideological one, and also as relevant to *all* researchers in the social sciences.

Either way, at the end of this chapter I really hope you have come to terms with these key ideas:

- That qualitative data is data which in a general sense is or can be transformed into *words* rather than numbers.
- That such data can be very rich, and analysis can be helped by *reducing* it to key ideas and concepts.
- Qualitative analysis can be described as a process of extracting and presenting these key ideas, themes and concepts in various ways.
- Key tasks in this process are coding, data displaying, and drawing conclusions.
- Concern for reliability and validity should pervade this process.

[2] After all, I don't own *every* analysis book in existence (and if you keep it quiet, I'll let you in on the secret that I haven't read all the books on my shelves either!)

Why is it Important to Know This Stuff?

Many of the points I raised in the corresponding section of Chapter 9 of course remain relevant here, so there seems little point repeating them (go back and read them if you must!) Naturally, this chapter will hopefully be extremely useful to those students setting out on a path of qualitative research. In particular, I think the concepts in this chapter provide a solid 'framework' to the researcher, helping to ensure they do not get lost in the data, or become seduced by its richness into anecdotalism. Remember, we are dealing with many of the same issues as we will be in later chapters – how do we go about looking at data from the real world and drawing conclusions relating back to the theoretical world (see Figure 10.1).

However, knowledge of qualitative analysis methods is particularly important to all researchers who wish to become strong, well-rounded contributors to their discipline. First of all, to the quantitatively oriented researcher, looking at things from a qualitative perspective takes you out of your 'comfort-zone' extremely effectively. It allows you to see possible new ways of looking at a problem, which will almost definitely lead to interesting and useful viewpoints and solutions. It also exercises your mind. Furthermore, I always find the flexibility and scope for originality in qualitative analysis extremely refreshing, especially after a long session of adhering to a quantitative methodological framework. Essentially, for me at least, they seem to exercise different parts of my mind, which always leads to new and often useful approaches to a given problem.

If you want to be an effective member of your discipline you will need to have the confidence and competence to fairly evaluate qualitative analysis – whether this is in existing research articles, ones you have been asked to review, grant proposals, theses, or anything else. Without a knowledge of what makes 'good' qualitative analysis, you will either tend to consider all qualitative analysis 'bad' or be unable to recognise when it is good – or worse when it really *is* bad!

Finally, I have found a solid understanding of qualitative analysis has opened up huge vistas of projects that I have been lucky enough to work on, and collaborators who I have been blessed to work with. Without that knowledge (and my usual tendency to let everyone know about it) I would never had participated in many of the interesting research projects and teams that I have.

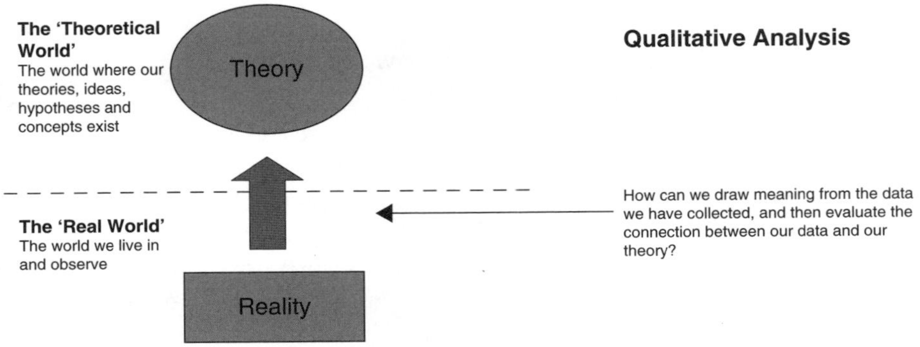

Figure 10.1 The Place of quallitative analysis

A perspective on qualitative analysis

When considering how to analyse 'qualitative' data, the first question that needs to be answered is 'exactly what is it that defines a set of data as qualitative?' In fact, in the social sciences it can be argued that *all* data begins as qualitative – as one of Locke's or Berkeley's sensory experiences[3] – and is subsequently transformed into words, images, sounds or numbers. An interesting question is exactly who this transformation is done by. On one level, it can be argued that in qualitative research the subject of the research (e.g. the interviewee) transforms their experience into words which are then uttered to the interviewer. By contrast one can suggest that quantitative research *imposes* the transformation onto subjects (say the respondents to your questionnaires) by asking them to express their experiences by way of working out which rigid box they fall into, or how much they agree or disagree with an 'objective' statement. However, the very act of transforming a raw set of qualitative data (e.g. transcribing an interview recording) can also impose the researcher's own conceptualisations on to that data. This is particularly relevant when recording observational data; separating out pure recording of the experience from the researcher's own interpretation of that experience can be a key issue to keep in mind when collecting qualitative data to analyse.

A very simple way of looking at the nature of qualitative data is to consider it as data in the form of words or, more pertinently, meaningful collections of words. Admittedly, this excludes things like visual data, but if we extend the definition to include data that can be transformed into words, that problem is solved for the moment. Qualitative data has some key strengths which have a major impact on the way in which qualitative analysis methods have evolved, and for the way you should think about qualitative analysis. We've covered

[3] If you don't recognise these names, you probably need to read Chapters 2 and 3.

many of these strengths in previous chapters, but let's recap a little, especially as they are more useful than rigid definitions of what qualitative data is. Firstly, remember how a lot of qualitative work is focused on exploring events as they occur naturally, and is grounded within the context? This allows analysis to really get to grips with the underlying meanings and layers of the social world. We should try not to strip all of this 'context' away when we analyse the data. Of course, qualitative data is also 'rich and thick'. This again means that our analysis methods should play to this strength, while recognising that the richer the data, the easier it can be to get lost in it – even though it can make our findings really compelling to the reader. And perhaps my favourite strength is the flexibility of qualitative data – there are literally limitless ways you can design analysis methods for qualitative data. This of course makes it difficult for the beginner as there are few 'textbook' approaches available. But when you take advantage of this strength, you can create fantastic and enlightening analysis tools which allow you to see the world in entirely different ways.

A general approach to qualitative data analysis

Although there are many and varied approaches to qualitative analysis available to the researcher, there are few that are actually set down clearly, allowing the novice researcher a good starting point from which to move forwards. The approach set out here is indebted to that of Miles and Huberman (1994), who's work provided my own initiation into qualitative analysis. Much of the balance of this chapter will be devoted to providing detail on this general process.

The first step in analysis occurs even before the collection of data is started, in a pre-planning process involving a theoretical appreciation; which questions to ask, how to ask them and the like. These issues were covered in the previous chapter, and they have an important impact on the analysis you can do later. Immediately following the data collection should come a brief process of summarising the interaction, which can be a key influence on your more detailed analysis. The first major part of post-collection analysis is concerned with data reduction. Miles and Huberman (1994, p. 10) define data reduction as 'the process of selecting, focusing, simplifying, abstracting, and transforming the data', and I am yet to find a better definition. I tend to explain it to my students as trying to reduce the rich data set down to its core ideas, although we will go into this in more detail later. Following and concurrent (at least in part) with reduction is what I consider to be the fun part of qualitative analysis – data displays. While displays can simply be selections of text (like quotes), it is often helpful to draw a parallel with quantitative information. Not all quantitative data is displayed in numbers, often charts and other visual displays are used to help understanding of the data. The concept is exactly the same with qualitative data. Finally, and again this often occurs along with reduction and displaying, is the drawing of conclusions. I often find students have problems with this stage. This is basically the process of deciding what your data 'means', and can be difficult for all researchers. For example, a problem that one of my students is having as I write this is exactly where to stop; the data is so interesting that she is tempted to keep adding to the conclusions.

One key point to keep in mind here is that you shouldn't think of this as necessarily a sequential process. In particular, I generally advocate where possible the beginning of preliminary analysis during the data collection. For many people, waiting until after all the data is collected can result in an intimidating and demotivating pile of thousands of pages of text to analyse. Analysis during collection can also help modify later data collection efforts (the iterative process mentioned in the previous chapter). Furthermore, in the process of reduction the analyst often develops ideas for displays, and begins to get tentative ideas for conclusions as well. These things should never be ignored simply because you are 'not at that stage yet'.

Reliability and validity in qualitative analysis

You'll remember that notions of reliability and validity were raised early on in the previous chapter – and you were warned that they would occur again. Indeed, the analysis of your data is yet another key point in a piece of qualitative research where questions of reliability, validity (I used the term *justifiability* as well) raise their heads. Silverman (2005, pp. 209–210) sums up the importance of these concepts to analysis with the strongly worded statement that 'short of reliable methods and valid conclusions, research descends into a bedlam where the only battles that are won are by those who shout the loudest'. Although it was suggested in the previous chapter that qualitative data collection was not inherently unreliable or invalid, concern still needs to be given to how that data is analysed, and whether we can justify the conclusions we draw from that data.[4] However, there are, of course, dissenters, and some opposing views are presented in Alternative View 10.1.

Beginning with reliability, in analysis this can generally be considered to concern the manner in which the raw data is transformed into 'analysable form'. This can involve things like transcribing, but also issues such as coding. In particular, how much of the researchers' own inference has gone into, say, summarising or transforming that raw data into a transcript, and that transcript into a set of codes? In fact, a number of scholars argue that extended swathes of raw data be included in research write-ups, including such things as the interviewer's questions and prompts (Bryman, 1988; Silverman, 2005). This allows readers to get a better picture of the respondents' own concepts and categories, without relying solely on the interpretation of the researcher. It also helps readers determine whether the researcher's interpretation is able to be relied upon. When transcribing or otherwise transforming the raw data, it is important to have consistent methods (especially when multiple team members are working with the data) and notation styles. For instance, do you transcribe all utterances,

---

[4]Of course, you've already seen in Chapter 6 and 7 (and it will be covered again later) that qualitative researchers do not have the monopoly on reliability and validity problems – these are relevant to quantitative research too.

even things like 'mm', 'um', and other various tics and pauses? In fact, there are many more details involved in conversation which you could record, and newer developments in *conversation analysis* (a variant of discourse analysis, which will be discussed later) are good examples of this approach. The way in which you record your raw data will have a major impact on your ability to reliably represent the perspectives of your respondents.

Validity, on the other hand, is an altogether more nebulous concept in this context. Drawing from the previous chapter, we can consider it to be concerned with how well your conclusions reflect the data you drew them from – how justifiable are your conclusions? Of course, whether these conclusions reflect some kind of underlying truth or reliability (external validity) is a philosophical question which may or may not have relevance to you; but it is my view that the concern for internal validity or what Guba and Lincoln (1994) called **credibility** is important to all qualitative analysts. Although we covered many of these issues in Chapter 9, there are specific concerns for the qualitative analyst. Most pertinent is the issue of **anecdotalism**, which refers to the temptation to base your conclusions on a small number of quotes or examples which epitomise key points, rather than a thorough investigation of the data. As you are about to discover, qualitative analysis is *not* about simply extracting a good quote which exemplifies a theoretical idea. For example, why was one quote included and another not? Were there alternative interpretations of the same material? Was there data which contradicted your chosen example? If so, how common was it? How much were your interpretations and selections influenced by prior theory? Answers and reassurances about these issues provide the real meat on the bones of the validity concept as it refers to qualitative research.

Alternative View 10.1: A Counterpoint to Reliability and Validity Concerns

A full discussion of those viewpoints which essentially reject the notions of validity explored in this chapter is of course far beyond my remit (and my capability – I've already tied myself in knots trying to explain postmodernism in Chapter 3!) However, if we consider the social world to be constantly in flux and ever-changing, it has been said that it's somewhat nonsensical to spend time worrying whether our methods are reliable, since they can never truly be replicated (e.g. Marshall and Rossman, 1999). In terms of validity, postmodern thinkers would argue that the very nature of qualitative research renders any criteria for judging it irrelevant (Hammersley, 1992). Postmodern thought rejects the idea that there is a set of privileged criteria which can be used to judge one piece of research as 'better' than another; all representations are equal. Poststructuralist positions (such as feminism, ethnic and other critical studies) would also argue that our existing notions of validity are not relevant. Oftentimes, the criteria for such work involves concepts such as whether it is somehow emancipatory, or otherwise helpful to its subjects and wider constituents; does it break down existing barriers, or raise awareness of problems? Is it humane and socially informed? Of course, criticism from traditional quarters stresses the inherent impossibility of then telling whether such research is in fact 'good or bad'. This is rebutted by poststructuralists, with the argument that the very concept of 'good and bad science' is the problem, as it has been used in the past as a way of maintaining control on knowledge and progress by a minority, and that traditional scientific criticism is irrelevant as poststructuralism is concerned with a completely different set of aims and objectives. It is usually at this point when I am inclined to refer to the quote by Silverman that I gave earlier.

There are many ways of providing information which can reassure readers that your conclusions are valid. **Triangulation** is one way in which you can try to enhance validity. It involves looking at the issue from different angles (maybe using different types of method, or different analysis techniques, and the like). Whereas this works well if you assume there is some kind of external reality which you can get a 'fix' on, it is quite incompatible with the more interpretive ideas presented in Chapter 3. If there is no 'truth', then how can looking at different perspectives get you closer to it? Triangulation can certainly be useful to enhance the richness of your data set, but you do need to be careful when you employ it to enhance validity. Another commonly advocated method is that of **respondent validation**, which involves taking your early results back to the people you studied, and asking basically whether you are on the right track. Although I have always been a bit of a fan of this method, others are not so sure (e.g. Bryman, 1988). Of course, it is not really in question that respondents can provide interesting insights; the crux of the objection relates to whether you give the views of the respondents more weight than any other view. Why should their interpretation be more valuable than yours, for example? Nevertheless, I still feel respondent validation can be useful if you wish to make sure you have recorded respondents' perspectives accurately – if that was your goal. While I have poured a little cold water on some oft-cited bulwarks to validity, there are some other ways of thinking about validity which may be used with more confidence, and these are presented in IDE 10.1.

IDE 10.1: Refutability

Silverman (2005) develops the concept of **refutability**, which draws from Popper's ideas of falsification (see Chapter 2) as a defence against charges of anecdotalism. While it should be clear to you that this kind of approach may be anathema to some of the philosophical standpoints expressed in Chapter 3 (and in Alternative

View 10.1), it does provide a very solid set of principles for thinking about how valid your conclusions are. Basically, the principle of refutability implies that you should always seek to *refute* your initial assumptions about the data. You will undoubtedly recognise this principle from the Popperian emphasis on hypothesis falsification (if not, Chapter 2 is calling you). Of course, we are usually hoping that we *won't be able to* refute our original ideas, but equally, we cannot accept them as 'knowledge' unless we have done our utmost to do so. There are a number of more specific techniques which can be drawn from qualitative methodology which can help us do this. For example, researchers should always look to explore their ideas by comparing their findings from one case to those for another. In my Doctoral work, I studied sales managers, and then took those tentative theories to a set of salespeople. Within the data set, it is also useful to begin with a small part (say one transcript), and then slowly snowball out until you have incorporated and compared your findings with all parts of the set, constantly flipping between the various parts of your data, and modifying your conclusions as new insights emerge. This *constant comparative method* is similar to that advocated in the Grounded Theory approach I have already mentioned. It also involves what Silverman (2005) calls *comprehensive data treatment*, or making sure every single piece of data is somehow analysed. More specific is the search for *deviant cases*, or cases which seem to exhibit relevant characteristics at odds with the rest of your data set. For example, in my Doctoral study of sales manager problem resolution, I was aware that existing knowledge suggested that disciplinary activities were emotionally stressful and difficult for managers to carry out, and this was borne out in many of my interviews. However, I made concerted efforts to interview managers who admitted that they *didn't* have any problems carrying out such activity. The principles of refutability incorporated into the qualitative work allowed me to have more confidence in the validity of my conclusions regarding the antecedents to and consequences of sales managers' problem resolution.

Preparatory steps in analysis

The first step in analysis can be considered to be the design of the study – before you even get out into the field, let alone collect data. Although we considered many of these issues in the previous chapter on data collection, they still have relevance here. One key decision you need to make is how to bound your efforts. Do you go into the field with virtually no preconceptions or do you have a tightly structured framework? Of course, there are pros and cons to both sides of this debate. A pre-existing conceptual framework or set of categories allows you to 'see' more clearly what is useful or not to your study; but then again it could also restrict you from developing any new insights inductively. Of course, if you are studying something completely new, then you will not be able to develop too much of an existing framework anyway, but this is not often the case. In fact, as Miles and Huberman (1994) point out, we are almost always furnished with some kind of pre-existing knowledge, and it is somewhat silly to try to deny this. At a minimum, our skills as researchers influence us to interpret events in different ways from others. On the other hand, having some kind of framework allows you to structure your later analysis methods more easily – you have a good idea of what concepts and categories are going to be there, but you have to be careful to 'let the data speak' for itself, and not bend it to fit your existing model. If this sounds like a trade-off, that's because it is, and you need to be careful to find the right balance (which can be influenced by such mundane political things as your funder or supervisor).

Your research questions and sampling methods will also influence later analysis. You need to make certain at a minimum that your sampling strategy will give you enough data to answer those research questions, and the notions of refutability presented in IDE 10.1 are also relevant here. For example, if you don't look for deviant cases, you will not be able to take that particular approach to validity. Also, the instruments you use to collect data have a major influence on the data you collect. If you go in with few prepared instruments (e.g. interview questions, observation log books and schedules, and the like) you run the risk of not being able to differentiate between useful data and irrelevance – leading to data overload at minimum. However, again too much structure can leave you blind to the situational context and overly influenced by previous models. It's usually best to settle somewhere in the middle; the more exploratory your study, the less instrumentation you will be able to create. If you are looking to compare multiple cases or situations, however, instrumentation will be of considerable help in comparative analysis.

Your decisions on how to manage your data will also have a major bearing on analysis. When I began qualitative work, in 1998, I used no special qualitative software, but I did maintain all my work on computer. Others I know managed their data by hand, using sticky labels and card files. As I moved on, I incorporated qualitative data analysis (QDA) software such as QSR NUD*IST[5] and its updated version, called NVIVO. Interestingly, I think my approach to analysis has been quite strongly influenced by the ease of coding and retrieving information in these packages. Some would undoubtedly argue that this is A Bad Thing, perhaps removing the ultimate creativity from qualitative analysis. However, tools are not the reason for such a problem. In fact, a lack of creativity is the researcher's fault, not the fault of the tools. What is not in doubt is that in a qualitative project of any reasonable scale (say over five to ten interviews), the use of QDA software at a minimum to organise and manage your data can make your life a lot easier. There are a number of key issues you need to think about regarding data management, and these are summarised in IDE 10.2.

[5] I'll be honest, it was mainly the name that attracted me first, and the fact that my institution paid money to send me on a 'NUD*IST Course', which wasn't as much fun as I was expecting!

IDE 10.2: Data Management

The first thing you need to think about is how you will gain access to your data. This may seem easy at first, but when you have a large project which goes on for an extended time period this is not so easy. Also, it's not just about gaining access to the entire transcript or case notes. What about specific parts within that unit? You'll also need to record what analysis you did and how it developed. This can be incredibly important for later writing up – especially in light of the iterative process of qualitative work, and the need to document your methods for validity and reliability purposes.

Finally, it's necessary to think about what you will do with the data and records after you are finished – you will at minimum need to keep them for some period of time. This could be because you are going to write up your dissertation into some articles, or to have the data on hand for examiners or funders to look at for themselves. It is for all these reasons that having your data in electronic format, with the use of some kind of QDA package, is probably the most helpful in the contemporary environment.

Lastly, one piece of advice. **Back up your data regularly!!!!** I say this from bitter experience!

The first thing I usually do after a piece of qualitative data collection (say an interview, or maybe a key event in an observation), after spending some time reflecting on it, is write up a short **contact summary**. The contact summary form I often use is shown in Figure 10.2, and as you can see it is a pretty simplistic sheet of paper. The detail you go into on this form is up to you, but you should always try to keep it to one page. It is meant to be a simple sheet which allows you to focus on the key issues which came out of the contact. It can be drawn from your conceptual framework (e.g. which key concepts were mentioned), be more exploratory (e.g. what were the main overall themes), or more usually both. It should be driven by the research questions you are trying to answer. Another useful idea is to leave some space for writing down ideas for future data collection efforts which were suggested by this contact (e.g. did some questions prove difficult, can they be rephrased?)

The contact summary should be done as soon as practical after the contact; its aim is to record those overarching observations and feelings about the contact, which can prove of immense help in later analysis. A set of these sheets can give you a good impression of what was going on in your data, and help you design a further scheme of data reduction. It can also be used as part of a hermeneutic type of analysis (see IDE 3.2 and related material), as a good way of getting a first impression of 'the whole' of your contact. That said, Miles and Huberman (1994, p. 52) suggest that you shouldn't do a contact summary immediately after

Interview details: *Here, record things like name, position, time and date*

Salient Points	**Themes**
Here, write down any interesting points you can remember	*Here, try to think about what overall themes they could represent.*

Figure 10.2 Example contact summary sheet

the contact, as you can be overwhelmed by what they call 'vivid incidents', and that you should always write-up first. As implied above, my personal feeling is that this misses the point a little, as it seems to me that a contact summary should get the *first impressions* of a contact, before anything else. However, my opinion is based on interview research, where you have a verbatim record of the contact available (the tape). In an observational context, Miles and Huberman's concerns are very relevant, in that a pre-write-up contact summary can influence your later write-up of the field notes.

Coding and data reduction

It is not overstating things to say that **coding** is at the very core of the analysis approach I usually utilise. Strangely, it is also the idea which I have found most difficult to explain to students. I have always suspected that this may be because I am just not very good at explaining it, but I imagine we are all about to find out whether or not this is the case. In essence, coding begins as data preparation, and moves you forward into truly beginning to analyse your data. First, imagine the amount of information you might begin to build up in a typical qualitative study: interview transcripts, field notes, miscellaneous documents, and the like. This can get rather difficult to handle; for example, how can you retain all that information in your head in order to compare various parts of it? Or how are you to quickly retrieve important pieces of data from the pile? Even worse, the words in your data will often have different meanings across different people, or people will say different words when they mean the same thing. What we need is a way of encoding the key ideas of the data, as well as reducing the sheer amount of it, and allowing it to be quickly retrieved and rearranged. Coding helps us do this, and then builds from there to draw meaningful conclusions about our data.

A code is simply a *label* which you attach to a bit of text, whether it be a single word, a whole paragraph, or even an entire document (e.g. a transcript). They are designed to capture the *meaning* of that unit of text – not just the words (remember, different people use different words for the same underlying meanings). Once raw data is coded, it can be retrieved, compared, and used to answer the research questions – and if QDA software is used this process is almost ridiculously easy, although the *thinking and interpretation* behind it is still complex. There are many different styles of coding, ranging from very unstructured right up to extremely structured. It's probably best to begin with a somewhat structured approach to help you understand the basic process of coding, and to this end, IDE 10.3 demonstrates some different types of codes, but these are not the 'only' way of coding. In a qualitative project, you should feel free to be creative, once you understand the basics. Figure 10.3 is a screenshot of a coded paragraph from QSR NVIVO, which demonstrates the basic coding idea.

IDE 10.3: Four Types of Code

Miles and Huberman (1994) give good examples of three types of codes, *descriptive, interpretive, and pattern,* to which I add another, *organisational.* They operate in a rather nice hierarchical structure. I think it's a good idea to begin with 'big' or high-level codes which describe the whole interview and help you organise your data, which I term 'organisational' codes. You can see one in Figure 10.3 which is called 'Sales Manager', which told me the whole interview was with a sales manager. Such things are often concerned with demographics, e.g. the interview was done with a 'sales manager', who was 'female'.[6] These codes are of course driven by your objectives and likely analysis. For example, I anticipated comparing sales managers with salespeople, and males with females, thus I needed an easy way of retrieving relevant data from these groups. It may sound

[6] My 'actual' codes were simply those words, since from the beginning I used software to do my qualitative analysis. In the past a code such as 'sales manager' would often be expressed by something like 'SM' – which is of course where the name 'coding' comes from.

trivial, but if you are doing a large-scale study with many interviews over a year or more, let me assure you these things are necessary. A descriptive code simply describes what's going on in a piece of text – e.g. is the sales manager talking about her salespeople's prior performance? A code of 'prior-perf' may be used here. Interpretive codes are used when you have gone beyond merely describing what's happening to making your interpretation of what's going on 'behind the words'. They are often used more in research which allows you to get deeply involved in a context, such as observation or case study. For example, was the sales manager using poor prior performance to justify disciplinary activities for salespeople she in fact had personal problems with? The code in this case could be 'ext-just' for external justification. Pattern codes are used when (usually through continued iterative readings and data collection) you are able to detect underlying patterns, themes, and links in the data. For example, sales manager's disciplinary activities within a firm may in fact be part of an underlying political struggle between different teams, notated by the code 'pol-strug'.

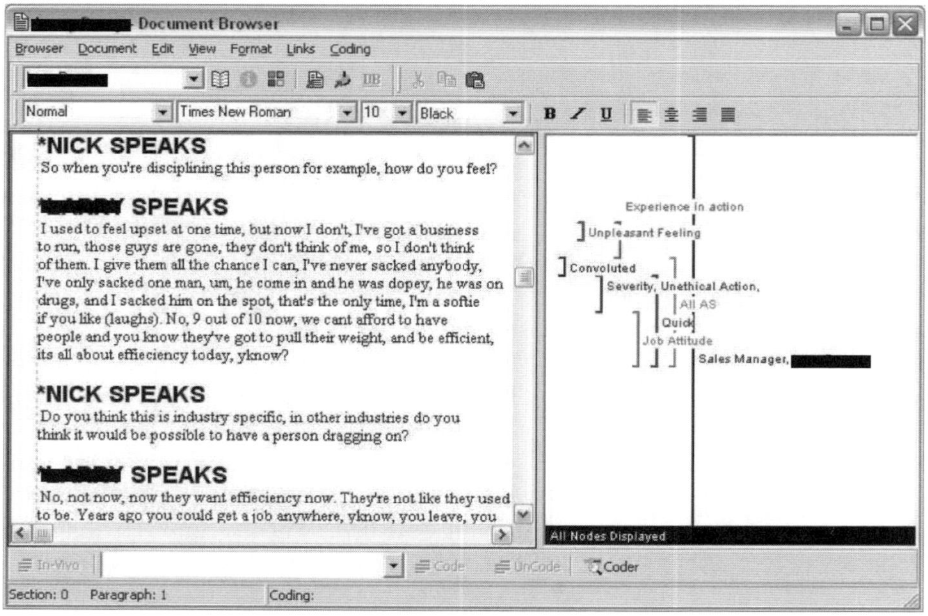

Figure 10.3 Example coded paragraph from QSR NVIVO
Source: Used with kind permission of QSR International: www.qsrinternational.com.

Coding is quite a complex process, and one thing which should be mentioned is that it is iterative just like many other aspects of the qualitative process. You often start by simply describing the data with codes, and then as you get more of a holistic picture of what's going on underneath, you recognise patterns, concepts and links between them. This then necessitates you returning to previously coded sections and re-evaluating them, adding interpretive layers on top of the basic description. You should recognise this concept as somewhat hermeneutic. There is some disagreement (of course) over how much of a pre-structure of codes you should begin with. For most people, their conceptual work will have suggested at least a preliminary set of concepts and categories to work with. For example, in my study of sales manager problem resolution I began with the idea that disciplinary activity comprised the actual 'action' and also the 'interpersonal style' with which it was delivered. Thus, I created two master codes ('action style' and 'interpersonal style), which had subcodes, such as 'AS-fast' or 'IP-aggressive'. There were also codes for antecedents and consequences, such as 'prior-perf' and 'team-respect'. Thus, I had a starting list of maybe 40 codes, which is quite possible to keep in memory. Of course, I had it stuck up on my computer monitor, and it got modified as the coding process proceeded. That said, it is important not to generate too complex a scheme, as in the end you will not really be reducing the data too much. A more inductive approach, such as true grounded theory, for example, would not start with such a list, but instead try to generate codes from the data. This can be difficult for the inexperienced researcher, but a good place to start is to look at a piece of data in great detail, marking out ideas in the margins, and then looking to combine those ideas into more abstract ideas, which you then attach codes to. Phrases which were used by the respondents when you interviewed them are also useful starting points for codes (which is called *in-vivo* coding). I think most researchers fall somewhere in the middle, beginning with a tentative structure, but allowing it to evolve in ways suggested by the data.

You'll probably find as I did, that once you actually start coding, you'll get the hang of it pretty quickly and at first your list will snowball into silly numbers of codes. Try to avoid this. Use the benchmark of keeping your structure on a single piece of paper if possible. Also, try to work with an overall structure, not just a set of unrelated codes – this is one of the reasons a theoretical appreciation can help your analysis. One of you main aims is usually to find some kind of structure in the data, so it makes good sense to keep this in mind. Also, try to make the code labels 'sensitising', by which I mean give them easy-to-understand names, not numbers. This helps you to think about things, and also eases the teamworking process if that's relevant. Speaking of which, it can also be useful to have a second analyst check your coding once in a while, just to see if you are being consistent in your coding. Also, don't forget that good qualitative work is iterative and evolving, not rigidly structured, so try not to wait until the end of data collection before beginning the coding process. Finally, do try to keep in mind that the coding process can be argued as one of placing your own interpretation on the data, and therefore you should be very careful that you 'let the data speak', rather than get drawn in to 'making it fit' your earlier theoretical ideas.

Data displays

A data display is another central pillar of qualitative analysis. It's another concept which many have trouble understanding. It is however, quite simple when you think about it. Think about a set of numbers about people's preferences, you can display this in any number of forms, for example as a spreadsheet. However, it is more insightful usually to display it as a graph. Qualitative data is in the same boat here. Simply displaying large swathes of textual data is not often insightful (although can provide compelling context when used appropriately), nor is simply lifting out a few quotes (running the risk of anecdotalism). Also, the qualitative research report (another large body of text) can be difficult for readers to comprehend, especially if they are pressed for time. Combined and done well, these things can comprise a fairly useful piece of research analysis. But is there a way of doing what quantitative analysts do as a matter of course, creating those pretty diagrams, models, graphs and charts? In this section the concept of qualitative data displays will be introduced, and some examples given. However, you should always keep in mind that qualitative displays are a forum for creativity in analysis; design them in the way you think helps understand the data best, not by slavishly following examples.

One way I have found useful to think of data displays is as small lamps. Imagine a statue in a museum, your data is the statue, and the data displays are the lamps that let the public see the key parts of interest of that statue. If you have a set of qualitative data, it can be lit up in a number of ways. Each different way helps the reader to understand the findings differently. So our task is to illuminate the data set with lamps (i.e. displays) in such a way that the reader can see it more clearly. Sometimes certain aspects are so important they need multiple lamps, and other times we need a single lamp to illuminate a part of the data. Of course, if you extend the metaphor, lamps can also cast interesting shadows, and be used to point out some parts and hide others; but this kind of thing is not what we will talk about here.

There are a number of ways of classifying data displays. Firstly, there is the display which is focused on a single case (be it an interview, focus group, observational site or the like), which are termed **within-case** displays. But we also like to compare across different cases, perhaps in an attempt to increase generalisability, or to deepen our understanding of the situation, which is called **cross-case** analysis. We can also think about the aims of the displays. Some displays are focused on **describing** the data, while others are focused on **explaining** what is happening, which usually involves some kind of causality-based thinking. We'll focus here on the actual displays, as they are often applicable to many of the various classifications given above. If you want to know more, it would be a good idea to look at the references given at the end of this chapter.

The design of a display can usually be considered to fall into one of two main camps: the *matrix* or the *network*; although you can possibly think of the network as the *diagram* as well. There are other types of display, such as the poem (yes really), but there isn't enough space to go into them here. You should always think about the purpose of your display.

Is it for your purposes, to let you get a picture of the data set as a whole, or challenge your assumptions? Or is it for the final reader, to actually illuminate or justify some aspect of your conclusions? For example, sometimes you just want to create a matrix which pulls all the relevant data together and compares it, say, by gender. If you are doing this for yourself, it can be as detailed as you want, but for a final display you need to work out whether it is going to provide the reader with any additional 'illumination power' when condensed into a format suitable for publication.

A matrix is exactly what it sounds like, one concept crossed over with another. Figure 10.4 shows a matrix of 'action speed' crossed over with 'locus of comments', where I was trying to figure out whether my respondents were only describing *others* as quick to punish salespeople, not themselves. Doing this for each individual helped me begin to infer that quick punishment could be seen as a negative characteristic by many. Matrices can be even more ordered than this, for example, you could order them by time, or key events, such as in a purchase decision process. One decision to make is what to put in the cells – direct

	Personal Comments	**'Other Managers'**
General		
Responsive	23-29: 'if they don't suit then they're out, you with me?...we cant afford to have people...linger on'. 63-64: 'I can tell within a week whether they're going to be any good' 165-167: 'if I'm going to get rid of someone [then I do it], but I prefer to try and coax them to do a better job, but you can only go so far' 237-238: 'if they don't pull their weight they're gone, its that simple, no matter how well they get on with the others' 242: 'if I notice I put my foot on it straight away, you can't be everywhere' 327-328: 'give me a week and I'll sort him out and he's gone if he's no good' 352-357: 'I asked them for all the help I could...[and]...they couldn't care that much so I closed it down' 489-490: 'I got rid of him, I didn't want to but I had to'	138-140: 'other people wouldn't give the lad the chances I gave him, they'd have had him out quicker' 167: 'a lot of managers...have got no mercy' 190-191: 'if they don't pull their weight they're gone' 301-302: 'if they don't pull their weight then they have to go' 467-469: 'are [managers] sympathetic today? No...my son is nothing like me, if he's got to get rid of someone he does it'.
Non-responsive	40-41: we give him about 4 chances and in the end...I just kicked him out, we were wasting our time' 111: 'I give him that many chances, he'd upset a few of the personnel'. 177-178: 'I'm a softie if you like' 271-272: 'I said you come back in 6 months and [if] you're alright I'll give you your job back' 330-331: 'if I think he's got potential I'll extend his...trial' 371-374: 'I'd do anything to keep these [employees], put my own house up for mortgage...these blokes are good blokes, they've worked for me a long time'.	

Figure 10.4 Example within-case matrix

quotes, descriptions, inferences or something else? You'll note in Figure 10.4 that I have described what's going on, and then put line numbers for the transcript. This wouldn't have been useful for a published display, where no transcripts are available. Nevertheless, you should be careful not to over-infer when constructing matrices, nor to taking small quotes out of context. Doing so can divorce you from your data rather effectively.

I always seem to find diagrams more interesting than matrices, perhaps it's because I am a frustrated artist, or not. Probably it's because I think in very visual terms, as most of my students will tell you. There is an almost infinite variety of diagrams which can be drawn which help illuminate what's going on in your data. It's difficult to really overstate the variety of diagrams that are possible in qualitative analysis. In fact, what you can do is driven purely by your research objectives and the data you have collected. So, of course, it is surely needless to say that you have to be very clear about your objectives, and what data you need, *before* you go and collect it!

A classic example of a data display, which I haven't had the chance to use yet, is the time line, say of a consumer decision process for a new car. Time could be on a horizontal axis, and another key variable (perhaps 'amount of information searched') on a vertical axis. Another interesting format is exemplified in Figure 10.5, which was developed by one of my students (Jennifer Walker, who appeared at the start of Chapter 9). It shows the evaluation process of consumers to information about a company's ethical behaviour. This display came from a single focus group of highly ethically aware consumers. It helped illuminate a number of things, most specifically the key importance of a concept termed the 'moment of scepticism', where individuals doubted the authenticity of the information.

Displays play a hugely important role. They can allow you to see things in the data which are not obvious simply by examining the text, they can help readers understand the conclusions more easily, and they can condense huge amounts of data into manageable and illuminating formats. You should be thinking about how to display the data very early on, drawing tentative diagrams, designing matrices and the like. However, take care not to become wedded to certain displays too early. Displays are always evolving, and if you remove yourself from the raw data too early your thinking is then going to be basically driven by what you put in your display. Remember, the data should drive the display, don't try to force the data to fit a display which you really like.

The displays above were essentially *descriptive*, but we can also use displays to begin to develop explanatory links in our findings. Now is not the time and the place to discuss causality, but it should not be in question that displays can help us get a handle on the concepts which seem to be influencing other concepts in our data. While matrices can be used in this context, I have always found diagrams to be more intuitive – probably because I tend to draw them myself to explain theories to others. Figure 10.6 shows a within-case diagram designed to illuminate the set of antecedents and consequences to a sales manager's speed to punish a problem salesperson. It was based on the coding and other processes already explored above. Such diagrams can be very simple, or very complex, depending on

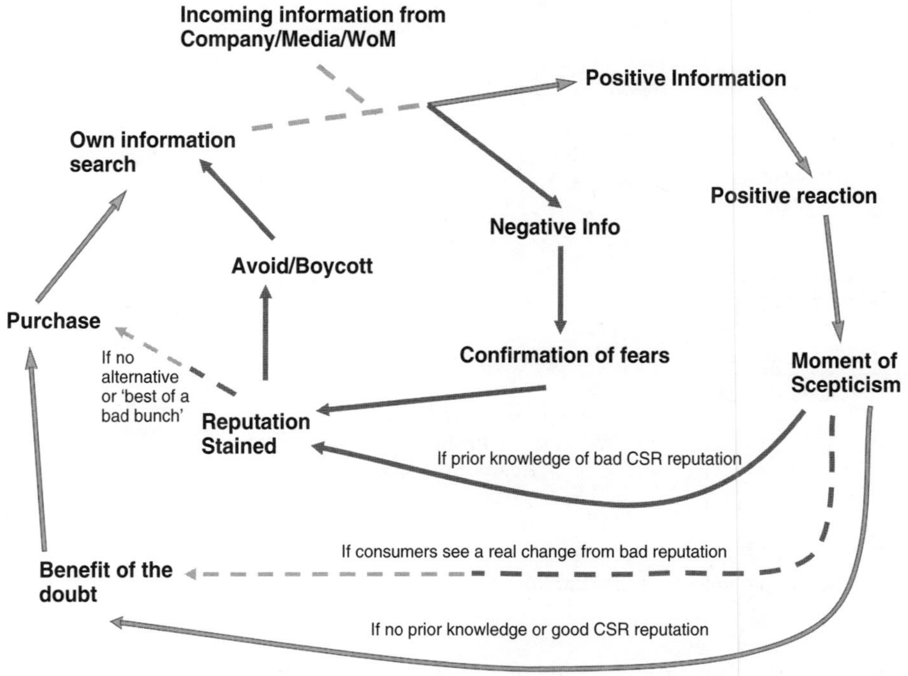

Figure 10.5 Example cyclical diagram
Source: Used with kind permission of Jennifer Walker, from an unpublished Msc Dissertation (Aston Business School, 2006).

the complexity of the situation itself, as well as the amount of information in the case. I also expect that I could have made the diagram more complex myself, by incorporating more of my own inference rather than relying as I did on descriptive coding. You can develop these diagrams by beginning with a theoretical conceptual framework, or purely from the data itself. Of course, most people fall somewhere in the middle, such as in Figure 10.6. But it does depend on your data collection – if you are basing your data collection on theoretical frameworks, you are more likely to end up with a diagram that looks like an existing theoretical model.

All of the concepts referred to above can be applied to a cross-case situation as well. Here, we are usually looking for patterns across cases. Are there uniform antecedents to quick punishment, for example? If there are differences, what are the specific aspects of those cases which may be influencing differences? You can see that yet again these kinds of conclusions are bound up inextricably with data collection. If you don't have the right kind of cases, you can't draw conclusions about their similarities or differences. One way of doing cross-case

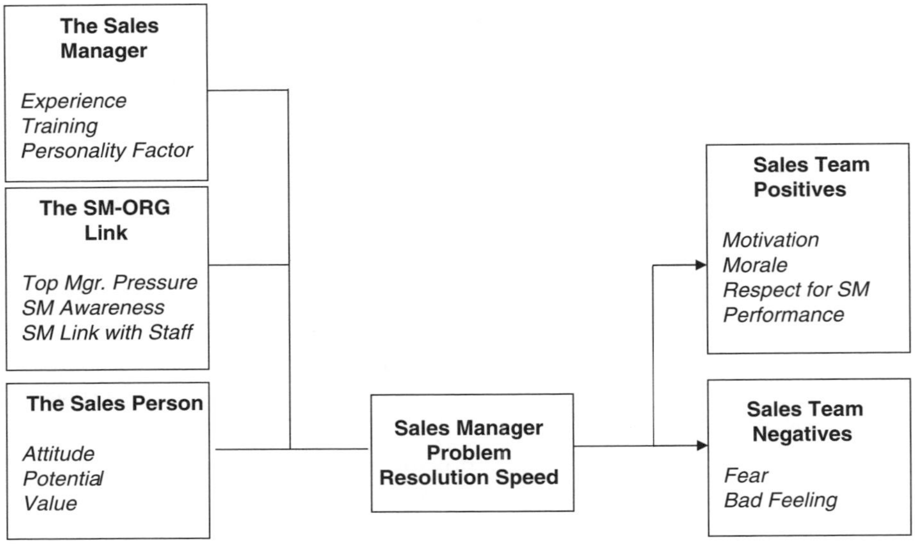

Figure 10.6 Example within-case conceptual framework

analysis is to develop a framework from one case, and then examine subsequent cases to see whether they 'fit the pattern' or not. Or you could look for key themes or variables which occur repeatedly across many cases. I combined these approaches when generating a cross-case model from multiple within-case diagrams like Figure 10.6.

Another common approach is the 'meta-matrix', where one can directly compare, say, different types of respondent (e.g. males versus females) on various factors. It could be expected that such matrices can be unwieldy, and this is indeed the case. In fact, Miles and Huberman (1994) refer to them as 'monster-dogs' for this reason. But when used properly, they can be a powerful way of exploring your data.

An example of a cross-case diagram is given in Figure 10.7, where the designers were looking to explain why consumers chose to resist adopting innovations. You can see the numbers refer to the proportions of times respondents from the eight focus groups discussed each concept. This display led to a rethink on how different factors may influence different types of resistance, from passive to active.

Beginning to draw conclusions

As you begin to code and display your data, you will naturally begin to draw some conclusions, and think about what your data 'means'. It is here we start to get to the nub

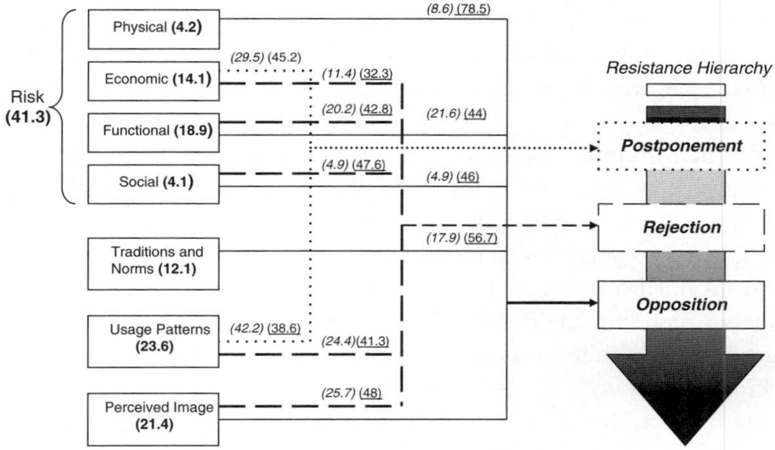

Bold numbers refer to the percentage per antecedent of the total number of quotes forall focus groups
Italicised numbers refer to the percentage of quotes within each set of focus groups(e.g. the rejection groups)
Underlined numbers refer to the percentage of the total number of quotes regarding that antecedent within all focus group

Used with kind permission of Mirella Kleijnen and Martin Wetzels, from an un published manuscript co-written by Mirella Lee, and Martin Wetzels.

Figure 10.7 Example of cross-case conceptual framework

of qualitative analysis; how do we know what that data means? However, it's vital to avoid 'over-interpreting' your data. What I mean is that you should guard very carefully against putting your own ideas 'on to' the data and not letting the data speak for itself. There's a fine line between interpreting data in light of prior theory and your ideas, and biasing your conclusions. Qualitative analysts generally present their conclusions in the third major component of good qualitative research, extended text – the first part being appropriate selection of quotes and raw data to exemplify your points, and the second being good displays. I sometimes call this section of the analysis *creating a narrative* for your research, as you are essentially telling a story. However, this term can be a bit confusing for those who are in fact conducting the specific form of narrative research (which none of my students do) so I won't use it again here. In creating the text, you should understand that your displays don't stand alone for the reader, you need to explain them, pick out key points and patterns, and ultimately build a convincing evidence-based argument as to what you are trying to say.

There are various approaches to generating conclusions and meaning from your data and its displays, but I will focus on one particular higher-level issue you need to keep in mind; **plausibility**. In other words, do your conclusions intuitively feel right? This is dangerous ground. Most of us can almost always pick out some plausible explanation for even the most random events – as the continuing attention paid to astrology demonstrates so clearly (I'm a Leo if you're interested). If the only justification for a finding you can give is that it seems intuitively correct, you are in trouble. Similarly, do not dismiss potential conclusions simply because they are implausible, or fly in the face of existing wisdom. Some of the world's greatest discoveries were made after researchers closely investigated their implausible original findings.

Essentially, rather than thinking solely in terms of intuition, which was the 'black box' at the heart of qualitative analysis for far too long, start looking at your data for patterns, and explaining those patterns. Maybe these patterns are across multiple sites, people, or multiple examples given by a single participant. Compare these patterns, look for situations where they do and do not hold – which could be called *boundary conditions*. Some people like to use numbers to represent the comparative importance of ideas and variables, which was done in Figure 10.7. While coding has taken you right down into the data, try to raise your level of abstraction to one which takes in all of the data. Think in terms of general concepts or variables and their relationships, not always individual people or cases.

Verifying your conclusions and their validity

Of course, anyone can draw some conclusions from a set of data, the real task is to convince yourself and your readers of the 'goodness' of those conclusions. Validity is something which has cast a long shadow over the last two chapters, and it remains a key concept here. But first we will consider a few areas which you need to examine to convince *yourself* of your work, which you should find intimately bound with all of the issues we've covered so far.

First is you as the research instrument. How can you be sure that you were an unbiased tool? In the previous chapter we spoke at length about the inherent *reflexivity* of qualitative work, in that the researcher can influence the respondents, and the respondents can influence the way the researcher works. There are few solutions which can be offered at the analysis stage though – you can't 'remove' many of these influences here. It is simply a case of good research design and careful practice. Nevertheless, it is relevant to the analyst, as you really want to be clear on the likelihood of bias in your work, especially when writing it up. Look for feelings of 'betrayal' of your respondents, and try to maintain an ethical stance throughout.

We've already spoken about tools for exploring validity earlier in the chapter, such as the refutability concept. But overall you need to be concerned with looking at whether you are being overly anecdotal in your conclusions. Do your patterns really explain *all* the data? Sometimes, it can be useful to get an outside party to comment on your findings, a colleague or supervisor, for example. This can help you step back a little. But remember, these people may be even more likely to be seduced by the 'plausibility' issue, as they are less inclined to look at the whole data set.

As already mentioned, looking for extreme or contradictory examples of your conclusions can help. Can you find reasons for why they did not agree? Were they special cases, are they ignorable reasons, or do they necessitate re-evaluation of your conclusions? Try really hard to look for contradictory explanations, and see whether your conclusions still hold more water than them. Sometimes, this can actually necessitate collecting more data which is specifically targeted at deviant cases or contradictory explanations. Of course, I realise that very few people ever want to do this at the 'end' of a project. But remember you should not think about a qualitative project in stages, but as iterative and cyclical. In this context it therefore makes perfect sense to collect some more data late in the day, to provide some confirmatory evidence.

Finally, we come to the question of validity, which ties pretty much everything together which has been mentioned in the past two chapters. By now you should have a good understanding of the concept, and it is unnecessary to go through it here yet again. Suffice it to say that simply doing 'good' research may not lead to valid conclusions. Your research doesn't operate in a vacuum, if that were the case you would conduct it, write it up and then spend the rest of your life reading it in your bedroom, never showing it to anyone else (rather like Gollum with his 'precious' ring)[7]. If we wish it to be read, and possibly used, by other parties, we owe it to them and ourselves to consider criteria for its quality. I remember Eddie Vedder, lead singer of the band Pearl Jam, petulantly accepting a Grammy Award with the simple speech 'you can't judge art'. Unfortunately for us, while Pearl Jam's Grammy-winning song 'Spin the Black Circle' may be a work of art, research is not,[8] and it needs to be judged as to its quality. Whatever those quality criteria are – and there are many as the previous chapters have shown – the qualitative analyst needs to consider them when conducting their work and presenting it to the outside world. With specific relevance to the processes discussed here, you need to be concerned with the **internal validity**, or credibility, or justifiability (whatever you want to call it) of your conclusions. How well do they reflect the social situation or issue which you examined and collected data about? Ignoring data collection issues, *how well does your analysis reflect the data?* Whatever you believe about the eternal flux of the social world, how it is constructed between actors, or the existence of an underlying 'truth' and our likelihood of gaining access to it, this question **must** be answered convincingly.

A brief introduction to some other issues

This section will contain some brief 'sketches' of a number of other qualitative issues. Some of these issues are specific types of methodology, others are more conceptual, but I think it is useful for all researchers to realise that the methods presented above are not the 'only' methods, nor are they necessarily the 'best'. They have certainly worked well for me, resulting

[7] If you don't know what I am talking about, stop reading this book and go and read *The Lord of the Rings*. If you don't own a copy swap this – actually, swap another book – for a copy.

[8] Although doubtless many postmodernists and poststructuralists will disagree.

in quite a lot of good work, but there are others. This section should give you a set of directions to go in if you wish to expand your knowledge of qualitative approaches.

Content analysis

Content analysis is something which I've always found a little confusing. On the one hand, it is often considered a qualitative technique, probably because it primarily works with textual data. On the other hand, it can be considered as quantitative in essence, as you are counting the occurrence of certain distinct phrases. Nevertheless, in contrast to most qualitative techniques, the focus of content analysis is on objectively identifying and usually counting given features of the data. You can use content analysis on all kinds of data, from text (e.g. newspapers, advertising, transcripts) to visual data (perhaps TV programmes, advertising again). It can be particularly useful in analysing published text, such as studying trends in media reactions to a key issue, or in exploring advertising content. A good introduction to content analysis is in Franzosi (2004). Altheide (1996) proposed a more 'qualitative' content analysis (which I employed myself in my first ever 'real' research project), where the analyst takes a less structured approach, allowing the categories to emerge more inductively and recognising context – rather than imposing a rigid 'objective' structure on the data.

Semiotics

In contrast with the structured approach of content analysis is semiotics, which is the study of 'signs'. It can be somewhat arcane, but the basics are reasonably simple. Semiotics is essentially concerned with the analysis of documents – although it can be applied to other data as it considers everything to be a 'text' – and explicitly recognises that that most signs have underlying meaning. It is the researcher's task to uncover this meaning. By way of explanation, semiotics considers every *sign* to be made up of a *signifier* (something which points to an underlying or hidden meaning), and the *signified* (the hidden meaning). A strength of semiotics is that it encourages us to look beyond the obvious in analysis, but it could be argued that the results can be somewhat analyst-dependent. It has been employed in many situations, wherever the interest is in looking beyond surface manifestations (e.g. advertising research). A useful introduction is given by Manning (2004).

Discourse analysis

Discourse analysis (often referred to as DA) is heavily based on some of the 20th century philosophers who appeared in Chapter 3, particularly Michel Foucault (1926–1984), who considered discourse to essentially create the ways in which we look at objects and phenomena. Like many such qualitative methods, it can be impenetrable for the uninitiated – as attendance at a DA-focused conference will show – and really refers to a set of different approaches. DA is fundamentally opposed to the idea of independent reality, and is wedded to the idea of social constructionism. In this framework, DA looks to explore the underlying objectives of a discourse – what are the parties trying to achieve and how? DA treats almost everything as a discourse, so it can be applied to most data sources. In contrast to my own feelings, DA researchers seem to be somewhat shy of documenting their exact methods, preferring to consider it a 'craft' (e.g. Potter, 1997). DA is also related to conversation analysis (CA) in some ways. However, CA is focused on 'naturally-occurring' conversations (i.e. not really interviews), and also employs detailed analysis techniques to uncover the structure of interaction in talk. These methods can be usefully employed in many situations, and it really does depend on your research objectives and (to some extent) philosophical assumptions, particularly in the case of DA. Useful introductions to DA and CA are Potter (2004) and Clayman and Gill (2004) respectively.

Narrative analysis

Narrative analysis is really a set of different methods, which all share a concern for the 'stories' that we and others use to describe, understand and explain the world and their place in it. Therefore, it can be seen that it is not so much interested in the objective 'facts' of the situation, but how people interpreted it and their position/role within it. Of course, this necessitates a natural concern with temporal order, as well as an interest in the social construction of meaning. It is naturally suited to research about people's lives and biographies, but it is not difficult to see how 'smaller' events can be approached in this way – such as purchase decisions, disciplinary activities (I'm always talking about that aren't I?) or other organisation and consumer topics. Data is often collected through dedicated narrative interviews, the approach can be applied to other interview data or data from observations. The approach can be criticised as potentially subject to biases from the respondent – for example they may wish to present themselves in a positive light rather than tell their 'real' story. But by now you should be capable of rebutting that argument with some of the concepts in Chapter 3, and this one too. In fact, try it as a little thought experiment.[9] A useful introduction to narrative methods is in Andrews *et al.* (2004).

Feminism: An example of the political influence in qualitative research

I debated for some time whether or not to write this brief section. I don't want to imply that feminism is either (a) some kind of special set of techniques and methods (although some will disagree), or (b) that feminism is the most important of the 'critical' traditions of qualitative research. However, it does provide a nice example of how political positions can be used as bases for research traditions – so I am willing to risk it. In brief, feminist research could be considered to be subsumed within general critical and poststructuralist traditions. Here, as I mentioned earlier, our cherished notions of validity are called into question. However, the point I want to make here is that not all research traditions are in

---

[9]Hint: start by thinking about (a) who is doing the defining of 'real' here anyway, and (b) are such biases interesting in their own right regardless?

fact aimed at uncovering 'the truth' (in realist terms), or even 'a truth'. In fact, many critical research traditions (of which feminism is one) have the goal of bringing about some kind of positive or emancipatory change in the context, or society as a whole. Within the research tasks themselves, the focus would be on allowing respondents' own voices to be heard without imposing control, and in reciprocating during fieldwork (giving as well as taking data). While this is a gross simplification, it is easy to see how considerations such as this would influence the research questions, data collection, analysis, conclusions and ultimate reporting of feminist research. For example, such traditions are clearly very amenable to an 'action research' methodology, where you participate in the context while researching it, with the aim of 'changing' the context for the better as the research outcome. The goals here are very different from what we might implicitly expect from a 'research project'. More information can be found in Kitzinger (2004).

The Internet

In putting this section at the end, I don't mean to imply that the Internet should be treated as an afterthought. Indeed, a consideration of the Internet as an environment to study and utilise to collect data should pervade your thinking. The Internet does offer some interesting advantages and opportunities that deserve special mention though. One thing I have found fascinating is the prevalence of interpersonal contact on the Internet – for example there are masses of social networks based around things like TV shows, computer games, music and products. People use these as hubs for their own social interaction in some ways – not just sad people with no 'real' friends, but regular people like you. Even better, this interaction is generally archived, so you can track it. Also, today there is a rising trend for 'virtual worlds' where you can even purchase 'land' to 'build' on using real money. The possibilities for ethnography and other types of qualitative research here are endless. The Internet is also a useful medium for more 'traditional' research. For example, it can be used to enhance your ability to contact geographically diverse respondents, using email, live messaging, audio, or even video. A useful introduction to the issues involved in online qualitative research is Mann and Stewart (2000), although bear in mind the evolution of the Internet means such material often dates quickly.

Summary

At various points throughout this chapter I have characterised qualitative analysis as being traditionally a 'black-box'. This may be fine for experienced qualitative researchers who are comfortable with their interpretive philosophical standpoints, and readers who share the same views and are willing to take on faith any conclusions of a research project. However, it is of precisely zero value to a beginning researcher, or the analyst who wishes to engage with the link between research findings and some kind of outside standards of 'quality'. Such a standpoint also runs the risk of leaving qualitative analysis in the hands of an 'elite' who know what they are doing, and who then essentially control the dissemination of that knowledge. In recent times such opinions have become less prevalent, and great books on qualitative analysis are beginning to appear more regularly. This chapter was an attempt primarily to introduce a basic framework for qualitative analysis in the context of a wider appreciation of research in general, linking it where necessary to various philosophical assumptions while also giving solid practical tools. An appreciation of 'quality' in qualitative analysis should also be considered to run as a seam through this chapter. In light of this, I hope that you now have at the very least a respect for qualitative analysis, and something of a springboard from which to investigate it further if necessary.

Key points to take from this chapter:

- All data can be considered as originally 'qualitative' in some ways, but qualitative data for most intents and purposes is that which is or could be transformed into words.
- The qualitative analysis process is generally that of reducing the vast amount of data to themes, ideas and concepts. However there is a tension between this and retaining the fundamental richness of qualitative data.
- Most qualitative analysts should not ignore considerations of reliability and validity, although there are a number of different perspectives on these ideas.
- Coding is the starting point of analysis, allowing you to closely explore the underlying themes and concepts in your data.
- Data displays allow you to see and present the data in many different lights, which provides a far richer and more useful analysis.
- Be careful when drawing conclusions not to be seduced by the 'plausibility' of your findings, nor of relying solely on intuition, researchers should also consider the 'quality' of their findings.

Further reading

There are many great books out there that I've already referred to, in particular the ones in Chapter 3 (especially Chris Hackley's one) and of course Chapter 9, here are a few more specifically about analysis:

- *Qualitative Data Analysis* by Matthew B. Miles and A. Michael Huberman: A wonderful book which goes farther than I ever could. Anyone who wishes to analyse qualitative data and does not fundamentally disagree with the general approach of this chapter should get a copy.
- *Collecting and Interpreting Qualitative Materials* edited by Norman K. Denzin and Yvonna S. Lincoln: A good collection of interesting material, particularly strong on the more interpretive side of things.

EXERCISES

1. What is 'qualitative' data? How can you determine whether data is qualitative or quantitative?
2. Think about and explain some possible uses that numbers can have in a qualitative project.
3. Considering validity, go back to Chapter 3 and try to write a counterpoint to IDE 10.1 from the perspective of Nietzche.
4. Speaking of validity concerns, respond to the argument that 'a concern for validity within qualitative research is nothing more than a cringe towards "traditional" notions of science which is irrelevant in contemporary social science'. Begin by explaining exactly what this argument may mean.
5. Consider how the Internet could have an impact on a qualitative research project, in terms of data collection and data analysis. What are the potential advantages and dangers of this?
6. At this point, I think it would be valuable if you went and learnt a tune on a musical instrument – try an Irish whistle if you don't already play something (I once had a Ph.D. student who could play virtually any tune on that, the show off!).

11 Designing Case Studies

ROBERT K. YIN

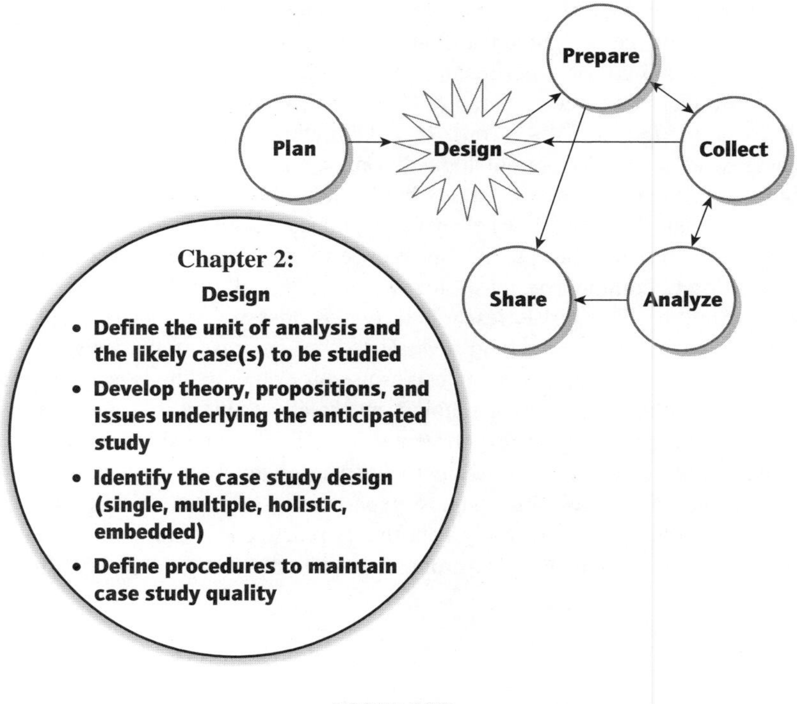

ABSTRACT

A research design is the logic that links the data to be collected (and the conclusions to be drawn) to the initial questions of study. Every empirical study has an implicit, if not explicit, research design. Articulating "theory" about what is being studied and what is to be learned helps to operationalize case study designs and make them more explicit.

Case study designs need to maximize their quality through four critical conditions related to design quality: (a) construct validity, (b) internal validity, (c) external validity, and (d) reliability. How investigators can deal with these aspects of quality control in doing case studies is discussed in Chapter 2 but also is a major theme throughout the remainder of the book.

Among the actual case study designs, four major types are relevant, following a 2 × 2 matrix. The first pair consists of single-case and multiple-case designs. The second pair, which can occur in combination with either of the first pair, is based on the unit or units of analysis to be covered—and distinguishes between holistic and embedded designs. Among these designs, most multiple-case designs are likely to be stronger than single-case designs. Trying to use even a "two-case" design is therefore a worthy objective, compared to doing a single-case study. Case studies also can be part of a larger mixed methods study.

GENERAL APPROACH TO DESIGNING CASE STUDIES

In identifying the method for your research project, Chapter 1 has shown when you might choose to use the case study method, as opposed to other methods. The next task is to design your case study. For this purpose, as in designing any other type of research investigation, you need a plan or *research design.*

The development of this research design is a difficult part of doing case studies. Unlike other research methods, a comprehensive "catalog" of research designs for case studies has yet to be developed. There are no textbooks, like those in the biological and psychological sciences, covering such design considerations as the assignment of subjects to different "groups," the selection of different stimuli or experimental conditions, or the identification of various response measures (see Cochran & Cox, 1957; Fisher, 1935, cited in Cochran & Cox, 1957; Sidowski, 1966). In a laboratory experiment, each of these choices reflects an important logical connection to the issues being studied. Similarly, there are not even textbooks like the well-known volumes by Campbell and Stanley (1966) or by Cook and Campbell (1979) that summarize the various research designs for quasi-experimental situations. Nor have there emerged any common designs—for example, "panel" studies—such as those recognized in doing survey research (see L. Kidder & Judd, 1986, chap. 6).

One pitfall to be avoided, however, is to consider case study designs to be a subset or variant of the research designs used for other methods, such as experiments. For the longest time, scholars incorrectly thought that the case study was but one type of quasi-experimental design (the "one-shot post-test-only" design). This misperception has finally been corrected, with the following statement appearing in a revision on quasi-experimental designs (Cook & Campbell, 1979): "Certainly the case study as normally practiced should not be demeaned by identification with the one-group post-test-only design" (p. 96). In other words, the one-shot post-test-only design as a quasi-experimental design still may be considered flawed, but the case study has now been recognized as something different. In fact, the case study is a separate research method that has its own research designs.

Unfortunately, case study research designs have not been codified. The following chapter therefore expands on the new methodological ground broken by earlier editions of this book and describes a basic set of research designs for doing single- and multiple-case studies. Although these designs will need to be continually modified and improved in the future, in their present form they will nevertheless help you to design more rigorous and methodologically sound case studies.

Tip: *How should I select the case(s) for my case study?*

You need sufficient access to the potential data, whether to interview people, review documents or records, or make observations in the "field." Given such access to more than a single candidate case, you should choose the case(s) that will most likely illuminate your research questions. Absent such access, you should consider changing your research questions, hopefully leading to new candidates to which you do have access.

Do you think access should be so important?

Definition of Research Designs

Every type of empirical research has an implicit, if not explicit, research design. In the most elementary sense, the design is the logical sequence that connects the empirical data to a study's initial research questions and, ultimately, to its conclusions. Colloquially, a research design is *a logical plan for getting from here to there,* where *here* may be defined as the initial set of questions to be answered, and *there* is some set of conclusions (answers) about these questions. Between "here" and "there" may be found a number of major steps, including the collection and analysis of relevant data. As a summary definition, another textbook has described a research design as a plan that

> guides the investigator in the process of collecting, analyzing, and interpreting observations. It is a *logical model of proof* that allows the researcher to draw inferences concerning causal relations among the variables under investigation. (Nachmias & Nachmias, 1992, pp. 77-78, emphasis added)

Another way of thinking about a research design is as a "blueprint" for your research, dealing with at least four problems: what questions to study, what data are relevant, what data to collect, and how to analyze the results (Philliber, Schwab, & Samsloss, 1980).

Note that a research design is much more than a work plan. The main purpose of the design is to help to avoid the situation in which the evidence does not address the initial research questions. In this sense, a research design deals with a *logical* problem and not a *logistical* problem. As a simple example, suppose you want to study a single organization. Your research questions, however, have to do with the organization's relationships with other organizations—their competitive or collaborative nature, for example. Such questions can be answered only if you collect information directly from the other organizations and not merely from the one you started with. If you complete your study by examining only one organization, you cannot draw unbiased conclusions about interorganizational partnerships. This is a flaw in your research design, not in your work plan. The outcome could have been avoided if you had developed an appropriate research design in the first place.

Components of Research Designs

For case studies, five components of a research design are especially important:

1. a study's questions;
2. its propositions, if any;
3. its unit(s) of analysis;
4. the logic linking the data to the propositions; and
5. the criteria for interpreting the findings.

Study questions. This first component has already been described in Chapter 1, which suggested that the *form* of the question—in terms of "who," "what," "where," "how," and "why"—provides an important clue regarding the most relevant research method to be used. The case study method is most likely to be appropriate for "how" and "why" questions, so your initial task is to clarify precisely the nature of your study questions in this regard.

More troublesome may be coming up with the substance of the questions. Many students take an initial stab, only to be discouraged when they find the same question(s) already well covered by previous research. Other less desirable questions focus on too trivial or minor parts of an issue. A helpful hint is to move in three stages. In the first, try to use the literature to narrow your interest to a key topic or two, not worrying about any specific research questions. In the second, examine closely—even dissect—a few key studies on your topic of interest. Identify the questions in those few studies and whether they conclude with new questions or loose ends for future research. These may then stimulate your own thinking and imagination, and you may find yourself articulating some potential questions of your own. In the third stage, examine another set of studies on the same topic. They may provide support for your potential questions or even suggest ways of sharpening them.

EXERCISE 2.1 Defining the Boundaries of a Case Study

Select a topic for a case study you would like to do. Identify some research questions to be answered or propositions to be examined by your case study. How does the naming of these questions or propositions clarify the boundaries of your case study with regard to the time period covered by the case study; the relevant social group, organization, or geographic area; the type of evidence to be collected; and the priorities for data collection and analysis?

Study propositions. As for the second component, each proposition directs attention to something that should be examined within the scope of study. For instance, assume that your research, on the topic of interorganizational partnerships, began with the following question: How and why do organizations collaborate with one another to provide joint services (for example, a manufacturer and a retail outlet collaborating to sell certain computer products)? These "how" and "why" questions, capturing what you are really interested in answering, led you to the case study as the appropriate method in the first place. Nevertheless, these "how" and "why" questions do not point to what you should study.

Only if you are forced to state some propositions will you move in the right direction. For instance, you might think that organizations collaborate because they derive mutual benefits. This proposition, besides reflecting an important theoretical issue (that other incentives for collaboration do not exist or are unimportant), also begins to tell you where to look for relevant evidence (to define and ascertain the extent of specific benefits to each organization).

At the same time, some studies may have a legitimate reason for not having any propositions. This is the condition—which exists in experiments, surveys, and the other research methods alike—in which a topic is the subject of "exploration." Every exploration, however, should still have some purpose. Instead of propositions, the design for an exploratory study should state this purpose, as well as the criteria by which an exploration will be judged successful. Consider the analogy in BOX 4 for exploratory case studies. Can you imagine how you would ask for support from Queen Isabella to do your exploratory study?

BOX 4

"Exploration" as an Analogy for an Exploratory Case Study

When Christopher Columbus went to Queen Isabella to ask for support for his "exploration" of the New World, he had to have some reasons for asking for three ships (Why not one? Why not five?), and he had some rationale for going westward (Why not south? Why not south and then east?). He also had some (mistaken) criteria for recognizing the Indies when he actually encountered it. In short, his exploration began with some rationale and direction, even if his initial assumptions might later have been proved wrong (Wilford, 1992). This same degree of rationale and direction should underlie even an exploratory case study.

Unit of analysis. This third component is related to the fundamental problem of defining what the "case" is—a problem that has plagued many investigators at the outset of case studies (e.g., Ragin & Becker, 1992). For instance, in the classic case study, a "case" may be an individual. Jennifer Platt (1992) has noted how the early case studies in the Chicago school of sociology were life histories of such persons as juvenile delinquents or derelict men. You also can imagine case studies of clinical patients, of exemplary students, or of certain types of leaders. In each situation, an individual person is the case being studied, and the individual is the primary unit of analysis. Information about the relevant individual would be collected, and several such individuals or "cases" might be included in a multiple-case study.

You would still need study questions and study propositions to help identify the relevant information to be collected about this individual or individuals. Without such questions and propositions, you might be tempted to cover "everything" about the individual(s), which is impossible to do. For example, the propositions in studying these individuals might involve the influence of early childhood or the role of peer relationships. Such seemingly general topics nevertheless represent a vast narrowing of the relevant data. The more a case study contains specific questions and propositions, the more it will stay within feasible limits.

Of course, the "case" also can be some event or entity other than a single individual. Case studies have been done about decisions, programs, the implementation process, and organizational change. Feagin et al. (1991) contains some classic examples of these single cases in sociology and political science. Beware of these types of cases—none is easily defined in terms of the beginning or end points of the "case." For example, a case study of a specific program may reveal (a) variations in program definition, depending upon the perspective of different actors, and (b) program components that preexisted the formal designation of the program. Any case study of such a program would therefore have to confront these conditions in delineating the unit of analysis.

As a general guide, your tentative definition of the unit of analysis (which is the same as the definition of the "case") is related to the way you have defined your initial research questions. Suppose, for example, you want to study the role of the United States in the global economy. Years ago, Peter Drucker (1986) wrote a provocative essay (not a case study) about fundamental changes in the world economy, including the importance of "capital movements" independent of the flow of goods and services. Using Drucker's work or some similar theoretical framework, the unit of analysis (or "case") for your case study might be a country's economy, an industry in the world marketplace, an economic policy, or the trade or capital flow between countries. Each unit of analysis and its related questions and propositions would call for a slightly different research design and data collection strategy.

Selection of the appropriate unit of analysis will start to occur when you accurately specify your primary research questions. If your questions do not lead to the favoring of one unit of analysis over another, your questions are probably either too vague or too numerous—and you may have trouble doing a case study. However, when you do eventually arrive at a definition of the unit of analysis, do not consider closure permanent. Your choice of the unit of analysis, as with other facets of your research design, can be revisited as a result of discoveries during your data collection (see discussion and cautions about flexibility throughout this book and at the end of this chapter).

Sometimes, the unit of analysis may have been defined one way, even though the phenomenon being studied actually follows a different definition. Most frequently, investigators have confused case studies of neighborhoods with case studies of small groups (as another example, confusing a new technology with the workings of an engineering team in an organization; see BOX 5A). How a geographic *area* such as a neighborhood copes with racial transition, upgrading, and other phenomena can be quite different from how a small *group* copes with these same phenomena. For instance, *Street Corner Society* (Whyte, 1943/1955; see BOX 2A in Chapter 1 of this book) and *Tally's Corner* (Liebow, 1967; see BOX 9, this chapter) often have been mistaken for being case studies of neighborhoods when in fact they are case studies of small groups (note that in neither book is the neighborhood geography described, even though the small groups lived in a small area with clear neighborhood implications). BOX 5B, however, presents a good example of how units of analyses can be defined in a more discriminating manner—in the field of world trade.

BOX 5
Defining the Unit of Analysis

5A. What Is the Unit of Analysis?

The Soul of a New Machine (1981) was a Pulitzer Prize–winning book by Tracy Kidder. The book, also a best seller, is about the development of a new minicomputer, produced by Data General Corporation, intended to compete with one produced by a direct competitor, Digital Equipment Corporation (also see BOX 28, Chapter 5, p. 142).

This easy-to-read book describes how Data General's engineering team invented and developed the new computer. The book begins with the initial conceptualization of the computer and ends when the engineering team relinquishes control of the machine to Data General's marketing staff.

The book is an excellent example of a case study. However, the book also illustrates a fundamental problem in doing case studies—that of defining the unit of analysis. Is the "case" being studied the minicomputer, or is it about the dynamics of a small group—the engineering team? The answer is critical for understanding how the case study might relate to any broader body of knowledge—that is, whether to generalize to a technology topic or to a group dynamics topic. Because the book is not an academic study, it does not need to, nor does it, provide an answer.

5B. A Clearer Choice among Units of Analysis

Ira Magaziner and Mark Patinkin's (1989) book, *The Silent War: Inside the Global Business Battles Shaping America's Future*, presents nine individual case studies (also see BOX 35, Chapter 5, p. 161). Each case helps the reader to understand a real-life situation of international economic competition.

Two of the cases appear similar but in fact have different main units of analysis. One case, about the Korean firm Samsung, is a case study of the critical policies that make the firm competitive. Understanding Korean economic development is part of the context, and the case study also contains an embedded unit—Samsung's development of the microwave oven as an illustrative product. The other case, about the development of an Apple computer factory in Singapore, is in fact a case study of Singapore's critical policies that make the country competitive. The Apple computer factory experience—an embedded unit of analysis—is actually an illustrative example of how the national policies affected foreign investments.

These two cases show how the definition of the main and embedded units of analyses, as well as the definition of the contextual events surrounding these units, depends on the level of inquiry. The main unit of analysis is likely to be at the level being addressed by the main study questions.

Most investigators will encounter this type of confusion in defining the unit of analysis or "case." To reduce the confusion, one recommended practice is to discuss the potential case with a colleague. Try to explain to that person what questions you are trying to answer and why you have chosen a specific case or group of cases as a way of answering those questions. This may help you to avoid incorrectly identifying the unit of analysis.

Once the general definition of the case has been established, other clarifications in the unit of analysis become important. If the unit of analysis is a small group, for instance, the persons to be included within the group (the immediate topic of the case study) must be distinguished from those who are outside it (the context for the case study). Similarly, if the case is about local services in a specific geographic area, you need to decide which services to cover. Also desirable, for almost any topic that might be chosen, are specific time boundaries to define the beginning and end of the case (e.g., whether to include the entire or only some part of the life cycle of the entity that is to be the case). Answering all of these types of questions will help to determine the scope of your data collection and, in particular, how you will distinguish data about the subject of your case study (the "phenomenon") from data external to the case (the "context").

These latter cautions regarding the need for spatial, temporal, and other concrete boundaries underlie a key but subtle aspect in defining your case. The desired case should be some real-life phenomenon, not an abstraction such as a topic, an argument, or even a hypothesis. These abstractions, absent the identification of specific examples or cases, would rightfully serve as the subjects of research studies using other kinds of methods but not case studies. To justify using the case study method, you need to go one step further: You need to define a specific, real-life "case" to represent the abstraction. (For examples of more concrete and less concrete case study topics, see Figure 2.1.)

Take the concept of "neighboring." Alone, it could be the subject of research studies using methods other than the case study method. The other methods might include a survey of the relationships among neighbors, a history of the evolution of the sense of neighboring and the setting of boundaries, or an experiment in which young children do tasks next to each other to determine the distracting effects, if any, of their neighbors. These examples show how the abstract concept of "neighboring" does not alone produce the grounds for a case study. However, the concept could readily become a case study topic if it were accompanied by your selecting a specific neighborhood ("case") to be studied and posing study questions and propositions about the neighborhood in relation to the concept of "neighboring."

One final point pertains to the role of the available research literature and needs to be made about defining the case and the unit of analysis. Most researchers will want to compare their findings with previous research. For

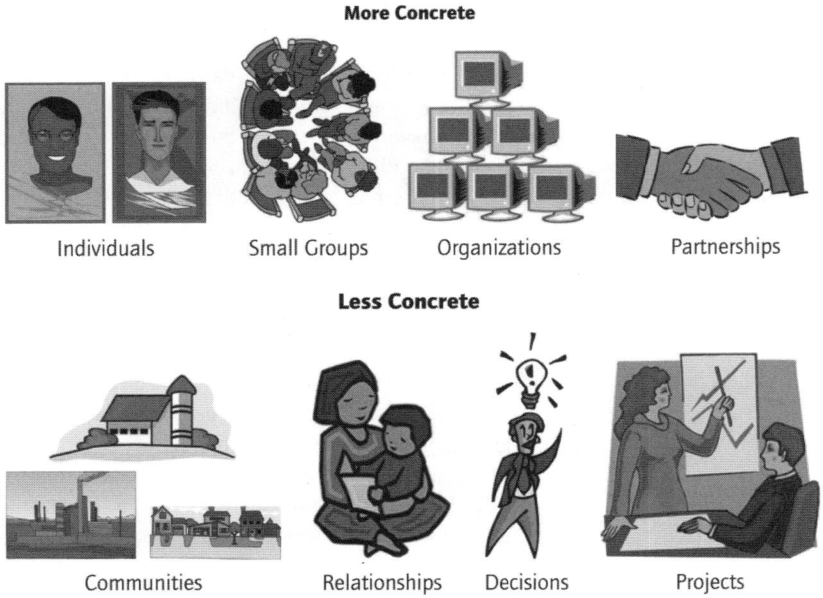

Figure 2.1 Illustrative Case Study Topics

this reason, the key definitions used in your study should not be idiosyncratic. Rather, each case study and unit of analysis either should be similar to those previously studied by others or should innovate in clear, operationally defined ways. In this manner, the previous literature also can become a guide for defining the case and unit of analysis.

EXERCISE 2.2 Defining the Unit of Analysis (and the "Case") for a Case Study

Examine Figure 2.1. Discuss each subject, which illustrates a different unit of analysis. Find a published case study on at least one of these subjects, indicating the actual "case" that was being studied. Understanding that each subject illustrates a different unit of analysis and involves the selection of different cases to be studied, do you think that the more concrete units might be easier to define than the less concrete ones? Why?

Linking data to propositions and criteria for interpreting the findings. The fourth and fifth components have been increasingly better developed in doing case studies. These components foreshadow the data analysis steps in case study research. Because the analytic techniques and choices are covered in detail in Chapter 5, your main concern during the design phase is to be aware of the main choices and how they might suit your case study. In this way, your research design can create a more solid foundation for the later analysis.

All of the analytic techniques in Chapter 5 represent ways of *linking data to propositions:* pattern matching, explanation building, time-series analysis, logic models, and cross-case synthesis. The actual analyses will require that you combine or calculate your case study data as a direct reflection of your initial study propositions. For instance, knowing that some or all of your propositions cover a temporal sequence would mean that you might eventually use some type of time-series analysis. Noting this strong likelihood during the design phase would call your attention to the need to be sure you had sufficient procedures to collect time markers as part of your data collection plans.

If you have had limited experience in conducting empirical studies, you will not easily identify the likely analytic technique(s) or anticipate the needed data to use the techniques to their full advantage. More experienced researchers will note how often they have either (a) collected too much data that were not later used in any analysis or (b) collected too little data that prevented the proper use of a desired analytic technique. Sometimes, the latter situation even may force researchers to return to their data collection phase (if they can), to supplement the original data. The more you can avoid any of these situations, the better off you will be.

Criteria for interpreting a study's findings. Statistical analyses offer some explicit criteria for such interpretations. For instance, by convention, social science considers a p level of less than .05 to demonstrate that observed differences were "statistically significant." However, much case study analysis will not rely on the use of statistics and therefore calls attention to other ways of thinking about such criteria.

A major and important alternative strategy is to identify and address rival explanations for your findings. Again, Chapter 5 discusses this strategy and how it works more fully. At the design stage of your work, the challenge is to anticipate and enumerate the important rivals, so you will include information about them as part of your data collection. If you only think of rival explanations after data collection has been completed, you will be starting to justify and design a *future* study, but you will not be helping to complete your *current* case study. For this reason, specifying important rival explanations is a part of a case study's research design work.

Summary. A research design should include five components Although the current state of the art does not provide detailed guidance on the last two, the complete research design should indicate what data are to be collected—as indicated by a study's questions, its propositions, and its units of analysis. The design also should tell you what is to be done after the data have been collected—as indicated by the logic linking the data to the propositions and the criteria for interpreting the findings.

The Role of Theory in Design Work

Covering these preceding five components of research designs will effectively force you to begin constructing a preliminary theory related to your topic of study. This role of theory development, prior to the conduct of any data collection, is one point of difference between case studies and related methods such as ethnography (Lincoln & Guba, 1985; Van Maanen, 1988) and "grounded theory" (Corbin & Strauss, 2007). Typically, these related methods deliberately avoid specifying any theoretical propositions at the outset of an inquiry. As a result, students confusing these methods with case studies wrongly think that, by having selected the case study method, they can proceed quickly into the data collection phase of their work, and they may have been encouraged to make their "field contacts" as quickly as possible. No guidance could be more misleading. Among other considerations, the relevant field contacts depend upon an understanding—or theory—of what is being studied.

Theory development. For case studies, theory development as part of the design phase is essential, whether the ensuing case study's purpose is to develop or to test theory. Using a case study on the implementation of a new management information system (MIS) as an example (Markus, 1983), the simplest ingredient of a theory is a statement such as the following:

> The case study will show why implementation only succeeded when the organization was able to re-structure itself, and not just overlay the new MIS on the old organizational structure. (Markus, 1983)

The statement presents the nutshell of a theory of MIS implementation—that is, that organizational restructuring is needed to make MIS implementation work.

Using the same case, an additional ingredient might be the following statement:

> The case study will also show why the simple replacement of key persons was not sufficient for successful implementation. (Markus, 1983)

This second statement presents the nutshell of a *rival* theory—that is, that MIS implementation fails because of the resistance to change on the part of individual people and that the replacement of such people is the main requirement for implementation to succeed.

You can see that as these two initial ingredients are elaborated, the stated ideas will increasingly cover the questions, propositions, units of analysis, logic connecting data to propositions, and criteria for interpreting the findings—that is, the five components of the needed research design. In this sense, the complete research design embodies a "theory" of what is being studied.

This theory should by no means be considered with the formality of grand theory in social science, nor are you being asked to be a masterful theoretician. Rather, the simple goal is to have a sufficient blueprint for your study, and this requires theoretical propositions, usefully noted by Sutton and Staw (1995) as "a [hypothetical] story about why acts, events, structure, and thoughts occur" (p. 378). Then, the complete research design will provide surprisingly strong guidance in determining what data to collect and the strategies for analyzing the data. For this reason, theory development prior to the collection of any case study data is an essential step in doing case studies. As noted for nonexperimental studies more generally, a more elaborate theory desirably points to a more complex pattern of expected results (P. R. Rosenbaum, 2002, pp. 5–6 and 277–279). The benefit is a stronger design and a heightened ability to interpret your eventual data.

However, theory development takes time and can be difficult (Eisenhardt, 1989). For some topics, existing works may provide a rich theoretical framework for designing a specific case study. If you are interested in international economic development, for instance, Peter Drucker's (1986) "The Changed World Economy" is an exceptional source of theories and hypotheses. Drucker claims that the world economy has changed significantly from the past. He points to the "uncoupling" between the primary products (raw materials) economy and the industrial economy, a similar uncoupling between low labor costs and manufacturing production, and the uncoupling between financial markets and the real economy of goods and services. To test these propositions might require different studies, some focusing on the different uncouplings, others focusing on specific industries, and yet others explaining the plight of specific countries. Each different study would likely call for a different unit of analysis. Drucker's theoretical framework would provide guidance for designing these studies and even for collecting relevant data.

In other situations, the appropriate theory may be a descriptive theory (see BOX 2A in Chapter 1 for another example), and your concern should focus on such issues as (a) the purpose of the descriptive effort, (b) the full but realistic range of topics that might be considered a "complete" description of what is to be studied, and (c) the likely topic(s) that will be the essence of the description. Good answers to these questions, including the rationales underlying the answers, will help you go a long way toward developing the needed theoretical base—and research design—for your study.

For yet other topics, the existing knowledge base may be poor, and the available literature will provide no conceptual framework or hypotheses of note. Such a knowledge base does not lend itself to the development of good theoretical statements, and any new empirical study is likely to assume the characteristic of an "exploratory" study. Nevertheless, as noted earlier with the illustrative case in BOX 4, even an exploratory case study should be preceded by statements about what is to be explored, the purpose of the exploration, and the criteria by which the exploration will be judged successful.

Overall, you may want to gain a richer understanding of how theory is used in case studies by reviewing specific case studies that have been successfully completed. For instance, Yin (2003, chap. 1) shows how theory was used in exploratory, descriptive, and explanatory situations by discussing five actual case studies.

Illustrative types of theories. In general, to overcome the barriers to theory development, you should try to prepare for your case study by doing such things as reviewing the literature related to what you would like to study (also see Cooper, 1984), discussing your topic and ideas with colleagues or teachers, and asking yourself challenging questions about what you are studying, why you are proposing to do the study, and what you hope to learn as a result of the study.

As a further reminder, you should be aware of the full range of theories that might be relevant to your study. For instance, note that the MIS example illustrates MIS "implementation" theory and that this is but one type of theory that can be the subject of study. Other types of theories for you to consider include

- individual theories—for example, theories of individual development, cognitive behavior, personality, learning and disability, individual perception, and interpersonal interactions;
- group theories—for example, theories of family functioning, informal groups, work teams, supervisory-employee relations, and interpersonal networks;
- organizational theories—for example, theories of bureaucracies, organizational structure and functions, excellence in organizational performance, and interorganizational partnerships; and
- societal theories—for example, theories of urban development, international behavior, cultural institutions, technological development, and marketplace functions.

Other examples cut across these illustrative types. Decision-making theory (Carroll & Johnson, 1992), for instance, can involve individuals, organizations, or social groups. As another example, a common topic of case studies is the evaluation of publicly supported programs, such as federal, state, or local programs. In this situation, the development of a theory of how a program is supposed to work is essential to the design of the evaluation. In this situation, Bickman (1987) reminds us that the theory needs to distinguish between the substance of the program (e.g., how to make education more effective) and the process of program implementation (e.g., how to install an effective program). The distinction would avoid situations where policy makers might want to know the desired substantive remedies (e.g., findings about a newly effective curriculum) but where an evaluation unfortunately focused on managerial issues (e.g., the need to hire a good project director). Such a mismatch can be avoided by giving closer attention to the substantive theory.

Generalizing from case study to theory. Theory development does not only facilitate the data collection phase of the ensuing case study. The appropriately developed theory also is the level at which the generalization of the case study results will occur. This role of theory has been characterized throughout this book as "analytic generalization" and has been contrasted with another way of generalizing results, known as "statistical generalization." Understanding the distinction between these two types of generalization may be your most important challenge in doing case studies.

Let us first take the more commonly recognized way of generalizing—*statistical* generalization—although it is the less relevant one for doing case studies. In statistical generalization, an inference is made about a population (or universe) on the basis of empirical data collected about a sample from that universe. This is shown as a Level One inference in Figure 2.2.[1] This method of generalizing is commonly recognized because research investigators have ready access to quantitative formulas for determining the confidence with which generalizations can be made, depending mostly upon the size and internal variation within the universe and sample. Moreover, this is the most common way of generalizing when doing surveys (e.g., Fowler, 1988; Lavrakas, 1987) or analyzing archival data.

A fatal flaw in doing case studies is to conceive of statistical generalization as the method of generalizing the results of your case study. This is because your cases are not "sampling units" and should not be chosen for this reason. Rather, individual case studies are to be selected as a laboratory investigator selects the topic of a new experiment. Multiple cases, in this sense, resemble multiple experiments. Under these circumstances, the mode of generalization is *analytic* generalization, in which a previously developed theory is used as a template with which to compare the empirical results of the case study.[2] If two or more cases are shown to support the same theory, replication may be

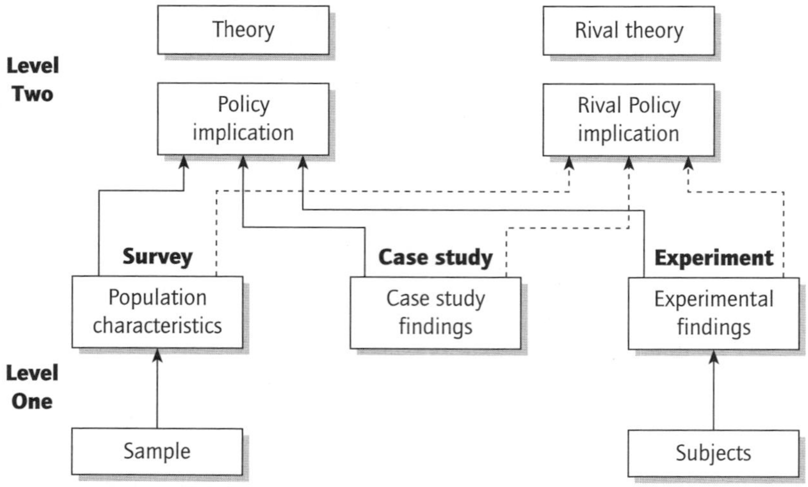

Figure 2.2 Making Inferences: Two Levels

claimed. The empirical results may be considered yet more potent if two or more cases support the same theory but do not support an equally plausible, *rival* theory. Graphically, this type of generalization is shown as a Level Two inference in Figure 2.2.

Analytic generalization can be used whether your case study involves one or several cases, which shall be later referenced as single-case or multiple-case studies. Furthermore, the logic of replication and the distinction between statistical and analytic generalization will be covered in greater detail in the discussion of multiple-case study designs. The main point at this juncture is that you should try to aim toward analytic generalization in doing case studies, and you should avoid thinking in such confusing terms as "the sample of cases" or the "small sample size of cases," as if a single-case study were like a single respondent in a survey or a single subject in an experiment. In other words, in terms of Figure 2.2, you should aim for Level Two inferences when doing case studies.

Because of the importance of this distinction between the two ways of generalizing, you will find repeated examples and discussion throughout the remainder of this chapter as well as in Chapter 5.

Summary. This subsection has suggested that a complete research design, covering the four components described earlier, in fact requires the development of a theoretical framework for the case study that is to be conducted. Rather than resisting such a requirement, a good case study investigator should make the effort to develop this theoretical framework, no matter whether the study is to be explanatory, descriptive, or exploratory. The use of theory, in doing case studies, is an immense aid in defining the appropriate research design and data collection. The same theoretical orientation also becomes the main vehicle for generalizing the results of the case study.

CRITERIA FOR JUDGING THE QUALITY OF RESEARCH DESIGNS

Because a research design is supposed to represent a logical set of statements, you also can judge the quality of any given design according to certain logical tests. Concepts that have been offered for these tests include trustworthiness, credibility, confirmability, and data dependability (U.S. Government Accountability Office, 1990).

Four tests, however, have been commonly used to establish the quality of any empirical social research. Because case studies are one form of such research, the four tests also are relevant to case studies. An important innovation of this book is the identification of several tactics for dealing with these four tests when doing case studies. Figure 2.3 lists the four widely used tests and the recommended case study tactics, as well as a cross-reference to the phase of research when the tactic is to be used. (Each tactic is described in detail in the referenced chapter of this book.)

Because the four tests are common to all social science methods, the tests have been summarized in numerous textbooks (see L. Kidder & Judd, 1986, pp. 26–29):

- *Construct validity:* identifying correct operational measures for the concepts being studied
- *Internal validity* (for explanatory or causal studies only and not for descriptive or exploratory studies): seeking to establish a causal relationship, whereby certain conditions are believed to lead to other conditions, as distinguished from spurious relationships
- *External validity:* defining the domain to which a study's findings can be generalized
- *Reliability:* demonstrating that the operations of a study—such as the data collection procedures—can be repeated, with the same results

Each item on this list deserves explicit attention. For case studies, an important revelation is that the several tactics to be used in dealing with these tests

TESTS	Case Study Tactic	Phase of research in which tactic occurs
Construct validity	♦ use multiple sources of evidence ♦ establish chain of evidence ♦ have key informants review draft case study report	data collection data collection composition
Internal validity	♦ do pattern matching ♦ do explanation building ♦ address rival explanations ♦ use logic models	data analysis data analysis data analysis data analysis
External validity	♦ use theory in single-case studies ♦ use replication logic in multiple-case studies	research design research design
Reliability	♦ use case study protocol ♦ develop case study database	data collection data collection

Figure 2.3 Case Study Tactics for Four Design Tests

should be applied throughout the subsequent conduct of the case study, not just at its beginning. Thus, the "design work" for case studies may actually continue beyond the initial design plans.

Construct Validity

This first test is especially challenging in case study research. People who have been critical of case studies often point to the fact that a case study investigator fails to develop a sufficiently operational set of measures and that "subjective" judgments are used to collect the data.[3] Take an example such as studying "neighborhood change"—a common case study topic (e.g., Bradshaw, 1999; Keating & Krumholz, 1999).

Over the years, concerns have arisen over how certain urban neighborhoods have changed their character. Any number of case studies has examined the types of changes and their consequences. However, without any prior specification of the significant, operational events that constitute "change," a reader cannot tell whether the claimed changes in a case study genuinely reflect the events in a neighborhood or whether they happen to be based on an investigator's impressions only.

Neighborhood change can cover a wide variety of phenomena: racial turnover, housing deterioration and abandonment, changes in the pattern of urban services, shifts in a neighborhood's economic institutions, or the turnover from low- to middle-income residents in revitalizing neighborhoods. The choice of whether to aggregate blocks, census tracts, or larger areas also can produce different results (Hipp, 2007).

To meet the test of construct validity, an investigator must be sure to cover two steps:

1. define neighborhood change in terms of specific concepts (and relate them to the original objectives of the study) and
2. identify operational measures that match the concepts (preferably citing published studies that make the same matches).

For example, suppose you satisfy the first step by stating that you plan to study neighborhood change by focusing on trends in neighborhood crime. The second step now demands that you select a specific measure, such as police-reported crime (which happens to be the standard measure used in the FBI Uniform Crime Reports) as your measure of crime. The literature will indicate certain known shortcomings in this measure, mainly that unknown proportions of crimes are not reported to the police. You will then need to discuss how the shortcomings nevertheless will not bias your study of neighborhood crime and hence neighborhood change.

As Figure 2.3 shows, three tactics are available to increase construct validity when doing case studies. The first is the use of *multiple sources of evidence,* in a manner encouraging convergent lines of inquiry, and this tactic is relevant during data collection (see Chapter 4). A second tactic is to establish a *chain of evidence,* also relevant during data collection (also Chapter 4). The third tactic is to have the draft case study report reviewed by key informants (a procedure described further in Chapter 6).

Internal Validity

This second test has been given the greatest attention in experimental and quasi-experimental research (see Campbell & Stanley, 1966; Cook & Campbell, 1979). Numerous "threats" to validity have been identified, mainly dealing with spurious effects. However, because so many textbooks already cover this topic, only two points need to be made here.

First, internal validity is mainly a concern for explanatory case studies, when an investigator is trying to explain how and why event *x* led to event *y*. If the investigator incorrectly concludes that there is a causal relationship between *x* and *y* without knowing that some third factor—*z*—may actually have caused *y*, the research design has failed to deal with some threat to internal validity. Note that this logic is inapplicable to descriptive or exploratory studies (whether the studies are case studies, surveys, or experiments), which are not concerned with this kind of causal situation.

Second, the concern over internal validity, for case study research, extends to the broader problem of making inferences. Basically, a case study involves an inference every time an event cannot be directly observed. An investigator will "infer" that a particular event resulted from some earlier occurrence, based on interview and documentary evidence collected as part of the case study. Is the inference correct? Have all the rival explanations and possibilities been considered? Is the evidence convergent? Does it appear to be airtight? A research design that has anticipated these questions has begun to deal with the overall problem of making inferences and therefore the specific problem of internal validity.

However, the specific tactics for achieving this result are difficult to identify. This is especially true in doing case studies. As one set of suggestions, Figure 2.3 shows that the analytic tactic of *pattern matching,* described further in Chapter 5, is one way of addressing internal validity. Three other analytic tactics, *explanation building, addressing rival explanations,* and *using logic models,* also are described in Chapter 5.

External Validity

The third test deals with the problem of knowing whether a study's findings are generalizable beyond the immediate case study. In the simplest example, if a study of neighborhood change focused on one neighborhood, are the results applicable to another neighborhood? The external validity problem has been a major barrier in doing case studies. Critics typically state that single cases offer a poor basis for generalizing. However, such critics are implicitly contrasting the situation to survey research, in which a sample is intended to generalize to a larger universe. *This analogy to samples and universes is incorrect when dealing with case studies.* Survey research relies on *statistical* generalization, whereas case studies (as with experiments) rely on *analytic* generalization. In analytical generalization, the investigator is striving to generalize a particular set of results to some broader theory (see three examples in BOX 6).

For example, the theory of neighborhood change that led to a case study in the first place is the same theory that will help to identify the other cases to which the results are generalizable. If a study had focused on population transition in an urban neighborhood (e.g., Flippen, 2001), the procedure for selecting a neighborhood for study would have begun with identifying a neighborhood within which the hypothesized transitions were occurring. Theories about transition would then be the domain to which the results could later be generalized.

BOX 6
How Case Studies Can Be Generalized to Theory: Three Examples

6A. The Origins of Social Class Theory

The first example is about the uncovering and labeling of a social class structure based on a case study of a typical American city, *Yankee City* (Warner & Lunt, 1941). This classic case study in sociology made a critical contribution to social stratification theory and an understanding of social differences among "upper," "upper-middle," "middle-middle," "upper-lower," and "lower" classes.

6B. Contributions to Urban Planning Theory

The second example is Jane Jacobs and her famous book, *The Death and Life of Great American Cities* (1961). The book is based mostly on experiences from a single case, New York City. However, the chapter topics, rather than reflecting the single experiences of New York, cover broader theoretical issues in urban planning, such as the role of sidewalks, the role of neighborhood parks, the need for primary mixed uses, the need for small blocks, and the processes of slumming and unslumming. In the aggregate, these issues in fact represent Jacobs's building of a theory of urban planning.

Jacobs's book created heated controversy in the planning profession. As a partial result, new empirical inquiries were made in other locales, to examine one or another facet of her rich and provocative ideas. Her theory, in essence, became the vehicle for examining other cases, and the theory still stands as a significant contribution to the field of urban planning.

6C. A More Contemporary Example

A third example covers a 5-year ethnographic study of a single neighborhood at the edge of Chicago (Carr, 2003). The study shows how the neighborhood successfully thwarted undesirable youth-related crime. The experience, in the author's view, challenged existing theories claiming that strong social ties are crucial to effective neighborhood control. Instead, the author offers newer theories of informal social control that he believes may be especially pertinent to youth crime prevention in contemporary suburban neighborhoods.

The generalization is not automatic, however. A theory must be tested by replicating the findings in a second or even a third neighborhood, where the theory has specified that the same results should occur. Once such direct replications have been made, the results might be accepted as providing strong support for the theory, even though further replications had not been performed. This *replication logic* is the same that underlies the use of experiments (and allows scientists to cumulate knowledge across experiments). The logic will be discussed further in this chapter in the section on multiple-case designs.

Reliability

Most people are probably already familiar with this final test. The objective is to be sure that, if a later investigator followed the same procedures as described by an earlier investigator and conducted the same case study all over again, the later investigator should arrive at the same findings and conclusions. (Note that the emphasis is on doing the *same* case over again, not on "replicating" the results of one case by doing another case study.) The goal of reliability is to minimize the errors and biases in a study.

One prerequisite for allowing this other investigator to repeat an earlier case study is the need to document the procedures followed in the earlier case. Without such documentation, you could not even repeat your own work (which is another way of dealing with reliability). In the past, case study research procedures have been poorly documented, making external reviewers suspicious of the reliability of the case study method.[4] Figure 2.3 indicates two specific tactics to overcome these shortcomings—the use of a *case study protocol* to deal with the documentation problem in detail (discussed in Chapter 3) and the development of a *case study database* (discussed in Chapter 4).

The general way of approaching the reliability problem is to make as many steps as operational as possible and to conduct research as if someone were always looking over your shoulder. Accountants and bookkeepers always are aware that any calculations must be capable of being audited. In this sense, an auditor also is performing a reliability check and must be able to produce the same results if the same procedures are followed. A good guideline for doing case studies is therefore to conduct the research so that an auditor could in principle repeat the procedures and arrive at the same results.

Summary

Four tests may be considered relevant in judging the quality of a research design. In designing and doing case studies, various tactics are available to deal with these tests, though not all of the tactics occur at the formal stage of designing a case study. Some of the tactics occur during the data collection, data analysis, or compositional phases of the research and are therefore described in greater detail in subsequent chapters of this book.

EXERCISE 2.3 Defining the Criteria for Judging the Quality of Research Designs

Define the four criteria for judging the quality of research designs: (a) construct validity, (b) internal validity, (c) external validity, and (d) reliability. Give an example of each type of criterion in a case study you might want to do.

CASE STUDY DESIGNS

These general characteristics of research designs serve as a background for considering the specific designs for case studies. Four types of designs will be discussed, based on a 2 × 2 matrix (see Figure 2.4). The matrix first shows that every type of design will include the desire to analyze contextual conditions in relation to the "case," with the dotted lines between the two signaling that the boundaries between the case and the context are not likely to be sharp. The matrix then shows that single- and multiple-case studies reflect different design situations and that, within these two variants, there also can be unitary or multiple units of analysis. The resulting four types of designs for case studies are (Type 1) single-case (holistic) designs, (Type 2) single-case (embedded)

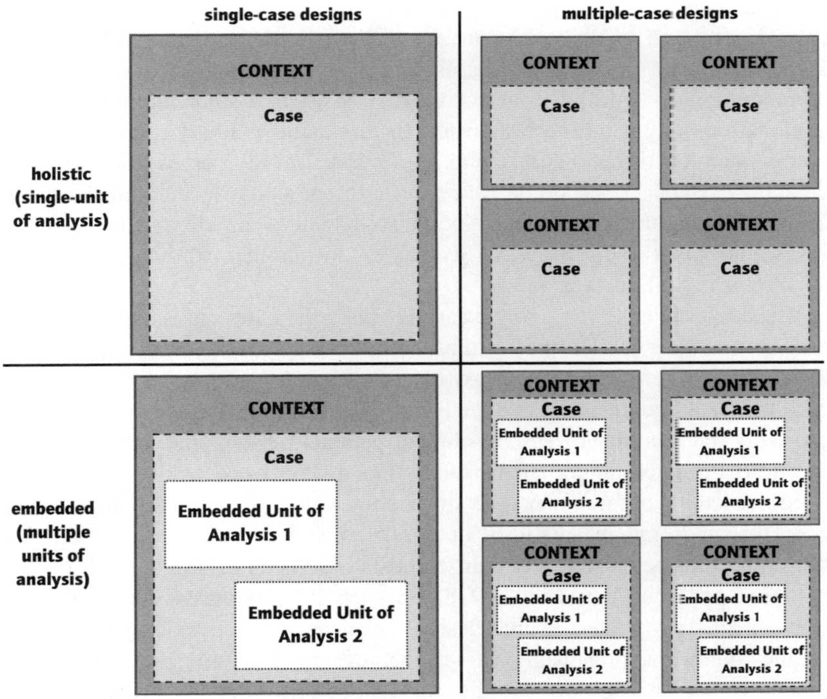

Figure 2.4 Basic Types of Designs for Case Studies
SOURCE: COSMOS Corporation.

designs, (Type 3) multiple-case (holistic) designs, and (Type 4) multiple-case (embedded) designs. The rationale for these four types of designs is as follows.

What Are the Potential Single-Case Designs (Types 1 and 2)?

Rationale for single-case designs. A primary distinction in designing case studies is between *single-* and *multiple-*case designs. This means the need for a decision, prior to any data collection, on whether a single case or multiple cases are going to be used to address the research questions. The single-case study is an appropriate design under several circumstances, and five rationales are given below. Recall that a single-case study is analogous to a single experiment, and many of the same conditions that justify a single experiment also justify a single-case study.

One rationale for a single case is when it represents the *critical case* in testing a well-formulated theory (again, note the analogy to the critical *experiment*). The theory has specified a clear set of propositions as well as the circumstances within which the propositions are believed to be true. A single case, meeting all of the conditions for testing the theory, can confirm, challenge, or extend the theory. The single case can then be used to determine whether a theory's propositions are correct or whether some alternative set of explanations might be more relevant. In this manner, like Graham Allison's comparison of three theories and the Cuban missile crisis (described in Chapter 1, BOX 2), the single case can represent a significant contribution to knowledge and theory building. Such a study can even help to refocus future investigations in an entire field. (See BOX 7 for another example, in the field of organizational innovation.)

A second rationale for a single case is where the case represents an *extreme* case or a *unique* case. Either of these situations commonly occurs in clinical psychology, where a specific injury or disorder may be so rare that any single case is worth documenting and analyzing. For instance, one rare clinical syndrome is the inability of certain clinical patients to recognize familiar faces. Given visual cues alone, such patients are unable to recognize loved ones, friends, pictures of famous people, or (in some cases) their own image in a mirror. This syndrome appears to be due to some physical injury to the brain. Yet the syndrome occurs so rarely that scientists have been unable to establish any common patterns (Yin, 1970, 1978). In such circumstances, the single-case study is an appropriate research design whenever a new person with this syndrome—known as prosopagnosia—is encountered. The case study would document the person's abilities and disabilities, determine the precise nature of the face recognition deficit, but also ascertain whether related disorders exist.

BOX 7
The Critical Case as a Single-Case Study

One rationale for selecting a single-case rather than a multiple-case design is that the single case can represent the critical test of a significant theory. Gross, Bernstein, and Giacquinta (1971) used such a design by focusing on a single school in their book, *Implementing Organizational Innovations* (also see BOX 19B, Chapter 3, p. 110).

The school was selected because it had a prior history of innovation and could not be claimed to suffer from "barriers to innovation." In the prevailing theories, such barriers had been prominently cited as the major reason that innovations failed. Gross et al. (1971) showed that, in this school, an innovation also failed but that the failure could not be attributed to any barriers. Implementation processes, rather than barriers, appeared to account for the failure.

In this manner, the book, though limited to a single case, represented a watershed in organizational innovation theory. Prior to the study, analysts had focused on the identification of barriers to innovation; since the study, the literature has been much more dominated by studies of the implementation process.

Conversely, a third rationale for a single case is the *representative* or *typical* case. Here, the objective is to capture the circumstances and conditions of an everyday or commonplace situation (see BOX 8; also see BOX 14, p. 75). The case study may represent a typical "project" among many different projects, a manufacturing firm believed to be typical of many other manufacturing firms in the same industry, a typical urban neighborhood, or a representative school, as examples. The lessons learned from these cases are assumed to be informative about the experiences of the average person or institution.

A fourth rationale for a single-case study is the *revelatory* case. This situation exists when an investigator has an opportunity to observe and analyze a phenomenon previously inaccessible to social science inquiry, such as Whyte's

BOX 8
The Average Case as a Single-Case Study

A famous community case study in sociology, *Middletown*, is about an average American city. The investigators, Robert and Helen Lynd (1929), deliberately chose to study a small town in middle America during the early 20th century (also see BOX 14, p. 75). Their purpose was to show how the transition from an agricultural to an industrial economy occurred in the average town—and thereby to provide a case study about a significant development in all of American history.

(1943/1955) *Street Corner Society,* previously described in Chapter 1, BOX 2A. Another example is Elliot Liebow's (1967) famous case study of unemployed men, *Tally's Corner* (see BOX 9). Liebow had the opportunity to meet the men in an African American neighborhood in Washington, D.C. and to learn about their everyday lives. His observations of and insights into the problems of unemployment formed a significant case study, because few social scientists had previously had the opportunity to investigate these problems, even though the problems were common across the country. When other investigators have similar types of opportunities and can uncover some prevalent phenomenon previously inaccessible to social scientists, such conditions justify the use of a single-case study on the grounds of its revelatory nature.

BOX 9
The Revelatory Case as a Single-Case Study

Another rationale for selecting a single-case rather than a multiple-case design is that the investigator has access to a situation previously inaccessible to scientific observation. The case study is therefore worth conducting because the descriptive information alone will be revelatory.

Such was the situation in Elliot Liebow's (1967) sociological classic, *Tally's Corner.* The book is about a single group of African American men living in a poor, inner-city neighborhood. By befriending these men, the author was able to learn about their lifestyles, their coping behavior, and in particular their sensitivity to unemployment and failure. The book provided insights into a subculture that has prevailed in many U.S. cities for a long period of time, but one that had been only obscurely understood. The single case showed how investigations of such topics could be done, thus stimulating much further research and eventually the development of policy actions.

A fifth rationale for a single-case study is the *longitudinal* case: studying the same single case at two or more different points in time. The theory of interest would likely specify how certain conditions change over time, and the desired time intervals would presumably reflect the anticipated stages at which the changes should reveal themselves.

These five serve as major reasons for conducting a single-case study. There are other situations in which the single-case study may be used as a pilot case that is the first of a multiple-case study. However, in these latter instances, the single-case study cannot be regarded as a complete study on its own.

Whatever the rationale for doing single-case studies (and there may be more than the five mentioned here), a potential vulnerability of the single-case design is that a case may later turn out not to be the case it was thought to be at the outset. Single-case designs therefore require careful investigation of the potential case to minimize the chances of misrepresentation and to maximize the access needed to collect the case study evidence. A fair warning is not to commit yourself to any single-case study until all of these major concerns have been covered.

Holistic versus embedded case studies. The same single-case study may involve *more than one unit of analysis*. This occurs when, within a single case, attention is also given to a subunit or subunits (see BOX 10). For instance, even though a case study might be about a single organization, such as a hospital, the analysis might include outcomes about the clinical services and staff employed by the hospital (and possibly even some quantitative analyses based on the employee records of the staff). In an evaluation study, the single case might be a public program that involves large numbers of funded projects—which would then be the embedded units. In either situation, these embedded units can be selected through sampling or cluster techniques (McClintock, 1985). No matter how the units are selected, the resulting design would be called an *embedded case study design* (see Figure 2.4, Type 2). In contrast, if the case study examined only the global nature of an organization or of a program, a *holistic design* would have been used (see Figure 2.4, Type 1).

These two variants of single-case studies both have their strengths and weaknesses. The holistic design is advantageous when no logical subunits can be identified or when the relevant theory underlying the case study is itself of a holistic nature. Potential problems arise, however, when a global approach allows an investigator to avoid examining any specific phenomenon in operational detail. Thus, a typical problem with the holistic design is that the entire case study may be conducted at an unduly abstract level, lacking sufficiently clear measures or data.

BOX 10
An Embedded, Single-Case Design

Union Democracy (1956) is a highly regarded case study by three eminent academicians—Seymour Martin Lipset, Martin Trow, and James Coleman. The case study is about the inside politics of the International Typographical Union and involves several units of analysis (see "Kinds of Data" table). The main unit was the organization as a whole, the smallest unit was the individual member, and several intermediary units also were important. At each level of analysis, different data collection techniques were used, ranging from historical to survey analysis.

Kinds of Data (BOX 10 Continued)

	Total System	*Intermediate Units*		*Individuals*	
Unit Being Characterized	*Issues, Data on Occupation; Union Laws; Policies; Historical Data; Convention Reports*	*Locals' Histories and Voting records; Issues on Local Level; size of Locals*	*Shops' Voting Records; Shop Size*	*Interviews with Leaders*	*Interviews of the Sample of Men*
ITU as a whole	Structural, environmental, behavioral properties	By inference, communication network (structural)			
Locals	Behavioral properties (militancy, etc.)	Behavioral properties, size	By inference, communication network (structural)	Structural, environmental, behavioral properties	
Shops			Behavioral properties, size		Distributions of individual properties
Other immediate social environment of men	The social climate, by inference from dominant issues and election outcome	The social climate, by inference from dominant issues and election outcome			Chapel chairman's attributes; friends' attributes
Men	By inference, dominant values and interests	By inference: values, interests, and loyalties (e.g., local over international)	By inference: values, interests, loyalties (e.g., to shop over local)	By inference: values	Behavior, background, values, attitudes

SOURCE: Lipset, Trow, & Coleman (1956, p. 422). Reprinted by permission.

A further problem with the holistic design is that the entire nature of the case study may shift, unbeknownst to the researcher, during the course of study. The initial study questions may have reflected one orientation, but as the case study proceeds, a different orientation may emerge, and the evidence begins to address different research questions. Although some people have claimed such flexibility to be a strength of the case study approach, in fact the largest criticism of case studies is based on this type of shift—in which the implemented research design is no longer appropriate for the research questions being asked (see COSMOS Corporation, 1983). Because of this problem, you need to avoid such unsuspected slippage; if the relevant research questions really do change, you should simply start over again, with a new research design. One way to increase the sensitivity to such slippage is to have a set of subunits. Thus, an embedded design can serve as an important device for focusing a case study inquiry.

An embedded design, however, also has its pitfalls. A major one occurs when the case study focuses only on the subunit level and fails to return to the larger unit of analysis. For instance, an evaluation of a program consisting of multiple projects may include project characteristics as a subunit of analysis. The project-level data may even be highly quantitative if there are many projects. However, the original evaluation becomes a project study (i.e., a multiple-case study of different projects) if no investigating is done at the level of the original case—that is, the program. Similarly, a study of organizational climate may involve individual employees as a subunit of study. However, if the data focus only on individual employees, the study will in fact become an employee and not an organizational study. In both examples, what has happened is that the original phenomenon of interest (a program or organizational climate) has become the context and not the target of study.

Summary. Single cases are a common design for doing case studies, and two variants have been described: those using holistic designs and those using embedded units of analysis. Overall, the single-case design is eminently justifiable under certain conditions—where the case represents (a) a critical test of existing theory, (b) a rare or unique circumstance, or (c) a representative or typical case, or where the case serves a (d) revelatory or (e) longitudinal purpose.

A major step in designing and conducting a single case is defining the unit of analysis (or the case itself). An operational definition is needed, and some caution must be exercised—before a total commitment to the whole case study is made—to ensure that the case in fact is relevant to the issues and questions of interest.

Within the single case may still be incorporated subunits of analyses, so that a more complex—or embedded—design is developed. The subunits can often add significant opportunities for extensive analysis, enhancing the insights into the single case. However, if too much attention is given to these subunits, and if the larger, holistic aspects of the case begin to be ignored, the case study itself will have shifted its orientation and changed its nature. If the shift is justifiable, you need to address it explicitly and indicate its relationship to the original inquiry.

What Are the Potential Multiple-Case Designs (Types 3 and 4)?

The same study may contain more than a single case. When this occurs, the study has used a multiple-case design, and such designs have increased in frequency in recent years. A common example is a study of school innovations (such as the use of new curricula, rearranged school schedules, or a new educational technology), in which individual schools adopt some innovation. Each school might be the subject of an individual case study, but the study as a whole covers several schools and in this way uses a multiple-case design.

Multiple- versus single-case designs. In some fields, multiple-case studies have been considered a different "methodology" from single-case studies. For example, both anthropology and political science have developed one set of rationales for doing single-case studies and a second set for doing what have been considered "comparative" (or multiple-case) studies (see Eckstein, 1975; Lijphart, 1975). This book, however, considers single- and multiple-case designs to be variants within the same methodological framework—and no broad distinction is made between the so-called classic (that is, single) case study and multiple-case studies. The choice is considered one of research design, with both being included under the case study method.

Multiple-case designs have distinct advantages and disadvantages in comparison to single-case designs. The evidence from multiple cases is often considered more compelling, and the overall study is therefore regarded as being more robust (Herriott & Firestone, 1983). At the same time, the rationale for single-case designs cannot usually be satisfied by multiple cases. By definition, the unusual or rare case, the critical case, and the revelatory case all are likely to involve only single cases. Moreover, the conduct of a multiple-case study can require extensive resources and time beyond the means of a single student or independent research investigator. Therefore, the decision to undertake multiple-case studies cannot be taken lightly.

Selecting the multiple cases also raises a new set of questions. Here, *a major insight is to consider multiple cases as one would consider multiple experiments*—that is, to follow a "replication" design. This is far different from a mistaken analogy in the past, which incorrectly considered multiple cases to be similar to the multiple respondents in a survey (or to the multiple subjects within an experiment)—that is, to follow a "sampling" design. The methodological differences between these two views are revealed by the different rationales underlying the replication as opposed to sampling designs.

Replication, not sampling logic, for multiple-case studies. The replication logic is analogous to that used in multiple experiments (see Hersen & Barlow, 1976). For example, upon uncovering a significant finding from a single experiment, an ensuing and pressing priority would be to replicate this finding by conducting a second, third, and even more experiments. Some of the replications might attempt to duplicate the exact conditions of the original experiment. Other replications might alter one or two experimental conditions considered unimportant to the original finding, to see whether the finding could still be duplicated. Only with such replications would the original finding be considered robust.

The logic underlying the use of multiple-case studies is the same. Each case must be carefully selected so that it either (a) predicts similar results (a *literal replication*) or (b) predicts contrasting results but for anticipatable reasons (a *theoretical replication*). The ability to conduct 6 or 10 case studies, arranged effectively within a multiple-case design, is analogous to the ability to conduct 6 to 10 experiments on related topics; a few cases (2 or 3) would be literal replications, whereas a few other cases (4 to 6) might be designed to pursue two different patterns of theoretical replications. If all the cases turn out as predicted, these 6 to 10 cases, in the aggregate, would have provided compelling support for the initial set of propositions. If the cases are in some way contradictory, the initial propositions must be revised and retested with another set of cases. Again, this logic is similar to the way scientists deal with conflicting experimental findings.

An important step in all of these replication procedures is the development of a rich, theoretical framework. The framework needs to state the conditions under which a particular phenomenon is likely to be found (a literal replication) as well as the conditions when it is not likely to be found (a theoretical replication). The theoretical framework later becomes the vehicle for generalizing to new cases, again similar to the role played in cross-experiment designs. Furthermore, just as with experimental science, if some of the empirical cases do not work as predicted, modification must be made to the theory. Remember, too, that theories can be practical and not just academic.

For example, one might consider the initial proposition that an increase in using a new technology in school districts will occur when the technology is used for both administrative and instructional applications, but not either alone. To pursue this proposition in a multiple-case study design, 3 or 4 cases might be selected in which both types of applications are present, to determine whether, in fact, technology use did increase over a period of time (the investigation would be predicting a literal replication in these 3 or 4 cases). Three or

4 additional cases might be selected in which only administrative applications are present, with the prediction being little increase in use (predicting a theoretical replication). Finally, 3 or 4 other cases would be selected in which only instructional applications are present, with the same prediction of little increase in use, but for different reasons than the administrative-only cases (another theoretical replication). If this entire pattern of results across these multiple cases is indeed found, the 9 to 12 cases, in the aggregate, would provide substantial support for the initial proposition.

Another example of a multiple-case replication design comes from the field of urban studies (see BOX 11). You also can find examples of three entire case studies, all following a replication design but covering HIV/AIDS prevention, university administration, and the transformation of business firms, in the companion text (Yin, 2003, chaps. 8–10).

This replication logic, whether applied to experiments or to case studies, must be distinguished from the sampling logic commonly used in surveys. The sampling logic requires an operational enumeration of the entire universe or pool of potential respondents and then a statistical procedure for selecting a

BOX 11
A Multiple-Case, Replication Design

A common problem in the 1960s and 1970s was how to get good advice to city governments. Peter Szanton's (1981) book, *Not Well Advised*, reviewed the experiences of numerous attempts by university and research groups to collaborate with city officials.

The book is an excellent example of a multiple-case, replication design. Szanton starts with eight case studies, showing how different university groups all failed to help cities. The eight cases are sufficient "replications" to convince the reader of a general phenomenon. Szanton then provides five more case studies, in which nonuniversity groups also failed, concluding that failure was therefore not necessarily inherent in the academic enterprise. Yet a third group of cases shows how university groups have successfully helped business, engineering firms, and sectors other than city government. A final set of three cases shows that those few groups able to help city government were concerned with implementation and not just with the production of new ideas, leading to the major conclusion that city governments may have peculiar needs in receiving but also then putting advice into practice.

Within each of the four groups of case studies, Szanton has illustrated the principle of literal replication. Across the four groups, he has illustrated theoretical replication. This potent case study design can and should be applied to many other topics.

specific subset of respondents to be surveyed. The resulting data from the sample that is actually surveyed are assumed to reflect the entire universe or pool, with inferential statistics used to establish the confidence intervals for which this representation is presumed accurate. The entire procedure is commonly used when an investigator wishes to determine the prevalence or frequency of a particular phenomenon.

Any application of this sampling logic to case studies would be misplaced. First, case studies are not the best method for assessing the prevalence of phenomena. Second, a case study would have to cover both the phenomenon of interest and its context, yielding a large number of potentially relevant variables. In turn, this would require an impossibly large number of cases—too large to allow any statistical consideration of the relevant variables.

Third, if a sampling logic had to be applied to all types of research, many important topics could not be empirically investigated, such as the following problem: Your investigation deals with the role of the presidency of the United States, and you are interested in doing a multiple-case study of a (few) presidents to test your theory about presidential leadership. However, the complexity of your topic means that your choice of a small number of cases could not adequately represent all the 44 presidents since the beginning of the Republic. Critics using a sampling logic might therefore deny the acceptability of your study. In contrast, if you use a replication logic, the study is eminently feasible.

The replication approach to multiple-case studies is illustrated in Figure 2.5. The figure indicates that the initial step in designing the study must consist of theory development, and then shows that case selection and the definition of specific measures are important steps in the design and data collection process. Each individual case study consists of a "whole" study, in which convergent evidence is sought regarding the facts and conclusions for the case; each case's conclusions are then considered to be the information needing replication by other individual cases. Both the individual cases and the multiple-case results can and should be the focus of a summary report. For each individual case, the report should indicate how and why a particular proposition was demonstrated (or not demonstrated). Across cases, the report should indicate the extent of the replication logic and why certain cases were predicted to have certain results, whereas other cases, if any, were predicted to have contrasting results.

An important part of Figure 2.5 is the dashed-line feedback loop. The loop represents the situation where important discovery occurs during the conduct of one of the individual case studies (e.g., one of the cases did not in fact suit the original design). Such a discovery even may require you to reconsider one or more of the study's original theoretical propositions. At this point,

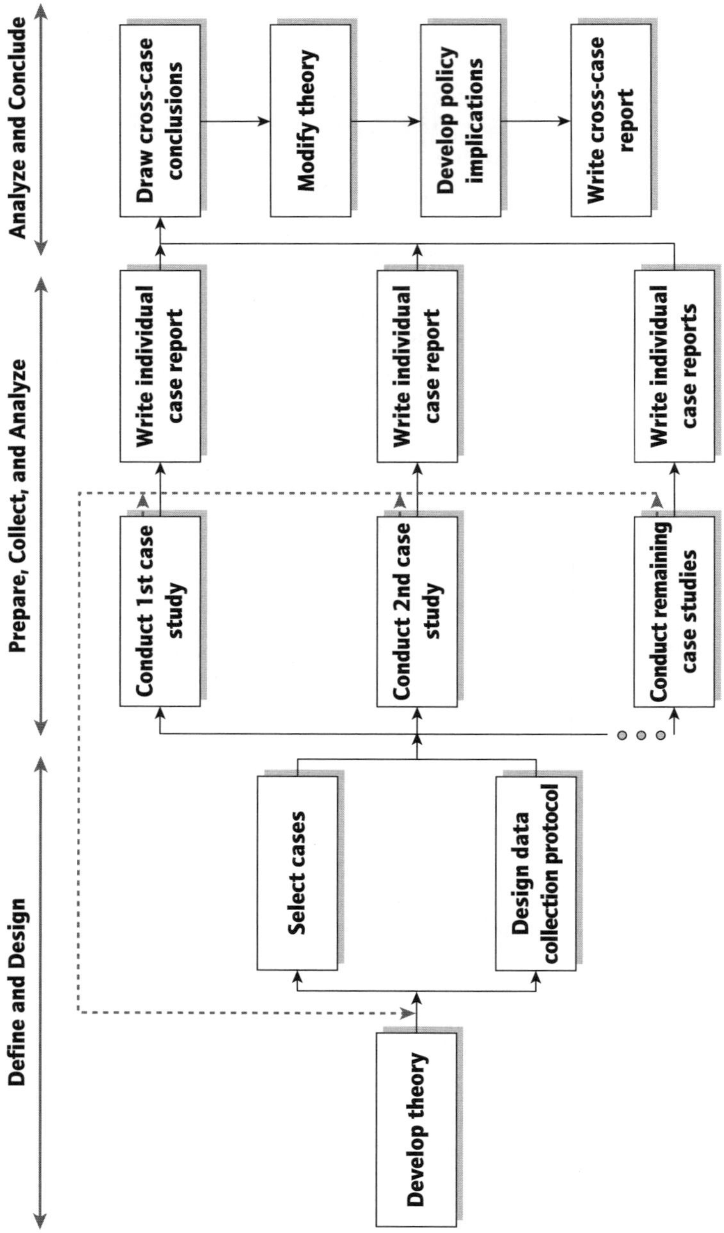

Figure 2.5 Case Study Method
SOURCE: COSMOS Corporation.

"redesign" should take place before proceeding further. Such redesign might involve the selection of alternative cases or changes in the case study (i.e., data collection) protocol (see Chapter 3). Without such redesign, you risk being accused of distorting or ignoring the discovery, just to accommodate the original design. This condition leads quickly to a further accusation—that you have been selective in reporting your data, to suit your preconceived ideas (i.e., the original theoretical propositions).

Overall, Figure 2.5 depicts a very different logic from that of a sampling design. The logic as well as its contrast with a sampling design may be difficult to follow and is worth extensive discussion with colleagues before proceeding with any multiple case study.

When using a multiple-case design, a further question you will encounter has to do with the *number* of cases deemed necessary or sufficient for your study. However, because a sampling logic should not be used, the typical criteria regarding sample size also are irrelevant. Instead, you should think of this decision as a reflection of the number of case replications—both literal and theoretical—that you need or would like to have in your study.

For the number of literal replications, an appropriate analogy from statistics is the selection of the criterion for establishing the sample size desired to detect an "effect." Designating a "$p < .05$" or "$p < .01$" likelihood of detection as part of a power analysis is not based on any formula but is a matter of discretionary, judgmental choice. Analogously, designating the number of replications depends upon the certainty you want to have about your multiple-case results (as with the higher criterion for establishing the likelihood of detection, the greater certainty lies with the larger number of cases). For example, you may want to settle for two or three literal replications when your theory is straightforward and the issue at hand does not demand an excessive degree of certainty. However, if your theory is subtle or if you want a high degree of certainty, you may press for five, six, or more replications.

For the number of theoretical replications, the important consideration is related to your sense of the importance of rival explanations. The stronger the rivals, the more additional cases you might want, each case showing a different result when some rival explanation had been taken into account. For example, your original hypothesis might be that summer reading programs improve students' reading scores, and you already might have shown this result through several cases that served as literal replications. A rival explanation might be that parents also work more closely with their children during the summer and that this circumstance can account for improved reading scores. You would then find another case, with parent participation but no summer reading program, and in this theoretical replication you would predict that the scores would not improve.

Rationale for multiple-case designs. In short, the rationale for multiple-case designs derives directly from your understanding of literal and theoretical replications. The simplest multiple-case design would be the selection of two or more cases that are believed to be literal replications, such as a set of cases with exemplary outcomes in relation to some evaluation questions, such as "how and why a particular intervention has been implemented smoothly." Selecting such cases requires prior knowledge of the outcomes, with the multiple-case inquiry focusing on how and why the exemplary outcomes might have occurred and hoping for literal (or direct) replications of these conditions from case to case.[5]

More complicated multiple-case designs would likely result from the number and types of theoretical replications you might want to cover. For example, investigators have used a "two-tail" design in which cases from both extremes (of some important theoretical condition, such as good and bad outcomes) have been deliberately chosen. Multiple-case rationales also can derive from the prior hypothesizing of different types of conditions and the desire to have subgroups of cases covering each type. These and other similar designs are more complicated because the study should still have at least two individual cases within each of the subgroups, so that the theoretical replications across subgroups are complemented by literal replications within each subgroup.

Multiple-case studies: Holistic or embedded. The fact that a design calls for multiple-case studies does not eliminate the variation identified earlier with single cases: Each individual case may still be holistic or embedded. In other words, a multiple-case study may consist of multiple holistic cases (see Figure 2.4, Type 3) or of multiple embedded cases (see Figure 2.4, Type 4).

The difference between these two variants depends upon the type of phenomenon being studied and your research questions. In an embedded design, a study even may call for the conduct of a survey at each case study site. For instance, suppose a study is concerned with the impact of the same type of curriculum adopted by different schools. Each school may be the topic of a case study, with the theoretical framework dictating that nine such schools be included as case studies, three to replicate a direct result (literal replication) and six others to deal with contrasting conditions (theoretical replications).

For all nine schools, an embedded design is used because surveys of the students (or, alternatively, examination of students' archival records) are needed to address research questions about the performance of the schools. However, the results of each survey will *not* be pooled across schools. Rather, the survey data will be part of the findings for each individual school, or case. These data may be highly quantitative, focusing on the attitudes and behavior of individual students, and the data will be used along with archival information to interpret the success and operations at the given school. If, in contrast, the survey data are pooled across schools, a replication design is no longer being used. In fact, the study has now become a single-case study, in which all nine schools and their students have now become part of some larger, main unit of analysis. Such a new case study would then require a complete redefinition of the main unit of analysis, with extensive revisions to the original theories and propositions of interest also a likely need.

Summary. This section has dealt with situations in which the same investigation may call for multiple-case studies. These types of designs are becoming more prevalent, but they are more expensive and time-consuming to conduct.

Any use of multiple-case designs should follow a replication, not a sampling logic, and an investigator must choose each case carefully. The cases should serve in a manner similar to multiple experiments, with similar results (a literal replication) or contrasting results (a theoretical replication) predicted explicitly at the outset of the investigation.

The individual cases within a multiple-case study design may be either holistic or embedded. When an embedded design is used, each individual case study may in fact include the collection and analysis of quantitative data, including the use of surveys within each case.

EXERCISE 2.4 Defining a Case Study Research Design

Select one of the case studies described in the BOXES of this book, reviewing the entire case study (not just the material in the BOX). Describe the research design of this case study. How did it justify the relevant evidence to be sought, given the basic research questions to be answered? What methods were used to draw conclusions, based on the evidence? Is the design a single- or multiple-case design? Is it holistic or does it have embedded units of analysis?

MODEST ADVICE IN SELECTING CASE STUDY DESIGNS

Now that you know how to define case study designs and are prepared to carry out design work, three pieces of advice may be offered.

Single- or Multiple-Case Designs?

The first word of advice is that, although all designs can lead to successful case studies, when you have the choice (and resources), multiple-case designs may be preferred over single-case designs. Even if you can do a "two-case"

case study, your chances of doing a good case study will be better than using a single-case design. Single-case designs are vulnerable if only because you will have put "all your eggs in one basket." More important, the analytic benefits from having two (or more) cases may be substantial.

To begin with, even with two cases, you have the possibility of direct replication. Analytic conclusions independently arising from two cases, as with two experiments, will be more powerful than those coming from a single case (or single experiment) alone. Alternatively you may have deliberately selected your two cases because they offered contrasting situations, and you were not seeking a direct replication. In this design, if the subsequent findings support the hypothesized contrast, the results represent a strong start toward theoretical replication—again vastly strengthening your findings compared to those from a single case alone (e.g., Eilbert & Lafronza, 2005; Hanna, 2005; also see BOX 12).

BOX 12
Two, "Two-Case" Case Studies

12A. Contrasting Cases for Community Building

Chaskin (2001) used two case studies to illustrate contrasting strategies for capacity building at the neighborhood level. The author's overall conceptual framework, which was the main topic of inquiry, claimed that there could be two approaches to building community capacity—using a collaborative organization to (a) reinforce existing networks of community organizations or (b) initiate a new organization in the neighborhood. After thoroughly airing the framework on theoretical grounds, the author presents the two case studies, showing the viability of each approach.

12B. Contrasting Strategies for Educational Accountability

In a directly complementary manner, Elmore, Abelmann, and Fuhrman (1997) chose two case studies to illustrate contrasting strategies for designing and implementing educational accountability (i.e., holding schools accountable for the academic performance of their students). One case represented a lower cost, basic version of an accountability system. The other represented a higher cost, more complex version.

In general, criticisms about single-case studies usually reflect fears about the uniqueness or artifactual conditions surrounding the case (e.g., special access to a key informant). As a result, the criticisms may turn into skepticism about your ability to do empirical work beyond having done a single-case study. Having two cases can begin to blunt such criticism and skepticism. Having more than two cases will produce an even stronger effect. In the face of these benefits, having at least two cases should be your goal. If you do use a single-case design, you should be prepared to make an extremely strong argument in justifying your choice for the case.

EXERCISE 2.5 Establishing the Rationale for a Multiple-Case Study

Develop some preliminary ideas about a "case" for your case study. Alternatively, focus on one of the single-case studies presented in the BOXES in this book. In either situation, now think of a companion "case" that might augment the single case. In what ways might the companion case's findings supplement those of the first case? Could the data from the second case fill a gap left by the first case or respond better to some obvious shortcoming or criticism of the first case? Would the two cases together comprise a stronger case study? Could yet a third case make the findings even more compelling?

Closed Designs or Flexible Designs?

Another word of advice is that, despite this chapter's details about design choices, you should not think that a case study's design cannot be modified by new information or discovery during data collection. Such revelations can be enormously important, leading to your altering or modifying your original design.

As examples, in a single-case study, what was thought to be a critical or unique case might have turned out not to be so, after initial data collection had started; ditto a multiple-case study, where what was thought to be parallel cases for literal replication turn out not to be so. With these revelations, you have every right to conclude that your initial design needs to be modified. However, you should undertake any alterations only given a serious caution. The caution is to understand precisely the nature of the alteration: Are you merely selecting different cases, or are you also changing your original theoretical concerns and objectives? The point is that the needed flexibility should not lessen the rigor with which case study procedures are followed.

Mixed Methods Designs: Mixing Case Studies with Other Methods?

Researchers have given increasing attention to "mixed methods research"—a "class of research where the researcher mixes or combines quantitative and qualitative research techniques, methods, approaches, concepts or language into a *single* study" (Johnson & Onwuegbuzie, 2004, p. 17, emphasis added). Confinement to a single study forces the methods being mixed into an integrated mode. The mode differs from the conventional situation whereby different methods are used in *separate* studies that may later be synthesized.

Mixed methods research forces the methods to share the same research questions, to collect complementary data, and to conduct counterpart analyses (e.g., Yin, 2006b)—in short, to follow a mixed methods design. As such, mixed methods research can permit investigators to address more complicated research questions and collect a richer and stronger array of evidence than can be accomplished by any single method alone. Depending upon the nature of your research questions and your ability to use different methods, mixed methods research opens a class of research designs that deserve your consideration.

The earlier discussion of embedded case study designs in fact points to the fact that certain kinds of case studies already represent a form of mixed methods research. The embedded case studies rely on more holistic data collection strategies for studying the main case but then call upon surveys or other more quantitative techniques to collect data about the embedded unit(s) of analysis. In this situation, other research methods are embedded within your case study.

The opposite relationship also can occur. Your case study may be part of a larger, mixed methods study. The main investigation may rely on a survey or other quantitative techniques, and your case study may help to investigate the conditions within one of the entities being surveyed. The contrasting relationships (survey within case or case within survey) are illustrated in Figure 2.6.

At the same time, mixed methods research need not include the use of the case study strategy at all. For instance, much historical work embraces the quantitative analysis of archival records, such as newspapers and other file material. And, in an even broader sense, mixed methods research need not be limited to combinations of quantitative and qualitative methods. For instance, a study could employ a survey to describe certain conditions, complemented by an experiment that tried to manipulate some of those conditions (e.g., Berends & Garet, 2002).

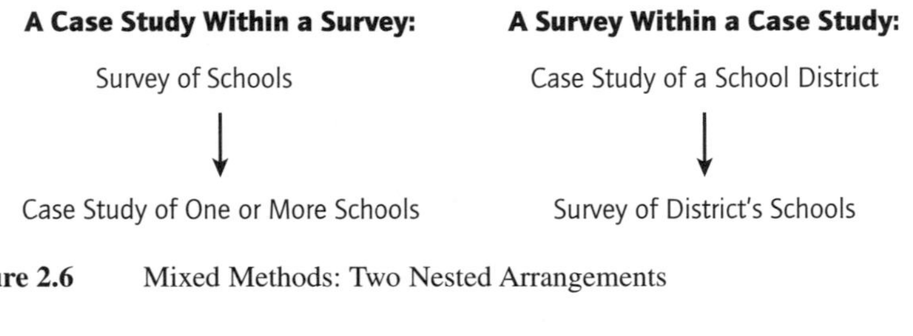

Figure 2.6 Mixed Methods: Two Nested Arrangements

By definition, studies using mixed methods research are more difficult to execute than studies limited to single methods. However, mixed methods research can enable you to address broader or more complicated research questions than case studies alone. As a result, mixing case studies with other methods should be among the possibilities meriting your consideration.

NOTES

1. Figure 2.2 focuses only on the formal research design process, not on data collection activities. For all three types of research (survey, case study, and experiment), data collection techniques might be depicted as the level below Level One in the figure. For example, for case studies, this might include using multiple sources of evidence, as described further in Chapter 4. Similar data collection techniques can be described for surveys or experiments—for example, questionnaire design for surveys or stimulus presentation strategies for experiments.

2. See Gomm, Hammersley, and Foster (2000) for more explanation of *analytic* generalization, though their work uses different labels for the same concept.

3. One of the anonymous reviewers of the third edition of this book pointed out that construct validity also has to do with whether interviewees understand what is being asked of them.

4. For other suggested guidelines for reviewers of case study proposals or manuscripts, see Yin (1999).

5. Strictly quantitative studies that select cases with known outcomes follow the same design and have alternatively been called "case-control," "retrospective," or "case referent" studies (see P. R. Rosenbaum, 2002, p. 7).

REFERENCE TO EXPANDED CASE STUDY MATERIALS FOR CHAPTER 2

For selected case studies cited in the text of this chapter, two anthologies contain either a more extensive excerpt or the full case study. The table on the next page crosswalks the reference in this book to the location of the excerpt or full rendition.

Chapter 2 *Chapter Topic and Page Number*	*Topics of Illustrative Case Studies*	*Reference to Lengthier Material*
General Approach to Designing Case Studies		
BOX 4, p. 2-6	Exploratory study	None
BOX 5A, p. 2-9	Computers and technology	None
BOX 5B, p. 2-9	Business and industry	CSA-6
p. 2-15 text	Five different case studies	ACSR-1
Criteria for Judging the Quality of Research Designs		
BOX 6A, p. 2-23	Cities and towns	CSA-4
BOX 6B, p. 2-23	Urban planning	None
BOX 6C, p. 2-23	Neighborhoods	None
Case Study Designs		
BOX 7, p. 2-27	Schools	CSA-9
BOX 8, p. 2-28	Cities and towns	CSA-3
BOX 9, p. 2-28	Neighborhoods	None
BOX 10, p. 2-29	Business and industry	CSA-10
BOX 11, p. 2-35	Government agencies	None
p. 2-35 text	Health (HIV/AIDS) care	ACSR-8
p. 2-35 text	University administration	ACSR-9
p. 2-35 text	Business and industry	ASCR-10
Modest Advice in Selecting Case Study Designs		
BOX 12A, p. 2-41	Community organizations	None
BOX 12B, p. 2-41	Schools	None

NOTE: CSA = *Case Study Anthology* (Yin, 2004). ACSR = *Applications of Case Study Research* (Yin, 2003). The number denotes the chapter number in the book.

12 Case Study Research

MICHAEL D. MYERS

Objectives

By the end of this chapter, you will be able to:

- Understand the purpose of case study research
- Appreciate the difference between teaching cases and research cases
- Distinguish between different approaches to conducting case study research
- Be more confident in doing case study research
- Identify the advantages and disadvantages of case study research
- Evaluate case study research
- See how case study research has been used in business and management

INTRODUCTION

In all of the business disciplines, case studies are used in many different ways. The two most popular uses of case studies in business schools are, first, in teaching, and, second, in research.

In teaching, case studies are tremendously helpful to students in allowing them to understand better the theory and principles that are relevant to business. Case studies illustrate a principle or a particular point that the instructor wishes to make. They show that the theory has a practical application and bring the subject matter to life. Probably the most famous case studies of this type – in business schools at least – are the Harvard cases published by the Harvard Business School. These cases describe actual situations that the instructor and students explore together. The idea is for the students to figure out by themselves the 'correct' answer or answers to the discussion

Table 7.1 A comparison of teaching and research cases

Teaching cases	Research cases
Written primarily for students	Written primarily for researchers
Designed to illustrate an existing theory or principle	Designed to contribute to a new theory or explore/test an existing theory
Published on its own as a teaching case, often with notes for the instructor	Published as part of a research article in a journal, conference, or book

questions. As students study more cases, hopefully they get better at identifying current business problems and solutions, and how such solutions might be implemented.

Teaching case studies are thus written for students of business. They are designed to illustrate a more general point or a theory that is already well known to most, if not all, instructors in the subject. The purpose of teaching cases is to help students learn. The cases themselves may be based on real life or they may be fictional.

By contrast, research case studies are written primarily for researchers, not students. Research cases are used as empirical evidence to convince other researchers of the applicability (or inapplicability) of a particular theory or proposition. If the case is first published as part of a research article, the particular point that the research article makes is likely to be new to those reviewing the paper (i.e. other experts in the same field). The purpose of research cases is thus to contribute to knowledge in a particular field. Teaching and research cases are compared in Table 7.1.

This chapter is concerned with the use of case studies in research, but does not deal with the use of case studies in teaching. Although the writing of teaching cases for business students is a very worthwhile activity and one that I fully support, the preparation and writing of case studies for teaching purposes is outside the scope of this book. Instead, this book focuses on the use of case studies for research in business, hence the name of this chapter.

Writing a research case requires different skills and knowledge than when writing a teaching case. To write a teaching case, an author needs to be familiar with the subject matter of the course being taught: for example, the textbook and readings that are used in that course. The author also needs to gain access to or to create an interesting scenario that illustrates the point to be made. However, the theory or the guidelines that the case is designed to illustrate may or may not be explicitly mentioned in the write-up of the case itself. As a general rule, the write-up will include few, if any, citations of the relevant research literature. This is because the very idea of a teaching case is often for students to 'discover' the applicable theory or principles for themselves. One of the key things about creating teaching cases is that the case needs to be written in an engaging manner such that students are inspired and encouraged to learn.

To write a research case, the author needs to have a much higher and more detailed knowledge of the subject matter. The author needs to be familiar with, and cite, the latest research on the particular topic in question. The author also needs to write up a case that directly relates to that research topic. The case needs to be written in such a way that the story is plausible and convinces other researchers that the research article is indeed a new contribution to knowledge in the field. The case also needs to be written in an engaging manner, such that fellow researchers will find the story interesting.

THEORY BUILDING FROM CASE STUDIES IN MANAGEMENT

Following the logic of inductive case study methods, Dutta, Zbaracki, and Bergen (2003) analysed the data collected from a study of the pricing process of a large manufacturing firm in an iterative manner: first, they analysed the data and compared the data with existing theory; second, they developed a new theory; third, they returned to the data to see how the emergent theory matched the data; lastly, they returned to the theory for yet another revision (Dutta et al., 2003).

Research case studies can be used in the exploratory phase of a research topic, to discover the relevant features, factors, or issues that might apply in other similar situations. In this way, case studies are used in the early stages of research on a particular topic. Research cases can also be used in explanatory research, when there is already a large body of literature on the subject. In this way, case studies can be used to test theory, to develop causal explanations, or even to compare theories. It is mistake to suggest, as some do, that research cases can only be used in an exploratory way.

RESEARCH CASES CAN BE USED:

- In exploratory research – to discover.
- In explanatory research – to test, to explain, or to compare.

Case study research is thus applicable at any stage of the research on a particular topic. The key defining feature of case study research is not *when* in the research process it should be used, but *what* is studied. The 'what' are contemporary real-life situations where there is no control on the part of the researcher and where everything might happen all at once. Real life is sometimes messy, but then business theories that are unable to deal with messy real-life situations are probably of little value.

In a business discipline, case study research uses empirical evidence from real people in contemporary real-life organizations. The specific topics vary widely, from current marketing practices in marketing through to the implementation of enterprise resource planning (ERP) systems in the field of information systems. But a defining feature of case study research is its focus on asking 'how' and 'why' questions. The case study researcher seeks to understand how and why a particular business decision was made, or how and why a business process works the way it does. Unlike action research, the case study researcher does not deliberately intervene in a situation but seeks, at least in the first instance, simply to describe it. And as was mentioned earlier, as distinct from teaching cases, the primary audience for the case study write-up is fellow researchers in a particular discipline, not students. The case study write-up has to convince these fellow researchers that the case study is an original contribution to knowledge. These fellow researchers might be the examiners of your Masters or PhD thesis, or reviewers from a peer-reviewed research conference or journal.

The purpose of case study research in business and management is to use empirical evidence from real people in real organizations to make an original contribution to knowledge.

A CLASSIC THEORY-TESTING CASE STUDY

One of the most cited articles in the field of information systems is a theory-testing case study written by Markus (1983). Markus compared three theories of resistance with the implementation of computer-based information systems (IS), using an in-depth case study to test the predictions of each theory.

The first theory of IS implementation is what she calls a 'people-determined' theory. This theory assumes that people resist IS because of factors internal to the person or group. An example of this is when it is said that 'people resist change'.

(Cont'd)

The second theory of IS implementation is what she calls a 'system-determined' theory. This theory assumes that people resist IS because of factors inherent in the system itself. In this second theory, resistance is determined externally by the environment or the technology.

The first theory thus suggests that 'people' are the primary cases of resistance, whereas the second theory suggests that 'systems' or the technology are the primary cases of resistance.

Markus suggested a third theory – a theory of interaction. The third theory holds that people resist IS because of an interaction between characteristics related to the people and characteristics related to the system.

Using empirical data from a case study of the implementation of a financial information system, Markus showed that the interaction theory has superior explanatory and predictive power (Markus, 1983).

Defining Case Study Research

The word 'case study' has multiple meanings. The simplest idea of 'a case' is that the phenomenon described is of a more general category. That is, the description of a particular case or situation is used to draw some conclusions about the phenomenon more generally. For example, a medical journal might describe the case of an asthma patient who showed certain symptoms after taking a particular medication. The particular case might be new and unique, but the case is still an example of a more general phenomenon (e.g. asthma).

A somewhat narrower definition of a case study, one that is more applicable for the social sciences, is that it is a detailed study of a single social unit: 'The social unit is usually located in one physical place, the people making up the unit being differentiated from others who are not part of it. In short, the unit has clear boundaries which make it easy to identify' (Payne & Payne, 2004: 31). A case study can be of a social process, an organization, or any collective social unit.

Along similar lines, Yin (2003) defines a case study in two parts, as follows:

1 A case study is an empirical inquiry that

- Investigates a contemporary phenomenon within its real-life context, especially when
- The boundaries between phenomenon and context are not clearly evident

2 The case study inquiry

- Copes with the technically distinctive situation in which there will be many more variables of interest than data points, and as one result
- Relies on multiple sources of evidence, with data needing to converge in a triangulating fashion, and as another result
- Benefits from the prior development of theoretical propositions to guide data collection and analysis. (pp. 13–14)

The first part of Yin's definition specifies the scope of a case study. The real-life context of a case means that the phenomenon of interest is not studied divorced from its context. In case study research, it is in fact very difficult to separate the phenomenon of interest from the context, because the context itself is part and parcel of the story. Also, in a case study the researcher has no control over the situation. This contrasts with the use of some other research methods such as a laboratory experiment, where the whole idea is for the researcher to maintain control of certain specified variables and to separate clearly the context from the phenomenon.

The second part of Yin's definition specifies the data collection and data analysis strategies. Yin advocates using multiple sources of evidence, triangulating these data, and using theoretical propositions from the research literature to guide the research.

Although Yin's definition of a case study is very helpful – and I thoroughly recommend his book as one of the best books available on case study research – the definition does not necessarily fit all case studies within the business disciplines. In one respect it is too broad, in another it is too narrow.

Yin's definition is too broad in the sense that case studies in business are usually restricted to studies of one or more business organizations. A 'case study' in business is almost always synonymous with a study of some business aspect of an organization. This organizational focus is an important identifying feature of most case studies in the business disciplines, and distinguishes case study research in business from case study research in other fields. In other fields, there can be case studies of educational programmes, or case studies of communities in a local neighbourhood. But as these are not studies of a business-related issue in an organization, they would not qualify as being called case study research in business.

Yin's definition is too narrow in the sense that he advocates just one type of case study research. This is perhaps best described as a positivist approach to case study research. Like most positivist researchers, Yin recommends the prior development of theoretical propositions or hypotheses. He also suggests that the quality of case study research designs can be judged by paying attention to four design tests, namely, construct validity, internal validity, external validity, and reliability. However, there are other types of case studies such as interpretive and critical case study research that do not require or recommend the use of propositions or hypotheses in research. Also, these other types of case study research do not use the words 'validity' or 'reliability' as part of their quality assessment.

> The aim of Buxey's (2005) research project was to document how the Australian textiles, clothing, and footwear industry has responded to the forces of globalization. Given the high level of competition within the industry, the objective of the study was to discover what strategies the survivors employed.
>
> Buxey conducted three representative cases of firms in the industry. He describes the strategy that each firm employed in responding to the forces of globalization (Buxey, 2005).

Hence, while Yin's (2003) book can be regarded as one of the most useful books on case study research – and it is widely cited by researchers in most business disciplines – his definition of case study research is not entirely appropriate for all qualitative researchers in business. Therefore I propose my own definition of case study research as follows:

> Case study research in business uses empirical evidence from one or more organizations where an attempt is made to study the subject matter in context. Multiple sources of evidence are used, although most of the evidence comes from interviews and documents.

There are three important points to note about this definition:

1. **This definition draws attention to the fact that case study research in business *almost always involves a firm or organization*, even if the main issue, topic, or subject matter being studied is something else. For example, a case study of a joint venture might focus primarily on the joint venture – its governance, its financial or marketing success – but the researcher would still use empirical evidence from one or more of the organizations concerned; a case study in information systems might focus on an information systems development project, but the project will be situated within one or more organizations; or a case study in marketing might focus primarily on the development of brands, but these brands would still involve one or more firms. The most common**

research cases in business, therefore, have an explicit organizational focus and tell the story of that organization.

2 This definition also distinguishes case study research from ethnographic research. Case study research, even in-depth case study research, *does not normally involve participant observation or fieldwork.* Most of the empirical evidence in case study research in business comes from interviews and documents. Ethnographic research, on the other hand, relies extensively on data from fieldwork. Fieldwork is the defining feature of ethnography.

3 Lastly, this definition of case study research is philosophically neutral. That is, it allows for the fact that *case study research can be conducted according to positivist, interpretive, or critical tenets* of what is considered to be 'good' research. These different types of case study research are discussed next.

APPROACHES TO CASE STUDY RESEARCH

Just like action research, case study research can take positivist, interpretive, or critical forms. These three types correspond to the three main philosophical approaches to research discussed in Chapter 3.

Positivist case study research was the norm in business schools some 10 or 15 years ago. However, interpretive case studies have become more accepted over the past decade and now appear on a reasonably regular basis in the top journals and conferences of most business disciplines. There are still very few critical case studies, but I predict that these will increase over the next decade.

The first type of case study research, positivist case study research, attempts to meet the requirements of positivist social science. Work of this kind is often justified in positivistic terms – case study research is seen as a method for testing and refining hypotheses or propositions in the real world. An example of this approach is Yin (2003), who discusses the importance of propositions and emphasizes construct validity, internal validity, external validity, and reliability. The concern with 'validity' and 'reliability' represents an attempt to ensure that the case meets the quality standards expected of a positivistic study. Another example of a positivistic approach to case study research is Benbasat, Goldstein, and Mead's (1987) approach to case study research in information systems. Essentially, they apply Yin's approach to the field of information systems and advocate case study research along positivistic lines.

The second type of case study research is of an interpretive nature. Interpretive case study research relies on an underlying interpretive and constructivist epistemology, i.e. social reality is socially constructed. Interpretive case studies generally attempt to understand phenomena through the meanings that people assign to them. Unlike positivist case studies, which define quality in terms of validity and reliability, interpretive case studies define quality in terms of the plausibility of the story and the overall argument. An example of an interpretive case study in business is Corley and Gioia's study of organizational identity change in the spin-off of a Fortune 100 company's top-performing organizational unit into an independent organization (Corley & Gioia, 2004). Another example is Walsham and Waema's study of information systems strategy development in a building society in the United Kingdom (Walsham & Waema, 1994). Both case studies focus on the social construction of reality – how and why people see the world the way they do. Both cases are plausible, and the authors do not justify their research in positivistic terms.

The third type of case study research, critical case study research, involves critical reflection on current practices, questions taken-for-granted assumptions, and critiques the status quo based on the theories of one or more critical theorists. An example of a critical case study is Myers' study of the failed implementation of an information system in the health sector. Myers (1994) used the critical hermeneutics of Gadamer and Ricoeur to help explain the findings. Like interpretive case studies, the author does not justify the quality of the research in positivist terms. Words such as 'validity' and 'reliability', which imply an objective reality independent of social reality, are not normally used in interpretive or critical studies.

Some Practical Suggestions

One of the most important things in doing case study research is finding an 'interesting' case in the first place. If your case is boring, then it does not matter how well you do the research, or how meticulous you are in recording your interviews, or how well you write it up; a boring case is really just a waste of everyone's time. So what makes an interesting case?

An interesting case study is one which tells us something new. That is, it tells researchers in a particular field something that they did not know before. For example, if it is an exploratory case, then it provides the vehicle for exploring a new subject area. If it is a theory-testing case, then perhaps it is a critical case which disconfirms existing theory and suggests an alternative. At the very least both you and your supervisors should find the story and the implications of the case interesting.

One of the biggest challenges in doing case study research is to find a company in which you can do the research. Some of my students have found that it can take a good few attempts before permission is obtained.

One way of finding a suitable company is to read the local newspaper or business magazines. If the story in a magazine includes quotations from some of the people in a relevant organization, then you already have one or more contact names. Another way is to explore existing personal or corporate friendships. For example, if you have already worked for a company or have friends or relatives working there, they might be more likely to be receptive to the idea of case study research. In particular I have found that previous graduates of the university are much more likely to be receptive to case study research than complete strangers. I suspect this is because they feel some obligation to the university which educated them, and because they are more open to the idea of research being done on them. Also they may be less threatened by the idea of the researcher finding out some bad news about the organization. In fact, they may well welcome such findings and treat them as an opportunity to learn and improve.

Once you have been given access to an organization, then you need to gather as much evidence as possible that is relevant to your topic. There are various techniques for gathering data (these are discussed in more detail in Part IV); however, the most common technique – and probably the most important – used for gathering data in business is the interview. Interviews are an excellent 'window' into an organization, and can help you to find out what people are thinking. They are particularly useful for finding out people's motivations, and their rationale as to why they did certain things.

Of course, there is a need for those doing interviews to have good people skills. If you are not good at relating to people or empathizing with them, then it is highly unlikely that you will learn much. Not everyone is suited to doing case study research. Although people skills can be taught, it might be easier and less time consuming for some budding researchers to choose another research method altogether, one that does not rely so heavily on people interaction. Case study research is not a soft option, particularly for those who are socially challenged.

It is possible to conduct a case study that is based almost entirely on a few interviews with key people. However, a more in-depth case study will rely on interviews with many people in the organization, and these people will represent diverse perspectives.

Either way, it is extremely important to identify and interview 'key' informants. Key informants are those who know the most about a particular topic in the organization and have decision-making authority for the general area in which you are interested. For example, if you are doing a case study about the marketing strategy of a particular company, then you will definitely want to interview the marketing manager. The marketing manager is the one who is likely to know the most about the whys and wherefores of the company's approach.

A more in-depth case study will use other sources of evidence besides interviews. Written documents can be extremely valuable as they often provide evidence for things which people sometimes have difficulty remembering, e.g. exact dates of a particular event, or the attendee list at a particular meeting, and so forth. Documentary evidence includes items such as annual reports, newspaper clippings, reports, memos, organization charts, and minutes of meetings. In some cases, physical artefacts such as devices, tools, or systems might provide additional sources of evidence.

TIPS FOR SUCCESS IN DOING CASE STUDY RESEARCH

- Find an interesting case.
- Make sure you have good people skills.
- Gather rich data and try to establish the context.

CRITIQUE OF CASE STUDY RESEARCH

Advantages and Disadvantages of Case Study Research

Case study research is the most popular qualitative research method used in the business disciplines. It is popular because one of the main advantages of case study research is what I would call its 'face validity'. By 'face validity', I mean that a well-written case study based on empirical research in an organization represents a real story that most researchers can identify with. This is especially the case with well-known organizations, where everyone is already familiar with the company or its products. Most cases are also contemporary stories, which means that the case documents one or more firms' attempt to deal with issues of current importance to other firms, many of which are likely to be in the same boat.

Another advantage of case study research is that it allows researchers to explore or test theories within the context of messy real-life situations. These situations are never as neat and tidy as our theories. For example, there may be multiple, equally valid interpretations of the same situation, or a chief executive officer (CEO) may have many reasons for doing a particular action, some personal, some professional, and some based on rational business principles (this is not to say that personal reasons are not rational reasons). These kinds of complexities can only be brought out in a research method that allows a researcher to get 'close to the action', as the case study research method does.

IMPLEMENTING ACTIVITY-BASED COSTING: A CASE STUDY IN MANAGEMENT ACCOUNTING

Consultants, business schools, and the business media have promoted activity-based accounting (ABC), claiming that it gives more accurate product costs and helps managers understand cost causation. However, there have been few empirical studies of the implementation of ABC. Doubts about the benefits and impact of ABC remain.

Therefore Major and Hopper (2005) decided to conduct an in-depth, interpretive case study of Marconi, a Portuguese telecommunications company, investigating ABC implementation and usage. They decided they wanted to identify and explore issues from the perspective of the actors involved, cast light on previous findings, and aid theory development. Like most case study research, they focused on exploring 'how' and 'why' research questions.

The data were obtained mostly from interviews and documents. Semi-structured interviews were conducted with managers and employees of Marconi, its parent company, the consultants that implemented ABC, the Portuguese telecommunications regulator, and managers from other telecommunication companies in Portugal. Their aim was to gain a rich description of Marconi's ABC system, its implementation, and managers' usage and evaluation of ABC.

Their research case makes three important contributions to the management accounting literature on ABC implementation:

1. Technical issues arose, in that there were technical problems associated with joint and common costs. These are significant in telecommunications. The ABC system did not meet the stringent conditions for providing valid data.
2. Implementing ABC in firms beset by conflict is difficult. As it turned out, only parts of the company used ABC. The production engineers resisted using ABC. They saw ABC as threatening their autonomy, threatening their employment prospects, and increasing their work load. Generally, they regarded it as a confusing and meaningless exercise.
3. Outside production the ABC implementation was judged a 'success' (in terms of evaluations and usage). This was associated with top management support, adequate resources, clear goals, and employee commitment. The implementer tried to give employees ownership of the project (Major & Hopper, 2005).

One of the main disadvantages of doing case study research, particularly in business settings, is that it can be difficult to gain access to the particular company or group of companies that you want to study. This is because firms may be sceptical of the value of the research for themselves. In fact they may worry that not only will the researcher take up too much of their valuable time in interviews, but also that the findings may be unflattering and lead to some unwelcome publicity. The last thing a company wants is bad PR. For these reasons it can sometimes take you months to find a suitable company and one that gives you the required permissions.

Another disadvantage of case study research is that the researcher has no control over the situation. In practice, this means that if the company you are studying is suddenly taken over by another company halfway through your study, there is very little that you can do about it. Alternatively, if your key sponsor (e.g. the chief operating officer) resigns just as you are starting to conduct your interviews, you may find that you have too few friends within the firm to continue your research.

Yet another disadvantage of case study research is that it can be difficult, particularly for younger, inexperienced researchers, to focus on the most important issues. As the context of the study can be as large or as small as you want, a real danger is that an inexperienced researcher will think everything is relevant. Therefore such a person ends up with a huge amount of data, most of which turns out to be irrelevant in the final analysis.

The last disadvantage of case study research is that it takes a long time, even for experienced researchers. It takes time to gain access, it takes time to do the empirical research, and it takes even more time to do the write-up. From start to finish, case study research is time consuming

If we put all these disadvantages together, it means that only those who are enthusiastic and committed, and only those who have the required people skills, should consider doing case study research. It is a serious mistake to think that case study research is an easy or a soft option. It is not easy at all.

However, for those who are keen, case study research can be very rewarding. It gives you the opportunity to find out at first hand whether or not your concepts or theories have any value in the business world.

How to Evaluate Case Study Research

Like all qualitative research methods, it is important that case study research should be evaluated in an appropriate way. In other words, it is important to evaluate case study research according to its fundamental tenets, and not by the assumptions or tenets of some other method. It would be inappropriate to evaluate case study research by criteria used in evaluating survey research, just as it would be inappropriate to evaluate survey research by criteria used in evaluating a case study.

Keeping this comment in mind, it is important to note that conducting just one case study is fine. Many budding qualitative researchers make the mistake of thinking that one case study is not enough. They think that if only they had three or more cases, then this would increase the 'validity' of the findings.

However, this way of thinking confuses things. Researchers who think this way are making the common mistake, of using sampling logic to judge the validity of the case method. But case study research does not use sampling logic. Sampling logic is based on statistics. Sampling logic and statistical theory are what are used when you conduct a survey.

In a survey, the larger your sample size, the better. The larger the sample, the more sure you can be that the results truly reflect the population as a whole. Most statistical concepts such as significance tests and confidence intervals assume you have a truly random sample.

But in case study research, statistical concepts such as confidence levels and confidence intervals are meaningless. Using three or four cases is no better than using one case when it comes to increasing the confidence in your findings. First of all, the sample size is still far too small; second, you do not have a truly random sample in the first place. A case study is not one instance of a much larger random sample!

Instead of using sampling logic to justify case study research, which generalizes from a sample to a population, it is much better to generalize one or more cases to theory, as Yin (2003) points out. Just as it is possible to generalize from a single experiment, so it is possible to generalize from a single case (Lee, 1989; Yin, 2003).

So what makes an exemplary case study? The following criteria are offered as general guidelines for evaluating a research case in business:

1 **The case study must be 'interesting'.**
2 **The case study must display sufficient evidence.**
3 **The case study should be 'complete'.**
4 **The case study must consider alternative perspectives.**
5 **The case study should be written in an engaging manner.**
6 **The case study should contribute to knowledge.**

First of all, the case study must be 'interesting'. As was mentioned earlier, this means that the case study should tell the researchers in a particular field something new that they did not know before. At the very least both you and your supervisors should find the story of the case interesting.

Second, the case study must display sufficient evidence. If you are writing a research article for a journal, this means that it is usually a good idea to include some supporting quotations from those who were interviewed. Quotes that are verbatim bring the case to life. The general idea is that you need to include sufficient evidence such that your argument makes sense and is plausible.

Third, the case study should be 'complete'. By complete, I do not mean that everything that it is possible to say about the case has been said. Rather,

I mean that all the relevant evidence to prove or disprove a particular theoretical point has been collected.

Fourth, the case study must consider alternative perspectives. This may mean considering different theories, alternative cultural views, or disagreements among the subjects. The key point here is that cases that document real-life situations should reflect real life. Since real life is never neat and tidy, the story that is presented in your case study should not be so neat and tidy either. A 'perfect story' where there is a hero or heroine and everyone lives happily ever after is a fairy story, not a research case. Hence it may be advisable to include evidence which does not necessarily support your own theory.

Fifth, the case study should be written in an engaging manner. The key test here is whether you are enthusiastic about it. If you are not captivated by the story, then it is almost guaranteed that others will not be enthusiastic either. The write-up requires some creative energy.

Sixth, the case study should contribute to knowledge. This is fairly similar to the first criterion, except that it emphasizes the contribution to scientific knowledge rather than the case's intrinsic interest value. As a general rule, this means that a research case will be generalized to one or more theories or concepts.

These six criteria for evaluating a research case apply to all kinds of case study research. However, it is also possible to add additional quality criteria for evaluating case study research depending upon the type of such research that is conducted. These quality criteria will vary depending upon whether this research is positivist, interpretive, or critical.

For positivist research, good case study design is vital (Dubé & Paré, 2003; Yin, 2003). Yin (2003) suggests five components of good case study design:

1 **A study's questions.**
2 **Its propositions, if any.**
3 **Its unit(s) of analysis.**
4 **The logic linking the data to the propositions.**
5 **The criteria for interpreting the findings.**

For interpretive research, the plausibility of the case is far more important than its design. That is, fellow researchers in a particular field will need some confidence in the case, and its story should be believable. The plausibility of a case is improved by many things, such as using multiple sources of evidence, and having a clear description of what you did and how.

Klein and Myers (1999) suggest seven principles for evaluating interpretive case studies (although these principles also apply to interpretive ethnographies):

1 **The Fundamental Principle of the Hermeneutic Circle**
2 **The Principle of Contextualization**
3 **The Principle of Interaction between the Researchers and Subjects**
4 **The Principle of Abstraction and Generalization**
5 **The Principle of Dialogical Reasoning**
6 **The Principle of Multiple Interpretations**
7 **The Principle of Suspicion.**

These seven principles are summarized in Figure 7.1. They apply to interpretive work that is of a hermeneutic nature, but other criteria or principles might be more applicable to interpretive work that takes a different approach.

For critical research, the case should question taken-for-granted assumptions, and open to scrutiny possible hidden agendas, power centres, and assumptions that inhibit, repress, and constrain (cf. Thomas, 1993). Most critical case studies will use one or more critical theories such as from Habermas or Foucault.

EXAMPLES OF CASE STUDY RESEARCH

Open-Book Accounting in Networks: A Case Study in Management Accounting

Many manufacturing companies have developed close cooperative relationships with their key suppliers and buyers in recent years. This has led to the emergence of manufacturing networks, where there is a more comprehensive sharing of information among supply chain members.

In their research, Kajuter and Kulmala (2005) looked at the issue of manufacturing networks providing a platform for inter-organizational cost management. Compared with traditional cost management in single companies, they say that additional opportunities for cost reduction arise through collaborative efforts of network members. However, in order to reveal such opportunities, transparency of cost structures is essential. Open-book accounting can play a key role in inter-organizational cost management.

The authors, using an interpretive type of case study research, investigated the reasons why open-book accounting is successful in some cases and often fails in others. They examined the main obstacles hindering firms from exchanging cost data in networks.

This interpretive study consisted of two parts. First, a single case study of a German car manufacturing network – the Eurocar case – was conducted. Second, a multi-site case study of three Finnish manufacturing networks was

1 **The Fundamental Principle of the Hermeneutic Circle**

Suggests that all human understanding is achieved by iterating between considering the interdependent meaning of parts and the whole that they form. This principle of human understanding is fundamental to all the other principles.
Example: Lee's (1994) study of information richness in email communications. It iterates between the separate message fragments of individual email participants as parts and the global context which determines the full meanings of the separate messages to interpret the message exchange as a whole.

2 **The Principle of Contextualization**

Requires critical reflection on the social and historical background of the research setting, so that the intended audience can see how the current situation under investigation emerged.
Example: After discussing the historical forces which led to Fiat establishing a new assembly plant, Ciborra, Patriotta, and Erlicher (1996) show how old Fordist production concepts still had a significant influence despite radical changes in work organization and operations.

3 **The Principle of Interaction Between the Researchers and the Subjects**

Requires critical reflection on how the research materials (or "data") were socially constructed through the interaction between the researchers and participants.
Example: Trauth (1997) explains how her understanding improved as she became self-conscious and started to question her own assumptions.

4 **The Principle of Abstraction and Generalization**

Requires relating the idiographic details revealed by the data interpretation through the application of Principles 1 and 2 to theoretical, general concepts that describe the nature of human understanding and social action.
Example: Monteiro and Hanseth's (1996) findings are discussed in relation to Latour's actor–network theory.

5 **The Principle of Dialogical Reasoning**

Requires sensitivity to possible contradictions between the theoretical preconceptions guiding the research design and actual findings ("the story which the data tell") with subsequent cycles of revision.
Example: Lee (1991) describes how Nardulli (1978) came several times to revise his preconceptions of the role of case load pressure as a central concept in the study of criminal courts.

6 **The Principle of Multiple Interpretations**

Requires sensitivity to possible differences in interpretations among the participants as are typically expressed in multiple narratives or stories of the same sequence of events under study. Similar to multiple witness accounts even if all tell it as they saw it.
Example: Levine and Rossmore's (1993) account of the conflicting expectations for the Threshold system in the Bremerton Inc. case.

7 **The Principle of Suspicion**

Requires sensitivity to possible 'biases' and systematic 'distortions' in the narratives collected from the participants.
Example: Forester (1992) looks at the facetious figures of speech used by city planning staff to negotiate the problem of data acquisition.

Figure 7.1 The seven principles of interpretive research as suggested by Klein and Myers (1999) conducted. In these studies the contextual factors influencing the implementation, utilization, and outcome of open-book accounting in networks were analysed.

Most of the data were obtained by conducting 61 semi-structured interviews with key personnel. At Eurocar and at the Finnish main contractors, manager-level personnel responsible for product development, purchasing, production, and accounting were interviewed. In the Finnish networks, at least one person from each supplier's top management, either the managing director or the entrepreneur, was interviewed. These people were assumed to have a good overview of their entire company and its relationships to network partners.

The interviews included mainly open questions. Due to the confidential nature of some of the issues discussed, the interviews were not recorded on tape. Non-recording was expected to encourage the respondents to answer as freely and openly as possible. The interviews took from 1.5 to 3 hours each.

All firms were visited at least once in order to gain an understanding of the operations and business environment. In addition, content analysis was used for both official and internal documents.

The authors' analysis was based upon the contingency theory of management accounting. As this theory suggests, many, or even most, of the changes and improvements in management accounting can be explained through contingencies in the external environment and internal structure, strategy, and culture of companies.

On the basis of a contingency model, the authors found that open-book accounting is most likely to work in long-term hierarchical networks that manufacture functional products, provide a sound infrastructure for open-book practice, and comprise trust-based network relationships (Kajuter & Kulmala, 2005).

Mergers and Acquisitions: Multiple Interpretive Cases Telling the Seller's Side of the Story

Graebner and Eisenhardt (2004) say that most of the research literature in the area of corporate governance in management has taken the buyer's perspective. Most acquisition studies have focused on the acquirer as the decision maker of importance and have ignored the seller.

Therefore, the authors chose to explore acquisition from the seller's perspective. Specifically, they wanted to know when and to whom company leaders sell their firms. Given that this research was exploratory, they decided to conduct 12 case studies of entrepreneurial firms. They chose entrepreneurial firms because they say these firms 'are a primary engine of growth' whose acquisition has emerged as central to the corporate strategy of many corporations.

The research design they chose to use was a multiple case, inductive study involving 12 entrepreneurial firms in the United States. Four firms (three acquired, one not acquired) were chosen in each of three industries: networking hardware, infrastructure software, and online commerce. These industries have significant entrepreneurial activity and yet differ along key dimensions such as cost structure, sales and distribution channels, and customer characteristics. The time period was 1999–2000.

Most of the data were obtained from semi-structured interviews with key acquisition decision makers from both sellers and buyers. The authors also used emails and phone calls to follow up interviews and track real-time acquisition processes, and used archival data, including company websites, business publications, and materials provided by informants. Lastly, the authors used quantitative data on financing rounds. This study illustrates that interpretive case study research can use quantitative as well as qualitative data.

More than 80 interviews were conducted over 14 months. The interviews were 60–90 minutes long. All interviews were tape recorded and transcribed.

The first phase included 15 pilot interviews with managers who had sold their companies, managers who had purchased companies, investors in companies that were sold, and acquisition intermediaries. The pilot interviews indicated that the selling firm's acquisition decisions are usually made by a very small set of people, typically the CEO and two or three key executives and/or board members. Other individuals at the selling firm will have limited, if any, awareness of the events taking place. This pattern reflects the sensitive nature of acquisition decisions and is consistent with prior evidence that awareness of a firm's strategy declines rapidly below the top management team.

In the second phase, multiple senior-level informants in the selling and buying firms were interviewed. The pilot interviews provided guidance in identifying the most influential informants in the acquisition process. To ensure further that the sample included the most important individuals, 'snowball sampling' was used. The initial entry was made through either the CEO of the selling firm or the head of business development at the buying firm, if applicable. This contact then identified other individuals who had been actively involved in the acquisition with both the buyer and seller. These individuals then identified others, as appropriate.

As is typical in inductive research, the data were analysed by first building individual case studies synthesizing the interview transcripts and archival data. A central aspect of case writing was 'triangulation' between each interview and archival sources to create a richer, more reliable account.

The case histories were used for two analyses: within-case and cross-case. The within-case analysis focused on developing constructs and relationships to describe the process experienced by a single focal firm. A core aspect of the inductive process was that it allowed constructs to emerge from the data during this process, rather than being guided by specific hypotheses.

Cross-case analysis began after all cases were finished. Using standard cross-case analysis techniques, similar constructs and relationships across multiple cases were looked for. Tentative propositions were developed by grouping the firms according to the potential variables of interest. Case pairs were compared to identify similarities and differences. Emerging relationships were refined through replication logic, revisiting the data often to see if each separate case demonstrated the same pattern, using charts and tables to facilitate comparisons. The analysis process was iterative and lasted six months. From this process a framework emerged describing when acquisitions occur from the seller's perspective.

The key contribution of this study was to propose an emergent framework of when acquisition occurs from the seller's perspective. The authors framed acquisition as a courtship, emphasizing that acquisition is a process of mutual agreement between buyer and seller, and encompasses timing and strategic and emotional factors, not just price (Graebner & Eisenhardt, 2004).

Responding to Schedule Changes in Supply Chains: Multiple Case Studies in Operations Management

A supply chain is a network of plants and logistical resources producing the materials, components, assemblies, and final product for various customers. With the trend of mass customization and personalization, more and more products – from personal computers and customized bicycles to automobiles – are being made through build-to-order (BTO) supply chains. Krajewski, Wei, and Tang (2005) say that, unlike a typical assembly-to-order environment where customers can only choose from a small set of pre-configured end products, a BTO supply chain allows each customer to configure a final product from a personalized subset of components.

In this study, the authors focused on the short-term dynamics in BTO supply chains brought on by changes in the replenishment shipping schedules of members in the chain. They explored the reaction strategies that suppliers use to respond to short-term dynamics in BTO supply chains, and also looked at the power relations between a buyer and supplier.

The authors studied five firms in the microcomputer industry involved in the production of notebook computers and their components in Taiwan. The microcomputer industry was selected because of the prevalent use of BTO supply chains and because short-term dynamics in this industry create a challenging environment.

As can be seen, the authors decided to use multiple cases to address the research question. In this multiple case study design, the cases were treated as a series of experiments that confirm or disconfirm the emerging conceptual insights. Data were obtained primarily via structured interviews.

With regard to their data analysis, the authors first of all conducted within-case analysis, where members of the research team discussed the elements of reaction strategies and the short-term process flexibility and supplier power relationships. Then a cross-case analysis was conducted to denote the differences and similarities between the cases. The cross-case analysis provided the basis for developing the study's propositions.

In their research article, the authors describe the various reaction strategies of the various firms in the BTO supply chain and make some recommendations for best practice. In summary, the study shows that high short-term process flexibility can be used to competitive advantage by offering flexible supply contracts and supporting that linkage with frequent schedule revisions, even though finished goods inventories must be maintained (Krajewski et al., 2005).

EXERCISES

1. Look in the business pages of your local newspaper and find an interesting story about a new company, product, or service. Try to find other related articles in the paper and obtain as much publicly available information related to your story as you can (e.g. the latest annual report of the company). Are there one or more theories that you think might be relevant to the story? Write up a mini-case that attempts to explain your data in the light of your chosen theory.
2. Conduct a brief literature search using Google Scholar or some other bibliographic database and see if you can find some case study research articles in your chosen field. What kinds of topics appear?
3. Now narrow your search to one of the top journals in your field that has a reputation for publishing qualitative research (e.g. *Academy of Management Review*, *Accounting, Organizations and Society*, *Journal of Consumer Research*, *MIS Quarterly*, etc.). How many articles using case study research can you find over the past 2–3 years?
4. Evaluate some of the articles you found earlier. Do the articles adopt a positivist, interpretive, or critical approach?
5. Evaluate some of these same articles. Did the authors rely mostly on data from interviews? Did the authors use data from the use of other data-gathering techniques? What approach to data analysis did they use?

6 Brainstorm to come up with a list of three or four possible practical research topics. How could these topics be studied using case study research?

7 Find one or more faculty members at your institution or at a conference who conducts case study research. Ask them what topics they are working on right now, and why.

Further Reading

Articles

An article by Walsham (1995) discusses how interpretive case studies can be evaluated. The article by Klein and Myers (1999), as mentioned earlier, suggests a set of principles by which interpretive field studies (both case studies and ethnographies) can be evaluated.

Books

One of the best books on case study research is the classic book entitled *Case Study Research: Design and Methods* by Yin (2003). This book provides an excellent introduction to the case study research method. However, you should keep in mind that Yin, by and large, adopts a positivistic approach to case study research.

Another book by Yin entitled *Applications of Case Study Research* provides a companion to the first (Yin, 2002). This book discusses numerous completed case studies on a variety of topics and includes examples using specific case study techniques and principles.

Websites on the Internet

- The Qualitative Report includes a few useful articles on case study research. This resource is freely available at http://www.nova.edu/ssss/QR/index.html
- More references are available at www qual.auckland.ac.nz

13 Implementing and Sustaining Empowerment: Lessons Learned from Comparison of a For-Profit and a Non-Profit Organization

SETH SILVER, W. ALAN RANDOLPH and SCOTT SEIBERT

This article explores the experiences of two organizations, one nonprofit and the other for-profit, seeking to create a culture of empowerment. Both organizations make a strong start and achieve significant change that is reflected in qualitative observations, quantitative measures of empowerment, and organizational performance results. The for-profit organization manages to sustain ongoing change in the direction of greater empowerment; however, the nonprofit loses focus and eventually drops the change effort. The article compares the two cases paying particular attention to contextual factors to better understand what may have lead to the different outcomes and then closes with ten lessons for sustaining empowerment efforts.

Keywords: *empowerment implementation; case study; comparison of for-profit to nonprofit; best practices*

In 1999, two very different organizations began a formal process of organizational change focused on helping their employees become more "empowered." Both embarked on this journey because of a desire to increase productivity and quality, and to enhance employee motivation and retention. Throughout the next 3 years, both made significant progress despite numerous challenges in their respective environments, including the pressures exerted by the events of September 11, 2001. However, by 2002, one organization had successfully sustained its culture change and was continuing to experience positive business results, whereas the other had lost focus and all but given up on even sustaining the improvements it had once experienced. Given the fact that both organizations held similar goals and pursued similar organizational change strategies, why did one succeed and the other fail? What roles do context and the nature of the work environment play when managers try to create and maintain an empowered workplace? What can be learned from these two organizations' experiences that might help other managers and consultants in their efforts to foster employee empowerment?

THE INTERVENTION MODEL

The intervention in these two consulting cases was built on the concept of organizational empowerment. Well-known management authors such as Block (1987), Byham (1988), and Blanchard, Carlos, and Randolph (2001) have popularized the idea of empowerment as a compelling leadership strategy that involves sharing control with employees to allow decisions to be made and actions to be taken at the lowest level in the organization that is appropriate. Randolph (1995) and Blanchard et al. (2001) identified three key management practices associated with empowerment. *Information sharing* refers to the managerial practice of giving employees information about such important issues as competitor activities, firm financial performance, problems and emerging opportunities, and new business plans. The premise is that providing people with more complete information allows them to better appreciate how their activities contribute to the attainment of organizational goals. It also communicates trust and a sense of ownership that should lead to more responsible goal-directed action. *Developing clear boundaries* refers to an unambiguous shared understanding of work unit goals, policies, processes, and operational values among employees. The purpose of clear boundaries is somewhat paradoxically—it is not to place limits on employees but to better enable employees to take autonomous action. Because employees know and understand the goals and procedures of their work unit and the parameters within which they may take autonomous action, they will, in fact, come to rely less on their manager for direction and more on their own initiative. It is also necessary to provide extensive training opportunities to ensure that employees have the right skills to do such things as manage a project team, set and follow a budget, or run information and decision making meetings. Finally, the *use self-managed teams* refers to the extensive use of teams at all levels of the organization to replace the traditional hierarchy. Within the self-managed team, team members take on many of the responsibilities formerly held by supervisors or work-unit managers. For example, the team will work as a unit that sets its own goals, makes its own decisions regarding the allocation of team resources and workload, measures its own results, rewards and disciplines its own members, and even interacts with its own key suppliers and customers. The replacement of the traditional organizational hierarchy with self-managed teams serves to flatten the organization, redistribute power, and move decision making downward to the employees most immediately involved in the work of the organization.

Following a classic survey feedback approach to organizational change, we administered a questionnaire instrument to the employees of both organizations at the beginning of the interventions to motivate the change effort and followed up with at least one subsequent administration to assess progress and provide additional direction. The survey instrument we used was the Empowerment Barometer, a 30-item questionnaire developed by Blanchard, Carlos, and Randolph (1995) that is specifically designed to measure these three dimensions of organizational empowerment outlined above. Aggregated to the organizational level, the Empowerment Barometer can be thought of as a measure of organizational climate. *Organizational climate* has been defined as a set of shared employee perceptions regarding the policies, practices, and procedures of an organization (Schneider & Reichers, 1983). Recent research has shown the Empowerment Barometer to be a reliable and valid instrument related to individual attitudes and organizational outcomes (Seibert, Silver, & Randolph, 2004). We also followed up with a set of qualitative interviews of participants within the organizations. These interviews and observations were conducted by students completing their master's thesis with the first author in the area of human resource development (Keefe, 2003; Thompson, 2003).

THE NONPROFIT'S EMPOWERMENT STORY

The nonprofit organization is a 350-person blood collection group that supplies blood and blood products (e.g. platelets, apheresis, etc.) to hospitals and clinics in upstate New York in a geographical territory spanning almost 400 miles from east to west. The key jobs within this organization include the senior management team, collection supervisors who manage small teams of about 15, blood collection technicians who actually work with donors to collect blood, drivers who transport equipment and blood to and from blood drives, account managers who work in the community to recruit donors and sponsoring organizations, and administrative assistants who work in an office capacity, at the region's six district office locations.

When we first starting working with the nonprofit, it was ranked in the bottom quartile of the 39 regions that made up the entire organization. This performance rating was based on "production levels," that is, the number of units of blood collected monthly from donors compared to the general population of the region, as well as Food and Drug Administration (FDA)–mandated quality measures for the collection, processing, and storage of the blood and related blood products. The nonprofit's regional director, we'll call him *Mike*, had a vision of his group improving productivity to become one of the top-five producing regions in the country. His vision also included improving employee morale, which was mediocre at best, and decreasing union organizing efforts. He also wanted to decrease turnover among blood technicians and supervisors, which was disruptively high at about 25% annually. Mike initiated the empowerment strategy in mid-1999. He wanted empowerment to help change the culture so that employees were better at solving their own problems, teams were more cohesive, and people at all levels took more initiative and were more positive in their attitudes. Working with one of the authors, Mike sponsored a day-long senior management team workshop focused on understanding the theory, application, and implementation of empowerment.

Following the 1-day program for the senior team, Mike sponsored a half-day "kick-off" meeting, facilitated by the same consultant-author, with the 40 other managers, supervisors, and account representatives of the region. This meeting was specifically designed to introduce the participants to Randolph's (1995) model of organizational empowerment as outlined above and included three key components: (a) an opportunity for subgroups to define what empowerment would "look like" in their area if implemented well, (b) a chance to discuss how they would address the challenges of getting there, and (c) the opportunity to fill out the Empowerment Barometer.

At a follow-up meeting, each manager and supervisor was asked to set "empowerment goals," which identified key changes in their work processes that would encourage sharing information, establish and communicate boundaries, and clarify how to use teams to make more managerial decisions. Managers and supervisors were also asked to summarize some of the training they had received on empowerment for their direct reports. Finally, in this first phase, the remaining 300 employees of the region were asked to fill out anonymously the Empowerment Barometer to establish a baseline set of measures for the region and its respective job categories and districts.

Throughout the next year and a half, a great deal of effort and attention was focused on creating a culture of empowerment. Mike made a point of visiting each of the five districts quarterly to hold "Town Hall meetings" and roundtables with local managers and employees. These sessions were designed to allow Mike to share his thoughts on empowerment, provide recognition for accomplishments related to empowerment and other priorities, and answer questions and listen to ideas relative to the region or local district. Mike and the other senior managers preferred the word *ownership* when talking with employees, as opposed to *empowerment*, as they thought the "e-word" had fallen out of favor and that *ownership* better captured what they wanted from employees. They encouraged groups to solve problems on their own and come up with workable solutions; they encouraged supervisors to create new recognition strategies and use them more frequently; and they engaged a number of "empowered" committees to make recommendations on region-wide issues, such as donor satisfaction, facilities, blood drives scheduling, and inner-city donor recruitment.

In an effort to keep the process moving forward, Mike asked about "ownership" often, talked about it at communications meetings, and rewarded and sanctioned, in part, based on progress with empowerment. He also followed up and reviewed the empowerment-related goals set by the top 20 managers, and he sponsored a region-wide follow-up survey with the Barometer 1 year after the baseline survey. Based on their team's results, managers were then required to develop detailed action plans to address the weak areas. Mike continued to meet quarterly with the extended management group, sometimes with outside facilitation, to discuss empowerment-related process changes and to get updates from them on progress.

Progress

Without question, the nonprofit organization made progress implementing empowerment during this initial period. From a quantitative perspective, as seen in Table 1, a comparison of Time 1 (Fall 1999) to Time 2 (late 2000) Empowerment Barometer results reveal statistically significant movement toward a more empowered culture. The mean scores for all three scales increased significantly, with the largest gain in the scale of Self-Managed Teams, followed by Sharing Information.

From a qualitative perspective, based on three research interviews (Thompson, 2003), with Mike, the human relations (HR) director, and one of the five district managers who reported to Mike, employees' day-to-day work behavior did change in the ways hoped for from 1999 to 2000. Problems were more often resolved by front-line employees instead of being passed up the hierarchy; communications increased across departments and up from employees to the senior team; people seemed more energized and enthusiastic; employee turnover fell below 18% among blood technicians and supervisors; two unionized areas were decertified, and union-organizing efforts essentially stopped in the remaining areas, reflecting, we believe, higher levels of satisfaction and positive morale among employees. In terms of organizational performance, this region did become one of the top-five blood-producing regions in the country: the numbers of units of blood collected monthly increased by more than 15% on average; and quality compliance improved significantly based on National Headquarters Quality Assurance audits. It appears that sharing strategic and operational information and the development of self-managed teams created a greater sense of enthusiasm and problem ownership among employees. The employees exerted greater effort and worked more creatively to meet or exceed blood-collection targets and worked more carefully and cooperatively to conform to established quality standards. In short, organizational empowerment led to employees working harder, smarter, and more cooperatively. and the positive effects of the new culture were apparent in the performance of the region.

Table 1
Comparison of Barometer Mean Scores on the Three Scales of Organizational Empowerment, 1999, 2000 and 2002 for the Nonprofit Organization

	Time 1 1999 (n = 284)	*Time 2* 2000 (n = 276)	*Time 3* 2002 (n = 227)	F *Value*	p *Value*
Sharing information	3.84^a (1.05)	4.14^b (.82)	4.23^b (.97)	12.64	< .001
Clear boundaries	3.75^a (1.09)	3.97^b (.80)	4.13^b (1.01)	9.50	.001
Self-managed teams	3.50^a (1.18)	3.99^b (.86)	4.03^b (1.00)	22.41	.001

Note: This table reports the results from a repeated measures ANOVA. Values are overall mean scores (and standard deviations) for each scale, aggregated for the six employee groups across the region's five districts.
a, b. Indicate the results of planned comparisons. Means for the same scale with different superscripts are significantly different ($p < .01$), means with the same superscript are not significantly different from each other.

Losing Focus

What happened next, from early 2001 to 2002 is, unfortunately, common for many organizations working with an empowerment strategy. Although progress was made, statistically significant behavioral results were recorded, and production and quality levels were up, the nonprofit began to decrease its focus on empowerment-related efforts. The leadership training and review sessions became more infrequent; managers' action plans, reviewed twice in 2000, were hardly checked in 2001; communication sessions with employees were increasingly cancelled as other priorities and crises emerged; and the senior team grew complacent with respect to empowerment. Perhaps not coincidentally, it was in summer 2001 that Mike was recruited by another region for the top position. After several weeks of discussion, he accepted the new job and was gone by early fall. Mike's former right-hand person, Jane, was promoted to take over his old position. During this transitional "changing of the guard," the tragic events of September 11, 2001, occurred. The crisis sent shock waves, operationally and politically, to all blood-collection regions across the country, leading to an intense period of chaos and high stress. National Headquarters dictates meant that everything was managed more tightly: Budgets were frozen, scrutiny intensified on regulatory and blood safety procedures, work rules were strictly enforced, and training virtually ceased as people dealt with being in "crisis mode." Adding to the pressure, public trust in the national organization was at an all-time low, and collection goals in all regions became harder to meet. Employee turnover within the region rose, and union efforts became active again, reflecting perhaps a lack of satisfaction on the part of employees.

By early 2002, when some of the pressure had calmed, Jane commissioned a third distribution of the Empowerment Barometer to all employees. As before, the surveys were filled out anonymously and analyzed by the consultant-author. As the third column of Table 1 shows, scale means from Time 3 are significantly higher than they were in Time 1; however, they were not significantly higher than the Time 2 means. In other words, the empowerment change effort had reached a plateau. In one sense, this can be seen as an accomplishment, given the challenges of the previous year. Changes in management systems and practices instituted in 1999 and 2000 were apparently still evident to employees in 2002, suggesting a certain degree of robustness to the change effort. However, a lack of forward progress can itself become a source of confusion, fatigue, discouragement, and disillusionment. Randolph (2000) described this period in implementing empowerment as "Stage 2: making changes and dealing with discouragement." It is at this stage that managerial leadership becomes critical, supporting and role modeling the way that the practices of empowerment—information sharing, developing clear boundaries, and relying on self-managed teams—can be used to deal with emerging problems and used to extend the empowerment effort itself. However, if this period is not well managed, most organizations at this stage will revert back to the old ways of doing things.

The 2002 scores on the Empowerment Barometer were presented to Jane and her senior team at a 2-day leadership retreat in early 2002. The group dialogued at length on how to proceed with empowerment in light of the new September 11 realities. However, as other priorities and crises continued to emerge, and people adjusted to Jane's new role as leader, the nonprofit essentially dropped empowerment as an organizational strategy. No further training sessions were held, no empowerment action plans were required of the managers, and communications forums with employees became rare and largely crisis driven. When asked about empowerment in February 2003, a year after all formal empowerment change efforts from top management had ceased, Jane stated that she believed empowerment would always be difficult to achieve in this organization as the regulatory requirements related to collecting blood, dictated by the FDA, made meaningful employee discretion and responsibility quite limited, if not even unrealistic. She was resigned to the fact that empowerment was no longer a region priority, and that it was probably an unreachable goal from the outset. The Empowerment Barometer was not administered in 2003, so we do not know how the region would have scored at this point; however, the region's production numbers had dropped, moving it down from one of the top-five performers to the bottom half of the 39 regions.

THE FOR-PROFIT'S EMPOWERMENT STORY

The for-profit organization is a 90-person department in the engineering division of a *Fortune* 500 technology company. The key jobs within this department are the senior management team of 10, and the 80 software, hardware and computer engineers who report to members of the senior team. Since 1997, this group has been focused on the development and launch of a new advanced product, involving breakthrough software and the challenging integration of new and existing technologies.

From 1997 through 1999, the senior manager of the department, call him *Roy*, sponsored a number of half-day training sessions for employees on interactive and group process skills. These "interactive skills" workshops, delivered by one of the authors of this article, were focused on teaching concepts and behaviors related to communications, teamwork, problem solving, self-management, and negotiation. The sessions were designed to address the engineers' needs for improved "people skills," a key factor to the success of the "multifunctional teams" (MFTs) that constituted the organization. In many ways, these MFTs were a precursor to self-managing teams. In late 1997, in line with his interest on the success of MFTs, Roy volunteered his software group, about 30 at the time, to participate in some research on organizational empowerment using the Empowerment Barometer. The results of this research, and the related debrief session, were a catalyst for Roy to think about how to develop the managers in his group to become more "empowering," so that they, in turn, would help to create a more productive and "self-managing" work environment.

Although conversations about empowerment had taken place during 1998 to 1999, Roy formally began developing his team's change strategy in 2000. He decided to begin with a broad focus on leadership development, assuming that empowerment would naturally be one of the leadership competency areas to be developed. Roy had several goals in mind with this focus. First, he believed strongly in the personal value of continuous learning and wished to provide some form of ongoing leadership development for his immediate team, particularly given that Corporate had stopped its support for all management training because of budget cuts. Second, Roy hoped that leadership excellence on the part of his managers would enable his organization to develop the new product and meet engineering targets related to quality, cost, and delivery, while maintaining high employee morale. Given that the larger company was well known for schedule slips (i.e., delays in development and launch), cost overruns, quality problems, and had been going through difficult layoffs during the previous 2 years, these were actually quite ambitious goals. Finally, Roy wanted the leadership development strategy to be a means of building teamwork and cohesion within his senior team. He believed that if his senior team was working well and had high trust in one another, then the rest of his organization would stand a better chance of success.

The process began in summer 2000 with a 360-degree feedback assessment of the leadership skills of each member of the senior team. A set of open-ended questions was asked related to each manager; for example, "What are this manager's three key strengths?" "What are this manager's three key development areas?" "What five adjectives would you use to describe this manager?" and "What advice do you have for this manager to become a more effective leader?" A 2-day leadership training workshop followed, at which the individual feedback reports were presented, corresponding action plans were created, and key leadership concepts, including empowerment, were presented. Roy had each of his managers prepare detailed "personal leadership development action plans" to address weak areas identified by the 360 feedback, which then had to be reviewed by him.

In early 2001, as the next step in the leadership strategy, the Empowerment Barometer was anonymously completed by the members of the 90-person department. It was coded by the team so that each senior staff member could get the personal results from his or her team. Roy and the senior staff then attended a half-day workshop on empowerment that focused on understanding the theory and implementation of organizational empowerment, reviewing their Barometer results, and developing team action plans. To provide some context on the 2001 results, the 1997 Barometer results that were obtained from seven of the managers and their teams, were also presented for purposes of comparison.

Table 2 below presents the results from Time 1 (1997) and Time 2 (2001). Note that the same seven managers were now responsible for more than twice as many employees as the project had been scaled up. As can be seen, there was significant progress on the three empowerment dimensions from 1997 to 2001. These results are particularly interesting because, at this point in the consultation, the training and development activities were not specifically built around an empowerment framework. It appears that perceptions of organizational empowerment can be positively affected by working on related and important factors like "people skills," teamwork, and transformational leadership.

Table 2
Comparison of Barometer Mean Scores on the Three Scales of Organizational Empowerment, 1997 vs. 2001 for the For-Profit Organization

	Time 1	*Time 2*		
	1997 (n = 28)	*2001* (n =60)	t	p *Value*
Sharing information	3.22[a] (.96)	4.36[b] (.75)	6.11	< .001
Clear boundaries	3.44[a] (1.03)	4.34[b] (.75)	4.79	< .001
Self-managed teams	4.01[a] (.85)	4.50[b] (.76)	2.67	< .01

Note: This table reports the results from a *t* test. Values are overall mean scores (and standard deviations) for each scale aggregated for all employees. The different *n* reflects that in 1997 the software group was smaller; in 2001 the same seven managers from 1997 were managing more engineers.
a, b. Means for the same scale with different superscripts are significantly different ($p < .01$), means with the same superscript are not significantly different from each other.

What is particularly noteworthy, however, is the way that the consultation progressed with the for-profit organization from this point on as distinct from events in the nonprofit. Instead of reacting to the initial positive results with complacency or discouragement, the senior team of the for-profit organization assumed that more progress was possible and necessary. During the next 2 years, Roy and his staff went through a number of training sessions and organization development interventions designed to foster learning and sustain progress on leadership development and empowerment.

First, Roy commissioned a series of three "keynote talks," 90 minutes each, presented during a 5-month period in 2001 to the entire organization. The first was on teamwork, the second on improving employee retention, and the third on empowerment, which was presented as a refresher for the senior team and an introduction for the larger organization. Concurrent with the keynote talks, Roy also commissioned quarterly "Bridge-Building" sessions with groups of employees. These Bridge-Building sessions were forums in which 15 to 30 employees, facilitated by the consultant author, would prepare answers as a group to a set of open-ended questions designed to encourage upward communication, common understanding on key issues, and problem ownership within the groups. The groups developed responses to questions such as "What is going well in our work? What is not going well?" "What can we, as engineers, do to address our own problems and concerns?" "What recommendations do we have for Roy and the senior team to help us become more effective and satisfied?" and "What questions do we have for the senior team?" The employees' answers were then presented to the senior team, who were required to respond to the group's output, with guarantees of no retribution or negative consequence for whatever was shared. The senior team also had to answer all questions posed as candidly as possible. These sessions were actually a good example of Randolph's (1995) first key, sharing information to build trust and responsibility, structured into a process that enabled the senior staff to learn what the "rank and file" were thinking and feeling, and that strengthened the relationship between the managers and engineers through dialogue, mutual feedback, and listening. The sessions also produced literally a hundred suggestions for Roy and his staff to consider relative to the operation of the department, and the behavior of his managers and himself.

It should be noted that although Roy initiated the leadership development strategy and "drove" the activities associated with it in the first year, it was the senior staff that later made most of the decisions about training and organization development; that is, by mid 2001, when the staff had "bought in" and experienced some of the benefits of becoming better leaders and empowering the engineers, it was the staff who determined what was needed next quarter, how much time would be allotted, who would be involved, and what follow-up was appropriate. Roy continued to lead by raising the issue, asking the questions, and offering his opinion as appropriate; however, the team made the decisions.

Progress

The overall strategy in the for-profit organization was simple: As the various sessions and interventions developed the managers, they in turn applied the ideas, concepts, and feedback within their areas, which in turn energized, engaged, and empowered the engineers. Although Empowerment Barometer results were not available subsequent to 2001, other survey results and qualitative observations make it clear that this organization made progress toward a culture of empowerment. For example, the senior team of 10 managers has had no turnover in 5 years, which is virtually unheard of in high-tech organizations and certainly within this company. Roy's organization of 90 had the highest ratings in the entire company on the annual employee attitude survey in 2001 and 2002. Given that the company has approximately 70,000 employees, this was quite an achievement. These outcomes suggest that Roy's organization was one where the developmental needs of managers and employees were met.

To add descriptive detail to these outcomes, one of our graduate students observed empowerment-related management practices within Roy's organization during a 2-month period during 2002 (Keefe, 2003). She concluded that many of the senior staff routinely practice effective ways to foster the three key empowerment practices outlined above within their own teams. For example, consistent with the practice of information sharing, she observed that most of the managers dedicate a regular portion of their weekly staff meetings to sharing important performance information, reviewing and revising group goals and values, and soliciting reactions and questions. Most use a "round-robin" approach at their meetings, having each engineer share good news, bad news, and technical concerns that may affect others in the team. A technique related to the development of clear boundaries was practiced by two of the managers, who use a team Web site to list the responsibilities and tasks of their team throughout the upcoming 4 to 6 months, then allow the individual engineers to vote on-line for the activities they most wish to do. This version of "job-assignment democracy" allows the engineers to choose the top two projects they want to work on, within the boundaries of what the team is responsible for, thereby making them more committed and satisfied doing those tasks. Consistent with the goal of clear boundaries and greater team responsibility, some managers were observed to use a "team covenant" with their staff, a type of behavioral contract outlining mutual expectations and obligations between the team and the manager. Some of the managers send an engineer in their place to important meetings for purposes of development and to understand better the "big picture" and virtually all the managers routinely use subteams, committees, and group consensus to make critical decisions, rather than autocratically deciding on issues that could affect the whole group.

Finally, we can report several indicators that suggest that Roy's department is performing at a high level. Because the organization is working on the development and launch of a new product, such outcomes as revenue or profit are not relevant. We can, however, report that Roy's group is an outstanding performer on the measures that are considered the most important in this organization. For example, Roy's group is the only department associated with the new advanced product (there are about 800 people in total working on this product) that has consistently met its software deliverables on time, on budget, and within acceptable quality parameters. This department has the internal reputation of being among the best led in the company, and arguably of being the most desirable place in the company for engineers wanting to work on challenging projects, in an empowered environment.

SOME IMPORTANT COMPARISON ISSUES

The for-profit organization has clearly achieved and sustained something unusual in terms of empowerment and a commitment to continuous improvement, whereas the nonprofit organization stalled after a strong start. This leads to several important questions that are at the core of this article: How did the for-profit group sustain the process of learning and development while the nonprofit did not? Was it solely a function of the senior leader's continued commitment and involvement, or is there more to the story? How important is budget and the ability to pay for ongoing outside help? What role does context and the preexisting culture of the larger organization play? Does being a for-profit or nonprofit make a difference? And finally, what can be learned from both organizations to help others succeed in sustaining the empowerment process?

Summary Overview of Both Approaches

Before exploring the differences in approach that might have led to the different results noted above, it is important to note that there were many similarities in how the two organizations implemented empowerment. On the positive side, both had strong leaders with a vision and set of goals, and both used outside expertise to help define, teach, and measure empowerment. Both organizations assumed the process had to begin with the senior team and that managers had to change first; hence, both required their managers to get involved, set goals, and develop personal action plans. The leaders in both organizations communicated often with employees about cultural changes and the "new way of doing things"; both used premeasures and postmeasures to assess progress and make changes; and both did a reasonable job at recognizing and praising employees as they advanced toward empowerment goals.

On the negative side, neither organization provided much training focused directly on empowerment issues for the employees. Neither organization used much in the way of formal rewards or incentives to encourage change. Both organizations may have placed too much accountability for the strategy on the leader and senior team as opposed to getting employee groups more involved. Both were negatively affected by September 11, one politically, the other more financially. Finally, incredibly, both leaders received essentially no recognition, reward, or even much praise from their management on the many productivity and morale successes that came from empowering employees. So, what were the differences in implementation and culture that made the difference?

Overcoming the Change of Leadership

The first obvious disparity was the fact that the nonprofit lost its visionary leader, Mike, after fewer than 2 years into the empowerment strategy. The aftermath of September 11 notwithstanding, Jane clearly did not seem as committed to empowerment as her predecessor. By contrast, in the for-profit, Roy has been in the same role for almost 5 years, with the exception of 11 months, military leave, and apparently has not lost his commitment to improving empowerment and leadership.

It is tempting to conclude that the primary reason the nonprofit lost focus and derailed from its empowerment strategy was the departure of the visionary leader. Admittedly, this was a major event for the organization; however, could it have been overcome? The answer, we think, is yes. On examination, there were a number of other key factors that better help to explain how the for-profit sustained its efforts while the nonprofit did not.

Empowerment as a Part of Leadership

The first key difference in approach was that the for-profit did not explicitly aim to create an "empowerment strategy" per se. Their focus was always more broadly on leadership development, in which the knowledge and practice of empowering others was viewed as an important component. This wider focus was helpful because although implementing organizational empowerment may be sufficiently multifaceted and stimulating for those who have studied it, the reality for most managers less familiar with it is, "OK, three strategies, that's easy enough. I get it . . . now what?" The fact that the empowerment effort in the for-profit was "bundled" into a broader change effort that had a number of dimensions added variety to what was being learned and measured, and helped to keep the group's interest. As so often happens, a focus on one approach is quickly lost as managers search for the next new topic. Perhaps a broader array of topics helps maintain people's attention for a longer period of time.

Senior Team Involvement

A second key difference was the role of the senior team. At first, Mike and Roy were the driving forces behind their respective empowerment and leadership efforts. However, as noted earlier, after the 1st year, Roy in the for-profit shared decisions on the leadership strategy with his staff, whereas Mike in the nonprofit continued to direct and decide on behalf of his organization. Both leaders would be considered highly intelligent, confident, and good judges of people. Hence, both may have made the right decision in terms of delegation, given the maturity and readiness of their staff and the culture of their organization. However, the fact remains that Roy involved his team, and this transfer of power has served to strengthen the staff's commitment and energy to the process, and to lighten the load on him. By contrast, Mike did not involve his senior team to the same degree, and when he departed, his senior team was simply not as prepared or as committed to the change effort.

Employee Feedback

A third difference concerned the use of employee feedback. Feedback in this case does not refer to the scores on the Empowerment Barometer but rather to direct verbal feedback from employees on the behavior and style of the senior team, and upward suggestions from the "troops" on the operation itself, empowerment issues, and the work environment generally. As noted earlier, the nonprofit leadership team did receive some employee feedback at the Town Hall meetings, through supervisors who reported up on ideas they received from employees, and they received some input from employee roundtables. However, this feedback was ad hoc, and not systematically or routinely solicited.

By contrast, the for-profit team proactively sought input on a regular basis. They used the Bridge-Building sessions to get opinions and suggestions from employee groups. Roy and the managers received outside executive coaching as a form of personal feedback and development, and the managers were asked to present their 360-degree feedback and action plan to their individual teams so that the engineers themselves could understand the plan and provide input on their boss's development plan. In addition, most of the managers routinely asked their engineers at team meetings for comments and suggestions relative to the work of their team. For this senior staff, feedback was not viewed as something to avoid or fear but rather as something that could genuinely enhance satisfaction and the overall effectiveness of the organization.

Certainly, one factor that probably influenced employee feedback is the different size of the two organizations and, related to this, the hierarchical structure of the two organizations. The structure in the nonprofit was four layers of management between Mike and the front-line employees, thus making direct input from staff more difficult. By contrast, in the for-profit, all 80 engineers report directly or "dotted line" to members of Roy's senior staff. Hence, their input could be received in a more direct and efficient manner. It may be that opening up more direct channels of communication across levels, and finding multiple ways to enable upward feedback to the senior team, regardless of the size of the organization, are key ingredients of establishing a culture of empowerment.

Continued Use of Outside Resources

A fourth difference relates to the use of outside resources. Both organizations used external consultants to advise the leaders on the empowerment strategy and provide training and coaching during the first 1½ years of the respective efforts. However, after September 11 and the change in leadership, the nonprofit essentially discontinued using the external resources.

By comparison, the for-profit engaged outside training, facilitation, and coaching for 2 years, "rode out" a 1-year budget freeze after September 11, and then resumed use of these services.

It may be tempting to assume that the reason for this difference is that for-profits have more funds for consulting services than do nonprofits. However, in this case, it was actually the for-profit that was in worse financial shape. After September 11, the budget freezes in the nonprofit were in place for a relatively short period of time and actually began to loosen by mid-2002. From that point forward, the nonprofit continued to be in good financial shape; after all, even in a bad economy, hospitals still buy blood. By contrast, at the for-profit company, revenues had been down considerably and spending very tight since 1998, well before Roy's leadership strategy began, and the reduced budgets continued well beyond early 2002. Roy, who was committed to using outside expertise, simply worked his budget out so that he could pay for the 8 to 10 consulting days a year to help his organization's leadership and empowerment efforts.

Preexisting Culture

Without question, the preexisting "culture" of the two organizations was quite different. The nonprofit's culture emphasized supreme concern for donor safety and public trust, strong identification with the mission of collecting blood, begrudging respect for National Headquarters and FDA rules, sincere appreciation of volunteers, professionalism among managers, and a noteworthy focus on effective budget management. Their culture also contained rigid deference to hierarchy, and feelings of entitlement, frustration, and overwork among front-line workers. There was an acceptance of poor customer service to donors and a certain bureaucratic style from the many managers who had never worked outside of this organization or other nonprofits.

The for-profit's culture emphasized teamwork and helpfulness, regular use of measurement, and TQM (Total Quality Management) principles; acceptance of disagreement and "push back" from direct reports; comfort with accountability, "taking ownership" and "driving the solution"; openness to outside suggestions and feedback; and a high respect for individual technical competence (Keefe, 2003). The culture also contained occasionally sharp teasing and condescending humor; obsession with detail and planning; an unhealthy praise for those who stay the longest, work weekends, and make the greatest sacrifices for work; and some degree of sexism. There was also an odd tolerance for cynics who often said such things as "This organization will never change," "We are not capable of delivering on time," and "Once again we are too late to market."

In terms of developing and sustaining empowerment, the for-profit's cultural comfort with process improvement, measurement, feedback, and people being held accountable were huge assets. Certainly, some of these qualities existed in the nonprofit as well, but not to the same extent. Recall that the for-profit is an engineering department. It is part of their routine practice to share information regularly, establish decision boundaries for individuals and groups, assign work to teams, document processes, use project plans, measure progress regularly, and value structure. In this respect, organizational empowerment found highly fertile ground with these engineers. A culture without some of these preexisting practices and orientations might well find the transition much more difficult—not impossible, just more difficult. This observation suggests that basic accountability practices might need to be developed before introducing more advanced practices related to empowerment.

The Right Level of Leader

Finally, one other key difference between the organizations concerns the level of the leader who is seen as the "champion" and active spokesperson for the empowerment strategy. Some authors (Keefe, 2003; Silver, 1999) have suggested that a leader who is too high up the management chain, for example, a division president or vice president in a for-profit or the executive director of a larger nonprofit, may be too far removed from the day-to-day decisions concerning the three keys to empowerment. They simply do not have enough contact with front-line employees to be knowledgeable on the details of how empowerment can actually be applied. Meaningful opportunities to share information, set specific boundaries, and work with and coach self-managing teams are more frequently controlled by the second-level or perhaps the third-level manager. Hence these middle levels of management probably make the most effective change agents (Huy, 2001). By contrast, the first-level manager or immediate supervisor does not usually have enough authority to make many of the important decisions related to the three key practices of empowerment. So, if the champion is too low or too high on the management chain, they are less likely to be effective.

In the nonprofit organization, Mike was the senior director of the 350-person organization. Although someone at his level could more easily change policy and direct resources, his role-modeling of empowerment and use of empowerment principles with his own staff largely went unnoticed by the "rank and file." Furthermore, despite attempts to interact with front-line employees at various Town Hall meetings and focus groups, the reality is that these amounted to a few meetings a quarter. Most of his time was, legitimately, spent in high-level meetings unseen by most.

In the for-profit, Roy is a third-level manager, one step down from vice president. He is high enough to manage a multimillion-dollar budget, direct considerable human and capital resources, and have influence on organizational policy. However, he is close enough to the 80 engineers doing the work to know everyone by name, to participate in meetings with many of them over the course of a given month, to have his behaviors routinely visible for most to observe, and to know in detail about the work of each team and engineer.

Thoughts on Sustaining Empowerment

Despite the overall conclusion that the nonprofit work environment may be harder for empowerment, two key questions remain: Are there ways to make empowerment work in both types of organizations and what lessons can be gleaned from these two cases that can help any organization wishing to sustain empowerment? Based on the experiences of the two case organizations, we close with a "Top 10" list of important factors to consider.

- Lesson 1: Be clear on why empowerment is important, what improvements are expected, and use these to develop a working change strategy. Consider making empowerment a part of a broader strategy, such as leadership, quality, or customer service focus and include multiple metrics to assess progress.
- Lesson 2: Involve, if only for a defined period, external experts who can help the leadership team understand their role and what to expect from the "journey." If possible, continue to bring them in at key points to provide feedback, training, and an objective perspective.
- Lesson 3: Start at the top. Train the senior managers first and expect behavior change from them. Establish baseline measures for the organization and set improvement goals. Have the senior managers develop personal action plans.
- Lesson 4: Involve the senior team as early as possible. Push decision making for the strategy onto the senior team so that they come to model what is expected throughout the organization. Then if the visionary leader does leave, the team will be committed to continuing the strategy
- Lesson 5: Train the employees. Although they may not need as much training as the managers, they will need to learn about the three empowerment keys for change, what new behaviors are expected from them and the managers, new skills to take on the new responsibilities, and why all this is being done.
- Lesson 6: Solicit employee feedback and ideas. Have the senior team, or members of it, routinely meet with groups of employees to dialogue and obtain input on how the organization is doing and what needs to change at all levels. Bridge-Building sessions are a good approach to this.
- Lesson 7: Share the lessons learned, innovative practices, and successes that come from the group. Ensure that every manager is engaging in new practices and behaviors that support the cultural change. Recognize achievements but do not overuse rewards lest they become the focus instead of the changes themselves.
- Lesson 8: Recycle. Retrain the managers, retake the Barometer, redo action plans, and continue with the regular employee forums.
- Lesson 9: Leverage the helpful aspects of the organization's culture as much as possible. If the organization is in the service sector, use the language of customer care and loyalty; if it is in the technology sector, use TQM tools and processes.
- Lesson 10: Make sure the right levels are the champions. Although the initial vision may come from the very top, it is the middle level, that is second- or third-level management, that is best placed to actually lead and typically most knowledgeable about what needs to change.

REFERENCES

Blanchard, K., Carlos, J. P., & Randolph, A. (1995). *The Empowerment Barometer*. San Diego: Blanchard Companies.

Blanchard, K., Carlos, J. P., & Randolph, A. (2001). *Empowerment takes more than a minute* (2nd ed.). San Francisco: Berrett-Koehler.

Block, P. (1987). *The empowered manager: Positive political skills at work*. San Francisco: Jossey-Bass.

Byham, W. (1988). *Zapp: The lightning of empowerment*. New York: Fawcett Columbine.

Hackman, J. R., & Oldham, G. R. (1980). *Work redesign*. Reading, MA: Addison-Wesley.

Huy, Q. N. (2001, September). In praise of middle managers. *Harvard Business Review, 79*(8), 73-79.

Keefe, T. (2003). *I'll believe it when I see it: Observing organizational empowerment in a high performing team*. Unpublished master's thesis, St. John Fisher College, Rochester, NY.

Randolph, W. A. (1995). Navigating the journey to empowerment. *Organizational Dynamics*, *23*, 19-32.

Randolph, W. A. (2000). Re-thinking empowerment: Why is it so hard to achieve? *Organizational Dynamics*, *29*, 94-107.

Schneider, B., & Reichers, A. E. (1983). On the etiology of climates. *Personnel Psychology*, *36*, 19-39.

Seibert, S., Silver, S., & Randolph, W. A. (2004). Taking empowerment to the next level: A multiple-level model of empowerment, performance, and satisfaction. *Academy of Management Journal*, *47*(3), 332-349.

Silver, S. R. (1999). *Perceptions of empowerment in engineer workgroups: The linkage to transformational leadership and performance*. Unpublished doctoral dissertation, George Washington University, Washington, DC.

Silver, S. R. (2001, October). Power to the people. *Training Magazine*, *38*(10), 88.

Thompson, L. L. (2003). *Changes in empowerment over a period of time: A quantitative and qualitative analysis*. Unpublished master's thesis, St. John Fisher College, Rochester, NY.

SETH SILVER *is an assistant professor in the Graduate Human Resource Development Program at St. John Fisher College in Rochester, New York, and provides consulting services through Fulcrum Consulting, Inc. He received his EdD in human resource development from George Washington University. His research and consulting work focuses on transformational leadership, empowerment, and "team covenants" or behavioral contracts between managers and their organizations. He can be reached at Seth1701@aol.com.*

W. ALAN RANDOLPH *is a professor of management and Director of the Global Business Practicum Program at the Robert G. Merrick School of Business, University of Baltimore, in Maryland. He received his PhD in business administration from the University of Massachusetts. His current research interests focus on the processes for effectively creating cultures of empowerment, the relationship between dimensions of empowerment and bases of power, and the effects of national culture on the creation of cultures of empowerment. He can be reached at wrandolph@ubalt.edu.*

SCOTT SEIBERT *is an associate professor at the Melbourne Business School. He earned his PhD in organizational behavior at the New York State School of Industrial and Labor Relations at Cornell University. His interest in personality, climate, and social networks informs his research on careers, empowerment, groups, and workplace safety. He can be reached at sseibert@mbs.edu.*

14 Theory, Conceptualisation and Hypothesis

NICK LEE and IAN LINGS

SUPERVISOR'S VIEW: DR NICK LEE

I got a bit antsy not saying anything for two whole chapters, so I thought I would put my two cents in here. Seriously, theory has been one of the major thorns in my side since I graduated with my Doctorate and began publishing my work – or more accurately trying to. I remember getting many rejection letters from top level journals with the same criticism each time; 'this work has no theory'. For a very long time I couldn't understand this criticism – 'after all', I thought 'this manuscript has about 10 theories in it, one for each hypothesis!' The more experienced among you will already have seen my naive error. However, it took me a long time to come to grips with the idea that having a strong theoretical foundation for your work is not the same as throwing as many theories as possible together without any logic behind *why* those theories are linked. Basically, and I admit I am still working on really becoming comfortable with this, your work should have some kind of overall coherence linking the various concepts together. There are many general theories of social behaviour (or whatever it is that you study) which you could use as fundamental foundations of your work. In turn this will inform the development of your more specific theory – perhaps by adding new ideas and theories to extend its explanatory power, or solve a weakness in it. In other words, most of the time social scientists are working at the margins of existing theory, but not creating completely new theories.

Unfortunately, this kind of thing takes a while for a keen researcher with visions of changing the world to come to grips with! It's very easy to go into a research career thinking that in order to make a contribution and become famous (or whatever drives you) you must create or discover something entirely new. After all, that's what all the scientists you've ever heard of did, isn't it? But eventually, you'll come to realise that virtually no researcher has *ever* come up with something completely new. In fact, you can probably trace back the lineage of almost all of the major discoveries or theories to earlier theories and ideas. The famous researchers who discovered something 'new' usually did so by working at extending, or solving a problem with, an existing theory. Or, perhaps, they were looking for an explanation for something which they saw or experienced, and then discovered that none existed. Another common way which seemingly 'new' theories get developed is the application of ideas from outside the relevant field. This kind of thing can happen through pure luck, you may meet a fascinating colleague from another department over coffee, or something stronger, and get talking. Most of my best work has started in this way actually. So, I guess if I were to conclude, I would say that the best way to do something original is *not to try to*! What I mean is; don't go into your career specifically trying to come up with something new. Go in with the goal of answering important questions, and if you need to create something new to do this, then you will do so. My other advice would be to keep an open mind in *all* respects. Expose yourself to as many different ideas, people, and situations as possible, read anything that interests you – as well as the stuff specifically related to your area. But before you go off creating new things, make *absolutely certain* you are completely well-versed on the theory which is already out there!

VIEW FROM THE TRENCHES: DR JOHN RUDD

The process of conceptualising a theoretical model and developing sound hypotheses is fraught with opportunities for you to get ahead of yourself. Try to avoid this as it will only cause a great wringing of the hands further down the line. Focus on the theory, and develop your model and your hypotheses from this. Remember, while you may be very clear on why your overall model looks the way it does, where is the supporting theory/ evidence that says that hypotheses 'x' may be worth further investigation? Why does factor 'a' impact on factor 'b' positively? Why not the other way? Why not negatively? If you do not know then how do you expect a reader, or a reviewer, of your work to believe in it?

A theoretical model is not a process diagram! This is bad! Let me explain. Coming from a background in industry, I was very much used to buzzwords like 'brainstorming', 'blue skies thinking' and 'imagineering'. These techniques allow teams of managers to, very quickly, consolidate the complexities of the competitive environment into a process diagram on a couple of well-thumbed flip charts. Usually there are various arrows and feedback loops, accompanied by a smattering of exclamation marks and well-placed smiley faces and cash signs; presumably signifying success of some kind. While these have proven to be extremely valuable in applied circumstances, they will be of little, or no, use to those of you interested in an academic career. 'Why'? I hear you cry. 'They are woolly', I reply. Also, and more importantly within a research framework, they are based on experience and 'gut feel', not on theory. While an arrow here and an arrow there (dotted or otherwise) may convey to the drawer, and his immediate audience, a very specific nuance of management action, to anyone else they may very well be interpreted as the daubings of a lunatic. In developing a theoretical model it is important to avoid the trap of the process diagram! Make me happy, don't do it.

Theory is the foundation on which much academic research is based. Without it, researchers are in the dark about **how** phenomena relate to each other and **why** they relate to each other in the way that they do. Think about some of the common statistics that we see reported by firms and governments: 'socially deprived individuals engage in more crime than socially advantaged individuals'; 'young people drive faster and are more reckless on the road than older people'; people in certain parts of the country are 'happier than others'. These reported relationships are often presented just so, especially in the tabloid press. Although they may make an interesting topic of discussion, the fact that crime is related to social deprivation, speeding related to age or happiness related to location, does not offer us any insights into *why this may be so*. Without an understanding of why, it is impossible to make any meaningful recommendations to manage these issues (a particularly relevant issue in the applied social sciences). The role of theory is bound up with the 'why' question. Without theory all we can say are things like: 'maybe young people shouldn't drive', or 'social deprivation needs to be addressed if we want to manage crime'. However, if we have an underlying theory to explain *why* such relationships between factors like age and reckless driving are observed, then we can say so much more. For example, if we theorise and later find support for the idea that young people drive fast because they believe that nothing bad can happen to them – that they are invincible – then we can address this underlying perception of invincibility to manage the problem, maybe through education. In research, we can interrogate the theory, and other competing theories that explain the same thing, and conduct research projects to see if it is really perceptions of invincibility that are driving this behaviour or if it is something else. In other words, we test the theories to see which is the better at explaining what is happening.

One thing is for certain, if you do not understand what theory is and what it does, you cannot conduct credible research. Furthermore, it becomes difficult for you to articulate your contribution to academic knowledge. With this in mind, read on, this chapter will hopefully answer your questions about theory and its role in research. At the end of this chapter I really hope you have come to terms with these key ideas:

1. What theory is and its role in social science.
2. The philosophical underpinnings of theory.
3. The difference between laws, theories, concepts, models, measures and hypotheses.
4. How to construct and recognise a theory, extend it, and contribute to the theoretical foundations of your subject.
5. How to represent your theory in a conceptual model, and how to develop hypotheses from it.

Why is it Important to Know This Stuff?

Theory is the foundation of science, both the natural sciences like chemistry and physics, and social sciences like business, sociology, and political science. Many people view the natural sciences as 'better' at developing and testing theory than the social sciences. However, this is not really true. Certainly, natural sciences are often better at defining and controlling the conditions under which a theory applies, and typically inanimate matter behaves more consistently than do people (this links back to what Professor Clegg said at the beginning of Chapter 3). Theory helps us to explain what has happened and to predict what will happen. When an apple fell from the tree, supposedly on Sir Isaac Newton's head, he theorised from the observation that the earth attracted the apple towards it, his head just happened to be in the way. From this observation (and many more I suspect) Sir Isaac eventually developed a theory which argued that all objects with mass attract each other. This eventually, after a great deal of work, became his *Universal Law of Gravitation.* It is important to note the difference between a law and a theory, which will be discussed in depth later. In common usage, most people consider laws to relate primarily to the natural sciences, and to always hold under the right conditions. Theories however, are more provisional. Of course, interesting as it is to have an explanation for why the apple fell on his head, Newton's theory serves a more important role. Having developed his theory and repeatedly tested it, leading to the Law of Gravitation, Sir Isaac could now *apply* the Law to *predict* the behaviour of any object in relation to another object; such as which will move the furthest, how fast, at what point will the objects collide, and how much energy is needed to make sure that the force of attraction is overcome. Pretty useful if you want to put a satellite in orbit around the earth, for example. In other words, theory itself exists (obviously) in the theoretical world, as Figure 5.1 shows. However, scientists and others use theories and laws to predict events in the 'real world'. If we observe those events, then our theories have support.

In the social sciences theories serve the same purpose. They are used to explain events, like behaviours, and perhaps to predict them. Unfortunately for social scientists, people do not always behave as predictably as apples. If a planet has enough mass to also have gravity, the apple will always fall towards the ground at a given rate, the apple cannot decide that it doesn't like the ground and so will decide to fall towards the stars. This inherent awkwardness of the human race poses several challenges for social scientists, but more of this later in the book. Unfortunately, beginning researchers commonly have difficulty when developing theory. In fact it is hard for many to even come to grips with what theory actually is. Even worse, there are few resources available to help the confused researcher understand what theory is, and for many it is therefore a process of trial and error (and reams of criticism) before something finally 'clicks'. This chapter is aimed at giving you a broad introduction to the idea of theory in social science, and from then on you should be able to build on it using your own experiences. So needless to say, I think that everyone should read this, because without theory, science is merely a technical exercise with questionable relevance.

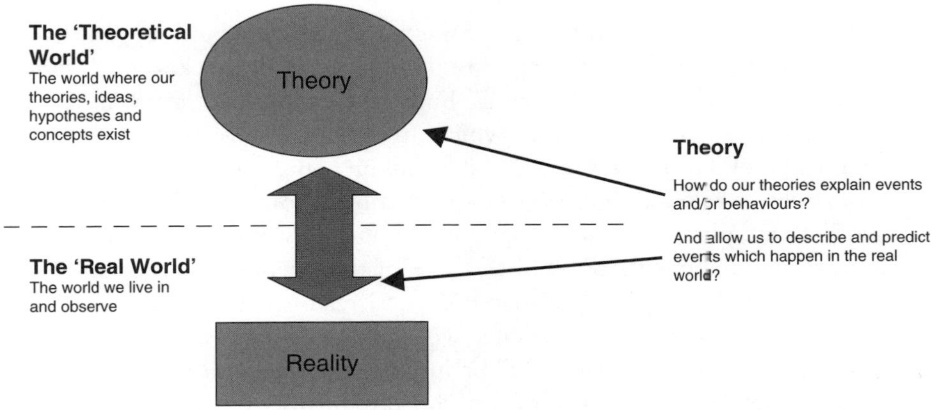

Figure 5.1 The place of theory

Some philosophical assumptions

Before we together embark on the voyage of discovery that will hopefully illuminate the nature of theories to you, it is important to explore the underlying assumptions of theory in general, and the basic philosophical approach that is a prerequisite to theory development and testing in the social sciences. Science is an important label here. The word *science* derives from the Latin verb *scire*, 'to know'. Although it is possible to 'know' through faith or intuition, the scientific method (as described in Chapter 2 for example) requires that it should be possible for other investigators to establish the credibility of any knowledge claims we make. This credibility is typically approached, although never finally 'proved', through empirical replication of work, and comparison of the observations of different researchers studying the same phenomena. However, pure logic and mathematics can also be used to provide evidence of knowledge claims (for example, many cutting-edge physical theories have never been directly tested using real-world data). But the ultimate test of any theory is whether the events it predicts in the 'real world' are actually observed.

This brings me to the next assumption of the scientific method. That there is an objective 'truth' to be observed. An objective truth is something that, no matter what we believe to be the case, will always be true. It is related to the idea of an objective reality, one which exists independent of us. Remember questions like: 'Do you see the same colour orange as I do?'; 'Does a tree falling in a forest make a noise, even if there is no one there to hear it?' These are questions to do with the objective reality of the world, whether it exists independently of us or is a construct of our minds. Objective truth is contingent on a philosophy that suggests that our beliefs, whatever they are, have no bearing on the facts of the world around us. That which is true is always true – even if we stop believing it and even if we stop existing at all. This is a notion of *epistemological objectivity*; truth can be determined inter-subjectively by generally agreed methods or procedures.

Contrast this to a purely subjective view of the world, which would suggest that there is no reality independent of people's perceptions. This extreme view is known as *metaphysical idealism*, and suggests that so-called 'physical' things don't really exist at all, in fact nothing exists independently of our experiences, which are in our minds, and therefore nothing exists independently of our minds and reality depends on being experienced. This leads us to the notion of a subjective truth or *epistemological subjectivity*. Somewhere towards the middle of these two extreme philosophical standpoints lie the views of critical realists and critical relativists. Your views about theory and the role of the scientific method in developing knowledge will depend on where you stand. Critical realists believe that we must *assume* the existence of an objective reality so that we can make claims about cause and effect relationships; even though these claims will be imperfect, while critical relativists argue that there is no single knowable reality waiting 'out there' to be discovered. Even though critical relativists accede that there may well be a single social and natural reality, they do not believe that science can reveal it. The critical relativist view has given rise to criticisms of the scientific method and the development of other approaches to knowledge creation, such as postmodernism, discussed elsewhere in the book. However, in this chapter, as in most of the rest of the book, I have taken an objective view of reality and adopt a predominantly critical realist view of the world. This will become important later. For the relativistic researcher, however, the concept of theory as an explanation for events is still important, although not all relativists will consider it necessary to have any *a priori* theory behind their work at all.

Laws and theories: What they are and what they are not

In your readings for the literature review, you will need to decide what constitutes laws, theories, frameworks, conceptual models, hypotheses and arguments; and which of these are theoretic or not, logical or not, or both or neither. The first stage in being able to do this is to understand what each of these is. This is much easier said than done! Definitions, especially of theories, laws and conceptualisations, are somewhat confused and confusing in the literature. Here, I will try to make sense of the different opinions about just what these things are, and importantly, what they are not.

Laws

In scientific research, laws are most commonly encountered in the natural sciences and consequently I won't spend too long discussing them here. However, it is important to consider the differences between what most laypeople think of as 'laws', and what a law is in actual practice. To the average person, natural laws have several characteristics, among which are:

1. They are true; there have never been repeatable contradicting observations.
2. They are universal; they appear to apply everywhere in the universe.
3. They are simple; typically expressed in terms of a single mathematical equation.
4. They are stable, and have not changed since first discovered.

In this sense then, laws are considered to be universal truths, things that are *always true*. However, let's take, for example, a very simple law, which most people would recognise at least in some way: Newton's Universal Law of Gravitation. Newton's theory (briefly) states that every object in the universe attracts every other object by a force pointing along a straight line combining the two. This can be represented by a law in the form of an equation:

$$F_g = G\frac{M_1 M_2}{R^2}$$

F_g = the force of gravity, M_1 and M_2 are the masses of the objects and R is their separation. G is a constant.

The equation translates as the force of gravity is a function of the masses of the two objects and the distance between them. From Newton's first publication of *Philosophiae Naturalis Principia Mathematica* in 1687 until Einstein's development of general relativity, this was generally considered a law. At that time, Newton's theory had the characteristics of a law to most people, in that there had never been repeatable contradicting observations, it appeared to apply everywhere in the universe, it was expressed in terms of a single mathematical equation, and it was stable, and had not changed since it was first discovered. However, as science and measuring technology moved on (Nick will discuss measurement in the next two chapters), Newton's description of gravity began to exhibit some inconsistencies. In fact, Newton's 'law' is *not* accurate under certain conditions (e.g. approaching the speed of light). Instead, Einstein's general relativity is a much better expression of gravity. Even so, Newton's description is accurate for many 'practical' purposes, and therefore is widely used. So, from being considered to be a universal 'law', Newton's equation has really become more of a practical tool – and is not really considered to be a good explanation of how the universe 'works' today. In fact, this is a great example of how scientific progress works. Most of the time, a law is only a law until something better comes along which shows that the existing law does not hold. Nevertheless, Newton's equation is still generally considered a 'law' as it does predict accurately under a specific set of conditions. This example also illuminates another characteristic of laws – they are not an explanation of *why* or *how* things happen, they are just descriptions of *what* happens. Newton's law by itself does not explain anything about why or how bodies attract each other, it just describes what actually happens. One needs more than just this law for a theory of *why*.

So, you have seen that even in the realm of non-sentient entities like apples and planets, it is extremely difficult to formulate natural laws that are always true. What hope then do we have in the messy social world, where the players in our laws have consciousness and free will? Unsurprisingly, laws are not generally encountered in the social sciences, perhaps reflecting this difficulty of identifying universal truths within human phenomena. But also, it should not be forgotten that most social sciences are far younger than the natural sciences. That said, many social disciplines do tend to use the *language* of laws, such as economics (e.g. the law of supply and demand). It is a common assumption among social scientists though, that laws are not able to be formulated about the social world. It would seem that this argument may often be founded on a naive idea of what a law actually is. As you saw above, a scientific law is *not* necessarily something which holds absolutely and always, and almost all natural scientific laws have exceptions, and tend to hold only under distinct, defined, conditions.

If one accepts this more realistic definition of what a law can be, then the idea of laws in the social sciences becomes less fanciful. A law can be an expression of a theoretical principle – such as the laws of supply and demand – or they can be mathematical formulae such as Newton's above. Laws can also be regularities which have been established through repeated empirical replications (these are often called *empirical generalisations*). So, if you accept the idea that there are at least *some* regularities (which are not purely accidental) in the social world, it seems to be unavoidable to accept that it is at minimum *possible* in principle to create laws in social sciences. Remember, a law does not have to be something which is **always true**, all laws have defined exceptions. However, this brings up what may be the real problem with the idea of social laws. More specifically, the exceptions to physical laws are well defined and regular (e.g. Newton's law does not hold at velocities nearing the speed of light), but the exceptions to social laws are far more dependent on the unique social context in existence at the time of observation (Kincaid, 1994). So when a social law does not hold under empirical observation, is it possible to clearly define the local conditions which caused this failure? If not, then it is impossible to determine whether the exception to the law was caused by local conditions, or a fault of the law itself.

In fact, one wonders whether the question of whether there can be social laws is even of particular importance. Certainly, we have evidence that indicates that there do exist non-accidental regularities in the social world, and perhaps this is the closest social scientists can ever get to a 'law'. Instead, social scientists tend to couch their statements about regularities in the language of **theory**. In contrast to laws, theories are generally characterised by being more complex. Theories generally have several component parts, and are more likely to be changed as the body of available experimental data and analysis develops. Most importantly, unlike physical laws, which summarise and describe empirical events, theories *account for events, explain them and relate them to other events*, often making predictions which may subsequently be tested. To finalise this point, **a law simply describes what happens (e.g. apples fall to the earth); a theory explains why it happens.**

Theories (Origin Greek theoria 'contemplation, speculation')

What then, is a theory? This question is more difficult to answer than one might think. The word theory has several meanings, depending on which field you are working in and what philosophical viewpoint you favour. A definition of theory is made even more difficult by the fact that its common usage is different to its scientific usage; worse still, usage in the natural sciences also differs from usage in the social sciences; and to cap the whole thing off, usage within the social sciences differs between individuals! These confusions about the nature of theory can be seen in definitions offered by both the Oxford and Cambridge English dictionaries.

The Cambridge Advanced Learner's Dictionary has this to say:

Theory: noun

1. *a formal statement of the rules on which a subject of study is based.*
2. *or of ideas which are suggested to explain a fact or event .*
3. *or, more generally, an opinion or explanation.*

The Oxford English dictionary:

Theory: noun (pl. theories)

1. *A supposition or a system of ideas intended to explain something, especially one based on general principles independent of the thing to be explained.*
2. *An idea accounting for or justifying something.*
3. *A set of principles on which an activity is based.*

In common usage (i.e. conversations between non-scientists), many people use 'theory' to mean 'opinion' or 'conjecture', suggesting that a theory is not necessarily based on facts; in other words, it is not required to be consistent with descriptions of reality. However, this usage is not what I mean when I talk about 'theory' in the social sciences. When a social researcher talks of a theory, he or she is not referring to a guess or hunch, as might be the case in everyday speech. For a scholar, a theory is a logically self-consistent model or framework that describes and explains how related phenomena behave; it is generally based on, and may be supported by, some kind of observations. A defining characteristic of a *scientific* theory is that it makes falsifiable or testable predictions about things not yet observed. According to Stephen Hawking in *A Brief History of Time,* 'theory is always provisional', in this sense one can never prove a theory. No matter how many observations agree with the theory, one can never be sure that the next observation will not contradict it. To disprove a theory, only a single repeatable observation that disagrees with the predictions of the theory is necessary. You should remember this basic concept from Chapter 2, when Nick talked about Karl Popper and the black swans.

Using existing theory to explain behaviour

In most social science research we are trying to explain some aspect of behaviour; the behaviour of individuals (customers, employees, politicians, individual team members, fanatics, etc.); or the behaviour of groups (teams, families, companies, nations, societies, political or religious parties); sometimes we are exploring the behaviour of systems of management, such as manufacturing systems, HR practices or government policies. Most commonly, in the applied fields of social research (like business), general theories explaining these phenomena are drawn from disciplines like psychology or economics, but occasionally theories from other disciplines such as physics, philosophy or mathematics are also relevant. It is important when examining your research topic to understand those theories that explain what is going on in the small aspect of the world that you are interested in. For example, if you are trying to explain and understand how people behave in response to certain stimuli, you may wish to explore some of the theories discussed in psychology (e.g. the theory of planned behaviour, game theory, expectancy theory), and you may also wish to explore the economic theories that attempt to explain the same phenomena (such as utility theory). Of course, there are other general theories that also attempt to explain human behaviours in different contexts, and these should also be explored fully.

This is one of the key areas where beginning researchers get confused. In particular, the novice researcher will often not actually build their work on an existing general theory at all – as Nick related at the start of this chapter. In fact, even many more experienced researchers (especially in the applied social research disciplines) fail to solidly ground their work in an existing theory, and then are often confused when they are criticised for not doing so. The difficulty is that grounding your work in existing theory is *not the same* as picking and choosing a cornucopia of theories from all over the place to justify your work. Unfortunately for me, this is a very hard concept to get across right now. Many research students especially, assume that they should create some kind of new grand theory rather than base their work on existing theory, but this is not usually the case. Perhaps an example will help. Imagine your research is looking to examine the relationship or interaction between a buyer and a seller, which is quite common in many different fields of research. In a general sense, one can explore this in various different ways, each based on a different general theory. One way is *social exchange* theory, which considers that relationships between people are essentially exchanges of various resources. People stay in relationships because the benefits they get exceed the benefits they would get if they left the relationship. Another way of exploring relationships is *social network theory*. In the present context, this perspective would conceptualise individual buyers and sellers as being part of a 'web' of relationships of various types, some stronger than others. One could also explore *transaction cost* theory, which would consider the various costs to the buyer of purchasing from a given seller. Of course, there are many other ways of looking at relationships, and each one of these general theories would influence you to look at a different set of concepts and ideas. Within your general theory you would probably look to add something new or original somewhere, to make a contribution to knowledge. There are many ways of doing this, and it is something you need to think about very carefully in the early stages of any piece of scholarly research. In other words, **where does your work make a contribution to existing theory**?

What you should *not* do is simply toss a whole bunch of concepts and ideas together, mixing and matching theories without an overall framework. As I have already said though, it is quite common for new researchers to do this, and I have made the same mistake myself (and you can see Nick has too from the beginning of this chapter). The problem is that, without an overall theoretical framework, there is no reason for those concepts and ideas to all appear in your model, and to be related to each other, apart from your own 'intuition'. While intuition can be a major help to a researcher, it should not really be the whole basis for a theory. The common retort I hear to this is 'so how am I supposed to contribute to theory without adding new theories to it?' Indeed this is a fair question, and deserves an answer. Simply put, you can modify and change existing theories using ideas from other theories, but this has to be clearly and logically justified. Using additional theoretical ideas to *add to* existing theory is not the same as throwing loads of different theories into some kind of witch's brew without an overall structure.

This is not to say that all research must follow existing theory. Certainly there is room for researchers to create entirely new theories. However, creating a new theory is not for the faint-hearted, and is never a risk-free proposition. This means it is rarely a good choice for a research student or inexperienced researcher.[1] Again though, creating a new theory is not the same as throwing together a bunch of others. A new theory must be self-contained and consistent with itself, it must offer a general explanation for the phenomena at hand. Furthermore, it must explain things **better than previous theories**. Going back to the buyer–seller relationship example, a new theory must either: (a) be a general theory of relationships (not just buyer–seller), or (b) show why existing general theories are not adequate to explain the unique situation of buyer–seller relationships. From here, your new theory must *then* go on to show how it explains the phenomena in some kind of materially superior way to existing theories. Needless to say, it is usually easier to show how existing theory should be **augmented** by new ideas, rather than thrown out completely. However, this is not always the case – sometimes existing theory is just plain wrong (do you still believe the Earth is flat?), and if you are truly convinced of this, then I, and I trust Nick, would say *go for it*. But don't expect an easy life (in fact, Nick will touch on this in Chapter 15).

So moving on, assuming you have an overarching theoretical perspective, it's time to see how it relates to your research. One of the defining characteristics of a scientific theory is that it *makes falsifiable or testable predictions about things which can be observed*. It is these predictions that allow the theory to be tested over and over in different contexts. With continual testing, the body of evidence supporting the theory builds up, and the theory gets modified (by the contributions of newer research) to overcome the limitations identified by such repeated testing in different contexts. Also, the existence of several theories that explain similar phenomena in different ways, based on differing assumptions and sometimes different underlying philosophical views, allows for comparisons of the explanatory and predictive ability of these competing theories to be made, essentially testing them against each other in different contexts. Of course, sometimes contradictory evidence builds up to such a stage that a given theory is discredited, and this can be a long and painful process for adherents to that theory. More on this in Chapter 15.

Developing theory

As I touched on above, in most instances scholarly research aims to make some contribution to theory, not necessarily a large contribution, but some advancement of the theory in

[1]On the other hand, it could be argued that only research students and inexperienced researchers have the time to dedicate to creating new theory, and also are not totally immersed in existing theory yet either.

some manner. Of course, different research contexts require different types of contribution. Masters and Doctoral level research certainly needs to make some kind of contribution, and research by full-time academics is often held to very high standards in this regard. Undergraduate research may have a more modest aim (perhaps to apply an existing theory to a new context and provide new information or additional evidence for a theory) but this still requires an understanding of what theory is. Consequently, theory relates to your literature review inasmuch as your theory is a systematic and formalised expression of all previous observations (found from reviewing previous work) that is predictive, logical and testable (I will come to this later). *However*, when conducting the literature review, and looking at previous observations in the field that you are interested in, it is most usually the case that reported observations contradict each other, contradict other theories and generally appear to be inconsistent. But what should you do when this happens?

The art of critical evaluation of these inconsistent findings or observations is for you to evaluate what is going on with the results that previous researchers have reported. Take for example two studies examining a similar situation and reporting different or even conflicting observations. Your job, as a reviewer of these studies, is to try to work out if the conflicting results support, modify, or challenge the existing theory that you are interested in. There are many reasons why conflicting results may be reported (and you will become very knowledgeable about these as you move through this book). The results may be inconsistent because one or other of them is plain wrong; or maybe they are inconsistent because there are other factors at work which have not been accounted for in the explanation of the observations; they could be inconsistent because there is error which is masking what is really being observed, or they could be inconsistent because the researcher is interpreting similar data yet coming to different conclusions. In this instance the observations may actually be the same, just the interpretation different. So how much confidence do you have in the reported results? This will depend on how well you think the researchers have applied particular methods to collect and interpret the data, (remember, no method is perfect), where the data were collected, perhaps the results are sample-specific and not sufficiently generalisable to be considered as either supporting the theory or not. Consider the example of Newton's Law given above: you may read many articles that report that gravitational force always works the same way; this may have been tested in a variety of ways with a variety of objects at many different times and in many different locations. It may be reported by many esteemed researchers. Then you come across a paper that reports that this is not true, that in some instances objects do *not* attract each other in the same way. In fact, this really happened, although it was more that the law did not accurately predict some events than that apples started falling upwards! So, what do you do? Ignore the anomaly? This is a tempting option, and one that many people will engage in when given information that contradicts their view of the world. However, we are scholars so should not allow ourselves to bury our heads and ignore the contradictory information. What then? Well we can examine the research paper; look at the methods, conditions under which the observations were made, methods used to make these observations, and ultimately come to a conclusion about the validity of the observations. Bear in mind that even though we are scholars, we are also human, and humans have a tendency to place more importance on information that supports their existing views than information which challenges those views. Even if we do not allow ourselves the comfort of ignoring contradictory advice, we must ensure that we do not find ways of dismissing it simply because we do not know what to do with it. The challenge is to look at the information provided and work out whether: (a) it is justified, and therefore that our universal law or theory is not quite so universal, or (b) the research is flawed in some way and so we can legitimately argue that the observations, although contradictory, probably do not challenge the validity of our theory. Our third option is to accept (a), but to argue that it is not really that important a departure. This is kind of what has happened with Newton's example. We know that it is not accurate near the speed of light, but we also accept that it remains a useful predictive device within its strictly defined conditions.

Another explanation of the existence of contradictory evidence is the possibility that the theory is *based on an incorrect assumption*. All theories are based to some degree on assumptions, at the most philosophical level these may be to do with the nature of reality as discussed at the start of this chapter. Other assumptions may be included in a theory because they were thought to be 'true' at the time that the theory was developed but have subsequently been shown to be untrue (or at least replaced with an alternative truth). It is worth remembering when you are reading about theories that they *always* contain some assumptions, which, by definition, are accepted without proof. The more assumptions a theory has the more complex it is. In fact, a commonly cited argument for simple theories is known as **Occam's Razor**, which is discussed in IDE 5.1.

IDE 5.1: Occam's Razor

Occam's Razor is a general principle of theoretical development and interpretation that is credited to William of Ockham (1288-1348). Thus, it is sometimes referred to as 'Ockham's Razor'. You can also see the basic idea of Occam's Razor echoed in many other areas of methodology, particularly statistical methods. Occam's Razor is essentially the principle that a theory should rely on as few assumptions, and propose as few hypothetical entities, as possible. It is often expressed as the maxim that 'the simplest explanation is usually the best'. Or at least that's how Lisa Simpson referred to it in episode 6 of 'The Simpsons' season 7. Occam's Razor is a way of choosing between competing theories, as long as they are all equally 'good'. This, of course, depends on what you define as good. Some theorists use the criteria of 'correctness', so, for example, Newton's Law is simpler than Einstein's General Relativity – but we shouldn't prefer it since we know it to be incorrect. The problem occurs when we don't know whether theories are correct or not – commonly the case when we are developing theories! In this case we should use Occam's Razor as a general principle to guide our theoretical development. In other words, we should certainly never make our theories unnecessarily complicated, but nonetheless, we should never over-simplify them to the point where they are obviously not accurate. Speaking of Newton, he stated it nicely when he said that, 'we are to admit no more causes of natural things than such as are both true and sufficient to explain their appearances'. In other words, our theories should first be aimed at providing an accurate and realistic explanation, but should never be *unnecessarily* complex. When you are developing your own models and theories, you would do well to take this advice to heart.

An illustration of how theories are based on assumptions, and also of how **models** can be derived from theories, can be found in early astronomy. The Greek astronomer Ptolemy created a planetary model based on the prevailing astronomy theory, and its assumptions, at the time. Some of these assumptions were based on the idea that the Earth, being God's creation, was naturally at the centre of the entire universe. So, the observed motion of the stars and Sun were explained by assuming that the Earth was at the centre of the planetary and solar system, and theorising that the planets and the Sun made circular orbits around the Earth, and the stars were on a sphere outside of these orbits. Retrograde motion of the planets was explained by smaller circular orbits of individual planets. This astronomical theory could be illustrated as a mathematical model, and could even be built into a physical model, an *orrery*. In fact, even today mathematical calculations based on Ptolemy's model can predict, to a great degree of accuracy, where the planets will be at a given time. All this evidence suggests that the theory and the model are good representations of the real world. This example also illustrates the idea that a theory is a *model of reality*, one that describes and predicts certain measurable occurrences, yet may not be a good description of what the world is actually like (just like Newton's so-called Law). Another, more accurate, theory can later replace the previous model, just as this model of the planetary system was replaced 1,500 years later at the time of Copernicus, although not without much wailing and gnashing of teeth (being as it destroyed the assumption that the Earth was necessarily the centre of the Universe).

Assumptions are the weak points in any theory, as they have to be accepted on faith, which is quite contrary to most philosophies of science. However, a given theory can never explain absolutely everything down to the finest detail, so it must to some greater or lesser extent rely on assumptions about those parts of the world which it does not directly relate to. Thus, assumptions are essential in the development of theory, but while they cannot be removed completely, we can at least aim to base our theories on as few assumptions as possible. When examining the assumptions upon which a theory is based, it is important to remember that *assumptions* themselves can be neither true nor false, since there is no way of proving them to be either. If there were a way, they would no longer be assumptions. For example, the assumption of Earth being the centre of the Universe was no longer an assumption once it was discovered to be untrue. Nevertheless, we can comment on the usefulness or uselessness of assumptions, depending on whether deductions made from them correspond to actual events. To take a more social scientific example, many classical economic theories depend on the assumption that the decision maker in any situation is both (a) rational (i.e. always makes the best decision to maximise benefit) and (b) has access to perfect information about every situation. It is up to you to judge whether these assumptions are realistic, or more importantly whether models relying on them are still able to usefully predict or explain economic behaviour.

Doubtless you have noticed that so far I have focused mostly on the natural sciences to explore the notion of theory. This is because, in the physical world, it is often easier to see the relationship between physical events and theory, to show how theories can be incorrect, and how the assumptions on which the theory is based can be wrong. Within the social sciences, understanding the nature of theory is complicated by the fact that the behaviour of people is generally less predictable than objects in the physical world and the factors that influence behaviour are more varied, often less measurable and less well understood. This gives rise to an interesting debate in the field of social science about what theory is, and there is considerable disagreement. When does an 'idea' become a theory, and then when does a theory become a law. If ever?

Despite this, there seems to be more agreement about what theory isn't. Most importantly, when reading a theoretical work (maybe a literature review, an article, a research monograph, etc.) there are many different components which might be confused with theory by the unwary. For example, in such work you will probably see lots of *references*, *variables*, *data*, *conceptual definitions*, *models* and *hypotheses*. While all of these may be relevant to theory in a supporting role, they should not be thought of as actually *being* theory. Instead, as Sutton and Staw (2003) show in their excellent book chapter, theory is that part of the work which shows the patterns of interconnectedness between phenomena; providing details about the mechanisms of causality in these relationships; and answering questions about **why** these phenomena are related, and **why** the relationships operate as they do. Furthermore, a strong theory should be more than an explanation of historical events (typically your observations), it should also be able to predict future events and outcomes.

If theory is not references, variables, data, conceptual definitions, models or hypotheses, this is probably a good place to have a look at these to see what they are and how they relate to theory. References, variables, data and concepts are the topic of later chapters in the book so I won't deal with these in detail here. In the next paragraphs we will deal with models and hypotheses, since they are very often confused with theory itself.

Models

Like so much in the academic literature examining theory, the distinction between a theory and a model is not always clear. Often the two terms are used synonymously. I will draw a distinction between theories and models here which I hope will help you to think about the theories that you are working with, and may wish to develop. Theories attempt to **explain** phenomena, whereas models by themselves are like laws in that they can only **describe**. Both can be used to predict future phenomena, but in slightly different ways. A good model should be *based on* a solid theory, but the model is just a descriptive representation of the theory, and by itself offers no explanatory power. Think about Newton's Law – which can also be considered to be a mathematical model describing the behaviour of bodies. It offers no description or explanation of why those bodies are attracted, just a mathematical description of what does happen, allowing you to predict what might happen in the future. The theoretical component would be a detailed thesis on *how* bodies attract each other according to their mass and distance. Of course, as we now 'know', theoretical explanations of gravity are elusive.

In many instances, when we create a theory we are also constructing a model of reality. A model is a representation (literally, 're-presentation') of the real world; but it is not the real world. For instance, a scale model of a Ferrari, no matter how detailed and intricate, is clearly not the Ferrari itself; the aspects of the car represented in the scale model are, only in certain limited ways, representative of the actual entity. However, in most ways that matter, the scale model of the car is not an actual car. It *describes a car* to a greater or lesser extent. But to explain how a car actually worked, you would need to refer to a detailed theoretical description of the internal combustion engine, electronic control systems, transmissions, aerodynamics, and many other things. Take a look at Figures 5.2a and 5.2b, which both represent the same model of the relationship between consumer satisfaction and behaviour. One is a graphical model, and the other is the same thing represented in mathematical form.

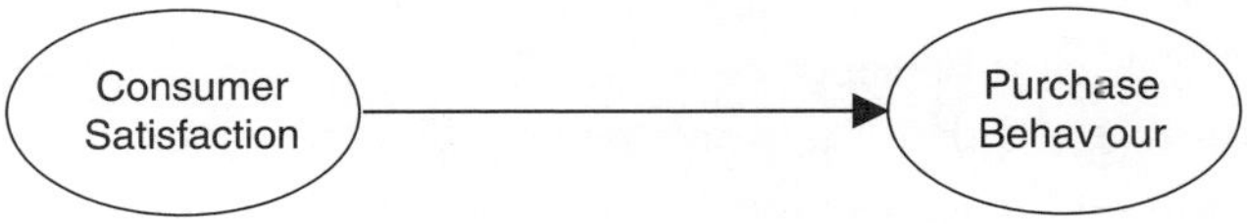

Figure 5.2a A graphical model

$P = f(CS)$

(purchase behaviour = a function of consumer satisfaction)

Figure 5.2b A mathematical model

Both these models are only representations of the real world. Such models are **based on** corresponding underlying theories, of which there are several. Different theories give rise to different models, each of which may be able to describe the same phenomenon to a greater or lesser extent. As a representation of behaviour in consumer markets such competing models and theories are useful, but all of them are incomplete. They are based on their own sets of assumptions, which may be different, and these assumptions may or may not be true (we do not know if they are or not).

For example, let us look at two competing theories that predict the behaviour of consumers. I have grossly simplified these theories to illustrate the point and apologise to both economists and psychologists who may well cringe at the lack of detail in the explanations of these two theories. The first theory has its foundations in economics (utility theory), the second in psychology (theory of reasoned action). From economics, utility theory states that an individual's utility is a measure of the relative satisfaction gained from engaging in a behaviour (perhaps buying a car) to satisfy their wants and needs. Accordingly, utility (relative satisfaction with the car) can increase or decrease. Utility theory explains people's behaviour in terms of their attempts to increase their utility (relative satisfaction) with the behaviour (car purchase) given the economic constraints which they endure (buy the car that provides the most satisfaction, given limitations on the amount of money one can spend). It is also generally accepted that products have several salient attributes (the car's colour, brand, power and fuel economy). Utility theory would predict that the individual would weigh up the cost of each of these attributes against the satisfaction gained by having different levels of each. Their choice of car will be the one that provides the most overall satisfaction. This utility maximising behaviour is based on the assumptions of rationality and perfect information, which I touched on above. Assumptions such as this dominate classical theories in microeconomics. Yet they are still assumptions because they cannot be directly tested, so have to be taken on faith.

Clearly an assumption such as rationality may be incorrect in certain circumstance, most notably where the preferences of the individual are not stable, such as when they are not sure of the consequences of making a particular choice. A competing model of human behaviour derived from a psychological perspective is the Theory of Reasoned Action. The Theory of Reasoned Action suggests that a person's behaviour is determined by their intention to perform the behaviour and that this intention is, in turn, a function of their attitude toward the behaviour and their subjective norms. According to the theory of reasoned action the behaviour of an individual can be predicted by understanding the beliefs that they hold about themselves and their environment. These beliefs are thought to underlie the person's attitudes and subjective norms, and ultimately determine their intentions and their behaviour. Simply put, the Theory of Reasoned Action suggests that a person's intention to perform a behaviour is predicted by their attitude toward that behaviour and how they think other people would view them if they performed the behaviour. This intention to perform a behaviour then predicts the actual behaviour itself. The Theory of Reasoned Action has its own set of assumptions, most notably that the behaviour of the individual is voluntary and decision making is a conscious activity. In certain circumstances these assumptions may be incorrect, such as when the decision is not a conscious one, perhaps because it is impulsive or habitual, or the behaviour is not voluntary, perhaps because it is determined by a third party such as an employer.

Proponents of both these theories concede that the assumptions made are not a totally accurate description of reality, but would argue that both theories are good inasmuch as they help researchers to reason, and provide help in formulating falsifiable hypotheses. In other words, theories do not necessarily have to be perfectly accurate explanations of what happens in the world. Instead, the criteria for the usefulness of a theory is whether those departures from reality invalidate the theory. Of course this is a thorny question, and leads to significant disagreement because different researchers have different criteria for what makes a theory valid. For some, to assume that individuals have perfect information and are rational is so patently incorrect that any theories drawn from such assumptions can not be of any use at all. For others, the fact that such theories give us the basic mental tools to explore a lot of human decision-making, and allow the development of models which *do* seem to describe human behaviour with a reasonable level of accuracy, is enough to retain such theories. Many critics of social science theories do tend to make the error of assuming that to be useful, a theory has to be a perfect representation of what happens. This is of course not really the case, and scientific progress has to start somewhere. It is up to the individual to determine whether they consider a theory to be useful, even though it may contain some unrealistic assumptions. If we had to ignore theories unless they were perfect representations of the world, would we have any theories at all?

Moving on, from these different theories it is possible to develop different conceptual models. A conceptual model is one which is based on theory, in this instance we have two competing conceptual models because we have two competing theories to explain and predict behaviour. The conceptual model represents the theory as applied to the real world; it consists of a set of variables and a set of logical and quantitative relationships between them. Typically the conceptual model refers to only some aspects of the phenomenon in question (in the Utility Theory and Theory of Reasoned Action examples, these aspects are a small set of determinants of an individual's behaviour). This means that two models of the same phenomenon may be fundamentally different, as they are based on different theoretical backgrounds and underlying assumptions. This is illustrated in Figure 5.3.

Remember from the previous discussion that models by their very nature are incomplete and, like theory, are based on some explicit assumptions, which are also often incomplete (or even false). It is nearly always necessary to make assumptions in order to simplify the real world into a theory and then further into a model; however, we also need to make sure that we don't include so many assumptions that acceptably accurate solutions are not produced. Other reasons why conceptual models may differ, even if they are based on the

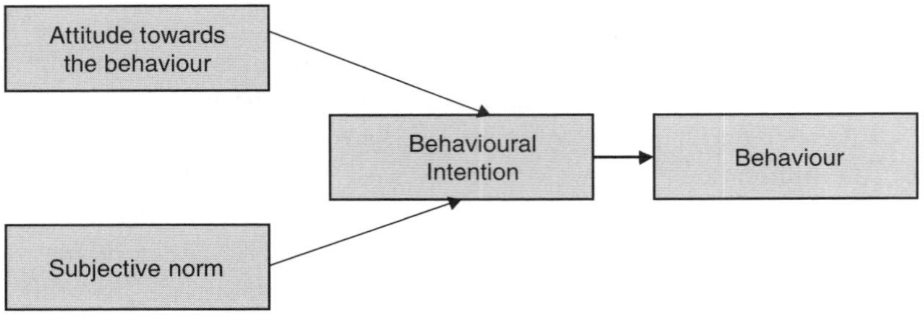

(a) A conceptual model of the theory of planned behaviour

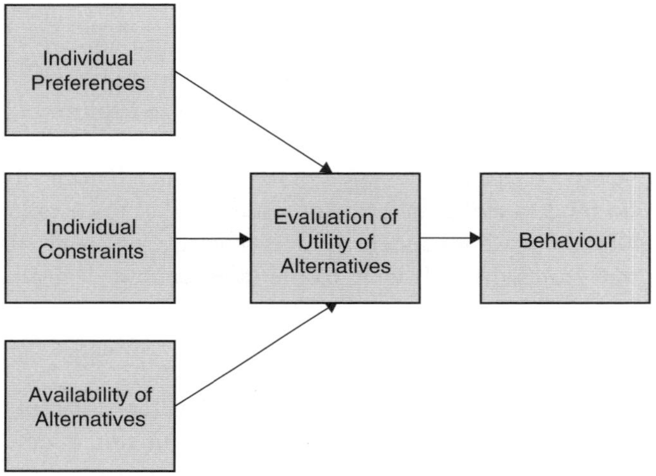

(b) A conceptual model of utility theory

Figure 5.3 Different theoretical models

same theoretical background, include the preferences of the person developing the model, the use to which they want to put it and the other assumptions that they have made regarding the nature of the world. For example, a researcher using a utility framework to examine satisfaction may decide to use a general framework such as the one in Figure! 5.2 shown earlier, or alternatively they may decide that they have sufficient information to 'know' what the alternatives are and the attributes that the individual uses to evaluate these alternatives, as shown in Figure 5.4. This could than be represented as a more specific conceptual model describing the influence of the satisfaction with each attribute with the overall utility of the product chosen.

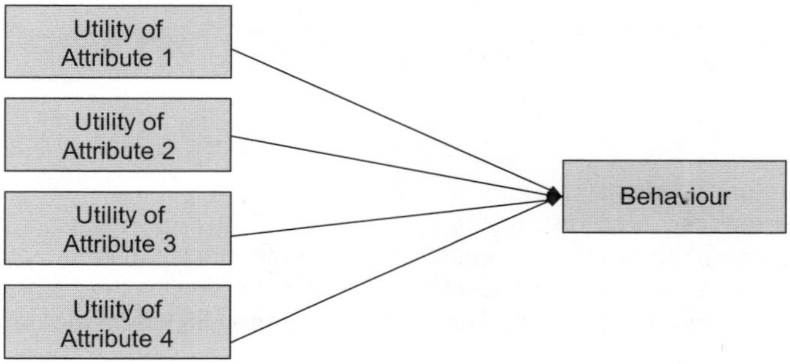

Figure 5.4 A more detailed model

The fact that two models attempting to represent the same element of reality may be essentially different, presents opportunities and challenges to the researcher. First, it means that if you wish to use a model you need to understand its original purpose and the assumptions that it is based on. This is particularly important when putting the critical literature review together. Examining, and explaining, the assumptions of the underlying theory that a model is based on is an essential element of commenting on the applicability of certain theories and their associated models to different contexts and for different purposes. When critiquing the work of one researcher in comparison to others, comparing the assumptions and simplifications that have been made to create the conceptual models used, is an effective way in which to comment on the applicability of different research to the context in which it has been applied and its suitability for the context in which you are interested.

Hypotheses and propositions

But once you have developed a model, this is only half the job. It is now possible to derive formal hypotheses or propositions from it. For example, you could think of every 'link' in the models presented in Figures 5.3 and 5.4 as needing a formal hypothesis or proposition linked to it. Many people get hypotheses and propositions confused with theory, which is understandable, so let me clear this up right from the start. First, it is necessary to differentiate between the terms **hypothesis** and **proposition**, which often get confused.

The Oxford English Dictionary defines hypotheses and propositions as follows.

hypothesis n. (pl. hypotheses)

1. a proposition made as a basis for reasoning, without the assumption of its truth.
2. a supposition made as a starting-point for further investigation from known facts (cf. THEORY).

3. a groundless assumption.
   [LL f. Gk hypothesis foundation (as HYPO-, THESIS)]

proposition noun

1. a statement or assertion.
2. a scheme proposed; a proposal.
3. Logic a statement consisting of subject and predicate that is subject to proof or disproof.
4. colloq. a problem, opponent, prospect, etc. that is to be dealt with (a difficult proposition).
5. Math. a formal statement of a theorem or problem, often including the demonstration.

On first reading, hypotheses and propositions appear to be very similar, and they are in many ways. But there are some important differences too. Yet in the social sciences confusion abounds about the exact usage of the two terms. A proposition is, strictly speaking, a **statement that predicts a relationship between two or more variables**, one that answers research questions and makes predictions. These predictions are of the type: *A* ***causes*** *B*, or *an increase in the amount of A will* ***lead to*** *an increase/decrease the amount of B*. Important to note here, is that if the statement does not offer any causality, and merely indicates that A and B are correlated, then it should technically be called a hypothesis. However, in common social scientific usage, a *hypothesis* is used to describe a proposition that will be tested in the study being reported, irrespective of whether there is causality inferred, and *proposition* is used when there will not be a test of the relationship between the constructs. Nevertheless, this is not strictly correct.

A more correct and useful distinction would define a hypothesis as simply **a statement which predicts what you expect to observe in your empirical data**. By itself, it has no theoretical content.[2] Of course, hypotheses should be *supported* by detailed theoretical arguments and logic, but the hypothesis itself is just a prediction of what you will observe in your data. This is the source of the distinction between correlation (hypothesis) and causality (proposition) made above. Causality is actually a theoretical concept, and as you can never actually *see* causation in your data, a hypothesis should never state it. A proposition, on the other hand, is kind of like a summary statement about a given theoretical idea, which may or may not relate to actual empirical data or tests.

Hypotheses are derived from the theory on which your research is based. This theory will usually provide an indication of the direction of causality; for example, A causes B, or B causes A, and the size and sign of the causality A increases or decreases B and by how much. Hypotheses should be closely related to your conceptual model, inasmuch as they typically describe the arrows in the model. The scientific method, specifically the hypothetico-deductive method, requires that hypotheses be **falsifiable**. This means that they must be written in such a way that other researchers can show them to be false (usually by

---

[2]There will be more about hypotheses in Chapter 14 about quantitative testing.

using empirical data, but sometimes from pure logic). For this reason, hypotheses predicting a relationship between two variables are accompanied by a **null hypothesis** which predicts *no* relationship between the variables. Normally the null hypothesis is not stated in journal articles as it can easily be derived from the hypothesis that is presented.

Using the example of the Theory of Reasoned Action above, it is possible to derive several hypotheses about the relationships between the constructs in the study. For instance, the theory tells us that the *more positive the person's attitude* towards a behaviour, the *more they will intend to perform* that behaviour. Similarly, the *more the person's subjective norms support* the behaviour the *more the person will intend to perform* the behaviour; and finally the *more the person intends to perform* a behaviour; the *more they will display* the behaviour.

These statements may be written as formal hypotheses:

H_1: A person's attitude towards a given behaviour will be positively associated with their intention to undertake that behaviour.

And the associated null hypothesis:

H_0: A person's attitude towards a given behaviour will have no association with their intention to undertake that behaviour.

Similarly the relationship between subjective norms and intentions to behave can be written as a formal hypothesis thus:

H_2: A person's subjective norms about a given behaviour will be positively associated with their intention to undertake that behaviour.

And the associated null hypothesis:

H_0: A person's subjective norms about a given behaviour will have no association with their intention to undertake that behaviour.

For the relationship between behavioural intentions and behaviour the formal hypotheses would be:

H_3: A person's intention to perform a given behaviour will be positively associated with their behaviour.

H_0: A person's intention to perform a given behaviour will have no association with their behaviour.

Note that the hypotheses only state an *association*, not any causal relationship or effect. Your theoretical logic which leads up to your hypotheses may well propose causal influences (indeed we tend to think in this manner all the time), but since you cannot ever observe causality, your hypotheses should not make any predictions regarding it. Remember, stick to exactly what tests of your empirical data can provide evidence of. Once the hypotheses, and the associated null hypotheses, have been formally stated they can be tested. Typically this is done by collecting and analysing empirical data to establish support for either the hypothesis or the null hypothesis. You will get to looking at what data are and how to collect and analyse them later in this book.

Supporting a hypothesis

Once tested, retested and further tested, a supported hypothesis may become a well-accepted part of a theory, or occasionally may grow to become a theory itself. It may be tempting to think of such well-validated hypotheses as laws. They are not! One should more accurately refer to repeatedly supported hypotheses simply as adequately verified, or as dependable. However, even dependable hypotheses remain provisional, as by their very nature hypotheses cannot be proven to be true. Observations which support a hypothesis *fail to falsify* it rather than prove it to be true. As both myself and Nick have mentioned already at various points, a single, non-confirming observation can prove a hypothesis to be false.

An appropriate example of the provisional nature of hypotheses would be my first visit to what is in my opinion[3] the most beautiful place on Earth, New Zealand. New Zealand is famous for having more sheep than people, and on my first visit, I noticed that all the sheep I saw were white. From this I could have formed the hypothesis that *all sheep in New Zealand are white*. Even though it does not predict any association, this is still a hypothesis, as it predicts *something* I could test, and it is falsifiable. In fact, anyone could falsify my hypothesis by observing a single black sheep. If someone with nothing better to do were to try to do this though, there are some considerations that are required for good science to be conducted.

Firstly, I myself have to correctly define and communicate the statement of my hypothesis and define the variables in my hypothesis. Without this, it is impossible for any other researcher to examine my hypothesis in a meaningful way. What exactly do I mean by 'sheep'? Does this include lambs and rams? What do I mean by New Zealand? Does this include only the two main islands, or the smaller offshore islands as well? Provided that I have clearly and unambiguously defined my variables (more about this in later chapters) and clearly stated my hypothesis, any researcher can come along and test my hypothesis. Some researchers will be better at this than others, and much of that depends on the methods that they use to make the observations, and therefore how confident we can be in the observations that they make. In order to have confidence in the findings of these imaginary researchers that wish to examine my hypothesis, we need to be assured that measurement errors are sufficiently small. Have they adequately distinguished black sheep from goats or llamas, or

[3]Honestly, I am not just putting this in here for Nick's benefit!

the many other animals that look like black sheep but are not really black sheep? If we are confident that the method was suitable and the error sufficiently small, then finding a black sheep falsifies the 'white sheep only' hypothesis.

There are other types of hypothesis which are more common in social sciences research than the type used in the sheep example above. For example, many of the hypotheses I've already given you assert associations between variables, such as *A is positively associated with B*. For example, if one observes a particular independent variable change, then one will also observe a certain dependent variable change. This formulation, also known as an **if-then** statement, applies whether or not a proposition or theory asserts a direct cause-and-effect relationship (remember, hypotheses can only state what can be observed).

Beware! Not all if-then statements are hypotheses. For example, 'If you warm yeast, then more gas will be produced' is not a hypothesis. It is instead a simple prediction. The problem with this statement is that there is no theoretical proposition to test. What is related to what? Is temperature a variable? Is yeast a variable? Is gas production a variable? Which gas? A better hypothesis along these lines would be 'The temperature of yeast is positively associated with the amount of carbon dioxide produced'. This hypothesis clearly states what we expect to observe, and the key variables. However, it does not make clear the assumptions – which in this case are that the yeast is present in a mixture of flour, salt, water and milk, which provide the fermentable sugars which are converted to carbon dioxide. This context would be discussed fully in the theory which preceded the hypothesis.

Hypotheses about possible correlation do not stipulate the cause and effect *per se,* they only state that A is related to B. Among other key philosophical and technical issues, verifying causal relationships is complicated by *intervening variables*. Observations may give the appearance of a direct cause-and-effect relationship between A and B, but further investigation may reveal other factors not mentioned in the proposition. Also, observing that changes in A are correlated with changes in B, does not provide any information about the cause and effect. In such circumstances it is possible, and often common, to mistake the effect for the cause, and vice versa (i.e. potentially get the hypothesised cause and effect backwards).

Summary

At various points throughout this chapter I have characterised laws, theories, models and hypotheses. This discussion was based on a critical realist philosophical view of the world. This is not to suggest that critical relativism is not 'as good' or that metaphysical idealism is not valid though, just that the idea of developing theory is most easily discussed from the critical realist (or positivistic) viewpoint. This is the first challenge that you will have to face. You need to decide which philosophical standpoint you intend to take (this will also be influenced by your supervisors' views of the world too). You have also seen the relationship between laws, models, and theories: laws are supposedly always true (in their context), theories are always tentative, models describe, theories explain. You have seen how the same theory can give rise to different models and how different theories can give rise to competing models to explain the same phenomena. These differences arise, in part, from the assumptions that researchers make in developing and adopting a theory to a particular problem.

You have also seen how the hypothetico-deductive method can be used to develop and test hypotheses (and associated null hypotheses) and have explored the nation of proving a hypothesis correct (or more specifically we have noted that this is not possible). Finally, one of the aims of this chapter was to illustrate the need for strong theory and the need to understand what theories are (and what they are not) if you are to do this. Most academic research projects aim to make a contribution to knowledge in some way, and one way of doing this is to contribute to theory. This does not mean developing a whole new theory, but more usually means examining existing theories and making an incremental advancement to them, maybe by challenging some of the underlying assumptions or by developing alternative conceptualisations of the theory and testing these.

Key points to take from this chapter:

- Strong theory provides a foundation on which to build your research and is the cornerstone of a well-considered project.
- There may be several different theories that attempt to explain the same phenomena, typically these will be based on different assumptions and may derive from different areas of social science.
- Understanding the assumptions of a theory is important to evaluate the usefulness of that theory.
- Theories can often be represented in conceptual models; competing conceptual models arise from competing theories explaining the same phenomena.
- Theories, and the scientific method, are by definition based on a philosophy of epistemological objectivity.
- In the Hypothetico-Deductive Method, it is impossible to prove a scientific theory true by means of induction, because no amount of evidence assures us that contrary evidence will not be found. Instead, a process of deduction involving the process of falsification is used.

Further reading

There aren't too many sources specifically about theory, but a book I have always found helpful is *Evaluating Social Science Research* by Paul C. Stern and Linda Kalof. This book gives a lot of attention to theory, and how to evaluate it. One can move from here (with the help of other sources) to come to terms with actually creating theory.

There are also some great articles on theory, and doubtless you will come across many in your own fields. In marketing, some great works are:

- Hunt. S (1990), 'Truth in marketing theory and research.' *Journal of Marketing,* 54 (July), 1–15.
- Zinkhan, G. M., and Hirschheim, R. (1992), 'Truth in marketing theory and research: An alternative perspective'. *Journal of Marketing,* 56 (April), 80–88.
- Stewart, D. W. and Zinkhan, G. M. (2006), 'Enhancing marketing theory in academic research' *Journal of the Academy of Marketing Science,* 34 (4), 477–480.

EXERCISES

1. What are epistemological objectivity, and metaphysical idealism? How do these concepts influence theory development in the scientific method?
2. What is the difference between a law, a theory, a model and a hypothesis?
3. For your research project:

   a. What phenomena are you interested in?
   b. Think about different theories that aim to explain the relationships between the phenomena that you are interested in.
   c. What are the assumptions of these theories?

4. Identify two or three journal articles that describe the relationships between the phenomena that you are interested in.

   a. Can you identify conceptual models that are presented in these papers?
   b. How well do these conceptual models relate to the underlying theory?
   c. Do the authors explicitly state what theoretical foundations they are basing their work on?

15

Concepts, Constructs and Measurement

NICK LEE and IAN LINGS

SUPERVISOR'S VIEW: PROFESSOR DENNY BORSBOOM

Stuck in Psychometrics: I work in a psychometrics department, and I guess many people think of me as some sort of statistician – but I really don't feel that way. As far as I'm concerned, I am a psychologist who has gotten stuck in psychometrics. Why? Because, even though I am more interested in psychology than in psychometric models *per se*, I do not think that you can do much in the way of worthwhile science if you haven't found out how to connect theoretical terms – intelligence, extraversion, self-efficacy, etc. – to empirical observations. To do that properly, you have to solve the measurement problem. And psychology (and many related or similar disciplines), in my personal view, hasn't so far done a very convincing job in this respect.

Now, the fact that the measurement problem, in most areas of psychology, is basically unsolved is not widely recognised. People – researchers as well as laypersons – are often quite uncritical in accepting statements like 'IQ-tests measure intelligence'; often they will even equate 'intelligence' (the theoretical concept) with 'IQ' (the score that you get from an IQ-test). Researchers do this because they are interested primarily in relations between variables (e.g. 'does breast feeding increase a child's intelligence?'). They don't want to spend their whole life figuring out the measurement issues (and learning all the difficult mathematical models) before they can get to what they perceive as the really interesting stuff. So they just substitute IQ for intelligence when it comes to statistically analysing their data. However, the commingling of, say, IQ and intelligence, is a little too quick for my taste, and the same holds for most other important variables in psychology. For instance, IQ is a single number. To substitute 'IQ-score' for 'intelligence' in empirical research one therefore has to assume that intelligence can also be represented as a single number. Why should we believe that? How should we investigate whether this assumption is justified?

What, by the way, is intelligence? How does it relate to IQ-scores? How do we mathematically formalise such a relation, and how do we test whether we are on the right track? These issues, to me, are not problems that merely need to be solved before we can do the really interesting work. They *are* the really interesting work. And that's why I'm happy to be stuck in psychometrics.

VIEW FROM THE TRENCHES: WALTER HERZOG

I have just completed my Ph.D. in consumer behaviour at the University of St. Gallen (Switzerland). My dissertation manuscript comprises papers on topics in consumer psychology and psychometric theory. However, a question I often had to deal with was: 'Why are psychometric or measurement issues relevant for 'applied' researchers?' Let me begin with the following story: I will probably never forget a comment of a reviewer of one of my conference papers. About one-third of the paper consisted of an appendix with statistical results. Although the reviewer was quite positive and highlighted the 'practical relevance' of my findings, (s)he closed the review with the following sentence: 'It would have been desirable to empirically test the proposed model'. The reviewer obviously did not recognise any of the numbers in the appendix, even though I referred to it throughout the manuscript! So, how could (s)he then conclude that my model was of practical value or 'relevance'?

Now, the point that I want to make here is not that reading reviews can be quite funny (although they can be). It is about the relation of 'relevance' and 'rigour'. Most applied researchers would agree (especially after two or three pints of beer in a relaxed atmosphere at a conference dinner) that a nice 'story' (i.e. theory) brings you through the review process of almost any journal – despite methodological weaknesses. In other words, 'relevance compensates rigour'. However, how can a result be relevant *without* rigour in testing the hypothesised relations among the variables under study? In my view, rigour is a **necessary condition** for the relevance of research findings. Of course, rigour itself cannot produce relevant results, but a good idea or an interesting research topic without rigour in theory-testing is of limited worth.

In this perspective, the role of measurement becomes immediately clear. Measurement of the variables under study is not just a 'bonus', or something you have to do to get your research published. It is the central step in the research process that gives you access to the concepts, and relations among the concepts, under study – thereby translating good ideas into relevant results, and identifying bad ideas as such. Without measurement, good ideas will remain merely ideas, and will not be differentiable from bad ideas. I always conceived this important function of measurement theory for applied research as a motivation to deal with psychometric issues. And after a while, when you realise the immense value of psychometrics for your applied research, this seemingly nerdy stuff gets more and more exciting.

However, during your studies you are likely to come across people (maybe reviewers) who are less excited about measuring variables or statistical issues, and might be of the opinion that fooling around with statistics is wasting time that could be invested in more interesting 'applied' issues. I remember several such encounters during the last three years, and sometimes I thought that it might be the case that these people are much more clever than I am and therefore, they do not need to test their theories in a proper way since their hypotheses are correct anyway. Such people must be very impressive applied scientists!

Measurement is completely ubiquitous in today's world, whether you know it or not. In order to get to the stage of your education where you are reading this book, you have almost certainly been subjected to a battery of measures, from your IQ, your reading ability, perhaps SATs (standard aptitude tests), the GMAT (graduate management admission test), or various other exams. Perhaps you learnt a music instrument when you were younger, or danced; if so, you would have probably been measured on your ability to do such things, and given various gradings. If you're ill, you'll be taking some kind of carefully measured amount (or dose) of medicine; if you are not ill, you might be going out to a bar tonight for a carefully measured pint of beer. Furthermore, measurement properties and theories impact our lives almost constantly. Virtually none of the technology used to write this book, for example, would be possible without measurement. Recipes for dishes are, of course, full of measurements as well. However, we hardly ever think about measurement until something goes wrong. I once had a flatmate who misread teaspoons for tablespoons of salt when making guacamole. Fortunately, there was a large supply of drinks on hand. Speaking of drinks, I remember learning the hard way that English beer was in rather larger 'pints' than those I used to drink in New Zealand. If you are thinking of petrol consumption, you better work out the units you are concerned with (how many litres are in a gallon?), and many London market-traders are still working out how to use grams and kilos instead of ounces and pounds. Although we survived for thousands of years without formalised measurement theories, the advent of measurement was one of the key factors in the rise of technology and science. In a social science context, the massive advances made since the beginning of the 20th century would have been impossible without accompanying advances in measurement theory.

By now you should be well aware of my fetish for the theory that lies behind the methods we use to do research (trust me, there are worse fetishes to have), as well as the historical development of these theories. I'm hoping that by now you are beginning to realise how an appreciation of these things can help us better understand how and why we do research. I'm hoping this because this chapter contains some pretty difficult concepts to grasp if it's your first time thinking about them, and I really want you to make the effort to become comfortable with them. If you do this, then you'll be able to use the practical sections of this and the next chapter much more effectively – if not, you will become (yet) another automaton, plugging numbers into a formula and not realising why or even how you are getting it wrong. In reading this chapter I want you to get a flavour of the importance of measurement theory, and perhaps be inspired to find out more. But even if you don't get interested in measurement itself, I want you to take away a real appreciation for the importance of good measurement to your research, and a commitment to actually doing it properly as much as possible. Because in the past, have I *ever* seen some bad measurement. Please, don't contribute to this yourself, especially after reading this and the next chapter (boy that would make me mad!)

At the end of this chapter I really hope you have come to terms with these key ideas:

- What measurement is, and the importance of rigorous measurement.
- The different rules by which we assign numbers to qualities.
- The difference between direct and indirect measurement, and what a 'latent construct' is.
- The difference between constructs and concepts, and the importance of defining your constructs very clearly.
- What a dimension is, and how to decide whether your constructs are 'multidimensional'.

Why is it Important to Know This Stuff?

At this point, I am hoping that you are beginning to understand many of the ideas relating to the 'theoretical side' of research. Many of you will also have actually got a tentative idea of the theoretical model you may wish to examine. However, this model is exactly that – theoretical. It doesn't exist in the real world. In order to investigate it, we need somehow to collect data which allows us to detect the presence and amount of the concepts which make up our model. In fact, this process is critical to the success of your project. Unfortunately it is also a process which is often little understood and poorly managed by researchers.

So far, we've been talking about developing the theoretical side of our research – the philosophies, concepts, and arguments which make up our theories. However, we now need to think about how to link that theory to the real world, which is what now need to think about how to link that theory to the real world, which is what we can actually observe. This chapter marks the first point where we really look at **how** to link theory and reality. We've been building up to this throughout the first five chapters of this book, but here we begin to put together both sides of the coin, theoretical and real. Understanding this link will put you in a great position to conduct good research, as well as to evaluate the quality of your and others' research. Figure 6.1 should look quite familiar to you.

The material in this chapter should also help you critically analyse other research, such as that you are reviewing in the conceptual development of your own research. In doing so, you may save yourself a lot of heartache later on in the process of research, and may actually help yourself do considerably better research. It will also allow you to have a ready source of questions when you view presentations of research, say in your faculty or at a conference – which can really help you look clever (or irritating, take your pick).

Plus, I think it's really interesting – honest!

Measurement and the theory behind it

Before we take a look at some of the major concepts of measurement, it's a good idea to have a think about exactly *why* we measure things, or even *what* measurement actually means. One thing which may surprise you is that measurement as a formal area of study is quite a recent idea, in fact Savage and Ehrlich (1992) seem to imply that it was less than 30 years

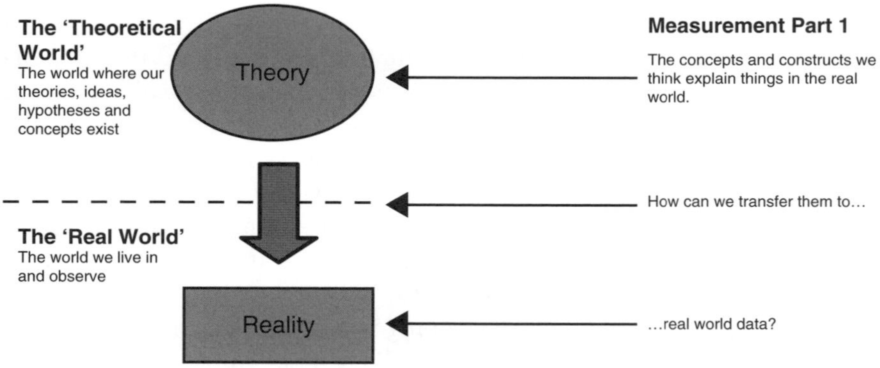

Figure 6.1 The place of measurement

old at the time of their writing.[1] Of course, concepts relating to measurement itself have appeared throughout human history, and both the Bible and the Koran include references to measurement, particularly as they relate to commerce (see Hand, 2004). Interestingly, many of the great philosophers you've already met in these pages (if you are reading the book in order) have been contributors to measurement theory. Aristotle wrote about quantities in his work, and the ancient Greeks were often concerned with such matters. Furthermore, Descartes was one of the first to theorise that one could assign a numerical value to length, area, and volume by counting how many standard units most closely approximated the object. In other words, to measure the length of a line segment, for example, you could count the amount of standard units (i.e. of the same standard length) which end-on-end came closest to the length of the line segment. I'm not sure about you, but it seems almost unbelievable that we could be well into the Enlightenment before someone came up with this idea. Related to this, while you're reading this chapter, remember that measurement theory is still evolving and by no means 'set in stone', no matter what your colleagues think.

With that in mind, let's begin by exploring just what the purpose of measurement is, or even what measurement itself it. First and foremost, measurement can be thought of as the business of quantifying attributes, i.e., *assigning numbers to represent their magnitude.* For example, you as an individual possess many qualities or attributes. Some of these are easily observable and obvious, such as your height, your weight, the length of your hair, the size of your feet and the like. However, you also possess many more subtle attributes, such as intelligence, extraversion, motivation, self-esteem and such. Many of these latter attributes have been developed by social scientists from theory and can't actually be 'seen' by us. Measurement is the process of assigning numbers to represent the amount of any given attribute which is present. Note that I said we measure the *attribute*, not the person (or organisation, or whatever). You don't measure a person, you measure their height, or their self-esteem.

Try to remember the points made above as you move through this chapter, as they imply some interesting and important things which I will point out subsequently. Firstly, measurement is fundamentally *quantitative* as opposed to qualitative. What I mean by this is that measurement is explicitly concerned with numbers. If you read various other chapters of this book you should be clear that there is something of a divide between qualitative (which focuses on gaining direct access to words, thoughts, and feelings, and immersion in the research context) and quantitative (which tends to focus on abstracting oneself from the research context, and converting qualities into numbers to standardise them) research. Chapters 2 and 3 looked at some of the philosophical backgrounds to such approaches. While qualitative data have some unique benefits which will be discussed in later chapters

---

[1] I'm not so sure I agree with this, but they are definitely a lot smarter than me, so I will just go with it.

(Chapter 9 and 10 especially), they are fundamentally inappropriate for manipulation using many of the tools which have been developed in or adopted by the social sciences, such as mathematics and statistics. For one thing, qualitative attributes are difficult to standardise, and easy to confuse. Take height, for example. Due to some great cosmic joke, I am a mere 5 feet 7 inches tall, but does this mean I am 'tall' or 'short' – well that depends whether you compare me to Snow White, or the Seven Dwarfs, doesn't it? But I am 5′7″ whoever you compare me to. This allows a consistent interpretation of my height, whatever the context I find myself in – be it Lilliput or the Land of the Giants. Using the qualitative terms 'tall' and 'short' can lead to confusion, for example in my family I am actually one of the tallest; if we lived in a small village where average height was quite low, I may in fact come across as quite tall. Now if I were to be set up by my mum on a blind date with a girl who liked 'tall men' from a neighbouring village where average height was much greater, things would clearly not work out well (although my charming personality may carry the day). The use of standard quantitative measures would avoid such confusion and heartache.

Similarly, think of 'numerical ability' – many students of mine over the years have insisted they were 'rubbish with numbers'. In my experience this tends to be a function of the fact they compare themselves with people who are very very good. Essentially, in a University environment, average levels of numerical ability (and most intelligence-related factors) are clearly higher than the general population. Furthermore, a student also is commonly exposed to those who are numeric experts – the tutors who are teaching the course, and the top students as well. This tends to lead the less numerically-strong students to think they are far worse than they actually are in relation to the general population. In fact, in a quantitative test, most of these students would be far above the norm for the population in quantitative ability, not 'rubbish' at all. One perspective on measurement is that quantifying attributes allows us to place them in an artificial, numerical, objective world, where the mess and subjectivity of the 'real' world is removed. And once attributes are mapped on to numerical values, we are able to manipulate the numbers with mathematical and statistical tools – which is incredibly useful. However, this mapping of 'real to artificial' is a concept which seems to fit best with the idea of measuring things which are 'real' and 'observable' themselves – such as height. Height is a real, objective, observable attribute, which we map onto numbers. But as we shall see later, when we come to think about the things we measure most often in the social sciences (self-esteem, personality traits, etc.), the *opposite* is a more helpful way of thinking. But hold that thought for now, that's just a heads-up.

Either way though, **measurement is the process of mapping the magnitude of an attribute to a numerical value – or transferring the amount of a *quality* to a *quantity*.** It is this mapping process that measurement theory is concerned with. The idea of quantifying qualities (which has a nice ring to it) also relies on some key assumptions – many of which have been criticised from certain perspectives. First of all, once we quantify these qualities, our numerical operations are performed on *them* and not the qualities themselves. For example, when you translate two people's heights to numbers, you may get 172 cm and 186 cm.

These two numbers are just that, numbers. It is only in our heads that we know they represent the heights of two people (say me and my tall blind date from above). I can technically do anything I want to mathematically to those numbers, and nothing will of course happen to my actual height itself. For example, if I divide 172 in half and get 86, it doesn't mean that all of a sudden I become even shorter (God forbid!) We must always maintain the link between the attribute and the number which represents it – this requires a set of rules to make sure we are doing it right. Firstly, if the mapping of the attributes on to the numbers is done poorly, or is somehow defective, then any conclusions we draw from our numerical manipulations are also defective. For example, I would usually measure height with some kind of solid ruler, but what if I used a rubber rope? This would mean that according to the tension on the rope, I would get a different number each time I measured the same object! This would of course mean my measurement was meaningless – one day I would be 179 cm tall (brilliant!) and another day 168 cm tall (awful!) In that case I might as well just give up trying to measure things and go back to saying 'short'. In a nutshell, this is the challenge of measurement, and the more complex the attribute we are trying to measure, the more complex and debatable the rules of measurement are. This is important because, once we manipulate our numbers and come up with some answers, we must then map these answers *back* to the things we were trying to measure. Poor measurement means we have no basis with which to map our numerical results back to the things we were trying to measure – so our results are meaningless. Secondly, we must have rules by which we can manipulate the numbers which are appropriate to the attribute we are trying to measure. Basically, numbers themselves have mathematical properties of their own. Sometimes these properties are not held by the attribute in question, and sometimes the numbers are unable to fully represent some quality of the attribute. If you look at IDE 6.1, you'll see what I mean, and we'll fully discuss this when we talk about **scales of measurement** later on.

IDE 6.1: Numerical Representations of Qualities

By this stage of your education, I assume you have some knowledge of numbers themselves – even if you don't *think* you do. For example, you know that numbers have certain properties – e.g. '10' is a bigger number than '9', and is 10 times bigger than '1'. But many of the qualities we want to map to numbers do not even share this basic 'order of magnitude' attribute. Take gender for example. If we allocate '1' to represent males and '2' to represent females this should not be taken to mean that females are twice as 'big', or 'good', or whatever, as males – even though their numerical representation is. In this case the number is just a label for each gender. So in this particular case, the raw number is *more powerful* in terms of properties than the attribute it is measuring. We have created different **scales** to deal with this problem, which I'll discuss very soon.

More interesting to me (and less often talked about) is that many attributes we wish to measure are *more powerful than the numbers we use.* For example, one property of most number systems is that they are discrete. In other words each numerical value is separate from the one below and the one above. Many attributes we may wish to measure are instead *continuous* – there is no demarcation between one value and the next. Think of a bar graph (discrete) versus a line graph (continuous). We could divide a line up into five segments, for example, and number them 1–5. But each of these five segments would therefore represent a **range** of values of the line. This would mean that our numerical measure of 1–5 was less powerful than the actual attribute we were trying to measure – we've lost some information. I like to think of this in terms of music (as usual). I remember when CDs came out, there was (and still is) a lot of controversy over whether they sounded better than vinyl LPs (ask your parents – or maybe your grandparents – if you are wondering what an LP is). CDs represent the sound by cutting it up into thousands (around 16,000 per second in fact) of tiny bits (discrete), whereas on an LP there is a groove cut which is a direct representation of the original sound wave (continuous). CDs are more convenient, and sound really good in most situations, but if you have the correct equipment and the right situation, most audiophiles agree that LPs actually sound better.

Bringing it back to a social science context, a variable like 'satisfaction' is theoretically continuous, but we usually measure it with a range of numerical values (say 1–5). In cutting it up into these discrete segments, we have lost some of the information in the actual variable. It is our job as researchers to work out the appropriate trade-off between information lost, and the need for numerical representation. What this also means, is that – like CDs' representation of music – measures are almost always only an *approximation* of the actual value of the quality or attribute within our subject. In other words, there is always some kind of error involved. The concept of **measurement error** is a vital consideration in measurement theory, and research in general.

Measurement theory is complex and substantial in size, and it is a difficult task to even give a short introduction without raising more questions than answers. Nevertheless, some important distinctions can be made which should serve to provide a theoretical context to the rest of this chapter. This should in turn allow you to (a) gain a fuller understanding of what you are doing, and why, when you measure, and (b) impress the uninitiated – which I find is surprisingly important in life. First, it should be clear that *counting* is different from *measuring* – although both are essentially concerned with quantities and numbers.[2] Whereas it is simple to count the amount of observable, discrete objects (such as students in a class, or phone numbers in your address book), how do you count attributes like time, area or – even more obscurely – attitude and satisfaction? Some attributes, like time or area, can be divided into standard units, and we can then count how many of these units (or *quanta*) which most closely approximate the size/amount of the attribute you want to measure (see IDE 6.1 for a discussion of measurement as approximation). When you are a child at school, you learn measurement by actually physically doing this, laying short rods end-on-end next to a longer rod to measure length, for example. Normally as adults though, we are able to do this automatically, or I guess we would have to carry around rather a lot of small rods and other stuff with us just in case we ever needed to measure something.

Of course, this measurement process depends on a number of things. Firstly, we must have discrete, standardised quanta to use. Even such a basic concept as this is subject to international debate. For example, the US uses imperial quanta such as miles, pounds and gallons, while Europe (supposedly) uses kilometres, kilograms, and litres. Even worse, when it *is* used, a UK gallon is different from a US gallon! Fundamentally, we must also recognise that measurement is necessary, that more than one quanta must be used to measure the extent of our attribute. Finally, we must have rules for *concatenation*. This basically means how we 'add up' the quanta to represent the quantity of the attribute. When measuring length, would you lay your standard length quanta end-on-end or in parallel? In practical terms, if you had 10 standard quanta rods (say they were a foot long each), how would you use them to measure a 5 foot length of rope? Of course, you would lay the rope down, and lay the rods next to it until you reached 5. What about a 5 and a half foot length of rope? What about a 15 foot length? Concatenation rules seem simple in this context, but as we go on to measure more and more complex attributes they become correspondingly complex and also highly important (plus, the word makes you sound really clever). For example, how do you 'add up' the various elements which make up a measure of the 'quality of life' in a particular country? Is average salary more important than levels of pollution?

The discussion above also brings into relief one of the absolutely key concepts of this chapter (and the next one) – the distinction between **direct** and **indirect** measurement. Direct measurement is essentially what I have been referring to so far – i.e. giving numbers to the actual attributes we wish to measure, like weight or height. We can only directly measure things that we can actually observe in some way (e.g., age, speed, etc.). Nevertheless, many of the things that are of interest to psychological, organisational or social researchers are not observable at all. Now, before I go on, turn off the stereo or TV and prepare to think about

[2] The history of numbers and mathematics is far too long and complex to even begin to detail here, but it is certainly interesting enough for me to recommend you investigating it. Some references are given at the end of this chapter, and Hand (2004) has a nice introduction in the context of measurement.

this concept carefully, as the rest of this chapter, and the next, is based on it. Think back to the previous chapters about theory development and conceptual models. Such models often consist of concepts such as intelligence, customer satisfaction, love, commitment, trust, motivation and the like. How do we observe such things? Even if I were to cut your head open and spoon around in it, I would be unable to find the bit in there marked 'motivation', and measure its size.[3] What about intelligence, as mentioned in Professor Borsboom's viewpoint at the beginning of this chapter? 'IQ' you say? Well, it is a mistake to think of your IQ score as a direct measure of your intelligence (which is a shame if yours is really big). Instead, theorists have argued that IQ (which is the ability to answer certain types of questions to a time frame) should be related in some way to intelligence. But this is definitely not the same thing as saying IQ *is* intelligence. We can't measure things like intelligence, motivation, or other attitudes and psychological factors directly, so we must use **indirect** measurement. In other words, we need a model to relate the amount of intelligence, or motivation, or whatever, to the *measures* we are using, and therefore we derive the score for motivation from the scores of our subject on these measures. As you move through this chapter, you'll often see references to these latter measures – which are combined in some way to get the measure of our actual attribute – as **observed variables**, although in other work you may find them referred to as 'manifest' variables, 'items', 'indicators', or similar things. The thing we are actually interested in (e.g. motivation) will be termed a **construct** for the most part, and in other work you may find it called a 'concept', a 'latent construct', an 'unobservable', or various other combinations.[4] But the important thing to remember from this paragraph is that *a measurement of an attribute is not the attribute itself.* This will become highly relevant in a few pages, but for now, look at Figure 6.2 for an example.

Scales of measurement

The previous section introduced the idea of 'models' of measurement, which are essentially rules as to how measures can represent unobservable attributes. However, even in direct measurement applications, we need rules to help us decide how to assign numbers to attributes. Remember the earlier discussion, and also IDE 6.1, where I talked about how numbers may possess properties that the attributes we are trying to measure do not? **Scales of measurement** can be thought of as the basic rules which tell us what properties we can allow our measurements to have, due to the properties they are trying to measure, and what

[3] Of course, as science marches on, brain imaging techniques such as functional Magnetic Resonance Imaging may be able to help us begin to directly measure things such as emotions or attitudes (assuming they do in fact exist physically, which is far from agreed-upon), but we are a long way from this right now. Nevertheless, if you are interested in measurement, I suggest keeping your eye on this over the next decade or so!

[4] I actually believe there should be distinctions made between these terms, but now is not the place to go into that.

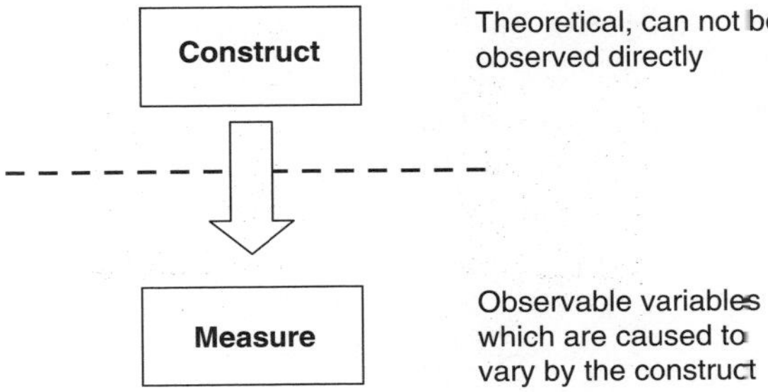

Figure 6.2 Constructs and measures

analysis we can therefore perform. There are four different scales each of which is more 'powerful' than the last. By 'power' I mean that the scale gets closer and closer to having the properties of the real number system. If you don't quite get this, then read on and it should all make sense in the end. Either way, the four scales are called in ascending power order; **nominal**, **ordinal**, **interval**, and **ratio**. A little trick to remember these is to think of *NOIR* as an acronym, which of course is French for black (I think this is quite clever, but to be honest all my students seem to think it's a bit lame).

Nominal scales

Nominal scales simply represent categories with numeric labels. For example, the variable 'gender' could be labelled as '1' for male and '2' for female, or vice versa. It could just as well be labelled '0.111' for male and 'π' for female. The numbers themselves are solely labels. This means the order of the numbers means absolutely nothing in terms of the attribute you are measuring. Another good example of a nominal scale could be for the variable 'country of birth', with a number assigned to the country given by the respondent. Nominal scales are used when the variable we wish to measure has no order of magnitude. For example, one gender is not bigger or better than another. So we must use nominal rules when analysing the measurement. Nominal rules tell us that the only thing we can do is to count the occurrence of each value (how many are in each group). So we can say 'there were 20 males and 10 females'. We can also take the 'mode' of the variable – the most common value. So if males are '1' and females are '2' we can say '1' is the mode. It makes no sense to do anything else (such as take the mean or median), as there is no order to the values under nominal rules. If we find the mean to be around '1.25', this value means nothing of any sense to us does it? Is the typical value therefore some kind of part male-part female super-creature? Nominal scales are of course the least powerful, but for variables like gender, country of origin, industry, and others where there is no order of magnitude to the categories, they are all we have. Nominal scales tend to be generally ignored or quickly passed over in many situations. However, they are actually quite important and understanding them can save you a bit of time and trouble when you first learn how to use statistics packages like SPSS. Basically, never get into the habit of giving your nominal variables non-numeric labels (e.g. **m** for male and **f** for female, or **y** for yes and **n** for no), learning how to use numbers to label such things is a great exercise in beginning measurement and statistics.

Ordinal scales

Ordinal scales add the idea of 'order' to the categories of a nominal scale – hence the name. They are very commonly used in social research. To use them, your variable must have some kind of order of magnitude. For example, we could measure wealth with the scale 'poor = 1, average = 2, rich = 3'. This variable clearly has some kind of order, but what is the difference between 1 and 2, or 2 and 3? In this case we can't really tell, other than the fact that 'rich' is more wealthy than 'poor' and 'average', but we have no way of telling how much, or whether the difference between 'rich' and 'average' is the same as between 'average' and 'poor'. Ordinal rules do, however, let us take the median – or the middle value – since the order of numbers does make some sense. The property of order also allows us to use ranking techniques on the data – which opens up a whole range of statistical tests (covered in later chapters). We still can't take the mean though, since the gaps between the numbers in an ordinal scale have no meaning. But remember, to use an ordinal scale, your attribute must posses the order of magnitude quality – wealth does have order, gender does not.

Interval scales

Interval scales add a consideration of the 'interval' between the numeric values to ordinal rules. A classic example of an interval scale is that of the Celsius temperature scale. For example, the difference between 10 and 20 degrees C is the same as the difference between 30 and 40. In other words – the *gaps between the numbers* finally represent something. This has major implications for interval rules, because at last we are able to take the mean of an interval scale, which opens up huge vistas of statistical testing, which you'll be delighted to know are coming up in a few chapters. Because the leap in usefulness between ordinal and interval rules is so big, social scientists are very keen to argue that their scales are interval at least. However, it's not always as simple as all that. You must be able to argue that the difference between the points of your scale is equal across the whole range of the scale. When we measure temperature in Celsius this is easy, but when we measure say self-esteem on a 5-point 'Likert-type' scale such as that shown in Figure 6.3, it's arguable at best. My advice here is to consult some additional sources (like those at the end of this chapter) and come to your own conclusions about this issue. In most practical situations, however, researchers tend to go with the assumption that such scales are interval, unless it is very obvious that the gaps are not equidistant.

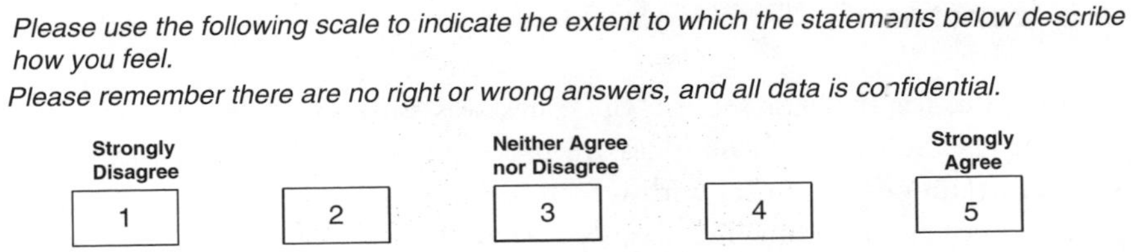

Figure 6.3 A 5-point Likert-type scale

Ratio scales

Finally, we come to ratio scales. Ratio scales have all the properties of interval scales plus the idea of an absolute zero. For example, what does zero in the Celsius scale mean? It doesn't mean 'no temperature', it means 'water freezes'. It's certainly possible to get colder than this. A ratio scale of temperature would have a zero which occurred at the complete absence of temperature. In fact, this is termed the 'Kelvin' scale of temperature, where 0 K is the coldest temperature possible (for fact fans, that's –273.15 degrees Celsius). In order to use a ratio scale, your quality or attribute must possess an absolute zero; attributes such as age, wealth, and company sales do so, but it's harder to argue that many psychological attributes do. The advantages of the ratio scale over the interval one to social scientists are not as great as the advantages of interval over ordinal though. You can perform proportional transformations (feet to centimetres, for example), and you can take the geometric and harmonic means of the variable. And anyone who finds a use for the latter should drop me a line.[5]

There are a few things to remember about scaling which are quite important. Firstly, remember that the attribute you are measuring determines the most powerful scale you can use (remember, I defined 'power' at the beginning of this section). Gender possesses no order, therefore you can only use a nominal scale. Self-esteem does possess order, and it is probably continuous, therefore you could divide it up into equally spaced intervals and use an interval scale. Or you could use an ordinal scale if you weren't confident in designing equal intervals. Company sales has an absolute zero, therefore you could use a ratio scale if you wanted, or you could use interval or ordinal if you would rather. Why would you use a less powerful scale? Well it's usually the case that more powerful scales are harder for respondents to fill in, and sometimes you just don't need that extra information. The extra information you get from a ratio scale is not often going to be that important, compared with the information you could get anyway from an interval scale. This also suggests a need to understand what you are going to do with your data *before* you collect it! You'll be glad you paid attention to that sentence one day in the future, trust me!

[5] Well, I am being facetious here. The geometric and harmonic means are used in a number of situations, it's just that *I* haven't had a use for them so far.

What is a 'construct'?

I have to apologise, for that last section on scales was somewhat dry, I hope you haven't given up on me. Nonetheless, those ideas are pretty important because they show us how we govern measurement using rules with which to assign numbers to measures of attributes. This section also covers that, but in a slightly different way. What I'm interested in here is rules which show us how we should assign measures to the sort of unobservable concepts social scientists like us are usually interested in, such as motivation, attitudes, and the like. Theoretically speaking, it's the key section of the chapter. So pay attention.

Remember above, when I talked about measuring things like motivation and IQ, which we couldn't actually observe, and therefore couldn't measure directly (say by putting a measuring device next to them)? Well, unfortunately these sorts of things appear to be the ideas which most interest us in the organisational and social sciences. If you go and read almost any article in a relevant journal, you'll find that it will usually be concerned with the relationships between **unobservable**, also called **latent**, **constructs**. We call these things latent or unobservable precisely because we cannot see them directly. We call them 'constructs' because they are exactly that – they are *constructed* within the minds of researchers because they appear likely to be a useful explanatory device in some theory which is being examined. What do I mean here? Well I think a little history will help (sound familiar yet?)

The idea of constructs can probably best be traced back to psychological research in the early part of the 20th century. At this point psychological researchers were developing many theories with which to explain human behaviours, or *why* people do certain things. Now of course, the only thing we can directly measure is the behaviour itself, but this does not often help explain why it happened. Theoretical psychologists looked to explain why behaviours occurred, by constructing hypothetical variables such as 'motivation', which were theorised to influence your performance of some behaviour. Figure 6.4 shows this idea in diagrammatic form. What you have here is a latent, unobservable construct of 'motivation', which is considered to influence a number of behavioural consequences, which we *can* observe. Also, have a glance at Alternative View 6.1 for a brief picture of the debates which went on at this time.

Alternative View 6.1: Are Constructs 'Real'?

During the early part of the 20th century, you will remember that the positivist/empiricist philosophy was having a large impact on science, and psychology was no exception. Factor analysis (you'll hear about this later) was being developed as well, and statistically inclined psychologists were using this to explore whether underlying concepts could explain our behaviour. Some of this work still influences psychology today. At the same time, psychoanalysts were explaining behaviour using concepts such as *libido*, *ego*, and *superego*.

Empiricist psychologists were vocal on the subject that nothing which is not directly measurable can exist, and that entities must be reducible to empirical equations in order to have value (this position is called **operationalism** which you'll also briefly hear about at the beginning of the next chapter). However, other theoretical psychologists argued that certain constructs could never be reduced simply to observed data. Much of this debate is summarised and explored in MacCorquodale and Meehl's (1948) brilliant (but difficult for the beginner) paper in the *Psychological Review*, which argues that unobservable constructs can indeed be `real', even though they are not directly observable. Nevertheless, they make the point that no unobservable construct should specify something which is `impossible' in light of what we already know. For example, libido could be considered as a term for a set of sexual needs – which is the type of construct which is indeed reducible to empirical observation (e.g. need1 + need2...). However, one could *not* specify an unobservable construct of libido as some kind of liquid which `flows', or becomes `dammed' (as was being implied by psychoanalysts at the time), since existing knowledge of physiology suggested that the nervous system did not consist of a set of tubes with various liquids in them (see MacCorquodale and Meehl, 1948).

So it is quite acceptable to think of constructs as `real', even though we can not observe them directly, but we must be careful as to exactly what properties we specify our constructs as having.

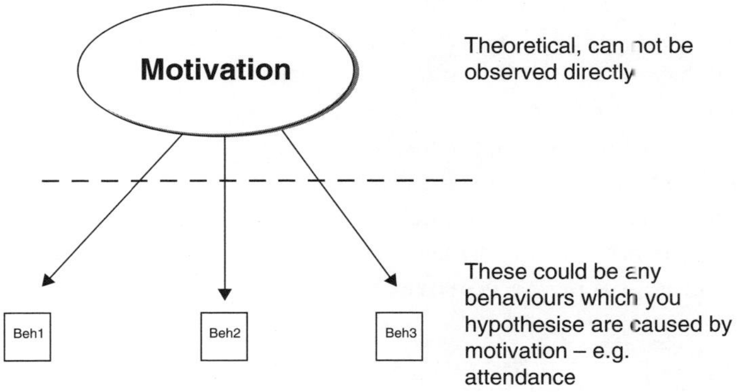

Figure 6.4 Hypothetical construct

The idea of unobservable variables – essentially 'inside our minds'[6] – which have observable impacts, quickly caught on in the social sciences. Much of this had to do with Nunnally's (1967) seminal book on the theory of how to measure these concepts. But even more so, the idea of constructs is extremely appealing to most social researchers, since we are ultimately looking to explain why things happen, yet we can't see inside the mind of individuals. However, instead of using actual behaviours as observable items, researchers now commonly use questions or statements on a questionnaire. You've probably already come across many such measures (sometimes they are called 'multi-item scales' or just 'scales') in your work. While the theory is called 'psychometric' theory, and was originally used to measure psychological constructs, it has also caught on as a way of measuring organisational variables and the like, such as a firm's 'market orientation'. Although I don't want to start a debate on the rights and wrongs of this, I do want to clearly make the point that theories of latent constructs were originally designed solely to measure unobservable psychological factors.

Concepts and constructs

All of the previous theory in this chapter has been building up to this small section. We've been talking about the basics of measurement, and then trying to transfer those concepts to the situation which is most common in social research – measuring unobservable concepts. This section will explicitly define exactly what such unobservable concepts actually are, and give you a consistent language to use for the next chapter, where we talk about the practicalities of developing measures of such concepts, and also hopefully when you conduct your own research. It's important to clarify a set of terms, or language for these purposes, because there are all kinds of terms bandied around in the literature, which tends to confuse things somewhat. This section therefore puts a little cap on the theory presented so far. Firstly, let's define the term **concept** as meaning a general idea in our heads about a variable which has a part to play in one of our theories about human behaviour, organisational performance, or whatever it is we are interested in. For example, I might think that an employee's satisfaction with their job will have an important influence on their absenteeism. But then I need to ask myself; 'just *what is* this concept of satisfaction with one's job?' It is when I start putting words to that concept, and defining what it means, that I *construct* its meaning within the framework of my theory, and also therefore within the wider context of other relevant theories. I will also give this concept a more formal name – say 'job satisfaction'. The concept is no longer a vague idea, but it is now more formally defined, i.e. 'job satisfaction' means something consistent and specific, it is now a **construct**.

[6]Note I said minds not brains – if these variables are simply reducible to brain signals then we will be able eventually to directly measure them with new technology. The *mind*, however, now that is a more interesting concept!

Interestingly, some theorists don't make the distinction between concept and construct, considering them to be pretty much the same thing (e.g. Bryman, 2004). However, I like to clearly separate out the vague ideas we have in our heads about things (concepts) from the more formalised definitions of them (constructs). Perhaps this is because I tend to walk around this world with my head full of vague ideas which need defining, but I think its valuable to delineate between mere 'ideas' and the things that are actually components of our theories. I base my distinction on a great example that my Ph.D. supervisor once gave me; you can think of a concept as sort of like an invisible idea in the air in front of you – you basically know what it is, and that it's 'there', but you can't really pin it down – nor can you explain it to anyone else. However, what you could do was throw a tin of paint in the air, and it would cover the concept and make it visible, and it then becomes easy to see and describe. The concept becomes a *construct*. Think of the paint as the words you use to pin down the concept and make it easy to see, and so others can see the same thing as you.[7]

Anyway, once we have a construct, everyone knows what we are talking about, and also how it relates to existing work in the area. Because of this, *the construct definition process is the most important step in measure development*. Get this right, and the rest will almost always work out (if you do it properly). In fact assuming the data and technical side are OK, I can usually trace almost all problems with measures 'not working' back to a flawed construct definition and conceptualisation process. Most commonly, researchers do a poor job of working out just where their construct differs from other already existing constructs, or whether there are separate and distinct aspects of the construct which need to be treated separately. In fact, we'll take a special look at the latter aspect in the next section. This doesn't just apply to constructs you develop, but existing ones as well – most of the problems you'll find with existing constructs and measures are because they were defined and conceptualised poorly, and the next chapter will provide some good advice as to how you might avoid such things.

A note on dimensionality

As a final note on the idea of construct definition, I think it's important to talk about an issue in the construct definition process which you will almost definitely have to grapple with in some way, be it for your own new constructs, or evaluating other people's. This is the issue of **dimensionality**. Or more specifically, **multidimensionality**. I'll say more about the technical side of dimensionality in the next chapter on developing measures of constructs, but here I want to talk about it in a more theoretical sense.

When you are developing a construct definition, you often come up against the idea that your construct is actually very complex. And the more you think about it, the more

[7] Credit of course goes to Prof. John Cadogan for this example.

complex it seems. As an example, think about the concept of 'job satisfaction'; what does it really mean? It could be argued that it is in fact made up of many different aspects, such as 'satisfaction with working conditions', 'satisfaction with management style', 'satisfaction with promotion prospects' and many others. Your first decision in this case is to be absolutely certain in what you are interested in, and what job satisfaction really is. If you continue to think all these aspects are important (and it seems that many people do tend to think in this way when they define constructs), what often happens is that you will tend to say 'job satisfaction is multidimensional, and I need to measure all these dimensions and combine them'. Before I go further, I would just like to say that *this almost never works well in a technical sense.* In my experience most multidimensional scales have major problems when they are being developed. But this is by-the-by, I want to talk in conceptual terms. There are plenty of good articles on the technical side (e.g. Law *et al.*, 1998), but not much on the conceptual side.

Conceptually, there are three ways of representing a construct, such as job satisfaction which you have decided has multiple 'aspects'. They are shown in Figure 6.5a–c: 6.5a shows an individual item capturing each aspect, 6.5b shows a classic 'multidimensional' measure, and 6.5c shows each dimension represented as a completely separate construct. My personal feeling is that most of the time what people decide to represent as multidimensional constructs could much more effectively be represented by separate constructs for each dimension. However, for some reason, students (and researchers in general) appear to be very easily seduced by the multidimensional model. Who knows why? Maybe it just looks cooler? And of course, everyone knows a cool-looking model is half the battle (I wish I were joking).

Although there is not much theory available on how you should choose which model (a–c) to use, I as usual have a few thoughts. Firstly, Model a should be your primary one, which you should find conceptual reasons to reject. For example, when you think in more depth and you decide the construct which you thought was just one 'thing' actually has multiple aspects, you will need to decide between b and c. One thing you should think about is the relationship between your 'second order' construct, and the 'first-order' dimensions. Specifically, what does the 'second-order' construct actually mean? According to model b[8] morale is a 'real' thing, which influences the dimensions' occurrence. The dimensions also can not occur independently of each other since they are caused by the same common source, so we are expecting them to be intercorrelated in some way. As the second-order factor increases or decreases, the first-order ones must necessarily also move. Can your theory support these assertions? Most of the time it cannot! If not, you can look for other models of multidimensional constructs (e.g. Law *et al.*, 1998), or you could consider the dimensions as

[8] There are other models which are covered in the references I have given, but this one is a good illustration, and my point here still stands as key. Furthermore, this model is the one implicitly used by most researchers when they create multidimensional constructs.

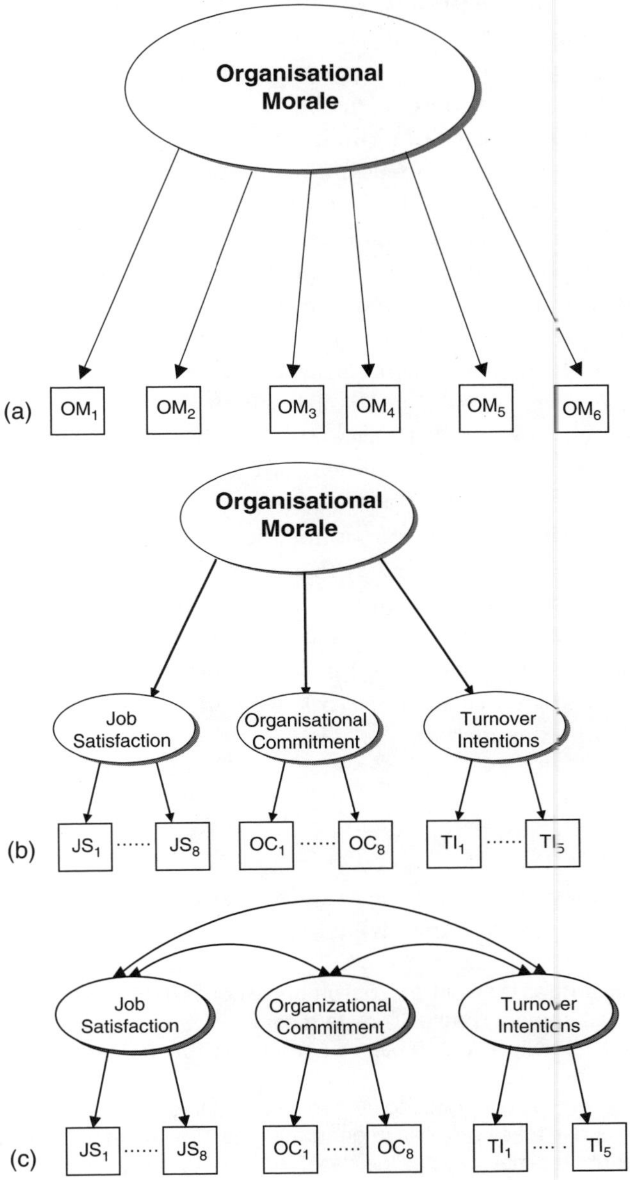

Figure 6.5 (a) A single construct; (b) A multidimensional measure; (c) Three separate constructs

separate constructs (6.5c) since you could argue they have their own conceptual 'meaning' and deserve to be individual constructs.

The other common issue (I hesitate to say mistake, because it is very common and I can see that it's easy to slip into this way of thinking) is that individual relationships are hypothesised from each dimension to various consequences. For example, thinking about Figure 6.5b, one could hypothesise that 'job satisfaction' influences citizenship behaviours, while 'turnover intentions' cause absenteeism, and 'morale' influences performance. If you find yourself doing this, it is almost always a good sign that you should be going with model 6.5c rather than b. Why? Well it seems to me logically difficult to argue that individual dimensions can have their own relationships with consequences according to model 6.5b. For example, if second-order morale influences all dimensions (which it should) then how can one dimension but not another have an individual influence on a consequence? And how can the dimensions have different influences than the main construct? Remember, the dimensions are merely aspects of the construct, *not constructs in their own right*. It's like saying that individual manifest items used to measure a construct can have relationships with consequences. This kind of thinking is normally indicative that the dimensions are in fact separate constructs, with their own relationships.

Now, it should be clear that this section is not a set of rules regarding multidimensionality. Better thinkers than me have grappled with this issue. And besides, there is a lot more thinking to be done here. What I want you to do is take this section as a set of tools to help you *think* about dimensionality, and a caution to be very careful what you want to do, because I commonly see problems where Ph.D. students (for example) have conceptualised multidimensional constructs that do not work well after they have collected their data – causing endless difficulties in analysis.

Summary

As this chapter is critically linked with the next, there's not much point in summarising now, but some key points to take from this chapter are:

- Measurement as an idea is an old one, but probably not as old as you think, and the formalisation and study of measurement is actually quite recent.
- Measurement is actually evolving as you read this, be prepared to keep modifying your assumptions and methods.
- Measurement is the process of linking numerical quantities to the attributes we want to examine in our theories, and is a key process in generating confidence in your findings.
- However, the attributes may have properties that the numbers we use to measure them do not, and vice versa, which means we need rules to tell us how to treat measurement.
- There are many key assumptions and rules which tell us how we are able to link numbers to the attributes we want to measure. Scales of measurement are one such set of rules, which tell us how we can manipulate the numbers we have used to measure an attribute.

- In a social science context, we are usually concerned with the *indirect* measurement of *latent constructs*. Constructs are formal definitions of ideas we have in our minds about key concepts which make up our theories.
- Construct definition is extremely important, and it will be one of the major influences on the success of your research.

Further reading

- *Measurement: Theory and Practice* by David Hand: This is a great book on measurement in general. It's not really a textbook or instruction manual, but more of an overview of measurement from its beginnings to the current state-of-the-art. I think it's absolutely fascinating and very useful. It will definitely help you understand the importance of measurement, and the theory and philosophy behind it.
- *Conceptualization and Measurement in the Social Sciences* by Hubert M. Blalock: One of the key texts on defining constructs – especially the first two chapters. It doesn't often get read too much these days but I think it is still highly relevant for all researchers who wish to measure 'stuff' somehow.
- *Measuring the Mind* by Denny Borsboom: You should remember Professor Borsboom from the start of this chapter. Once you have got the hang of the theory I've introduced here, you should go on to this book, which is a really excellent consideration of measuring latent constructs in psychology.

There are also a number of great journal articles which have appeared over the last 50 or 60 years on constructs and the like, such as:

- Bagozzi, Richard P. and Edwards, Jeffrey R. (1998) A general approach for representing constructs in organisational research, *Organisational Research Methods* 1 (1): 45–87.
- Bollen, Kenneth A. (2002) Latent variables in psychology and the social sciences. *Annual Review of Psychology* 53: 605–634.
- MacCorquodale Kenneth and Meehl, Paul E. (1948) 'On a distinction between hypothetical constructs and intervening variables,' *Psychological Review* 55: 95–107.

EXERCISES

1. What is measurement?
2. Think about the last time measurement caused some kind of problem or confusion to you in everyday life. What was it? Why did this confusion arise? Can you relate it to any of the concepts in this chapter?
3. Thinking now about scales of measurement (remember – NOIR), explain the most powerful scale which can be used to measure the following attributes and why:

   a. Market share
   b. Motivation
   c. Country of birth
   d. Attraction
   e. Relationship quality

4. In fact, if you have some time, why don't you try to define a construct of relationship quality from the existing literature?[9]
5. Is measurement as discussed in this chapter incompatible with any of the various schools of thought explored in Chapter 3? Why?
6. Finally, don't you think you should get out into the fresh air and enjoy yourself a little?

---

[9] Not as easy as you thought was it?

16 The Process of Measure Development

NICK LEE and IAN LINGS

SUPERVISOR'S VIEW: PROFESSOR JOHN CADOGAN

Like many academics, I first experienced the joys of measure development during my Ph.D. In fact, a major contribution of my Doctoral work was the development of a new measurement scale to capture 'export market orientation'. Strange as it sounds, the process really was good fun, and I enjoyed it.

It relies on you being able to develop one or more 'item banks' (basically, bunches of questions that will constitute the new measures). You do this using a variety of sources, including your own imagination, other published scales, and qualitative enquiry, perhaps by speaking to potential respondents for clues. At this stage, there is a strong element of creativity involved in the process. You have to develop the wording carefully to ensure that the meaning of the questions is just right, that you nuance things so that you direct people to provide the right kind of information. Consequently, the initial stages of the measure development process are certainly more art than science. I remember thinking that perhaps I was going over the top, developing item banks that were far too large: 'How would I fit all these questions on a questionnaire? Wouldn't it be too long and too repetitive?' I needn't have worried. Some students find this part of the measure development process easy (perhaps because it involves playing with words, not numbers) and dread the bit that will follow (because that involves 'doing statistics').

And yes, once you've created the questionnaire, and collected the data, you get to spend hours and hours poring over descriptive statistics (e.g., means and variances), correlation tables, factor analysis tables and reliability analysis tables. The thing is, you are looking for elegant solutions to measure development problems – and when you get it right, exploratory factor analysis can produce tabular outputs that show off these solutions quite nicely. Likewise, confirmatory factor analysis packages can produce path diagrams that look quite impressive. So you find yourself proudly showing off your 'elegant' factor analysis results to fellow students and family members (who usually put up with you the first few times). It is also at this stage that it begins to dawn on most novice measure developers that it would have been useful if they had made their item banks even bigger. About now, when measures have started to emerge, I tend to find that students who were once nervous of 'statistics' begin to blossom. Statistical approaches that once were unfathomable, and statistical language that once was gibberish, are both used freely. The students have unknowingly become statisticians.

VIEW FROM THE TRENCHES: DR AARTI SOOD

Developing a measure can be extremely tempting and, almost, exciting – as it virtually guarantees that your Ph.D. will make a significant contribution. However, it is vital for you to understand exactly what you are trying to measure before you embark upon this process, otherwise it can be an extremely stressful and time-wasting experience. It sounds obvious but you can only measure something once you know exactly what it is that you are trying to measure. Thus, take you time when specifying and defining your construct as it is arguably the most important step. A starting point for me was to look at how previous researchers had operationalised constructs that were similar to what I wanted to develop a measure for. This not only helped me define my construct but was also useful for generating an initial pool of items for my measure as well.

Although adding to your item pool, as there is some debate in the literature about this, I think it is a good idea to include negatively worded items at this stage. Hopefully these will go towards strengthening your measure, and giving you one line of defence against the dreaded 'common method bias' criticism. This will prove to be a great plus point for you in your viva! Trust me. Following generation of your item pool, it is extremely important to carefully choose expert judges to evaluate your measure. Remember, you want to end up with a set of items that best reflect the construct you want to measure. Therefore it is preferable to choose experts who are from your area of research. They will also be helpful in assessing any problem items such as ambiguous or double-barrelled items.

If you are in the position to be able to collect a separate set of data to evaluate your measure then that is great and you are very lucky. However, seeing that many of us have both time and financial restrictions, the best piece of advice I can offer you is to **make sure you include a 'back-up' measure in your questionnaire.** What I mean is, include a measure that is the closest to what you want to measure. It is perfectly possible that – even after all the blood, sweat and (yes) tears that have gone into developing your measure – it simply will not work. I say with some understatement (since Nick told me I couldn't swear in this) that this will be frustrating and somewhat depressing, but at least you will have *something* to work with! So, in a nutshell be extremely patient in understanding what you want to measure and ALWAYS include a back-up measure!

The previous chapter dealt with a lot of the foundational ideas about measurement. After reading it you should have a good idea about what measurement actually is, and the types of things social scientists often measure. Also, you should be comfortable with the idea that we need rules to connect our constructs to our measures of them, and tell us how we are able to manipulate those numbers.

This chapter, on the other hand, is where you'll start looking at the theory and practice of actually connecting numbers to your constructs. It's all very well having very elegant and well-defined constructs, but how should you actually go about designing measures of them? It is this part of measurement theory which has received the most attention from scholars in the last 50 years, which has resulted in a proliferation of different ideas and theories about how to construct measures. I'll focus on arguably the most influential of these theories throughout this chapter, but will also introduce some other ideas towards the end. But remember, measurement theories are always evolving, so it pays to keep up with the relevant literature to make sure you are always knowledgeable about current thinking.

Moving on, at the end of this chapter I really hope you have come to terms with these key ideas:

- What an 'auxiliary theory' is, and how it connects real world data to theoretical concepts.
- What validity is, and why it is important.
- 'Psychometric' theory as a key example of auxiliary theory.
- How you should go about developing a measure of a latent construct using the psychometric approach.
- Some examples of alternative theories of measurement, such as Item Response Theory.

Why is it Important to Know This Stuff?

By now I expect you all to understand what measurement is and why we need to measure things. You should also know about latent constructs, and how they are unobservable, even though we need somehow to measure them to transfer them into the real world. You also know that – because constructs are unobservable – it's really important to define your constructs clearly. But what do you do now?

What you need to do is work out how to transfer that theoretical latent construct into real-world measures. We covered the concepts behind that in the last chapter, but now we talk about the technical side of things. This of course then has implications for what the real world results you find (i.e. the 'numbers') mean in relation to the theoretical world concepts you are trying to measure. Figure 7.1 expresses this key idea. Try to think about measurement as a whole in terms of combining Figures 6.1 and 7.1.

Without understanding this key link, between theoretical concepts and real world data (expressed here in terms of measurement) it's no exaggeration to say that you will never really be able to do good research, and you will certainly never be able to measure anything well. If you can't be confident about how you measure your concepts, you will never be able to be confident in what your findings mean for your theory. Needless to say, this is A Bad Thing. How can you conclude your research project if you are unsure of what you have actually found? For example, if your theory argues that compliments from the manager influence employee self-esteem, you are unable to find any support for this theory unless you are confident you have measured self-esteem correctly.

Thus (and I don't want to labour the point), without good measurement, no one can ever take your findings seriously; not your supervisor, your colleagues, journal reviewers, or even yourself.

I think that makes it pretty important.

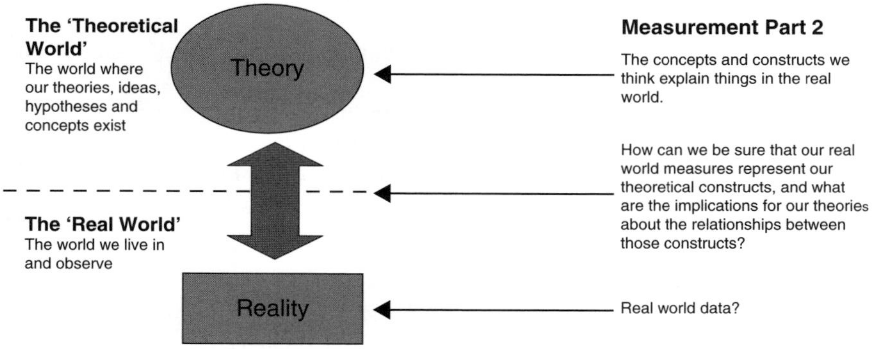

Figure 7.1 The importance of measurement, part II

Moving from the theoretical to the real world

In the previous chapter, we talked a lot about what constructs were, and how to define them. That said, however well you describe your construct, you should be aware that it is still only *theoretical*, that is it is located in what we've so far called the 'theoretical world'. In other words, you have defined something which you think has an important place in a theory of some kind. We've introduced this idea before in the book, when we talked about theory construction and in other places, but until now we've solely been located in the theoretical world. For the purposes of this book, the measurement of latent constructs can be thought of as the process of moving our theoretical constructs into the 'real world' – i.e. collecting data about them.[1] Remember, we can't *see* these constructs, that's why we must 'construct' them! Unfortunately the theoretical world is just that, theoretical. Instead, we live and operate in the real world (well most of us do), and therefore must somehow transfer our constructs into things we can actually work with. Once we work out exactly how we can represent our construct in the real world, we have what can be called an **operational definition**. There are actually multiple theories which propose to explain how we can link real world data to theoretical constructs. Blalock (1982) termed this 'auxiliary theory' to distinguish it from theories which link theoretical constructs to other theoretical constructs. We're usually most interested in the latter theory (which could be called structural theory), but without the auxiliary theory, our real-world measurements may bear no relation to our theoretical world constructs. In case you're *still* wondering, this would be A Bad Thing. Remember back to the previous chapter, when I talked about indirect measurement. No matter how elegant our measure may be numerically, we must still be able to justify *why* it represents the theoretical construct we say it does.

The operational definition is the outward manifestation of our auxiliary theory. It defines exactly what in the real world we say represents our theoretical construct. I say it is a manifestation of the auxiliary theory because (whether you realise it or not) it rests upon some idea or theory of how to connect real-world data to theoretical world latent constructs. The auxiliary theory I have been implicitly referring to so far, and will continue to do so for the most part, is called 'psychometric' theory,[2] which was mentioned in the previous chapter (take a refresher look at Figures 6.2 and 6.4 as well), and it developed from the roots introduced in Alternative View 6.1 in the previous chapter.

[1] You'll remember from the previous chapter that when we are measuring observable things like height and weight, it pays to think about measurement as moving them on to a more abstract mathematical plane. However, when we talk about measuring latent constructs, it helps to consider measurement as moving our consideration to a more 'real', empirical, world.

[2] You might see it – or parts of it – termed 'classical test theory' sometimes, or even 'domain sampling theory', depending on what other books you read.

However, it's important that you realise this theory is not the only one available, nor is it unquestioned among social scientists. I'll briefly cover some alternatives towards the end of the chapter. Nevertheless, it is very widely used in the social sciences, and provides a solid base from which to work. Indeed, most alternative theories have psychometrics as their fundamental roots – even if it is only as something to react against.

Although a full discussion of psychometric theory is outside the scope of this book (some good references are given at the end of the chapter), it is appropriate to cover some key points. Firstly, psychometrics makes the underlying assumption that latent constructs actually exist, but are unobservable. This is kind of a weird idea, but it is quite intuitive to most of us that a construct like 'motivation' actually exists somehow, so let's just go with it for now. Of course, those who were paying attention earlier will note that this must therefore be a realist sort of theory, rather than an empiricist or positivist theory (if you're unsure why, go back and hit Chapter 2 again).

The next key thing is that psychometric theory makes the assumption that the 'real' thing, which we call a construct, influences some things which we can actually observe. We could argue, for example, that university students' motivation influences their classroom attendance (see Figure 6.2). We therefore could take attendance as a manifest or observable **indicator** of the unobservable motivation construct. However, this kind of indicator would have some problems. For example, your attendance may be influenced by many things other than motivation – such as your health, the weather, the traffic, your alcohol consumption the night before and all kinds of other things. Thus, should I take low attendance levels as indicating low levels of motivation, or that the traffic on the way to school was heavier? A good indicator should be influenced primarily by the construct we are trying to measure, not anything else. Furthermore, attendance would need to be recorded by actual physical observation at the time, so what if I can't be there then? Instead of using that type of measuring instrument, we should think of something which is a little easier to administer if possible. Whereas there are many different ways of doing this, what normally happens is that we define a *set of multiple questions* which can be filled out on a questionnaire, varying answers to which we argue are directly caused by the level of motivation of a student. One example could be asking a student their level of agreement with the statement 'I attend class because I enjoy it', or something like that. IDE 7.1 shows how in my Doctoral research, I moved from theoretical construct to a set of manifest indicators for the construct 'sales manager caring'. We use multiple indicators (rather than just asking a single question) for many reasons. Arguably the most important reason is that we can get an idea of how 'well' the indicators represent a common construct (which they should) by examining their inter-correlations. On a more practical level, multiple items 'average out' errors by respondents, and allow us to capture more of the full 'meaning' of the construct in our measure.

IDE 7.1: Developing the Construct of Sales Manager Caring

After extensive qualitative research, the construct of sales manager caring was defined as concerning **the degree to which sales managers invest *emotional* and *affective* resources into the social process of problem resolution**.

From here, it was decided to measure the construct by tapping the perceptions of salespeople – the subject of the caring, rather than those who were displaying the caring. Conceptually speaking, this was because it was felt that caring was a construct which at its heart was concerned with the subject, and that the giver may have inaccurate estimations of how they were perceived by the subject of their activities. For example, you may think you are being very caring to a friend, but they in fact may not think that at all.

The construct was operationalised by way of a number of items which were given to salespeople. Salespeople were asked to rate how strongly they agreed with the items on a 1–5 scale, which is displayed in Figure 6.3 in the previous chapter.

The original set of items numbered 13; after the process detailed in Figure 7.2, the items finally settled upon (presented here in shortened form) included items such as:

Manager is friendly
Manager is empathetic
Manager can put himself in others' shoes
Manager is something of a counsellor

So, moving to a slightly wider frame of reference, the term **operational definition** can be thought of as referring to exactly what manner in which we mean to measure the construct. In other words, referring to IDE 7.1, the operational definition of sales manager caring concerns the items, but also how they are used to create the final measure. Are they summed? Averaged? Or something more complicated? If you think back to the early sections of Chapter 6, we are in the general area of rules of concatenation here. At this point, dealing with actual numbers, we are now fully in the real world, and must be extremely careful not to lose touch with what we really want to do – that is look at relationships between constructs in the theoretical world. Interestingly, as a side note, the term operational definition has been co-opted from an empiricist auxiliary theory called *operationalism*. According to this theory, a construct is nothing more than its measurement (see Alternative View 6.1 in the previous chapter). This throws psychometrics into nice relief, being as psychometrics defines the latent construct to be something independent of its measurement – with the items merely being caused by the latent construct. Operationalism has been generally discredited, so I won't

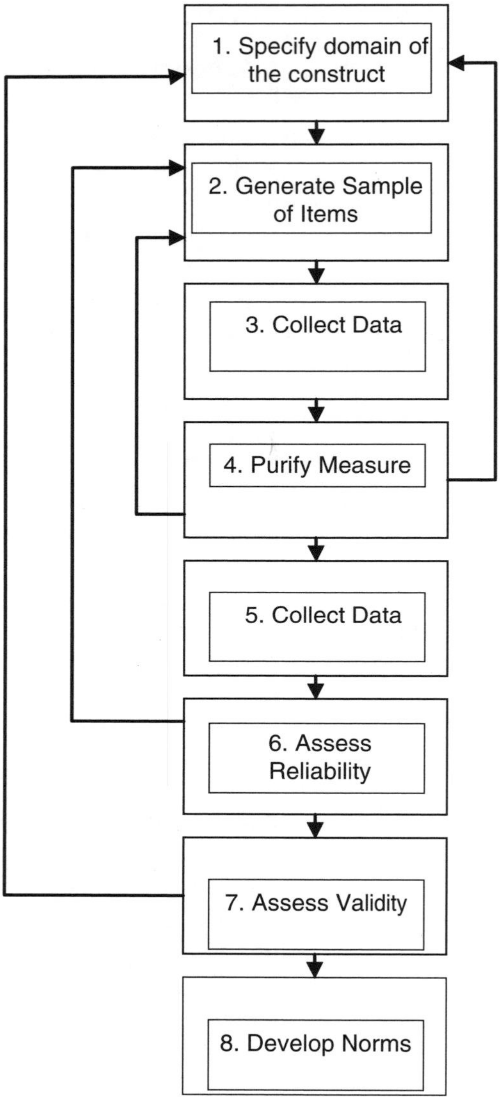

Figure 7.2 A traditional process of measure development
Source: Lee and Hooley (2005), adapted from Churchill (1979).

spend any more time on it right now, but it is probably worth your keeping it in mind, even if it is just as a counterpoint to other theories.

Developing a measure

This section is designed to give you a brief introduction to the process of developing a new measure for an unobservable construct, according to what could be called 'traditional' theory (i.e. psychometric). Of course, it is impossible within the context of such a book to give you fine details of the process – and in fact there are many great books on the subject which will be referenced throughout. Use this section as an overview, a basic source from which you can go into more detail when required using other sources. Figure 7.2 shows a diagram of this process, which I will use to structure the following discussion. What can be seen here is that the process is a technical one – in that you are assumed to understand the relevant auxiliary theory prior to beginning, which should drive how you do the stages. Unfortunately, many have and continue to use such models as this without thinking about the theory of measurement (see Lee and Hooley, 2005 for a discussion of this).

We've already talked a lot about the first stage; *specify the domain of the construct*, so I won't repeat myself other than to say it is arguably the most important stage, so please take note of the earlier discussions in Chapter 6. Once you've done this, you must develop indicators from which to make up your measure. Remember that earlier, I briefly mentioned that you generally need to use multiple items to measure a latent construct? Well these items have to come from somewhere! There are many sources of items, such as existing theory and academic experts. However, it is also common to use qualitative exploratory research to discover key aspects of constructs which you can use to develop items from – like interviews, focus groups, observations, etc. For example, you might want to interview managers and employees in a wide variety of contexts in order to develop items about a type of leadership. Of course, you don't simply ask your respondents 'so, how should I measure leadership then?' It's a little more complicated than that. Chapters 9 and 10 are good introductions to qualitative research, but on a very basic level getting respondents to relate key stories and incidents which relate to leadership, and just talk about their feelings, observations and opinions on leadership is a great start. You could also spend some time within an organisation, observing how managers lead their employees, and how employees react to that. Reviewing the existing literature on leadership is also a great way of developing items. What you normally get from this process is a large set of items, which may or may not be good measures of your construct. This is a good thing, because the rest of the process is essentially one of reducing that large pool to the smaller set of 'best' indicators of your construct, through a number of stages.

The first thing I like to do is 'ask the experts'. Basically, what I mean here is to find a bunch of academic experts in your area (say six or seven professors and lecturers who know a bit about the field you are working in) and ask them to look at your items to see if they think they could represent the relevant construct. I use a worksheet which contains the construct definitions, and a table where the experts can rate how well they think a given indicator represents a given construct. Usually, you are developing more than one measure, so the experts should do them all at the same time which means they can compare how well each item measures different constructs. You can see part of such a worksheet in Figure 7.3, which I actually designed for my Doctoral work. If you are developing only a single measure, it might be an idea to include 'dummy' items which you *don't* think measure the construct, to check whether your experts are paying attention. Interestingly, I tend to find that this process is nearly as accurate as statistical procedures in detecting 'good' or 'bad' items.

Once you've done this, you'll find a few of your items are clearly poor indicators, so drop them from your consideration. For example if you look at Figure 7.3, I found that some of the items which I thought were pretty clear indicators of 'aggressiveness' were actually rated as indicators of 'responsiveness'. Now, although you might think your 'experts' either made some mistakes, or are simply stupid, this is not often the case. In fact it's more likely that things

Sales Person Item Bank:

Please place a number (1–5) in the relevant column if you think an item relates to that construct.

Item	Responsiveness	Aggressiveness	Caring
In general, when a problem needs dealing with, my manager deals with it quickly.			
My manager can often see the reason for a problem, and is very concerned with helping the sales person correct it .			
My manager could be described as 'fiery'.			
My manager doesn't accept excuses for causing problems.			
My manager doesn't seem to have the confidence to take the necessary action to solve a problem.			
My manager doesn't seem to take the initiative when dealing with a problem.			
My manager doesn't waste any time when dealing with a problem.			

Figure 7.3 A section of an expert analysis form

you thought were good indicators in fact weren't. On the other hand, you might find that some items are questionable, for example perhaps one or two experts thought they indicated the 'wrong' construct, but others didn't. I think it's normally best to keep these items at this stage – you can always drop them later. That said, keep an eye on them, and I bet you find they are the first ones to fail subsequent tests. Strictly speaking, we should then go out and collect data to see how good our measure is (stages 3 and 4). However, in a lot of social research we skip to stage 5 for various (usually pragmatic – like time) reasons.[3] What this means is that you move directly to a test of your measure and the theory associated with it – so you do both tests together, using the same data. However, this is frankly poor practice, and we should really collect preliminary data and evaluate the measure before including it in our full questionnaires. Also, if it *is* done, stage 3 often uses student samples. But unless you are looking to measure a general population, or student, sample with your final measure, this is *also* poor practice, and pretty much a waste of time. For example, if your measure is designed to measure sales manager performance – what valid information can a student sample tell you about it? Alternative View 7.1 discusses the relevant issues concerning sampling for measure development. Either way, the technical process of purification in stage 4 is the same as stage 6, so there is no reason to repeat the discussion.

Alternative View 7.1: Sampling in Measure Development

I'll be covering the issue of sampling and representativeness in much more detail in Chapter 11, but it's appropriate here to look at a few key issues. If you look at a lot of psychological research, you'll find that much measure development (essentially stage 3 and 4 of Figure 7.2) is done by collecting data from student samples. For example, I could hand out a set of items to one of my undergraduate classes and get 150 sets of data back, which I could then analyse and purify. Of course, this would be very easy in practical terms. Furthermore, because a lot of organisational researchers have psychology backgrounds, you can also find quite a lot of this practice throughout organisational research.

Nevertheless the question must be asked as to whether this is in fact good practice. Any potential criticism is based around the idea that students may be inappropriate because they have little knowledge of the construct in question. For example, if you wish to develop a measure of salesperson role conflict, students are essentially unable to answer questions on such a construct from a position of knowledge. In such cases

[3]That said, some fields have more tradition of using the 'full' process, such as psychology, and this is unarguably a superior and more rigorous methodology.

they will either not answer or simply put random answers down. This is likely to lead to biased data and thus any statistical purification you do will be meaningless. Any measure development for such constructs (which most organisational research uses) must be done on a sample of the intended final population – one reason which separate measure development samples are not often taken in organisational research.

However, if you are developing a measure designed to be used on a general population – such as self-esteem or many other general psychological characteristics – students may be just as good as any other segment of the population. In such a case, you need to consider whether students may be systematically different from other groups of the population, and whether this may influence your data. If not, there is little reason to avoid student samples in measure development. The issue of using student samples in organisational research is covered in a general sense by Calder *et al.* (1982) in their interesting paper, which will be discussed in more depth in Chapter 11, and this has plenty of implications in the present context too.

If we aren't taking a separate measure development sample (which we really *should*), what normally happens is that after the expert analysis stage, we include the measure in a questionnaire with all the other measures we are using to test our theoretical model (see Chapter 5 for more discussion of models). We then send out the sample and wait with bated breath for it to return (see Chapter 11 for information on collecting quantitative data).

After the few weeks of stress about whether you will ever get enough responses, and the inevitable panic when none arrive in the first week, you'll probably end up with a bunch of responses. How many responses you need is an interesting question, most authors recommend that you need around 150–250 responses to be confident in any measure development activity. There are many reasons for this, though. Firstly, many of the analysis techniques we need to use to assess the measure rely on large samples for confidence in their findings (you'll learn more about this in Chapters 13 and 14). The more items you have in your measures, the more responses you will need of course. This is a key consideration. Also, the larger your sample, the more confident you can be that it is not overly influenced by chance fluctuations, such as over-large representation of small sub-groups. Once you have your data, you can then spend a long and boring week entering them into your analysis package of choice (although I discuss software in Chapter 13, since no one is paying me, I won't recommend one way or the other!). Now you have some data, and you should do some preliminary analysis along the lines of that discussed in Chapter 13 – i.e. cleaning your data, and descriptive analysis.

Moving on, we usually at this stage want to assess the 'quality' of our measurement. This process is usually concerned with assessing the *reliability* and *validity* of our measures.

Validity is covered in the next section, but reliability basically refers to how consistent your measurement is. For example, if you were to measure the same person twice, one week apart, would the measurement be pretty much the same (assuming their level of the latent construct remained the same)? If not, then it could be argued that the measure captures some kind of random error rather than what you want it to catch. The difference between reliability and validity can be summed up by the classic example of the faulty measuring scales which weigh every person 5 kg too heavy (nightmare, I know). These scales always give a weight which is exactly 5 kg too heavy, so they are reliable in that they are consistent and not randomly incorrect. However, they are not valid as they do not give the 'correct' measurement. For something like weight and height this is easy to understand and discover, because there are pre-existing standards of weight which we can test our measuring instruments against. But what about a latent construct like job satisfaction? It's an altogether more difficult question.

Although there is some debate about how to measure reliability for latent constructs, we usually capture it by measuring the *internal consistency* of the items in our measure. In other words, if all the items are caused by a latent construct, they should also be inter-correlated to some extent. Theoretically speaking, therefore, the less random error there is in our measure, the more inter-correlated our items should be. There are many measures of internal consistency, but the most popular one has been Cronbach's coefficient *alpha* (see DeVellis 1991 for example). Cronbach's alpha essentially measures the proportion of variation within a set of items which can be attributed to some kind of common cause. Theoretically, of course, we think this 'common cause' is our construct, but we have no real proof of that. If you are really unlucky you could be developing a great measure of something completely different! At this point, it's really important that you never lose touch with the fact that you are trying to work out whether your set of items is a good measure of some construct which you defined previously. Never get lost in the statistics to the extent that you forget the construct itself! Going back to Cronbach's alpha, its popularity can probably be attributed to the fact that Nunnally (1967) gave some 'cut-off' values which he suggested indicated reliable measures. And we all know how much researchers love stuff like that. Although this approach has been vastly popular since the 1970s, there have been some concerns, which I would advise you to check out (see Cattell and Kline, 1977; Kline, 2000).

Validity of measures

Validity is an interesting idea, it's essentially the most important characteristic of any measure, yet misconceptions abound about it. It's primarily a conceptual issue, yet we tend to assess it using statistical tools and rules of thumb, some of which actually detract from validity (see Lee and Hooley, 2005). Ultimately, a measure of a construct is valid if it accurately measures the construct (Carmines and Zeller, 1979). But what does this actually mean?

For most situations, in practical terms this means that variation on the latent construct should be accurately captured by the measure. So if my level of 'motivation' is lower than yours, my score on a valid measure of motivation should be lower than yours. The more accurately the measure tracks variation in the construct, the more valid it is. One step further on is to actually map point values of the measure to point values of the construct. For example, what does a score of '4' on a 1–7 scale of motivation mean in terms of your actual level of motivation? This is a whole other issue, but one which we are not often concerned with in theoretical research.[4] Nevertheless, if you are a clinical psychologist, for example, or someone else who uses indirect measures to assess individuals, it will be important to you.

However, as you should be aware, we can never actually measure the latent construct directly – so how do we ascertain whether our indirect measure accurately reflects variation in the true latent construct? This question has occupied the minds of many over the last century. Firstly, in order to be valid, a measure also has to be reliable – which we must also assess (see above). Secondly, we should also realise that we can never get a perfectly valid measure, and even if we did we would never actually know this because we can't see the latent construct. Also, consider that validity is essentially a property of the purpose you are putting your measure to. In other words, a measure of motivation may be a valid measure of an underlying trait of motivation, but not of their work performance. Again, construct definition is highly important here!

There are various different 'types' of validity which have been discussed over the years, of which I will introduce a few. Firstly, *criterion-related* validity is a test of whether your measure accurately estimates or predicts the value of some criterion (it could also be termed *predictive* validity). It really is as simple as that and is actually quite an intuitive concept to most of us. It's very useful when we are looking to develop scales to test individuals (like the psychologist example above). For example, does the GMAT (Graduate Management Admission Test) accurately predict how well an MBA student will perform on the course? Or how well does a pregnancy test predict actual pregnancy? In situations like this, criterion-related validity is of huge importance! The correlation between the measure and the criterion is the only thing relevant to criterion-related validity, and selection and measurement of the criterion is obviously key. Also, this should suggest to you that criterion-related validity is highly empirical, rather than theoretical. However, a limitation is that for most situations in the theoretical social sciences, there is no criterion with which to assess validity. We could assess, say, motivation with the criterion of 'class attendance', but is this really a good criterion? I suppose it may be if we want to measure motivation for the purpose solely of predicting attendance, but this is not often the case in theoretical research. Remember, validity is about

[4]This is because theoretical research tends to look at relationships between theoretical constructs, not individual scores on measures. In order to explore the former, we must be confident in how close the variation in a construct maps to the measure, but not the individual point score.

the purpose of the measure, so if we want to measure an underlying latent construct of role ambiguity, or organisational loyalty, criterion-related validity may not be the best approach.

Another type of validity is *content validity*. This is essentially how well a measure represents a specific area of content. Of course, this is bound up with your construct definition. This is easy if you are trying to measure something simple like mathematical ability of nine-year-olds, or in an organisational context something like share price performance. We just work out what the construct consists of, and construct a test which covers all, or a sufficient sample of, these issues (obviously this is a simplification). But what about Self-Esteem? Satisfaction? Relationship Quality? Unfortunately, in the social sciences we rarely have exact and agreed-upon definitions of content for our constructs to draw from. Thus, content validity usually relies on some kind of judgement that we have got the 'right stuff' in our measure, or whether it 'looks right'. In my opinion this process would be better called *face validity*, and is similar to the expert judgement process I talked about earlier. That said, sometimes face and content validity are considered the same. So content validity in this sense is a great idea, but not one which can be rigorously assessed in general (although a dissenting voice will be heard later in this chapter).

Finally, we come to *construct validity*. It is similar to, but should never be confused with, criterion-related validity. Construct validity essentially requires you to specify theoretical relationships between your latent construct and other things which you think are related to it (e.g. antecedents and/or consequences). Sometimes this is called 'nomological' validity (how's that for a word?) Basically, what you do is specify some theoretical hypotheses around your latent construct, and assess these relationships with your data. So if you think motivation will have a positive impact on class participation, you can collect data on both, assess the results of your analysis, and if you find a positive relationship, then a small piece of evidence exists for the validity of your motivation measure. The more elaborate your network of hypotheses, the more rigorous the test of construct validity. Furthermore, the more repeated studies support the predictions, then the stronger the evidence of construct validity. However, we must be pretty confident in our theoretical hypotheses, and in the measures of our other constructs – not to mention the quality of our data and analysis – in order to be confident in the strength of this method of testing.

As you can see, assessing validity for the type of latent constructs we normally want to measure in the social sciences is not an easy task. You should take the previous discussion as a set of pointers from which to investigate the issue of validity in some more depth, as well as to help you in assessing prior work and guiding your own.

Other approaches and models

This section is aimed at giving a very brief flavour of some other models of measurement – or 'auxiliary theories' as they were termed previously – which have developed in the latter part of the 20th century. In general they are adaptations of psychometrics, and were designed to counter specific criticisms of the psychometric model. Although it is beyond the scope of this book to give full details on each theory, I hope to give you an idea of their strengths and how they relate to the general approach given earlier, as well as some directions to shape your future reading. You will then be in a better position to judge how you should measure the constructs in your own research.

Formative and causal models[5]

You should have noticed that the psychometric model we have discussed so far considers variations in the underlying latent construct to cause the variation in the indicators. However, in recent times, social scientists – including many in the organisational and management sciences – have argued that this direction of causality may in fact be reversed in some cases. In other words, it seems that in some cases indicators can be argued to cause the presence of constructs. A classic example (see Diamantopoulos and Winklhofer, 2001 for an excellent introduction) is socioeconomic status (SES). If one considers SES to be a combination of measures like education, income, employment and place of residence, then the presence of these items *causes* your level of SES. If any single item was to change, SES would also change, even if the others remained the same. Variation in the indicators therefore drives variation in the construct. By contrast, the psychometric (called 'reflective' in this type of discussion) model assumes that the indicators are driven by the construct, and thus if the level of the construct changes, then all the indicators must also change. Deciding between formative and reflective models is a conceptual decision based on a number of criteria. Firstly, think about your construct; is it something in existence (although unobservable) which you consider to cause the appearance of certain items (e.g. a personality trait)? If this is the case, your model should be reflective. However, if the individual items are in fact separate components which together cause the existence of the construct (e.g. SES, or Advertising Expenditure), then you should explore the formative model. This decision is becoming more and more important in social science as the formative model becomes more accepted. The downside is technical, it is in fact rather difficult to create and assess formative measures. But this should not stop you if formative measurement is the right conceptual decision.

The C-OAR-SE method

The C-OAR-SE method (it stands for Construct definition, Object classification, Attribute classification, Rater identification, Scale formation, and Enumeration) was developed by Professor John Rossiter (e.g. 2002) as a reaction against what he saw as increasing reliance on the blind application of statistics to the process of measurement. This model does illuminate

---

[5]Note, there can be argument about whether there is a difference between formative and causal measurement. However, at present the literature seems to treat them as synonymous.

some interesting issues and problems within measure development, and is thus well worth a look. It's certainly been the source of some interesting and fun debates between myself and Professor Rossiter. The C-OAR-SE model is based around the idea that not all constructs can be captured by traditional psychometric, or formative, models, and in fact some do not need to. Instead, C-OAR-SE argues that the only type of validity of use is 'content validity', which can not be assessed statistically, only by agreement of experts on whether or not the measure is valid. While the C-OAR-SE procedure itself is long and involved, it can be summarised by a concern for construct definition (which in fact is similar in spirit at least to what I have said in this, and especially the previous, chapters). However, C-OAR-SE splits construct definition into a number of sections, including the object (e.g. Coca-Cola), the attribute (e.g. quality), and the rater (e.g. consumer). All three of these can vary, implying different models of measurement. Prof. Rossiter considers this to be a rationalist rather than empiricist (which he considers psychometrics to be) theory, in that it relies on judgement not empirical validation. However, it seems to me that it is strongly pragmatist as well.[6] While C-OAR-SE makes some important points, it hasn't really caught on. This is probably because many of the constructs we measure do fit within the psychometric or formative models, and we already have theories which deal with them – and what's more these theories provide us with tools to assess the quality of our measures independent of expert judgement. However, it is unarguable that C-OAR-SE provides a strong critique of existing measurement, and is worth investigating.

Item response theory

Item response theory (IRT) appears superficially very similar to the psychometric model explored in the main part of this chapter. It shares the assumption that items are caused by underlying constructs (although IRT terms them 'latent traits'), but where psychometric theory focuses on the construct level in the main, IRT focuses on the individual properties of the items in more depth. Furthermore, the properties of an individual item are not dependent on the respondent or on the group of items used. This is in contrast to psychometrics, where item properties depend on the group of people who are tested as well as the collection of items themselves. The upshot of this is that IRT allows a more rigorous test of measurement across different groups – e.g. cross-cultural – since the item statistics are independent of the group. In addition, IRT allows one to select items which are most accurate to each individual's ability and level of the latent trait – so conceivably each person could fill in a different test which is customised to most accurately measure their level of the latent trait. The downside of all of this is complexity for one thing. IRT models are much more complex than traditional psychometric models. Also, it has always struck me that for many social science research purposes, customising tests to individual populations is not as important as

---

[6] And of course, as you will know by now, psychometric theory is in fact Realist not Empiricist, but now is not the time to get into that.

being able to send out a consistent 'pretty good' scale to many respondents – for example, on mail-out surveys. So sometimes IRT may be a little impractical. Nevertheless, I think it is definitely worth investigating in situations where you are measuring multiple different sub-groups, testing individuals (such as in a clinical or educational context), or in other face-to-face measurement contexts.

Final words and summary

To cap off the end of my discussion on measurement, which I have to admit has grown somewhat longer than I'd hoped, I just want to make a few notes from my own experience about measurement. These notes are primarily to do with practicalities of measurement, especially where Ph.D. and other dissertations are concerned. First I want to deal with the issue of 'other people's measures'. If you are developing your own measures for new constructs, then you should go through the most thorough process possible – drawing from this chapter. However, for most projects, you will be using measures which have been developed by others for at least some of the constructs. Here I think you can take a slightly different approach. In particular, most existing measures should have gone through a process similar to that suggested herein already (well you would hope so if they have been published in reputable journals). That said, I still feel it is necessary to look at the reliability and validity of these measures along with your own new ones. It could be the case that prior work has not been able to use techniques as sophisticated as those available to you, and it is also necessary to assess how well these measures work with your sample. The major confusion occurs when (as is often the case) these existing measures don't actually work as well as they did in the past. What do you do? Well the first thing to *not* do is panic. If you have done your research well (i.e. collected good data, used good analyses), then it can hardly be argued as your fault that these measures don't work. In many cases, if you look closely at the existing measure and construct, you may find it wasn't conceptualised or developed in the past as rigorously as you hoped. Therefore, to some extent you are fighting a losing battle and can only do your best with what you have. My advice is really to try to anticipate such issues, by including alternative measures of key constructs, just in case the existing measures do not work so well.

Also, one should consider that individuals who answer questionnaires may not be telling the whole truth, and may in fact be biased. One key bias which has received plenty of attention is *social desirability* bias (e.g. King and Bruner, 2000). This refers to the idea that individuals to a greater or lesser extent tend to try to present themselves in the best light possible. Therefore they may answer some questions in a way which makes them look smarter, nicer, kinder, or whatever. This can be a major problem if you are measuring many psychological constructs. The first thing to do is try to avoid it at the source, assure respondents that their answers are anonymous if possible, or confidential at minimum.

Make it clear that they are not being 'assessed', and that there are no 'right or wrong' answers. Even so, there are measures of socially desirable response tendencies, and I recommend including one in your questionnaire. You can then correlate items and scales with this measure, to see whether social desirability bias is a problem. More recent research has explored many other types of bias, and I would advise any researcher becoming familiar with such literature (e.g. Baumgartner and Steenkamp, 2001; Podsakoff *et al.*, 2003).

Cross-cultural measurement is also a key issue. My main point here is that it is not as simple as merely translating your measures into the language of another culture and expecting them to work. Many researchers actually recommend going through the concept and measure development process anew when you wish to transfer one measure to a new culture. However, in many cases researchers need to measure the same thing in multiple cultures, which necessitates some kind of comparability of the measurements. In this case, there is substantial advice on how to develop measures which are what is called *invariant* across cultures (e.g. Steenkamp and Baumgartner, 1998). Whereas much of this literature is quite technical, it is very important that researchers consult it very early in the development process.

So, by now you should have a pretty good grasp of the key ideas of measurement as they have developed within the social sciences, and particularly organisational research. However, what's probably even more important is that you recognise that measurement is a vital process in itself, and should never be treated as an afterthought. Without good measurement you will never be able to be confident that your findings bear any relationship to the theories you so dearly wish to explore. You should leave this chapter with an appreciation of the importance of measurement, as well as hopefully some level of interest in what is a really interesting (and under-rated) area of methodology. Finally, try to take Figure 7.1 as a model in some way for the whole research process. The idea of linking the theoretical world to the real world is a key one, and upon it depends the validity of the whole social research process. The rest of the chapters will to a greater or lesser extent be concerned with this process in one way or the other – whether it be linking theoretical concepts to real-world data, or real-world findings back to theoretical world concepts and relationships.

The key things to take from this specific chapter are:

- The operational definition of a construct is the set of rules which link your theoretical-world construct to the real-world measurement of it.
- An auxiliary theory is one which sets out exactly how constructs relate to measures. Without solid auxiliary theory, our structural theories (i.e. those which relate constructs to each other) can not be tested with real-world data.
- In order to generate a good measure of a construct, you must define that construct very clearly. You can then follow a process to generate and assess the validity of that construct's measure.
- Validity refers to how well your measure captures variation in the latent construct. You can assess this in a number of ways, including exploring your measure's relationships with other measures.

- Alternative measurement (also termed auxiliary) theories are formative measurement and IRT, these can be appropriate in certain situations.
- There are differences between developing entirely new measures and assessing existing ones. You should also make yourself aware of the chances of response biases, and various cross-cultural issues if they are relevant to your research.

Further reading

- *Scale Development: Theory and Applications* by Robert DeVellis (1991), and *Summated Rating Scale Construction: An Introduction* by Paul Spector (1992). These two little books were my own introduction to the practicalities of developing measures. I still consult them from time to time, and I think they are a great introduction to measurement.
- *Psychometric Theory* (3edn) by Jum Nunnally and Ira Bernstein: The 1967 first edition (written solely by Nunnally) is generally considered 'the' classic text on psychometric scale development, but it's pretty hard to get hold of now. Being the weird obsessive I am, I hunted high and low for mine (well, on the Internet anyway). If you can't get hold of the original, or don't have my strange desire for such things, this third edition is updated and revised, and pretty much just as good. However, to be totally honest, I do rather like the original version since I feel a few key ideas have changed a bit in this latest revision. I also just love old books like that.
- *Reliability and Validity* by Edward Carmines and Richard Zeller. This is an excellent introduction to validity, and really helps in understanding what can be quite difficult concepts. You can buy it separately, but it also available as part of a single-volume collection of four measurement titles (including the Spector one above). What a great idea for a birthday present!

There are many other sources of information on measurement available, lots of which are articles in the academic literature. Below is a selection I think are really good which cover the psychometric approach:

- Churchill, Gilbert A., Jr. (1979) 'A paradigm for developing better measures of marketing constructs', *Journal of Marketing Research*, XVI (February), 64–73.
- Gerbing, David W. and Anderson, Janet C. (1988) 'An updated paradigm for scale development incorporating unidimensionality and its assessment'. *Journal of Marketing Research*, XXV (May), 186–192.
- Gerbing, David W. and Hamilton, Janet G. (1996) 'Viability of exploratory factor analysis as a precursor to confirmatory factor analysis', *Structural Equation Modeling*, 3 (1), 62–72.
- Lee, Nick and Hooley, Graham (2005) 'The evolution of "classical mythology" within marketing measure development'. *European Journal of Marketing*, Vol. 39 (3/4) (if I do say so myself!)

And here's a few which look at alternatives:

- Diamantopoulos, Adamantios and Winklhofer, Heidi M. (2001) 'Index construction with formative indicators: An alternative to scale development', *Journal of Marketing Research*, 38 (2), 269–277.

- Rossiter, John R. (2002) 'The C-OAR-SE procedure for scale development in marketing', *International Journal of Research in Marketing*, 305–336.

EXERCISES

1. Going back to question 3 in Chapter 6 about defining relationship quality, explain the process you would go through to create a measure of relationship quality.
2. Explain what 'auxiliary theory' is, how it relates to 'structural theory', and why it is so important.
3. For the following constructs, explain whether (or in what situation) a student sample would be appropriate to develop their measures, and why or why not[7]:
    a. Self-esteem
    b. Attitude towards an advertisement
    c. Sales manager caring (see IDE 7.1)
    d. Brand loyalty
    e. Job satisfaction
4. What is reliability, how can something be reliable but not valid?
5. Explain what construct validity is, how it differs from criterion-related validity.
6. What is social-desirability bias and how could it influence your measures?
7. Put this book down and go read a work of fiction for a while.

[7] Have a look for research on these topics if you want to get some examples.

17 Collecting Quantitative Data

NICK LEE and IAN LINGS

SUPERVISOR'S VIEW: DR IAN LINGS

If you are conducting a quantative study, collecting your data is another major milestone in your research process, and one that can be fraught with anxiety. Generally your data collection resources (time, money and respondents) are limited. This means that often in reality you have only one bite at this cherry, despite what so many research methods books will tell you. You may be anxious as you question yourself; do my models and frameworks adequately reflect the real world? Have I designed my collection instruments appropriately? Have I chosen appropriate respondents that will provide me with the data I require? Will they agree to provide me with this data, either through their own efforts (if you use a self-response method) or if I observe them (using an observational technique)? *Oh my God,* what if I forget to ask a question or make an observation, what if I ask the wrong question, etc? WHAT IF IT DOESN'T WORK? Well, calm down, panic will never help you run a good data collection programme.

The panic of data collection, in my experience, tends to lead first-time researchers down one of two paths. Either a lack of confidence causes them to refuse to move to the data collection stage by procrastinating endlessly over their conceptual frameworks and models, eternally refining them to make sure they haven't missed anything. Or, they are so keen to finish, graduate, get a job and earn some money (at last), that they want to rush into data collection, seeing it as the last major hurdle to finishing the thesis, leading to corners which are cut, and poor data. Unsurprisingly, I would advocate an approach somewhere between these two extremes – and working through the material in the *other* chapters of this book will have just as positive an impact on your data collection as this dedicated one will!

The objective of your quantitative data collection is to provide you with a source of 'evidence' against which you can test your hypotheses. If you never collect the data you cannot test your hypotheses and the project will not progress; if you collect the wrong data, you will have to repeat the exercise once you discover that you have the wrong data. This is one of the main problems that first-time researchers face. You won't truly know if your conceptual framework is missing something important or if you have forgetten to collect an important variable until you have analysed your data. So data collection and analysis are inextricably linked. You *must* have an idea about what you intend to do with the data before you collect it. Both your intended analysis technique and your theoretical framework should give you a good idea of the data you need, but you don't know until you have analysed your data. So what are you to do?

Professor Gummesson highlighted the need for researchers to *practise*, and to use their experience, wisdom, insights and judgement and to reflect on their work. But as a first-time researcher you may not have experiences to reflect on. This is where practise comes in; I cannot emphasise enough the value of *practising your research*. Conduct a small-scale pilot study, collect the data, analyse it and interpret the results. Even a relatively small sample will give you important information about how well your full study will work. *It is not wasted time*, it will not slow down and it will almost definitely prevent you from making easily rectified mistakes that can cost you a lot of time, effort and money to put right.

What I am advocating is, from this point onwards, complete your project on a small scale first; gain some experience of the data collection, analysis and interpretation; reflect on this, and redesign your study if necessary. If you identify some problems you will be glad that you did; if it all works well, you can sleep more soundly in your (or someone else's) bed at night, knowing that you are on the way to a successful project.

VIEW FROM THE TRENCHES: ANDREW FARRELL

Firstly, let me just say that the majority of my comments refer to questionnaires. This is because it's what I mainly employ, and in my experience it's what the majority of people who say they are collecting quantitative data for their research actually mean. Now, I'll begin with something sinister. Quantitative data collection is a daunting process as it remains largely out of your control. You can study your sample with the greatest of precision, you can design the most easily completed, interesting, novel and downright pretty questionnaire ever, but if the respondents don't want to fill it in, they won't. *And there is nothing you can do about it!*

Well, that's not entirely true. There is something you can do. In order to combat respondent inertia, you need to arm yourself with an in-depth understanding of quantitative data collection procedures. It isn't possible to know 'too much' about quantitative data collection. If other people at your institution have been involved in the process before, ask them about it. Ask what went wrong, what went right, what they would do differently the next time. Everyone has at least one piece of advice that you will probably find indispensable.

The hardest part of quantitative data collection is getting the involvement of your participants. Due to the larger sample sizes that are often found (some would say required) in quantitative data collection, you generally don't have the option of personally contacting each participant and building up a rapport with them, as you tend to have when attempting qualitative data collection. Therefore, it is crucial that you are able to 'sell' your project to potential participants. Make them *want* to be involved. Make them worry about what they could miss out on if they are not involved. But, while doing this, don't forget that your participants are doing you a favour, and not the other way around. Participants are busy people. Shorter questionnaires mean more responses. Easy questions mean more responses. It's very tempting when designing a questionnaire to try and measure too much, to sneak a few extra questions in there so you can add another variable to your model that you are interested in. We all dream of being able to test the most comprehensive model ever conceptualised in our particular area, but that's all it normally is, a dream. It's nice to be able to achieve a healthy balance between the amount of data collected and the length of your questionnaire, but sometimes you've just got to be ruthless. Don't forget, a simple model is easier to explain, and easier to sell to your respondents.

Just remember, quantitative data collection can seduce you, with promises that more data means more power and more testing, which means better publications. However, a model, and by association a Ph.D., doesn't need to be complicated to make a contribution, but it does need sufficient data available to test it. If I'm asked if I'd like a complicated model with a small sample size, or a simple model with a large sample size, I know which one I'd choose every time (hint, it's the latter!)

Quantitative data is often what beginning researchers assume they are going to be collecting when they begin a research degree or career in most departments. Nevertheless, there are contrasting traditions and viewpoints towards different types of quantitative data collection, depending on what field you are involved in. In my own field, marketing, as well as a lot of other business disciplines, there is a prevalence of questionnaire survey designs – especially in the UK (Saunders and Lee, 2005). In the psychological disciplines (including consumer psychology) there is a tradition of experimental designs. In many finance, economics, and related disciplines, the approach is often based around collecting longitudinal secondary quantitative data.

These different approaches each offer contrasting strengths and weaknesses, meaning they are more or less appropriate for different research objectives. For example, if you wish to look at the influence of motivation on performance, utilising a longitudinal analysis of secondary data may be less useful than collecting experimental data. Therefore it is of course necessary to understand the basic link between your research question and the data you need to collect. This chapter will begin with the logic of sampling for surveys, as this is probably the fundamental theory of quantitative data collection. Following this, I will outline some key issues which need to be considered if you are using a different data collection method, or research design. Finally, some hints and tips about instrument design will be given.

After the previous few chapters, you're probably under the impression that if you choose to collect quantitative data, you won't have to deal with any criticism of your approach, as it is 'accepted'. Although this is in many ways true, choosing to collect a set of quantitative data poses its own problems. For one thing, you are choosing to be bound by a far more rigid set of principles and guidelines, so you had better spend some serious time learning these principles. In fact, this chapter is designed to provide a springboard into the sometimes deep waters of quantitative data collection, from which you can determine the appropriate methods to employ, and get a basic appreciation of what these methods entail. It is primarily concerned with the theory behind the practice of quantitative data collection – as there are many other excellent resources which tell you 'how' to collect data (e.g. how to design telephone surveys, etc.), and some of these are given at the end of the chapter.

In keeping with this, one important point to make at the outset concerns the Internet. As technology and society evolves, the Internet is becoming a vitally important tool to collect quantitative data. However, the Internet does not make the basic theories and principles outlined here invalid. Instead it augments your options with which to apply them. Consequently, the Internet will receive little explicit attention in this chapter, except where specific pieces of advice need to be given.

At the end of this chapter I really hope you have come to terms with these key ideas:

- That sampling is of key importance to statistics and the generalisability of our findings.
- What representativeness means, and the different ways of looking at the issues involved.
- That while probability sampling is seen as the 'gold standard' of sampling, in practice non-probability samples are more often used.
- The differences between interactive or non-interactive data collection methods.
- The key issues involved in instrument design.

Why is it Important to Know This Stuff?

As I have already mentioned, choosing to collect quantitative data involves an implicit choice to accept the basic principles and assumptions that underlie quantitative research. You are going to need a good appreciation of the underlying theory and its implications before you are capable of doing a good project. For one thing, a lack of understanding about quantitative data collection will make it really hard for you to truly grasp the basic principles of quantitative analysis – which is a common problem I am faced with among so many of my students.

While there are fewer political issues to deal with when compared to qualitative and interpretive approaches, the quantitative researcher will probably still face criticism from others for their stance. Just as the qualitative researcher should have a good knowledge of the reasoning behind their position, so should the quantitative researcher. You owe it to yourself and others to understand the bases of your chosen approach – or else how do you know 'why' you chose to collect quantitative data? Why should qualitative researchers be the only ones who need to justify themselves? As well as this, understanding the theory of quantitative data collection will allow you to determine when criticism of your work is justified, and when it is not.

Basically, what I am saying is that for quantitative researchers, it is important to know and accept the principles behind the approach. Furthermore, you will need to know this kind of information in order to interpret the quality of other pieces of quantitative research – which can have a huge impact on your theoretical work. For example, knowledge of sampling theory can have a big influence on how important you consider a given set of findings are to your own work.

Of course, we are dealing with the same basic issues as in other chapters (such as Chapter 9), the gathering of real-world data with which to examine our theory, and Figure 11.1 is almost identical to Figure 9.1. Finally, for those who truly know without doubt that they will never use quantitative data, they had better work out some reasons why – and this chapter would be a good starting point.

Quantitative sampling

Earlier in this book, I spent some time discussing the logic behind qualitative sampling. If you wanted to characterise this process, you could probably say that it was concerned with selecting 'appropriate' sampling units (or cases), with the benefit of some kind of criteria – whether it be theoretical, practical, or analysis-based. Hopefully, you also saw the link between this kind of approach and the underlying interpretive philosophy, and also the

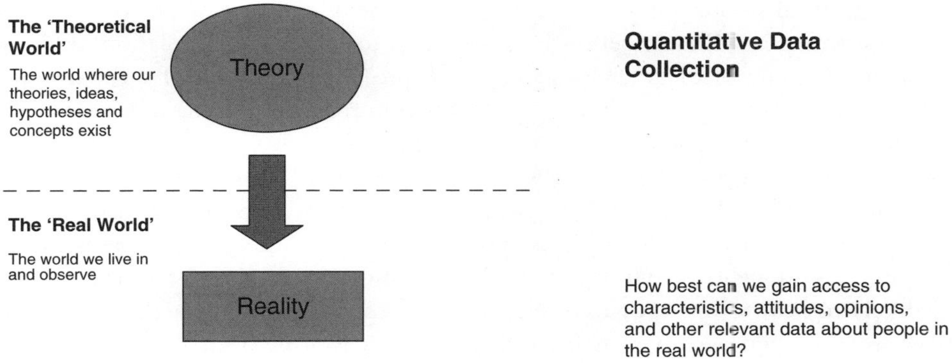

Figure 11.1 The place of quantitative data collection

needs of qualitative analysis techniques. However, the logic behind quantitative sampling is fundamentally different, which is why students often get confused between the two. The logic of quantitative sampling is also absolutely fundamental to statistical analysis, as hopefully you will grasp by the end of the next couple of chapters. So understanding this will give you a great start to learning about statistics – which I imagine you are not looking forward to if you are anything like most of my students.

First, to imagine the following scenario let's go back to the Milesians from Chapter 2 (again, you can use swirling colours and whooshing sounds if you want). If you remember, they wanted to know the answer to the question 'what is reality made of?' Let's pretend that instead of sitting around philosophising about it, they wanted to get the opinions of the Milesian population. Now Miletus was a small city in our modern terms, so it is easy to imagine that our Milesian researcher could feasibly go around the entire place and get the thoughts of every single person – a **census**. Our researcher would then be confident that all opinions were taken into account. However, what if some Milesians were busy when our hero called on them, or couldn't be bothered to reply? Does this introduce some error into the answer? Also, what if we were actually interested in the opinions of the entire population of what is now called Turkey – are the opinions of Miletus an adequate substitute? If not, surely it is impossible to collect opinions from the entirety of 'Turkey', so how would we decide who to collect data from? Perhaps we could go to the biggest city, stand in a central plaza and ask whoever comes past (and whoever will stop and talk to us)? Or maybe our intrepid researcher could get on a horse and ride around 'Turkey', looking for people to ask opinions of? Or instead, maybe we could employ say 1,000 people to each ride off and get the opinion of one person, then come back?

Now, let's make clear that none of these data collection strategies is inherently 'wrong' – they should all result in some data of interest to the researcher. The problem comes when we wish to **generalise** our results to situations and contexts *outside the data*. For example, can the findings from our Milesian census be generalised to the entire population of 'Turkey'? It is unlikely that any of the strategies above will provide what we call a **representative** (see Alternative View 11.1) sample – i.e. one which mirrors the population (within limits). Firstly, those who participated in our Milesian census (which you could also consider to be a sample of the population of 'Turkey') seem likely to be different from the rest of the population – after all, they were a distinct colony, who were interested in philosophy when no one else in the world appeared to be. Both the standing in the plaza and riding around strategies depend on who is around at the time, and who the researcher selects. This is likely to lead to bias. For example, if I were the researcher I might be more likely to select attractive women than men (well, I might as well be honest about it, I would). Also, not all members of the population have an equal chance of being selected in the sample. If all we are interested in is the findings as they apply to the individuals we have questioned (e.g. when we were only interested in Miletus), this is no problem. But when we need to generalise our results to a larger population, how can we know whether this is appropriate?

Alternative View 11.1: Representativeness

Representativeness is a thorny problem in my opinion. The common perception is that to truly generalise your findings to the population, you must have a *representative* sample, but what does this actually mean? Does it mean that if your population is 50 per cent male and 50 per cent female, so should your sample be? Even if this is so, how do you ever know the characteristics of your population in such detail? Calder *et al.*, (1982) provide an interesting perspective on this issue. Essentially they define two types of generalisation: (a) *effects* generalisation, where you are interested in applying your findings directly to some specific population or interest, and (b) *theory* generalisation where you are trying to find basic theories which apply to a variety of real-world contexts, i.e. a general understanding of the real world. According to Calder *et al.*, the latter situation does not require you to be concerned about the specific context you have sampled, nor the actual effects you observe (e.g. correlation sizes), but only in their potential to support or refute your theory (you should recognise Popper's influence here). In an effects generalisation situation however you *are* interested in whether the specific findings are applicable to the specific population – for example the size of the correlation between advertising and sales for a specific target market. It is reasonably clear that in *most* academic research, we are more interested in our theories as a whole rather than their specific effects.

Calder *et al.* consider that one can not be very confident in effects generalisations without a representative sample of the population. However, this is not the case for theory generalisations. In fact, the only criterion is that your sample is able to provide a test of your theory, not whether it is representative of some hypothetical population. Interestingly, they argue that strong tests of theory are *usually* best done with homogeneous samples (those which don't vary on characteristics which may influence your variables of interest), as you are less likely to detect false relationships. The upshot of this is that Calder *et al.* (p. 200) argue that representative samples are not necessarily required for theory generalisation purposes, as 'statistical generalisation of the findings is not the goal. It is the theory that is applied beyond the research setting ... and, any sample within the theory's domain (e.g. any relevant sample), not just a representative one, can provide such a test'. This of course does not excuse one from thinking seriously about the type of sample which is able to provide a good test of your theory – e.g. if your study is about sales managers' actions, a student sample is not necessarily able to provide a good theory test.[1]

In fact, such approaches can lead to various types of **error** in your sample. If you do not use what is called a *probability sample*, then some members of the population are more or less likely to be selected than others, which can cause statistical problems, as we shall see later. However, many (if not most) social science research projects don't use probability samples, even though the very logic of statistical analysis depends on it. I'll talk about this later on. Even if you do manage to use a probability sample, there are still other possible problems. For example, your sample may still not be representative by some unfortunate chance, which is called *sampling error*. The latter is difficult for the researcher to deal with, however, so most time is spent on *non-sampling error*, which concerns things which are caused by problems in your methods. For example, you might have selected your sample from an incomplete sampling frame (e.g. if you use the telephone directory, non-listed numbers have no chance of being selected), or those you do select may not respond (like when someone rings you for a market research survey in the middle of your favourite TV programme), or you may not be able to contact some members of your sample. You can see there are many problems which can arise in the sampling process. But even though it is virtually impossible to get a representative sample in 'real' social research, you need to understand why it is important. It is certainly not adequate just to collect data from 'whoever is around at the time'.

[1] One interesting perspective on this is that it moves quite close to parts of the qualitative sampling logic in Chapter 9, doesn't it?

Probability sampling

The probability sample is the 'gold standard' of quantitative sampling. In fact, this can be considered from two angles. Firstly, quantitative methodologists (i.e. those of us who actually study methods themselves) consider it to be the 'ideal' method of sampling, and the only one which allows you to draw statistical generalisations from your sample to the population. On the other hand, many quantitative researchers (i.e. those of us who actually *conduct* quantitative research) tend to consider it something of an unrealistic ideal in practice, one to aim at but hardly ever achieve.[2] Later, IDE 11.1 will show how the demands of research practice can make it difficult to achieve the perfect probability sample in many contexts.

IDE 11.1: Is Probability Sampling Realistic?

As already mentioned, probability sampling is the 'gold standard' for quantitative data collection. But in practical terms it is extremely difficult to conduct. Of course, if you have a well-defined population and a perfect list of it, then it is actually easy. And if any of you ever find yourselves in such a situation then I would be very surprised! Let's deal with the population issue first. In fact, many researchers don't really even seem to think about the population to which they wish to generalise at all. To test this, go and ask one of your colleagues about a research project they are doing, and then ask what population they are going to generalise to. You'll probably get some kind of vague answer like 'ummm, sales managers'[3] or 'ahhhh, Internet users'. What does this actually mean? All sales managers? Internet users between 25 and 40? Without a good idea of the population, it is impossible to take a probability sample. However, even if we do have a good idea of our population, it is almost never the case that we also have a perfect list of that population! Imagine our population is 'all chocolate consumers in the US', how do we find a list of those people? What about 'all UK small business owners'? We can possibly get a list of those registered companies, but what about those who are not registered – are they included in our theoretical reasoning? Even for as simple a population as 'the entire population of London' it is practically impossible to obtain a list. In most cases – especially in applied social research – we have to do the best we can to generate a useful sample. But we should be under no illusions that we have a 'true' probability sample. Does this mean our work is invalid? In a purely technical sense I guess it does!

[2] Those of us who are both methodologists *and* researchers can sometimes get confused over just what we think!

[3] I say this because I have given that very answer in the past!

However, the logic outlined in Alternative View 11.1 is not in agreement here. Furthermore, if we know the rules and theories behind sampling and why it is important, we can be in an informed position to judge the value of our non-probability sample-based conclusions. That's why it's important to read this and the next chapter of course!

The first key issue to be concerned with is deciding exactly what your **population** is. The population is who you wish to generalise your results to. Consider the Milesian example above. Do we wish to generalise to the population of Miletus, or 'Turkey', or the World? This has important implications for your sampling strategy, as well as for your findings and conclusions. Although larger or more general populations can make your theoretical conclusions seem more 'weighty', this is only the case if you are justified in generalising to that population. In other words, generalising our findings to the whole World rather than just Miletus might make us feel we did a more important piece of research, but this generalisation would be untrustworthy or nonsensical without a coherent sampling strategy. For the purposes of illustration, let's imagine we are solely interested in generalising to the population of Miletus at this point. However, before we start, you should never forget that no matter how rigorous your probability sample is, there is still the chance that it is subject to random sampling error. In fact, some form of sampling error is always evident.

The most basic type of probability sample is the **simple random sample**. This is essentially a perfectly random selection from a perfect list of all members of the population (the sampling frame). To conduct this, you must have a perfect sampling frame of all members of the population, and randomly select your sample elements from this list (e.g. numbering each element and selecting via a random number generator). Thus there is no bias, and I can't select just the attractive women, because the random number generator does the selecting for me. However, this necessitates numbering the entire population list, which can be laborious. A slight modification is **systematic sampling** where you begin at a random point between 1 and *n* by using a random number generator, then selecting every *n*th member systematically. You define *n* by dividing the number in your sampling frame by the sample size you wish to take. But, if your sampling frame is ordered in some way (e.g. alphabetically), this can cause bias, so it's best to somehow rearrange it. Of course, this may be just as laborious as numbering each element!

However, in some cases I might want to make sure I select the right proportions for various groups – say citizens and servants in the Milesian example. This *might* happen in a random sample, but it's not guaranteed. In this case I can use a **stratified random sample**, which involves breaking my population into relevant strata, and then randomly or systematically sampling within these strata to achieve sample proportions which accurately mirror the population. This is useful when you think that the strata might be relevant. For example, whether you are a citizen or a servant might be associated with many personal traits which are relevant to your study of perceptions of reality. However, it's only feasible when you can get the right information about your population.

But what if my rich Milesian sponsor (well, someone has to pay for this research!) actually wants to study the perceptions of the entirety of 'Turkey'? We've already seen how this could involve a lot of travel, and if we just randomly select elements from a (hypothetical) list of the entire population, it will most likely be virtually impossible to get to all these people within a reasonable time frame (quite apart from the practicalities of travel). A **multi-stage cluster sample** can be used in this case. If we decide we want a sample of say 1,000 people (we'll deal with sample size later), we could divide 'Turkey' into an exhaustive set of 'provinces' and randomly sample five provinces, then randomly sample 200 people in each province. There are many other ways of dividing up the overall population, but the key is to maintain the randomness of the sampling method. This method can also be combined with the stratification method above.

Non-probability sampling

As seen in IDE 11.1, the probability sample is more often an ideal than a reality, and as we know, these ideals can be extremely seductive (Hollywood has been trading on that for nearly a century so far). It is far more common to see organisational and other social research projects using non-probability samples than probability ones. While there are many different strategies available, I will focus here on the most common, which is termed the **convenience sample**. Convenience samples have a bad reputation, in fact the very name carries connotations of lazy research and a lack of concern over exactly who you sample. However, I believe convenience sampling can be looked at from at least two perspectives. In fact I think it is important to recognise that convenience samples do not necessarily denote bad research, not least because they are so commonly used! It is far better for researchers to admit they are using a convenience sample and justify why their research remains useful, than to ignore completely this fact and 'pretend' they are using a probability sample.

While I am going to introduce some positive ways of thinking about convenience sampling in this section, I'll begin with the dark side of this practice. Let's go back to Miletus again (I think I am beginning to like it there). Say that I couldn't find a good list of the Milesian population, which naturally causes me some panic. So, like most days I am sitting in the 'Milesian Arms' tavern thinking about my problems,[4] and in a blinding flash of inspiration decide to just collect data from whoever enters the bar during the next week, which turns out to be a sample of 200 people. Because I am a pretty likeable and well-known figure in Miletus, almost everyone answers my survey so I've got a good solid set of data, problem

[4]OK, OK, I admit that I am taking artistic licence here, but just go with the flow. Besides, this story is starting to resemble my life quite closely now.

solved! The problem is with generalisation of course. Those people in the tavern are almost definitely different from the general Milesian population. Even worse, I can think of plenty of reasons why their opinions about reality would be different too! This is purely lazy research, which I could never advocate as a good strategy. That's not to say you can never sample from a tavern, just that in this case it is lazy and inappropriate.

But there are plenty of other sampling strategies which are technically 'convenience' but still allow us to generalise our theoretical results to other contexts – as long as we are comfortable with the logic described in Alternative View 11.1. This is of course very lucky since we are almost never able to generate perfectly representative samples. Essentially, we need to make the best efforts to generate samples which are able to test our theories. Understandably, this kind of approach is only relevant to the theory generalisation task, not the effects generalisation task – so in some contexts we are bound by the representativeness logic detailed above. But most academic projects are theory-based, particularly in the social sciences.

There are two key criteria you need to think about when you are looking to take a non-probability sample for theoretical purposes. Firstly, can your population give you any data of interest in order to test your theory? For example, if you are interested in influences on managerial choices of different punishment activity, many would consider a sample of typical first year just-out-of-school undergraduate students inappropriate. This is simply because I fail to see how they could answer any questions from a perspective which is informed by any experience of the situation you are theorising about. However, if you wish to study the experience of *receiving* managerial punishment, the same typical 18–19-year-old first-year undergraduate sample might be more appropriate, since almost all of them should have worked as subordinates before (and you could screen the others out). Of course, if the typical first-year undergraduate in your institution is more mature, then perhaps this argument may differ. The second issue is whether those you select as your sample should have any systematic differences on any variables or characteristics of interest from the population you are interested in. Or if you are not interested in a specific population (e.g. you might be interested in a general consumer population), does your sample have any specific characteristics which would influence how you interpret your results? Let's take the undergraduate example again, if I am interested in sales executives, will the opinions of undergraduates (who have probably worked primarily in menial jobs) about experiencing punishment be systematically different? Or would they differ from a more general sample of employees on characteristics of interest? For example, undergraduates tend to be younger – is this likely to bias my conclusions?

These questions are also relevant when you make an attempt to collect a more general sample – such as when you stand in the car park of a shopping mall and try to get 250 responses. You need to work out whether your sample is likely to be systematically different from the population you are interested in (in this case probably general consumers). Or when you go through the telephone directory and select companies in an attempt to interview administrative assistants about their motivation. If you follow the theoretical logic of Alternative View 11.1, you are perfectly justified in using such a sample, and also generalising your theoretical conclusions (although not the specific effect sizes). However, this is only justifiable if you can show that the characteristics of your sample are not likely to have biased your results in some way. You can do this by appealing to demographic characteristics – showing you don't have any unusual groupings compared to your theoretical population (e.g. all males, or all over 65, etc.). Also, you should provide theoretical justifications as to why your sample is unlikely to be systematically different on any characteristics of interest.

Nevertheless, this section should not be taken as a *carte blanche* to collect any old data and generalise it to any setting. Instead, my argument is that it is probably better to bring the process of non-probability sampling 'into the open', and admit that it is far more common than probability sampling in practice. It is preferable to base our non-probability samples on some kind of theoretical logic, than blindly ignore them, or even worse desperately try to conceal the fact that we are not using probability sampling. Even more so, it is by far the best strategy in practice to 'try your best' to get a sample as close to probability as possible, and to make it as 'representative' as possible as well. But as already said, if you can't get the perfect sample, this does not necessarily invalidate your research – just make sure you understand why representative probability samples are seen as desirable.

Error in samples

As alluded to earlier, there are two main sources of error in samples: **sampling error** and **non-sampling error**. Sampling error is the difference between the sample and the population (i.e. how 'non-representative' is the sample?), and is something that is present to a greater or lesser extent in all samples. Using a probability sample is no guarantee against sampling error, but a well-designed probability sample does minimise the chances of it occurring to any great extent. Of course, to assess the degree of sampling error, you do need to have a good appreciation of what your population is.

Non-sampling error, on the other hand, is error which arises either because your sampling strategy was inadequate or biased, or your data collection and/or analysis techniques were poor. *Non-response* is one possible source of error here, which is when some of the people you try to contact either refuse to respond, can't be found (e.g. their addresses are wrong) or just can't give you the information you need. You will also have non-sampling error if your sampling frame is not an accurate reflection of the population. Some other sources of error are subsumed within the technical processes of data collection and processing – e.g. poor questionnaire design, incorrect administration (perhaps caused by bias in sample selection), or mistakes in data entry.

Dealing with these problems is not straightforward, nor in some cases is even assessing whether you have a problem. For example, how can you tell whether non-response is a problem? For it to be a problem you need to expect that non-responders are systematically different in some important ways to those who do respond. Of course to do this you would need to somehow get data from non-respondents! One popular way of getting a picture of non-response is to compare those who respond very quickly to those who respond very late to a mail survey, the logic being late responders are likely to be more similar to non-responders (Armstrong and Overton, 1977). But this is only applicable to mail surveys, and has also been criticised on a number of levels, even by its originators! Another way is to try to get a sample of non-responders to answer a very short set of questions in order to compare these answers with those who have responded. But there are no easy answers here. In terms of technical and administrative errors, these need to be minimised by careful data collection and analysis techniques, which are covered in various other chapters throughout this book. This is relatively easy if you are the sole researcher, but you need to be much more careful if you are working with others – say if you are employing people to collect data for you. In this case you have to be very clear in your instructions, and also do at least some monitoring and checking. I always found that paying your research assistants well (and being nice to them) helped too!

How big should a sample be?

This is a common question from students to supervisors, and it's one I have grappled with on many occasions. Some textbooks give calculations for desired sample size with a given level of *precision*, which basically means your sample mean is *more likely* to be closer to the population mean (I'll discuss sample means and stuff a bit more in the next chapter). I will refer to some of these books at the end of this chapter. However, these formulas are arguably rather unrealistic in practice. Firstly, you tend to never focus on one simple value (e.g. the mean), but instead your data set will be trying to get many different estimates of population values at the same time. Also, such considerations ignore non-sampling error, which is often a more major issue. Quite apart from any formulae, a larger sample makes it more likely that your sample will be a better representation of the population (assuming it is a probability sample). The ultimate size of the population has no bearing on this; a sample of 500 people from a population of 1 million is theoretically the same in terms of 'accuracy' as a sample of 500 from a population of 10 million. Strange I know. Just go with it. Thus, in practical research terms there are more important considerations which you need to deal with in terms of sample size than this hypothetical idea of precision.

First is pure practicality – how big can you get your sample to be within the limits of time and resources? This needs to be balanced with the research considerations below, but there comes a point when you just have to settle for your sample and make the best of it (or you will be collecting data forever). Of course, you can only do this as long as you have a good argument as to why your sample is going to give you useful and trustworthy findings. Along the same lines you will need to factor in an expectation of non-response. For example, industrial mail surveys in the UK tend to get response rates between 15 and 30 per cent, so you will need to sample a correspondingly larger number of people to get the same amount of data. To judge this you will need to get into the literature in your field and try to get a picture of the average response to data collections efforts similar to yours. You can boost your response rates in various ways, such as by pre-notifying your sample and getting their agreement (I have found this to be the most effective), offering incentives, sending out repeated waves of questionnaires until you get a response, and the like. That said, this can be rather expensive and time consuming. But I guess it comes down to the question of 'how much do you want the data?'

Another consideration is the intended analysis techniques you want to use. Most quantitative techniques are squarely based around large-sample theories. Thus, if you want to employ such techniques you will need to understand how much data you need to collect. Although there is considerable debate over exactly how large a sample you need for various techniques, in most cases larger is better. For example, if you want to use cross-tabulation tables, you will need to have a certain number of data elements in each cell. Sample size issues are relevant to methods like analysis or variance, multiple regression, correlation, and even more so for iteration-based techniques, such as factor analysis and structural equation modelling. Of course, if those terms mean nothing to you, then you will be looking forward to Chapter 14!

In essence, sample size selection is a combination of all these factors, mixed in with a political understanding of what is expected in your field (we'll look at this issue a bit more later on). It's very unlikely to be the precise and objective business talked about in many research textbooks, simply because research itself is often not the same thing as the idealised models that those books write about. Just like most real research, sample size decisions are practical and sometimes political. But you need to understand the 'rules' even if you want to bend them a little.

Other considerations

The information so far in this chapter has been based on the survey sampling methodology, but this is not the only type of quantitative data one may collect. In particular, the logic behind collecting data for experiments contains some additional concerns. First, it can be seen that most of the concern so far has been on issues of generalisability, or what we could call *external validity*. But we should also be concerned with the *internal validity* of our research, especially in the experimental context. This basically means we need to design our sample so that it can actually provide a good test of our theory (whether or not we can justifiably generalise those results). A great example of this is in the way of data collection for a typical experiment. Imagine we want to test a theory that positive reinforcement increases performance of students. In order to test this, we might use two groups of students, one which was subjected to positive reinforcement, and one which was not (a control group). However, we need to make sure that the groups are equal with regard to any other independent variables which might have an effect on performance, such as intelligence, motivation, and the like. In order to do this we need to assign each student to one of the two groups *at random*.

This process of **randomisation** (discussed in Chapter 8) is key to the logic of experimental research, and in theory it 'spreads out' the varying characteristics of your subjects across the experimental groups so that any possible confounding influences should be approximately equal across the groups. Of course, just like probability sampling can not guarantee zero sampling error, randomisation can not guarantee that all groups are equal on their level of confounding variables, but at least we have given ourselves the best chance. Yet, as you can see, randomisation cares little for the external validity of the population, it is simply a method of avoiding confounds *within* your sample. In order to generalise your findings, you still need to have some concern for the sampling theories discussed above.

Another way of controlling for possible confounding variables in experimental (and other) designs is to simply remove that variable. For example, if you think that gender will have an impact on your dependent variable (and you don't want to test this), then you can use subjects of only one gender. While this removes the chance that gender differences will confound your results, it also means you have lost the ability to generalise to both genders. This is even the case if you work with the logic in Alternative View 11.1. Why is this? Well, you have just told me that you *expect* gender to influence the results, thus the genders are systematically different in some way – so your findings can not really be seen as relevant to both genders. You can't have it both ways! You could also employ this method in a mail survey if you are willing to put up with the lack of generalisability. Nevertheless, in an experimental design, randomisation is usually a superior method.

Another key consideration for experimental data collection is the time factor, and of course this also has relevance for any type of data collection which extends over multiple time periods. In essence, your subjects change over time – just like anyone else does. There are two ways in which these changes can be thought about. First is what is called a **history** effect. Basically, between two measurement periods (say a pre-treatment and post-treatment in an experiment, or two time periods in a longitudinal study) there is a good chance that other variables will have some impact on the subjects. If you are researching the effect of a promotional discount on sales, then if another product also introduces a promotion, this will naturally affect your dependent variable of sales. Of course, the longer between the two measurements (pre- and post-promotion), the more likely that such events will occur. Also, this kind of thing is far more likely if you are in a field setting than a laboratory setting, where many things can be controlled. That said, if your research needs long time periods between measurements, you can hardly keep your experimental subjects locked up for days on end. Well, not since ethics committees started to take an interest in our research!

The other way that time can impact on your dependent variables is through a **maturation** effect. This effect refers to how people (or any other organism) naturally change and grow over time, and there isn't much you can do about it no matter how you try to control for it. For example, people learn over time, and this learning may influence your dependent variable. Cognitive ability increases and then decreases as we age, and you need to take this into account if your research is over a long time period, and if cognitive function is likely to be a confound. Similarly, people's work motivations change naturally as their life situation changes. Many other factors are also subject to such natural growth and change. While it's unlikely that you will be doing studies which last many years, it is not entirely out of the question. Nor is it impossible that some variables may change far quicker than that – especially in some situations. For example, if you are studying students at the start and end of a year of study, their learning will (hopefully) have changed at a far higher rate than a general population. You need to take this effect into account in your research design.

Methods of collecting your data

Of course, all of that stuff about sampling is just so much theory without your own knowledge of how you are going to go about collecting your data. There are many different individual methods, but they can be broken up into two main types – those which are interactive, and those which are not. **Interactive** methods involve the subjects of your research in some way, usually by questioning them and recording their answers. For example, by sending them a questionnaire, or stopping them on the street to ask them questions. By contrast, **non-interactive** methods simply involve the researcher recording information about the subjects, normally by way of observation. For example, you may sit in a shop and count the number of people who look at a given product, then how many subsequently purchase. Of course, each method has its own advantages and disadvantages, and in fact different traditions of research tend to use different methods. For example, in my field (sales management) interactive methods are more common, but in other fields, such as consumer psychology, non-interactive methods play a big role. Figure 11.2 displays examples of the major different methods of each category of research. However, it's important to realise that the decision to use each kind of research is normally taken in light of the characteristics of data you need, and I'll try to give a picture of the considerations you'll need to take into account below.

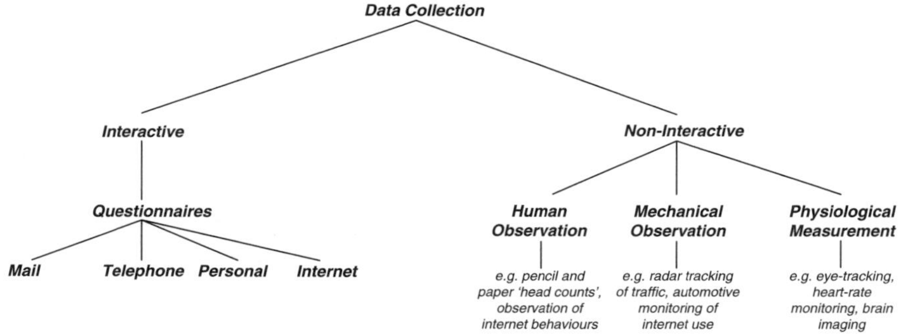

Figure 11.2 Interactive and non-interactive data collection methods

First of all, interactive methods are usually far more flexible. If you can think of a specific question about a piece of information you need, then you can normally collect that information. For example, information on internal constructs such as motivation, purchase intentions, attitudes and the like can be obtained via interactive questioning methods. That said, it's not quite as easy as that, and much of the information in Chapters 6 and 7 deals with how we should measure such concepts. Nevertheless, in terms of flexibility interactive methods are a clear winner, and you could sum them up with the rather snazzy slogan: 'If you want to know, just ask'. By contrast, non-interactive methods are pretty much bound to collect data about those things we can see. Furthermore, we are limited to those things we can see *right now*. There is no way you can get information about what happened in the past, nor what is likely to happen in the future. So basically, you are often stuck with information about observable behaviour, which is fine if you are interested in that, but not so good if you are not. However, technological advancement has led to a grey area here, which is explored in Alternative View 11.2.

Alternative View 11.2: Using Technology in Non-Interactive Research

The inexorable march of technology has allowed researchers to investigate all kinds of issues which in the past would have been incredibly difficult. One area where modern computers have allowed us to look into areas which would have been previously out of bounds concerns the observation of past behaviours. Firstly, the Internet is a goldmine of prior behaviour. In fact, almost every activity that you undertake on the Internet is recorded for posterity, and the well-informed researcher can reconstruct your behaviour with some degree of accuracy. Also, you'll find that people record their own behaviours, in settings like online communities, which the researcher can use to reconstruct the social behaviour of the community grouping. Of course, this type of thing often inhabits the grey area between qualitative and quantitative research. Another area which is proving to be of major utility to researchers is the vast amount of purchase behaviour data collected by retail scanners (like those ones at the supermarket). This data is in essence a record of your purchasing, and when combined with a loyalty card it is possible to reconstruct the patterns of a household over a given time period. Ignoring the somewhat worrying Big Brother connotations here, it is easy to see how fantastic such a set of data could be to a research. In the terms of this chapter, it is essentially a set of non-interactive data that can in fact record past behaviour (although when the behaviour was recorded, it was in the present I suppose). This type of data straddles the boundary between primary and secondary, sharing some characteristics of each. Of course, it is still unable to go beyond the surface-level issues, but for many research projects this is not important. One possible disadvantage is that it may be very difficult for academic researchers to get hold of, being as it is usually proprietary data collected by major research corporations, or retailers.

Interestingly, while interactive methods are by far the most flexible, an argument can be made for non-interactive methods being more objective – when used appropriately. Firstly, interactive methods rely on the willingness of the subject to give you the 'true' information after you have asked for it. In some situations, subjects may not be willing to do this, especially if you are asking them embarrassing questions. Furthermore, I've often found that subjects are desperate to give what they see as the 'right answer', no matter how many times you insist that you are only interested in their opinions. Thus, sometimes, subjects give what they think is the right answer, even if it bears little relation to their own knowledge or opinions. Furthermore, interactive questioning methods rely on the recall of participants if they are to measure past behaviour or opinions, and of course the longer into the past you wish to look, the harder it is for people to remember. The researcher or research instrument may play a role too (remember the idea of reflexivity in qualitative research, it's also relevant here). More specifically, in a personal interview situation a subject's responses may be influenced by the interviewer. This may also be relevant when you use a mail or other self-administered questionnaire; your question design may somehow influence the response (I'll touch on this in the next section). Non-interactive methods suffer less from these problems, they record objective behaviour as it actually happens, and do not depend on subjects to recall it. Furthermore, it may even be the case that subjects don't even realise they are being studied, which of course eliminates the chances of them modifying their behaviour to suit the researcher. Finally, the fact that non-interactive data collection is unable to measure non-observable things means that the data they *can* collect is more objective by definition.

A brief introduction to instrument design

Once you have decided how you are going to collect your data, you will then need to design the data collection instrument. This can be a difficult and frustrating exercise, and it's necessary for you to realise that careful instrument design is a very important part of a good research project. Without a good instrument, your data will never be of high quality, and of course this means that your research will also be less than adequate. Within the context of this book, it is completely impossible to give you all the information you will need to design top-quality data collection instruments, and therefore I am going to restrict this section to some general information about the design of self-administered surveys. The major reason for this is that design is probably *most* important for questionnaire surveys where the subject fills in the questionnaire themselves, as the researcher doesn't have a chance to correct any errors or help the respondent at all. However, at the end of this chapter I will discuss a few books which go into far more detail about design. You really should check these out if you want to be confident in your design.

The first issue to contend with is length. In fact, the length of the questionnaire is probably the single most important factor in influencing how many people are going to respond to your questionnaire. You need to balance out the need to cover everything you require for your research project with your desire to minimise length, and this issue is also bound up with issues of design and structure too. There is no minimum or maximum length of questionnaire, in all honesty, and the type of research you are conducting is also a major factor here. For example, in commercial surveys which are randomly mailed to consumers, length must be very short, but if a commercial research firm is paying the respondents, length can be longer. In an academic context, people will generally try to help you out if you write a good cover letter (i.e. begging them!), so you can get away with a bit of extra length, especially if you stress that you are a student and *really, really* need the data. If you get agreement from your respondents to fill in the questionnaire before sending it to them you can also make it longer – but remember to be (reasonably) honest about how long your questionnaire will take to fill in when you get agreement. It is counterproductive to tell people to expect a 10 minute survey when it is more like a 30 minute one. In fact, the more time you spend with people gaining their agreement, and the more relevant to them the topic is, the longer you can make the survey. I have run surveys of over 30 pages which gained quite good response rates, but the topic was very relevant to a select group of executives, and we spent a very long time with them gaining their agreement and convincing them of the benefits of participation. Most of my academic industrial mail surveys have hovered around 8–10 pages of questions, which is rather long compared to the recommendations of many research textbooks. However, respondents were pre-notified, and I spent a long time drafting good cover letters which stressed how much I needed this data. You should also balance the need to get lots of information which you don't *really* require here. More specifically, you should have some back-up measures and concepts in a survey, just in case your main model doesn't work out. You may also wish to collect data for multiple projects in one instrument. All of these considerations need to be balanced out – not an easy process.

Tied in with this is the issue of design. A better-designed survey can be longer in page terms. In fact, one thing you should *always* avoid is to 'artificially' decrease page length by cramming questions into tiny spaces; your questionnaire needs to be clear and easy to read. It's far better to have an extra page or two than to have a confusing and hard to read questionnaire. Modern word-processors allow you to do really neat things regarding the design of your questionnaire, and you should take advantage of these capabilities as much as possible. Unfortunately, I have seen far too many astoundingly poorly designed questionnaires, which do more to put off respondents than encourage them to complete the questionnaire. In particular, you *must* spend time proof-reading your questionnaire to avoid errors creeping in, like duplicate questions, spelling mistakes, poor wording and the like. Give it to someone else as well, although it can get a bit soul-destroying when it comes back with corrections all over it. However, in design terms try to balance out the need for good design with cost and practicality implications. For example, it might be great in design terms to print your questionnaire in all the colours of the rainbow, but this will cost a huge amount compared to simple black and white. Similarly, it's usually better to have your questionnaires professionally printed in booklet form so they open out flat; but if you can only afford photocopying and a staple in the top corner, that's what you will have to go with.

Another key issue bound up with all of this is the structure of the questionnaire itself. There are various theories on where you should put the different types of questions, which could be considered a bit contradictory (surprise surprise!) So what I will try to do here is give you an overview of the things you need to balance out. First and foremost, try to give your questionnaire a logical structure of some kind. For example, you might want to ask general questions first and then more specific questions later on. This allows the respondent to get their brain 'primed' for your more complex questions. Some theories also suggest you should keep questions on the same topic together, which allows the respondent to focus their mind on one topic at a time. Furthermore, there's nothing worse than filling out questions on one topic, then getting a few pages down the line and the same topic coming up again. I tend to follow this line of reasoning myself, but on the other hand it could be said that respondents can get lazy if they are answering the same topic consistently, leading to them not reading the questions thoroughly, making assumptions, and ultimately leading to poor data. Thus, the other view is to mix up your questions to keep the respondent thinking. Theory also suggests that you should keep more personal questions until the end of the questionnaire. Your respondents are probably more likely to answer personal questions if they've already invested their time to get that far. However, another unavoidable fact of questionnaire surveys is that some people do stop part-way through. If your important questions are at the end of the questionnaire, then this means that more people will miss these out than if they are at the beginning. You therefore need to balance this out with the other considerations. Personally, I tend to put key measures reasonably close to the front, after basic questions which just focus the mind of my respondent. At the end I tend to have a page of demographic questions. For most of my work these questions are not essential, so if a respondent gets bored and ignores them, I can still use the response in some ways as my most important data is usually still there.

Tips on writing good questions

There is a vast body of literature available on the specifics of scaling techniques, different forms of questioning, the appropriate type of response form for each type of information you require, and many other issues. I'm not even going to try to cover all the ground in this area. Instead I am going to discuss a few good and bad ideas when you are designing the actual questions you intend to use to collect your data.

The first thing you need to consider is whether to use open ended or closed questions. An open question such as: 'What is your opinion on advertising legislation in this country?' gives the respondent the chance to answer in their own words, but also has the disadvantage of a lack of comparability and consistency across respondents. Such questions can be useful to start things off, or when you are not sure of your topic right now, but more usually you will use closed questions, where you give the respondent a set of responses, and the respondent will choose the response which most closely matches their position. There are many different types of closed questions (also known as fixed alternative questions), and some of the various types are shown in Figure 11.3.

There are a number of considerations when you design the choices on closed questions. Firstly you must make sure the choices are mutually exclusive and exhaustive. That is, each respondent must be able to choose one and only one alternative, and for every respondent there must be an appropriate alternative. In practice, this means that there must be no overlap between your choices, and you should almost always include an 'other (please specify)' option in your questions when necessary. Another decision you must make regards how many alternatives you will give the respondent. Think about the Likert-type scale example

What is your highest educational qualification?
(please tick one)

_______ Postgraduate degree
_______ University degree
_______ Some university courses
_______ Trade qualifications
_______ 'O' or 'A' levels
_______ GCSE or equivalent
_______ High school
_______ Other

Please indicate your team's average level of performance on:

	Excellent		Neither Good nor Bad		*Poor*
Sales commissions.......................................	1	2	3	4	5

How often do you purchase a newspaper?
(please tick one)
_______ Once a day or more often
_______ Between six times and four times a week inclusive
_______ Between three times and once a week inclusive
_______ Less than once a week

Figure 11.3 Different question response types

in Figure 11.3. Should you use a 5-point scale, or a 9-point scale? A 9-point scale is certainly more fine-grained, but you need to think whether respondents can really distinguish between information at that level. For some concepts they may be, but for other they may not be. Furthermore, the more alternatives there are, the more difficult it is for respondents to answer the question. It has always been my feeling that one should attempt to minimise the effort required by the respondent. Therefore I try to use the least amount of choices necessary to get my information. However, sometimes you need to give a wider range of possible responses. This is particularly relevant if you think your responses will be clustered at the extreme ends of the scales. In this case you need to spread the responses out by giving them more options. For example, if a typical 5-point Likert-type scale has 'strongly disagree' as its extreme end, a 7-point may have 'very strongly disagree', while a 9-point might have 'very, very strongly disagree'. While this may not be an ideal method, it does tend to have some effect on spreading extreme responses out.

The next issue you have to consider is the wording of your questions. This is a key influence on your results, as poor wording is highly likely to result in poor data. First and foremost you need to remember that you are designing your questionnaire for your sample, not to impress your colleagues with big words, or anything like that. You must always remember to write your questions as simply as possible within the bounds of your topic. In fact, if you find that it is impossible to write your questions in such a form as can be understood by the least well-educated of your likely sample, you may wish to reconsider the use of a questionnaire. You also need to avoid accidental ambiguity in the wording – your questions have to be completely clear. Similarly, make sure each question refers to one and only one issue. For example, double-barrelled questions such as 'are you impressed by my wit and intelligence?' are never advisable, as it is impossible to interpret what an answer of 'yes' (or more likely 'no') would mean. You must also never lead your respondents down a particular track with your question wording, keep the wording objective and factual. You should, in addition, avoid making the respondent make difficult estimates or assumptions as well. While an entire chapter could be devoted to this topic alone, the basic rule is to try to make your questions as clear as possible, and reduce the workload on your respondents. This allows them to give you the information you need as easily as possible, which in turn should increase the accuracy of that information.

Testing your draft questionnaire

Once you have designed a questionnaire or other data collection instrument, what should you do next? No, the answer is not 'rush out and collect all your data'! In fact you need to go through a series of tests first before you can be certain that you have a good instrument. This is important, because one of the worst things that can happen to a researcher is to throw away a bunch of data because the questionnaire contained key errors. I think the ideal sequence consists of three main stages. Firstly, you should get your supervisor or colleagues to look at the questionnaire. This usually results in a whole bunch of demoralising questions that make you think your work isn't as good as you thought it was. You need to take all these comments seriously, and if they are helpful take them into account But don't forget that no one except you knows *exactly* what you are trying to do, so don't be afraid to counter-argue sometimes if you don't think a change is necessary. After this, I think it is useful to take your questionnaire out into the field and test it on the people who are going to answer it for real. The best way of doing this is to run some personal interviews with potential respondents, which have been called 'protocol' interviews (e.g. Diamantopoulos *et al.*, 1994). Sit down with them, and ask them to fill in your questionnaire while you watch. As they go through, ask them to comment on things that they found difficult, and record these comments so you can modify your questionnaire accordingly. This stage often shows up wording and other question design problems. Finally, you should run a **pilot study**, which is a mini version of your full study. Take a small sample of your population, and administer everything exactly as you would in your full study, to see if everything works out well. Please, don't avoid this step, as you can get into heaps of trouble if you do. It's never nice if you send out 1,000 questionnaires in your full study only to find out that some problem with your method results in no one sending them back! Much better to find this out in a small sample of 50 or 100. Furthermore, if your pilot works out Ok, then you can incorporate that data into your main study.

Cross-national instrument design

Cross-national research is becoming increasingly popular for many reasons, not least of which is the realisation that traditional US or Western theories and research may not be able to explain what happens in other societies. However, conducting cross-national research is fraught with difficulties for many reasons. In particular, the design of your questionnaire can be extremely difficult when you try to translate it to another country. In fact, translation itself is not as simple as it sounds. It's usually not enough just to get your questionnaire translated into another language, you should then get it 'back-translated' by someone else into its original language. This is a very basic check on the adequacy of your translation. However, any researcher experienced in translated questionnaires will know that even with the best translation in the world some concepts are unable to be translated accurately. I came across this when I had some of my salesperson questionnaires translated to be used in Thailand, discovering that some of my key concepts simply did not exist in that culture in the same way. In such situations you need to be very careful in making decisions about how to compare the data from different countries. Another line of thinking suggests that you should not even try to transfer concepts and measures from one culture to another, but instead you should go through the development process completely separately for each culture you wish to study. This is fine if you are studying countries in isolation, but it makes things virtually impossible when you want to study and compare multiple cultures, as you no longer have consistent measures. The two contrasting approaches can be considered to be polar extremes of a continuum. The *emic* approach argues that cultures are unique and are thus best studied in isolation, while the *etic* approach counters that there are universal concepts in existence, and thus one should focus on developing measures which can be used in multiple cultural contexts (see Craig and Douglas, 2005). The best position here is probably somewhere in the middle. Certainly, it seems plausible that there are at least some common attitudinal or behavioural factors across cultures. However, researchers should be careful not to assume that *every* concept they are interested in is the same across cultures, nor that one can unthinkingly apply measures developed in one culture to another. Overall, cross-national research can be a minefield, so you should think carefully about conducting it if you are an inexperienced researcher. Those who do wish to conduct such research should begin by consulting some of the specialist books on the subject.

Summary

This chapter was designed for you to use as an introduction into the field of qualitative data collection. Each topic in this chapter is worthy of its own book, and indeed each topic has many books available on it which contain far more detail and should be consulted in addition if you are serious about conducting quantitative research. This chapter presents key issues and decisions which need to be made in the design of a quantitative data collection project, as well as some viewpoints which have sometimes been ignored by other sources. It is also an attempt to put quantitative data collection in the context of a wider appreciation of research in general, rather than just as a technical process. Too often are beginning researchers indoctrinated into the technical process of quantitative research without understanding why they are conducting such work. Hopefully this chapter, when read in conjunction with the rest of this book – will go some way towards helping researchers think about quantitative work in a wider context, rather than just as a process to follow.

Key points to take from this chapter:

- Quantitative sampling is of key importance to statistics.
- It is particularly important to the generalisability of our findings.
- The representativeness of samples is not a straightforward issue, and there are various ways of approaching it.
- Probability sampling is the 'gold standard' of sampling, but in practical terms it is hard to employ perfectly.
- Non-probability samples are not inherently poor, but you do need to think carefully about how you use them.
- Sample size is also a complex issue, and you need to take many factors into account when designing your sample.
- Your data needs determine whether you use interactive or non-interactive data collection methods.
- Questionnaire design is a complex business, with many conflicting issues which need to be balanced out.

Further reading

- *Mail and Internet Surveys: The Tailored Design Method* by Don A. Dillman. This is generally thought of as 'the' book on survey design. The first edition was actually called *The Total Design Method*, but Dillman has extended this approach and renamed it to reflect the changes. All told it is a classic of its kind.
- *Marketing Research: Methodological Foundations* by Gilbert A. Churchill and Dawn Iacobucci. Already mentioned in Chapter 8, this book is also a great introduction to general data collection issues. It contains excellent information on sampling and general research methods and is a fine example of a 'textbook' approach to research methods.
- *International Marketing Research* by C. Samuel Craig and Susan P. Douglas. This is a great starting point for exploring the techniques and concepts relating to doing international and cross-cultural research.

EXERCISES

1. What is the difference between a sample and a population?
   - Why don't we always use the population?
2. What does 'representative' mean in the context of sampling?
   - Do we always have to have a representative sample? Why or why not?
3. Design a method of taking a simple random sample of household shoppers in the UK.
   - What factors would effect your methodology?
   - How could you stratify the population and why might you want to do this?
   - How would a cluster sample help your research method?
4. What are the key factors you need to take into account when you design non-probability samples?
5. What is the difference between sampling and non-sampling error?
6. What factors can influence the internal validity of a quantitative study?
7. Describe a topic ideally suited to interactive data collection methods, and explain why.
8. Describe a topic ideally suited to non-interactive data collection methods and explain why.
9. Imagine I wanted to design a questionnaire with the following sets of questions:
   - Demographic information
   - Job satisfaction
   - Work motivation
   - Opinions on how much of a 'bully' their boss was
   - Work stress

   What would be the 'best' way of arranging these questions, and why?
10. I think now you should go out with your friends (I hope you still have some!) and have a nice meal. Personally, I am always partial to a curry.

18

The SPSS Environment

ANDY FIELD

FIGURE 3.1 All I want for Christmas is … some tasteful wallpaper

3.1. What will this chapter tell me? ①

At about 5 years old I moved from nursery (note that I moved, I was not 'kicked out' for showing my …) to primary school. Even though my older brother was already there, I remember being really scared about going. None of my nursery school friends were going to the same school and I was terrified about meeting all of these new children. I arrived in my classroom and, as I'd feared, it was full of scary children. In a fairly transparent ploy to make me think that I'd be spending the next 6 years building sand castles, the teacher told me to play in the sand pit. While I was nervously trying to discover whether I could build a pile of sand high enough to bury my head in it, a boy came and joined me. He was Jonathan Land,

and he was really nice. Within an hour he was my new best friend (5 year olds are fickle ...) and I loved school. Sometimes new environments seem more scary than they really are. This chapter introduces you to a scary new environment: SPSS. The SPSS environment is a generally more unpleasant environment in which to spend time than your normal environment; nevertheless, we have to spend time there if we are to analyse our data. The purpose of this chapter is, therefore, to put you in a sand pit with a 5 year old called Jonathan. I will orient you in your new home and everything will be fine. We will explore the key windows in SPSS (the **data editor**, the **viewer** and the **syntax editor**) and also look at how to create variables, enter data and adjust the properties of your variables. We finish off by looking at how to load files and save them.

3.2. Versions of SPSS ①

This book is based primarily on version 17 of SPSS (at least in terms of the diagrams); however, don't be fooled too much by version numbers because SPSS has a habit of releasing 'new' versions fairly regularly. Although this makes SPSS a lot of money and creates a nice market for people writing books on SPSS, there are few differences in these new releases that most of us would actually notice. Occasionally they have a major overhaul (version 16 actually looks quite different to version 15, and the output viewer changed quite a bit too), but most of the time you can get by with a book that doesn't explicitly cover the version you're using (the last edition of this book was based on version 13, but could be used easily with all subsequent versions up to this revision!). So, this third edition, although dealing with version 17, will happily cater for earlier versions (certainly back to version 10). I also suspect it'll be useful with versions 18, 19 and 20 when they appear (although it's always a possibility that SPSS may decide to change everything just to annoy me). In case you're very old school there is a file called **Field2000(Chapter1).pdf** on the book's website that covers data entry in versions of SPSS before version 10, but most of you can ignore this file.

3.3. Getting started ①

SPSS mainly uses two windows: the data editor (this is where you input your data and carry out statistical functions) and the viewer (this is where the results of any analysis appear).[1] There are several additional windows that can be activated such as the SPSS Syntax Editor (see section 3.7), which allows you to enter SPSS commands manually (rather than using the window-based menus). For many people, the syntax window is redundant because you can carry out most analyses by clicking merrily with your mouse. However, there are various additional functions that can be accessed using syntax and in many situations it can save time. This is why sick individuals who enjoy statistics find numerous uses for syntax and start dribbling excitedly when discussing it. Because I wish to drown in a pool of my own excited dribble, there are some sections of the book where I'll force you to use it.

Once SPSS has been activated, a start-up window will appear (see Figure 3.2), which allows you to select various options. If you already have a data file on disk that you would like to open then select *Open an existing data source* by clicking on the ○ so that it looks like ◉: this is the default option. In the space underneath this option there will be a list of recently used data files that you can select with the mouse. To open a selected file click on OK. If you want to open a data file that isn't in the list then simply select *More Files ...*

[1] There is also the SmartViewer window, which actually isn't very smart, but more on that later.

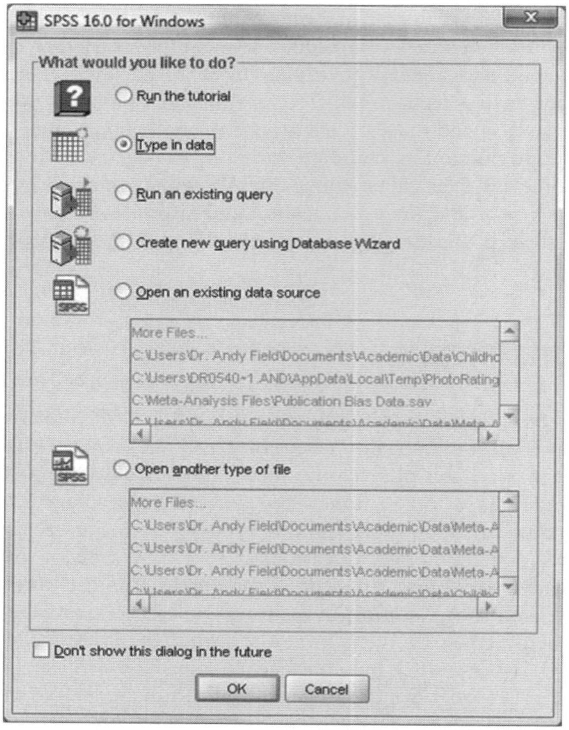

FIGURE 3.2 The start-up window of SPSS

with the mouse and click on OK. This will open a standard explorer window that allows you to browse your computer and find the file you want (see section 3.9). Now it might be the case that you want to open something other than a data file, for example a *viewer* document containing the results of your last analysis. You can do this by selecting *Open another type of file* by clicking on the ○ (so that it looks like ◉) and either selecting a file from the list or selecting *More Files* ... and browsing your computer. If you're starting a new analysis (as we are here) then we want to type our data into a new data editor. Therefore, we need to select *Type in data* (by again clicking on the appropriate ○) and then clicking on OK. This will load a blank data editor window.

3.4. The data editor ①

The main SPSS window includes a data editor for entering data. This window is where most of the action happens. At the top of this screen is a menu bar similar to the ones you might have seen in other programs. Figure 3.3 shows this menu bar and the data editor. There are several menus at the top of the screen (e.g. File Edit View) that can be activated by using the computer mouse to move the on-screen arrow onto the desired menu and then pressing the left mouse button once (I'll refer to pressing this button as *clicking*). When you have clicked on a menu, a menu box will appear that displays a list of options that can be activated by moving the on-screen arrow so that it is pointing at the desired option and then clicking with the mouse. Often, selecting an option from a menu makes a window appear; these windows are referred to as *dialog boxes*. When referring to selecting options in a menu I will use images to notate the menu paths; for example, if I were to say that you should select the *Save As* ... option in the *File* menu, you will see File Save As....

FIGURE 3.3 The SPSS Data Editor

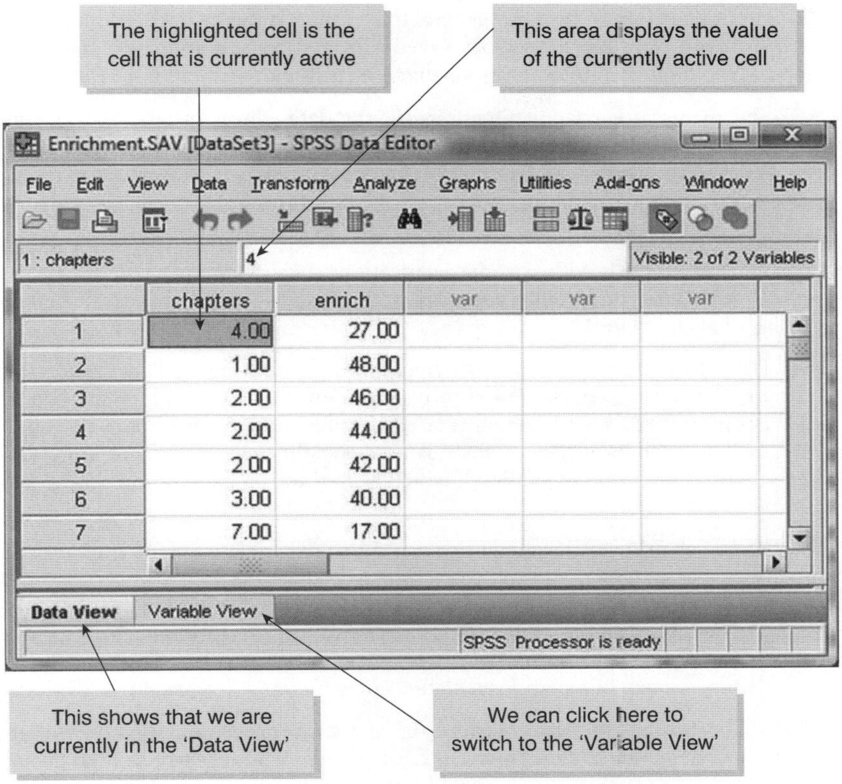

The data editor has two views: the **data view** and the **variable view**. The data view is for entering data into the data editor, and the variable view allows us to define various characteristics of the variables within the data editor. At the bottom of the data editor, you should notice that there are two tabs labelled 'Data View' and 'Variable View' (**Data View** | Variable View) and all we do to switch between these two views is click on these tabs (the highlighted tab tells you which view you're in, although it will be obvious). Let's look at some general features of the data editor, features that don't change when we switch between the data view and the variable view. First off, let's look at the menus.

In many computer packages you'll find that within the menus some letters are underlined: these underlined letters represent the *keyboard shortcut* for accessing that function. It is possible to select many functions without using the mouse, and the experienced keyboard user may find these shortcuts faster than manoeuvring the mouse arrow to the appropriate place on the screen. The letters underlined in the menus indicate that the option can be obtained by simultaneously pressing *Alt* on the keyboard and the underlined letter. So, to access the *Save As...* option, using only the keyboard, you should press *Alt* and F on the keyboard simultaneously (which activates the *File* menu), then, keeping your finger on the *Alt* key, press A (which is the underlined letter).[2]

Below is a brief reference guide to each of the menus and some of the options that they contain. This is merely a summary and we will discover the wonders of each menu as we progress through the book:

[2] If these underlined letters are not visible (in Windows XP they seemed to disappear, but in Vista they appear to have come back) then try pressing *Alt* and then the underlined letters should become visible.

- File This menu allows you to do general things such as saving data, graphs or output. Likewise, you can open previously saved files and print graphs data or output. In essence, it contains all of the options that are customarily found in *File* menus.
- Edit This menu contains edit functions for the data editor. In SPSS it is possible to *cut* and *paste* blocks of numbers from one part of the data editor to another (which can be very handy when you realize that you've entered lots of numbers in the wrong place). You can also use the Options... to select various preferences such as the font that is used for the output. The default preferences are fine for most purposes.
- View This menu deals with system specifications such as whether you have grid lines on the data editor, or whether you display value labels (exactly what value labels are will become clear later).
- Data This menu allows you to make changes to the data editor. The important features are Insert Variable, which is used to insert a new variable into the data editor (i.e. add a column); Insert Cases, which is used to add a new row of data between two existing rows of data; Split File..., which is used to split the file by a grouping variable (see section 5.4.3); and Select Cases..., which is used to run analyses on only a selected sample of cases.
- Transform You should use this menu if you want to manipulate one of your variables in some way. For example, you can use *recode* to change the values of certain variables (e.g. if you wanted to adopt a slightly different coding scheme for some reason) – see SPSS Tip 7.1. The *compute* function is also useful for transforming data (e.g. you can create a new variable that is the average of two existing variables). This function allows you to carry out any number of calculations on your variables (see section 5.7.3).
- Analyze The fun begins here, because the statistical procedures lurk in this menu. Below is a brief guide to the options in the statistics menu that will be used during the course of this book (this is only a small portion of what is available):
  - Descriptive Statistics ▸ This menu is for conducting descriptive statistics (mean, mode, median, etc.), frequencies and general data exploration. There is also a command called *crosstabs* that is useful for exploring frequency data and performing tests such as chi-square, Fisher's exact test and Cohen's kappa.
  - Compare Means ▸ This is where you can find *t*-tests (related and unrelated – Chapter 9) and one-way independent ANOVA (Chapter 10).
  - General Linear Model ▸ This menu is for complex ANOVA such as two-way (unrelated, related or mixed), one-way ANOVA with repeated measures and multivariate analysis of variance (MANOVA) – see Chapters 11, 12, 13, 14, and 16.
  - Mixed Models ▸ This menu can be used for running multilevel linear models (MLMs). At the time of writing I know absolutely nothing about these, but seeing as I've promised to write a chapter on them I'd better go and do some reading. With luck you'll find a chapter on it later in the book, or 30 blank sheets of paper. It could go either way.
  - Correlate ▸ It doesn't take a genius to work out that this is where the correlation techniques are kept! You can do bivariate correlations such as Pearson's *R*, Spearman's rho (ρ) and Kendall's tau (τ) as well as partial correlations (see Chapter 6).
  - Regression ▸ There are a variety of regression techniques available in SPSS. You can do simple linear regression, multiple linear regression (Chapter 7) and more advanced techniques such as logistic regression (Chapter 8).
  - Loglinear ▸ Loglinear analysis is hiding in this menu, waiting for you, and ready to pounce like a tarantula from its burrow (Chapter 13).

- Data Reduction ▸ You'll find factor analysis here (Chapter 17).
- Scale ▸ Here you'll find reliability analysis (Chapter 17).
- Nonparametric Tests ▸ There are a variety of non-parametric statistics available such as the chi-square goodness-of-fit statistic, the binomial test, the Mann–Whitney test, the Kruskal–Wallis test, Wilcoxon's test and Friedman's ANOVA (Chapter 15).

- Graphs SPSS has some graphing facilities and this menu is used to access the Chart Builder (see Chapter 4). The types of graphs you can do include: bar charts, histograms, scatterplots, box–whisker plots, pie charts and error bar graphs to name but a few.
- Window This menu allows you to switch from window to window. So, if you're looking at the output and you wish to switch back to your data sheet, you can do so using this menu. There are icons to shortcut most of the options in this menu so it isn't particularly useful.
- Utilities In this menu there is an option, Data File Comments..., that allows you to comment on your data set. This can be quite useful because you can write yourself notes about from where the data come, or the date they were collected and so on.
- Add-ons SPSS sells several add-ons that can be accessed through this menu. For example, SPSS has a program called *Sample Power* that computes the sample size required for studies, and power statistics (see section 2.6.5). However, because most people won't have these add-ons (including me) I'm not going to discuss them in the book.
- Help This is an invaluable menu because it offers you online help on both the system itself and the statistical tests. The statistics help files are fairly incomprehensible at times (the program is not designed to teach you statistics) and are certainly no substitute for acquiring a good book like this – erm, no, I mean acquiring a good knowledge of your own. However, they can get you out of a sticky situation.

SPSS TIP 3.1 Save time and avoid RSI ①

By default, when you try to open a file from SPSS it will go to the directory in which the program is stored on your computer. This is fine if you happen to store all of your data and output in that folder, but if not then you will find yourself spending time navigating around your computer trying to find your data. If you use SPSS as much as I do then this has two consequences: (1) all those seconds have added up and I have probably spent weeks navigating my computer when I could have been doing something useful like playing my drum kit; (2) I have increased my chances of getting RSI in my wrists, and if I'm going to get RSI in my wrists I can think of more enjoyable ways to achieve it than navigating my computer (drumming again, obviously). Well, we can get around this by telling SPSS where we'd like it to start looking for data files. Select Edit Options... to open the *Options* dialog box below and select the *File Locations* tab.

This dialog box allows you to select a folder in which SPSS will initially look for data files and other files. For example, I keep all of my data files in a single folder called, rather unimaginatively, 'Data'. In the dialog box here I have clicked on Browse... and then navigated to my data folder. SPSS will use this as the default location when I try to open files and my wrists are spared the indignity of RSI. You can also select the option for SPSS to use the *Last folder used*, in which case SPSS remembers where you were last time it was loaded and uses that folder when you try to open up data files.

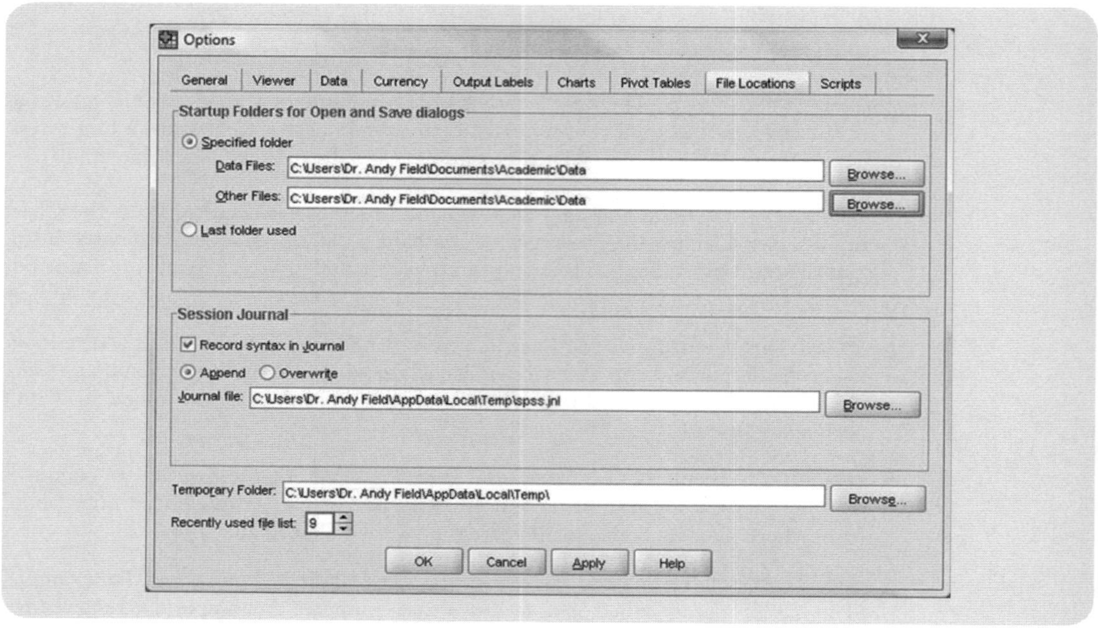

As well as the menus there is also a set of *icons* at the top of the data editor window (see Figure 3.3) that are shortcuts to specific, frequently used, facilities. All of these facilities can be accessed via the menu system but using the icons will save you time. Below is a brief list of these icons and their functions:

	This icon gives you the option to open a previously saved file (if you are in the data editor SPSS assumes you want to open a data file; if you are in the output viewer, it will offer to open a viewer file).
	This icon allows you to save files. It will save the file you are currently working on (be it data or output). If the file hasn't already been saved it will produce the *Save Data As* dialog box.
	This icon activates a dialog box for printing whatever you are currently working on (either the data editor or the output). The exact print options will depend on the printer you use. By default SPSS will print everything in the output window so a useful way to save trees is to print only a selection of the output (see SPSS Tip 3.4).
	Clicking on this icon will activate a list of the last 12 dialog boxes that were used. From this list you can select any box from the list and it will appear on the screen. This icon makes it easy for you to repeat parts of an analysis.
	This icon looks a bit like your data have had a few too many beers and have collapsed in the gutter by the side of the road. The truth is considerably less exciting: it enables you to go directly to a case (a case is a row in the data editor and represents something like a participant, an organism or a company). This button is useful if you are working on large data files: if you were analysing a survey with 3000 respondents it would get pretty tedious scrolling down the data sheet to find participant 2407's responses. This icon can be used to skip directly to a case. Clicking on this icon activates a dialog box in which you type the case number required (in our example 2407): 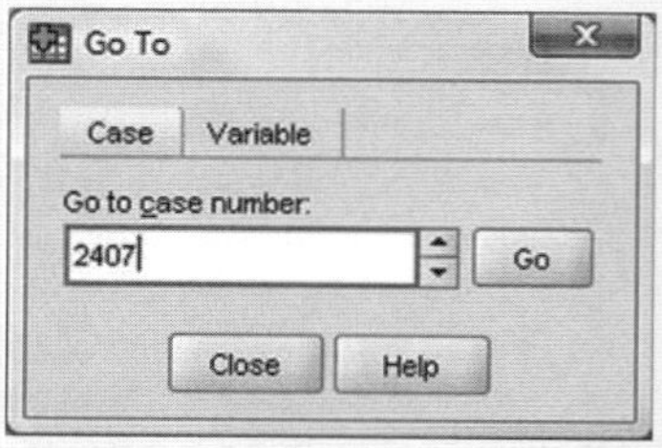

This icon activates a function that is similar to the previous one except that you can skip directly to a variable (i.e. a column in the data editor). As before, this is useful when working with big data files in which you have many columns of data. In the example below, we have a data file with 23 variables and each variable represents a question on a questionnaire and is named accordingly (we'll use this data file, **SAQ.sav**, in Chapter 17). We can use this icon to activate the *Go To* dialog box, but this time to find a variable. Notice that a drop-down box lists the first 10 variables in the data editor but you can scroll down to go to others.

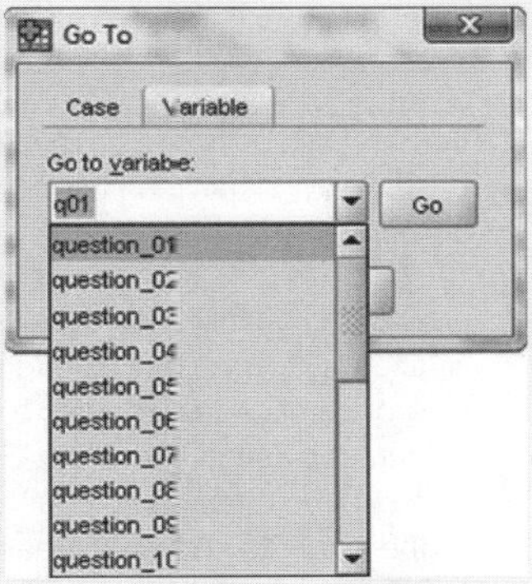

This icon implies to me (what with the big question mark and everything) that you click on it when you're looking at your data scratching your head and thinking 'how in Satan's name do I analyse these data?' The world would be a much nicer place if clicking on this icon answered this question, but instead the shining diamond of hope is snatched cruelly from you by the cloaken thief that is SPSS. Instead, clicking on this icon opens a dialog box that shows you the variables in the data editor and summary information about each one. The dialog box below shows the information for the file that we used for the previous icon. We have selected the first variable in this file, and we can see the variable name (question_01), the label (Statistics makes me cry), the measurement level (ordinal), and the value labels (e.g. the number 1 represents the response of 'strongly agree').

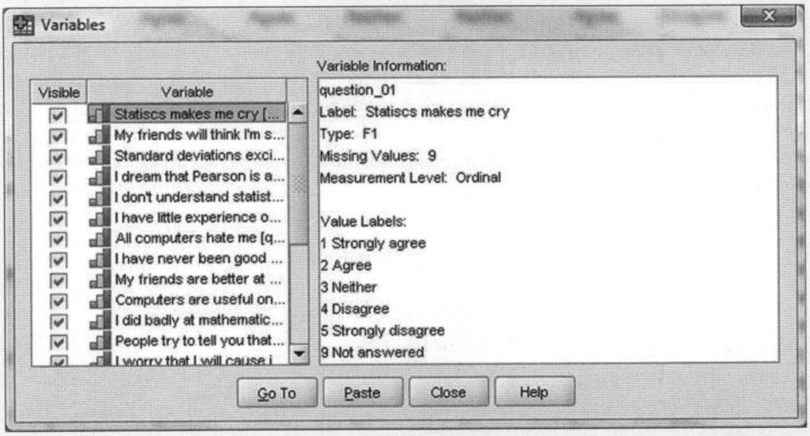

This icon doesn't allow you to spy on your neighbours (unfortunately), but it does enable you to search for words or numbers in your data file and output window. In the data editor it will search within the variable (column) that is currently active. This option is useful if, for example, you realize from a graph of your data that you have typed 20.02 instead of 2.02 (see section 4.4): you can simply search for 20.02 within that variable and replace that value with 2.02:

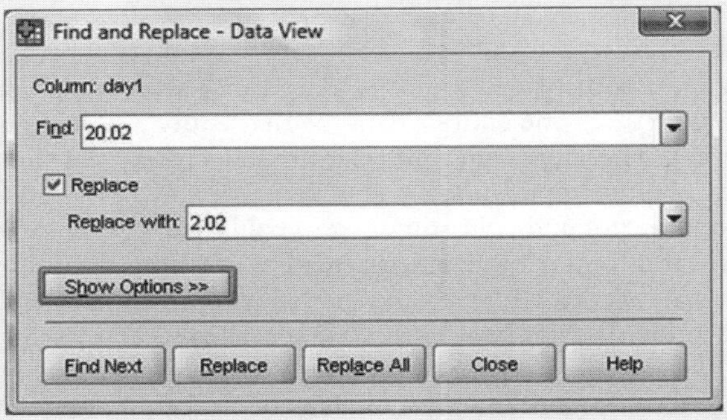

	Clicking on this icon inserts a new case in the data editor (so it creates a blank row at the point that is currently highlighted in the data editor). This function is very useful if you need to add new data at a particular point in the data editor.
	Clicking on this icon creates a new variable to the left of the variable that is currently active (to activate a variable simply click once on the name at the top of the column).
	Clicking on this icon is a shortcut to the Data Split File... function (see section 5.4.3). There are often situations in which you might want to analyse groups of cases separately. In SPSS we differentiate groups of cases by using a coding variable (see section 3.4.2.3), and this function lets us divide our output by such a variable. For example, we might test males and females on their statistical ability. We can code each participant with a number that represents their gender (e.g. 1 = female, 0 = male). If we then want to know the mean statistical ability of each gender we simply ask the computer to split the file by the variable **Gender**. Any subsequent analyses will be performed on the men and women separately. There are situations across many disciplines where this might be useful: sociologists and economists might want to look at data from different geographic locations separately, biologists might wish to analyse different groups of mutated mice, and so on.
	This icon shortcuts to the Data Weight Cases... function. This function is necessary when we come to input frequency data (see section 18.5.2) and is useful for some advanced issues in survey sampling.
	This icon is a shortcut to the Data Select Cases... function. If you want to analyse only a portion of your data, this is the option for you! This function allows you to specify what cases you want to include in the analysis. There is a Flash movie on the companion website that shows you how to select cases in your data file.
	Clicking on this icon will either display or hide the value labels of any coding variables. We often group people together and use a coding variable to let the computer know that a certain participant belongs to a certain group. For example, if we coded gender as 1 = female, 0 = male then the computer knows that every time it comes across the value 1 in the **Gender** column, that person is a female. If you press this icon, the coding will appear on the data editor rather than the numerical values; so, you will see the words *male* and *female* in the **Gender** column rather than a series of numbers. This idea will become clear in section 3.4.2.3.

3.4.1. Entering data into the data editor ①

When you first load SPSS it will provide a blank data editor with the title *Untitled1* (this of course is daft because once it has been given the title 'untitled' it ceases to be untitled!). When inputting a new set of data, you must input your data in a logical way. The SPSS Data Editor is arranged such that *each row represents data from one entity while each column represents a variable*. There is no discrimination between independent and dependent variables: both types should be placed in a separate column. The key point is that each row represents one entity's data (be that entity a human, mouse, tulip, business, or water sample). Therefore, any information about that case should be entered across the data editor. For example, imagine you were interested in sex differences in perceptions of pain created by hot and cold stimuli. You could place some people's hands in a bucket of very cold water for a minute and ask them to rate how painful they thought the experience was on a scale of 1 to 10. You could then ask them to hold a hot potato and again measure their perception of pain. Imagine I was a participant. You would have a single row representing my data, so there would be a different column for my name, my gender, my pain perception for cold water and my pain perception for a hot potato: Andy, male, 7, 10.

SPSS TIP 3.2 Entering data ①

There is a simple rule for how variables should be placed in the SPSS Data Editor: data from different things go in different rows of the data editor, whereas data from the same things go in different columns of the data editor. As such, each person (or mollusc, goat, organization, or whatever you have measured) is represented in a different row. Data within each person (or mollusc etc.) go in different columns. So, if you've prodded your mollusc, or human, several times with a pencil and measured how much it twitches as an outcome, then each prod will be represented by a column.

In experimental research this means that any variable measured with the same participants (a repeated measure) should be represented by several columns (each column representing one level of the repeated-measures variable). However, any variable that defines different groups of things (such as when a between-group design is used and different participants are assigned to different levels of the independent variable) is defined using a single column. This idea will become clearer as you learn about how to carry out specific procedures. This golden rule is broken in mixed models but until Chapter 19 we can overlook this annoying anomaly.

The column with the information about my gender is a grouping variable: I can belong to either the group of males or the group of females, but not both. As such, this variable is a between-group variable (different people belong to different groups). Rather than representing groups with words, in SPSS we have to use numbers. This involves assigning each group a number, and then telling SPSS which number represents which group. Therefore, between-group variables are represented by a single column in which the group to which the person belonged is defined using a number (see section 3.4.2.3). For example, we might decide that if a person is male then we give them the number 0, and if they're female we give them the number 1. We then have to tell SPSS that every time it sees a 1 in a particular column the person is a female, and every time it sees a 0 the person is a male. Variables that specify to which of several groups a person belongs can be used to split up data files (so in the pain example you could run an analysis on the male and female participants separately – see section 5.4.3).

Finally, the two measures of pain are a repeated measure (all participants were subjected to hot and cold stimuli). Therefore, levels of this variable (see SPSS Tip 3.2) can be entered in separate columns (one for pain to a hot stimulus and one for pain to a cold stimulus).

The data editor is made up of lots of *cells*, which are just boxes in which data values can be placed. When a cell is active it becomes highlighted in blue (as in Figure 3.3). You can move around the data editor, from cell to cell, using the arrow keys ← ↑ ↓ → (found on the right of the keyboard) or by clicking the mouse on the cell that you wish to activate. To enter a number into the data editor simply move to the cell in which you want to place the data value, type the value, then press the appropriate arrow button for the direction in which you wish to move. So, to enter a row of data, move to the far left of the row, type the value and then press → (this process inputs the value and then moves you into the next cell on the right).

The first step in entering your data is to create some variables using the 'Variable View' of the data editor, and then to input your data using the 'Data View' of the data editor. We'll go through these two steps by working through an example.

3.4.2. The 'Variable View' ①

Before we input any data into the data editor, we need to create the variables. To create variables we use the 'Variable View' of the data editor. To access this view click on the 'Variable View' tab at the bottom of the data editor (Data View | Variable View); the contents of the window will change (see Figure 3.4).

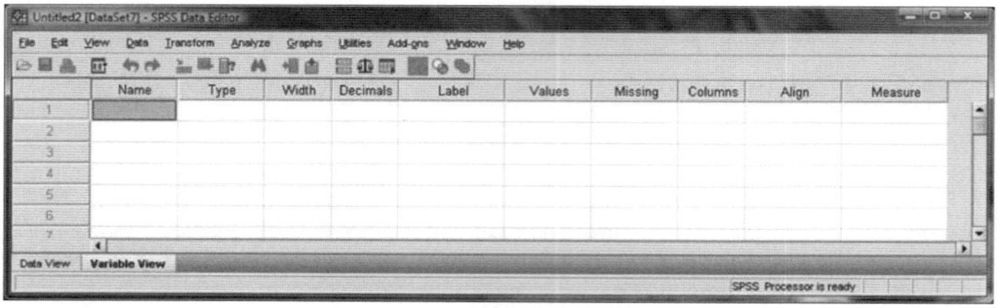

FIGURE 3.4 The 'Variable View' of the SPSS Data Editor

Every row of the variable view represents a variable, and you set characteristics of a particular variable by entering information into the labelled columns. You can change various characteristics of the variable by entering information into the following columns (play around and you'll get the hang of it):

Name	You can enter a name in this column for each variable. This name will appear at the top of the corresponding column in the data view, and helps you to identify variables in the data view. In current versions of SPSS you can more or less write what you like, but there are certain symbols you can't use (mainly symbols that have other uses in SPSS such as +, –, $, &) , and you can't use spaces. (Many people use a 'hard' space in variable names, which replaces the space with an underscore, for example, i.e. Andy_Field instead of Andy Field.) If you use a character that SPSS doesn't like you'll get an error message saying that the variable name is invalid when you click on a different cell, or try to move off the cell using the arrow keys.
Type	You can have different types of data. Mostly you will use **numeric variables** (which just means that the variable contains numbers – SPSS assumes this data type). You will come across **string variables**, which consist of strings of letters. If you wanted to type in people's names, for example, you would need to change the variable type to be string rather than numeric. You can also have **currency variables** (i.e. £s, $s, euro) and **date variables** (e.g. 21-06-1973)
Width	By default, when a new variable is created, SPSS sets it up to be *numeric* and to store 8 digits, but you can change this value by typing a new number in this column in the dialog box. Normally 8 digits is fine, but if you are doing calculations that need to be particularly precise you could make this value bigger.
Decimals	Another default setting is to have 2 decimal places displayed. (You'll notice that if you don't change this option then when you type in whole numbers to the data editor SPSS adds a decimal place with two zeros after it – this can be disconcerting initially!) If you want to change the number of decimal places for a given variable then replace the 2 with a new value or increase or decrease the values using ⇕, when in the cell that you want to change.
Label	The name of the variable (see above) has some restrictions on characters, and you also wouldn't want to use huge long names at the top of your columns (they become hard to read). Therefore, you can write a longer variable description in this column. This may seem pointless, but is actually one of the best habits you can get into (see SPSS Tip 3.3).
Values	This column is for assigning numbers to represent groups of people (see Section 3.4.2.3 below).
Missing	This column is for assigning numbers to missing data (see Section 3.4.3 below).
Columns	Enter a number into this column to determine the width of the column that is how many characters are displayed in the column. (This differs from Width, which determines the width of the variable itself – you could have a variable of 10 characters but by setting the column width to 8 you would only see 8 of the 10 characters of the variable in the data editor.) It can be useful to increase the column width if you have a string variable (section 3.4.2.1) that exceeds 8 characters, or a coding variable (section 3.4.2.3) with value labels that exceed 8 characters.
Align	You can use this column to select the alignment of the data in the corresponding column of the data editor. You can choose to align the data to the Left, Right or Center.
Measure	This is where you define the level at which a variable was measured (*Nominal*, *Ordinal* or *Scale* – section 1.5.1.2).

SPSS TIP 3.3 Naming variables ①

Why is it a good idea to take the time and effort to type in long variable names for your variables? Surely it's a waste of my time? In a way, I can understand why it would seem to be so, but as you go through your course accumulating data files, you will be grateful that you did. Imagine you had a variable called 'number of times I wanted to shoot myself during Andy Field's statistics lecture'; then you might have called the column in SPSS 'shoot'. If you don't add a label, SPSS will use this variable name in all of the output from an analysis. That's all well and good, but what happens in three weeks' time when you look at your data and output again? The chances are that you'll probably think 'What did shoot stand for? Number of shots at goal? Number of shots I drank?' Imagine the chaos you could get into if you had used an acronym for the variable 'workers attending new kiosk'. I have many data sets with variables called things like 'sftg45c', and if I didn't give them proper labels I would be in all sorts of trouble. Get into a good habit and label all of your variables!

Let's use the variable view to create some variables. Imagine we were interested in looking at the differences between lecturers and students. We took a random sample of five psychology lecturers from the University of Sussex and five psychology students and then measured how many friends they had, their weekly alcohol consumption (in units), their yearly income and how neurotic they were (higher score is more neurotic). These data are in Table 3.1.

TABLE 3.1 Some data with which to play

Name	Birth Date	Job	No. of Friends	Alcohol (Units)	Income	Neuroticism
Leo	17-Feb-1977	Lecturer	5	10	20,000	10
Martin	24-May-1969	Lecturer	2	15	40,000	17
Andy	21-Jun-1973	Lecturer	0	20	35,000	14
Paul	16-Jul-1970	Lecturer	4	5	22,000	13
Graham	10-Oct-1949	Lecturer	1	30	50,000	21
Carina	05-Nov-1983	Student	10	25	5,000	7
Karina	08-Oct-1987	Student	12	20	100	13
Doug	16-Sep-1989	Student	15	16	3,000	9
Mark	20-May-1973	Student	12	17	10,000	14
Mark	28-Mar-1990	Student	17	18	10	13

3.4.2.1. Creating a string variable ①

The first variable in our data set is the name of the lecturer/student. This variable consists of names; therefore, it is a *string variable*. To create this variable follow these steps:

1. Move the on-screen arrow (using the mouse) to the first white cell in the column labelled *Name*.
2. Type the word *Name*.
3. Move off this cell using the arrow keys on the keyboard (you can also just click on a different cell, but this is a very slow way of doing it).

You've just created your first variable! Notice that once you've typed a name, SPSS creates default settings for the variable (such as assuming it's numeric and assigning 2 decimal places). The problem is that although SPSS has assumed that we want a numeric variable (i.e. numbers), we don't; we want to enter people's names, namely a *string* variable. Therefore, we have to change the variable type. Move into the column labelled Type using the arrow keys on the keyboard. The cell will now look like this Numeric ... . Click on ... to activate the dialog box in Figure 3.5. By default, SPSS selects the numeric variable type (Numeric) – see the left panel of Figure 3.5. To change the variable to a string variable, click on String and the dialog box will change to look like the right panel of Figure 3.5. You can choose how many characters you want in your string variable (i.e. the maximum number of characters you will type for a given case of data). The default is 8, which is fine for us because our longest name is only six letters; however, if we were entering surnames as well, we would need to increase this value. When you have finished, click on OK to return to the variable view.

Now because I want you to get into good habits, move to the cell in the Label column and type a description of the variable, such as 'Participant's First Name'. Finally, we can specify the level at which a variable was measured (see section 1.5.1.2) by going to the column labelled *Measure* and selecting either *Nominal*, *Ordinal* or *Scale* from the drop-down list. In this case, we have a string variable, so they represent only names of cases and provide no information about the order of cases, or the magnitude of one case compared to another. Therefore, we need to select Nominal.

Once the variable has been created, you can return to the data view by clicking on the 'Data View' tab at the bottom of the data editor (Data View | Variable View). The contents of the window will change, and you'll notice that the first column now has the label *Name*. To enter the data, click on the white cell at the top of the column labelled *Name* and type the first name, 'Leo'. To register this value in this cell, we have to move to a different cell and because we are entering data down a column, the most sensible way to do this is to press the ↓ key on the keyboard. This action moves you down to the next cell, and the word 'Leo' should appear in the cell above. Enter the next name, 'Martin', and then press ↓ to move down to the next cell, and so on.

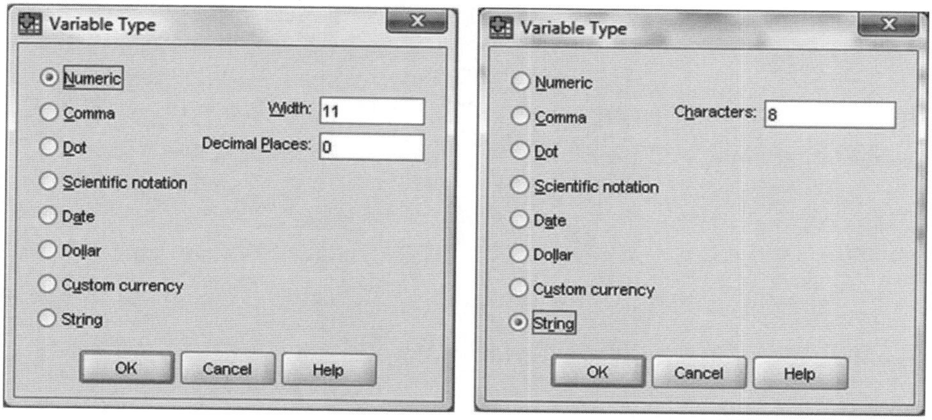

FIGURE 3.5 Defining a string variable in SPSS

3.4.2.2. Creating a date variable ①

Notice that the second column in our table contains dates (birth dates to be exact). To enter date variables into SPSS we use the same procedure as with the previous variable, except that we need to change the variable type. First, move back to the 'Variable View' using the tab at the bottom of the data editor (Data View | Variable View). As with the previous variable, move to the cell in row 2 of the column labelled *Name* (under the previous variable you created). Type the word 'Birth_Date' (note that we have used a hard space to separate the words). Move into the column labelled Type using the → key on the keyboard (SPSS will create default settings in the other columns). The cell will now look like this Numeric ... . Click on ... to activate the dialog box in Figure 3.6. By default, SPSS selects the numeric variable type (Numeric) – see the left panel of Figure 3.6. To change the variable to a date, click on Date and the dialog box will change to look like the right panel of Figure 3.6. You can then choose your preferred date format; being British, I am used to the days coming before the month and I have stuck with the default option of dd-mmm-yyyy (i.e. 21-Jun-1973), but Americans, for example, will be used to the month and date being the other way around and could select mm/dd/yyyy (06/21/1973). When you have selected a format for your dates, click on OK to return to the variable view. Finally, move to the cell in the column labelled *Label* and type 'Date of Birth'.

Now that the variable has been created, you can return to the data view by clicking on the 'Data View' tab (Data View | Variable View) and input the dates of birth. The second column now has the label *Birth_Date*; click on the white cell at the top of this column and type the first value, 17-Feb-1977. To register this value in this cell, move down to the next cell by pressing the ↓ key on the keyboard. Now enter the next date, and so on.

3.4.2.3. Creating coding variables ①

A coding variable (also known as a grouping variable) is a variable that uses numbers to represent different groups of data. As such, it is a *numeric variable*, but these numbers represent names (i.e. it is a nominal variable). These groups of data could be levels of a treatment variable in an experiment, different groups of people (men or women, an experimental group, or a control group, ethnic groups, etc.), different geographic locations, different organizations, etc.

In experiments, coding variables represent independent variables that have been measured between groups (i.e. different participants were assigned to different groups). If you were to run an experiment with one group of participants in an experimental condition and a different group of participants in a control group, you might assign the experimental group a code

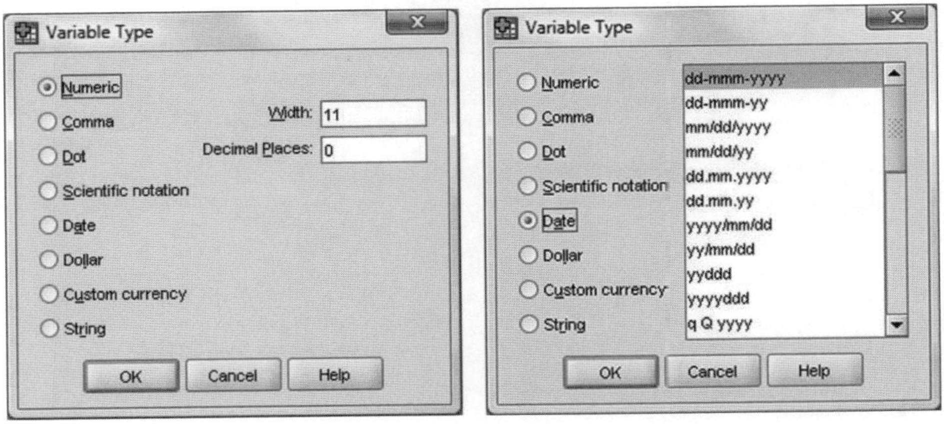

FIGURE 3.6 Defining variable types in SPSS

of 1 and the control group a code of 0. When you come to put the data into the data editor, you would create a variable (which you might call **group**) and type in the value 1 for any participants in the experimental group, and 0 for any participant in the control group. These codes tell SPSS that all of the cases that have been assigned the value 1 should be treated as belonging to the same group, and likewise for the cases assigned the value 0. In situations other than experiments, you might simply use codes to distinguish naturally occurring groups of people (e.g. you might give students a code of 1 and lecturers a code of 0).

We have a coding variable in our data: the one describing whether a person was a lecturer or student. To create this coding variable, we follow the steps for creating a normal variable, but we also have to tell SPSS which numeric codes have been assigned to which groups. So, first of all, return to the variable view (Data View | Variable View) if you're not already in it and then move to the cell in the third row of the data editor and in the column labelled *Name* type a name (let's call it **Group**). I'm still trying to instil good habits, so move along the third row to the column called *Label* and give the variable a full description such as 'Is the person a lecturer or a student?' Then to define the group codes, move along the row to the column labelled Values and into this cell: None ... . Click on ... to access the *Value Labels* dialog box (see Figure 3.7).

The *Value Labels* dialog box is used to specify group codes. This can be done in three easy steps. First, click with the mouse in the white space next to where it says *Value* (or press *Alt* and *u* at the same time) and type in a code (e.g. 1). These codes are completely arbitrary; for the sake of convention people typically use 0, 1, 2, 3, etc., but in practice you could have a code of 495 if you were feeling particularly arbitrary. The second step is to click the mouse in the white space below, next to where it says *Value Label* (or press *Tab*, or *Alt* and *e* at the same time) and type in an appropriate label for that group. In Figure 3.7 I have already defined a code of 1 for the lecturer group, and then I have typed in 2 as my code and given this a label of *Student*. The third step is to add this coding to the list by clicking on Add . When you have defined all of your coding values you can click on Spelling... and SPSS will check your variable labels for spelling errors (which can be very handy if you are as bad at spelling as I am). To finish, click on OK ; if you click on OK and have forgotten to add your final coding to the list, SPSS will display a message warning you that any pending changes will be lost. In plain English

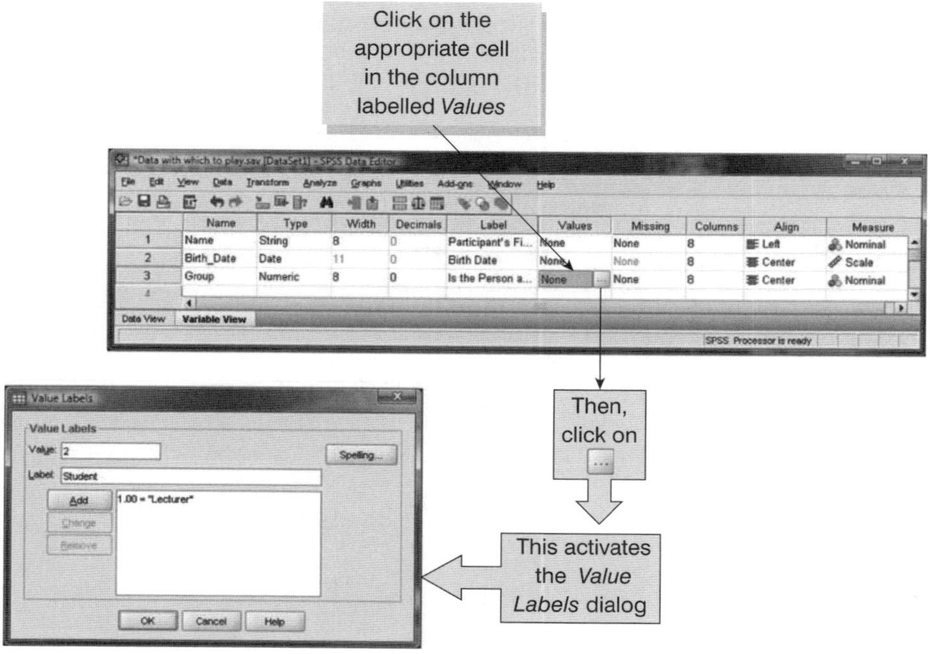

FIGURE 3.7 Defining coding variables and their values in SPSS

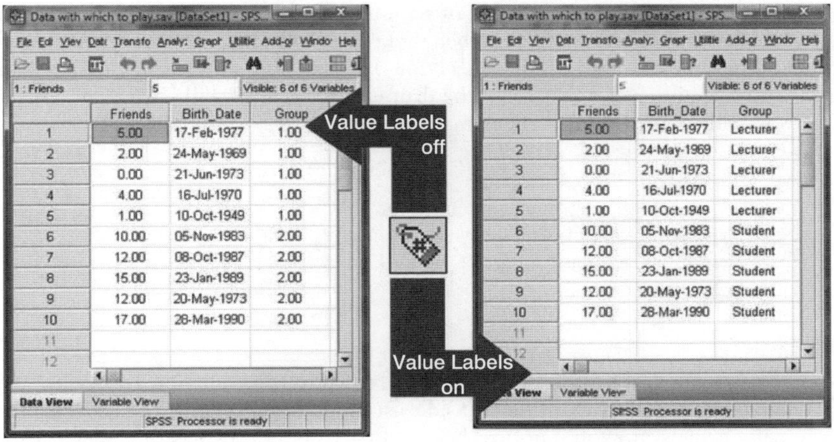

FIGURE 3.8 Coding values in the data editor with the value labels switched off and on

this simply tells you to go back and click on Add before continuing. Finally, coding variables always represent categories and so the level at which they are measured is nominal (or ordinal if the categories have a meaningful order). Therefore, you should specify the level at which the variable was measured by going to the column labelled *Measure* and selecting Nominal (or Ordinal if the groups have a meaningful order) from the drop-down list (see earlier).

Having defined your codes, switch to the data view and type these numerical values into the appropriate column (so if a person was a lecturer, type 1, but if they were a student then type 2). You can get SPSS to display the numeric codes, or the value labels that you assigned to them by clicking on (see Figure 3.8), which is pretty groovy. Figure 3.8 shows how the data should be arranged for a coding variable. Now remember that each row of the data editor represents data from one entity and in this example our entities were people (well, arguably in the case of the lecturers). The first five participants were lecturers whereas participants 6–10 were students.

This example should clarify why in experimental research grouping variables are used for variables that have been measured between participants: because by using a coding variable it is impossible for a participant to belong to more than one group. This situation should occur in a between-group design (i.e. a participant should not be tested in both the experimental and the control group). However, in repeated-measures designs (within subjects) each participant is tested in every condition and so we would not use this sort of coding variable (because each participant does take part in every experimental condition).

3.4.2.4. Creating a numeric variable ①

Numeric variables are the easiest ones to create because SPSS assumes this format for data. Our next variable is **No. of friends**; to create this variable we move back to the variable view using the tab at the bottom of the data editor (Data View | Variable View). As with the previous variables, move to the cell in row 4 of the column labelled *Name* (under the previous variable you created). Type the word 'Friends'. Move into the column labelled Type using the → key on the keyboard. As with the previous variables we have created, SPSS has assumed that this is a numeric variable, so the cell will look like this Numeric. We can leave this as it is, because we do have a numeric variable.

Notice that our data for the number of friends has no decimal places (unless you are a very strange person indeed, you can't have 0.23 of a friend). Move to the Decimals column and type '0' (or decrease the value from 2 to 0 using) to tell SPSS that you don't want any decimal places.

Next, let's continue our good habit of naming variables and move to the cell in the column labelled *Label* and type 'Number of Friends'. Finally, we can specify the level at which a variable was measured (see section 1.5.1.2) by going to the column labelled *Measure* and selecting Scale from the drop-down list (this will have been done automatically actually, but it's worth checking).

SELF-TEST Why is the 'Number of Friends' variable a 'scale' variable?

Once the variable has been created, you can return to the data view by clicking on the 'Data View' tab at the bottom of the data editor (Data View | Variable View). The contents of the window will change, and you'll notice that the first column now has the label *Friends*. To enter the data, click on the white cell at the top of the column labelled *Friends* and type the first value, 5. To register this value in this cell, we have to move to a different cell and because we are entering data down a column, the most sensible way to do this is to press the ↓ key on the keyboard. This action moves you down to the next cell, and the number 5 should appear in the cell above. Enter the next number, 2, and then press ↓ to move down to the next cell, and so on.

SELF-TEST Having created the first four variables with a bit of guidance, try to enter the rest of the variables in Table 3.1 yourself.

3.4.3. Missing values ①

Although as researchers we strive to collect complete sets of data, it is often the case that we have missing data. Missing data can occur for a variety of reasons: in long questionnaires participants accidentally (or, depending on how paranoid you're feeling, deliberately just to piss you off) miss out questions; in experimental procedures mechanical faults can lead to a datum not being recorded; and in research on delicate topics (e.g. sexual behaviour) participants may exert their right not to answer a question. However, just because we have missed out on some data for a participant doesn't mean that we have to ignore the data we do have (although it sometimes creates statistical difficulties). Nevertheless, we do need to tell SPSS that a value is missing for a particular case. The principle behind missing values is quite similar to that of coding variables in that we choose a numeric value to represent the missing data point. This value tells SPSS that there is no recorded value for a participant for a certain variable. The computer then ignores that cell of the data editor (it does not use the value you select in the analysis). You need to be careful that the chosen code doesn't correspond to any naturally occurring data value. For example, if we tell the computer to regard the value 9 as a missing value and several participants genuinely scored 9, then the computer will treat their data as missing when, in reality, they are not.

To specify missing values you simply click in the column labelled Missing in the variable view and then click on ... to activate the *Missing Values* dialog box in Figure 3.9. By default SPSS assumes that no missing values exist, but if you do have data with missing

FIGURE 3.9 Defining missing values

values you can choose to define them in one of three ways. The first is to select discrete values (by clicking on the circle next to where it says *Discrete missing values*) which are single values that represent missing data. SPSS allows you to specify up to three discrete values to represent missing data. The reason why you might choose to have several numbers to represent missing values is that you can assign a different meaning to each discrete value. For example, you could have the number 8 representing a response of 'not applicable', a code of 9 representing a 'don't know' response, and a code of 99 meaning that the participant failed to give any response. As far as the computer is concerned it will ignore any data cell containing these values; however, using different codes may be a useful way to remind you of why a particular score is missing. Usually, one discrete value is enough and in an experiment in which attitudes are measured on a 100-point scale (so scores vary from 1 to 100) you might choose 666 to represent missing values because (1) this value cannot occur in the data that have been collected and (2) missing data create statistical problems, and you will regard the people who haven't given you responses as children of Satan! The second option is to select a range of values to represent missing data and this is useful in situations in which it is necessary to exclude data falling between two points. So, we could exclude all scores between 5 and 10. The final option is to have a range of values and one discrete value.

3.5. The SPSS Viewer ①

Alongside the SPSS Data Editor window, there is a second window known as the *SPSS Viewer*. The viewer window has come a long way; not that you care, I'm sure, but in days of old, this window displayed statistical results in a rather bland and drab font, graphs appeared in a window called the carousel (not nearly as exciting as it sounds), and all of the computations were done by little nerdy dinosaurs that lived inside your computer. These days, the SPSS Viewer displays everything you could want (well, OK, it doesn't display photos of your cat) and it's generally prettier to look at than it used to be. Sadly, however, my prediction in previous editions of this book that future versions of SPSS will include a tea-making facility in the viewer have not come to fruition (SPSS Inc. take note!).

Figure 3.10 shows the basic layout of the output viewer. On the right-hand side there is a large space in which the output is displayed. SPSS displays both graphs and the results of statistical analyses in this part of the viewer. It is also possible to edit graphs and to do this

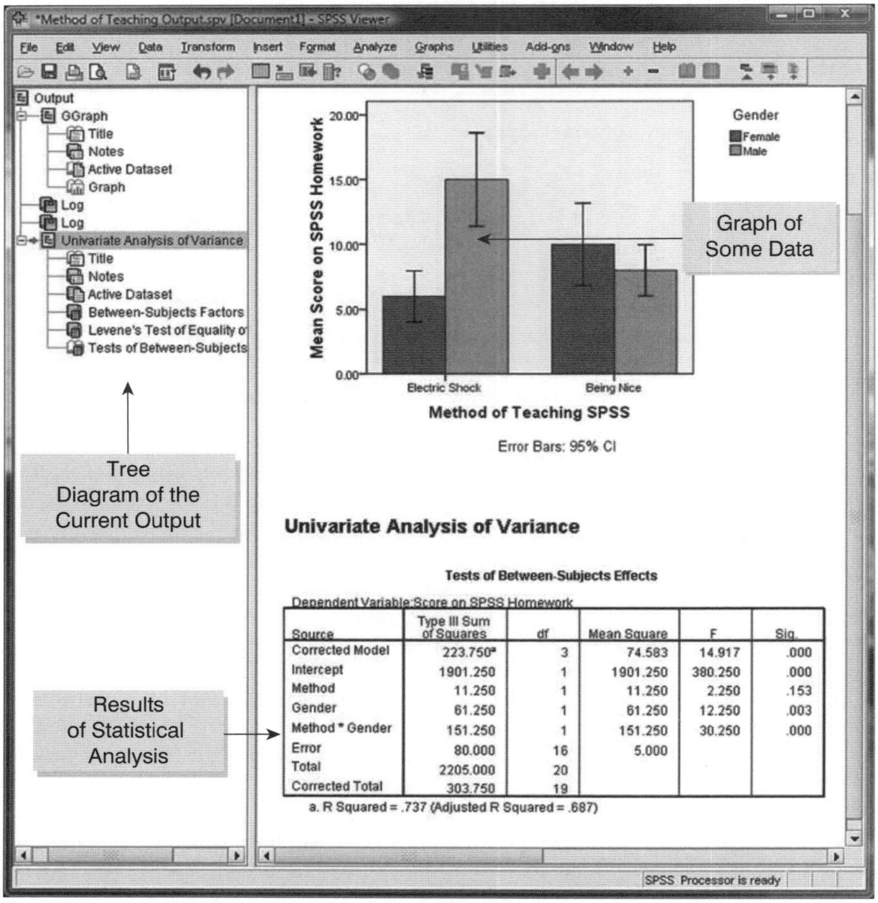

FIGURE 3.10 The SPSS Viewer

you simply double-click on the graph you wish to edit (this creates a new window in which the graph can be edited – see section 4.9). On the left-hand side of the output viewer there is a tree diagram illustrating the structure of the output. This tree diagram is useful when you have conducted several analyses because it provides an easy way of accessing specific parts of the output. The tree structure is fairly self-explanatory in that every time you do something in SPSS (such as drawing a graph or running a statistical procedure), it lists this procedure as a main heading.

In Figure 3.10 I conducted a graphing procedure followed by a univariate analysis of variance (ANOVA) and so these names appear as main headings. For each procedure there are a series of sub-headings that represent different parts of the analysis. For example, in the ANOVA procedure, which you'll learn more about later in the book, there are several sections to the output such as Levene's test (see section 5.6.1) and a table of the between-group effects (i.e. the *F*-test of whether the means are significantly different). You can skip to any one of these sub-components of the ANOVA output by clicking on the appropriate branch of the tree diagram. So, if you wanted to skip straight to the between-group effects you should move the on-screen arrow to the left-hand portion of the window and click where it says *Tests of Between-Subjects Effects*. This action will highlight this part of the output in the main part of the viewer (see SPSS Tip 3.4).

SPSS TIP 3.4 Printing and saving the planet ①

Rather than printing all of your SPSS output on reams of paper, you can help the planet by printing only a selection of the output. You can do this by using the tree diagram in the SPSS Viewer to select parts of the output for printing. For example, if you decided that you wanted to print out a graph but you didn't want to print the whole output, you can click on the word *GGraph* in the tree structure and that graph will become highlighted in the output. It is then possible through the print menu to select to print only the selected part of the output.

It is worth noting that if you click on a main heading (such as *Univariate Analysis of Variance*) then SPSS will highlight not only that main heading but all of the sub-components as well. This is useful for printing the results of a single statistical procedure.

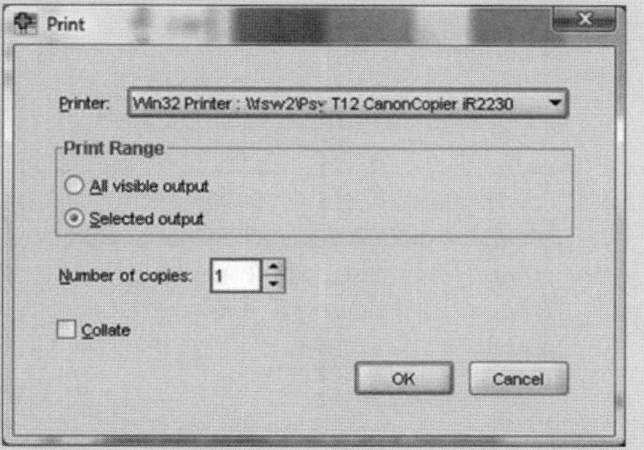

There are several icons in the output viewer window that help you to do things quickly without using the drop-down menus. Some of these icons are the same as those described for the data editor window so I will concentrate mainly on the icons that are unique to the viewer window:

	As with the data editor window, this icon activates the print menu. However, when this icon is pressed in the viewer window it activates a menu for printing the output (see SPSS Tip 3.4).
	This icon returns you to the data editor in a flash!
	This icon takes you to the last output in the viewer (so it returns you to the last procedure you conducted).
	This icon *promotes* the currently active part of the tree structure to a higher branch of the tree. For example, in Figure 3.10 the *Tests of Between-Subjects Effects* are a sub-component under the heading of *Univariate Analysis of Variance*. If we wanted to promote this part of the output to a higher level (i.e. to make it a main heading) then this is done using this icon.
	This icon is the opposite of the above in that it *demotes* parts of the tree structure. For example, in Figure 3.10 if we didn't want the *Univariate Analysis of Variance* to be a unique section we could select this heading and demote it so that it becomes part of the previous heading (the *Graph* heading). This button is useful for combining parts of the output relating to a specific research question.
	This icon collapses parts of the tree structure, which simply means that it hides the sub-components under a particular heading. For example, in Figure 3.10 if we selected the heading *Univariate Analysis of Variance* and pressed this icon, all of the sub-headings would disappear. The sections that disappear from the tree structure don't disappear from the output itself; the tree structure is merely condensed. This can be useful when you have been conducting lots of analyses and the tree diagram is becoming very complex.
	This icon expands any collapsed sections. By default all of the main headings are displayed in the tree diagram in their expanded form. If, however, you have opted to collapse part of the tree diagram (using the icon above) then you can use this icon to undo your dirty work.
	This icon and the following one allow you to show and hide parts of the output itself. So you can select part of the output in the tree diagram and click on this icon and that part of the output will disappear. It isn't erased, but it is hidden from view. This icon is similar to the collapse icon listed above except that it affects the output rather than the tree structure. This is useful for hiding less relevant parts of the output.

	This icon undoes the previous one, so if you have hidden a selected part of the output from view and you click on this icon, that part of the output will reappear. By default, all parts of the output are shown, so this icon is not active; it will become active only once you have hidden part of the output.
	Although this icon looks rather like a paint roller, unfortunately it does not paint the house for you. What it does do is to insert a new heading into the tree diagram. For example, if you had several statistical tests that related to one of many research questions you could insert a main heading and then demote the headings of the relevant analyses so that they all fall under this new heading.
	Assuming you had done the above, you can use this icon to provide your new heading with a title. The title you type in will actually appear in your output. So, you might have a heading like 'Research question number 1' which tells you that the analyses under this heading relate to your first research question.
	This final icon is used to place a text box in the output window. You can type anything into this box. In the context of the previous two icons, you might use a text box to explain what your first research question is (e.g. 'My first research question is whether or not boredom has set in by the end of the first chapter of my book. The following analyses test the hypothesis that boredom levels will be significantly higher at the end of the first chapter than at the beginning').

SPSS TIP 3.5 **Funny numbers ①**

You might notice that SPSS sometimes reports numbers with the letter 'E' placed in the mix just to confuse you. For example, you might see a value such as 9.612 E–02 and many students find this notation confusing. Well, this notation means 9.61×10^{-2} (which might be a more familiar notation, or could be even more confusing). OK, some of you are still confused. Well think of E–02 as meaning 'move the decimal place 2 places to the left', so 9.612 E–02 becomes 0.09612. If the notation read 9.612 E–01, then that would be 0.9612, and if it read 9.612 E–03, that would be 0.009612. Likewise, think of E+02 (notice the minus sign has changed) as meaning 'move the decimal place 2 places to the right'. So 9.612 E+02 becomes 961.2.

3.6. The SPSS SmartViewer ①

Progress is all well and good, but it usually comes at a price and with version 16 of SPSS the output viewer changed quite dramatically (not really in terms of what you see, but behind the scenes). When you save an output file in version 17, SPSS uses the file extension **.spv**, and it calls it an SPSS Viewer file. In versions of SPSS before version 16, the viewer documents were saved as SPSS output files (**.spo**). Why does this matter? Well, it matters mainly because if you try to open an SPSS Viewer file in a version earlier than 16, SPSS won't know what the hell it is and will scream at you (well, it won't open the file). Similarly in versions after 16, if you try to open an output file (**.spo**) from an earlier version of SPSS you won't be able to do it. I know what you're thinking: 'this is bloody SPSS madness – statistics is hard enough as it is without versions of SPSS not being compatible with each other; is it trying to drive me insane?' Well, yes, it probably is.

This is why when you install SPSS on your computer you can install the SPSS SmartViewer. The SPSS SmartViewer looks suspiciously like the normal SPSS Viewer but without the icons. In fact, it looks so similar that I'm not even going to put a screenshot of it in this book – we can live on the edge, just this once. So what's so smart about the SmartViewer? Actually bugger all, that's what; it's just a way for you to open and read your old pre-version 17 SPSS output files. So, if you're not completely new to SPSS, this is a useful program to have.

The Syntax Editor ③

SMART ALEX ONLY

I've mentioned earlier that sometimes it's useful to use SPSS syntax. This is a language of commands for carrying out statistical analyses and data manipulations. Most of the time you'll do the things you need to using SPSS dialog boxes, but SPSS syntax can be useful. For one thing there are certain things you can do with syntax that you can't do through dialog boxes (admittedly most of these things are fairly advanced, but there will be a few places in this book where I show you some nice tricks using syntax). The second reason for using syntax is if you often carry out very similar analyses on data sets. In these situations it is often quicker to do the analysis and save the syntax as you go along. Fortunately this is easily done because many dialog boxes in SPSS have a Paste button. When you've specified your analysis using the dialog box, if you click on this button it will paste the syntax into a syntax editor window for you. To open a syntax editor window simply use the menus File New Syntax and a blank syntax editor will appear as in Figure 3.11. In this window you can type your syntax commands into the command area. The rules of SPSS syntax can be quite frustrating; for example, each line has to end with a full stop and if you forget this full stop you'll get an error message. In fact, if you have made a syntax error, SPSS will produce an error message in the Viewer window that identifies the line in the syntax window in which the error occurred; notice that in the syntax window SPSS helpfully numbers each line so that you can find the line in which the error occurred easily.

EVERYBODY

As we go through the book I'll show you a few things that will give you a flavour of how syntax can be used. Most of you won't have to use it, but for those that do this flavour will hopefully be enough to start you on your way. The window also has a navigation area (rather like the Viewer window). When you have a large file of syntax commands this navigation area can be helpful for negotiating your way to the bit of syntax that you actually need. Once you've typed in your syntax you have to run it using the Run menu. Run All will run all of the syntax in the window (clicking on ▶ will also do this), or you can highlight a selection of your syntax using the mouse and use Run Selection to process the selected syntax. You can also run the current command by using Run Current (or press *Ctrl* and *R* on the keyboard), or run all the syntax from the cursor to the end of the syntax window using Run To End. Another thing to note is that in SPSS you can have several data files open at once. Rather than have a syntax window for each data file, which could get confusing, you can use the same syntax window, but select the data set that you want to run the syntax commands on before you run them using the drop-down list DataSet3 ▾.

OLIVER TWISTED

Please, Sir, can I have some more … syntax?

'I want to drown in a puddle of my own saliva' froths Oliver, 'tell me more about the syntax Window'. Really? Well, OK, there is a Flash movie on the companion website that guides you through how to use the syntax window.

3.8. Saving files ①

Although most of you should be familiar with how to save files, it is a vital thing to know and so I will briefly describe what to do. To save files simply use the 💾 icon (or use the

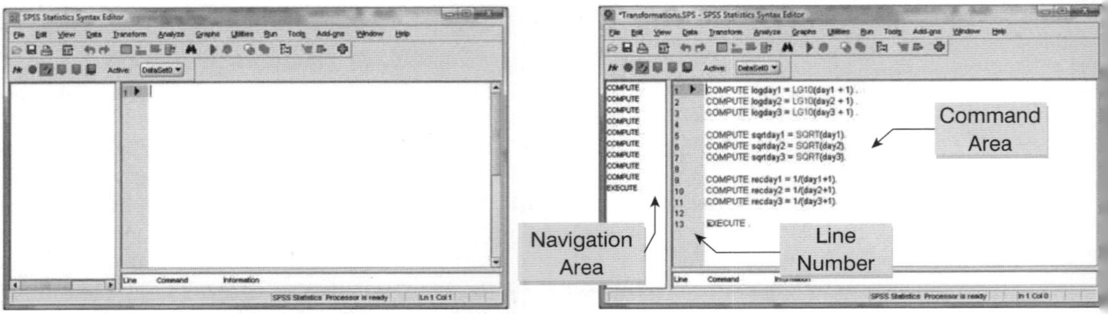

FIGURE 3.11 A new syntax window (top) and a syntax window with some syntax in it (bottom)

menus File Save or File Save As...). If the file is a new file, then clicking on this icon will activate the *Save As* ... dialog box (see Figure 3.12). If you are in the data editor when you select *Save As* ... then SPSS will save the data file you are currently working on, but if you are in the viewer window then it will save the current output.

There are several features of the dialog box in Figure 3.12. First, you need to select a location at which to store the file. There are many types of locations where you can save data: the hard drive (or drives), a USB drive, a CD or DVD, etc. (you could have many other choices of location on your particular computer). The first thing to do is select a main location by double-clicking on it: your hard drive ( ), a CD or DVD ( ), or a USB stick or other external drive ( ). Once you have chosen a main location the dialog box will display all of the available folders on that particular device. Once you have selected a folder in which to save your file, you need to give your file a name. If you click in the space next to where it says *File name*, a cursor will appear and you can type a name. By default, the file will be saved in an SPSS format, so if it is a data file it will have the file extension **.sav**, if it is a viewer document it will have the file extension **.spv**, and if it is a syntax file it will have the file extension

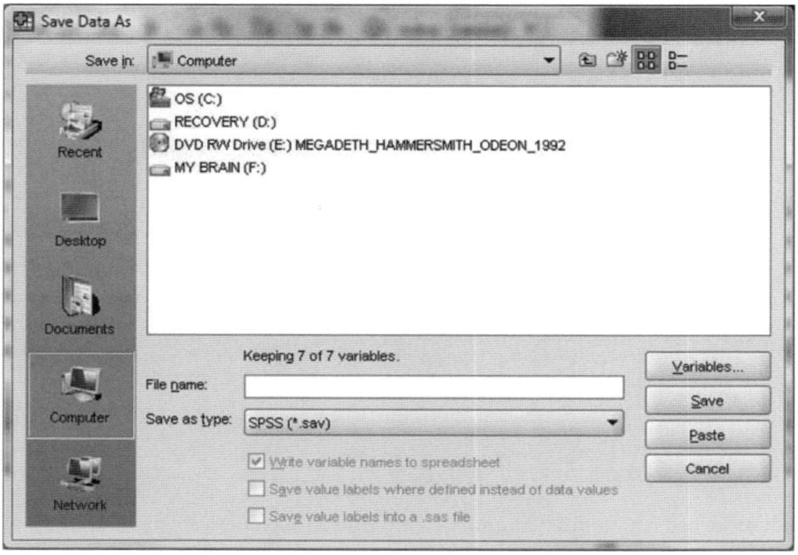

FIGURE 3.12 The *Save Data As* dialog box

.sps. However, you can save data in different formats such as Microsoft Excel files and tab-delimited text. To do this just click on SPSS (*.sav) and a list of possible file formats will be displayed. Click on the file type you require. Once a file has previously been saved, it can be saved again (updated) by clicking on the save icon. This icon appears in both the data editor and the viewer, and the file saved depends on the window that is currently active. The file will be saved in the location at which it is currently stored.

3.9. Retrieving a file ①

Throughout this book you will work with data files that you need to download from the companion website. It is, therefore, important that you know how to load these data files into SPSS. The procedure is very simple. To open a file, simply use the open icon (or use the menus File Open ▸ Data...) to activate the dialog box in Figure 3.13. First, you need to find the location at which the file is stored. Navigate to wherever you downloaded the files from the website (a USB stick, or a folder on your hard drive). You should see a list of files and folders that can be opened. As with saving a file, if you are currently in the data editor then SPSS will display only SPSS data files to be opened (if you are in the viewer window then only output files will be displayed). If you use the menus and used the path File Open ▸ Data... then data files will be displayed, but if you used the path File Open ▸ Output... then viewer files will be displayed, and if you used File Open ▸ Syntax... then syntax files will be displayed (you get the general idea). You can open a folder by double-clicking on the folder icon. Once you have tracked down the required file you can open it either by selecting it with the mouse and then clicking on Open, or by double-clicking on the icon next to the file you want (e.g. double-clicking on the data file icon). The data/output will then appear in the appropriate window. If you are in the data editor and you want to open a viewer file, then click on SPSS (*.sav) and a list of alternative file formats will be displayed. Click on the appropriate file type (viewer document (***.spv**), syntax file (***.sps**), Excel file (***.xls**), text file (***.dat**, ***.txt**)) and any files of that type will be displayed for you to open.

FIGURE 3.13 Dialog box to open a file

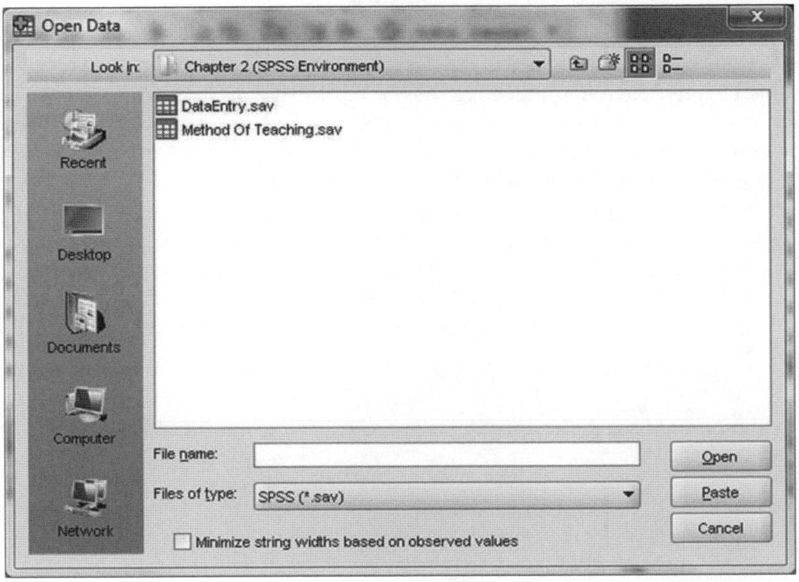

What have I discovered about statistics? ①

This chapter has provided a basic introduction to the SPSS environment. We've seen that SPSS uses two main windows: the data editor and the viewer. The data editor has both a data view (where you input the raw scores) and a variable view (where you define variables and their properties). The viewer is a window in which any output appears, such as tables, statistics and graphs. You also created your first data set by creating some variables and inputting some data. In doing so you discovered that we can code groups of people using numbers (coding variables) and discovered that rows in the data editor represent people (or cases of data) and columns represent different variables. Finally, we had a look at the syntax window and were told how to open and save files.

We also discovered that I was scared of my new school. However, with the help of Jonathan Land my confidence grew. With this new confidence I began to feel comfortable not just at school but in the world at large. It was time to explore.

Key terms that I've discovered

Currency variable
Data editor
Data view
Date variable
Numeric variable
SmartViewer
String variable
Syntax editor
Variable view
Viewer

Smart Alex's tasks

- **Task 1**: Smart Alex's first task for this chapter is to save the data that you've entered in this chapter. Save it somewhere on the hard drive of your computer (or a USB stick if you're not working on your own computer). Give it a sensible title and save it somewhere easy to find (perhaps create a folder called 'My Data Files' where you can save all of your files when working through this book).
- **Task 2**: Your second task is to enter the data that I used to create Figure 3.10. These data show the score (out of 20) for 20 different students, some of whom are male and some female, and some of whom were taught using positive reinforcement (being nice) and others who were taught using punishment (electric shock). Just to make it hard, the data should not be entered in the same way that they are laid out below:

Male		Female	
Electric Shock	Being Nice	Electric Shock	Being Nice
15	12	6	10
14	10	7	9
20	7	5	8
13	8	4	8
13	13	8	7

- **Task 3**: Research has looked at emotional reactions to infidelity and found that men get homicidal and suicidal and women feel undesirable and insecure (Shackelford, LeBlanc, & Drass, 2000). Let's imagine we did some similar research: we took some men and women and got their partners to tell them they had slept with someone else. We then took each person to two shooting galleries and each time gave them a gun and 100 bullets. In one gallery was a human-shaped target with a picture of their own face on it, and in the other was a target with their partner's face on it. They were left alone with each target for 5 minutes and the number of bullets used was measured. The data are below; enter them into SPSS and save them as **Infidelity.sav** (clue: they are not entered in the format in the table!).

Male		Female	
Partner's Face	Own Face	Partner's Face	Own Face
69	33	70	97
76	26	74	80
70	10	64	88
76	51	43	100
72	34	51	100
65	28	93	58
82	27	48	95
71	9	51	83
71	33	74	97
75	11	73	89
52	14	41	69
34	46	84	82

Answers can be found on the companion website.

Further reading

There are many good introductory SPSS books on the market that go through similar material to this chapter. Pallant's *SPSS survival manual* and Kinnear and Gray's *SPSS XX made simple* (insert a version number where I've typed XX because they update it regularly) are both excellent guides for people new to SPSS. There are many others on the market as well, so have a hunt around.

Online tutorials

The companion website contains the following Flash movie tutorials to accompany this chapter:

- Entering data
- Exporting SPSS output to Word
- Importing text data to SPSS
- Selecting cases
- The Syntax window
- The Viewer window
- Using Excel with SPSS

19

Exploring Assumptions

ANDY FIELD

FIGURE 5.1 I came first in the competition for who has the smallest brain

5.1. What will this chapter tell me? ①

When we were learning to read at primary school, we used to read versions of stories by the famous storyteller Hans Christian Andersen. One of my favourites was the story of the ugly duckling. This duckling was a big ugly grey bird, so ugly that even a dog would not bite him. The poor duckling was ridiculed, ostracized and pecked by the other ducks. Eventually, it became too much for him and he flew to the swans, the royal birds, hoping that they would end his misery by killing him because he was so ugly. As he stared into the water, though, he saw not an ugly grey bird but a beautiful swan. Data are much the same. Sometimes they're just big, grey and ugly and don't do any of the things that they're supposed to do. When we get data like these, we swear at them, curse them, peck them and hope that they'll fly away and be killed by the swans. Alternatively, we can try to force our data into becoming beautiful swans. That's what this chapter is all about: assessing how much of an ugly duckling of a data set you have, and discovering how to turn it into a swan. Remember, though, a swan can break your arm.[1]

5.2. What are assumptions? ①

Some academics tend to regard assumptions as rather tedious things about which no one really need worry. When I mention statistical assumptions to my fellow psychologists they tend to give me that raised eyebrow, 'good grief, get a life' look and then ignore me. However, there are good reasons for taking assumptions seriously. Imagine that I go over to a friend's house, the lights are on and it's obvious that someone is at home. I ring the doorbell and no one answers. From that experience, I conclude that my friend hates me and that I am a terrible, unlovable, person. How tenable is this conclusion? Well, there is a reality that I am trying to tap (i.e. whether my friend likes or hates me), and I have collected data about that reality (I've gone to his house, seen that he's at home, rang the doorbell and got no response). Imagine that in reality my friend likes me (he never was a good judge of character!); in this scenario, my conclusion is false. Why have my data led me to the wrong conclusion? The answer is simple: I had assumed that my friend's doorbell was working and under this assumption the conclusion that I made from my data was accurate (my friend heard the bell but chose to ignore it because he hates me). However, this assumption was not true – his doorbell was not working, which is why he didn't answer the door – and as a consequence the conclusion I drew about reality was completely false.

Enough about doorbells, friends and my social life: the point to remember is that when assumptions are broken we stop being able to draw accurate conclusions about reality. Different statistical models assume different things, and if these models are going to reflect reality accurately then these assumptions need to be true. This chapter is going to deal with some particularly ubiquitous assumptions so that you know how to slay these particular beasts as we battle our way through the rest of the book. However, be warned: some tests have their own unique two-headed, fire-breathing, green-scaled assumptions and these will jump out from behind a mound of blood-soaked moss and try to eat us alive when we least expect them to. Onward into battle …

5.3. Assumptions of parametric data ①

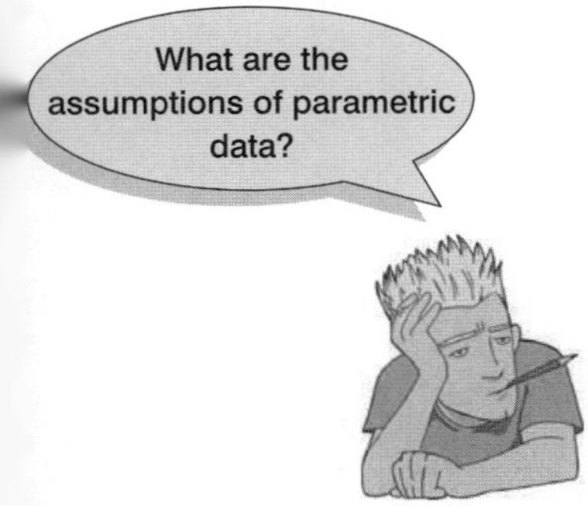

Many of the statistical procedures described in this book are **parametric tests** based on the normal distribution (which is described in section 1.7.4). A parametric test is one that requires data from one of the large catalogue of distributions that statisticians have described and for data to be parametric certain assumptions must be true. If you use a parametric test when your data are not parametric then the results are likely to be inaccurate. Therefore, it is very important that you check the assumptions before deciding which statistical test is appropriate. Throughout this book you will become aware of my obsession with assumptions and checking them. Most parametric tests based on the normal distribution have four basic assumptions that must be met for the test to be accurate. Many students find checking assumptions a pretty tedious affair, and often get confused about how to tell whether or not an assumption has been met. Therefore, this chapter is designed to take you on a step-by-step tour of the world of parametric assumptions (wow, how exciting!). Now, you may think that

[1] Although it is theoretically possible, apparently you'd have to be weak boned, and swans are nice and wouldn't do that sort of thing.

assumptions are not very exciting, but they can have great benefits: for one thing you can impress your supervisor/lecturer by spotting all of the test assumptions that they have violated throughout their careers. You can then rubbish, on statistical grounds, the theories they have spent their lifetime developing – and they can't argue with you[2] – but they can poke your eyes out! The assumptions of parametric tests are:

1 **Normally distributed data**: This a tricky and misunderstood assumption because it means different things in different contexts. For this reason I will spend most of the chapter discussing this assumption! In short, the rationale behind hypothesis testing relies on having something that is normally distributed (in some cases it's the sampling distribution, in others the errors in the model) and so if this assumption is not met then the logic behind hypothesis testing is flawed (we came across these principles in Chapters 1 and 2).

2 **Homogeneity of variance**: This assumption means that the variances should be the same throughout the data. In designs in which you test several groups of participants this assumption means that each of these samples comes from populations with the same variance. In correlational designs, this assumption means that the variance of one variable should be stable at all levels of the other variable (see section 5.6).

3 **Interval data**: Data should be measured at least at the interval level. This assumption is tested by common sense and so won't be discussed further (but do reread section 1.5.1.2 to remind yourself of what we mean by interval data).

4 **Independence**: This assumption, like that of normality, is different depending on the test you're using. In some cases it means that data from different participants are independent, which means that the behaviour of one participant does not influence the behaviour of another. In repeated-measures designs (in which participants are measured in more than one experimental condition), we expect scores in the experimental conditions to be non-independent for a given participant, but behaviour between different participants should be independent. As an example, imagine two people, Paul and Julie, were participants in an experiment where they had to indicate whether they remembered having seen particular photos earlier on in the experiment. If Paul and Julie were to confer about whether they'd seen certain pictures then their answers would *not* be independent: Julie's response to a given question would depend on Paul's answer, and this would violate the assumption of independence. If Paul and Julie were unable to confer (if they were locked in different rooms) then their responses should be independent (unless they're telepathic): Paul's responses should not be influenced by Julie's. In regression, however, this assumption also relates to the errors in the regression model being uncorrelated, but we'll discuss that more in Chapter 7.

We will, therefore, focus in this chapter on the assumptions of normality and homogeneity of variance.

5.4. The assumption of normality ①

We encountered the normal distribution back in Chapter 1; we know what it looks like and we (hopefully) understand it. You'd think then that this assumption would be easy to

[2] When I was doing my Ph.D., we were set a task by our statistics lecturer in which we had to find some published papers and criticize the statistical methods in them. I chose one of my supervisor's papers and proceeded to slag off every aspect of the data analysis (and I was being *very* pedantic about it all). Imagine my horror when my supervisor came bounding down the corridor with a big grin on his face and declared that, unbeknownst to me, he was the second marker of my essay. Luckily, he had a sense of humour and I got a good mark.☺

understand – it just means that our data are normally distributed, right? Actually, no. In many statistical tests (e.g. the *t*-test) we assume that the sampling distribution is normally distributed. This is a problem because we don't have access to this distribution – we can't simply look at its shape and see whether it is normally distributed. However, we know from the central limit theorem (section 2.5.1) that if the sample data are approximately normal then the sampling distribution will be also. Therefore, people tend to look at their sample data to see if they are normally distributed. If so, then they have a little party to celebrate and assume that the sampling distribution (which is what actually matters) is also. We also know from the central limit theorem that in big samples the sampling distribution tends to be normal anyway – regardless of the shape of the data we actually collected (and remember that the sampling distribution will tend to be normal regardless of the population distribution in samples of 30 or more). As our sample gets bigger then, we can be more confident that the sampling distribution is normally distributed (but see Jane Superbrain Box 5.1).

The assumption of normality is also important in research using regression (or general linear models). General linear models, as we will see in Chapter 7, assume that errors in the model (basically, the deviations we encountered in section 2.4.2) are normally distributed.

In both cases it might be useful to test for normality and that's what this section is dedicated to explaining. Essentially, we can look for normality visually, look at values that quantify aspects of a distribution (i.e. skew and kurtosis) and compare the distribution we have to a normal distribution to see if it is different.

5.4.1. Oh no, it's that pesky frequency distribution again: checking normality visually ①

We discovered in section 1.7.1 that frequency distributions are a useful way to look at the shape of a distribution. In addition, we discovered how to plot these graphs in section 4.4. Therefore, we are already equipped to look for normality in our sample using a graph. Let's return to the Download Festival data from Chapter 4. Remember that a biologist had visited the Download Festival (a rock and heavy metal festival in the UK) and assessed people's hygiene over the three days of the festival using a standardized technique that results in a score ranging between 0 (you smell like a rotting corpse that's hiding up a skunk's anus) and 5 (you smell of sweet roses on a fresh spring day). The data file can be downloaded from the companion website (**DownloadFestival.sav**) – remember to use the version of the data for which the outlier has been corrected (if you haven't a clue what I mean then read section 4.4 or your graphs will look very different to mine!).

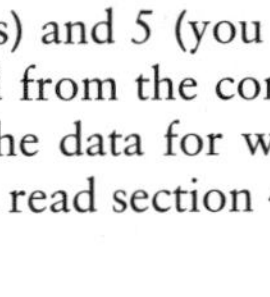

SELF-TEST Using what you learnt in section 4.4 plot histograms for the hygiene scores for the three days of the Download Festival.

There is another useful graph that we can inspect to see if a distribution is normal called a **P–P plot** (probability–probability plot). This graph plots the cumulative probability of a variable against the cumulative probability of a particular distribution (in this case we would specify a normal distribution). What this means is that the data are ranked and sorted. Then for each rank the corresponding z-score is calculated. This is the expected value that the score should have in a normal distribution. Next the score itself is converted

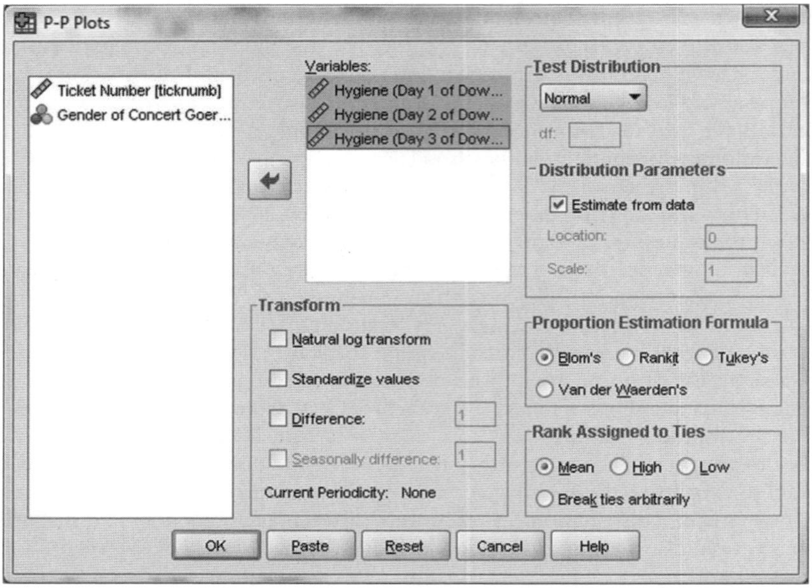

FIGURE 5.2 Dialog box for obtaining P–P plots

to a *z*-score (see section 1.7.4). The actual *z*-score is plotted against the expected *z*-score. If the data are normally distributed then the actual *z*-score will be the same as the expected *z*-score and you'll get a lovely straight diagonal line. This ideal scenario is helpfully plotted on the graph and your job is to compare the data points to this line. If values fall on the diagonal of the plot then the variable is normally distributed, but deviations from the diagonal show deviations from normality.

To get a P–P plot use Analyze Descriptive Statistics ▸ P-P Plots.. to access the dialog box in Figure 5.2. There's not a lot to say about this dialog box really because the default options will compare any variables selected to a normal distribution, which is what we want (although note that there is a drop-down list of different distributions against which you could compare your data). Select the three hygiene score variables in the variable list (click on the day 1 variable, then hold down *Shift* and select the day 3 variable and the day 2 scores will be selected as well). Transfer the selected variables to the box labelled *Variables* by clicking on ➡. Click on OK to draw the graphs.

Figure 5.3 shows the histograms (from the self-test task) and the corresponding P–P plots. The first thing to note is that the data from day 1 look a lot more healthy since we've removed the data point that was mis-typed back in section 4.5. In fact the distribution is amazingly normal looking: it is nicely symmetrical and doesn't seem too pointy or flat – these are good things! This is echoed by the P–P plot: note that the data points all fall very close to the 'ideal' diagonal line.

However, the distributions for days 2 and 3 are not nearly as symmetrical. In fact, they both look positively skewed. Again, this can be seen in the P–P plots by the data values deviating away from the diagonal. In general, what this seems to suggest is that by days 2 and 3, hygiene scores were much more clustered around the low end of the scale. Remember that the lower the score, the less hygienic the person is, so this suggests that generally people became smellier as the festival progressed. The skew occurs because a substantial minority insisted on upholding their levels of hygiene (against all odds!) over the course of the festival (baby wet-wipes are indispensable I find). However, these skewed distributions might cause us a problem if we want to use parametric tests. In the next section we'll look at ways to try to quantify the skewness and kurtosis of these distributions.

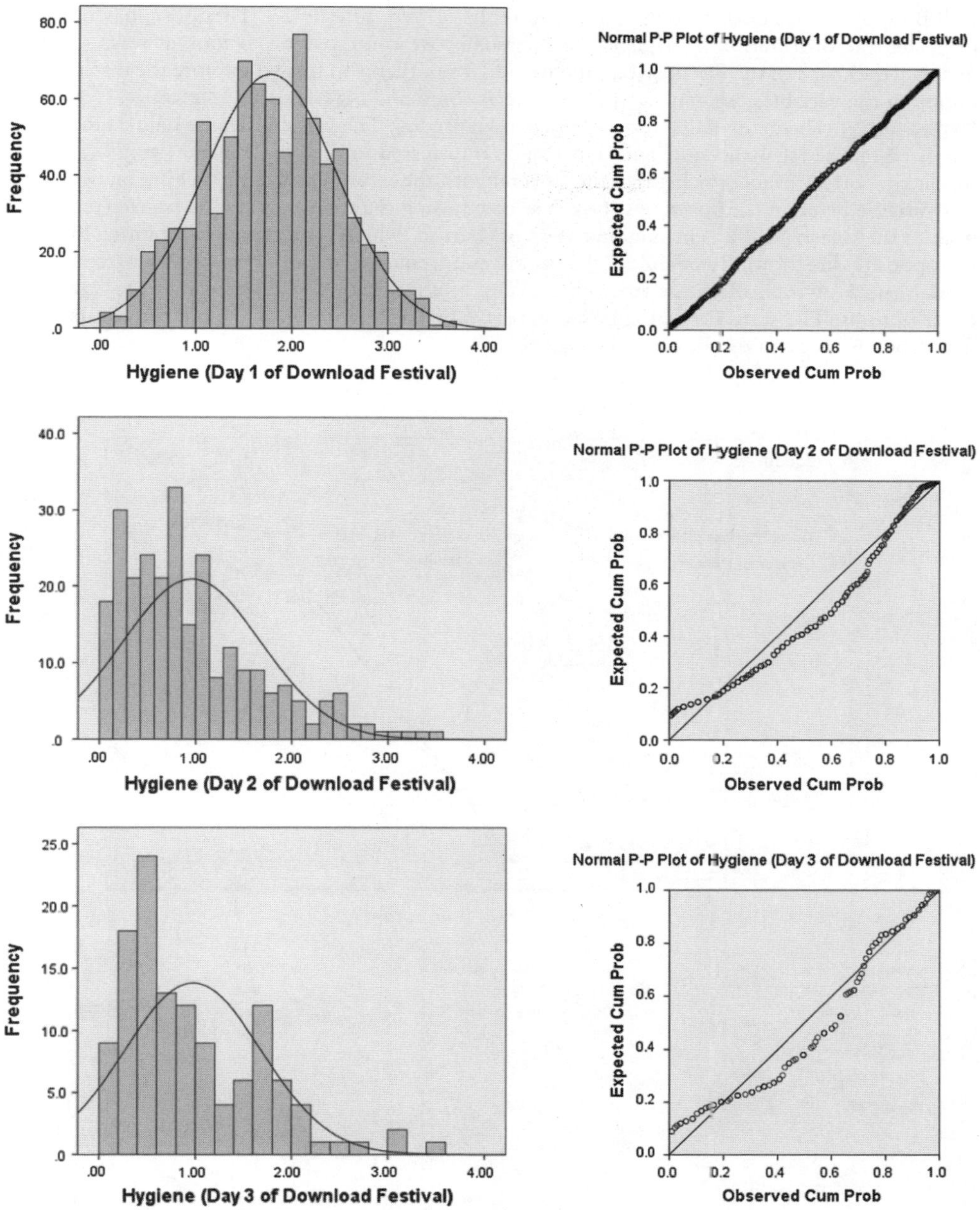

FIGURE 5.3 Histograms (left) and P–P plots (right) of the hygiene scores over the three days of the Download Festival

5.4.2. Quantifying normality with numbers ①

It is all very well to look at histograms, but they are subjective and open to abuse (I can imagine researchers sitting looking at a completely distorted distribution and saying 'yep, well Bob, that looks normal to me', and Bob replying 'yep, sure does'). Therefore, having inspected the distribution of hygiene scores visually, we can move on to look at ways to quantify the shape of the distributions and to look for outliers. To further explore the distribution of the variables, we can use the *frequencies* command (Analyze Descriptive Statistics ▸ 123 Frequencies...). The main dialog box is shown in Figure 5.4. The variables in the data editor are listed on the left-hand side, and they can be transferred to the box labelled *Variable(s)* by clicking on a variable (or highlighting several with the mouse) and then clicking on ➡. If a variable listed in the *Variable(s)* box is selected using the mouse, it can be transferred back to the variable list by clicking on the arrow button (which should now be pointing in the opposite direction). By default, SPSS produces a frequency distribution of all scores in table form. However, there are two other dialog boxes that can be selected that provide other options. The statistics dialog box is accessed by clicking on Statistics..., and the charts dialog box is accessed by clicking on Charts... .

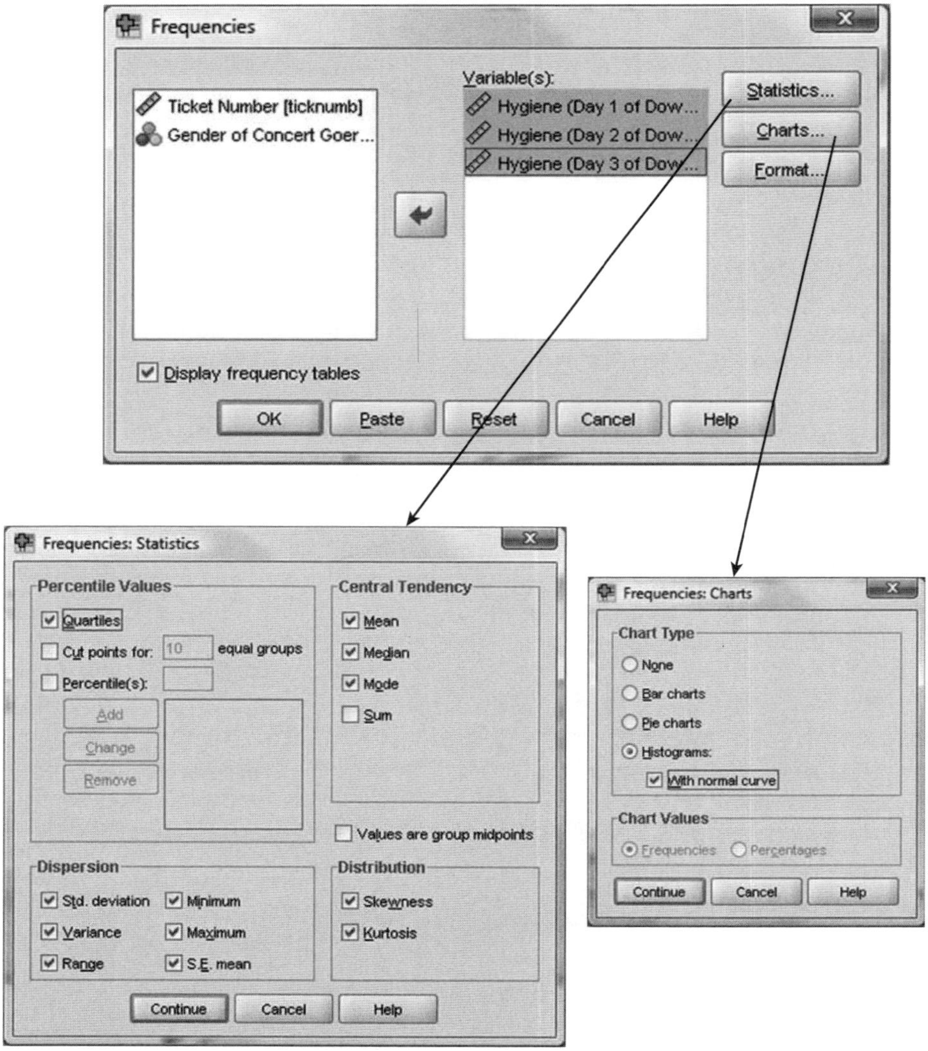

FIGURE 5.4 Dialog boxes for the *frequencies* command

The statistics dialog box allows you to select several ways in which a distribution of scores can be described, such as measures of central tendency (mean, mode, median), measures of variability (range, standard deviation, variance, quartile splits), measures of shape (kurtosis and skewness). To describe the characteristics of the data we should select the mean, mode, median, standard deviation, variance and range. To check that a distribution of scores is normal, we need to look at the values of kurtosis and skewness (see section 1.7.1). The *charts* option provides a simple way to plot the frequency distribution of scores (as a bar chart, a pie chart or a histogram). We've already plotted histograms of our data so we don't need to select these options, but you could use these options in future analyses. When you have selected the appropriate options, return to the main dialog box by clicking on Continue. Once in the main dialog box, click on OK to run the analysis.

SPSS OUTPUT 5.1

Statistics

		Hygiene (Day 1 of Download Festival)	Hygiene (Day 2 of Download Festival)	Hygiene (Day 3 of Download Festival)
N	Valid	810	264	123
	Missing	0	546	687
Mean		1.7711	.9609	.9765
Std. Error of Mean		.02437	.04436	.06404
Median		1.7900	.7900	.7600
Mode		2.00	.23	.44[a]
Std. Deviation		.69354	.72078	.71028
Variance		.481	520	.504
Skewness		-.004	1 095	1.033
Std. Error of Skewness		.086	150	.218
Kurtosis		-.410	.822	.732
Std. Error of Kurtosis		.172	.299	.433
Range		3.67	3.44	3.39
Minimum		.02	.00	.02
Maximum		3.69	3.44	3.41
Percentiles	25	1.3050	.4100	.4400
	50	1.7900	.7900	.7600
	75	2.2300	1.3500	1.5500

a. Multiple modes exist. The smallest value is shown

SPSS Output 5.1 shows the table of descriptive statistics for the three variables in this example. From this table, we can see that, on average, hygiene scores were 1.77 (out of 5) on day 1 of the festival, but went down to 0.96 and 0.98 on days 2 and 3 respectively. The other important measures for our purposes are the skewness and the kurtosis (see section 1.7.1), both of which have an associated standard error. The values of skewness and kurtosis should be zero in a normal distribution. Positive values of skewness indicate a pile-up of scores on the left of the distribution, whereas negative values indicate a pile-up on the right. Positive values of kurtosis indicate a pointy and heavy-tailed distribution, whereas negative values indicate a flat and light-tailed distribution. The further the value is from zero, the more likely it is that the data are not normally distributed. For day 1 the skew value is very close to zero (which is good) and kurtosis is a little negative. For days 2 and 3, though, there is a skewness of around 1 (positive skew).

Although the values of skew and kurtosis are informative, we can convert these values to *z*-scores. We saw in section 1.7.4 that a *z*-score is simply a score from a distribution that has a mean of 0 and a standard deviation of 1. We also saw that this distribution has known properties that we can use. Converting scores to a *z*-score is useful then because (1) we can compare skew and kurtosis values in different samples that used different measures, and (2) we can see how likely our values of skew and kurtosis are to occur. To transform any score to a *z*-score you simply subtract the mean of the distribution (in this case zero) and then divide by the standard deviation of the distribution (in this case we use the standard error). Skewness and kurtosis are converted to *z*-scores in exactly this way.

$$Z_{\text{skewness}} = \frac{S - 0}{SE_{\text{skewness}}} \qquad Z_{\text{kurtosis}} = \frac{K - 0}{SE_{\text{kurtosis}}}$$

In the above equations, the values of S (skewness) and K (kurtosis) and their respective standard errors are produced by SPSS. These z-scores can be compared against values that you would expect to get by chance alone (i.e. known values for the normal distribution shown in the Appendix). So, an absolute value greater than 1.96 is significant at $p < .05$, above 2.58 is significant at $p < .01$ and absolute values above about 3.29 are significant at $p < .001$. Large samples will give rise to small standard errors and so when sample sizes are big, significant values arise from even small deviations from normality. In smallish samples it's OK to look for values above 1.96; however, in large samples this criterion should be increased to the 2.58 one and in very large samples, because of the problem of small standard errors that I've described, no criterion should be applied! If you have a large sample (200 or more) it is more important to look at the shape of the distribution visually and to look at the value of the skewness and kurtosis statistics rather than calculate their significance.

For the hygiene scores, the z-score of skewness is –0.004/0.086 = 0.047 on day 1, 1.095/0.150 = 7.300 on day 2 and 1.033/0.218 = 4.739 on day 3. It is pretty clear then that although on day 1 scores are not at all skewed, on days 2 and 3 there is a very significant positive skew (as was evident from the histogram) – however, bear in mind what I just said about large samples! The kurtosis z-scores are: –0.410/0.172 = –2.38 on day 1, 0.822/0.299 = 2.75 on day 2 and 0.732/0.433 = 1.69 on day 3. These values indicate significant kurtosis (at $p < .05$) for all three days; however, because of the large sample, this isn't surprising and so we can take comfort in the fact that all values of kurtosis are below our upper threshold of 3.29.

CRAMMING SAM'S TIPS — Skewness and kurtosis

- To check that the distribution of scores is approximately normal, we need to look at the values of *skewness* and *kurtosis* in the SPSS output.
- Positive values of skewness indicate too many low scores in the distribution, whereas negative values indicate a build-up of high scores.
- Positive values of kurtosis indicate a pointy and heavy-tailed distribution, whereas negative values indicate a flat and light-tailed distribution.
- The further the value is from zero, the more likely it is that the data are not normally distributed.
- You can convert these scores to z-scores by dividing by their standard error. If the resulting score (when you ignore the minus sign) is greater than 1.96 then it is significant ($p < .05$).
- Significance tests of skew and kurtosis should not be used in large samples (because they are likely to be significant even when skew and kurtosis are not too different from normal).

OLIVER TWISTED

Please, Sir, can I have some more … frequencies?

In your SPSS output you will also see tabulated frequency distributions of each variable. This table is reproduced in the additional online material along with a description.

5.4.3. Exploring groups of data ①

Sometimes we have data in which there are different groups of people (men and women, different universities, people with depression and people without, for example). There are several ways to produce basic descriptive statistics for separate groups of people (and we will come across some of these methods in section 5.5.1). However, I intend to use this opportunity to introduce you to the *split file* function. This function allows you to specify a grouping variable (remember, these variables are used to specify categories of cases). Any subsequent procedure in SPSS is then carried out on each category of cases separately.

You're probably getting sick of the hygiene data from the Download Festival so let's use the data in the file **SPSSExam.sav**. This file contains data regarding students' performance on an SPSS exam. Four variables were measured: **exam** (first-year SPSS exam scores as a percentage), **computer** (measure of computer literacy in percent), **lecture** (percentage of SPSS lectures attended) and **numeracy** (a measure of numerical ability out of 15). There is a variable called **uni** indicating whether the student attended Sussex University (where I work) or Duncetown University. To begin with, open the file **SPSSExam.sav** (see section 3.9). Let's begin by looking at the data as a whole.

5.4.3.1. Running the analysis for all data ①

To see the distribution of the variables, we can use the *frequencies* command, which we came across in the previous section (see Figure 5.4). Use this dialog box and place all four variables (**exam**, **computer**, **lecture** and **numeracy**) in the *Variable(s)* box. Then click on Statistics... to select the statistics dialog box and select some measures of central tendency (mean, mode, median), measures of variability (range, standard deviation, variance, quartile splits) and measures of shape (kurtosis and skewness). Also click on Charts... to access the charts dialog box and select a frequency distribution of scores with a normal curve (see Figure 5.4 if you need any help with any of these options). Return to the main dialog box by clicking on Continue and once in the main dialog box, click on OK to run the analysis.

SPSS Output 5.2 shows the table of descriptive statistics for the four variables in this example. From this table, we can see that, on average, students attended nearly 60% of lectures, obtained 58% in their SPSS exam, scored only 51% on the computer literacy test, and only 5 out of 15 on the numeracy test. In addition, the standard deviation for computer literacy was relatively small compared to that of the percentage of lectures attended and exam scores. These latter two variables had several modes (multimodal). The other important measures are the skewness and the kurtosis, both of which have an associated standard error. We came across these measures earlier on and found that we can convert these values to z-scores by dividing by their standard errors. For the SPSS exam scores, the z-score of skewness is $-0.107/0.241 = -0.44$. For numeracy, the z-score of skewness is $0.961/0.241 = 3.99$. It is pretty clear then that the numeracy scores are significantly positively skewed ($p < .05$) because the z-score is greater than 1.96, indicating a pile-up of scores on the left of the distribution (so, most students got low scores).

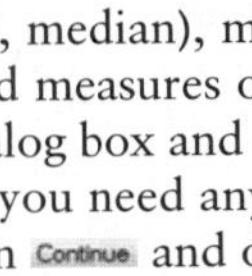

SELF-TEST Calculate and interpret the z-scores for skewness of the other variables (computer literacy and percentage of lectures attended).

SELF-TEST Calculate and interpret the z-scores for kurtosis of all of the variables.

The output provides tabulated frequency distributions of each variable (not reproduced here). These tables list each score and the number of times that it is found within the data set. In addition, each frequency value is expressed as a percentage of the sample (in this case the frequencies and percentages are the same because the sample size was 100). Also, the cumulative percentage is given, which tells us how many cases (as a percentage) fell below a certain score. So, for example, we can see that 66% of numeracy scores were 5 or less, 74% were 6 or less, and so on. Looking in the other direction, we can work out that only 8% (100 – 92%) got scores greater than 8.

SPSS OUTPUT 5.

Statistics

		Percentage on SPSS exam	Computer literacy	Percentage of lectures attended	Numeracy
N	Valid	100	100	100	100
	Missing	0	0	0	0
Mean		58.10	50.71	59.765	4.85
Std. Error of Mean		2.132	.826	2.1685	.271
Median		60.00	51.50	62.000	4.00
Mode		72[a]	54	48.5[a]	4
Std. Deviation		21.316	8.260	21.6848	2.706
Variance		454.354	68.228	470.230	7.321
Skewness		-.107	-.174	-.422	.961
Std. Error of Skewness		.241	.241	.241	.241
Kurtosis		-1.105	.364	-.179	.946
Std. Error of Kurtosis		.478	.478	.478	.478
Range		84	46	92.0	13
Minimum		15	27	8.0	1
Maximum		99	73	100.0	14

a. Multiple modes exist. The smallest value is shown

Finally, we are given histograms of each variable with the normal distribution overlaid. These graphs are displayed in Figure 5.5 and show us several things. The exam scores are very interesting because this distribution is quite clearly not normal; in fact, it looks suspiciously bimodal (there are two peaks indicative of two modes). This observation corresponds with the earlier information from the table of descriptive statistics. It looks as though computer literacy is fairly normally distributed (a few people are very good with computers and a few are very bad, but the majority of people have a similar degree of knowledge) as is the lecture attendance. Finally, the numeracy test has produced very positively skewed data (i.e. the majority of people did very badly on this test and only a few did well). This corresponds to what the skewness statistic indicated.

Descriptive statistics and histograms are a good way of getting an instant picture of the distribution of your data. This snapshot can be very useful: for example, the bimodal distribution of SPSS exam scores instantly indicates a trend that students are typically either very good at statistics or struggle with it (there are relatively few who fall in between these extremes). Intuitively, this finding fits with the nature of the subject: statistics is very easy once everything falls into place, but before that enlightenment occurs it all seems hopelessly difficult!

5.4.3.2. Running the analysis for different groups ①

If we want to obtain separate descriptive statistics for each of the universities, we can split the file, and then proceed using the *frequencies* command described in the previous section. To split the file, select Data Split File... or click on . In the resulting dialog box (Figure 5.6) select the option *Organize output by groups*. Once this option is selected, the *Groups Based on* box will activate. Select the variable containing the group codes by which you wish to repeat the analysis (in this example select **Uni**), and drag it to the box or click on . By default, SPSS will sort the file by these groups (i.e. it will list one category followed by the other in the data editor window). Once you have split the file, use the *frequencies* command (see the previous section). Let's request statistics for only **numeracy** and **exam** scores for the time being.

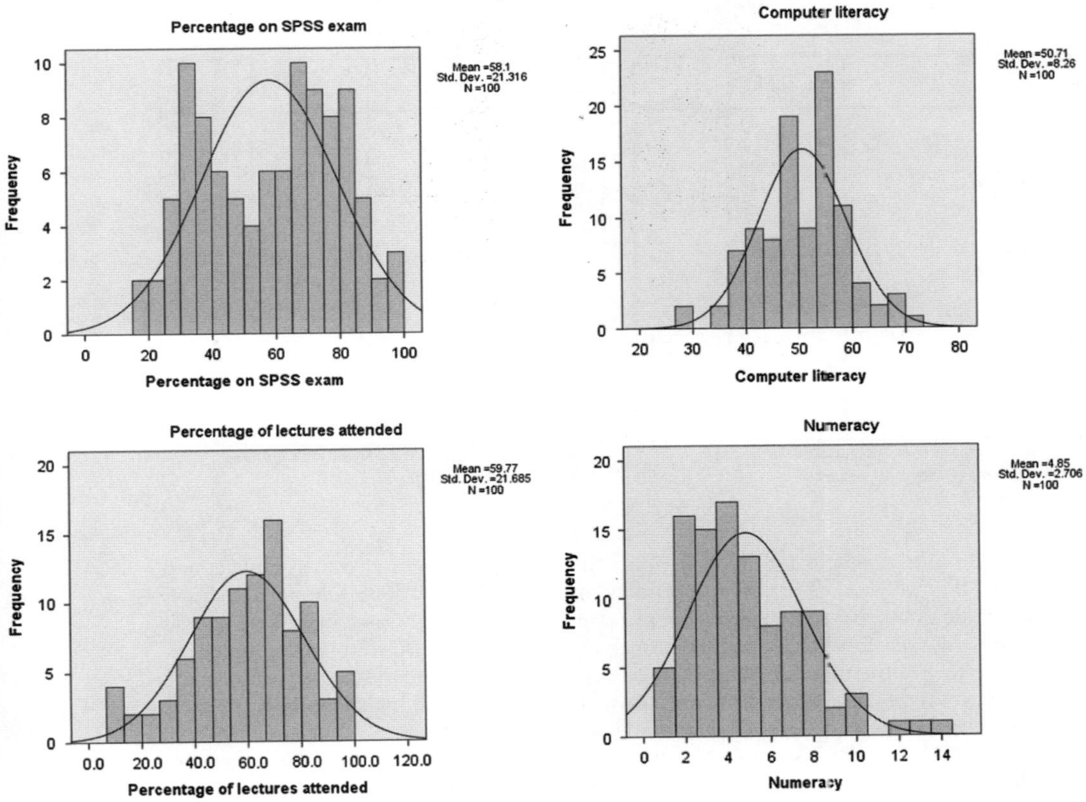

FIGURE 5.5 Histograms of the SPSS exam data

FIGURE 5.6 Dialog box for the *split file* command

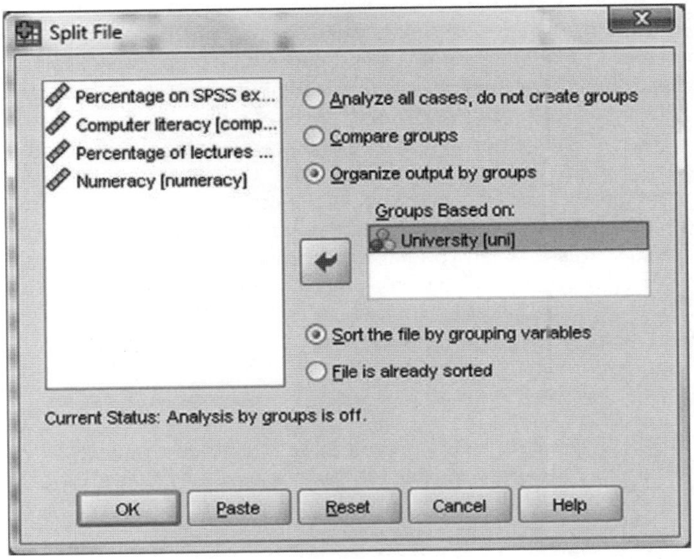

SPSS OUTPUT 5

Duncetown University
Statistics[b]

		Percentage on SPSS exam	Numeracy
N	Valid	50	50
	Missing	0	0
Mean		40.18	4.12
Std. Error of Mean		1.780	.292
Median		38.00	4.00
Mode		34[a]	4
Std. Deviation		12.589	2.067
Variance		158.477	4.271
Skewness		.309	.512
Std. Error of Skewness		.337	.337
Kurtosis		-.567	-.484
Std. Error of Kurtosis		.662	.662
Range		51	8
Minimum		15	1
Maximum		66	9

a. Multiple modes exist. The smallest value is shown
b. University = Duncetown University

Sussex University
Statistics[b]

		Percentage on SPSS exam	Numeracy
N	Valid	50	50
	Missing	0	0
Mean		76.02	5.58
Std. Error of Mean		1.443	.434
Median		75.00	5.00
Mode		72[a]	5
Std. Deviation		10.205	3.071
Variance		104.142	9.432
Skewness		.272	.793
Std. Error of Skewness		.337	.337
Kurtosis		-.264	.260
Std. Error of Kurtosis		.662	.662
Range		43	13
Minimum		56	1
Maximum		99	14

a. Multiple modes exist. The smallest value is shown
b. University = Sussex University

The SPSS output is split into two sections: first the results for students at Duncetown University, then the results for those attending Sussex University. SPSS Output 5.3 shows the two main summary tables. From these tables it is clear that Sussex students scored higher on both their SPSS exam and the numeracy test than their Duncetown counterparts. In fact, looking at the means reveals that, on average, Sussex students scored an amazing 36% more on the SPSS exam than Duncetown students, and had higher numeracy scores too (what can I say, my students are the best).

Figure 5.7 shows the histograms of these variables split according to the university attended. The first interesting thing to note is that for exam marks, the distributions are both fairly normal. This seems odd because the overall distribution was bimodal. However, it starts to make sense when you consider that for Duncetown the distribution is centred around a mark of about 40%, but for Sussex the distribution is centred around a mark of about 76%. This illustrates how important it is to look at distributions within groups. If we were interested in comparing Duncetown to Sussex it wouldn't matter that overall the distribution of scores was bimodal; all that's important is that each group comes from a normal distribution, and in this case it appears to be true. When the two samples are combined, these two normal distributions create a bimodal one (one of the modes being around the centre of the Duncetown distribution, and the other being around the centre of the Sussex data!). For numeracy scores, the distribution is slightly positively skewed (there is a larger concentration at the lower end of scores) in both the Duncetown and Sussex groups. Therefore, the overall positive skew observed before is due to the mixture of universities (the Duncetown students contaminate Sussex's normally distributed scores!). When you have finished with the *split file* command, remember to *switch it off* (otherwise SPSS will carry on doing every analysis on each group separately). To switch this function off, return to the *Split File* dialog box (Figure 5.6) and select *Analyze all cases, do not create groups.*

SELF-TEST Repeat these analyses for the computer literacy and percentage of lectures attended and interpret the results.

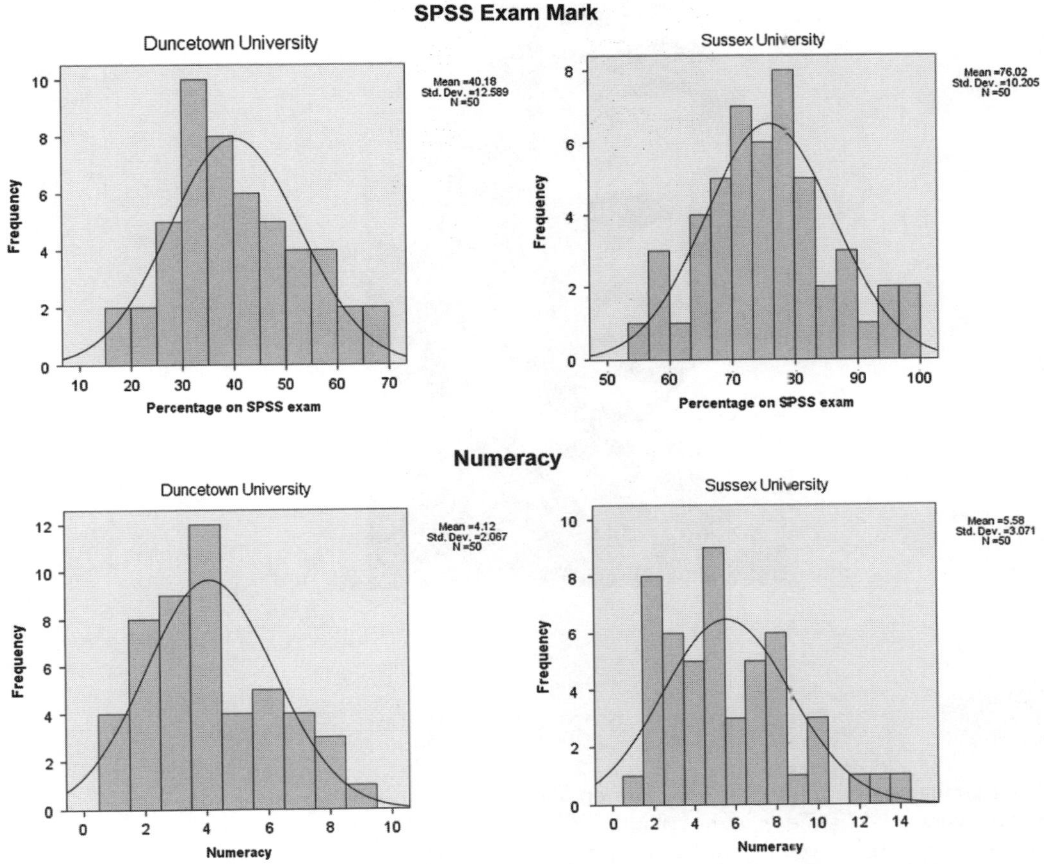

FIGURE 5.7 Distributions of exam and numeracy scores for Duncetown University and Sussex University students

5.5. Testing whether a distribution is normal ①

Another way of looking at the problem is to see whether the distribution as a whole deviates from a comparable normal distribution. The **Kolmogorov–Smirnov test** and **Shapiro–Wilk test** do just this: they compare the scores in the sample to a normally distributed set of scores with the same mean and standard deviation. If the test is non-significant ($p > .05$) it tells us that the distribution of the sample is not significantly different from a normal distribution (i.e. it is probably normal). If, however, the test is significant ($p < .05$) then the distribution in question is significantly different from a normal distribution (i.e. it is non-normal). These tests seem great: in one easy procedure they tell us whether our scores are normally distributed (nice!). However, they have their limitations because with large sample sizes it is very easy to get significant results from small deviations from normality, and so a significant test doesn't necessarily tell us whether the deviation from normality is enough to bias any statistical procedures that we apply to the data. I guess the take-home message is: by all means use these tests, but plot your data as well and try to make an informed decision about the extent of non-normality.

FIGURE 5.8 Andrei Kolmogorov, wishing he had a Smirnov

5.5.1. Doing the Kolmogorov–Smirnov test on SPSS ①

The Kolmogorov–Smirnov (K–S from now on; Figure 5.8) test can be accessed through the *explore* command (Analyze Descriptive Statistics ▸ Explore...). Figure 5.9 shows the dialog boxes for the *explore* command. First, enter any variables of interest in the box labelled *Dependent List* by highlighting them on the left-hand side and transferring them by clicking on ➡. For this example, just select the exam scores and numeracy scores. It is also possible to select a factor (or grouping variable) by which to split the output (so, if you select **Uni** and transfer it to the box labelled *Factor List*, SPSS will produce exploratory analysis for each group – a bit like the *split file* command). If you click on Statistics... a dialog box appears, but the default option is fine (it will produce means, standard deviations and so on). The more interesting option for our current purposes is accessed by clicking on Plots... . In this dialog box select the option ☑ Normality plots with tests, and this will produce both the K–S test and some graphs called *normal Q–Q plots*. A **Q–Q plot** is very similar to the P-P plot that we encountered in section 5.4.1 except that it plots the **quantiles** of the data set instead of every individual score in the data. Quantiles are just values that split a data set into equal portions. We have already used quantiles without knowing it because quartiles (as in the interquartile range in section 1.7.3) are a special case of quantiles that split the data into four equal parts. However, you can have other quantiles such as **percentiles** (points that split the data into 100 equal parts), **noniles** (points that split the data into nine equal parts) and so on. In short, then, the Q–Q plot can be interpreted in the same way as a P–P plot but it will have less points on it because rather than plotting every single data point it plots only values that divide the data into equal parts (so, they can be easier to interpret if you have a lot of scores). By default, SPSS will produce boxplots (split according to group if a factor has been specified) and stem and leaf diagrams as well. Click on Continue to return to the main dialog box and then click on OK to run the analysis.

GURE 5.9
alog boxes
r the *explore*
mmand

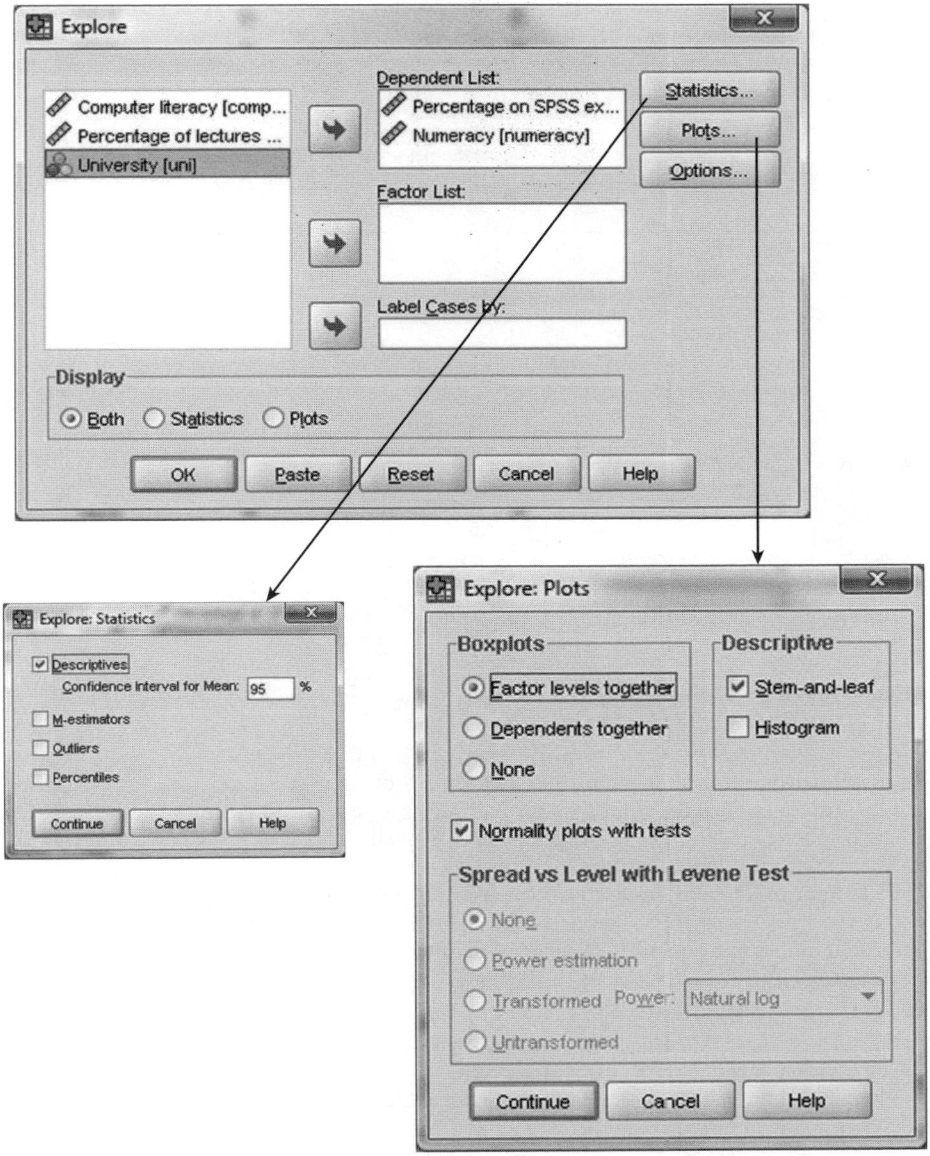

5.5.2. Output from the explore procedure ①

The first table produced by SPSS contains descriptive statistics (mean etc.) and should have the same values as the tables obtained using the frequencies procedure. The important table is that of the K–S test (SPSS Output 5.4). This table includes the test statistic itself, the degrees of freedom (which should equal the sample size) and the significance value of this test. Remember that a significant value (*Sig.* less than .05) indicates a deviation from normality. For both numeracy and SPSS exam scores, the K–S test is highly significant, indicating that both distributions are not normal. This result is likely to reflect the bimodal distribution found for exam scores, and the positively skewed distribution observed in the numeracy scores. However, these tests confirm that these deviations were *significant*. (But bear in mind that the sample is fairly big.)

SPSS OUTPUT 5

Tests of Normality

	Kolmogorov-Smirnov[a]			Shapiro-Wilk		
	Statistic	df	Sig.	Statistic	df	Sig.
Percentage on SPSS exam	.102	100	.012	.961	100	.005
Numeracy	.153	100	.000	.924	100	.000

a. Lilliefors Significance Correction

OLIVER TWISTED

Please, Sir, can I have some more … normality tests?

'There is another test reported in the table (the Shapiro–Wilk test)', whispers Oliver as he creeps up behind you, knife in hand, 'and a footnote saying that "Lilliefors' significance correction" has been applied. What the hell is going on?'. (If you do the K–S test through the non-parametric test menu rather than the explore menu this correction is not applied.) Well, Oliver, all will be revealed in the additional material for this chapter on the companion website: you can find out more about the K–S test, and information about the Lilliefor correction and Shapiro–Wilk test. What are you waiting for?

As a final point, bear in mind that when we looked at the exam scores for separate groups, the distributions seemed quite normal; now if we'd asked for separate tests for the two universities (by placing **Uni** in the box labelled *Factor List* as in Figure 5.9) the K–S test might not have been significant. In fact if you try this out, you'll get the table in SPSS Output 5.5, which shows that the percentages on the SPSS exam are indeed normal within the two groups (the values in the *Sig.* column are greater than .05). This is important because if our analysis involves comparing groups, then what's important is not the overall distribution but the distribution in each group.

SPSS OUTPUT 5

Tests of Normality

		Kolmogorov-Smirnov[a]			Shapiro-Wilk		
	University	Statistic	df	Sig.	Statistic	df	Sig.
Percentage on SPSS exam	Duncetown University	.106	50	.200*	.972	50	.283
	Sussex University	.073	50	.200*	.984	50	.715
Numeracy	Duncetown University	.183	50	.000	.941	50	.015
	Sussex University	.155	50	.004	.932	50	.007

*. This is a lower bound of the true significance.

a. Lilliefors Significance Correction

SPSS also produces a normal Q–Q plot for any variables specified (see Figure 5.10). The normal Q–Q chart plots the values you would expect to get if the distribution were normal (expected values) against the values actually seen in the data set (observed values). The expected values are a straight diagonal line, whereas the observed values are plotted as individual points. If the data are normally distributed, then the observed values (the dots on the chart) should fall exactly along the straight line (meaning that the observed values are the same as you would expect to get from a normally distributed data set). Any

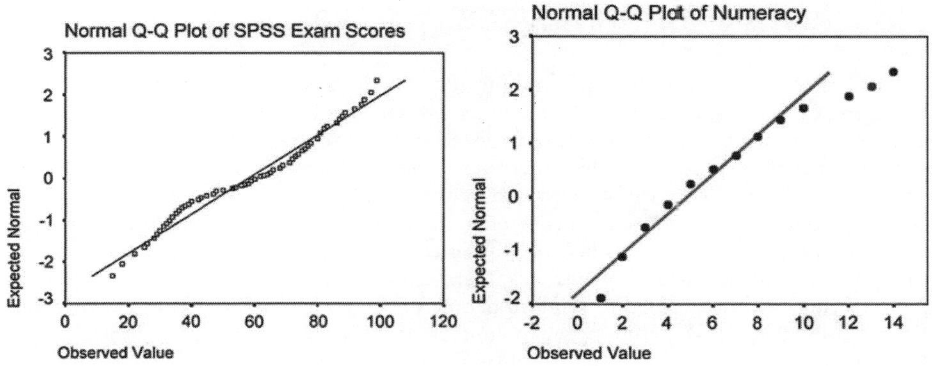

FIGURE 5.10 Normal Q–Q plots of numeracy and SPSS exam scores

deviation of the dots from the line represents a deviation from normality. So, if the Q–Q plot looks like a straight line with a wiggly snake wrapped around it then you have some deviation from normality! Specifically, when the line sags consistently below the diagonal, or consistently rises above it, then this shows that the kurtosis differs from a normal distribution, and when the curve is S-shaped, the problem is skewness.

In both of the variables analysed we already know that the data are not normal, and these plots confirm this observation because the dots deviate substantially from the line. It is noteworthy that the deviation is greater for the numeracy scores, and this is consistent with the higher significance value of this variable on the K–S test.

5.5.3. Reporting the K–S test ①

The test statistic for the K–S test is denoted by D and we must also report the degrees of freedom (df) from the table in brackets after the D. We can report the results in SPSS Output 5.4 in the following way:

✓ The percentage on the SPSS exam, $D(100) = 0.10$, $p < .05$, and the numeracy scores, $D(100) = 0.15$, $p < .001$, were both significantly non-normal.

CRAMMING SAM'S TIPS **Normality tests**

- The K–S test can be used to see if a distribution of scores significantly differs from a normal distribution.
- If the K–S test is significant (*Sig.* in the SPSS table is less than .05) then the scores are significantly different from a normal distribution.
- Otherwise, scores are approximately normally distributed.
- The Shapiro–Wilk test does much the same thing, but it has more power to detect differences from normality (so, you might find this test is significant when the K–S test is not).
- **Warning**: In large samples these tests can be significant even when the scores are only slightly different from a normal distribution. Therefore, they should always be interpreted in conjunction with histograms, P–P or Q–Q plots, and the values of skew and kurtosis.

5.6. Testing for homogeneity of variance ①

So far I've concentrated on the assumption of normally distributed data; however, at the beginning of this chapter I mentioned another assumption: homogeneity of variance. This assumption means that as you go through levels of one variable, the variance of the other should not change. If you've collected groups of data then this means that the variance of your outcome variable or variables should be the same in each of these groups. If you've collected continuous data (such as in correlational designs), this assumption means that the variance of one variable should be stable at all levels of the other variable. Let's illustrate this with an example. An audiologist was interested in the effects of loud concerts on people's hearing. So, she decided to send 10 people on tour with the loudest band she could find, Motörhead. These people went to concerts in Brixton (London), Brighton, Bristol, Edinburgh, Newcastle, Cardiff and Dublin and after each concert the audiologist measured the number of hours after the concert that these people had ringing in their ears.

Figure 5.11 shows the number of hours that each person had ringing in their ears after each concert (each person is represented by a circle). The horizontal lines represent the average number of hours that there was ringing in the ears after each concert and these means are connected by a line so that we can see the general trend of the data. Remember that for each concert, the circles are the scores from which the mean is calculated. Now, we can see in both graphs that the means increase as the people go to more concerts. So, after the first concert their ears ring for about 12 hours, but after the second they ring for about 15–20 hours, and by the final night of the tour, they ring for about 45–50 hours (2 days). So, there is a cumulative effect of the concerts on ringing in the ears. This pattern is found in both graphs; the difference between the graphs is not in terms of the means (which are roughly the same), but in terms of the spread of scores around the mean. If you look at the left-hand graph the spread of scores around the mean stays the same after each concert (the scores are fairly tightly packed around the mean). Put another way, if you measured the vertical distance between the lowest score and the highest score after the Brixton concert, and then did the same after the other concerts, all of these distances would be fairly similar. Although the means increase, the spread of scores for hearing loss is the same at each level of the concert variable (the spread of scores is the same after Brixton, Brighton, Bristol, Edinburgh, Newcastle, Cardiff and Dublin). This is what we mean by *homogeneity of variance*. The right-hand graph shows a different picture: if you look at the spread of scores after the Brixton concert, they are quite tightly packed around the mean (the vertical distance from

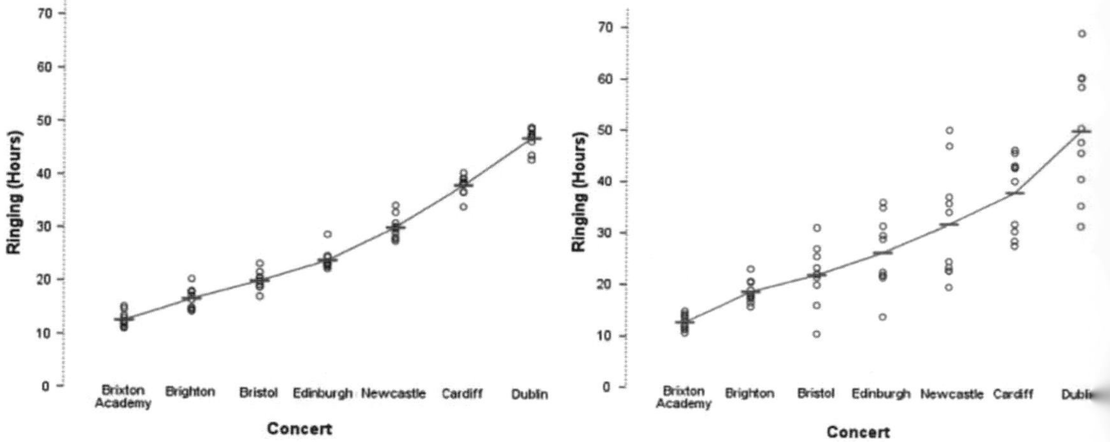

FIGURE 5.11 Graphs illustrating data with homogeneous (left) and heterogeneous (right) variances

the lowest score to the highest score is small), but after the Dublin show (for example) the scores are very spread out around the mean (the vertical distance from the lowest score to the highest score is large). This is an example of *heterogeneity of variance*: that is, at some levels of the concert variable the variance of scores is different to other levels (graphically, the vertical distance from the lowest to highest score is different after different concerts).

5.6.1. Levene's test ①

Hopefully you've got a grip of what homogeneity of variance actually means. Now, how do we test for it? Well, we could just look at the values of the variances and see whether they are similar. However, this approach would be very subjective and probably prone to academics thinking 'Ooh look, the variance in one group is only 3000 times larger than the variance in the other: that's roughly equal'. Instead, in correlational analysis such as regression we tend to use graphs (see section 7.8.7) and for groups of data we tend to use a test called **Levene's test** (Levene, 1960). Levene's test tests the null hypothesis that the variances in different groups are equal (i.e. the difference between the variances is zero). It's a very simple and elegant test that works by doing a one-way ANOVA (see Chapter 10) conducted on the deviation scores; that is, the absolute difference between each score and the mean of the group from which it came (see Glass, 1966, for a very readable explanation).[3] For now, all we need to know is that if Levene's test is significant at $p \leq .05$ then we can conclude that the null hypothesis is incorrect and that the variances are significantly different – therefore, the assumption of homogeneity of variances has been violated. If, however, Levene's test is non-significant (i.e. $p > .05$) then the variances are roughly equal and the assumption is tenable. Although Levene's test can be selected as an option in many of the statistical tests that require it, it can also be examined when you're exploring data (and strictly speaking it's better to examine Levene's test now than wait until your main analysis).

As with the K–S test (and other tests of normality), when the sample size is large, small differences in group variances can produce a Levene's test that is significant (because, as we saw in Chapter 1, the power of the test is improved). A useful double check, therefore, is to look at **Hartley's F_{Max}**, also known as the **variance ratio** (Pearson & Hartley, 1954). This is the ratio of the variances between the group with the biggest variance and the group with the smallest variance. This ratio was compared to critical values in a table published by Hartley. Some of the critical values (for a .05 level of significance) are shown in Figure 5.12 (see Oliver Twisted); as you can see the critical values depend on the number of cases per group (well, $n - 1$ actually), and the number of variances being compared. From this graph you can see that with sample sizes (n) of 10 per group, an F_{Max} of less than 10 is more or less always going to be non-significant, with 15–20 per group the ratio needs to be less than about 5, and with samples of 30–60 the ratio should be below about 2 or 3.

OLIVER TWISTED

Please, Sir, can I have some more … Hartley's F_{Max}?

Oliver thinks that my graph of critical values is stupid. 'Look at that graph,' he laughed, 'it's the most stupid thing I've ever seen since I was at Sussex Uni and I saw my statistics lecturer, Andy Fie…'. Well, go choke on your gruel you Dickensian bubo because the full table of critical values is in the additional material for this chapter on the companion website.

[3] We haven't covered ANOVA yet so this explanation won't make much sense to you now, but in Chapter 10 we will look in more detail at how Levene's test works.

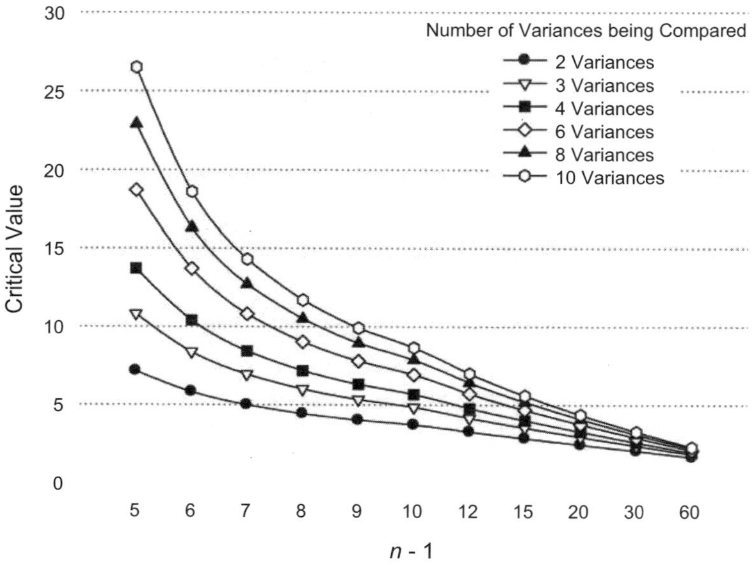

FIGURE 5.12 Selected critical values for Hartley's F_{Max} test

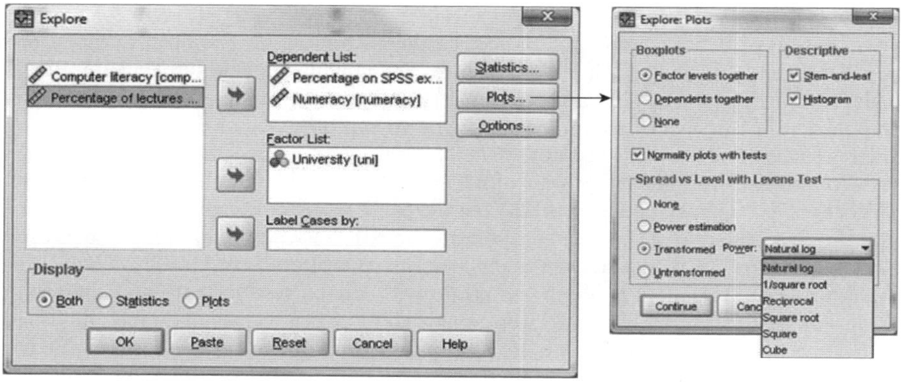

FIGURE 5.13 Exploring groups of data and obtaining Levene's test

We can get Levene's test using the *explore* menu that we used in the previous section. For this example, we'll use the SPSS exam data that we used in the previous section (in the file **SPSSExam.sav**). Once the data are loaded, use Analyze Descriptive Statistics ▶ Explore... to open the dialog box in Figure 5.13. To keep things simple we'll just look at the SPSS exam scores and the numeracy scores from this file, so transfer these two variables from the list on the left-hand side to the box labelled *Dependent List* by clicking on the ➡ next to this box, and because we want to split the output by the grouping variable to compare the variances, select the variable **Uni** and transfer it to the box labelled *Factor List* by clicking on the appropriate ➡. Then click on Plots... to open the other dialog box in Figure 5.13. To get Levene's test we need to select one of the options where it says *Spread vs. level with Levene's test*. If you select ⦿ Untransformed Levene's test is carried out on the raw data (a good place to start). When you've finished with this dialog box click on Continue to return to the main *Explore* dialog box and then click on OK to run the analysis.

SPSS Output 5.6 shows the table for Levene's test. You should read the statistics based on the mean. Levene's test is non-significant for the SPSS exam scores (values in the *Sig.*

column are more than .05) indicating that the variances are not significantly different (i.e. they are similar and the homogeneity of variance assumption is tenable). However, for the numeracy scores, Levene's test is significant (values in the *Sig.* column are less than .05) indicating that the variances are significantly different (i.e. they are not the same and the homogeneity of variance assumption has been violated). We can also calculate the variance ratio. To do this we need to divide the largest variance by the smallest. You should find the variances in your output, but if not we obtained these values in SPSS Output 5.3. For SPSS exam scores the variance ratio is 158.48/104.14 = 1.52 and for numeracy scores the value is 9.43/4.27 = 2.21. Our group sizes are 50 and we're comparing 2 variances so the critical value is (from the table in the additional material) approximately 1.67. These ratios concur with Levene's test: variances are significantly different for numeracy scores (2.21 is bigger than 1.67) but not for SPSS exam scores (1.52 is smaller than 1.67).

PSS OUTPUT 5.6

Test of Homogeneity of Variance

		Levene Statistic	df1	df2	Sig.
Percentage on SPSS exam	Based on Mean	2.584	1	98	.111
	Based on Median	2.089	1	98	.152
	Based on Median and with adjusted df	2.089	1	94.024	.152
	Based on trimmed mean	2.523	1	98	.115
Numeracy	Based on Mean	7.368	1	98	.008
	Based on Median	5.366	1	98	.023
	Based on Median and with adjusted df	5.366	1	83.920	.023
	Based on trimmed mean	6.766	1	98	.011

5.6.2. Reporting Levene's test ①

Levene's test can be denoted with the letter *F* and there are two different degrees of freedom. As such you can report it, in general form, as *F*(df1, df2) = value, *sig*. So, for the results in SPSS Output 5.6 we could say:

✓ For the percentage on the SPSS exam, the variances were equal for Duncetown and Sussex University students, $F(1, 98) = 2.58$, *ns*, but for numeracy scores the variances were significantly different in the two groups, $F(1, 98) = 7.37$, $p < .01$.

CRAMMING SAM'S TIPS Homogeneity of variance

- Homogeneity of variance is the assumption that the spread of scores is roughly equal in different groups of cases, or more generally that the spread of scores is roughly equal at different points on the predictor variable.
- When comparing groups, this assumption can be tested with Levene's test and the variance ratio (Hartley's F_{Max}).
- If Levene's test is significant (*Sig.* in the SPSS table is less than .05) then the variances are significantly different in different groups.
- Otherwise, homogeneity of variance can be assumed.
- The variance ratio is the largest group variance divided by the smallest. This value needs to be smaller than the critical values in Figure 5.12.
- **Warning:** In large samples Levene's test can be significant even when group variances are not very different. Therefore, it should be interpreted in conjunction with the variance ratio.

5.7. Correcting problems in the data ②

The previous section showed us various ways to explore our data; we saw how to look for problems with our distribution of scores and how to detect heterogeneity of variance. In Chapter 4 we also discovered how to spot outliers in the data. The next question is what to do about these problems?

5.7.1. Dealing with outliers ②

If you detect outliers in the data there are several options for reducing the impact of these values. However, before you do any of these things, it's worth checking that the data have been entered correctly for the problem cases. If the data are correct then the three main options you have are:

1 *Remove the case*: This entails deleting the data from the person who contributed the outlier. However, this should be done only if you have good reason to believe that this case is not from the population that you intended to sample. For example, if you were investigating factors that affected how much cats purr and one cat didn't purr at all, this would likely be an outlier (all cats purr). Upon inspection, if you discovered that this cat was actually a dog wearing a cat costume (hence why it didn't purr), then you'd have grounds to exclude this case because it comes from a different population (dogs who like to dress as cats) than your target population (cats).

2 *Transform the data*: Outliers tend to skew the distribution and, as we will see in the next section, this skew (and, therefore, the impact of the outliers) can sometimes be reduced by applying **transformations** to the data.

3 *Change the score*: If transformation fails, then you can consider replacing the score. This on the face of it may seem like cheating (you're changing the data from what was actually corrected); however, if the score you're changing is very unrepresentative and biases your statistical model anyway then changing the score is the lesser of two evils! There are several options for how to change the score:
   (a) *The next highest score plus one*: Change the score to be one unit above the next highest score in the data set.
   (b) *Convert back from a z-score*: A z-score of 3.29 constitutes an outlier (see Jane Superbrain Box 4.1) so we can calculate what score would give rise to a z-score of 3.29 (or perhaps 3) by rearranging the z-score equation in section 1.7.4, which gives us $X = (z \times s) + \bar{X}$. All this means is that we calculate the mean ($\bar{X}$) and standard deviation (s) of the data; we know that z is 3 (or 3.29 if you want to be exact) so we just add three times the standard deviation to the mean, and replace our outliers with that score.
   (c) *The mean plus two standard deviations*: A variation on the above method is to use the mean plus two times the standard deviation (rather than three times the standard deviation).

5.7.2. Dealing with non-normality and unequal variances ②

5.7.2.1. Transforming data ②

The next section is quite hair raising so don't worry if it doesn't make much sense – many undergraduate courses won't cover transforming data so feel free to ignore this section if you want to!

We saw in the previous section that you can deal with outliers by transforming the data and these transformations are also useful for correcting problems with normality and the assumption of homogeneity of variance. The idea behind transformations is that you do something to every score to correct for distributional problems, outliers or unequal variances. Although some students often (understandably) think that transforming data sounds dodgy (the phrase 'fudging your results' springs to some people's minds!), in fact it isn't because you do the same thing to all of your scores.[4] As such, transforming the data won't change the relationships between variables (the relative differences between people for a given variable stay the same), but it does change the differences between different variables (because it changes the units of measurement). Therefore, even if you only have one variable that has a skewed distribution, you should still transform any other variables in your data set if you're going to compare differences between that variable and others that you intend to transform.

Let's return to our Download Festival data (**DownloadFestival.sav**) from earlier in the chapter. These data were not normal on days 2 and 3 of the festival (section 5.4). Now, we might want to look at how hygiene levels changed across the three days (i.e. compare the mean on day 1 to the means on days 2 and 3 to see if people got smellier). The data for days 2 and 3 were skewed and need to be transformed, but because we might later compare the data to scores on day 1, we would also have to transform the day 1 data (even though scores were not skewed). If we don't change the day 1 data as well, then any differences in hygiene scores we find from day 1 to days 2 or 3 will be due to us transforming one variable and not the others.

There are various transformations that you can do to the data that are helpful in correcting various problems.[5] However, whether these transformations are necessary or useful is quite a complex issue (see Jane Superbrain Box 5.1). Nevertheless, because they *are* used by researchers Table 5.1 shows some common transformations and their uses.

5.7.2.2. Choosing a transformation ②

Given that there are many transformations that you can do, how can you decide which one is best? The simple answer is trial and error: try one out and see if it helps and if it doesn't then try a different one. Remember that you *must apply the same transformation to all variables* (you cannot, for example, apply a log transformation to one variable and a square root transformation to another if they are to be used in the same analysis). This can be quite time consuming. However, for homogeneity of variance we can see the effect of a transformation quite quickly. In section 5.6.1 we saw how to use the *explore* function to get Levene's test. In that section we ran the analysis selecting the raw scores (Untransformed). However, if the variances turn out to be unequal, as they did in our example, you can use the same dialog box (Figure 5.13) but select Transformed. When you do this you should notice a drop-down list that becomes active and if you click on this you'll notice that it lists several transformations including the ones that I have just described. If you select a transformation from this list (*Natural log* perhaps or *Square root*) then SPSS will calculate what Levene's test would be if you were to transform the data using this method. This can save you a lot of time trying out different transformations.

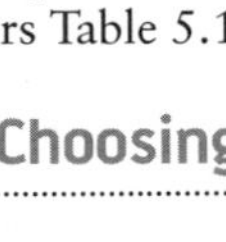

SELF-TEST Use the explore command to see what effect a natural log transformation would have on the four variables measured in **SPSSExam.sav** (section 5.6.1).

[4] Although there aren't statistical consequences of transforming data, there may be empirical or scientific implications that outweigh the statistical benefits (see Jane Superbrain Box 5.1).

[5] You'll notice in this section that I keep writing X_i. We saw in Chapter 1 that this refers to the observed score for the *i*th person (so, the *i* could be replaced with the name of a particular person, thus for Graham, $X_i = X_{Graham}$ = Graham's score, and for Carol, $X_i = X_{Carol}$ = Carol's score).

TABLE 5.1 Data transformations and their uses

Data Transformation	Can Correct For
Log transformation ($\log(X_i)$): Taking the logarithm of a set of numbers squashes the right tail of the distribution. As such it's a good way to reduce positive skew. However, you can't get a log value of zero or negative numbers, so if your data tend to zero or produce negative numbers you need to add a constant to all of the data before you do the transformation. For example, if you have zeros in the data then do $\log(X_i + 1)$, or if you have negative numbers add whatever value makes the smallest number in the data set positive.	Positive skew, unequal variances
Square root transformation ($\sqrt{X_i}$): Taking the square root of large values has more of an effect than taking the square root of small values. Consequently, taking the square root of each of your scores will bring any large scores closer to the centre – rather like the log transformation. As such, this can be a useful way to reduce positive skew; however, you still have the same problem with negative numbers (negative numbers don't have a square root).	Positive skew, unequal variances
Reciprocal transformation ($1/X_i$): Dividing 1 by each score also reduces the impact of large scores. The transformed variable will have a lower limit of 0 (very large numbers will become close to 0). One thing to bear in mind with this transformation is that it reverses the scores: scores that were originally large in the data set become small (close to zero) after the transformation, but scores that were originally small become big after the transformation. For example, imagine two scores of 1 and 10; after the transformation they become 1/1 = 1, and 1/10 = 0.1: the small score becomes bigger than the large score after the transformation. However, you can avoid this by reversing the scores before the transformation, by finding the highest score and changing each score to the highest score minus the score you're looking at. So, you do a transformation $1/(X_{Highest} - X_i)$.	Positive skew, unequal variances
Reverse score transformations: Any one of the above transformations can be used to correct negatively skewed data, but first you have to reverse the scores. To do this, subtract each score from the highest score obtained, or the highest score + 1 (depending on whether you want your lowest score to be 0 or 1). If you do this, don't forget to reverse the scores back afterwards, or to remember that the interpretation of the variable is reversed: big scores have become small and small scores have become big!	Negative skew

JANE SUPERBRAIN 5.1

To transform or not to transform, that is the question ③

Not everyone agrees that transforming data is a good idea; for example, Glass, Peckham, and Sanders (1972) in a very extensive review commented that 'the payoff of normalizing transformations in terms of more valid probability statements is low, and they are seldom considered to be worth the effort' (p. 241). In which case, should we bother?

The issue is quite complicated (especially for this early in the book), but essentially we need to know whether the statistical models we apply perform better on transformed data than they do when applied to data that violate the assumption that the transformation corrects. If a statistical model is still accurate even when its assumptions are broken it is said to be a **robust test** (section 5.7.4). I'm not going to discuss whether particular tests are robust here, but I will discuss the issue for particular tests in their respective chapters. The question of whether to transform is linked to this issue of robustness (which in turn is linked to what test you are performing on your data).

A good case in point is the *F*-test in ANOVA (see Chapter 10), which is often claimed to be robust (Glass et al., 1972). Early findings suggested that *F* performed as it should in skewed distributions and that transforming the data helped as often as it hindered the accuracy of *F* (Games & Lucas, 1966). However, in a lively but informative exchange Levine and Dunlap (1982) showed that transformations of skew did improve the performance of *F*; however, in a response Games (1983) argued that their conclusion was incorrect, which Levine and Dunlap (1983) contested in a response to the response. Finally, in a response to the response of the response, Games (1984) pointed out several important questions to consider:

1. The central limit theorem (section 2.5.1) tells us that in big samples the sampling distribution will be normal regardless, and this is what's actually important so the debate is academic in anything other than small samples. Lots of early research did indeed show that with samples of 40 the normality of the sampling distribution was, as predicted, normal. However, this research focused on distributions with light tails and subsequent work has shown that with heavy-tailed distributions larger samples would be necessary to invoke the central limit theorem (Wilcox, 2005). This research suggests that transformations might be useful for such distributions.
2. By transforming the data you change the hypothesis being tested (when using a log transformation and comparing means you change from comparing arithmetic means to comparing geometric means). Transformation also means that you're now addressing a different construct to the one originally measured, and this has obvious implications for interpreting that data (Grayson, 2004).
3. In small samples it is tricky to determine normality one way or another (tests such as K–S will have low power to detect deviations from normality and graphs will be hard to interpret with so few data points).
4. The consequences for the statistical model of applying the 'wrong' transformation could be worse than the consequences of analysing the untransformed scores.

As we will see later in the book, there is an extensive library of robust tests that can be used and which have considerable benefits over transforming data. The definitive guide to these is Wilcox's (2005) outstanding book.

5.7.3. Transforming the data using SPSS ②

5.7.3.1. The *Compute* function ②

To do transformations on SPSS we use the *compute* command, which enables us to carry out various functions on columns of data in the data editor. Some typical functions are adding scores across several columns, taking the square root of the scores in a column or calculating the mean of several variables. To access the *Compute Variable* dialog box, use the mouse to specify Transform ▸ Compute Variable... The resulting dialog box is shown in Figure 5.14; it has a list of functions on the right-hand side, a calculator-like keyboard in the centre and a blank space that I've labelled the command area. The basic idea is that you type a name for a new variable in the area labelled *Target Variable* and then you write some kind of command in the command area to tell SPSS how to create this new variable. You use a combination of existing variables selected from the list on the left, and numeric expressions. So, for example, you could use it like a calculator to add variables (i.e. add two columns in the data editor to make a third). However, you can also use it to generate data without using existing variables too. There are hundreds of built-in functions that SPSS has grouped together. In the dialog box it lists these groups in the area labelled *Function group*; upon selecting a function group, a list of available functions within that group will appear in the box labelled *Functions and Special Variables*. If you select a function, then a description of that function appears in the grey box indicated in Figure 5.14. You can enter variable names into the command area by selecting the variable required from the variables list and then clicking on ➡. Likewise, you can select a certain function from the list of available functions and enter it into the command area by clicking on ⬆.

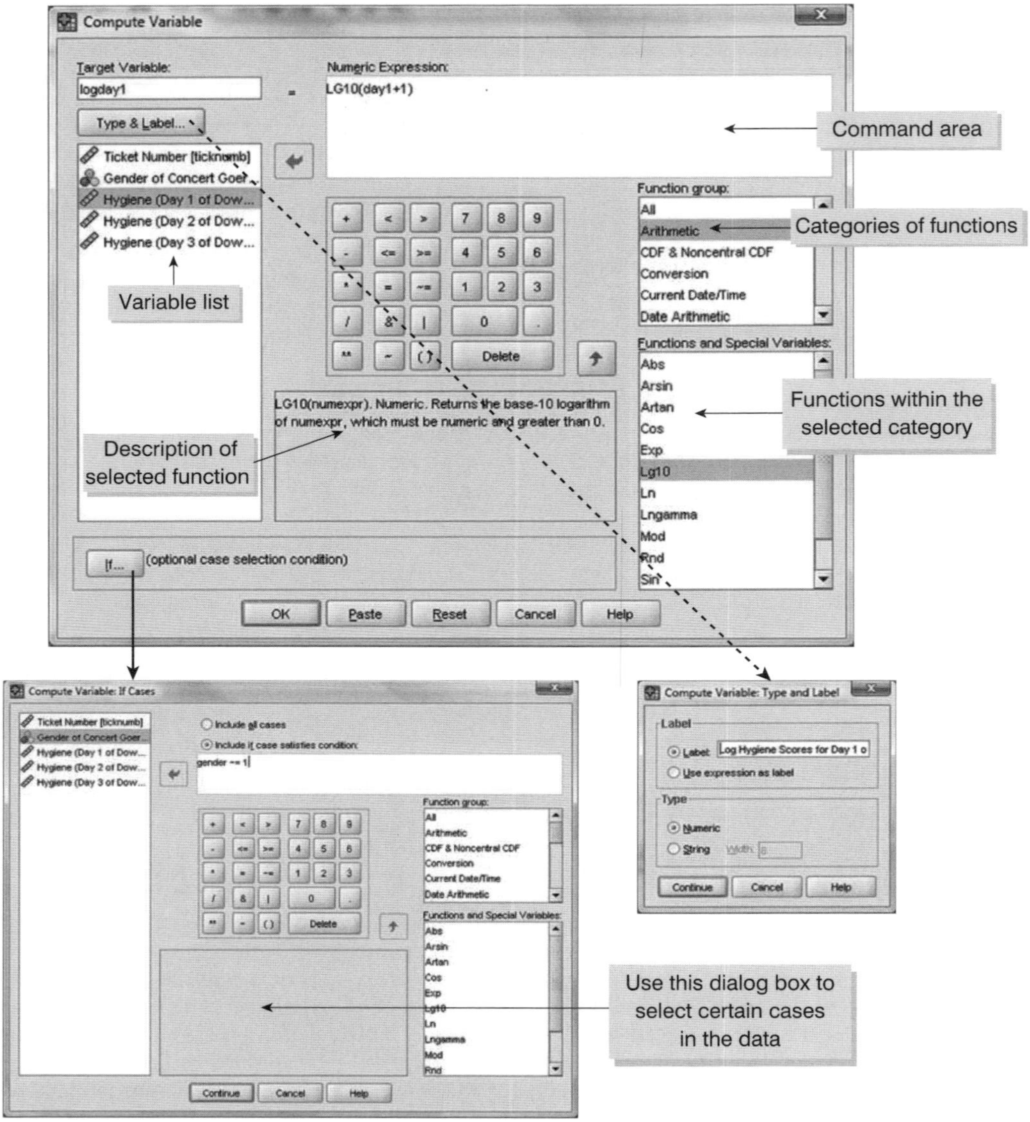

FIGURE 5.14 Dialog box for the *compute* function

The basic procedure is to first type a variable name in the box labelled *Target Variable*. You can then click on Type & Label... and another dialog box appears, where you can give the variable a descriptive label, and where you can specify whether it is a numeric or string variable (see section 3.4.2). Then when you have written your command for SPSS to execute, click on OK to run the command and create the new variable. If you type in a variable name that already exists in the data editor then SPSS will tell you and ask you whether you want to replace this existing variable. If you respond with *Yes* then SPSS will replace the data in the existing column with the result of the *compute* function; if you respond with *No* then nothing will happen and you will need to rename the target variable. If you're computing a lot of new variables it can be quicker to use syntax (see SPSS Tip 5.1).

+	**Addition**: This button places a plus sign in the command area. For example, with our hygiene data, 'day1 + day2' creates a column in which each row contains the hygiene score from the column labelled *day1* added to the score from the column labelled *day2* (e.g. for participant 1: 2.65 + 1.35 = 4).
-	**Subtraction**: This button places a minus sign in the command area. For example, if we wanted to calculate the change in hygiene from day 1 to day 2 we could type 'day2 – day1'. This creates a column in which each row contains the score from the column labelled *day1* subtracted from the score from the column labelled *day2* (e.g. for participant 1: 2.65 – 1.35 = –1.30). Therefore, this person's hygiene went down by 1.30 (on our 5-point scale) from day 1 to day 2 of the festival.
*	**Multiply**: This button places a multiplication sign in the command area. For example, 'day1 * day2' creates a column that contains the score from the column labelled *day1* multiplied by the score from the column labelled *day2* (e.g. for participant 1: 2.65 × 1.35 = 3.58).
/	**Divide**: This button places a division sign in the command area. For example, 'day1/day2' creates a column that contains the score from the column labelled *day1* divided by the score from the column labelled *day2* (e.g. for participant 1: 2.65/1.35 = 1.96).
**	**Exponentiation**: This button is used to raise the preceding term by the power of the succeeding term. So, 'day1**2' creates a column that contains the scores in the *day1* column raised to the power of 2 (i.e. the square of each number in the *day1* column: for participant 1, $(2.65)^2 = 7.02$). Likewise, 'day1**3' creates a column with values of **day1** cubed.
<	**Less than**: This operation is usually used for 'include case' functions. If you click on the If... button, a dialog box appears that allows you to select certain cases on which to carry out the operation. So, if you typed 'day1 < 1', then SPSS would carry out the *compute* function only for those participants whose hygiene score on day 1 of the festival was less than 1 (i.e. if **day1** was 0.99 or less). So, we might use this if we wanted to look only at the people who were already smelly on the first day of the festival!
<=	**Less than or equal to**: This operation is the same as above except that in the example above, cases that are exactly 1 would be included as well.
>	**More than**: This operation is used to include cases above a certain value. So, if you clicked on If... and then typed 'day1 > 1' then SPSS will carry out any analysis only on cases for which hygiene scores on day 1 of the festival were greater than 1 (i.e. 1.01 and above). This could be used to exclude people who were already smelly at the start of the festival. We might want to exclude them because these people will contaminate the data (not to mention our nostrils) because they reek of putrefaction to begin with so the festival cannot further affect their hygiene!
>=	**More than or equal to**: This operation is the same as above but will include cases that are exactly 1 as well.
=	**Equal to**: You can use this operation to include cases for which participants have a specific value. So, if you clicked on If... and typed 'day1 = 1' then only cases that have a value of exactly 1 for the **day1** variable are included. This is most useful when you have a coding variable and you want to look at only one of the groups. For example, if we wanted to look only at females at the festival we could type 'gender = 1', then the analysis would be carried out on only females (who are coded as 1 in the data).
~=	**Not equal to**: This operation will include all cases except those with a specific value. So, 'gender ~= 1' (as in Figure 5.14) will include all cases except those that were female (have a 1 in the gender column). In other words, it will carry out the *compute* command only on the males.

TABLE 5.2 Some useful compute functions

Function	Name	Example Input	Output
MEAN(?,?, ..)	Mean	Mean(day1, day2, day3)	For each row, SPSS calculates the average hygiene score across the three days of the festival
SD(?,?, ..)	Standard deviation	SD(day1, day2, day3)	Across each row, SPSS calculates the standard deviation of the values in the columns labelled *day1*, *day2* and *day3*
SUM(?,?, ..)	Sum	SUM(day1, day2)	For each row, SPSS adds the values in the columns labelled *day1* and *day2*
SQRT(?)	Square root	SQRT(day2)	Produces a column containing the square root of each value in the column labelled *day2*
ABS(?)	Absolute value	ABS(day1)	Produces a variable that contains the absolute value of the values in the column labelled *day1* (absolute values are ones where the signs are ignored: so –5 becomes +5 and +5 stays as +5)
LG10(?)	Base 10 logarithm	LG10(day1)	Produces a variable that contains the logarithmic (to base 10) values of the variable *day1*
RV.NORMAL (mean, stddev)	Normal random numbers	Normal(20, 5)	Produces a variable of pseudo-random numbers from a normal distribution with a mean of 20 and a standard deviation of 5

Some of the most useful functions are listed in Table 5.2, which shows the standard form of the function, the name of the function, an example of how the function can be used and what SPSS would output if that example were used. There are several basic functions for calculating means, standard deviations and sums of columns. There are also functions such as the square root and logarithm that are useful for transforming data that are skewed and we will use these functions now. For the interested reader, the SPSS help files have details of all of the functions available through the *Compute Variable* dialog box (click on Help when you're in the dialog box).

5.7.3.2. The log transformation on SPSS ②

Now we've found out some basic information about the *compute* function, let's use it to transform our data. First open the main Compute dialog box by selecting Transform Compute Variable.... Enter the name **logday1** into the box labelled *Target Variable* and then click on Type & Label... and give the variable a more descriptive name such as *Log transformed hygiene scores for day 1 of Download festival*. In the list box labelled *Function group* click on *Arithmetic* and then in the box labelled *Functions and Special Variables* click on *Lg10* (this is the log transformation to base 10, *Ln* is the natural log) and transfer it to the command area by clicking on ↑. When the command is transferred, it appears in the command area as 'LG10(?)' and the question mark should be replaced with a variable name (which can be typed manually or transferred from the variables list). So replace the question mark with the variable **day1** by either selecting the variable in the list and dragging it across, clicking on →, or just typing 'day1' where the question mark is.

For the day 2 hygiene scores there is a value of 0 in the original data, and there is no logarithm of the value 0. To overcome this we should add a constant to our original scores before we take the log of those scores. Any constant will do, provided that it makes all of the scores greater than 0. In this case our lowest score is 0 in the data set so we can simply add 1 to all of the scores and that will ensure that all scores are greater than zero. To do this, make sure the cursor is still inside the brackets and click on + and then 1. The final dialog box should look like Figure 5.14. Note that the expression reads LG10(day1 + 1); that is, SPSS will add one to each of the day1 scores and then take the log of the resulting values. Click on OK to create a new variable **logday1** containing the transformed values.

SELF-TEST Have a go at creating similar variables **logday2** and **logday3** for the day 2 and day 3 data. Plot histograms of the transformed scores for all three days.

5.7.3.3. The square root transformation on SPSS ②

To do a square root transformation, we run through the same process, by using a name such as **sqrtday1** in the box labelled *Target Variable* (and click on Type & Label... to give the variable a more descriptive name). In the list box labelled *Function group* click on *Arithmetic* and then in the box labelled *Functions and Special Variables* click on *Sqrt* and drag it to the command area or click on ↑. When the command is transferred, it appears in the command area as SQRT(?). Replace the question mark with the variable **day1** by selecting the variable in the list and dragging it, clicking on →, or just typing 'day1' where the question mark is. The final expression will read *SQRT(day1)*. Click on OK to create the variable.

SELF-TEST Repeat this process for **day2** and **day3** to create variables called **sqrtday2** and **sqrtday3**. Plot histograms of the transformed scores for all three days.

5.7.3.4. The reciprocal transformation on SPSS ②

To do a reciprocal transformation on the data from day 1, we could use a name such as **recday1** in the box labelled *Target Variable*. Then we can simply click on 1 and then /. Ordinarily you would select the variable name that you want to transform from the list and drag it across, click on → or just type the name of the variable. However, the day 2 data contain a zero value and if we try to divide 1 by 0 then we'll get an error message (you can't divide by 0). As such we need to add a constant to our variable just as we did for the log transformation. Any constant will do, but 1 is a convenient number for these data. So, instead of selecting the variable we want to transform, click on (). This places a pair of brackets into the box labelled *Numeric Expression*; then make sure the cursor is between these two brackets and select the variable you want to transform from the list and transfer it across by clicking on → (or type the name of the variable manually). Now click on + and then 1 (or type + 1 using your keyboard). The box labelled *Numeric Expression* should now contain the text *1/(day1 + 1)*. Click on OK to create a new variable containing the transformed values.

SELF-TEST Repeat this process for **day2** and **day3**. Plot histograms of the transformed scores for all three days..

SPSS TIP 5.1 Using syntax to compute new variables ③

If you're computing a lot of new variables it can be quicker to use syntax. For example, to create the transformed data in the example in this chapter. I've written the file **Transformations.sps** to do all nine of the transformations we've discussed in this section. Download this file from the companion website and open it. Alternatively, open a syntax window (see section 3.7) and type the following:

```
COMPUTE logday1 = LG10(day1 + 1) .
COMPUTE logday2 = LG10(day2 + 1) .
COMPUTE logday3 = LG10(day3 + 1) .
COMPUTE sqrtday1 = SQRT(day1).
COMPUTE sqrtday2 = SQRT(day2).
COMPUTE sqrtday3 = SQRT(day3).
COMPUTE recday1 = 1/(day1+1).
COMPUTE recday2 = 1/(day2+1).
COMPUTE recday3 = 1/(day3+1).
EXECUTE .
```

Each COMPUTE command above is doing the equivalent of what you'd do using the *Compute Variable* dialog box in Figure 5.14. So, the first three lines just ask SPSS to create three new variables (**logday1**, **logday2** and **logday3**), which are just the log transformations of the variables **day1**, **day2** and **day3** plus 1. The next three lines do much the same but use the SQRT function, and so take the square root of **day1**, **day2** and **day3** to create new variables called **sqrtday1**, **sqrtday2** and **sqrtday3** respectively. The next three lines do the reciprocal transformations in much the same way. The final line has the command EXECUTE without which none of the COMPUTE commands beforehand will be executed! Note also that every line ends with a full stop.

5.7.3.5. The effect of transformations ②

Figure 5.15 shows the distributions for days 1 and 2 of the festival after the three different transformations. Compare these to the untransformed distributions in Figure 5.3. Now, you can see that all three transformations have cleaned up the hygiene scores for day 2: the positive skew is reduced (the square root transformation in particular has been useful). However, because our hygiene scores on day 1 were more or less symmetrical to begin with, they have now become slightly negatively skewed for the log and square root transformation, and positively skewed for the reciprocal transformation![6] If we're using scores from day 2 alone then we could use the transformed scores; however, if we wanted to look at the change in scores then we'd have to weigh up whether the benefits of the transformation for the day 2 scores outweigh the problems it creates in the day 1 scores – data analysis can be frustrating sometimes!

[6] The reversal of the skew for the reciprocal transformation is because, as I mentioned earlier, the reciprocal has the effect of reversing the scores.

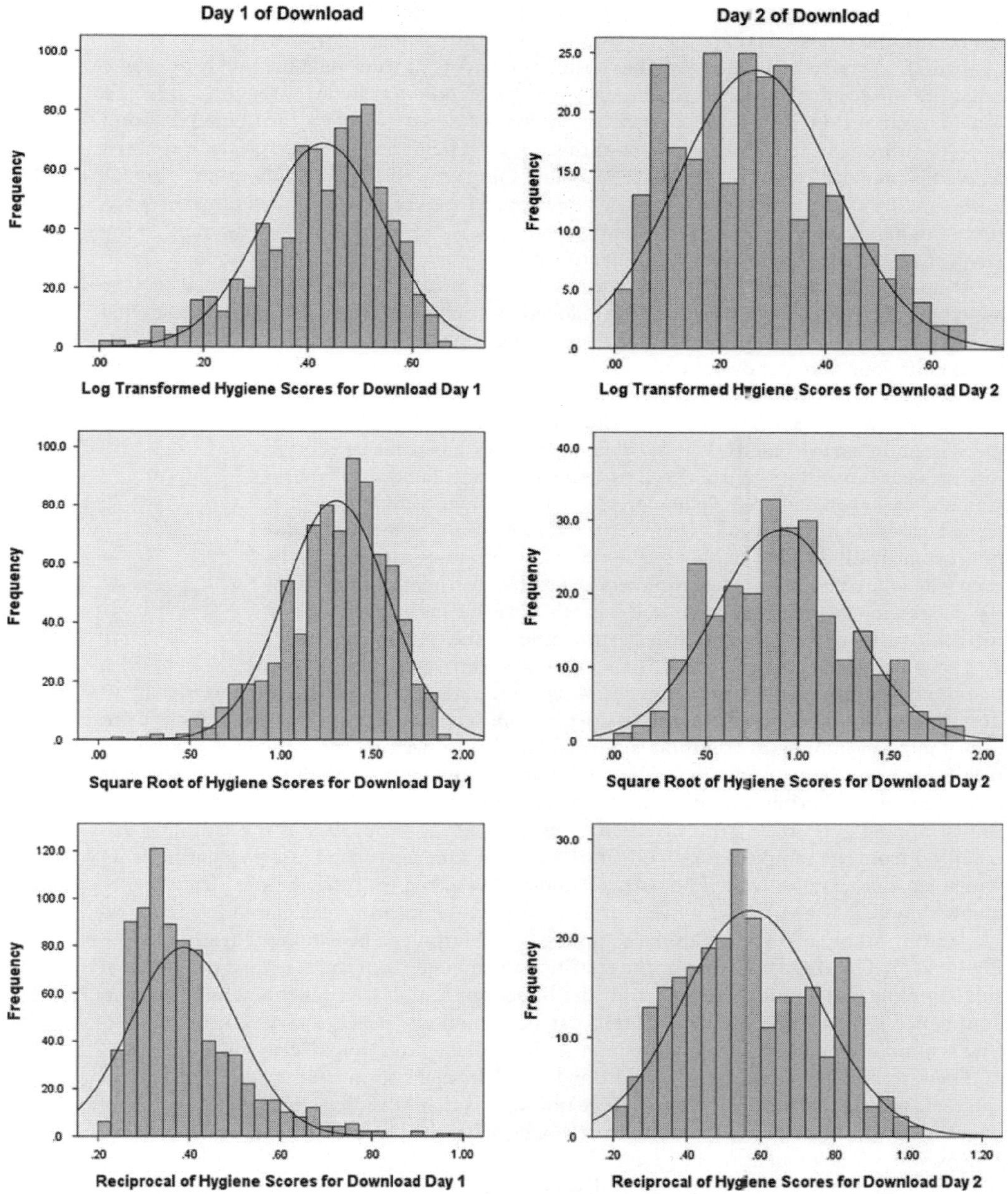

FIGURE 5.15 Distributions of the hygiene data on day 1 and day 2 after various transformations

5.7.4. When it all goes horribly wrong ③

It's very easy to think that transformations are the answers to all of your broken assumption prayers. However, as we have seen, there are reasons to think that transformations are not necessarily a good idea (see Jane Superbrain Box 5.1) and even if you think that they are they do not always solve the problem, and even when they do solve the problem they often create different problems in the process. This happens more frequently than you might imagine (messy data are the norm).

If you find yourself in the unenviable position of having irksome data then there are some other options available to you (other than sticking a big samurai sword through your head). The first is to use a test that does not rely on the assumption of normally distributed data and as you go through the various chapters of this book I'll point out these tests – there is also a whole chapter dedicated to them later on.[7] One thing that you will quickly discover about non-parametric tests is that they have been developed for only a fairly limited range of situations. So, happy days if you want to compare two means, but sad lonely days listening to Joy Division if you have a complex experimental design.

A much more promising approach is to use robust methods (which I mentioned in Jane Superbrain Box 5.1). These tests have developed as computers have got more sophisticated (doing these tests without computers would be only marginally less painful than ripping off your skin and diving into a bath of salt). How these tests work is beyond the scope of this book (and my brain) but two simple concepts will give you the general idea. Some of these procedures use a **trimmed mean**. A trimmed mean is simply a mean based on the distribution of scores after some percentage of scores has been removed from each extreme of the distribution. So, a 10% trimmed mean will remove 10% of scores from the top and bottom before the mean is calculated. We saw in Chapter 2 that the accuracy of the mean depends on a symmetrical distribution, but a trimmed mean produces accurate results even when the distribution is not symmetrical, because by trimming the ends of the distribution we remove outliers and skew that bias the mean. Some robust methods work by taking advantage of the properties of the trimmed mean.

The second general procedure is the **bootstrap** (Efron & Tibshirani, 1993). The idea of the bootstrap is really very simple and elegant. The problem that we have is that we don't know the shape of the sampling distribution, but normality in our data allows us to infer that the sampling distribution is normal (and hence we can know the probability of a particular test statistic occurring). Lack of normality prevents us from knowing the shape of the sampling distribution unless we have big samples (but see Jane Superbrain Box 5.1). Bootstrapping gets around this problem by estimating the properties of the sampling distribution from the sample data. In effect, the sample data are treated as a population from which smaller samples (called bootstrap samples) are taken (putting the data back before a new sample is drawn). The statistic of interest (e.g. the mean) is calculated in each sample, and by taking many samples the sampling distribution can be estimated (rather like in Figure 2.7). The standard error of the statistic is estimated from the standard deviation of this sampling distribution created from the bootstrap samples. From this standard error, confidence intervals and significance tests can be computed. This is a very neat way of getting around the problem of not knowing the shape of the sampling distribution.

These techniques sound pretty good don't they? It might seem a little strange then that I haven't written a chapter on them. The reason why is that SPSS does not do most of them, which is something that I hope it will correct sooner rather than later. However, thanks to Rand Wilcox you can do them using a free statistics program called R (www.r-project.org) and a non-free program called S-Plus. Wilcox provides a very comprehensive review of robust methods in his excellent book *Introduction to robust estimation and hypothesis testing* (2005) and has written programs to run these methods using R. Among many other things, he has files to run robust versions of many tests discussed in this book: ANOVA, ANCOVA, correlation and multiple regression. If there is a robust method, it is likely to be in his book, and he will have written a macro procedure to run it! You can also download these macros from his website.[8] There are

[7] For convenience a lot of textbooks refer to these tests as *non-parametric tests* or *assumption-free* tests and stick them in a separate chapter. Actually neither of these terms are particularly accurate (e.g. none of these tests is assumption-free) but in keeping with tradition I've put them in a chapter (15) on their own ostracized from their 'parametric' counterparts and feeling lonely.

[8] www.usc.edu/schools/college/psyc/people/faculty1003819.html

several good introductory books to tell you how to use R also (e.g. Dalgaard, 2002). There is also an SPSS plugin that you can download (http://www.spss.com/devcentral/index.cfm?pg=plugins) that allows you to use R commands from the SPSS syntax window. With this plugin you can analyse an open SPSS data file using the robust methods of R. These analyses are quite technical so I don't discuss them in the book, but if you'd like to know more see Oliver Twisted.

OLIVER TWISTED

Please, Sir, can I have some more … R?

'Why is it called R?', cackles Oliver 'Is it because using it makes you shout Arrghhh!!?' No, Oliver, it's not. The R plugin is a useful tool but it's very advanced. However, I've prepared a flash movie on the companion website that shows you how to use it. Look out for some other R-related demos on there too.

What have I discovered about statistics? ①

'You promised us swans,' I hear you cry, 'and all we got was normality this, homosomethingorother that, transform this – it's all a waste of time that. Where were the bloody swans?!' Well, the Queen owns them all so I wasn't allowed to have them. Nevertheless, this chapter did negotiate Dante's eighth circle of hell (Malebolge), where data of deliberate and knowing evil dwell. That is, data that don't conform to all of those pesky assumptions that make statistical tests work properly. We began by seeing what assumptions need to be met for parametric tests to work, but we mainly focused on the assumptions of normality and homogeneity of variance. To look for normality we rediscovered the joys of frequency distributions, but also encountered some other graphs that tell us about deviations from normality (P–P and Q–Q plots). We saw how we can use skew and kurtosis values to assess normality and that there are statistical tests that we can use (the Kolmogorov–Smirnov test). While negotiating these evildoers, we discovered what homogeneity of variance is, and how to test it with Levene's test and Hartley's F_{Max}. Finally, we discovered redemption for our data. We saw we can cure their sins, make them good, with transformations (and on the way we discovered some of the uses of the *transform* function of SPSS and the *split-file* command). Sadly, we also saw that some data are destined to always be evil.

We also discovered that I had started to read. However, reading was not my true passion; it was music. One of my earliest memories is of listening to my dad's rock and soul records (back in the days of vinyl) while waiting for my older brother to come home from school, so I must have been about 3 at the time. The first record I asked my parents to buy me was 'Take on the world' by Judas Priest which I'd heard on *Top of the Pops* (a now defunct UK TV show) and liked. This record came out in 1978 when I was 5. Some people think that this sort of music corrupts young minds. Let's see if it did …

Key terms that I've discovered

Bootstrap
Hartley's F_{Max}
Homogeneity of variance
Independence
Kolmogorov–Smirnov test
Levene's test
Noniles
Normally distributed data
Parametric test
Percentiles
P–P plot
Q–Q plot
Quantiles
Robust test
Shapiro–Wilk test
Transformation
Trimmed mean
Variance ratio

Smart Alex's tasks

- **Task 1**: Using the **ChickFlick.sav** data from Chapter 4, check the assumptions of normality and homogeneity of variance for the two films (ignore gender): are the assumptions met? ①
- **Task 2**: Remember that the numeracy scores were positively skewed in the **SPSSExam.sav** data (see Figure 5.5)? Transform these data using one of the transformations described in this chapter: do the data become normal? ②

Answers can be found on the companion website.

Online tutorial

The companion website contains the following Flash movie tutorial to accompany this chapter:

- Using the compute command to transform variables

Further reading

Tabachnick, B. G., & Fidell, L. S. (2006). *Using multivariate statistics* (5th ed.). Boston: Allyn & Bacon. (Chapter 4 is the definitive guide to screening data!)
Wilcox, R. R. (2005). *Introduction to robust estimation and hypothesis testing* (2nd ed.). Burlington, MA: Elsevier. (Quite technical, but this is the definitive book on robust methods.)

20 Comparing Two Means

ANDY FIELD

FIGURE 9.1 My (probably) 8th birthday. L–R: My brother Paul (who still hides behind cakes rather than have his photo taken), Paul Spreckley, Alan Palsey, Clair Sparks and me

9.1. What will this chapter tell me? ①

Having successfully slayed audiences at holiday camps around the country, my next step towards global domination was my primary school. I had learnt another Chuck Berry song ('Johnny B. Goode'), but also broadened my repertoire to include songs by other artists (I have a feeling 'Over the edge' by Status Quo was one of them).[1] Needless to say, when the opportunity came to play at a school assembly I jumped at it. The headmaster tried to have me banned,[2] but the show went on. It was a huge success (I want to reiterate my

[1] This would have been about 1982, so just before they became the most laughably bad band on the planet. Some would argue that they were *always* the most laughably bad band on the planet, but they were the first band that I called my favourite band.

[2] Seriously! Can you imagine, a headmaster banning a 10 year old from assembly? By this time I had an electric guitar and he used to play hymns on an acoustic guitar; I can assume only that he somehow lost all perspective on the situation and decided that a 10 year old blasting out some Quo in a squeaky little voice was subversive or something.

earlier point that 10 year olds are very easily impressed). My classmates carried me around the playground on their shoulders. I was a hero. Around this time I had a childhood sweetheart called Clair Sparks. Actually, we had been sweethearts since before my new-found rock legend status. I don't think the guitar playing and singing impressed her much, but she rode a motorbike (really, a little child's one) which impressed *me* quite a lot; I was utterly convinced that we would one day get married and live happily ever after. I was utterly convinced, that is, until she ran off with Simon Hudson. Being 10, she probably literally did run off with him – across the playground. To make this important decision of which boyfriend to have, Clair had needed to compare two things (Andy and Simon) to see which one was better; sometimes in science we want to do the same thing, to compare two things to see if there is evidence that one is different to the other. This chapter is about the process of comparing two means using a *t*-test.

9.2. Looking at differences ①

Rather than looking at relationships between variables, researchers are sometimes interested in looking at differences between groups of people. In particular, in experimental research we often want to manipulate what happens to people so that we can make causal inferences. For example, if we take two groups of people and randomly assign one group a programme of dieting pills and the other group a programme of sugar pills (which they think will help them lose weight) then if the people who take the dieting pills lose more weight than those on the sugar pills we can infer that the diet pills caused the weight loss. This is a powerful research tool because it goes one step beyond merely observing variables and looking for relationships (as in correlation and regression).[3] This chapter is the first of many that looks at this kind of research scenario, and we start with the simplest scenario: when we have two groups, or, to be more specific, when we want to compare two means. As we have seen (Chapter 1), there are two different ways of collecting data: we can either expose different people to different experimental manipulations (*between-group* or *independent* design), or take a single group of people and expose them to different experimental manipulations at different points in time (a *repeated-measures* design).

9.2.1. A problem with error bar graphs of repeated-measures designs ①

We also saw in Chapter 4 that it is important to visualize group differences using error bars. We're now going to look at a problem that occurs when we graph repeated-measures error bars. To do this, we're going to look at an example that I use throughout this chapter (not because I am too lazy to think up different data sets, but because it allows me to illustrate various things). The example relates to whether arachnophobia (fear of spiders) is specific to real spiders or whether pictures of spiders can evoke similar levels of anxiety. Twenty-four arachnophobes were used in all. Twelve were asked to play with a big hairy tarantula spider with big fangs and an evil look in its eight eyes. Their subsequent anxiety was measured. The remaining twelve were shown only pictures of the same big hairy tarantula and again their anxiety was measured. The data are in Table 9.1 (and **spiderBG.sav** if you're having difficulty entering them into SPSS yourself). Remember that each row in the data editor represents a

[3] People sometimes get confused and think that certain statistical procedures allow causal inferences and others don't (see Jane Superbrain Box 1.4).

TABLE 9.1 Data from **spiderBG.sav**

Participant	*Group*	*Anxiety*
1	0	30
2	0	35
3	0	45
4	0	40
5	0	50
6	0	35
7	0	55
8	0	25
9	0	30
10	0	45
11	0	40
12	0	50
13	1	40
14	1	35
15	1	50
16	1	55
17	1	65
18	1	55
19	1	50
20	1	35
21	1	30
22	1	50
23	1	60
24	1	39

different participant's data. Therefore, you need a column representing the group to which they belonged and a second column representing their anxiety. The data in Table 9.1 show only the group codes and not the corresponding label. When you enter the data into SPSS, remember to tell the computer that a code of 0 represents the group that were shown the picture, and that a code of 1 represents the group that saw the real spider (see section 3.4.2.3).

SELF-TEST Enter these data into SPSS. Using what you learnt in Chapter 4, plot an error bar graph of the spider data.

OK, now let's imagine that we'd collected these data using the *same* participants; that is, all participants had their anxiety rated after seeing the real spider, but also after seeing

TABLE 9.2 Data from **spiderRM.sav**

Subject	Picture (Anxiety score)	Real (Anxiety Score)
1	30	40
2	35	35
3	45	50
4	40	55
5	50	65
6	35	55
7	55	50
8	25	35
9	30	30
10	45	50
11	40	60
12	50	39

the picture (in counterbalanced order obviously!). The data would now be arranged differently in SPSS. Instead of having a coding variable, and a single column with anxiety scores in, we would arrange the data in two columns (one representing the **picture** condition and one representing the **real** condition). The data are displayed in Table 9.2 (and **spiderRM.sav** if you're having difficulty entering them into SPSS yourself). Note that the anxiety scores are identical to the between-group data (Table 9.1) – it's just that we're pretending that they came from the same people rather than different people.

SELF-TEST Enter these data into SPSS. Using what you learnt in Chapter 4, plot an error bar graph of the spider data.

Figure 9.2 shows the error bar graphs from the two different designs. Remember that the data are exactly the same, all that has changed is whether the design used the same participants (repeated measures) or different (independent). Now, we discovered in Chapter 1 that repeated-measures designs eliminate some extraneous variables (such as age, IQ and so on) and so can give us more sensitivity in the data. Therefore, we would expect our graphs to be different: the repeated-measures graph should reflect the increased sensitivity in the design. Looking at the two error bar graphs, can you spot this difference between the graphs?

Hopefully you're answer was 'no' because, of course, the graphs are identical! This similarity reflects the fact that when you create an error bar graph of repeated-measures data, SPSS treats the data as though different groups of participants were used! In other words, the error bars do not reflect the 'true' error around the means for repeated-measures designs. Fortunately we can correct this problem manually, and that's what we will discover now.

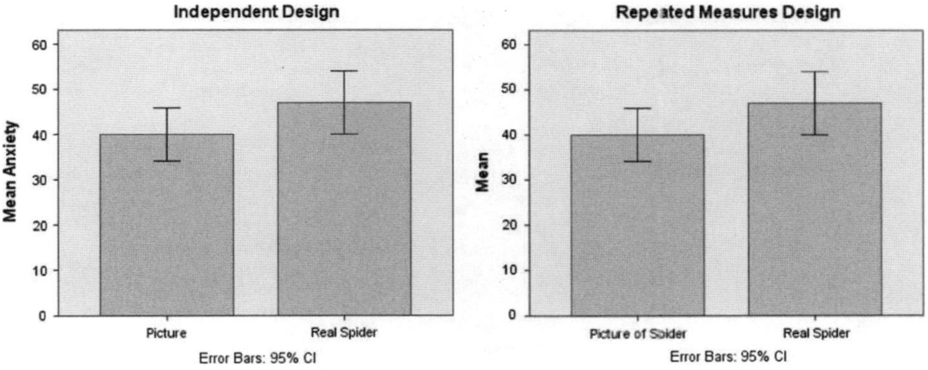

FIGURE 9.2 Two error bar graphs of anxiety data in the presence of a real spider or a photograph. The data on the left are treated as though they are different participants, whereas those on the right are treated as though they are from the same participants

9.2.2. Step 1: calculate the mean for each participant ②

To correct the repeated-measures error bars, we need to use the *compute* command that we encountered in Chapter 5. To begin with, we need to calculate the average anxiety for each participant and so we use the *mean* function. Access the main compute dialog box by selecting Transform Compute Variable.... Enter the name **Mean** into the box labelled *Target Variable* and then in the list labelled *Function group* select *Statistical* and then in the list labelled *Functions and Special Variables* select *Mean*. Transfer this command to the command area by clicking on ↑. When the command is transferred, it appears in the command area as *MEAN(?,?)*; the question marks should be replaced with variable names (which can be typed manually or transferred from the variables list). So replace the first question mark with the variable **picture** and the second one with the variable **real**. The completed dialog box should look like the one in Figure 9.3. Click on OK to create this new variable, which will appear as a new column in the data editor.

9.2.3. Step 2: calculate the grand mean ②

The **grand mean** is the mean of all scores (regardless of which condition the score comes from) and so for the current data this value will be the mean of all 24 scores. One way to calculate this is by hand (i.e. add up all of the scores and divide by 24); however, an easier way is to use the means that we have just calculated. The means we have just calculated represent the average score for each participant and so if we take the average of those mean scores, we will have the mean of all participants (i.e. the grand mean) – phew, there were a lot of means in that sentence! OK, to do this we can use a useful little gadget called the *descriptives* command (you could also use the *Explore* or *Frequencies* functions that we came across in Chapter 5, but as I've already covered those we'll try something different). Access the *descriptives* command by selecting Analyze Descriptive Statistics ▸ Descriptives.... The dialog box in Figure 9.4 should appear. The *descriptives* command is used to get basic descriptive statistics for variables and by clicking on Options... a second dialog box is activated. Select the variable **Mean** from the list and transfer it to the box labelled *Variable(s)* by clicking on ➡. Then, use the options dialog box to specify only the mean (you can leave the default settings as they are, but it is only the mean in which we are interested). If you run this analysis the output should provide you with

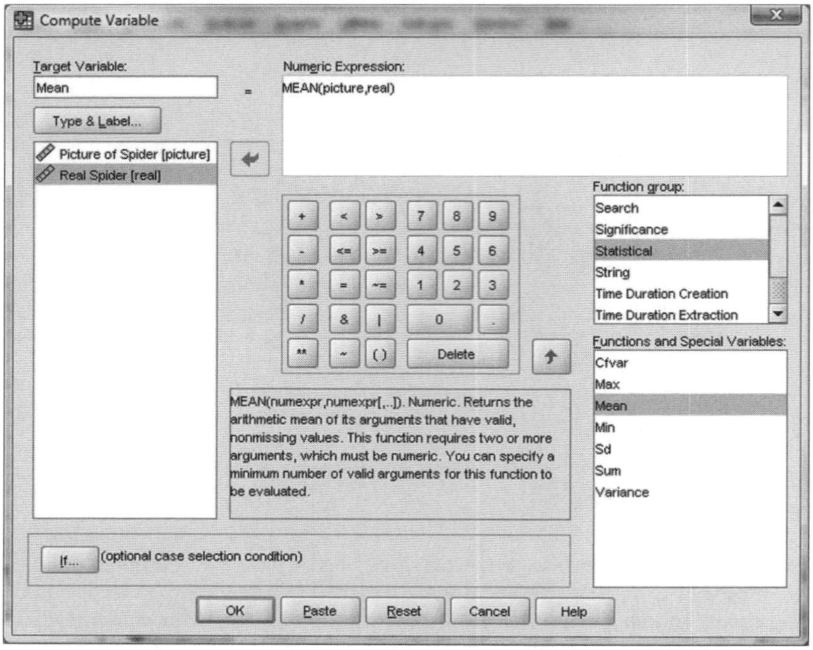

FIGURE 9.3 Using the compute function to calculate the mean of two columns

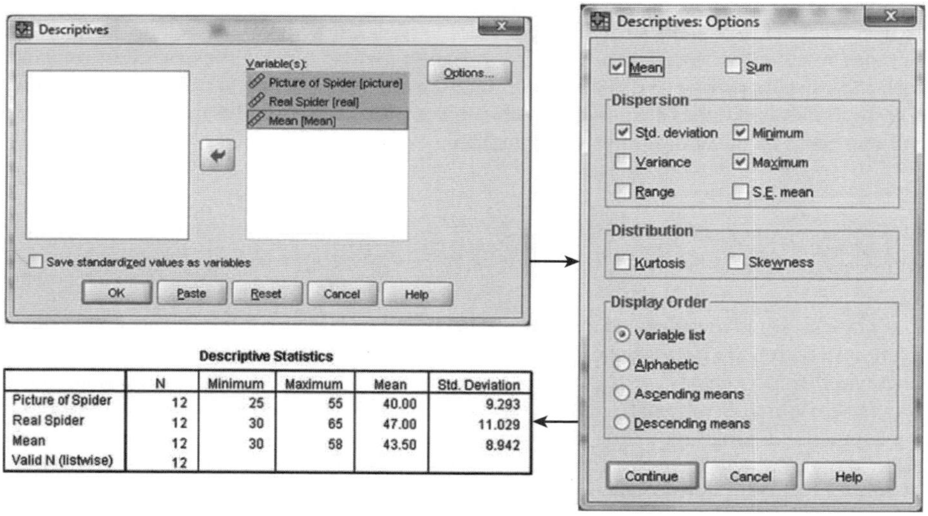

Descriptive Statistics

	N	Minimum	Maximum	Mean	Std. Deviation
Picture of Spider	12	25	55	40.00	9.293
Real Spider	12	30	65	47.00	11.029
Mean	12	30	58	43.50	8.942
Valid N (listwise)	12				

FIGURE 9.4 Dialog boxes and output for descriptive statistics

some self-explanatory descriptive statistics for each of the three variables (assuming you selected all three). You should see that we get the mean of the picture condition, and the mean of the real spider condition, but it's actually the final variable we're interested in: the mean of the picture and spider condition. The mean of this variable is the grand mean, and you can see from the summary table that its value is 43.50. We will use this grand mean in the following calculations.

9.2.4. Step 3: calculate the adjustment factor ②

If you look at the variable labelled **Mean**, you should notice that the values for each participant are different, which tells us that some people had greater anxiety than others did across the conditions. The fact that participants' mean anxiety scores differ represents individual differences between different people (so, it represents the fact that some of the participants are generally more scared of spiders than others). These differences in natural anxiety to spiders contaminate the error bar graphs, which is why if we don't adjust the values that we plot, we will get the same graph as if an independent design had been used. Loftus and Masson (1994) argue that to eliminate this contamination we should equalize the means between participants (i.e. adjust the scores in each condition such that when we take the mean score across conditions, it is the same for all participants). To do this, we need to calculate an adjustment factor by subtracting each participant's mean score from the grand mean. We can use the *compute* function to do this calculation for us. Activate the compute dialog box, give the target variable a name (I suggest **Adjustment**) and then use the command '43.5-mean'. This command will take the grand mean (43.5) and subtract from it each participant's average anxiety level (see Figure 9.5).

This process creates a new variable in the data editor called **Adjustment.** The scores in the column **Adjustment** represent the difference between each participant's mean anxiety and the mean anxiety level across all participants. You'll notice that some of the values are positive and these participants are one's who were less anxious than average. Other participants were more anxious than average and they have negative adjustment scores. We can now use these adjustment values to eliminate the between-subject differences in anxiety.

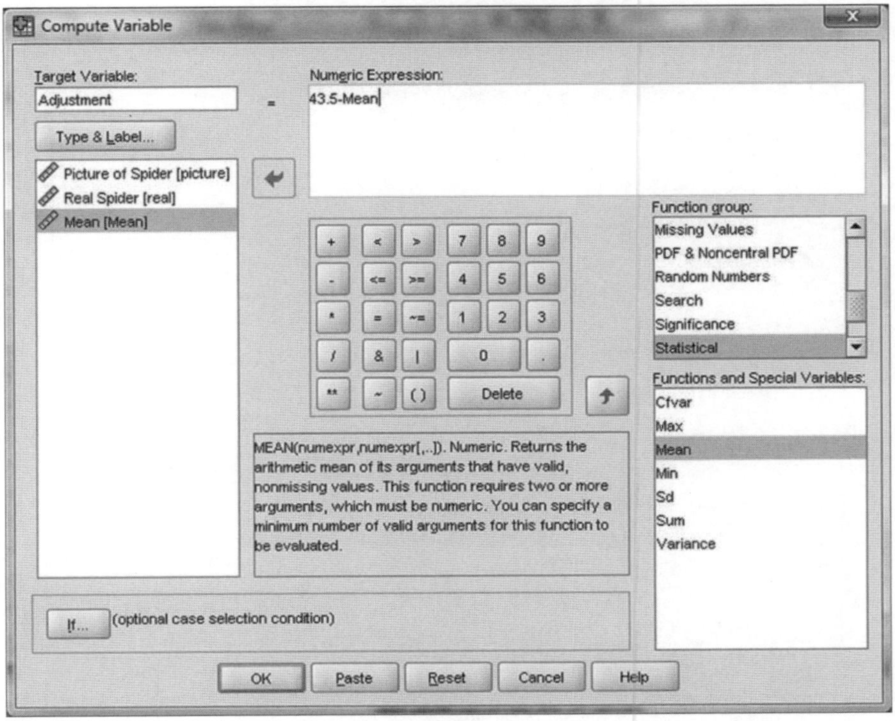

FIGURE 9.5 Calculating the adjustment factor

9.2.5. Step 4: create adjusted values for each variable ②

So far, we have calculated the difference between each participant's mean score and the mean score of all participants (the grand mean). This difference can be used to adjust the existing scores for each participant. First we need to adjust the scores in the **picture** condition. Once again, we can use the *compute* command to make the adjustment. Activate the compute dialog box in the same way as before, and then title our new variable **Picture_Adjusted** (you can then click on Type & Label... and give this variable a label such as 'Picture Condition: Adjusted Values'). All we are going to do is to add each participant's score in the **picture** condition to their adjustment value. Select the variable **picture** and transfer it to the command area by clicking on ➜, then click on + and select the variable **Adjustment** and transfer it to the command area by clicking on ➜. The completed dialog box is shown in Figure 9.6. Now do the same thing for the variable **real**: create a variable called **Real_Adjusted** that contains the values of **real** added to the value in the **Adjustment** column.

Now, the variables **Real_Adjusted** and **Picture_Adjusted** represent the anxiety experienced in each condition, adjusted so as to eliminate any between-subject differences. If you don't believe me, then use the *compute* command to create a variable **Mean2** that is the average of **Real_Adjusted** and **Picture_Adjusted** (just like we did in section 9.2.2). You should find that the value in this column is the same for every participant, thus proving that the between-subject variability in means is gone: the value will be 43.50 (the grand mean).

SELF-TEST Create an error bar chart of the mean of the adjusted values that you have just made (**Real_Adjusted** and **Picture_Adjusted**).

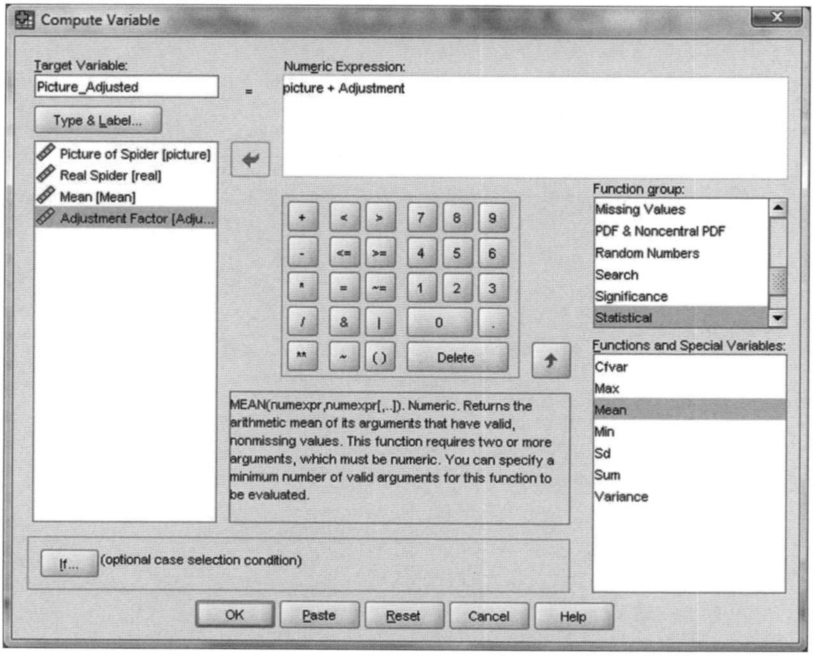

FIGURE 9.6 Adjusting the values of **picture**

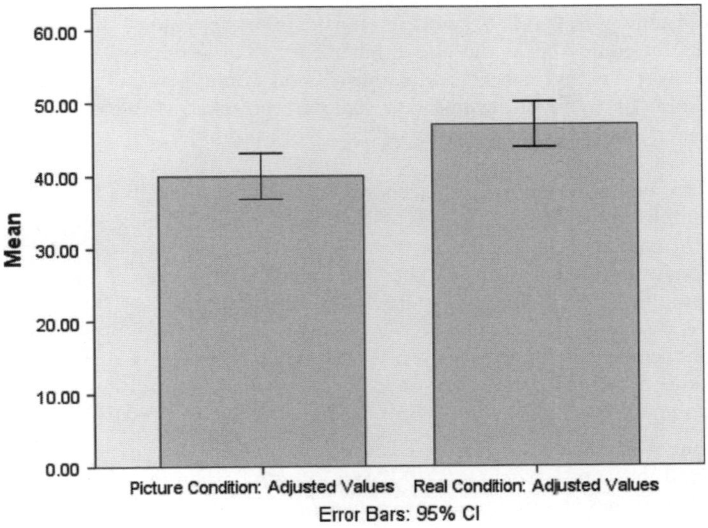

FIGURE 9.7 Error bar graph of the adjusted values of **spiderRM.sav**

The resulting error bar graph is shown in Figure 9.7. Compare this graph to the graphs in Figure 9.2 – what differences do you see? The first thing to notice is that the means in the two conditions have not changed. However, the error bars have changed: they have got smaller. Also, whereas in Figure 9.2 the error bars overlap, in this new graph they do not. In Chapter 2 we discovered that when error bars do not overlap we can be fairly confident that our samples have not come from the same population (and so our experimental manipulation has been successful). Therefore, when we plot the proper error bars for the repeated-measures data it shows the extra sensitivity that this design has: the differences between conditions appear to be significant, whereas when different participants are used, there does not appear to be a significant difference. (Remember that the means in both situations are identical, but the sampling error is smaller in the repeated-measures design.) I expand upon this point in section 9.6.

9.3. The *t*-test ①

We have seen in previous chapters that the *t*-test is a very versatile statistic: it can be used to test whether a correlation coefficient is different from 0; it can also be used to test whether a regression coefficient, *b*, is different from 0. However, it can also be used to test whether two group means are different. It is to this use that we now turn.

The simplest form of experiment that can be done is one with only one independent variable that is manipulated in only two ways and only one outcome is measured. More often than not the manipulation of the independent variable involves having an experimental condition and a control group (see Field & Hole, 2003). Some examples of this kind of design are:

- Is the movie *Scream 2* scarier than the original *Scream*? We could measure heart rates (which indicate anxiety) during both films and compare them.
- Does listening to music while you work improve your work? You could get some people to write an essay (or book!) listening to their favourite music, and then write a different essay when working in silence (this is a control group). You could then compare the essay grades!

- Does listening to Andy's favourite music improve your work? You could repeat the above but rather than letting people work with their favourite music, you could play them some of my favourite music (as listed in the acknowledgements) and watch the quality of their work plummet!

The *t*-test can analyse these sorts of scenarios. Of course, there are more complex experimental designs and we will look at these in subsequent chapters. There are, in fact, two different *t*-tests and the one you use depends on whether the independent variable was manipulated using the same participants or different:

- **Independent-means *t*-test**: This test is used when there are two experimental conditions and different participants were assigned to each condition (this is sometimes called the *independent-measures* or *independent-samples t*-test).
- **Dependent-means *t*-test**: This test is used when there are two experimental conditions and the same participants took part in both conditions of the experiment (this test is sometimes referred to as the *matched-pairs* or *paired-samples t*-test).

9.3.1. Rationale for the *t*-test ①

Both *t*-tests have a similar rationale, which is based on what we learnt in Chapter 2 about hypothesis testing:

- Two samples of data are collected and the sample means calculated. These means might differ by either a little or a lot.
- If the samples come from the same population, then we expect their means to be roughly equal (see section 2.5.1). Although it is possible for their means to differ by chance alone, we would expect large differences between sample means to occur very infrequently. Under the null hypothesis we assume that the experimental manipulation has no effect on the participants: therefore, we expect the sample means to be very similar.
- We compare the difference between the sample means that we collected to the difference between the sample means that we would expect to obtain if there were no effect (i.e. if the null hypothesis were true). We use the standard error (see section 2.5.1) as a gauge of the variability between sample means. If the standard error is small, then we expect most samples to have very similar means. When the standard error is large, large differences in sample means are more likely. If the difference between the samples we have collected is larger than what we would expect based on the standard error then we can assume one of two things:
  - There is no effect and sample means in our population fluctuate a lot and we have, by chance, collected two samples that are atypical of the population from which they came.
  - The two samples come from different populations but are typical of their respective parent population. In this scenario, the difference between samples represents a genuine difference between the samples (and so the null hypothesis is incorrect).
- As the observed difference between the sample means gets larger, the more confident we become that the second explanation is correct (i.e. that the null hypothesis should be rejected). If the null hypothesis is incorrect, then we gain confidence that the two sample means differ because of the different experimental manipulation imposed on each sample.

I mentioned in section 2.6.1 that most test statistics can be thought of as the 'variance explained by the model' divided by the 'variance that the model can't explain'. In other words, effect/error. When comparing two means the 'model' that we fit to the data (the effect) is the difference between the two group means. We saw also in Chapter 2 that means vary from sample to sample (sampling variation) and that we can use the standard error as a measure of how much means fluctuate (in other words, the error in the estimate of the mean). Therefore, we can also use the standard error of the differences between the two means as an estimate of the error in our model (or the error in the difference between means). Therefore, we calculate the *t*-test using equation (9.1) below. The top half of the equation is the 'model' (our model being the difference between means is bigger than the expected difference, which in most cases will be 0 – we expect the difference between means to be different to zero). The bottom half is the 'error'. So, just as I said in Chapter 2, we're basically getting the test statistic by dividing the model (or effect) by the error in the model. The exact form that this equation takes depends on whether the same or different participants were used in each experimental condition:

$$t = \frac{\begin{array}{c}\text{observed difference}\\ \text{between sample means}\end{array} - \begin{array}{c}\text{expected difference}\\ \text{between population means}\\ \text{(if null hypothesis is true)}\end{array}}{\begin{array}{c}\text{estimate of the standard error of the}\\ \text{difference between two sample means}\end{array}} \qquad (9.1)$$

9.3.2. Assumptions of the *t*-test ①

Both the **independent *t*-test** and the **dependent *t*-test** are *parametric tests* based on the normal distribution (see Chapter 5). Therefore, they assume:

- The sampling distribution is normally distributed. In the dependent *t*-test this means that the sampling distribution of the *differences* between scores should be normal, not the scores themselves (see section 9.4.3).
- Data are measured at least at the interval level.

The independent *t*-test, because it is used to test different groups of people, also assumes:

- Variances in these populations are roughly equal (*homogeneity of variance*).
- Scores are independent (because they come from different people).

These assumptions were explained in detail in Chapter 5 and, in that chapter, I emphasized the need to check these assumptions before you reach the point of carrying out your statistical test. As such, I won't go into them again, but it does mean that if you have ignored my advice and haven't checked these assumptions then you need to do it now! SPSS also incorporates some procedures into the *t*-test (e.g. Levene's test, see section 5.6.1, can be done at the same time as the *t*-test). Let's now look at each of the two *t*-tests in turn.

9.4. The dependent *t*-test ①

If we stay with our repeated-measures data for the time being we can look at the dependent *t*-test, or paired-samples *t*-test. The dependent *t*-test is easy to calculate. In effect, we use a numeric version of equation (9.1):

$$t = \frac{\bar{D} - \mu_D}{s_D / \sqrt{N}} \tag{9.2}$$

Equation (9.2) compares the mean difference between our samples ($\bar{D}$) to the difference that we would expect to find between population means (μ_D), and then takes into account the standard error of the differences ($s_D/\sqrt{N}$). If the null hypothesis is true, then we expect there to be no difference between the population means (hence $\mu_D = 0$).

9.4.1. Sampling distributions and the standard error ①

In equation (9.1) I referred to the lower half of the equation as the standard error of differences. The standard error was introduced in section 2.5.1 and is simply the standard deviation of the sampling distribution. Have a look back at this section now to refresh your memory about sampling distributions and the standard error. Sampling distributions have several properties that are important. For one thing, if the population is normally distributed then so is the sampling distribution; in fact, if the samples contain more than about 50 scores the sampling distribution should be normally distributed. The mean of the sampling distribution is equal to the mean of the population, so the average of all possible sample means should be the same as the population mean. This property makes sense because if a sample is representative of the population then you would expect its mean to be equal to that of the population. However, sometimes samples are unrepresentative and their means differ from the population mean. On average, though, a sample mean will be very close to the population mean and only rarely will the sample mean be substantially different from that of the population. A final property of a sampling distribution is that its standard deviation is equal to the standard deviation of the population divided by the square root of the number of observations in the sample. As I mentioned before, this standard deviation is known as the standard error.

We can extend this idea to look at the *differences* between sample means. If you were to take several pairs of samples from a population and calculate their means, then you could also calculate the difference between their means. I mentioned earlier that *on average* sample means will be very similar to the population mean: as such, most samples will have very similar means. Therefore, most of the time the difference between sample means from the same population will be zero, or close to zero. However, sometimes one or both of the samples could have a mean very deviant from the population mean and so it is possible to obtain large differences between sample means by chance alone. However, this would happen less frequently.

In fact, if you plotted these differences between sample means as a histogram, you would again have a sampling distribution with all of the properties previously described. The standard deviation of this sampling distribution is called the **standard error of differences**. A small standard error tells us that most pairs of samples from a population will have very similar means (i.e. the difference between sample means should normally be very small). A large standard error tells us that sample means can deviate quite a lot from the population mean and so differences between pairs of samples can be quite large by chance alone.

9.4.2. The dependent *t*-test equation explained ①

In an experiment, a person's score in condition 1 will be different to their score in condition 2, and this difference could be very large or very small. If we calculate the differences between each person's score in each condition and add up these differences we would get the total amount of difference. If we then divide this total by the number of participants we get the average difference (thus how much, on average, a person's score differed in condition 1 compared to condition 2). This average difference is $\bar{D}$ in equation (9.2) and it is an indicator

of the systematic variation in the data (i.e. it represents the experimental effect). We need to compare this systematic variation against some kind of measure of the 'systematic variation that we could naturally expect to find'. In Chapter 2 we saw that the standard deviation was a measure of the 'fit' of the mean to the observed data (i.e. it measures the error in the model when the model is the mean), but it does not measure the fit of the mean to the population. To do this we need the standard error (see the previous section, where we revised this idea).

The standard error is a measure of the error in the mean as a model of the population. In this context, we know that if we had taken two random samples from a population (and not done anything to these samples) then the means could be different just by chance. The standard error tells us by how much these samples could differ. A small standard error means that sample means should be quite similar, so a big difference between two sample means is unlikely. In contrast, a large standard error tells us that big differences between the means of two random samples are more likely. Therefore it makes sense to compare the average difference between means against the standard error of these differences. This gives us a test statistic that, as I've said numerous times in previous chapters, represents model/error. Our model is the average difference between condition means, and we divide by the standard error which represents the error associated with this model (i.e. how similar two random samples are likely to be from this population).

To clarify, imagine that an alien came down and cloned me millions of times. This population is known as Landy of the Andys (this would be possibly the most dreary and strangely terrifying place I could imagine). Imagine the aliens were interested in spider phobia in this population (because I am petrified of spiders). Everyone in this population (my clones) will be the same as me, and would behave in an identical way to me. If you took two samples from this population and measured their spider fear, then the means of these samples would be the same (we are clones), so the difference between sample means would be zero. Also, because we are all identical, then all samples from the population will be perfect reflections of the population (the standard error would be zero also). Therefore, if we were to get two samples that differed even very slightly then this would be very unlikely indeed (because our population is full of cloned Andys). Therefore, a difference between samples must mean that they have come from different populations. Of course, in reality we don't have samples that perfectly reflect the population, but the standard error gives an idea of how well samples reflect the population from which they came.

Therefore, by dividing by the standard error we are doing two things: (1) standardizing the average difference between conditions (this just means that we can compare values of *t* without having to worry about the scale of measurement used to measure the outcome variable); and (2) contrasting the difference between means that we have against the difference that we could *expect* to get based on how well the samples represent the populations from which they came. If the standard error is large, then large differences between samples are more common (because the distribution of differences is more spread out). Conversely, if the standard error is small, then large differences between sample means are uncommon (because the distribution is very narrow and centred around zero). Therefore, if the average difference between our samples is large, and the standard error of differences is small, then we can be confident that the difference we observed in our sample is not a chance result. If the difference is not a chance result then it must have been caused by the experimental manipulation.

In a perfect world, we could calculate the standard error by taking all possible pairs of samples from a population, calculating the differences between their means, and then working out the standard deviation of these differences. However, in reality this is impossible. Therefore, we estimate the standard error from the standard deviation of differences obtained within the sample (s_D) and the sample size (N). Think back to section 2.5.1 where we saw that the standard error is simply the standard deviation divided by the square root of the sample size; likewise the standard error of differences ($\sigma_{\bar{D}}$) is simply the standard deviation of differences divided by the square root of the sample size:

$$(\sigma_{\overline{D}}) = \frac{s_D}{\sqrt{N}}$$

If the standard error of differences is a measure of the unsystematic variation within the data, and the sum of difference scores represents the systematic variation, then it should be clear that the *t*-statistic is simply the ratio of the systematic variation in the experiment to the unsystematic variation. If the experimental manipulation creates any kind of effect, then we would expect the systematic variation to be much greater than the unsystematic variation (so at the very least, *t* should be greater than 1). If the experimental manipulation is unsuccessful then we might expect the variation caused by individual differences to be much greater than that caused by the experiment (so *t* will be less than 1). We can compare the obtained value of *t* against the maximum value we would expect to get by chance alone in a *t*-distribution with the same degrees of freedom (these values can be found in the Appendix); if the value we obtain exceeds this critical value we can be confident that this reflects an effect of our independent variable.

9.4.3. The dependent *t*-test and the assumption of normality ①

We talked about the assumption of normality in Chapter 5 and discovered that parametric tests (like the dependent *t*-test) assume that the sampling distribution is normal. This should be true in large samples, but in small samples people often check the normality of their data because if the data themselves are normal then the sampling distribution is likley to be also. With the dependent *t*-test we analyse the *differences* between scores because we're interested in the sampling distribution of these differences (not the raw data). Therefore, if you want to test for normality before a dependent *t*-test then what you should do is compute the differences between scores, and then check if this new variable is normally distributed (or use a big sample and not worry about normality!). It is possible to have two measures that are highly non-normal that produce beautifully distributed differences!

SELF-TEST Using the **spiderRM.sav** data, compute the differences between the picture and real condition and check the assumption of normality for these differences.

9.4.4. Dependent *t*-tests using SPSS ①

Using our spider data (**spiderRM.sav**), we have 12 spider-phobes who were exposed to a picture of a spider (**picture**) and on a separate occasion a real live tarantula (**real**). Their anxiety was measured in each condition (half of the participants were exposed to the picture before the real spider while the other half were exposed to the real spider first). I have already described how the data are arranged, and so we can move straight on to doing the test itself. First, we need to access the main dialog box by selecting Analyze Compare Means ▸ Paired-Samples T Test... (Figure 9.8). Once the dialog box is activated, you need to select pairs of variables to be analysed. In this case we have only one pair (**Real** vs. **Picture**). To select a pair you should click on the first variable that you want to select (in this case **Picture**), then hold down the *Ctrl* key on the keyboard and select the second (in this case **Real**). To transfer these

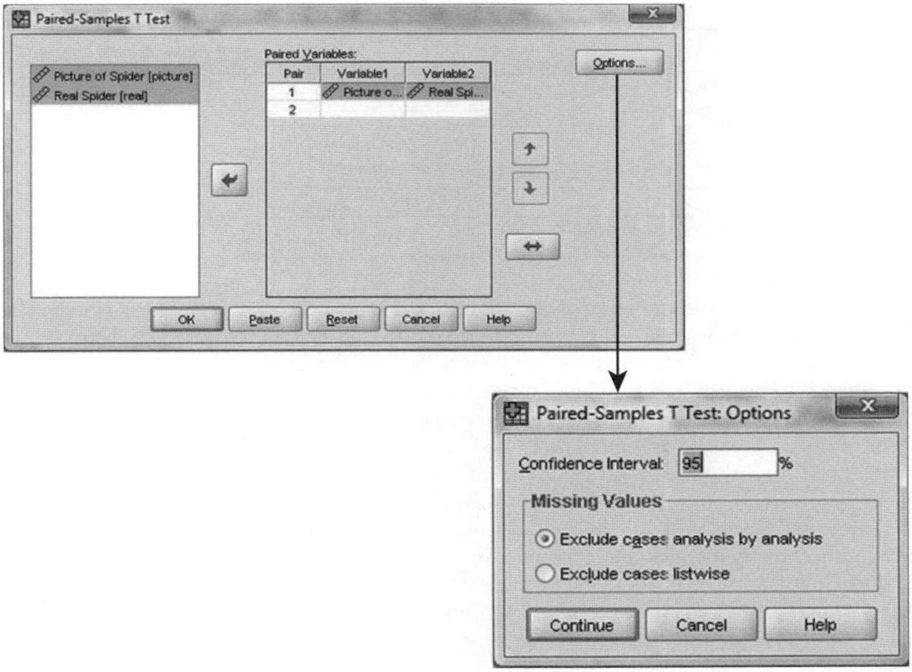

FIGURE 9.8 Main dialog box for paired-samples *t*-test

two variables to the box labelled *Paired Variables* click on . (You can also select each variable individually and transfer it by clicking on , but the method using the *Ctrl* key to select both variables is quicker.) If you want to carry out several *t*-tests then you can select another pair of variables, transfer them to the variables list, then select another pair and so on. In this case, we want only one test. If you click on Options... then another dialog box appears that gives you the chance to change the width of the confidence interval that is calculated. The default setting is for a 95% confidence interval and this is fine; however, if you want to be stricter about your analysis you could choose a 99% confidence interval but you run a higher risk of failing to detect a genuine effect (a Type II error). You can also select how to deal with missing values (see SPSS Tip 6.1). To run the analysis click on OK .

9.4.5. Output from the dependent *t*-test ①

The resulting output produces three tables. SPSS Output 9.1 shows a table of summary statistics for the two experimental conditions. For each condition we are told the mean, the number of participants (*N*) and the standard deviation of the sample. In the final column we are told the standard error (see section 9.4.1), which is the sample standard deviation divided by the square root of the sample size ($SE = s/\sqrt{N}$), so for the picture condition $SE = 9.2932/\sqrt{12} = 9.2932/3.4641 = 2.68$.

SPSS Output 9.1 also shows the Pearson correlation between the two conditions. When repeated measures are used it is possible that the experimental conditions will correlate (because the data in each condition come from the same people and so there could be some constancy in their responses). SPSS provides the value of Pearson's *r* and the two-tailed significance value (see Chapter 6). For these data the experimental conditions yield a fairly large correlation coefficient ($r = .545$) but are not significantly correlated because $p > .05$.

SPSS OUTPUT 9

Paired Samples Statistics

		Mean	N	Std. Deviation	Std. Error Mean
Pair 1	Picture of Spider	40.00	12	9.293	2.683
	Real Spider	47.00	12	11.029	3.184

Paired Samples Correlations

		N	Correlation	Sig.
Pair 1	Picture of Spider & Real Spider	12	.545	.067

SPSS Output 9.2 shows the most important of the tables: the one that tells us whether the difference between the means of the two conditions was large enough to *not* be a chance result. First, the table tells us the mean difference between scores (this value, i.e. $\bar{D}$ in equation (9.2), is the difference between the mean scores of each condition: $40 - 47 = -7$). The table also reports the standard deviation of the differences between the means and more important the standard error of the differences between participants' scores in each condition (see section 9.4.1). The test statistic, t, is calculated by dividing the mean of differences by the standard error of differences (see equation (9.2): $t = -7/2.8311 = -2.47$). The size of t is compared against known values based on the degrees of freedom. When the same participants have been used, the degrees of freedom are simply the sample size minus 1 ($df = N - 1 = 11$). SPSS uses the degrees of freedom to calculate the exact probability that a value of t as big as the one obtained could occur if the null hypothesis were true (i.e. there was no difference between these means). This probability value is in the column labelled *Sig.* By default, SPSS provides only the two-tailed probability, which is the probability when no prediction was made about the direction of group differences. If a specific prediction was made (e.g. we might predict that anxiety will be higher when a real spider is used) then the one-tailed probability should be reported and this value is obtained by dividing the two-tailed probability by 2 (see SPSS Tip 9.1). The two-tailed probability for the spider data is very low ($p = .031$) and in fact it tells us that there is only a 3.1% chance that a value of t this big could happen if the null hypothesis were true. We saw in Chapter 2 that we generally accept a $p < .05$ as statistically meaningful; therefore, this t is significant because .031 is smaller than .05. The fact that the t-value is a negative number tells us that the first condition (the **picture** condition) had a smaller mean than the second (the **real** condition) and so the real spider led to greater anxiety than the picture. Therefore, we can conclude that exposure to a real spider caused significantly more reported anxiety in spider-phobes than exposure to a picture, $t(11) = -2.47$, $p < .05$. This result was predicted by the error bar chart in Figure 9.7.

SPSS OUTPUT

Paired Samples Test

		Paired Differences					t	df	Sig. (2-tailed)
					95% Confidence Interval of the Difference				
		Mean	Std. Deviation	Std. Error Mean	Lower	Upper			
Pair 1	Picture of Spider - Real Spider	-7.000	9.807	2.831	-13.231	-.769	-2.473	11	.031

Finally, this output provides a 95% confidence interval for the mean difference. Imagine we took 100 samples from a population of difference scores and calculated their means ($\bar{D}$) and a confidence interval for that mean. In 95 of those samples the constructed confidence intervals contains the true value of the mean difference. The confidence interval tells us the boundaries within which the true mean difference is likely to lie.[4] So, assuming this sample's confidence interval is one of the 95 out of 100 that contains the population value,

[4] We saw in section 2.5.2 that these intervals represent the value of two (well, 1.96 to be precise) standard errors either side of the mean of the sampling distribution. For these data, in which the mean difference was -7 and the standard error was 2.8311, these limits will be $-7 \pm (1.96 \times 2.8311)$. However, because we're using the t-distribution, not the normal distribution, we use the critical value of t to compute the confidence intervals. This value is (with $df = 11$ as in this example) 2.201 (two-tailed), which gives us $-7 \pm (2.201 \times 2.8311)$.

SPSS TIP 9.1 **One- and two-tailed significance in SPSS ①**

Some students get a bit upset by the fact that SPSS produces only the two-tailed significance much of the time and are confused by why there isn't an option that can be selected to produce the one-tailed significance. The answer is simple: there is no need for an option because the one-tailed probability can be ascertained by dividing the two-tailed significance value by 2. For example, if the two-tailed probability is .107, then the one-tailed probability is .107/2 = .054.

we can say that the true mean difference lies between −13.23 and −0.77. The importance of this interval is that it does not contain zero (i.e. both limits are negative) because this tells us that the true value of the mean difference is unlikely to be zero. Crucially, if we were to compare pairs of random samples from a population we would expect most of the differences between sample means to be zero. This interval tells us that, based on our two samples, the true value of the difference between means is unlikely to be zero. Therefore, we can be confident that our two samples do not represent random samples from the same population. Instead they represent samples from different populations induced by the experimental manipulation.

9.4.6. Calculating the effect size ②

Even though our *t*-statistic is statistically significant, this doesn't mean our effect is important in practical terms. To discover whether the effect is substantive we need to use what we know about effect sizes (see section 2.6.4). I'm going to stick with the effect size *r* because it's widely understood, frequently used, and yes, I'll admit it, I actually like it! Converting a *t*-value into an *r*-value is actually really easy; we can use the following equation (e.g. Rosenthal, 1991; Rosnow & Rosenthal, 2005).[5]

$$r = \sqrt{\frac{t^2}{t^2 + df}}$$

We know the value of *t* and the *df* from the SPSS output and so we can compute *r* as follows:

$$r = \sqrt{\frac{-2.473^2}{-2.473^2 + 11}} = \sqrt{\frac{6.116}{17.116}} = .60$$

If you think back to our benchmarks for effect sizes this represents a very large effect (it is above .5, the threshold for a large effect). Therefore, as well as being statistically significant, this effect is large and so represents a substantive finding.

[5] Actually, this will overestimate the effect size because of the correlation between the two conditions. This is quite a technical issue and I'm trying to keep things simple here, but bear this in mind and if you're interested read Dunlap, Cortina, Vaslow, and Burke (1996).

9.4.7. Reporting the dependent *t*-test ①

There is a fairly standard way to report any test statistic: you usually state the finding to which the test relates and then report the test statistic, its degrees of freedom and the probability value of that test statistic. There has also been a recent move (by the American Psychological Association among others) to recommend that an estimate of the effect size is routinely reported. Although effect sizes are still rather sporadically used, I want to get you into good habits so we'll start thinking about effect sizes now. In this example the SPSS output tells us that the value of t was −2.47, that the degrees of freedom on which this was based was 11, and that it was significant at p = .031. We can also see the means for each group. We could write this as:

✓ On average, participants experienced significantly greater anxiety to real spiders (M = 47.00, SE = 3.18) than to pictures of spiders (M = 40.00, SE = 2.68), $t(11) = -2.47$, $p < .05$, $r = .60$.

Note how we've reported the means in each group (and standard errors) in the standard format. For the test statistic, note that we've used an italic t to denote the fact that we've calculated a t-statistic, then in brackets we've put the degrees of freedom and then stated the value of the test statistic. The probability can be expressed in several ways: often people report things to a standard level of significance (such as .05) as I have done here, but sometimes people will report the exact significance. Finally, note that I've reported the effect size at the end – you won't always see this in published papers but that's no excuse for you not to report it!

Try to avoid writing vague, unsubstantiated things like this:

× People were more scared of real spiders ($t = -2.47$).

More scared than what? Where are the *df*? Was the result statistically significant? Was the effect important (what was the effect size)?

CRAMMING SAM'S TIPS

- The dependent *t*-test compares two means, when those means have come from the same entities; for example, if you have used the same participants in each of two experimental conditions.
- Look at the column labelled *Sig.* If the value is less than .05 then the means of the two conditions are significantly different.
- Look at the values of the means to tell you how the conditions differ.
- SPSS provides only the two-tailed significance value; if you want the one-tailed significance just divide the value by 2.
- Report the *t*-statistic, the degrees of freedom and the significance value. Also report the means and their corresponding standard errors (or draw an error bar chart).
- If you're feeling brave, calculate and report the effect size too!

9.5. The independent *t*-test ①

9.5.1. The independent *t*-test equation explained ①

The independent *t*-test is used in situations in which there are two experimental conditions and different participants have been used in each condition. There are two different equations that can be used to calculate the *t*-statistic depending on whether the samples contain an equal number of people. As with the dependent *t*-test we can calculate the *t*-statistic by using a numerical version of equation (9.1); in other words, we are comparing the model or effect against the error. With the dependent *t*-test we could look at differences between pairs of scores, because the scores came from the same participants and so individual differences between conditions were eliminated. Hence, the difference in scores should reflect only the effect of the experimental manipulation. Now, when different participants participate in different conditions then pairs of scores will differ not just because of the experimental manipulation, but also because of other sources of variance (such as individual differences between participants' motivation, IQ, etc.). If we cannot investigate differences between conditions on a *per participant* basis (by comparing pairs of scores as we did for the dependent *t*-test) then we must make comparisons on a *per condition* basis (by looking at the overall effect in a condition – see equation (9.3)):

$$t = \frac{(\overline{X}_1 - \overline{X}_2) - (\mu_1 - \mu_2)}{\text{estimate of the standard error}} \tag{9.3}$$

Instead of looking at differences between pairs of scores, we now look at differences between the overall means of the two samples and compare them to the differences we would expect to get between the means of the two populations from which the samples come. If the null hypothesis is true then the samples have been drawn from the same population. Therefore, under the null hypothesis $\mu_1 = \mu_2$ and therefore $\mu_1 - \mu_2 = 0$. Therefore, under the null hypothesis the equation becomes:

$$t = \frac{\overline{X}_1 - \overline{X}_2}{\text{estimate of the standard error}} \tag{9.4}$$

In the dependent *t*-test we divided the mean difference between pairs of scores by the standard error of these differences. For the independent *t*-test we are looking at differences between groups and so we need to divide by the standard deviation of differences between groups. We can still apply the logic of sampling distributions to this situation. Now, imagine we took several pairs of samples – each pair containing one sample from the two different populations – and compared the means of these samples. From what we have learnt about sampling distributions, we know that the majority of samples from a population will have fairly similar means. Therefore, if we took several pairs of samples (from different populations), the differences between the sample means will be similar across pairs. However, often the difference between a pair of sample means will deviate by a small amount and very occasionally it will deviate by a large amount. If we could plot a sampling distribution of the differences between every pair of sample means that could be taken from two populations, then we would find that it had a normal distribution with a mean equal to the difference between population means ($\mu_1 - \mu_2$). The sampling distribution would tell us by how much we can expect the means of two (or more) samples to differ. As before, the standard deviation of the sampling distribution (the standard error) tells us how variable the differences between sample means are by chance alone. If the standard deviation is high then large differences between sample means can occur by chance; if it is small then only small differences between sample means are expected. It, therefore, makes sense that we use the standard error of the sampling distribution to assess whether the difference between two sample means is statistically meaningful or simply a chance result. Specifically, we divide the difference between sample means by the standard deviation of the sampling distribution.

So, how do we obtain the standard deviation of the sampling distribution of differences between sample means? Well, we use the **variance sum law**, which states that the variance of a difference between two independent variables is equal to the sum of their variances (see, for example, Howell, 2006). This statement means that the variance of the sampling distribution is equal to the sum of the variances of the two populations from which the samples were taken. We saw earlier that the standard error is the standard deviation of the sampling distribution of a population. We can use the sample standard deviations to calculate the standard error of each population's sampling distribution:

$$\text{SE of sampling distribution of population 1} = \frac{s_1}{\sqrt{N_1}}$$

$$\text{SE of sampling distribution of population 2} = \frac{s_2}{\sqrt{N_2}}$$

Therefore, remembering that the variance is simply the standard deviation squared, we can calculate the variance of each sampling distribution:

$$\text{variance of sampling distribution of population 1} = \left(\frac{s_1}{\sqrt{N_1}}\right)^2 = \frac{s_1^2}{N_1}$$

$$\text{variance of sampling distribution of population 2} = \left(\frac{s_2}{\sqrt{N_2}}\right)^2 = \frac{s_2^2}{N_2}$$

The variance sum law means that to find the variance of the sampling distribution of differences we merely add together the variances of the sampling distributions of the two populations:

$$\text{variance of sampling distribution of differences} = \frac{s_1^2}{N_1} + \frac{s_2^2}{N_2}$$

To find out the standard error of the sampling distribution of differences we merely take the square root of the variance (because variance is the standard deviation squared):

$$\text{SE of the sampling distribution of differences} = \sqrt{\left(\frac{s_1^2}{N_1} + \frac{s_2^2}{N_2}\right)}$$

Therefore, equation (9.4) becomes:

$$t = \frac{\overline{X}_1 - \overline{X}_2}{\sqrt{\left(\frac{s_1^2}{N_1} + \frac{s_2^2}{N_2}\right)}} \qquad (9.5)$$

Equation (9.5) is true only when the sample sizes are equal. Often in the social sciences it is not possible to collect samples of equal size (because, for example, people may not complete an experiment). When we want to compare two groups that contain different numbers of participants then equation (9.5) is not appropriate. Instead the pooled variance estimate *t*-test is used which takes account of the difference in sample size by *weighting* the variance of each sample. We saw in Chapter 1 that large samples are better than small ones because they more closely approximate the population; therefore, we weight the variance by the size of sample on which it's based (we actually weight by the number of degrees of freedom, which is the sample size minus 1). Therefore, the pooled variance estimate is:

$$s_p^2 = \frac{(n_1 - 1)s_1^2 + (n_2 - 1)s_2^2}{n_1 + n_2 - 2}$$

This is simply a weighted average in which each variance is multiplied (weighted) by its degrees of freedom, and then we divide by the sum of weights (or sum of the two degrees of freedom). The resulting weighted average variance is then just replaced in the *t*-test equation:

$$t = \frac{\overline{X}_1 - \overline{X}_2}{\sqrt{\frac{s_p^2}{n_1} + \frac{s_p^2}{n_2}}}$$

As with the dependent *t*-test we can compare the obtained value of *t* against the maximum value we would expect to get by chance alone in a *t*-distribution with the same degrees of freedom (these values can be found in the Appendix); if the value we obtain exceeds this critical value we can be confident that this reflects an effect of our independent variable. One thing that should be apparent from the equation for *t* is that to compute it you don't actually need any data! All you need are the means, standard deviations and sample sizes (see SPSS Tip 9.2).

The derivation of the *t*-statistic is merely to provide a conceptual grasp of what we are doing when we carry out a *t*-test on SPSS. Therefore, if you don't know what on earth I'm babbling on about then don't worry about it (just spare a thought for my cat: he has to listen to this rubbish all the time!) because SPSS knows how to do it and that's all that matters!

SPSS TIP 9.2 Computing *t* from means, *SDs* and *Ns* ③

Using syntax, you can compute a *t*-test in SPSS from only the two group means, the two group standard deviations and the two group sizes. Open a data editor window and set up six new variables: **x1** (mean of group 1), **x2** (mean of group 2), **sd1** (standard deviation of group 1), **sd2** (standard deviation of group 2), **n1** (sample size of group 1) and **n2** (sample size of group 2). Type the values of each of these in the first row of the data editor. Open a syntax window and type the following:

```
COMPUTE df = n1+n2-2.
COMPUTE poolvar = (((n1-1)*(sd1 ** 2))+((n2-1)*(sd2 ** 2)))/df.
COMPUTE t = (x1-x2)/sqrt(poolvar*((1/n1)+(1/n2))).
COMPUTE sig = 2*(1-(CDF.T(abs(t),df))) .
Variable labels sig 'Significance (2-tailed)'.
EXECUTE .
```

The first line computes the degrees of freedom, the second computes the pooled variance, s_p^2, the third computes *t* and the fourth its two-tailed significance. All of these values will be created in a new column in the data editor. The line beginning 'Variable labels' simply labels the significance variable so that we know that it is two-tailed. If you want to display the results in the SPSS Viewer you could type:

```
SUMMARIZE
 /TABLES= x1 x2 df t sig
 /FORMAT=VALIDLIST NOCASENUM TOTAL LIMIT=100
 /TITLE='T-test'
 /MISSING=VARIABLE
 /CELLS=NONE.
```

These commands will produce a table of the variables **x1**, **x2**, **df**, **t** and **sig** so you'll see the means of the two groups, the degrees of freedom, the value of *t* and its two-tailed significance.

You can run lots of *t*-tests at the same time by putting different values for the means, SDs and sample sizes in different rows. If you do this, though, I suggest having a string variable called **Outcome** in the file in which you type what was being measured (or some other information so that you can identify to what the *t*-test relates).

I have put these commands in a syntax file called **Independent t from means.sps**. My file is actually a bit more complicated because it calculates an effect size measure (Cohen's *d*). For an example of how to use this file see Labcoat Leni's Real Research 9.1.

LABCOAT LENI'S REAL RESEARCH 9.1

You don't have to be mad here, but it helps ③

In the UK you often see the 'humorous' slogan 'You don't have to be mad to work here, but it helps' stuck up in work places. Well, Board and Fritzon (2005) took this a step further by measuring whether 39 senior business managers and chief executives from leading UK companies were mad (well, had personality disorders, PDs). They gave them The Minnesota Multiphasic Personality Inventory Scales for DSM III Personality Disorders (MMPI-PD), which is a well-validated measure of 11 personality disorders: Histrionic, Narcissistic, Antisocial, Borderline, Dependent, Compulsive, Passive–aggressive, Paranoid, Schizotypal, Schizoid and Avoidant. They needed a comparison group and what better one to choose than 317 legally classified psychopaths at Broadmoor Hospital (a famous high-security psychiatric hospital in the UK).

The authors report the means and SDs for these two groups in Table 2 of their paper. Using these values and the syntax file **Independent t from means.sps** we can run *t*-tests on these means. The data from Board and Fritzon's Table 2 are in the file **Board and Fritzon 2005.sav**. Use this file and the syntax file to run *t*-tests to see whether managers score higher on personality disorder questionnaires than legally classified psychopaths. Report these results. What do you conclude?

Answers are in the additional material on the companion website (or look at Table 2 in the original article).

BOARD, B. J., & FRITZON, K. (2005). *PSYCHOLOGY, CRIME & LAW, 11*, 17–32.

9.5.2. The independent *t*-test using SPSS ①

I have probably bored most of you to the point of wanting to eat your own legs by now. Equations are boring and that is why SPSS was invented to help us minimize our contact with them. Using our spider data again (**spiderBG.sav**), we have 12 spider-phobes who were exposed to a picture of a spider and 12 different spider-phobes who were exposed to a real-life tarantula (the groups are coded using the variable **group**). Their anxiety was measured in each condition (**anxiety**). I have already described how the data are arranged (see section 9.2), so we can move straight on to doing the test itself. First, we need to access the main dialog box by selecting Analyze Compare Means ▸ Independent-Samples T Test... (see Figure 9.9). Once the dialog box is activated, select the dependent variable from the list (click on **anxiety**) and transfer it to the box labelled *Test Variable(s)* by clicking on ➔. If you want to carry out *t*-tests on several dependent variables then you can select other dependent variables and transfer them to the variables list. However, there are good reasons why it is not a good idea to carry out lots of tests (see Chapter 10).

Next, we need to select an independent variable (the grouping variable). In this case, we need to select **group** and then transfer it to the box labelled *Grouping Variable*. When your grouping variable has been selected the Define Groups... button will become active and you should click on it to activate the *Define Groups* dialog box. SPSS needs to know what numeric codes you assigned to your two groups, and there is a space for you to type the codes. In this example, we coded our picture group as 0 and our real group as 1, and so these are the codes that we type. Alternatively you can specify a *Cut point* in which case SPSS will assign all cases greater than or equal to that value to one group and all the values below the cut point to the second group. This facility is useful if you are testing different groups of participants based on something like a median split (see Jane Superbrain Box 9.1) – you would simply type the median value in the box labelled *Cut point*. When you have defined the groups, click on Continue to return to the main dialog box. If you click on Options... then another dialog box appears that gives you the same options as for the dependent *t*-test. To run the analysis click on OK .

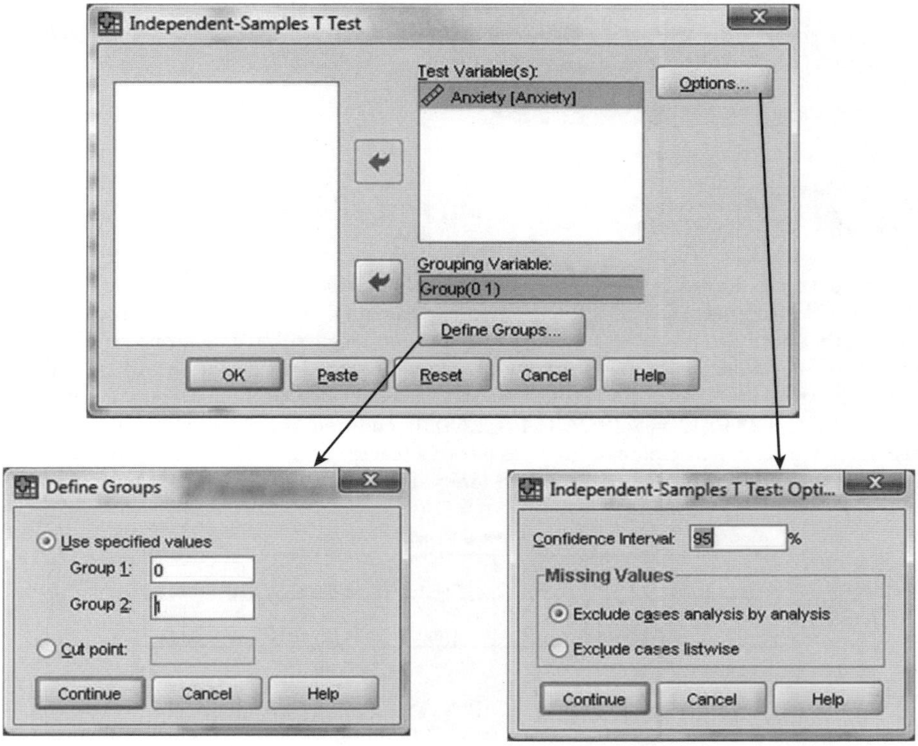

FIGURE 9.9 Dialog boxes for the independent-samples *t*-test

JANE SUPERBRAIN 9.1

Are median splits the devil's work? ②

Often in research papers you see that people have analysed their data using a 'median split'. In our spider phobia example, this means that you measure scores on a spider phobia questionnaire and calculate the median. You then classify anyone with a score above the median as a 'phobic', and those below the median as 'non-phobic'. In doing this you 'dichotomize' a continuous variable. This practice is quite common, but is it sensible?

MacCallum, Zhang, Preacher, and Rucker (2002) wrote a splendid paper pointing out various problems on turning a perfectly decent continuous variable into a categorical variable:

1. Imagine there are four people: Peter, Birgit, Jip and Kiki. We measure how scared of spiders they are as a percentage and get Jip (100%), Kiki (60%), Peter (40%) and Birgit (0%). If we split these four people at the median (50%) then we're saying that Jip and Kiki are the same (they get a score of 1 = phobic) and Peter and Birgit are the same (they both get a score of 0 = not phobic). In reality, Kiki and Peter are the most similar of the four people, but they have been put in different groups. So, median splits change the original information quite dramatically (Peter and Kiki are originally very similar but become very different after the split, Jip and Kiki are relatively dissimilar originally but become identical after the split).
2. Effect sizes get smaller: if you correlate two continuous variables then the effect size will be larger than if you correlate the same variables after one of them has been dichotomized. Effect sizes also get smaller in ANOVA and regression.
3. There is an increased chance of finding spurious effects.

So, if your supervisor has just told you to do a median split, have a good think about whether it is the right thing to do (and read MacCallum et al.'s paper). One of the rare situations in which dichotomizing a continuous variable is justified, according to MacCallum et al., is when there is a clear theoretical rationale for distinct categories of people based on a meaningful break point (i.e. not the median); for example, phobic versus not phobic based on diagnosis by a trained clinician would be a legitimate dichotomization of anxiety.

9.5.3. Output from the independent *t*-test ①

The output from the independent *t*-test contains only two tables. The first table (SPSS Output 9.3) provides summary statistics for the two experimental conditions. From this table, we can see that both groups had 12 participants (column labelled *N*). The group who saw the picture of the spider had a mean anxiety of 40, with a standard deviation of 9.29. What's more, the standard error of that group (the standard deviation of the sampling distribution) is 2.68 ($SE = 9.293/\sqrt{12} = 9.293/3.464 = 2.68$). In addition, the table tells us that the average anxiety level in participants who were shown a real spider was 47, with a standard deviation of 11.03 and a standard error of 3.18 ($SE = 11.029/\sqrt{12} = 11.029/3.464 = 3.18$).

Group Statistics

SPSS OUTPUT 9.3

	Spider or Picture?	N	Mean	Std. Deviation	Std. Error Mean
Anxiety	Picture	12	40.00	9.293	2.683
	Real Spider	12	47.00	11.029	3.184

The second table of output (SPSS Output 9.4) contains the main test statistics. The first thing to notice is that there are two rows containing values for the test statistics: one row is labelled *Equal variances assumed*, while the other is labelled *Equal variances not assumed*. In Chapter 5, we saw that parametric tests assume that the variances in experimental groups are roughly equal. Well, in reality there are adjustments that can be made in situations in which the variances are not equal. The rows of the table relate to whether or not this assumption has been broken. How do we know whether this assumption has been broken?

We saw in section 5.6.1 that we can use Levene's test to see whether variances are different in different groups, and SPSS produces this test for us. Remember that Levene's test is similar to a *t*-test in that it tests the hypothesis that the variances in the two groups are equal (i.e. the difference between the variances is zero). Therefore, if Levene's test is significant at $p \leq .05$, we can gain confidence in the hypothesis that the variances are significantly different and that the assumption of homogeneity of variances has been violated. If, however, Levene's test is non-significant (i.e. $p > .05$) then we do not have sufficient evidence to reject the null hypothesis that the difference between the variances is zero – in other words, we can assume that the variances are roughly equal and the assumption is tenable. For these data, Levene's test is non-significant (because $p = .386$, which is greater than .05) and so we should read the test statistics in the row labelled *Equal variances assumed*. Had Levene's test been significant, then we would have read the test statistics from the row labelled *Equal variances not assumed*.

SPSS OUTPUT 9.4

Independent Samples Test

		Levene's Test for Equality of Variances		t-test for Equality of Means					95% Confidence Interval of the Difference	
		F	Sig.	t	df	Sig. (2-tailed)	Mean Difference	Std. Error Difference	Lower	Upper
Anxiety	Equal variances assumed	.782	.386	-1.681	22	.107	-7.000	4.163	-15.634	1.634
	Equal variances not assumed			-1.681	21.385	.107	-7.000	4.163	-15.649	1.649

Having established that the assumption of homogeneity of variances is met, we can move on to look at the *t*-test itself. We are told the mean difference $(\bar{X}_1 - \bar{X}_2 = 40 - 47 = -7)$ and the standard error of the sampling distribution of differences, which is calculated using the lower half of equation (9.5):

$$\begin{aligned}\sqrt{\left(\frac{s_1^2}{N_1} + \frac{s_2^2}{N_2}\right)} &= \sqrt{\left(\frac{9.29^2}{12} + \frac{11.03^2}{12}\right)} \\ &= \sqrt{(7.19 + 10.14)} \\ &= \sqrt{17.33} \\ &= 4.16\end{aligned}$$

The *t*-statistic is calculated by dividing the mean difference by the standard error of the sampling distribution of differences ($t = -7/4.16 = -1.68$). The value of *t* is then assessed against the value of *t* you might expect to get by chance when you have certain degrees of freedom. For the independent *t*-test, degrees of freedom are calculated by adding the two sample sizes and then subtracting the number of samples ($df = N_1 + N_2 - 2 = 12 + 12 - 2 = 22$). SPSS produces the exact significance value of *t*, and we are interested in whether this value is less than or greater than .05. In this case the two-tailed value of *p* is .107, which is greater than .05, and so we would have to conclude that there was no significant difference between the means of these two samples. In terms of the experiment, we can infer that spider-phobes are made equally anxious by pictures of spiders as they are by the real thing.

Now, we use the two-tailed probability when we have made no specific prediction about the direction of our effect (see section 2.6.2). For example, if we were unsure whether a real spider would induce more or less anxiety, then we would have to use a two-tailed test. However, often in research we can make specific predictions about which group has the highest mean. In this example, it is likely that we would have predicted that a real spider would induce greater anxiety than a picture and so we predict that the mean of the real group would be greater than the mean of the picture group. In this case, we can use a one-tailed test (for more discussion of this issue see section 2.6.2). The one-tailed probability is .107/2 = .054 (see SPSS Tip 9.1). The one-tailed probability is still greater than .05 (albeit by a small margin) and so we would still have to conclude that spider-phobes' anxiety when presented with a real spider was not significantly different to spider-phobes who were presented with a picture of the same spider. This result was predicted by the error bar chart in Figure 9.2.

9.5.4. Calculating the effect size ②

To discover whether our effect is substantive we can use the same equation as in section 9.4.6 to convert the *t*-statistics into a value of *r*. We know the value of *t* and the *df* from the SPSS output and so we can compute *r* as follows:

$$\begin{aligned} r &= \sqrt{\frac{-1.681^2}{-1.681^2 + 22}} \\ &= \sqrt{\frac{2.826}{24.826}} \\ &= .34 \end{aligned}$$

If you think back to our benchmarks for effect sizes this represents a medium effect (it is around .3, the threshold for a medium effect). Therefore, even though the effect was non-significant, it still represented a fairly substantial effect. You may also notice that the effect has shrunk, which may seem slightly odd given that we used exactly the same data (but see section 9.6)!

9.5.5. Reporting the independent *t*-test ①

The rules that I made up, erm, I mean, reported, for the dependent *t*-test pretty much apply for the independent *t*-test. The SPSS output tells us that the value of *t* was −1.68, that the number of degrees of freedom on which this was based was 22, and that it was not significant at $p < .05$. We can also see the means for each group. We could write this as:

✓ On average, participants experienced greater anxiety to real spiders (M = 47.00, SE = 3.18) than to pictures of spiders (M = 40.00, SE = 2.68). This difference was not significant $t(22) = -1.68, p > .05$; however, it did represent a medium-sized effect $r = .34$.

Note how we've reported the means in each group (and standard errors) as before. For the test statistic everything is much the same as before except that I've had to report that *p* was greater than (>) .05 rather than less than (<). Finally, note that I've commented on the effect size at the end.

CRAMMING SAM'S TIPS

- The independent *t*-test compares two means, when those means have come from different groups of entities; for example, if you have used different participants in each of two experimental conditions.
- Look at the column labelled *Levene's Test for Equality of Variance*. If the *Sig*. value is less than .05 then the assumption of homogeneity of variance has been broken and you should look at the row in the table labelled *Equal variances not assumed*. If the *Sig.* value of Levene's test is bigger than .05 then you should look at the row in the table labelled *Equal variances assumed*.
- Look at the column labelled *Sig*. If the value is less than .05 then the means of the two groups are significantly different.
- Look at the values of the means to tell you how the groups differ.
- SPSS provides only the two-tailed significance value; if you want the one-tailed significance just divide the value by 2.
- Report the *t*-statistic, the degrees of freedom and the significance value. Also report the means and their corresponding standard errors (or draw an error bar chart).
- Calculate and report the effect size. Go on, you can do it!

9.6. Between groups or repeated measures? ①

The two examples in this chapter are interesting (honestly!) because they illustrate the difference between data collected using the same participants and data collected using different participants. The two examples in this chapter use the same scores in each condition. When analysed as though the data came from the same participants the result was a significant difference between means, but when analysed as though the data came from different participants there was no significant difference between group means. This may seem like a puzzling finding – after all the numbers were identical in both examples. What this illustrates is the relative *power* of repeated-measures designs. When the same participants are used across conditions the unsystematic variance (often called the error variance) is reduced dramatically, making it easier to detect any systematic variance. It is often assumed that the way in which you collect data is irrelevant, but I hope to have illustrated that it can make the difference between detecting a difference and not detecting one. In fact, researchers have carried out studies using the same participants in experimental conditions, then repeated the study using different participants in experimental conditions, then used the method of data collection as an independent variable in the analysis. Typically, they have found that the method of data collection interacts significantly with the results found (see Erlebacher, 1977).

9.7. The *t*-test as a general linear model ②

A lot of you might think it's odd that I've chosen to represent the effect size for my *t*-tests using *r*, the correlation coefficient. In fact you might well be thinking 'but correlations show relationships, not differences between means'. I used to think this too until I read a fantastic paper by Cohen (1968), which made me realize what I'd been missing; the complex, thorny, weed-infested and large Andy-eating tarantula-inhabited world of statistics suddenly turned into a beautiful meadow filled with tulips and little bleating lambs all jumping for joy at the wonder of life. Actually, I'm still a bumbling fool trying desperately to avoid having the blood sucked from my flaccid corpse by the tarantulas of statistics, but it was a good paper! What I'm about to say will either make no sense at all, or might help you to appreciate what I've said in most of the chapters so far: all statistical procedures are basically the same, they're just more or less elaborate versions of the correlation coefficient!

In Chapter 7 we saw that the *t*-test was used to test whether the regression coefficient of a predictor was equal to zero. The experimental design for which the independent *t*-test is used can be conceptualized as a regression equation (after all, there is one independent variable (predictor) and one dependent variable (outcome)). If we want to predict our outcome, then we can use the general equation that I've mentioned at various points:

$$\text{outcome}_i = (\text{model}) + \text{error}_i$$

If we want to use a linear model, then we saw that this general equation becomes equation (7.2) in which the model is defined by the slope and intercept of a straight line. Equation (9.6) shows a very similar equation in which A_i is the dependent variable (outcome), b_0 is the intercept, b_1 is the weighting of the predictor and G_i is the independent variable (predictor). Now, I've also included the same equation but with some of the letters replaced with what they represent in the spider experiment (so, A = **anxiety**, G = **group**). When we run an experiment with two conditions, the independent variable has only two values (group 1 or group 2). There are several ways in which these groups can be coded (in the spider example we coded group 1 with the value 0 and group 2 with the value 1). This coding variable is known as a *dummy variable* and values of this variable represent groups of entities. We have come across this coding in section 7.11:

$$\begin{aligned} A_i &= b_0 + b_1 G_i + \varepsilon_i \\ \text{Anxiety}_i &= b_0 + b_1 \text{group}_i + \varepsilon_i \end{aligned} \tag{9.6}$$

Using the spider example, we know that the mean **anxiety** of the picture group was 40, and that the **group** variable is equal to 0 for this condition. Look at what happens when the **group** variable is equal to 0 (the picture condition): equation (9.6) becomes (if we ignore the residual term):

$$\begin{aligned} \overline{X}_{\text{Picture}} &= b_0 + (b_1 \times 0) \\ b_0 &= \overline{X}_{\text{Picture}} \\ b_0 &= 40 \end{aligned}$$

Therefore, b_0 (the intercept) is equal to the mean of the picture group (i.e. it is the mean of the group coded as 0). Now let's look at what happens when the **group** variable is equal to 1. This condition is the one in which a real spider was used, therefore the mean **anxiety** ($\overline{X}_{\text{Real}}$) of this condition was 47. Remembering that we have just found out that b_0 is equal to the mean of the picture group ($\overline{X}_{\text{Picture}}$), equation (9.6) becomes:

$$\begin{aligned} \overline{X}_{\text{Real}} &= b_0 + (b_1 \times 1) \\ \overline{X}_{\text{Real}} &= \overline{X}_{\text{Picture}} + b_1 \\ b_1 &= \overline{X}_{\text{Real}} - \overline{X}_{\text{Picture}} \\ &= 47 - 40 \\ &= 7 \end{aligned}$$

b_1, therefore, represents the difference between the group means. As such, we can represent a two-group experiment as a regression equation in which the coefficient of the independent variable (b_1) is equal to the difference between group means, and the intercept (b_0) is equal to the mean of the group coded as 0. In regression, the t-test is used to ascertain whether the regression coefficient (b_1) is equal to 0, and when we carry out a t-test on grouped data we, therefore, test whether the difference between group means is equal to 0.

SELF-TEST To prove that I'm not making it up as I go along, run a regression on the data in **spiderBG.sav** with **group** as the predictor and **anxiety** as the outcome. **Group** is coded using zeros and ones and represents the dummy variable described above.

The resulting SPSS output should contain the regression summary table shown in SPSS Output 9.5. The first thing to notice is the value of the constant (b_0): its value is 40, the same as the mean of the base category (the picture group). The second thing to notice is that the value of the regression coefficient b_1 is 7, which is the difference between the two group means (47 – 40 = 7). Finally, the t-statistic, which tests whether b_1 is significantly different from zero, is the same as for the independent t-test (see SPSS Output 9.4) and so is the significance value.[6]

S OUTPUT 9.5
ression analysis
etween-group
er data

Coefficients[a]

Model		Unstandardized Coefficients		Standardized Coefficients	t	Sig.
		B	Std. Error	Beta		
1	(Constant)	40.000	2.944		13.587	.000
	Condition	7.000	4.163	.337	1.681	.107

a. Dependent Variable: Anxiety

This section has demonstrated that differences between means can be represented in terms of linear models and this concept is essential in understanding the following chapters on the general linear model.

9.8. What if my data are not normally distributed? ②

We've seen in this chapter that there are adjustments that can be made to the t-test when the assumption of homogeneity of variance is broken, but what about when you have non-normally distributed data? The first thing to note is that although a lot of early evidence suggested that t was accurate when distributions were skewed, the t-test *can be* biased when

[6] In fact, the value of the t-statistic is the same but has a positive sign rather than negative. You'll remember from the discussion of the point–biserial correlation in section 6.5.5 that when you correlate a dichotomous variable the direction of the correlation coefficient depends entirely upon which cases are assigned to which groups. Therefore, the direction of the t-statistic here is similarly influenced by which group we select to be the base category (the category coded as 0).

the assumption of normality is not met (Wilcox, 2005). Second, we need to remember that it's the shape of the sampling distribution that matters, not the sample data. One option then is to use a big sample and rely on the central limit theorem (section 2.5.1) which says that the sampling distribution should be normal when samples are big. You could also try to correct the distribution using a transformation (but see Jane Superbrain Box 5.1). Another useful solution is to use one of a group of tests commonly referred to as *non-parametric tests*. These tests have fewer assumptions than their parametric counterparts and so are useful when your data violate the assumptions of parametric data described in Chapter 5. Some of these tests are described in Chapter 15. The non-parametric counterpart of the *dependent t-test* is called the *Wilcoxon signed-rank Test* (section 15.4), and the independent *t*-test has two non-parametric counterparts (both extremely similar) called the *Wilcoxon rank-sum test* and the *Mann–Whitney test* (section 15.3). I'd recommend reading these sections before moving on.

A final option is to use robust methods (see section 5.7.4). There are various robust ways to test differences between means that involve using trimmed means or a bootstrap. However, SPSS doesn't do any of these directly. Should you wish to do these then plugin for SPSS. Look at the companion website for some demos of how to use the R plugin.

What have I discovered about statistics? ①

We started this chapter by looking at my relative failures as a human being compared to Simon Hudson before investigating some problems with the way SPSS produces error bars for repeated-measures designs. We then had a look at some general conceptual features of the *t*-test, a parametric test that's used to test differences between two means. After this general taster, we moved on to look specifically at the dependent *t*-test (used when your conditions involve the same entities). I explained how it was calculated, how to do it on SPSS and how to interpret the results. We then discovered much the same for the independent *t*-test (used when your conditions involve different entities). After this I droned on excitedly about how a situation with two conditions can be conceptualized as a general linear model, by which point those of you who have a life had gone to the pub for a stiff drink. My excitement about things like general linear models could explain why Clair Sparks chose Simon Hudson all those years ago. Perhaps she could see the writing on the wall! Fortunately, I was a ruthless pragmatist at the age of 10, and the Clair Sparks episode didn't seem to concern me unduly; I just set my sights elsewhere during the obligatory lunchtime game of kiss chase. These games were the last I would see of women for quite some time ...

Key terms that I've discovered

Dependent *t*-test
Grand mean
Independent *t*-test
Standard error of differences
Variance sum law

Smart Alex's tasks

These scenarios are taken from Field and Hole (2003). In each case analyse the data on SPSS:

- **Task 1**: One of my pet hates is 'pop psychology' books. Along with banishing Freud from all bookshops, it is my avowed ambition to rid the world of these rancid putrefaction-ridden wastes of trees. Not only do they give psychology a very bad name by stating the bloody obvious and charging people for the privilege, but they are also considerably less enjoyable to look at than the trees killed to produce them (admittedly the same could be said for the turgid tripe that I produce in the name of education but let's not go there just for now!). Anyway, as part of my plan to rid the world of popular psychology I did a little experiment. I took two groups of people who were in relationships and randomly assigned them to one of two conditions. One group read the famous popular psychology book *Women are from Bras and men are from Penis*, whereas another group read *Marie Claire*. I tested only 10 people in each of these groups, and the dependent variable was an objective measure of their happiness with their relationship after reading the book. I didn't make any specific prediction about which reading material would improve relationship happiness. The data are in the file **Penis.sav.** Analyse them with the appropriate *t*-test. ①
- **Task 2**: Imagine Twaddle and Sons, the publishers of *Women are from Bras and men are from Penis*, were upset about my claims that their book was about as useful as a paper umbrella. They decided to take me to task and design their own experiment in which participants read their book and one of my books (Field and Hole) at different times. Relationship happiness was measured after reading each book. To maximize their chances of finding a difference they used a sample of 500 participants, but got each participant to take part in both conditions (they read both books). The order in which books were read was counterbalanced and there was a delay of six months between reading the books. They predicted that reading their wonderful contribution to popular psychology would lead to greater relationship happiness than reading some dull and tedious book about experiments. The data are in **Field&Hole.sav.** Analyse them using the appropriate *t*-test. ①

Answers can be found on the companion website (or for more detail see Field and Hole, 2003).

Further reading

Field, A. P., & Hole, G. (2003). *How to design and report experiments*. London: Sage. (In my completely unbiased opinion this is a useful book to get some more background on experimental methods.)

Miles, J. N. V., & Banyard, P. (2007). *Understanding and using statistics in psychology: a practical introduction*. London: Sage. (A fantastic and amusing introduction to statistical theory.)

Rosnow, R. L., & Rosenthal, R. (2005). *Beginning behavioural research: a conceptual primer* (5th ed.). Englewood Cliffs, NJ: Pearson/Prentice Hall.

Wright, D. B., & London, K. (2009). *First steps in statistics* (2nd ed.) London: Sage. (This book has very clear introductions to the *t*-test.)

Online tutorial

The companion website contains the following Flash movie tutorial to accompany this chapter:

- *t*-tests using SPSS

Interesting real research

Board, B. J., & Fritzon, K. (2005). Disordered personalities at work. *Psychology, Crime & Law*, *11*(1), 17–32.

21

Correlation

ANDY FIELD

FIGURE 6.1 I don't have a photo from Christmas 1981, but this was taken about that time at my grandparents' house. I'm trying to play an 'E' by the looks of it, no doubt because it's in 'Take on the world'

6.1. What will this chapter tell me? ①

When I was 8 years old, my parents bought me a guitar for Christmas. Even then, I'd desperately wanted to play the guitar for years. I could not contain my excitement at getting this gift (had it been an *electric* guitar I think I would have actually exploded with excitement). The guitar came with a 'learn to play' book and after a little while of trying to play what was on page 1 of this book, I readied myself to unleash a riff of universe-crushing power onto the world (well, 'skip to my Lou' actually). But, I couldn't do it. I burst into tears and ran upstairs to hide.[1] My dad sat with me and said, 'Don't worry, Andy, everything is hard to begin with, but the more you practise the easier it gets.'

[1] This is not a dissimilar reaction to the one I have when publishers ask me for new editions of statistics textbooks.

In his comforting words, my dad was inadvertently teaching me about the relationship, or correlation, between two variables. These two variables could be related in three ways: (1) *positively related*, meaning that the more I practised my guitar, the better guitar player I would become (i.e. my dad was telling me the truth); (2) *not related* at all, meaning that as I practise the guitar my playing ability remains completely constant (i.e. my dad has fathered a cretin); or (3) *negatively related*, which would mean that the more I practised my guitar the worse a guitar player I became (i.e. my dad has fathered an indescribably strange child). This chapter looks first at how we can express the relationships between variables statistically by looking at two measures: *covariance* and the *correlation coefficient*. We then discover how to carry out and interpret correlations in SPSS. The chapter ends by looking at more complex measures of relationships; in doing so it acts as a precursor to the chapter on multiple regression.

6.2. Looking at relationships ①

In Chapter 4 I stressed the importance of looking at your data graphically before running any other analysis on them. I just want to begin by reminding you that our first starting point with a correlation analysis should be to look at some scatterplots of the variables we have measured. I am not going to repeat how to get SPSS to produce these graphs, but I am going to urge you (if you haven't done so already) to read section 4.8 before embarking on the rest of this chapter.

6.3. How do we measure relationships? ①

6.3.1. A detour into the murky world of covariance ①

The simplest way to look at whether two variables are associated is to look at whether they *covary*. To understand what **covariance** is, we first need to think back to the concept of variance that we met in Chapter 2. Remember that the variance of a single variable represents the average amount that the data vary from the mean. Numerically, it is described by:

$$\text{variance}(s^2) = \frac{\sum(x_i - \bar{x})^2}{N-1} = \frac{\sum(x_i - \bar{x})(x_i - \bar{x})}{N-1} \qquad (6.1)$$

The mean of the sample is represented by $\bar{x}$, x_i is the data point in question and N is the number of observations (see section 2.4.1). If we are interested in whether two variables are related, then we are interested in whether changes in one variable are met with similar changes in the other variable. Therefore, when one variable deviates from its mean we would expect the other variable to deviate from its mean in a similar way. To illustrate what I mean, imagine we took five people and subjected them to a certain number of advertisements promoting toffee sweets, and then measured how many packets of those sweets each person bought during the next week. The data are in Table 6.1 as well as the mean and standard deviation (s) of each variable.

TABLE 6.1

Subject	1	2	3	4	5	Mean	S
Adverts Watched	5	4	4	6	8	**5.4**	**1.67**
Packets Bought	8	9	10	13	15	**11.0**	**2.92**

If there were a relationship between these two variables, then as one variable deviates from its mean, the other variable should deviate from its mean in the same or the directly opposite way. Figure 6.2 shows the data for each participant (green circles represent the number of packets bought and blue circles represent the number of adverts watched); the green line is the average number of packets bought and the blue line is the average number of adverts watched. The vertical lines represent the differences (remember that these differences are called *deviations*) between the observed values and the mean of the relevant variable. The first thing to notice about Figure 6.2 is that there is a very similar pattern of deviations for both variables. For the first three participants the observed values are below the mean for both variables, for the last two people the observed values are above the mean for both variables. This pattern is indicative of a potential relationship between the two variables (because it seems that if a person's score is below the mean for one variable then their score for the other will also be below the mean).

So, how do we calculate the exact similarity between the pattern of differences of the two variables displayed in Figure 6.2? One possibility is to calculate the total amount of deviation but we would have the same problem as in the single variable case: the positive and negative deviations would cancel out (see section 2.4.1). Also, by simply adding the deviations, we would gain little insight into the *relationship* between the variables. Now, in the single variable case, we squared the deviations to eliminate the problem of positive and negative deviations cancelling out each other. When there are two variables, rather than squaring each deviation, we can multiply the deviation for one variable by the corresponding deviation for the second variable. If both deviations are positive or negative then this will give us a positive value (indicative of the deviations being in the same direction), but if one deviation is positive and one negative then the resulting product will be negative

FIGURE 6.2 Graphical display of the differences between the observed data and the means of two variables

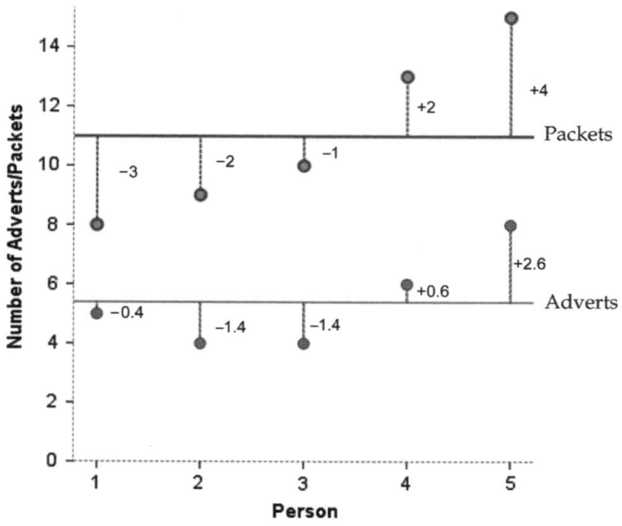

(indicative of the deviations being opposite in direction). When we multiply the deviations of one variable by the corresponding deviations of a second variable, we get what is known as the **cross-product deviations**. As with the variance, if we want an average value of the combined deviations for the two variables, we must divide by the number of observations (we actually divide by $N - 1$ for reasons explained in Jane Superbrain Box 2.3). This averaged sum of combined deviations is known as the covariance. We can write the covariance in equation form as in equation (6.2) – you will notice that the equation is the same as the equation for variance, except that instead of squaring the differences, we multiply them by the corresponding difference of the second variable:

$$\text{cov}(x, y) = \frac{\sum(x_i - \bar{x})(y_i - \bar{y})}{N - 1} \tag{6.2}$$

For the data in Table 6.1 and Figure 6.2 we reach the following value:

$$\begin{aligned}
\text{cov}(x, y) &= \frac{\sum(x_i - \bar{x})(y_i - \bar{y})}{N - 1} \\
&= \frac{(-0.4)(-3) + (-1.4)(-2) + (-1.4)(-1) + (0.6)(2) + (2.6)(4)}{4} \\
&= \frac{1.2 + 2.8 + 1.4 + 1.2 + 10.4}{4} \\
&= \frac{17}{4} \\
&= 4.25
\end{aligned}$$

Calculating the covariance is a good way to assess whether two variables are related to each other. A positive covariance indicates that as one variable deviates from the mean, the other variable deviates in the same direction. On the other hand, a negative covariance indicates that as one variable deviates from the mean (e.g. increases), the other deviates from the mean in the opposite direction (e.g. decreases).

There is, however, one problem with covariance as a measure of the relationship between variables and that is that it depends upon the scales of measurement used. So, covariance is not a standardized measure. For example, if we use the data above and assume that they represented two variables measured in miles then the covariance is 4.25 (as calculated above). If we then convert these data into kilometres (by multiplying all values by 1.609) and calculate the covariance again then we should find that it increases to 11. This dependence on the scale of measurement is a problem because it means that we cannot compare covariances in an objective way – so, we cannot say whether a covariance is particularly large or small relative to another data set unless both data sets were measured in the same units.

6.3.2. Standardization and the correlation coefficient ①

To overcome the problem of dependence on the measurement scale, we need to convert the covariance into a standard set of units. This process is known as **standardization**. A very basic form of standardization would be to insist that all experiments use the same units of measurement, say metres – that way, all results could be easily compared. However, what happens if you want to measure attitudes – you'd be hard pushed to measure them in metres! Therefore, we need a unit of measurement into which any scale of measurement can be converted. The unit of measurement we use is the *standard deviation*. We came across this measure in section 2.4.1 and saw that, like the variance, it is a measure of the average deviation from the mean. If we divide any distance from the mean by the standard deviation, it gives us that distance in standard deviation units. For example, for the data in Table 6.1, the standard deviation for the number of packets bought is approximately 3.0 (the exact value is 2.91). In Figure 6.2 we can see that the observed value for participant 1 was 3 packets less than the mean (so, there was an error of –3 packets of sweets). If we divide this deviation, –3, by the standard deviation, which is approximately 3, then we get a value of –1. This tells us that the difference between participant 1's score and the mean was –1 standard deviation. So, we can express the deviation from the mean for a participant in standard units by dividing the observed deviation by the standard deviation.

It follows from this logic that if we want to express the covariance in a standard unit of measurement we can simply divide by the standard deviation. However, there are two variables and, hence, two standard deviations. Now, when we calculate the covariance we actually calculate two deviations (one for each variable) and then multiply them. Therefore, we do the same for the standard deviations: we multiply them and divide by the product of this multiplication. The standardized covariance is known as a *correlation coefficient* and is defined by equation (6.3) in which s_x is the standard deviation of the first variable and s_y is the standard deviation of the second variable (all other letters are the same as in the equation defining covariance):

$$r = \frac{\text{cov}_{xy}}{s_x s_y} = \frac{\sum(x_i - \bar{x})(y_i - \bar{y})}{(N-1)s_x s_y} \tag{6.3}$$

The coefficient in equation (6.3) is known as the Pearson product-moment correlation coefficient or **Pearson correlation coefficient** (for a really nice explanation of why it was originally called the 'product-moment' correlation see Miles & Banyard, 2007) and was invented by Karl Pearson (see Jane Superbrain Box 6.1).[2] If we look back at Table 6.1 we see that the standard deviation for the number of adverts watched (s_x) was 1.67, and for the number of packets of crisps bought (s_y) was 2.92. If we multiply these together we get $1.67 \times 2.92 = 4.88$. Now, all we need to do is take the covariance, which we calculated a few pages ago as being 4.25, and divide by these multiplied standard deviations. This gives us $r = 4.25/4.88 = .87$.

By standardizing the covariance we end up with a value that has to lie between –1 and +1 (if you find a correlation coefficient less than –1 or more than +1 you can be sure that something has gone hideously wrong!). A coefficient of +1 indicates that the two variables are perfectly positively correlated, so as one variable increases, the other increases by a proportionate amount. Conversely, a coefficient of –1 indicates a perfect negative relationship: if one variable increases, the other decreases by a proportionate amount. A coefficient of zero indicates no linear relationship at all and so if one variable changes, the other stays the same. We also saw in section 2.6.4 that because the correlation coefficient is a standardized measure of an observed effect, it is a commonly used measure of the size of an effect and that values of ±.1 represent a small effect, ±.3 is a medium effect and ±.5 is a large effect (although I re-emphasize my caveat that these canned effect sizes are no substitute for interpreting the effect size within the context of the research literature).

[2] You will find Pearson's product-moment correlation coefficient denoted by both r and R. Typically, the uppercase form is used in the context of regression because it represents the multiple correlation coefficient; however, for some reason, when we square r (as in section 6.5.2.3) an upper case R is used. Don't ask me why – it's just to confuse me I suspect.

JANE SUPERBRAIN 6.1

Who said statistics was dull? ①

Students often think that statistics is dull, but back in the early 1900s it was anything but dull with various prominent figures entering into feuds on a soap opera scale. One of the most famous was between Karl Pearson and Ronald Fisher (whom we met in Chapter 2). It began when Pearson published a paper of Fisher's in his journal but made comments in his editorial that, to the casual reader, belittled Fisher's work. Two years later Pearson's group published work following on from Fisher's paper without consulting him. The antagonism persisted with Fisher turning down a job to work in Pearson's group and publishing 'improvements' on Pearson's ideas. Pearson for his part wrote in his own journal about apparent errors made by Fisher.

Another prominent statistician, Jerzy Neyman, criticized some of Fisher's most important work in a paper delivered to the Royal Statistical Society on 28 March 1935 at which Fisher was present. Fisher's discussion of the paper at that meeting directly attacked Neyman. Fisher more or less said that Neyman didn't know what he was talking about and didn't understand the background material on which his work was based. Relations soured so much that while they both worked at University College London, Neyman openly attacked many of Fisher's ideas in lectures to his students. The two feuding groups even took afternoon tea (a common practice in the British academic community of the time) in the same room but at different times! The truth behind who fuelled these feuds is, perhaps, lost in the mists of time, but Zabell (1992) makes a sterling effort to unearth it.

Basically then, the founders of modern statistical methods were a bunch of squabbling children. Nevertheless, these three men were astonishingly gifted individuals. Fisher, in particular, was a world leader in genetics, biology and medicine as well as possibly the most original mathematical thinker ever (Barnard, 1963; Field, 2005d; Savage, 1976).

6.3.3. The significance of the correlation coefficient ③

Although we can directly interpret the size of a correlation coefficient, we have seen in Chapter 2 that scientists like to test hypotheses using probabilities. In the case of a correlation coefficient we can test the hypothesis that the correlation is different from zero (i.e. different from 'no relationship'). If we find that our observed coefficient was very unlikely to happen if there was no effect in the population then we can gain confidence that the relationship that we have observed is statistically meaningful.

There are two ways that we can go about testing this hypothesis. The first is to use our trusty z-scores that keep cropping up in this book. As we have seen, z-scores are useful because we know the probability of a given value of z occurring, if the distribution from which it comes is normal. There is one problem with Pearson's r, which is that it is known to have a sampling distribution that is not normally distributed. This is a bit of a nuisance, but luckily thanks to our friend Fisher we can adjust r so that its sampling distribution *is* normal as follows (Fisher, 1921):

$$z_r = \frac{1}{2}\log_e\left(\frac{1+r}{1-r}\right) \qquad (6.4)$$

The resulting z_r has a standard error of:

$$\text{SE}_{z_r} = \frac{1}{\sqrt{N-3}} \qquad (6.5)$$

For our advert example, our $r = .87$ becomes 1.33 with a standard error of .71.

We can then transform this adjusted r into a z-score just as we have done for raw scores, and for skewness and kurtosis values in previous chapters. If we want a z-score that represents the size of the correlation relative to a particular value, then we simply compute a z-score using the value that we want to test against and the standard error. Normally we want to see whether the correlation is different from 0, in which case we can subtract 0 from the observed value of r and divide by the standard error (in other words, we just divide z_r by its standard error):

$$z = \frac{z_r}{\mathrm{SE}z_r} \tag{6.6}$$

For our advert data this gives us 1.33/.71 = 1.87. We can look up this value of z (1.87) in the table for the normal distribution in the Appendix and get the one-tailed probability from the column labelled 'Smaller Portion'. In this case the value is .0307. To get the two-tailed probability we simply multiply the one-tailed probability value by 2, which gives us .0614. As such the correlation is significant, $p < .05$ one-tailed, but not two-tailed.

In fact, the hypothesis that the correlation coefficient is different from 0 is usually (SPSS, for example, does this) tested not using a z-score, but using a t-statistic with $N - 2$ degrees of freedom, which can be directly obtained from r:

$$t_r = \frac{r\sqrt{N-2}}{\sqrt{1-r^2}} \tag{6.7}$$

You might wonder then why I told you about z-scores. Partly it was to keep the discussion framed in concepts with which you are already familiar (we don't encounter the t-test properly for a few chapters), but also it is useful background information for the next section.

6.3.4. Confidence intervals for r ③

I was moaning earlier on about how SPSS doesn't make tea for you. Another thing that it doesn't do is compute confidence intervals for r. This is a shame because as we have seen in Chapter 2 these intervals tell us something about the likely value (in this case of the correlation) in the population. However, we can calculate these manually. To do this we need to take advantage of what we learnt in the previous section about converting r to z_r (to make the sampling distribution normal), and using the associated standard errors. We can then construct a confidence interval in the usual way. For a 95% confidence interval we have (see section 2.5.2.1):

$$\text{lower boundary of confidence interval} = \overline{X} - (1.96 \times \mathrm{SE})$$
$$\text{upper boundary of confidence interval} = \overline{X} + (1.96 \times \mathrm{SE})$$

In the case of our transformed correlation coefficients these equations become:

$$\text{lower boundary of confidence interval} = z_r - (1.96 \times \mathrm{SE}_{z_r})$$
$$\text{upper boundary of confidence interval} = z_r + (1.96 \times \mathrm{SE}_{z_r})$$

For our advert data this gives us 1.33 – (1.96 × .71) = –0.062, and 1.33 + (1.96 × .71) = 2.72. Remember that these values are in the z_r metric and so we have to convert back to correlation coefficients using:

$$r = \frac{e^{(2z_r)} - 1}{e^{(2z_r)} + 1} \qquad (6.8)$$

This gives us an upper bound of $r = .991$ and a lower bound of -0.062 (because this value is so close to zero the transformation to z has no impact).

OLIVER TWISTED

Please, Sir, can I have some more … confidence intervals?

'These confidence intervals are rubbish,' says Oliver, 'they're too confusing and I hate equations, and the values we get will only be approximate. Can't we get SPSS to do it for us while we check Facebook?' Well, no you can't. Except you sort of can with some syntax. I've written some SPSS syntax which will compute confidence intervals for *r* for you. To find out more, read the additional material for this chapter on the companion website. Or check Facebook, the choice is yours.

CRAMMING SAM'S TIPS

- A crude measure of the relationship between variables is the *covariance*.
- If we standardize this value we get *Pearson's correlation coefficient, r*.
- The correlation coefficient has to lie between −1 and +1.
- A coefficient of +1 indicates a perfect positive relationship, a coefficient of −1 indicates a perfect negative relationship, a coefficient of 0 indicates no linear relationship at all.
- The correlation coefficient is a commonly used measure of the size of an effect: values of ±.1 represent a small effect, ±.3 is a medium effect and ±.5 is a large effect.

6.3.5. A word of warning about interpretation: causality ①

Considerable caution must be taken when interpreting correlation coefficients because they give no indication of the direction of *causality*. So, in our example, although we can conclude that as the number of adverts watched increases, the number of packets of toffees bought increases also, we cannot say that watching adverts *causes* us to buy packets of toffees. This caution is for two reasons:

- **The third-variable problem**: We came across this problem in section 1.6.2. To recap, in any correlation, causality between two variables cannot be assumed because there may be other measured or unmeasured variables affecting the results. This is known as the *third-variable* problem or the *tertium quid* (see section 1.6.2 and Jane Superbrain Box 1.1).

- **Direction of causality**: Correlation coefficients say nothing about which variable causes the other to change. Even if we could ignore the third-variable problem described above, and we could assume that the two correlated variables were the only important ones, the correlation coefficient doesn't indicate in which direction causality operates. So, although it is intuitively appealing to conclude that watching adverts causes us to buy packets of toffees, there is no *statistical* reason why buying packets of toffees cannot cause us to watch more adverts. Although the latter conclusion makes less intuitive sense, the correlation coefficient does not tell us that it isn't true.

6.4. Data entry for correlation analysis using SPSS ①

Data entry for correlation, regression and multiple regression is straightforward because each variable is entered in a separate column. So, for each variable you have measured, create a variable in the data editor with an appropriate name, and enter a participant's scores across one row of the data editor. There may be occasions on which you have one or more categorical variables (such as gender) and these variables can also be entered in a column (but remember to define appropriate value labels). As an example, if we wanted to calculate the correlation between the two variables in Table 6.1 we would enter these data as in Figure 6.3. You can see that each variable is entered in a separate column, and each row represents a single individual's data (so the first consumer saw 5 adverts and bought 8 packets).

SELF-TEST Enter the advert data and use the Chart Editor to produce a scatterplot (number of packets bought on the *y*-axis, and adverts watched on the *x*-axis) of the data.

FIGURE 6.3 Data entry for correlation

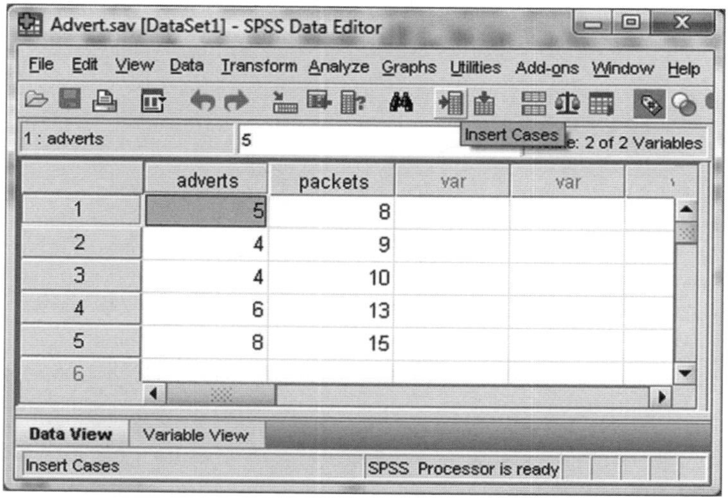

6.5. Bivariate correlation ①

6.5.1. General procedure for running correlations on SPSS ①

There are two types of correlation: *bivariate* and *partial*. A **bivariate correlation** is a correlation between two variables (as described at the beginning of this chapter) whereas a **partial correlation** looks at the relationship between two variables while 'controlling' the effect of one or more additional variables. Pearson's product-moment correlation coefficient (described earlier) and Spearman's rho (see section 6.5.3) are examples of bivariate correlation coefficients.

Let's return to the example from Chapter 4 about exam scores. Remember that a psychologist was interested in the effects of exam stress and revision on exam performance. She had devised and validated a questionnaire to assess state anxiety relating to exams (called the Exam Anxiety Questionnaire, or EAQ). This scale produced a measure of anxiety scored out of 100. Anxiety was measured before an exam, and the percentage mark of each student on the exam was used to assess the exam performance. She also measured the number of hours spent revising. These data are in **Exam Anxiety.sav** on the companion website. We have already created scatterplots for these data (section 4.8) so we don't need to do that again.

To conduct a bivariate correlation you need to find the *Correlate* option of the *Analyze* menu. The main dialog box is accessed by selecting Analyze Correlate ▸ Bivariate... and is shown in Figure 6.4. Using the dialog box it is possible to select which of three correlation statistics you wish to perform. The default setting is Pearson's product-moment correlation, but you can also calculate Spearman's correlation and Kendall's correlation – we will see the differences between these correlation coefficients in due course.

Having accessed the main dialog box, you should find that the variables in the data editor are listed on the left-hand side of the dialog box (Figure 6.4). There is an empty box

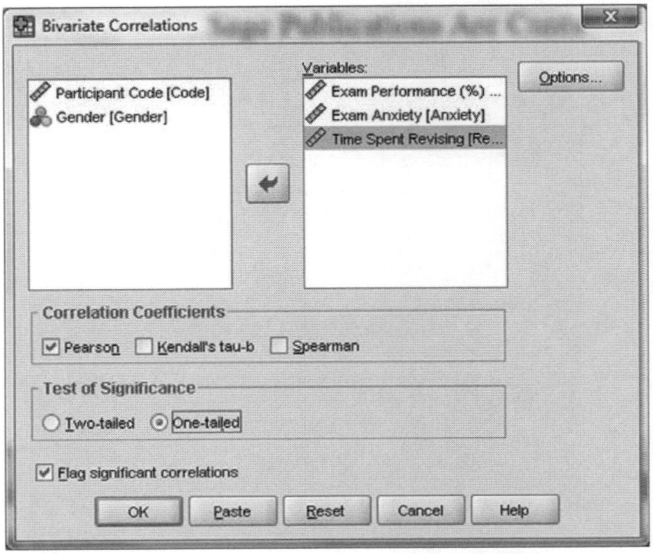

FIGURE 6.4 Dialog box for conducting a bivariate correlation

labelled *Variables* on the right-hand side. You can select any variables from the list using the mouse and transfer them to the *Variables* box by dragging them there or clicking on ➡. SPSS will create a table of correlation coefficients for all of the combinations of variables. This table is called a correlation matrix. For our current example, select the variables **Exam performance, Exam anxiety** and **Time spent revising** and transfer them to the *Variables* box by clicking on ➡. Having selected the variables of interest you can choose between three correlation coefficients: Pearson's product-moment correlation coefficient (Pearson) Spearman's rho (Spearman) and Kendall's tau (Kendall's tau-b). Any of these can be selected by clicking on the appropriate tick-box with a mouse.

In addition, it is possible to specify whether or not the test is one- or two-tailed (see section 2.6.2). To recap, a one-tailed test should be selected when you have a directional hypothesis (e.g. 'the more anxious someone is about an exam, the worse their mark will be'). A two-tailed test (the default) should be used when you cannot predict the nature of the relationship (i.e. 'I'm not sure whether exam anxiety will improve or reduce exam marks'). Therefore, if you have a directional hypothesis click on One-tailed, whereas if you have a non-directional hypothesis click on Two-tailed.

If you click on Options... then another dialog box appears with two *Statistics* options and two options for missing values (Figure 6.5). The *Statistics* options are enabled only when Pearson's correlation is selected; if Pearson's correlation is not selected then these options are disabled (they appear in a light grey rather than black and you can't activate them). This deactivation occurs because these two options are meaningful only for parametric data and the Pearson correlation is used with those kinds of data. If you select the tick-box labelled *Means and standard deviations* then SPSS will produce the mean and standard deviation of all of the variables selected for analysis. If you activate the tick-box labelled *Cross-product deviations and covariances* then SPSS will give you the values of these statistics for each of the variables in the analysis. The cross-product deviations tell us the sum of the products of mean corrected variables, which is simply the numerator (top half) of equation (6.2). The covariances option gives us values of the covariance between variables, which could be calculated manually using equation (6.2). In other words, these covariance values are the cross-product deviations divided by (N–1) and represent the unstandardized correlation coefficient. In most instances, you will not need to use these options but they occasionally come in handy (see Oliver Twisted). We can also decide how to deal with missing values (see SPSS Tip 6.1).

FIGURE 6.5 Dialog box for bivariate correlation options

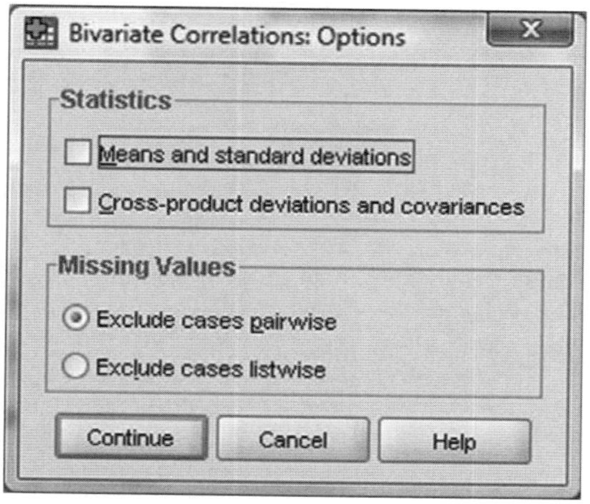

OLIVER TWISTED

Please, Sir, can I have some more … options?

Oliver is so excited to get onto analysing his data that he doesn't want me to spend pages waffling on about options that you will probably never use. 'Stop writing, you waffling fool,' he says. 'I want to analyse my data.' Well, he's got a point. If you want to find out more about what the Options... do in correlation, then the additional material for this chapter on the companion website will tell you.

SPSS TIP 6.1 Pairwise or listwise? ①

As we run through the various analyses in this book, many of them have additional options that can be accessed by clicking on Options... . Often part of the resulting *Options* dialog box will ask you if you want to exclude cases 'pairwise', 'analysis by analysis' or 'listwise'. First, we can exclude cases listwise, which means that if a case has a missing value for any variable, then they are excluded from the whole analysis. So, for example, in our exam anxiety data if one of our students had reported their anxiety and we knew their exam performance but we didn't have data about their revision time, then their data would not be used to calculate any of the correlations: *they would be completely excluded from the analysis*. Another option is to exclude cases on a pairwise or analysis-by-analysis basis, which means that if a participant has a score missing for a particular variable or analysis, then their data are excluded only from calculations involving the variable for which they have no score. For our student about whom we don't have any revision data, this means that their data would be excluded when calculating the correlation between exam scores and revision time, and when calculating the correlation between exam anxiety and revision time; however, the student's scores would be *included* when calculating the correlation between exam anxiety and exam performance because for this pair of variables we have both of their scores.

6.5.2. Pearson's correlation coefficient ①

6.5.2.1. Assumptions of Pearson's *r* ①

Pearson's correlation coefficient was described in full at the beginning of this chapter. Pearson's correlation requires only that data are interval (see section 1.5.1.2) for it to be an accurate measure of the linear relationship between two variables. However, if you want to establish whether the correlation coefficient is significant, then more assumptions are required: for the test statistic to be valid the sampling distribution has to be normally distributed and as we saw in Chapter 5 we assume that it is if our sample data are normally distributed (or if we have a large sample). Although typically, to assume that the sampling distribution is normal, we would want both variables to be normally distributed, there is one exception to this rule: one of the variables can be a categorical variable provided there are only two categories (in fact, if you look at section 6.5.5 you'll see that this is the same as doing a *t*-test, but I'm jumping the gun a bit). In any case, if your data are non-normal (see Chapter 5) or are not measured at the interval level then you should deselect the Pearson tick-box.

FIGURE 6.6
Karl Pearson

6.5.2.2. Running Pearson's *r* on SPSS ①

We have already seen how to access the main dialog box and select the variables for analysis earlier in this section (Figure 6.4). To obtain Pearson's correlation coefficient simply select the appropriate box (☑ Pearson) – SPSS selects this option by default. Our researcher predicted that (1) as anxiety increases, exam performance will decrease, and (2) as the time spent revising increases, exam performance will increase. Both of these are directional hypotheses, so both tests are one-tailed. To ensure that the output displays the one-tailed significance values select ⊙ One-tailed and then click on OK to run the analysis.

SPSS OUTPUT 6.1
Output for a Pearson's correlation

Correlations

		Exam performance (%)	Exam Anxiety	Time spent revising
Exam performance (%)	Pearson Correlation	1.000	-.441**	.397**
	Sig. (1-tailed)	.	.000	.000
	N	103	103	103
Exam Anxiety	Pearson Correlation	-.441**	1.000	-.709**
	Sig. (1-tailed)	.000	.	.000
	N	103	103	103
Time spent revising	Pearson Correlation	.397**	-.709**	1.000
	Sig. (1-tailed)	.000	.000	.
	N	103	103	103

**. Correlation is significant at the 0.01 level (1-tailed).

SPSS Output 6.1 provides a matrix of the correlation coefficients for the three variables. Underneath each correlation coefficient both the significance value of the correlation and the sample size (*N*) on which it is based are displayed. Each variable is perfectly correlated with itself (obviously) and so $r = 1$ along the diagonal of the table. Exam performance is negatively related to exam anxiety with a Pearson correlation coefficient of $r = -.441$ and the significance value is less than .001 (as indicated by the double asterisk after the coefficient). This significance value tells us that the probability of getting a correlation coefficient this big in a sample of 103 people if the null hypothesis were true (there was no relationship between these variables) is very low (close to zero in fact). Hence, we can gain confidence that there is a genuine relationship between exam performance and anxiety. Our criterion for significance is usually .05 (see section 2.6.1) so SPSS marks any correlation coefficient significant at this level with an asterisk. The output also shows that exam performance is positively related to the amount of time spent revising, with a coefficient of $r = .397$, which is also significant at $p < .001$. Finally, exam anxiety appears to be negatively related to the time spent revising, $r = -.709$, $p < .001$.

In psychological terms, this all means that as anxiety about an exam increases, the percentage mark obtained in that exam decreases. Conversely, as the amount of time revising increases, the percentage obtained in the exam increases. Finally, as revision time increases, the student's anxiety about the exam decreases. So there is a complex interrelationship between the three variables.

6.5.2.3. Using R^2 for interpretation ①

Although we cannot make direct conclusions about causality from a correlation, we can take the correlation coefficient a step further by squaring it. The correlation coefficient squared (known as the **coefficient of determination**, R^2) is a measure of the amount of variability in one variable that is shared by the other. For example, we may look at the relationship between exam anxiety and exam performance. Exam performances vary from person to person because of any number of factors (different ability, different levels of preparation and so on). If we add up all of this variability (rather like when we calculated the sum of squares in section 2.4.1) then we would have an estimate of how much variability exists in exam performances. We can then use R^2 to tell us how much of this variability is shared by exam anxiety. These two variables had a correlation of –0.4410 and so the value of R^2 will be $(-0.4410)^2 = 0.194$. This value tells us how much of the variability in exam performance is shared by exam anxiety.

If we convert this value into a percentage (multiply by 100) we can say that exam anxiety shares 19.4% of the variability in exam performance. So, although exam anxiety was highly correlated with exam performance, it can account for only 19.4% of variation in exam scores. To put this value into perspective, this leaves 80.6% of the variability still to be accounted for by other variables. I should note at this point that although R^2 is an extremely useful measure of the substantive importance of an effect, it cannot be used to infer causal relationships. Although we usually talk in terms of 'the variance in *y accounted for* by *x*', or even the variation in one variable *explained* by the other, this still says nothing about which way causality runs. So, although exam anxiety can account for 19.4% of the variation in exam scores, it does not necessarily cause this variation.

6.5.3. Spearman's correlation coefficient ①

Spearman's correlation coefficient (Spearman, 1910; Figure 6.7), r_s, is a non-parametric statistic and so can be used when the data have violated parametric assumptions such as non-normally distributed data (see Chapter 5). You'll sometimes hear the test referred to as Spearman's rho (pronounced 'row', as in 'row your boat gently down the stream'), which does make it difficult for some people to distinguish from the London lap-dancing club

FIGURE 6.7 Charles Spearman, ranking furiously

Spearmint Rhino.[3] Spearman's test works by first ranking the data (see section 15.3.1), and then applying Pearson's equation (equation (6.3)) to those ranks.

I was born in England, which has some bizarre traditions. One such oddity is The World's Biggest Liar Competition held annually at the Santon Bridge Inn in Wasdale (in the Lake District). The contest honours a local publican, 'Auld Will Ritson', who in the nineteenth century was famous in the area for his far-fetched stories (one such tale being that Wasdale turnips were big enough to be hollowed out and used as garden sheds). Each year locals are encouraged to attempt to tell the biggest lie in the world (lawyers and politicians are apparently banned from the competition). Over the years there have been tales of mermaid farms, giant moles, and farting sheep blowing holes in the ozone layer. (I am thinking of entering next year and reading out some sections of this book.)

Imagine I wanted to test a theory that more creative people will be able to create taller tales. I gathered together 68 past contestants from this competition and asked them where they were placed in the competition (first, second, third, etc.) and also gave them a creativity questionnaire (maximum score 60). The position in the competition is an ordinal variable (see section 1.5.1.2) because the places are categories but have a meaningful order (first place is better than second place and so on). Therefore, Spearman's correlation coefficient should be used (Pearson's r requires interval or ratio data). The data for this study are in the file **The Biggest Liar.sav**. The data are in two columns: one labelled **Creativity** and one labelled **Position** (there's actually a third variable in there but we will ignore it for the time being). For the **Position** variable, each of the categories described above has been coded with a numerical value. First place has been coded with the value 1, with positions being labelled 2, 3 and so on. Note that for each numeric code I have provided a value label (just like we did for coding variables). I have also set the *Measure* property of this variable to Ordinal.

The procedure for doing a Spearman correlation is the same as for a Pearson correlation except that in the *Bivariate Correlations* dialog box (Figure 6.4), we need to select Spearman and deselect the option for a Pearson correlation. At this stage, you should also specify whether you require a one- or two-tailed test. I predicted that more creative people would tell better lies. This hypothesis is directional and so a one-tailed test should be selected.

[3] Seriously, a colleague of mine asked a student what analysis she was thinking of doing and she responded 'a Spearman's Rhino'.

SPSS OUTPUT 6.2

Correlations

			Creativity	Position in Best Liar Competition
Spearman's rho	Creativity	Correlation Coefficient	1.000**	-.373**
		Sig. (1-tailed)	.	.001
		N	68	68
	Position in Best Liar Competition	Correlation Coefficient	-.373**	1.000**
		Sig. (1-tailed)	.001	.
		N	68	68

**. Correlation is significant at the 0.01 level (1-tailed).

SPSS Output 6.2 shows the output for a Spearman correlation on the variables **Creativity** and **Position.** The output is very similar to that of the Pearson correlation: a matrix is displayed giving the correlation coefficient between the two variables (–.373), underneath is the significance value of this coefficient (.001) and finally the sample size (68).[4] The significance value for this correlation coefficient is less than .05; therefore, it can be concluded that there is a significant relationship between creativity scores and how well someone did in the World's Biggest Liar Competition. Note that the relationship is negative: as creativity increased, position decreased. This might seem contrary to what we predicted until you remember that a low number means that you did well in the competition (a low number such as 1 means you came first, and a high number like 4 means you came fourth). Therefore, our hypothesis is supported: as creativity increased, so did success in the competition.

SELF-TEST Did creativity cause success in the World's Biggest Liar Competition?

6.5.4. Kendall's tau (non-parametric) ①

Kendall's tau, τ, is another non-parametric correlation and it should be used rather than Spearman's coefficient when you have a small data set with a large number of tied ranks. This means that if you rank all of the scores and many scores have the same rank, then Kendall's tau should be used. Although Spearman's statistic is the more popular of the two coefficients, there is much to suggest that Kendall's statistic is actually a better estimate of the correlation in the population (see Howell, 1997: 293). As such, we can draw more accurate generalizations from Kendall's statistic than from Spearman's. To carry out Kendall's correlation on the world's biggest liar data simply follow the same steps as for the Pearson and Spearman correlations but select ☑ Kendall's tau-b and deselect the Pearson and Spearman options. The output is much the same as for Spearman's correlation.

[4] It is good to check that the value of N corresponds to the number of observations that were made. If it doesn't then data may have been excluded for some reason.

SPSS OUTPUT 6.3

Correlations

			Creativity	Position in Best Liar Competition
Kendall's tau_b	Creativity	Correlation Coefficient	1.000**	-.300**
		Sig. (1-tailed)	.	.001
		N	68	68
	Position in Best Liar Competition	Correlation Coefficient	-.300**	1.000**
		Sig. (1-tailed)	.001	.
		N	68	68

**. Correlation is significant at the 0.01 level (1-tailed).

You'll notice from SPSS Output 6.3 that the actual value of the correlation coefficient is closer to zero than the Spearman correlation (it has increased from −.373 to −.300). Despite the difference in the correlation coefficients we can still interpret this result as being a highly significant relationship (because the significance value of .001 is less than .05). However, Kendall's value is a more accurate gauge of what the correlation in the population would be. As with the Pearson correlation, we cannot assume that creativity caused success in the World's Biggest Liar Competition.

SELF-TEST Conduct a Pearson correlation analysis of the advert data from the beginning of the chapter.

6.5.5. Biserial and point–biserial correlations ③

SMART ALEX ONLY

The biserial and point–biserial correlation coefficients are distinguished by only a conceptual difference yet their statistical calculation is quite different. These correlation coefficients are used when one of the two variables is dichotomous (i.e. it is categorical with only two categories). An example of a dichotomous variable is being pregnant, because a woman can be either pregnant or not (she cannot be 'a bit pregnant'). Often it is necessary to investigate relationships between two variables when one of the variables is dichotomous. The difference between the use of biserial and point–biserial correlations depends on whether the dichotomous variable is discrete or continuous. This difference is very subtle. A discrete, or true, dichotomy is one for which there is no underlying continuum between the categories. An example of this is whether someone is dead or alive: a person can be only dead or alive, they can't be 'a bit dead'. Although you might describe a person as being 'half-dead' – especially after a heavy drinking session – they are clearly still alive if they are still breathing! Therefore, there is no continuum between the two categories. However, it is possible to have a dichotomy for which a continuum does exist. An example is passing or failing a statistics test: some people will only just fail while others will fail by a large margin; likewise some people will scrape a pass while others will clearly excel. So although participants fall into only two categories there is clearly an underlying continuum along which people lie. Hopefully, it is clear that in this case there is some kind of continuum underlying the dichotomy, because some people passed or failed more dramatically than others. The **point–biserial correlation** coefficient (r_{pb}) is used when one variable is a discrete dichotomy (e.g. pregnancy), whereas the **biserial correlation** coefficient (r_b) is used when one variable is a continuous dichotomy (e.g. passing or failing an exam). The biserial correlation coefficient cannot be calculated directly in SPSS: first you must calculate the point–biserial correlation coefficient and then use an equation to adjust that figure.

Imagine that I was interested in the relationship between the gender of a cat and how much time it spent away from home (what can I say? I love cats so these things interest me). I had heard that male cats disappeared for substantial amounts of time on long-distance roams around the neighbourhood (something about hormones driving them to find mates) whereas female cats tended to be more homebound. So, I used this as a purr-fect (sorry!) excuse to go and visit lots of my friends and their cats. I took a note of the gender of the cat and then asked the owners to note down the number of hours that their cat was absent from home over a week. Clearly the time spent away from home is measured at an interval level – and let's assume it meets the other assumptions of parametric data – while the gender of the cat is discrete dichotomy. A point–biserial correlation has to be calculated and this is simply a Pearson correlation when the dichotomous variable is coded with 0 for one category and 1 for the other (actually you can use any values and SPSS will change the lower one to 0 and the higher one to 1 when it does the calculations). So, to conduct these correlations in SPSS assign the **Gender** variable a coding scheme as described in section 3.4.2.3 (in the saved data the coding is 1 for a male and 0 for a female). The **time** variable simply has time in hours recorded as normal. These data are in the file **pbcorr.sav**.

SELF-TEST Carry out a Pearson correlation on these data (as in 6.5.2.2).

Congratulations: if you did the self-test task then you have just conducted your first point–biserial correlation. See, despite the horrible name, it's really quite easy to do. You should find that you have the same output as SPSS Output 6.4, which shows the correlation matrix of **time** and **Gender**. The point–biserial correlation coefficient is $r_{pb} = .378$, which has a one-tailed significance value of .001. The significance test for this correlation is actually the same as performing an independent-samples t-test on the data (see Chapter 9). The sign of the correlation (i.e. whether the relationship was positive or negative) will depend entirely on which way round the coding of the dichotomous variable was made. To prove that this is the case, the data file **pbcorr.sav** has an extra variable called **recode** which is the same as the variable **Gender** except that the coding is reversed (1 = female, 0 = male). If you repeat the Pearson correlation using **recode** instead of **Gender** you will find that the correlation coefficient becomes −0.378. The sign of the coefficient is completely dependent on which category you assign to which code and so we must ignore all information about the direction of the relationship. However, we can still interpret R^2 as before. So in this example, $R^2 = (0.378)^2 = .143$. Hence, we can conclude that gender accounts for 14.3% of the variability in time spent away from home.

SPSS OUTPUT 6.4

Correlations

		Time away from home (hours)	Gender of cat
Time Away from Home (Hours)	Pearson Correlation	1.000	.378**
	Sig. (1-tailed)	.	.001
	N	60	60
Gender of Cat	Pearson Correlation	.378**	1.000
	Sig. (1-tailed)	.001	.
	N	60	60

**. Correlation is significant at the 0.01 level (1-tailed).

Imagine now that we wanted to convert the point–biserial correlation into the biserial correlation coefficient (r_b) (because some of the male cats were neutered and so there might be a continuum of maleness that underlies the gender variable). We must use equation (6.9) in which p is the proportion of cases that fell into the largest category and q is the proportion of cases that fell into the smallest category. Therefore, p and q are simply the number of male and female cats. In this equation y is the ordinate of the normal distribution at the point where there is p% of the area on one side and q% on the other (this will become clearer as we do an example):

$$r_b = \frac{r_{pb}\sqrt{pq}}{y} \tag{6.9}$$

To calculate p and q access the *Frequencies* dialog box using Analyze Descriptive Statistics ▸ 123 Frequencies... and select the variable **Gender**. There is no need to click on any further options as the defaults will give you what you need to know (namely the percentage of male and female cats). It turns out that 53.3% (0.533 as a proportion) of the sample were female (this is p because it is the largest portion) while the remaining 46.7% (0.467 as a proportion) were male (this is q because it is the smallest portion). To calculate y, we use these values and the values of the normal distribution displayed in the Appendix. Figure 6.8

FIGURE 6.8 Getting the 'ordinate' of the normal distribution

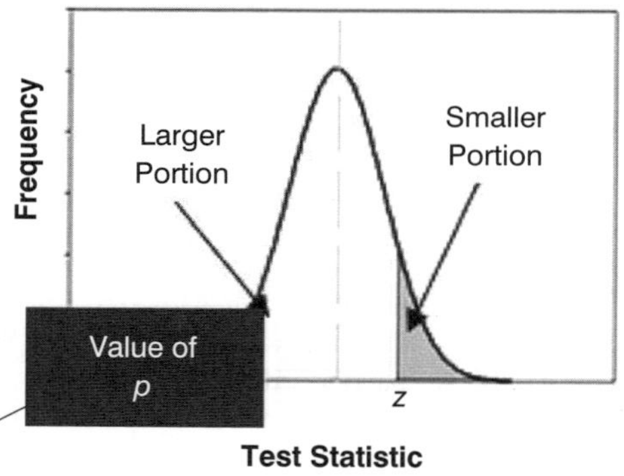

z	Larger Portion	Smaller Portion	y
.00	.50000	.50000	.3989
.01	.50399	.49601	.3989
.02	.50798	.49202	.3989
.03	.51197	.48803	.3988
.04	.51595	.48405	.3986
.05	.51994	.48006	.3984
.06	.52392	.47608	.3982
.07	.52790	.47210	.3980
.08	.53188	.46812	.3977
.09	.53586	.46414	.3973

z	Larger Portion	Smaller Portion	y
.23	.59095	.40905	.3885
.24	.59483	.40517	.3876
.25	.59871	.40129	.3867
.26	.60257	.39743	.3857
.27	.60642	.39358	.3847
.28	.61026	.38974	.3836
.29	.61409	.38591	.3825
.30	.61791	.38209	.3814
.31	.62172	.37828	.3802
.32	.62552	.37448	.3790

shows how to find the ordinate (the value in the column labelled y) when the normal curve is split with .467 as the smaller portion and .533 as the larger portion. The figure shows which columns represent p and q and we look for our values in these columns (the exact values of 0.533 and 0.467 are not in the table so instead we use the nearest values that we can find, which are .5319 and .4681 respectively). The ordinate value is in the column y and is .3977.

If we replace these values in equation (6.9) we get .475 (see below), which is quite a lot higher than the value of the point–biserial correlation (0.378). This finding just shows you that whether you assume an underlying continuum or not can make a big difference to the size of effect that you get:

$$r_{\mathrm{b}} = \frac{r_{\mathrm{pb}}\sqrt{pq}}{y} = \frac{(0.378)\sqrt{(0.533 \times 0.467)}}{0.3977} = 0.475$$

If this process freaks you out, you can also convert the point–biserial r to the biserial r using a table published by Terrell (1982b) in which you can use the value of the point–biserial correlation (i.e. Pearson's r) and p, which is just the proportion of people in the largest group (in the above example, .53). This spares you the trouble of having to work out y in the above equation (which you're also spared from using). Using Terrell's table we get a value in this example of .48 which is the same as we calculated to 2 decimal places.

To get the significance of the biserial correlation we need to first work out its standard error. If we assume the null hypothesis (that the biserial correlation in the population is zero) then the standard error is given by (Terrell, 1982a):

$$\mathrm{SE}_{r_{\mathrm{b}}} = \frac{\sqrt{pq}}{y\sqrt{N}} \tag{6.10}$$

This equation is fairly straightforward because it uses the values of p, q and y that we already used to calculate the biserial r. The only additional value is the sample size (N), which in this example was 60. So, our standard error is:

$$\mathrm{SE}_{r_{\mathrm{b}}} = \frac{\sqrt{(.533 \times .467)}}{.3977 \times \sqrt{60}} = .162$$

The standard error helps us because we can create a z-score (see section 1.7.4). To get a z-score we take the biserial correlation, subtract the mean in the population and divide by the standard error. We have assumed that the mean in the population is 0 (the null hypothesis), so we can simply divide the biserial correlation by its standard error:

$$Z_{r_{\mathrm{b}}} = \frac{r_{\mathrm{b}} - \bar{r}_{\mathrm{b}}}{\mathrm{SE}_{r_{\mathrm{b}}}} = \frac{r_{\mathrm{b}} - 0}{\mathrm{SE}_{r_{\mathrm{b}}}} = \frac{r_{\mathrm{b}}}{\mathrm{SE}_{r_{\mathrm{b}}}} = \frac{.475}{.162} = 2.93$$

EVERYBODY

We can look up this value of z (2.93) in the table for the normal distribution in the Appendix and get the one-tailed probability from the column labelled 'Smaller Portion'. In this case the value is .00169. To get the two-tailed probability we simply multiply the one-tailed probability value by 2, which gives us .00338. As such the correlation is significant, $p < .01$.

CRAMMING SAM'S TIPS

- We can measure the relationship between two variables using *correlation coefficients*.
- These coefficients lie between −1 and +1.
- *Pearson's correlation coefficient, r,* is a parametric statistic and requires interval data for both variables. To test its significance we assume normality too.
- *Spearman's correlation coefficient,* r_s, is a non-parametric statistic and requires only ordinal data for both variables.
- *Kendall's correlation coefficient,* τ, is like Spearman's r_s but probably better for small samples.
- *The point–biserial correlation coefficient,* r_{pb}, quantifies the relationship between a continuous variable and a variable that is a discrete dichotomy (e.g. there is no continuum underlying the two categories, such as dead or alive).
- *The biserial correlation coefficient,* r_b, quantifies the relationship between a continuous variable and a variable that is a continuous dichotomy (e.g. there is a continuum underlying the two categories, such as passing or failing an exam).

6.6. Partial correlation ②

6.6.1. The theory behind part and partial correlation ②

SMART ALEX ONLY

I mentioned earlier that there is a type of correlation that can be done that allows you to look at the relationship between two variables when the effects of a third variable are held constant. For example, analyses of the exam anxiety data (in the file **ExamAnxiety.sav**) showed that exam performance was negatively related to exam anxiety, but positively related to revision time, and revision time itself was negatively related to exam anxiety. This scenario is complex, but given that we know that revision time is related to both exam anxiety and exam performance, then if we want a pure measure of the relationship between exam anxiety and exam performance we need to take account of the influence of revision time. Using the values of R^2 for these relationships, we know that exam anxiety accounts for 19.4% of the variance in exam performance, that revision time accounts for 15.7% of the variance in exam performance, and that revision time accounts for 50.2% of the variance in exam anxiety. If revision time accounts for half of the variance in exam anxiety, then it seems feasible that at least some of the 19.4% of variance in exam performance that is accounted for by anxiety is the same variance that is accounted for by revision time. As such, some of the variance in exam performance explained by exam anxiety is not *unique* and can be accounted for by revision time. A correlation between two variables in which the effects of other variables are held constant is known as a partial correlation.

Let's return to our example of exam scores, revision time and exam anxiety to illustrate the principle behind partial correlation (Figure 6.9). In part 1 of the diagram there is a box for exam performance that represents the total variation in exam scores (this value would be the variance of exam performance). There is also a box that represents the variation in exam anxiety (again, this is the variance of that variable). We know already that exam anxiety and exam performance share 19.4% of their variation (this value is the correlation coefficient squared). Therefore, the variations of these two variables overlap (because they share variance) creating a third box (the one with diagonal lines). The overlap of the boxes representing exam performance and exam anxiety is the common variance. Likewise, in

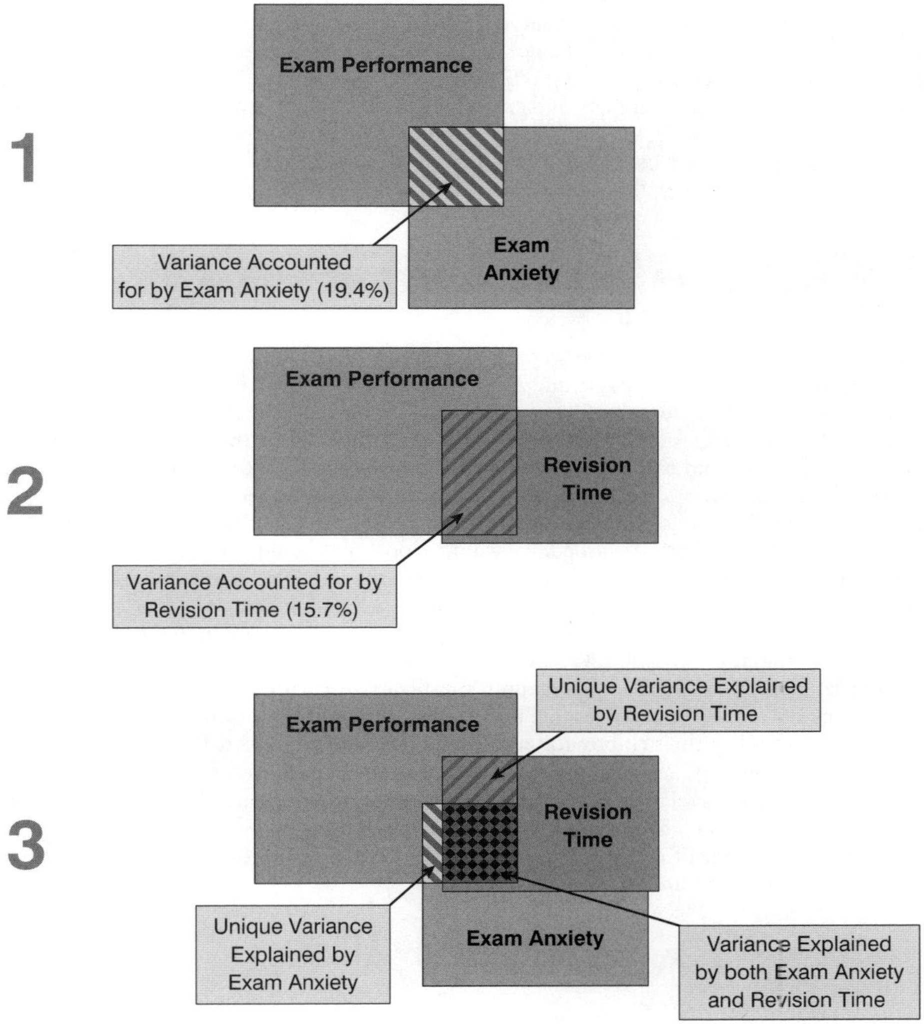

FIGURE 6.9 Diagram showing the principle of partial correlation

part 2 of the diagram the shared variation between exam performance and revision time is illustrated. Revision time shares 15.7% of the variation in exam scores. This shared variation is represented by the area of overlap (filled with diagonal lines). We know that revision time and exam anxiety also share 50% of their variation; therefore, it is very probable that some of the variation in exam performance shared by exam anxiety is the same as the variance shared by revision time.

Part 3 of the diagram shows the complete picture. The first thing to note is that the boxes representing exam anxiety and revision time have a large overlap (this is because they share 50% of their variation). More important, when we look at how revision time and anxiety contribute to exam performance we see that there is a portion of exam performance that is shared by both anxiety and revision time (the dotted area). However, there are still small chunks of the variance in exam performance that are unique to the other two variables. So, although in part 1 exam anxiety shared a large chunk of variation in exam performance, some of this overlap is also shared by revision time. If we remove the portion of variation that is also shared by revision time, we get a measure of the unique relationship between exam performance and exam anxiety. We use partial correlations to find out the size of the unique portion of variance. Therefore, we could conduct a partial correlation between exam anxiety and exam performance while 'controlling' for the effect of revision time. Likewise, we could carry out a partial correlation between revision time and exam performance while 'controlling' for the effects of exam anxiety.

6.6.2. Partial correlation using SPSS ②

Reload the **Exam Anxiety.sav** file so that, as I suggested above, we can conduct a partial correlation between exam anxiety and exam performance while 'controlling' for the effect of revision time.. To access the *Partial Correlations* dialog box (Figure 6.10) select Analyze Correlate $r_{12.3}$ Partial.... This dialog box lists all of the variables in the data editor on the left-hand side and there are two empty spaces on the right-hand side. The space labelled *Variables* is for listing the variables that you want to correlate and the space labelled *Controlling for* is for declaring any variables the effects of which you want to control. In the example I have described, we want to look at the unique effect of exam anxiety on exam performance and so we want to correlate the variables **exam** and **anxiety** while controlling for **revise**. Figure 6.10 shows the completed dialog box.

If you click on Options... then another dialog box appears as shown in Figure 6.11. These options are similar to those in bivariate correlation except that you can choose to compute zero-order correlations, which are simply the bivariate correlation coefficients without controlling for any other variables (i.e. they're Pearson's correlation coefficient). So, in our example, if we select the tick-box for zero-order correlations SPSS will produce a correlation matrix of **anxiety**, **exam** and **revise**. If you haven't conducted bivariate correlations before the partial correlation then this is a useful way to compare the correlations that haven't been controlled against those that have. This comparison gives you some insight into the contribution of different variables. Tick the box for zero-order correlations but leave the rest of the options as they are.

FIGURE 6.10
Main dialog box for conducting a partial correlation

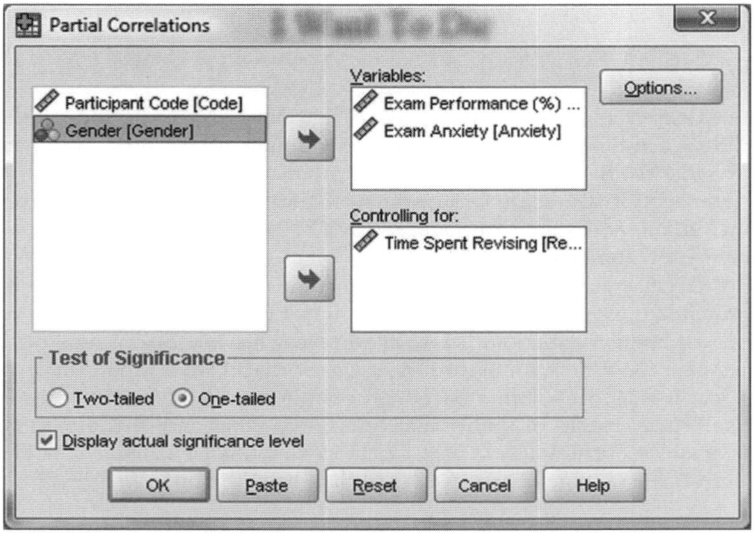

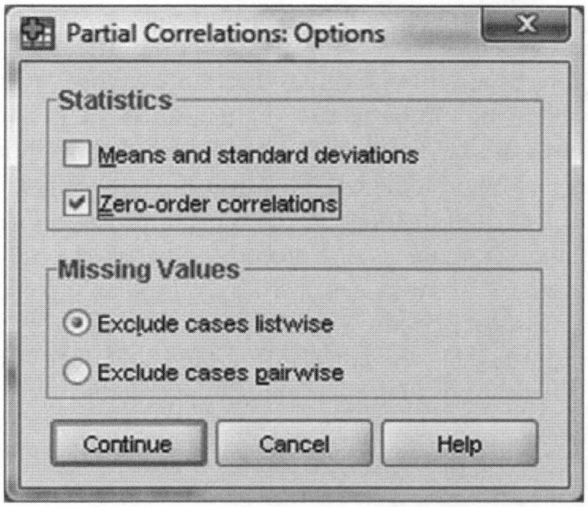

FIGURE 6.11 Options for partial correlation

Correlations

Control Variables			Exam Performance (%)	Exam Anxiety	Time Spent Revising
-none-[a]	Exam Performance (%)	Correlation	1.000	-.441	.397
		Significance (1-tailed)	.	.000	.000
		df	0	101	101
	Exam Anxiety	Correlation	-.441	1.000	-.709
		Significance (1-tailed)	.000	.	.000
		df	101	0	101
	Time Spent Revising	Correlation	.397	-.709	1.000
		Significance (1-tailed)	.000	.000	.
		df	101	101	0
Time Spent Revising	Exam Performance (%)	Correlation	1.000	-.247	
		Significance (1-tailed)	.	.006	
		df	0	100	
	Exam Anxiety	Correlation	-.247	1.000	
		Significance (1-tailed)	.006	.	
		df	100	0	

a. Cells contain zero-order (Pearson) correlations.

SPSS OUTPUT 6.5 Output from a partial correlation

SPSS Output 6.5 shows the output for the partial correlation of exam anxiety and exam performance controlling for revision time. The first thing to notice is the matrix of zero-order correlations, which we asked for using the options dialog box. The correlations displayed here are identical to those obtained from the Pearson correlation procedure (compare this matrix to the one in SPSS Output 6.1). Underneath the zero-order correlations is a matrix of correlations for the variables **anxiety** and **exam** but controlling for the effect of revision. In this instance we have controlled for one variable and so this is known as a first-order partial correlation. It is possible to control for the effects of two variables at the same time (a second-order partial correlation) or control three variables (a third-order partial correlation) and so on. First, notice that the partial correlation between exam performance and exam anxiety is −.247, which is considerably less than the correlation when the effect of revision time is not controlled for ($r = -.441$). In fact, the correlation coefficient is nearly half what it was before. Although this correlation is still statistically significant (its p-value is still below .05), the relationship is diminished. In terms of variance, the value of R^2 for the partial correlation is .06, which means that exam anxiety can now account for only 6% of the variance in exam performance. When the effects of revision time were not controlled for, exam anxiety shared 19.4% of the variation in exam scores and so the inclusion of revision time has severely diminished the amount of variation in exam scores shared by anxiety. As such, a truer measure of the role of exam anxiety has been obtained. Running this analysis has shown us that exam anxiety alone does explain some of the variation in exam scores, but there is a complex relationship between anxiety, revision and exam performance that might otherwise have been ignored. Although causality is still not certain, because relevant variables are being included, the third variable problem is, at least, being addressed in some form.

These partial correlations can be done when variables are dichotomous (including the 'third' variable). So, for example, we could look at the relationship between bladder relaxation (did the person wet themselves or not?) and the number of large tarantulas crawling up your leg controlling for fear of spiders (the first variable is dichotomous, but the second variable and 'controlled for' variables are continuous). Also, to use an earlier example, we could examine the relationship between creativity and success in the world's greatest liar contest controlling for whether someone had previous experience in the competition (and therefore had some idea of the type of tale that would win) or not. In this latter case the 'controlled for' variable is dichotomous.[5]

6.6.3. Semi-partial (or part) correlations ②

In the next chapter, we will come across another form of correlation known as a **semi-partial correlation** (also referred to as a part correlation). While I'm babbling on about partial correlations it is worth my explaining the difference between this type of correlation and a semi-partial correlation. When we do a partial correlation between two variables, we control for the effects of a third variable. Specifically, the effect that the third variable has on *both* variables in the correlation is controlled. In a semi-partial correlation we control for the effect that the third variable has on only one of the variables in the correlation. Figure 6.12 illustrates this principle for the exam performance data. The partial correlation that we calculated took account not only of the effect of revision on exam performance, but also of the effect of revision on anxiety. If we were to calculate the semi-partial correlation for the same data, then this would control for only the effect of revision on exam performance (the effect of revision on exam anxiety is ignored). Partial correlations are most useful for looking at the unique relationship between two variables when other variables are ruled out. Semi-partial correlations are, therefore, useful when trying to explain the variance in one particular variable (an outcome) from a set of predictor variables. (Bear this in mind when you read Chapter 7.)

FIGURE 6.12 The difference between a partial and a semi-partial correlation

CRAMMING SAM'S TIPS

- A *partial correlation* quantifies the relationship between two variables while controlling for the effects of a third variable on *both* variables in the original correlation.
- A *semi-partial correlation* quantifies the relationship between two variables while controlling for the effects of a third variable on only *one* of the variables in the original correlation.

[5] Both these examples are, in fact, simple cases of hierarchical regression (see the next chapter) and the first example is also an example of analysis of covariance. This may be confusing now, but as we progress through the book I hope it'll become clearer that virtually all of the statistics that you use are actually the same things dressed up in different names.

6.7. Comparing correlations ③

6.7.1. Comparing independent *r*s ③

Sometimes we want to know whether one correlation coefficient is bigger than another. For example, when we looked at the effect of exam anxiety on exam performance, we might have been interested to know whether this correlation was different in men and women. We could compute the correlation in these two samples, but then how would we assess whether the difference was meaningful?

SELF-TEST Use the *split file* command to compute the correlation coefficient between exam anxiety and exam performance in men and women.

If we did this, we would find that the correlations were $r_{Male} = -.506$ and $r_{Female} = -.381$. These two samples are independent; that is, they contain different entities. To compare these correlations we can again use what we discovered in section 6.3.3 to convert these coefficients to z_r (just to remind you, we do this because it makes the sampling distribution normal and we know the standard error). If you do the conversion, then we get z_r (males) = −.557 and z_r (females) = −.401. We can calculate a *z*-score of the differences between these correlations as:

$$Z_{Difference} = \frac{z_{r_1} - z_{r_2}}{\sqrt{\frac{1}{N_1 - 3} + \frac{1}{N_2 + 3}}} \qquad (6.11)$$

We had 52 men and 51 women so we would get:

$$Z_{Difference} = \frac{-.557 - (-.401)}{\sqrt{\frac{1}{49} + \frac{1}{48}}} = \frac{-.156}{0.203} = -0.768$$

We can look up this value of *z* (0.768, we can ignore the minus sign) in the table for the normal distribution in the Appendix and get the one-tailed probability from the column labelled 'Smaller Portion'. In this case the value is .221. To get the two-tailed probability we simply multiply the one-tailed probability value by 2, which gives us .442. As such the correlation between exam anxiety and exam performance is not significantly different in men and women. (see Oliver Twisted for how to do this on SPSS).

6.7.2. Comparing dependent *r*s ③

If you want to compare correlation coefficients that come from the same entities then things are a little more complicated. You can use a *t*-statistic to test whether a difference between two dependent correlations from the same sample is significant. For example, in our exam anxiety data we might want to see whether the relationship between exam anxiety (*x*) and exam performance (y) is stronger than the relationship between revision (z) and exam performance. To calculate this, all we need are the three *r*s that quantify the relationships between these variables: r_{xy}, the relationship between exam anxiety and exam performance (–.441); r_{zy}, the relationship between revision and exam performance (.397); and r_{xz}, the relationship between exam anxiety and revision (–.709). The t-statistic is computed as (Chen & Popovich, 2002):

$$t_{Difference} = \left(r_{xy} - r_{zy}\right)\sqrt{\frac{(n-3)(1+r_{xz})}{2\left(1 - r_{xy}^2 - r_{xz}^2 - r_{zy}^2 + 2r_{xy}r_{xz}r_{zy}\right)}} \tag{6.12}$$

Admittedly that equation looks hideous, but really it's not too bad: it just uses the three correlation coefficients and the sample size N. Place the numbers from the exam anxiety example in it (N was 103) and you should end up with:

$$t_{Difference} = (-.838)\sqrt{\frac{29.1}{2(1 - .194 - .503 - .158 + 0.248}} = -5.09$$

EVERYBODY

This value can be checked against the appropriate critical value in the Appendix with $N - 3$ degrees of freedom (in this case 100). The critical values in the table are 1.98 ($p < .05$) and 2.63 ($p < .01$), two-tailed. As such we can say that the correlation between exam anxiety and exam performance was significantly higher than the correlation between revision time and exam performance (this isn't a massive surprise given that these relationships went in the opposite directions to each other).

OLIVER TWISTED

Please, Sir, can I have some more … comparing of correlations?

'Are you having a bloody laugh with that equation?' yelps Oliver. 'I'd rather smother myself with cheese sauce and lock myself in a room of hungry mice.' Yes, yes, Oliver, enough of your sexual habits. To spare the poor mice I have written some SPSS syntax to run the comparisons mentioned in this section. For a guide on how to use them read the additional material for this chapter on the companion website. Go on, be kind to the mice!

6.8. Calculating the effect size ①

Calculating effect sizes for correlation coefficients couldn't be easier because, as we saw earlier in the book, correlation coefficients *are* effect sizes! So, no calculations (other than those you have already done) necessary! However, I do want to point out one caveat when using non-parametric correlation coefficients as effect sizes. Although the Spearman and Kendall correlations are comparable in many respects (their power, for example, is similar under parametric conditions), there are two important differences (Strahan, 1982).

First, we saw for Pearson's r that we can square this value to get the proportion of shared variance, R^2. For Spearman's r_s we can do this too because it uses the same equation as Pearson's r.

However, the resulting R_s^2 needs to be interpreted slightly differently: it is the proportion of variance in the *ranks* that two variables share. Having said this, R_s^2 is usually a good approximation of R^2 (especially in conditions of near-normal distributions). Kendall's τ, however, is not numerically similar to either r or r_s and so τ^2 does not tell us about the proportion of variance shared by two variables (or the ranks of those two variables).

Second, Kendall's τ is 66–75% smaller than both Spearman's r_s and Pearson's r, but r and r_s are generally similar sizes (Strahan, 1982). As such, if τ is used as an effect size it should be borne in mind that it is not comparable to r and r_s and should not be squared. A related issue is that the point–biserial and biserial correlations differ in size too (as we saw in this chapter, the biserial correlation was bigger than the point–biserial). In this instance you should be careful to decide whether your dichotomous variable has an underlying continuum, or whether it is a truly discrete variable. More generally, when using correlations as effect sizes you should remember (both when reporting your own analysis and when interpreting others) that the choice of correlation coefficient can make a substantial difference to the apparent size of the effect.

6.9. How to report correlation coefficents ①

Reporting correlation coefficients is pretty easy: you just have to say how big they are and what their significance value was (although the significance value isn't *that* important because the correlation coefficient is an effect size in its own right!). Five things to note are that: (1) there should be no zero before the decimal point for the correlation coefficient or the probability value (because neither can exceed 1); (2) coefficients are reported to 2 decimal places; (3) if you are quoting a one-tailed probability, you should say so; (4) each correlation coefficient is represented by a different letter (and some of them are Greek!); and (5) there are standard criteria of probabilities that we use (.05, .01 and .001). Let's take a few examples from this chapter:

- ✓ There was a significant relationship between the number of adverts watched and the number of packets of sweets purchased, $r = .87$, p (one-tailed) $< .05$.
- ✓ Exam performance was significantly correlated with exam anxiety, $r = -.44$, and time spent revising, $r = .40$; the time spent revising was also correlated with exam anxiety, $r = -.71$ (all ps $< .001$).
- ✓ Creativity was significantly related to how well people did in the World's Biggest Liar Competition, $r_s = -.37$, $p < .001$.
- ✓ Creativity was significantly related to how well people did in the World's Biggest Liar Competition, $\tau = -.30$, $p < .001$. (Note that I've quoted Kendall's τ here.)
- ✓ The gender of the cat was significantly related to the time the cat spent away from home, $r_{pb} = .38$, $p < .01$.
- ✓ The gender of the cat was significantly related to the time the cat spent away from home, $r_b = .48$, $p < .01$.

Scientists, rightly or wrongly, tend to use several *standard* levels of statistical significance. Primarily, the most important criterion is that the significance value is less than .05; however, if the exact significance value is much lower then we can be much more confident about the strength of the experimental effect. In these circumstances we like to make a big song and dance about the fact that our result isn't just significant at .05, but is significant at a much lower level as well (hooray!). The values we use are .05, .01, .001 and .0001. You are rarely ever going to be in the fortunate position of being able to report an effect that is significant at a level less than .0001!

TABLE 6.2 An example of reporting a table of correlations

	Exam Performance	*Exam Anxiety*	*Revision Time*
Exam Performance	1	−.44***	.40***
Exam Anxiety	101	1	−.71***
Revision Time	101	101	1

Ns = not significant (p > .05), *p < .05, ** p < .01, *** p < .001

When we have lots of correlations we sometimes put them into a table. For example, our exam anxiety correlations could be reported as in Table 6.2. Note that above the diagonal I have reported the correlation coefficients and used symbols to represent different levels of significance. Under the table there is a legend to tell readers what symbols represent. (Actually, none of the correlations were non-significant or had p bigger than .001 so most of these are here simply to give you a reference point – you would normally include symbols that you had actually used in the table in your legend.) Finally, in the lower part of the table I have reported the sample sizes. These are all the same (101) but sometimes when you have missing data it is useful to report the sample sizes in this way because different values of the correlation will be based on different sample sizes. For some more ideas on how to report correlations have a look at Labcoat Leni's Real Research 6.1.

LABCOAT LENI'S REAL RESEARCH 6.1

Why do you like your lecturers? ①

As students you probably have to rate your lecturers at the end of the course. There will be some lecturers you like and others that you hate. As a lecturer I find this process horribly depressing (although this has a lot to do with the fact that I tend focus on negative feedback and ignore the good stuff). There is some evidence that students tend to pick courses of lecturers who they perceive to be enthusastic and good communicators. In a fascinating study, Tomas Chamorro-Premuzic and his colleagues (Chamorro-Premuzic, Furnham, Christopher, Garwood, & Martin, 2008) tested a slightly different hypothesis, which was that students tend to like lecturers who are like themselves. (This hypothesis will have the students on my course who like my lectures screaming in horror.)

First of all the authors measured students' own personalities using a very well-established measure (the NEO-FFI) which gives rise to scores on five fundamental personality traits: Neuroticism, Extroversion, Openness to experience, Agreeableness and Conscientiousness. They also gave students a questionnaire that asked them to rate how much they wanted their lecturer to have each of a list of characteristics. For example, they would be given the description 'warm: friendly, warm, sociable, cheerful, affectionate, outgoing' and asked to rate how much they wanted to see this in a lecturer from –5 (they don't want this characteristic at all) through 0 (the characteristic is not important) to +5 (I really want this characteristic in my lecturer). The characteristics on the questionnaire all related to personality characteristics measured by the NEO-FFI. As such, the authors had a measure of how much a student had each of the five core personality characteristics, but also a measure of how much they wanted to see those same characteristics in their lecturer.

In doing so, Tomas and his colleagues could test whether, for instance, extroverted students want extrovert lecturers. The data from this study (well, for the variables that I've mentioned) are in the file **Chamorro-Premuzic.sav**. Run some Pearson correlations on these variables to see if students with certain personality characteristics want to see those characteristics in their lecturers. What conclusions can you draw?

Answers are in the additional material on the companion website (or look at Table 3 in the original article, which will also show you how to report a large number of correlations).

CHAMORRO-PREMUZIC, T., ET AL. (2008). *PERSONALITY AND INDIVIDUAL DIFFERENCES, 44*, 965–976.

What have I discovered about statistics? ①

This chapter has looked at ways to study relationships between variables. We began by looking at how we might measure relationships statistically by developing what we already know about variance (from Chapter 1) to look at variance shared between variables. This shared variance is known as *covariance*. We then discovered that when data are parametric we can measure the strength of a relationship using Pearson's correlation coefficient, *r*. When data violate the assumptions of parametric tests we can use Spearman's r_s, or for small data sets Kendall's τ may be more accurate. We also saw that correlations can be calculated between two variables when one of those variables is a dichotomy (i.e. composed of two categories); when the categories have no underlying continuum then we use the point–biserial correlation, r_{pb}, but when the categories do have an underlying continuum we use the biserial correlation, r_b. Finally, we looked at the difference between *partial correlations*, in which the relationship between two variables is measured controlling for the effect that one or more variables has on both of those variables, and *semi-partial correlations*, in which the relationship between two variables is measured controlling for the effect that one or more variables has on only one of those variables. We also discovered that I had a guitar and, like my favourite record of the time, I was ready to 'Take on the world'. Well, Wales at any rate ...

Key terms that I've discovered

Biserial correlation
Bivariate correlation
Coefficient of determination
Covariance
Cross-product deviations
Kendall's tau
Partial correlation
Pearson correlation coefficient
Point–biserial correlation
Semi-partial correlation
Spearman's correlation coefficient
Standardization

Smart Alex's tasks

- **Task 1**: A student was interested in whether there was a positive relationship between the time spent doing an essay and the mark received. He got 45 of his friends and timed how long they spent writing an essay **(hours)** and the percentage they got in the essay **(essay)**. He also translated these grades into their degree classifications **(grade)**: first, upper second, lower second and third class. Using the data in the file **EssayMarks.sav** find out what the relationship was between the time spent doing an essay and the eventual mark in terms of percentage and degree class (draw a scatterplot too!). ①

- **Task 2**: Using the **ChickFlick.sav** data from Chapter 3, is there a relationship between gender and arousal? Using the same data, is there a relationship between the film watched and arousal? ①

- **Task 3**: As a statistics lecturer I am always interested in the factors that determine whether a student will do well on a statistics course. One potentially important factor is their previous expertise with mathematics. Imagine I took 25 students and looked at their degree grades for my statistics course at the end of their first year at university. In the UK, a student can get a first-class mark (the best), an upper-second-class mark, a lower second, a third, a pass or a fail (the worst). I also asked these students what grade they got in their GCSE maths exams. In the UK GCSEs are school exams taken at age 16 that are graded A, B, C, D, E or F (an A grade is better than all of the lower grades). The data for this study are in the file **grades.sav**. Carry out the appropriate analysis to see if GCSE maths grades correlate with first-year statistics grades. ①

Answers can be found on the companion website.

Further reading

Chen, P. Y., & Popovich, P. M. (2002). *Correlation: Parametric and nonparametric measures*. Thousand Oaks, CA: Sage.

Howell, D. C. (2006). *Statistical methods for psychology* (6th ed.). Belmont, CA: Duxbury. (Or you might prefer his *Fundamental Statistics for the Behavioral Sciences,* also in its 6th edition, 2007. Both are excellent texts that are a bit more technical than this book so they are a useful next step.)

Miles, J. N. V., & Banyard, P. (2007). *Understanding and using statistics in psychology: a practical introduction*. London: Sage. (A fantastic and amusing introduction to statistical theory.)

Wright, D. B., & London, K. (2009). *First steps in statistics* (2nd ed.). London: Sage. (This book is a very gentle introduction to statistical theory.)

Online tutorial

The companion website contains the following Flash movie tutorial to accompany this chapter:

- Correlations using SPSS

Interesting real research

Chamorro-Premuzic, T., Furnham, A., Christopher, A. N., Garwood, J., & Martin, N. (2008). Birds of a feather: Students' preferences for lecturers' personalities as predicted by their own personality and learning approaches. *Personality and Individual Differences*, *44*, 965–976.

22

Chi-Square

ROBERT P. BURNS and RICHARD BURNS

Content list

By the end of this chapter you should be able to:

1 Understand the situations in which chi square is the appropriate statistic.
2 Use chi square in a goodness-of-fit test.
3 Use chi square to determine the degree of relationship between nominal variables in a cross-tabulation (contingency) format.
4 Use SPSS to calculate and interpret chi square goodness-of-fit and cross-tabulation printouts.

Introduction

In the previous two chapters we considered the testing of hypotheses that stated differences between groups. But testing for significant relationships is equally important. In this and the next chapter, we will look at how we test hypotheses that state relationships. The chi square test is a non-parametric test used when the variables are nominal.

What is chi square used for?

The chi square distribution uses nominal data such as counts or frequencies within categories. Many real world business situations produce a collection of count or frequency data and as a result chi square analysis is very common and useful.

For example, the nominal data may be:

- the number of people who indicate which one of three brands of toothpaste they prefer;
- membership or not of a trade union among full-time and part-time employees;
- number of investments by investment categories;
- different categories of responses made to a market research survey question by persons classified by age, sex, job classification or income age group;
- vehicles registered by the Department of Transport, classified and counted under headings such as cars, buses, commercial vehicles, motor bicycles;
- Immigration Department counts of the different type of immigrants, such as residents returning home, foreign work permit holders, business visitors and tourists.

For the chi square test, categories of responses are set up, such as Brands A, B and C of toothpaste, or 'member' and 'non-member' of the union, and the number of individuals, observations or events falling into each category of response.

Response distributions may be like those below:

1 Association between preferences for toothpaste brand and respondent gender:

Brand	*Male*	*Female*
Minty	21	46
Pegsave	83	14
Dentcool	27	63

2 The relationship between union membership and type of employment in the company:

Union member	*Full time*	*Part time*
Yes	68	13
No	10	74

In each of the above examples, both variables consist of a small number of categories containing the number or frequency of the sample found in each. This constitutes nominal data. With such data, the only analysis possible is to determine whether the frequencies observed in the sample differ significantly from hypothesized or expected frequencies.

Tables like those above are often called **cross-tabulation or contingency tables**. Each cell of the table is the intersection of a row and column and contains the frequency of individuals in that intersection. In Example 1 above, 46 females prefer Minty, while 27 males choose Dentcool. In Example 2, 13 out of 87 part-time employees are union members.

> ***Contingency table.*** *A two-dimensional table showing frequencies in each combination of categories for two dichotomous nominal variables, i.e. four cells.* ***Cross-tabulation*** *has more than four cells.*

Chi square is therefore the most common and simple non-parametric test of significance suitable for nominal data where observations can be classified into discrete categories and treated as frequencies. The symbol for this statistic is the Greek letter chi, which is pronounced 'ky' to rhyme with 'sky', and usually written as:

$$\chi^2$$

Chi square tests hypotheses about the independence (or alternatively the association) of frequency counts in various categories. The hypotheses for the chi square test are:

H_0 where the variables are statistically independent or no statistical association, and
H_1 where the variables are statistically dependent or associated.

In our examples above the null hypothesis would state that there is no significant association between your gender and which toothpaste you prefer; or that union membership is independent of (not associated with) type of employment, i.e. that the cross-categories from each variable are independent of each other.

The formula for chi square is the summation **for each cell** of:

$$\frac{(\text{observed frequency} - \text{expected frequency})^2}{\text{expected frequency}}$$

The mathematical formula is chi square $= \sum \frac{(O - E)^2}{E}$ where

O = observed frequency – the data observed in our research/survey
E = expected frequency, and
$\sum$ = the summation over all the cells in the table

There are two major uses of chi square:

1 As a *goodness-of-fit test* when it tells us how well an observed distribution fits a hypothesized or theoretical distribution. For example:
(a) Are some brands of frozen peas chosen by consumers more than others?

(b) Is absence through sickness regularly distributed through the working week or is 'sick leave' more frequent on some days than other days?

(c) Are choices on an item with a three-point response scale of '*yes*', '*no opinion*', '*no*', equally divided, or is there a significant preference for one choice to the item?

2 As a *cross-tabulation* between two categories, each of which can be divided into two or more sub-categories; for example, preference for type of music (classical, jazz, country and western, rock) against age group (below 21; 21–45; above 45); length of service in year groupings against position level.

But to whichever of these uses chi square is put, the general principle remains the same.

One compares the observed frequencies in a sample with the expected (chance) frequencies and applies the chi square test to determine whether a difference between observed and expected frequencies is likely to be a function of sampling error (non-significant – retaining the null hypothesis H0) or unlikely to be a function of sampling error (significant association – reject the null hypothesis and support alternative hypothesis – H1).

The observed frequency. *The number of observations classified in a particular category.*

The expected frequency. *The frequency value that is predicted from the null hypothesis and sample size, and is often the ideal sample distribution.*

Goodness-of-fit chi square

The whole idea of non-parametric tests is that they can be used when we do not know the distribution. In these situations, we often test any assumption we have about the shape of the distribution. Any test that compares the observations with the assumed or expected frequencies to see how well the latter 'fit' the observed frequencies, is called a **goodness-of-fit test**. Two major statistical assumptions are that the distribution is (i) uniform (equally split), or (ii) normally distributed.

The null hypothesis for the goodness-of-fit test states that the frequency distribution of one population does not differ from the known frequency distribution of another population or from chance expectancy. For example, it may be known that 60% of England's population favour the government's water conservation policy and 40% are in opposition. Does this same pattern exist in Scotland and Wales? The null hypothesis states that there is no difference between the populations, i.e. that the distribution in Scotland and Wales fits the national picture.

Because the null hypothesis in a goodness-of-fit test specifies an exact distribution, the alternative hypothesis simply states that the distribution is a different shape from that specified in the null hypothesis. For example, if a fair dice is rolled, we expect each of the six numbers to occur approximately one sixth of the time (H_0). If there is a significant deviation from this then we are entitled to conclude that the dice is biased (H_1). Or we may wish to determine whether the proportion of defective units produced on each of four parallel assembly lines producing computer boards would be the same for each of four different assembly line speeds. The defect rate is known to be 5%. Thus, by having the assembly lines run at different speeds the defect rates could be compared with the known uniform rate to determine whether it would be possible to run the system at some faster speed without sacrificing quality.

Goodness-of-fit test. *This measures how closely observed sample data fit a particular hypothesized distribution.*

Testing the assumption of uniform distribution

Example 1

Here is an example of a goodness-of-fit chi square using the assumption of a uniform distribution. Consider the question: *'Is more staff sick leave recorded on some days of the week rather than on other days?'* Here is some dummy observed data on number of staff off sick per day.

Monday	*Tuesday*	*Wednesday*	*Thursday*	*Friday*	*Total*
64	29	15	20	72	200

What sort of distribution would you expect if day of the week did not in fact have any influence? We would expect an even distribution. That is, one-fifth, or 20%, or 40 each day. The question is now:

> 'Is the fact that the observed frequencies are different from what we expected more likely due to chance, or does it more likely represent *actual differences* in absences on different days of the week?'

That is: is there an association between days of the week and sick leave? The null hypothesis claims that there is no such significant association and that the observed frequency distribution is simply due to chance. The chi square test permits us to estimate the probability that observed frequencies differ from expected frequencies through chance alone.

But how far can a departure from these frequencies go before we can say that such a discrepancy would occur so infrequently on a chance basis that our observations are significantly different from those expected and that there is relationship? Well, of course SPSS calculates this for us and produces the significance of the result.

Moreover, for small numbers, chi square can actually be easily calculated by hand; we need to enter our observed and expected data into a table of cells on the lines of the following model:

O	E
(O – E)	$(O - E)^2$

where O = Observed data and E = Expected data

We will now fill in the cells in our example by placing the observed and expected data into their respective cells and calculate (O – E) and $(O - E)^2$. Since we have observed 200 sick leave absences the expected uniform or equal frequency in each cell must be 40, i.e. 20% of the sample size for each of five days.

Monday		*Tuesday*		*Wednesday*		*Thursday*		*Friday*	
64	40	29	40	15	40	20	40	72	40
24	576	11	121	25	625	20	400	32	1024

$$\text{Chi square} = \sum \frac{(O - E)^2}{E} = \frac{576}{40} + \frac{121}{40} + \frac{625}{40} + \frac{400}{40} + \frac{1024}{40}$$

Chi square = 68.65

A relatively large chi square like this suggests that the 'O's' differed more from the 'E's' than is likely by chance. The raw data was inputed into SPSS and it calculated chi square as 68.65 as above and this is strongly significant ($p < .01$).

We can reject the null hypothesis with confidence, and accept the alternative hypothesis that sick leave is not randomly distributed through the week. To specify how it is distributed, you must return to inspect the original data where you can readily appreciate that absences are much higher on Mondays and Fridays and much lower on other days of the week. I leave the interpretation and speculation of why to you!

A chi square of zero indicates that the observed and expected frequencies match exactly. Chi square can never be negative since differences between the observed and expected are always squared.

Degrees of freedom in a goodness-of-fit chi square

SPSS uses degree of freedom (df) in its interpretation of the calculated chi square. For the goodness-of-fit chi square df = (number of categories – 1). The number of observations free to vary in our example is 4 because, once we have fixed the frequency of four days, the fifth day has to make the total 200. So the fifth category is fixed and the degree of freedom for that category is lost. The same principle holds true for any number of categories.

*The **degrees of freedom** in a **goodness-of-fit test** is one less than the number of categories.*

Example 2

The TEL-MOB company that sells mobile phones wants to make sure they have sufficient inventory level of their four types of phone to guard against the possibility of lost sales because one type of stock is exhausted. The company decides to test the null hypothesis of uniform demand. The alternative hypothesis is that demand is not uniform for all types of mobile phone.

The null hypothesis of uniform demand presumes purchase of an equal number of each type of phone over a fixed period, say of a month. The average number of phones sold each month over the last year was 480. If demand is uniform the company can expect 120 of each phone to be sold each month. This expectation, with the actual distribution of observed sales for the month just past, is shown below.

Phone type

type 1		type 2		type 3		type 4	
140	120	110	120	100	120	120	120
20	400	10	100	20	400	0	0

$$\text{Chi square} = \frac{400}{120} + \frac{100}{120} + \frac{400}{120} + \frac{0}{120}$$
$$= 7.49$$

Again, I put the data on SPSS and found with 3 df that our calculated value is not significant, therefore the null hypothesis that demand is uniform cannot be rejected and the company knows that it should maintain equal numbers of the four types of phone. The minor differences between observed and expected are attributed to chance variation in sales.

Testing for a specific pattern

In this goodness-of-fit approach, the distribution assumption has been fixed in advance, usually the result of a policy decision by a company, and the test is used to determine if policy is being followed.

Example 3

The PacAsia Bank wanted to ensure that it had a particular mix of loans in order to minimize the default rate from local business customers. They set a policy of 60% to business firms, 30% to individuals and 10% to foreign borrowers. One year later, to determine if this policy was being adhered to, the marketing manager randomly selected 85 loans approved in the last month. He finds 62 were extended to businesses, 10 to foreign borrowers and 13 to individuals. Is the bank's portfolio policy intact or in tatters?

If the null hypothesis that the pattern of loans is being maintained correctly, 60% of the 85 loans in the sample should be business loans (i.e. 85 × .60 = 51 loans), 30% would be individual loans (i.e. 25.5 loans) and loans to foreign customers would be 10% or 8.5 loans. The following are the expected frequencies:

Loan	observed	expected
Business	62	51
Individual	13	25.5
Foreign	10	8.5

$$\text{Chi square} = \frac{(62-51)^2}{51} + \frac{(13-25.5)^2}{25.5} + \frac{(10-8.5)^2}{8.5}$$
$$= 8.76$$

We placed the original data into chi square and with $df = 2$ and a 5% level of significance, this value of chi square is significant. In this situation, the null hypothesis should be rejected and the pattern of loans does not conform with established policy. There is only a 5% chance that the pattern observed would be produced if the policy was being observed.

***Goodness-of-fit chi square.** This measures how closely observed sample data fit a particular hypothesized distribution.*

SPSS activity – goodness-of-fit chi square

We will illustrate the computation of a goodness-of-fit chi square using SPSS Chapter 12 Data File B. We will test the hypothesis that the distribution of choices for soft drink is random, i.e. there is no significant preference for any specific drink.

How to proceed

1 ***Analyze* >> *Non-parametric Tests* >> *Chi square …*** which opens the ***Chi Square Test* dialogue** box.
2 Select the variable '*drink*' then click on the arrow button which transfers this variable to *the **Test Variable List*** box (Fig. 14.1).
3 ***OK***. The results of the analysis are then displayed as in Table 14.1.

How to interpret the output

- In the top box the four possible outcomes of the drink choice are listed vertically in the first column.
- The observed frequencies are presented in the second column.
- The expected frequencies of cases are displayed in the third column. These are all 10 since the expected frequency for each of the four drinks with 40 personal choices is 40/4.

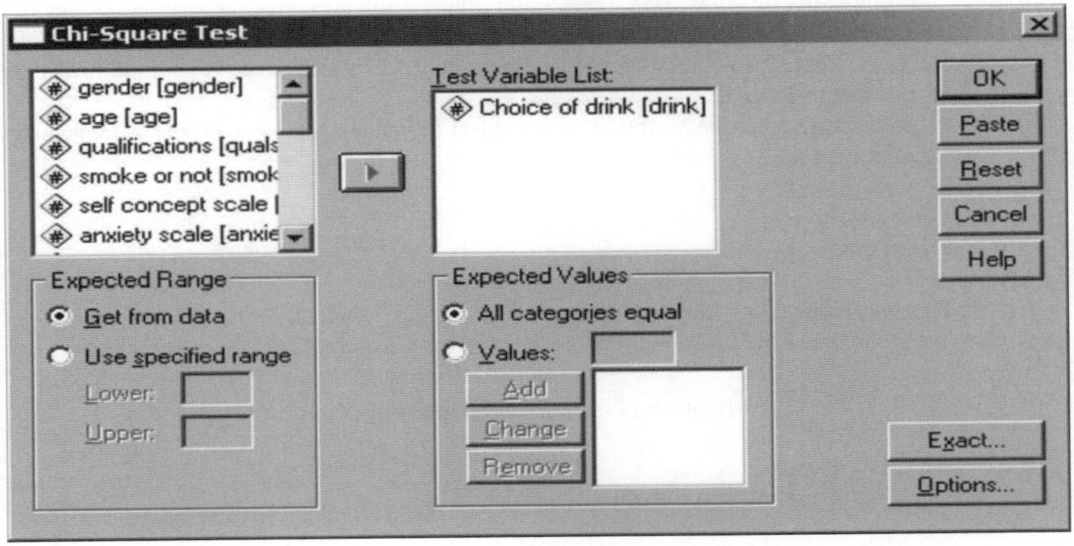

Figure 14.1 Chi square test.

Table 14.1 Chi square goodness-of-fit output

Choice of drink			
	Observed N	**Expected N**	**Residual**
Coke	17	10.0	7.0
Pepsi	11	10.0	1.0
Sprite	7	10.0	–3.0
Solo	5	10.0	–5.0
Total	40		

Test Statistics

	Choice of drink
Chi-Square(a)	8.400
df	3
Asymp. Sig.	.038

[a] 0 cells (0%) have expected frequencies less than 5. The minimum expected cell frequency is 10.0.

- The residual column displays the differences between the observed and expected frequencies.
- The value of chi square, its degrees of freedom and its significance are presented in the second box. Chi square is 8.4, its degrees of freedom are 3 (i.e. 4–1) and its significance level is .038. This latter figure indicates that there is a statistically significant deviation from the expected distribution of equality beyond $p < .05$. Coke is most popular while Solo and Sprite are much less preferred, i.e. not all drinks are equally preferred.
- Note the comment below the lower subtable. Chi square requires expected cell frequencies of at least 5.

Effect size

This is computed as

$$\text{Effect size} = \frac{\text{Chi square}}{\text{(Total sample size across all categories)(number of categories} - 1)}$$

$$= \frac{8.4}{(40)(3)} = .07$$

This is obviously minimal and in part due to the small sample.

How to report the results

'A goodness-of-fit chi square was conducted to determine whether free choice of four drinks by 40 persons would produce a distribution not significantly different from that expected by chance, i.e equality. There was a statistically significant difference between the observed and expected frequencies (chi square = 8.4, df = 3, p = .038). This suggests that Coke was the most popular choice while Solo was the least chosen. Effect size of .007 indicates that the observed frequencies deviated minimally from the expected frequencies and a stronger effect size would probably emerge if a larger sample was involved'.

Chi square test of the independence of categorical variables (cross-classification or cross-tabulation or contingency)

Another widely used application of the chi square procedure involves its use with data that are in the form of observations on two variables. For example, a sample of subjects is classified into categories on each of two variables and the question concerns the presence or absence of a relationship between the variables. One might ask:

- Is there a relationship between ethnic background and preference for watching different sports?
- Is there a relationship between income level and number of cars owned?
- Is there an association between consumers' age group and their preference or not for a product?
- Does the support of a strike call depend on national political voting intention?
- Do men and women prefer different levels of risk in making investment decisions?
- Does each factory in the company produce the same level of defective products?

Comparison of the independence of two variables is achieved as before by comparing observed frequencies with expected frequencies. When data of this type is gathered, they are recorded in a **contingency** *or* **cross-tabulation table**. The responses are categorized into cells organized by rows and columns.

Contingency tables

2 × 2 contingency table

One of the most common uses of the chi square test of the independence of categorical variables is with the 2 × 2 contingency table, in which there are two variables each divided into two categories only. Let use imagine our two categories are (i) adult/adolescent and (ii) approve of abortion/don't approve. The data is located in Table 14.2. The calculation produces:

Chi square = 122.78. $df = 1$ (always in a 2 × 2 table!)

Table 14.2 Example of a two by two table

	Adolescent	Adult	Total
Approve of abortion	120	18	138
Don't approve of abortion	20	98	118
Total	140	116	256

The result is extremely significant well beyond the .01 level. Hence the null hypothesis that there is only a chance association between age group and attitude to abortion is rejected for this sample. There is a significant relationship between the age group and its approval or disapproval of abortion. The two categories are not independent of each other for these samples, with adolescents approving more strongly and adults disapproving more strongly, from consideration of the raw data in Table 14.2.

N × N cross-tabulation

Cross-tabulation tables can have more than two rows and two columns, though as we increase each the interpretation of results becomes more complex and sample sizes need to be large so that sufficient observed counts occur in each cell.

As an example, consider whether there is an association between number of children in family and number of computers owned. Here is the observed data from our survey placed in a contingency or cross-tabulation format in a 3 × 3 table (Table 14.3).

We hypothesize that there is no significant association between number of computers owned and number of children. SPSS calculates the expected frequency values for each of the cells in the contingency table. Chi square in this example is 38.05, which far exceeds the .01 level. We are well justified in claiming that there is a significant association between family size and computer ownership, with a tendency for larger families to own more computers. We reject the null hypothesis that there is only a chance relationship between number of children in family and computer ownership, i.e. that both categories are independent.

The 'natural' application of the contingency table analysis is for cases in which each observation is measured by two categorical variables. However, quantitative variables may also be used to classify the observations into rows, or columns, or both, by recoding each quantitative variable arbitrarily into intervals so that each interval represents one row or

Table 14.3 Example of a cross-tabulation table

	Number of children in family		
No. of computers	One child	Two children	Three or more
Two	20	16	8
One	40	22	10
None	12	36	42

one column. If the quantitative variable is salary, the intervals may be set at *$10,000* with a final category that includes all salaries above a certain value. Age can be converted to a number of age group categories in this way too.

Computing effect size

SPSS provides a number of indices that assess the strength of the relationship between row and column variables. They include the contingency coefficient, phi, Cramer's V, and lambda. The two indices usually used are phi and Cramer's V. The phi coefficient for a 2×2 table is a special case of the Pearson product-moment correlation coefficient for a 2×2 contingency table. Because most social scientists have a reasonable understanding of the Pearson product-moment correlation coefficient (next chapter) they are likely to feel comfortable using its derivative, the phi coefficient. However, if both the row and the column variables have more than two levels, phi can exceed 1 and, therefore, is hard to interpret. Cramer's V rescales phi in these circumstances so that it ranges between 0 and 1.

SPSS activity – chi square for the independence of categorical variables (contingency tables)

Please access SPSS Chapter 12 Data File B. If you wish to calculate chi square with more than two categories in at least one variable then the procedure is the same. In this example, we will examine the null hypothesis that there is no significant relationship between gender and whether the person smokes or not. The procedure is as follows:

1 ***Analyze*** >> ***Descriptive Statistics*** >> ***Crosstabs***. This opens the ***Crosstabs: dialogue*** box.
2 Click on '*gender*' and then the arrow button beside Row[s]: which transfers it into the ***Rows box***.
3 Select '*smoke or not*' and then the arrow button beside Column[s] which moves it to the ***Columns box*** (Fig. 14.2). It does not matter which variable goes in row or columns.
4 If you wish to display bar charts check the box.
5 Choose ***Statistics*** at the bottom of the ***Crosstabs:*** **dialogue** box. This opens the ***Crosstabs: Statistics*** **dialogue** box.
6 Select ***Chi-square***, then ***phi*** and ***Cramer's V*** in the ***Nominal*** data box (Fig. 14.3).
7 ***Continue*** >> ***Cells***. This produces the ***Crosstabs: Cell Display*** **dialogue** box.
8 Choose ***Expected*** **in the** ***Counts*** box. (Observed should already be selected).
9 Click on ***Row, Column and Total*** in the ***Percentages*** box (Fig. 14.4).
10 ***Continue*** >> ***OK***.

Interpreting the output in Table 14.4

- Four subtables are produced. The top subtable lists the number of cases processed.
- The second subtable shows the observed and expected frequency of cases in each cell. The observed frequency (called *Count*) is presented first and the expected frequency (called *Expected count*) second.

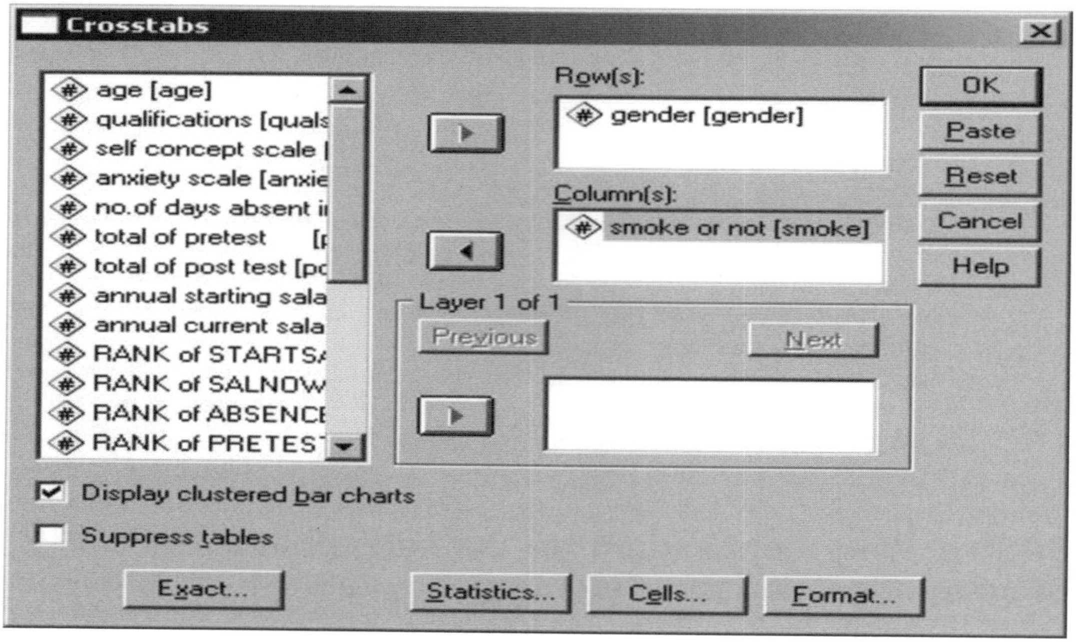

Figure 14.2 **Crosstabs.**

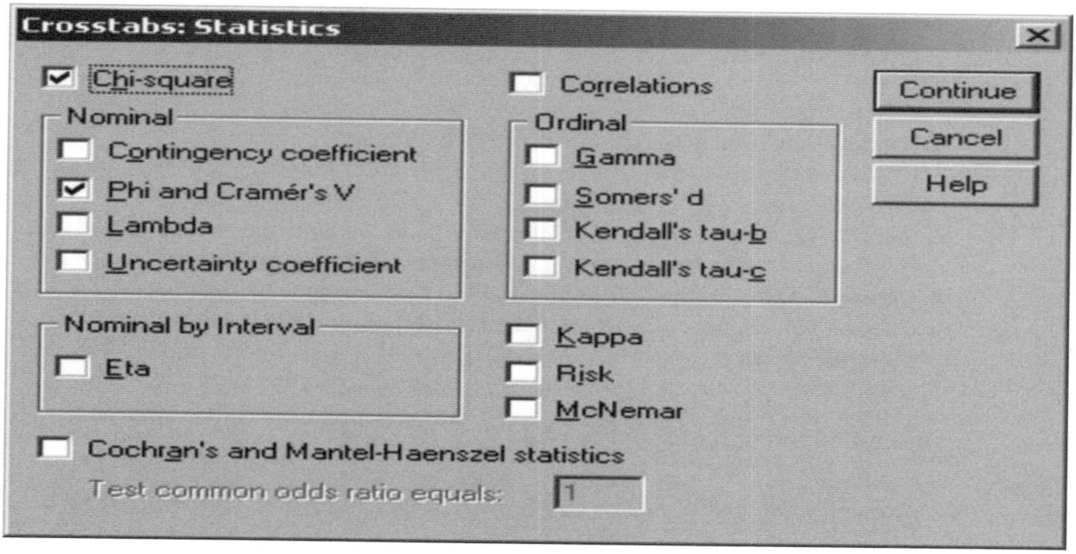

Figure 14.3 **Crosstabs: Statistics.**

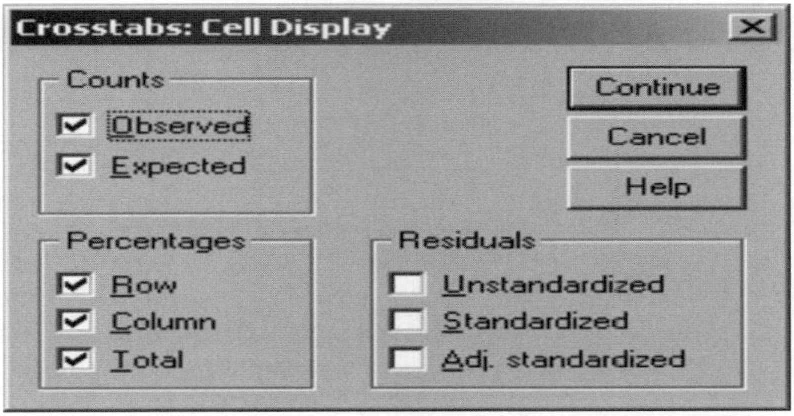

Figure 14.4 **Crosstabs cell display.**

Table 14.4 **Crosstabulation output**

Case Processing Summary

	Cases					
	Valid		Missing		Total	
	N	Percent	N	Percent	N	Percent
Gender* smoke or not	40	100.0%	0	.0%	40	100.0%

Gender* smoke or not Crosstabulation

			Smoke or not		
			Does not smoke	Smokes	Total
gender	male	Count	10	12	22
		Expected count	11.6	10.5	22.0
		% within gender	45.5%	54.5%	100.0%
		% within smoke or not	47.6%	63.2%	55.0%
		% of Total	25.0%	30.0%	55.0%
	female	Count	11	7	18
		Expected count	9.5	8.6	18.0
		% within gender	61.1%	38.9%	100.0%
		% within smoke or not	52.4%	36.8%	45.0%
		% of Total	27.5%	17.5%	45.0%

Table 14.4—cont'd

		Smoke or not		
		Does not smoke	Smokes	Total
Total	Count	21	19	40
	Expected Count	21.0	19.0	40.0
	% within gender	52.5%	47.5%	100.0%
	% within smoke or not	100.0%	100.0%	100.0%
	% of Total	52.5%	47.5%	100.0%

Chi Square Tests

	Value	df	Asymp. sig. (2-sided)	Exact sig. (2-sided)	Exact sig. (1-sided)
Pearson Chi-Square	.973(b)	1	.324		
Continuity Correction(a)	.447	1	.504		
Likelihood Ratio	.978	1	.323		
Fisher's Exact Test				.360	.252
Linear-by-Linear Association	.949	1	.330		
N of Valid Cases	40				

[a] Computed only for a 2×2 table.
[b] 0 cells (.0%) have expected count less than 5. The minimum expected count is 8.55.

Symmetric Measures

		Value	Approx. Sig.
Nominal by Nominal	Phi	−.156	.324
	Cramer's V	.156	.324
N of Valid Cases		40	

[a] Not assuming the null hypothesis.
[b] Using the asymptotic standard error assuming the null hypothesis.

- The observed frequencies are always whole numbers so they should be easy to spot. The expected frequencies are always expressed to one decimal place so they are easily identified. Thus the first cell of the table (defined as '*male*' and '*does not smoke*') has an observed frequency of 10 but an expected frequency of 11.6. The rest of the table is also easily interpretable.
- The next subtable displays the chi square value, its degrees of freedom and its significance level. Chi square is on the line labelled '*Pearson*', after the person who developed this test. The chi square value is .973. Its degrees of freedom are 1 and its two-tailed probability is .324. There is no significant association between whether a person smokes or not and their gender. The null hypothesis is retained.

- The likelihood ratio test has similar properties to chi square and is an alternative. The linear-by-linear association test is inappropriate for qualitative variables.
- The final table reports phi and Cramer's V as measures of effect size, namely, 0.324.
- Also shown in the output is the warning about the Minimum Expected Frequency of any cell in the table. If there are cells with a minimum expected frequency of 5.0 or less then we should be wary of using chi square and use Fisher's Exact test result instead, which will be produced by SPSS in such cases.
- The clustered bar chart (Fig. 14.5) provides a visual impression of the distribution of the frequencies.

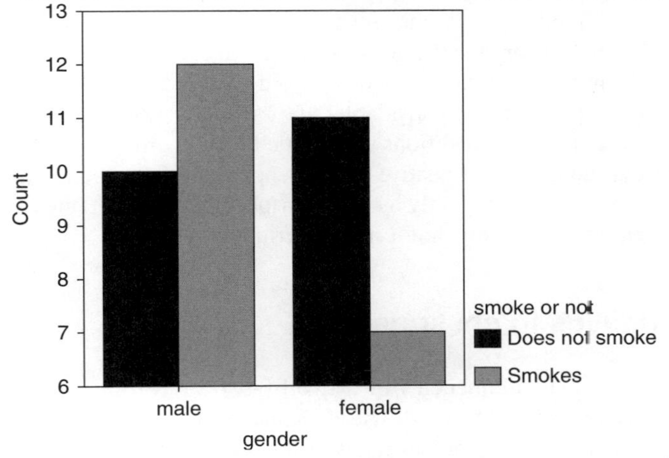

Figure 14.5 Bar chart of frequencies

How to report the results

You could write: '*A 2 × 2 contingency table analysis was conducted to determine whether there was an association between gender and whether the person smokes or not. A non-significant relationship was present with chi square = .973, df = 1, p = .324. The null hypothesis that there is no association between gender and smoking must be retained. The effect of .324 squared suggests that only around 11% of the variation in smoking can be explained by gender*'.

Restrictions in the use of the chi square

1 It is important to remember that chi square is only appropriate for the analysis of data that are classified as frequency of occurrence (counts) within categories (nominal data). When the data are ordinal or interval, other tests of significance are usually preferred. It must only be used on frequencies, *never on percentages*.

2 Categories for a chi square analysis must be mutually exclusive, which means that each response can be classified into only one cell. This is true because a fundamental assumption in the use of the chi square test is that each observation or frequency is independent of all others. For example, a person can only be in one age group and in one salary class.
3 Another restriction in the use of the chi square test is that when there are many categories within each variable, larger samples are needed. If N is small and consequently the expected frequency in any cell is small, the sample statistic may not approximate the theoretical chi square distribution very closely. A rule-of-thumb which one may follow is that in a two-by-two chi square analysis the expected frequency in all cells should at least equal or be greater than 5. With more than a two-by-two table, the expected frequency should be equal to or greater than 5 in at least 80% of the cells. If this condition is not fulfilled, it may be necessary to code together several low frequency categories so we have the larger expected frequencies in each cell or use Fisher's Exact Test result. The fusing of categories is not really desirable, since it involves a reduction in the amount of information available. If practically possible, we might obtain a larger sample so that the conditions are fulfilled for the original classification.
4 The chi square test is sensitive to difference but not direction of difference; it is therefore inherently two-tailed. Only by visual inspection of the obtained data can the direction of association in a significant test be determined.

Alternatives to chi square

If you have small frequencies in a two-by-two or two-by-three table the Fisher Exact Probability Test should be used. The chi square procedure computes Fisher's Exact Test for two-by-two tables when one or more of the four cells have an expected frequency of less than 5. SPSS output automatically provides the significance level for both a one- and two-tail test. These are placed near the bottom of the normal chi square output window as the last two significance levels quoted.

Summary of steps in chi square

- State the null and alternate hypotheses about the proposed relationship.
- Note the observed counts of data falling into different cells.
- Compute frequencies of occurrence of events that we expect under the null hypothesis to provide the expected frequencies for each cell.
- Evaluate the difference between the observed and expected to produce the chi square statistic.
- Observe the computed chi square in the SPSS printout and determine whether statistical significance is achieved.
- Inspect our original data to determine the direction of association if a significant result is obtained.

What you have learned in this chapter

Chi square tests are a non-parametric technique of testing hypotheses of association using nominal data. The two types of chi square tests are:

- the goodness-of-fit test; and
- the test for independence of two nominal variables.

The former compares how well the frequency distribution for a sample fits with the expected frequency distribution predicted by the null hypothesis. The latter assesses association between two variables, with the null hypothesis stating that there is no significant association between the two variables. Rejecting the null hypothesis implies a significant association between the two variables. Both tests are based on the assumption that each observation is independent of the others, and that one observation cannot be classified in more than one category.

The chi square statistic is distorted when there are less than five observations in a cell and the Fisher Exact test should be performed if this situation exists.

Review activities

SPSS Activity 14.1
Using SPSS Chapter 12 Data File B conduct a goodness-of-fit chi square on the variable 'house funding' to determine whether there is approximate equality in the types of funding used.

SPSS Activity 14.2
Access SPSS Chapter 12 Data File B. Test the null hypothesis that there is no significant association between qualifications held and type of house funding.

Now access Chapter 14 Web page and attempt the SPSS activities and other questions located there.

23 Regression

ANDY FIELD

FIGURE 7.1 Me playing with my ding-a-ling in the Holimarine Talent Show. Note the groupies queuing up at the front

7.1. What will this chapter tell me? ①

Although none of us can know the future, predicting it is so important that organisms are hard wired to learn about predictable events in their environment. We saw in the previous chapter that I received a guitar for Christmas when I was 8. My first foray into public performance was a weekly talent show at a holiday camp called 'Holimarine' in Wales (it doesn't exist anymore because I am old and this was 1981). I sang a Chuck Berry song called 'My ding-a-ling'[1] and to my absolute amazement I won the competition.[2] Suddenly other 8 year olds across the land (well, a ballroom in Wales) worshipped me (I made lots of friends after the competition). I had tasted success, it tasted like praline chocolate, and so I wanted to enter the competition in the second week of our holiday. To ensure success, I needed to know why I had won in the first week. One way to do this would have been to collect data and to use these data to predict people's evaluations of children's performances in the contest

[1] It appears that even then I had a passion for lowering the tone of things that should be taken seriously.

[2] I have a very grainy video of this performance recorded by my dad's friend on a video camera the size of a medium-sized dog that had to be accompanied at all times by a 'battery pack' the size and weight of a tank. Maybe I'll put it up on the companion website ...

from certain variables: the age of the performer, what type of performance they gave (singing, telling a joke, magic tricks), and maybe how cute they looked. A regression analysis on these data would enable us to predict future evaluations (success in next week's competition) based on values of the predictor variables. If, for example, singing was an important factor in getting a good audience evaluation, then I could sing again the following week; however, if jokers tended to do better then I could switch to a comedy routine. When I was 8 I wasn't the sad geek that I am today, so I didn't know about regression analysis (nor did I wish to know); however, my dad thought that success was due to the winning combination of a cherub-looking 8 year old singing songs that can be interpreted in a filthy way. He wrote me a song to sing in the competition about the keyboard player in the Holimarine Band 'messing about with his organ', and first place was mine again. There's no accounting for taste.

7.2. An introduction to regression ①

In the previous chapter we looked at how to measure relationships between two variables. These correlations can be very useful but we can take this process a step further and predict one variable from another. A simple example might be to try to predict levels of stress from the amount of time until you have to give a talk. You'd expect this to be a negative relationship (the smaller the amount of time until the talk, the larger the anxiety). We could then extend this basic relationship to answer a question such as 'if there's 10 minutes to go until someone has to give a talk, how anxious will they be?' This is the essence of regression analysis: we fit a model to our data and use it to predict values of the dependent variable (DV) from one or more independent variables (IVs).[3] Regression analysis is a way of predicting an **outcome variable** from one **predictor variable** (**simple regression**) or several predictor variables (**multiple regression**). This tool is incredibly useful because it allows us to go a step beyond the data that we collected.

In section 2.4.3 I introduced you to the idea that we can predict any data using the following general equation:

$$\text{outcome}_i = (\text{model}) + \text{error}_i \tag{7.1}$$

This just means that the outcome we're trying to predict for a particular person can be predicted by whatever model we fit to the data plus some kind of error. In regression, the model we fit is linear, which means that we summarize a data set with a straight line (think back to Jane Superbrain Box 2.1). As such, the word 'model' in the equation above simply gets replaced by 'things' that define the line that we fit to the data (see the next section).

With any data set there are several lines that could be used to summarize the general trend and so we need a way to decide which of many possible lines to choose. For the sake of making accurate predictions we want to fit a model that *best* describes the data. The simplest way to do this would be to use your eye to gauge a line that looks as though it summarizes the data well. You don't need to be a genius to realize that the 'eyeball' method is very subjective and so offers no assurance that the model is the best one that could have been chosen. Instead, we use a mathematical technique called the *method of least squares* to establish the line that best describes the data collected.

[3] I want to remind you here of something I discussed in Chapter 1: SPSS refers to regression variables as dependent and independent variables (as in controlled experiments). However, correlational research by its nature seldom controls the independent variables to measure the effect on a dependent variable and so I will talk about 'independent variables' as *predictors*, and the 'dependent variable' as the *outcome*.

7.2.1. Some important information about straight lines ①

I mentioned above that in our general equation the word 'model' gets replaced by 'things that define the line that we fit to the data'. In fact, any straight line can be defined by two things: (1) the slope (or gradient) of the line (usually denoted by b_1); and (2) the point at which the line crosses the vertical axis of the graph (known as the *intercept* of the line, b_0). In fact, our general model becomes equation (7.2) below in which Y_i is the outcome that we want to predict and X_i is the ith participant's score on the predictor variable.[4] Here b_1 is the gradient of the straight line fitted to the data and b_0 is the intercept of that line. These parameters b_1 and b_0 are known as the *regression coefficients* and will crop up time and time again in this book, where you may see them referred to generally as b (without any subscript) or b_i (meaning the b associated with variable i). There is a residual term, ε_i, which represents the difference between the score predicted by the line for participant i and the score that participant i actually obtained. The equation is often conceptualized without this residual term (so, ignore it if it's upsetting you); however, it is worth knowing that this term represents the fact our model will not fit the data collected perfectly:

$$Y_i = (b_0 + b_1 X_i) + \varepsilon_i \tag{7.2}$$

A particular line has a specific intercept and gradient. Figure 7.2 shows a set of lines that have the same intercept but different gradients, and a set of lines that have the same gradient but different intercepts. Figure 7.2 also illustrates another useful point: the gradient of the line tells us something about the nature of the relationship being described. In Chapter 6 we saw how relationships can be either positive or negative (and I don't mean the difference between getting on well with your girlfriend and arguing all the time!). A line that has a gradient with a positive value describes a positive relationship, whereas a line with a negative gradient describes a negative relationship. So, if you look at the graph in Figure 7.2

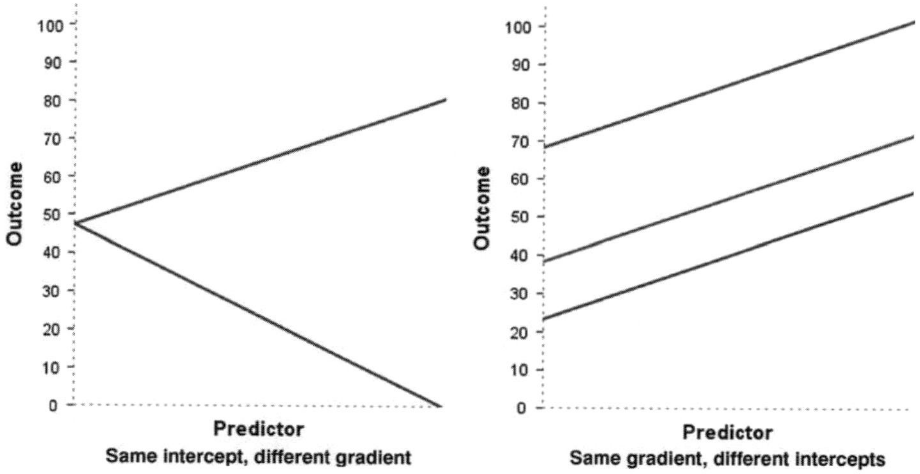

FIGURE 7.2 Lines with the same gradients but different intercepts, and lines that share the same intercept but have different gradients

[4] You'll sometimes see this equation written as:

$$Y_i = (\beta_0 + \beta_1 X_i) + \varepsilon_i$$

The only difference is that this equation has got βs in it instead of bs and in fact both versions are the same thing, they just use different letters to represent the coefficients. When SPSS estimates the coefficients in this equation it labels them b and to be consistent with the SPSS output that you'll end up looking at, I've used bs instead of βs.

in which the gradients differ but the intercepts are the same, then the red line describes a positive relationship whereas the green line describes a negative relationship. Basically then, the gradient (b) tells us what the model looks like (its shape) and the intercept (b_0) tells us where the model is (its location in geometric space).

If it is possible to describe a line knowing only the gradient and the intercept of that line, then we can use these values to describe our model (because in linear regression the model we use is a straight line). So, the model that we fit to our data in linear regression can be conceptualized as a straight line that can be described mathematically by equation (7.2). With regression we strive to find the line that best describes the data collected, then estimate the gradient and intercept of that line. Having defined these values, we can insert different values of our predictor variable into the model to estimate the value of the outcome variable.

7.2.2. The method of least squares ①

I have already mentioned that the method of least squares is a way of finding the line that best fits the data (i.e. finding a line that goes through, or as close to, as many of the data points as possible). This 'line of best fit' is found by ascertaining which line, of all of the possible lines that could be drawn, results in the least amount of difference between the observed data points and the line. Figure 7.3 shows that when any line is fitted to a set of data, there will be small differences between the values predicted by the line and the data that were actually observed.

Back in Chapter 2 we saw that we could assess the fit of a model (the example we used was the mean) by looking at the deviations between the model and the actual data collected. These deviations were the vertical distances between what the model predicted and each data point that was actually observed. We can do exactly the same to assess the fit of a regression line (which, like the mean, is a statistical model). So, again we are interested in the vertical differences between the line and the actual data because the line is our model: we use it to predict values of Y from values of the X variable. In regression these differences are usually called **residuals** rather than deviations, but they are the same thing. As with the mean, data points fall both above (the model underestimates their value) and below (the

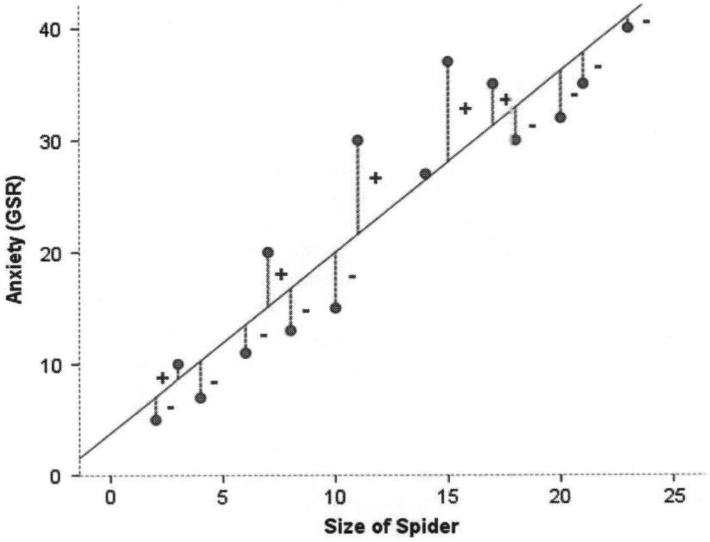

FIGURE 7.3 This graph shows a scatterplot of some data with a line representing the general trend. The vertical lines (dotted) represent the differences (or residuals) between the line and the actual data

model overestimates their value) the line yielding both positive and negative differences. In the discussion of variance in section 2.4.2 I explained that if we sum positive and negative differences then they tend to cancel each other out and that to circumvent this problem we square the differences before adding them up. We do the same thing here. The resulting squared differences provide a gauge of how well a particular line fits the data: if the squared differences are large, the line is not representative of the data; if the squared differences are small, the line is representative.

You could, if you were particularly bored, calculate the sum of squared differences (or SS for short) for every possible line that is fitted to your data and then compare these 'goodness-of-fit' measures. The one with the lowest SS is the line of best fit. Fortunately we don't have to do this because the method of least squares does it for us: it selects the line that has the lowest sum of squared differences (i.e. the line that best represents the observed data). How exactly it does this is by using a mathematical technique for finding maxima and minima and this technique is used to find the line that minimizes the sum of squared differences. I don't really know much more about it than that, to be honest, so I tend to think of the process as a little bearded wizard called Nephwick the Line Finder who just magically finds lines of best fit. Yes, he lives inside your computer. The end result is that Nephwick estimates the value of the slope and intercept of the 'line of best fit' for you. We tend to call this line of best fit a regression line.

7.2.3. Assessing the goodness of fit: sums of squares, *R* and R^2 ①

Once Nephwick the Line Finder has found the line of best fit it is important that we assess how well this line fits the actual data (we assess the **goodness of fit** of the model). We do this because even though this line is the best one available, it can still be a lousy fit to the data! In section 2.4.2 we saw that one measure of the adequacy of a model is the sum of squared differences (or more generally we assess models using equation (7.3) below). If we want to assess the line of best fit, we need to compare it against something, and the thing we choose is the most basic model we can find. So we use equation (7.3) to calculate the fit of the most basic model, and then the fit of the best model (the line of best fit), and basically if the best model is any good then it should fit the data significantly better than our basic model:

$$\text{deviation} = \sum(\text{observed} - \text{model})^2 \tag{7.3}$$

This is all quite abstract so let's look at an example. Imagine that I was interested in predicting record sales (*Y*) from the amount of money spent advertising that record (*X*). One day my boss came in to my office and said 'Andy, I know you wanted to be a rock star and you've ended up working as my stats-monkey, but how many records will we sell if we spend £100,000 on advertising?' If I didn't have an accurate model of the relationship between record sales and advertising, what would my best guess be? Well, probably the best answer I could give would be the mean number of record sales (say, 200,000) because on average that's how many records we expect to sell. This response might well satisfy a brainless record company executive (who didn't offer my band a record contract). However, what if he had asked 'How many records will we sell if we spend £1 on advertising?' Again, in the absence of any accurate information, my best guess would be to give the average number of sales (200,000). There is a problem: whatever amount of money is spent on advertising I always predict the same levels of sales. As such, the mean is a model of 'no relationship' at all between the variables. It should be pretty clear then that the mean is fairly useless as a model of a relationship between two variables – but it is the simplest model available.

So, as a basic strategy for predicting the outcome, we might choose to use the mean, because on average it will be a fairly good guess of an outcome. Using the mean as a model, we can calculate the difference between the observed values, and the values predicted by the mean (equation (7.3)). We saw in section 2.4.2 that we square all of these differences to give us the sum of squared differences. This sum of squared differences is known as the **total sum of squares** (denoted SS_T) because it is the total amount of differences present when the most basic model is applied to the data. This value represents how good the mean is as a model of the observed data. Now, if we fit the more sophisticated model to the data, such as a line of best fit, we can again work out the differences between this new model and the observed data (again using equation (7.3)). In the previous section we saw that the method of least squares finds the best possible line to describe a set of data by minimizing the difference between the model fitted to the data and the data themselves. However, even with this optimal model there is still some inaccuracy, which is represented by the differences between each observed data point and the value predicted by the regression line. As before, these differences are squared before they are added up so that the directions of the differences do not cancel out. The result is known as the *sum of squared residuals* or **residual sum of squares** (SS_R). This value represents the degree of inaccuracy when the best model is fitted to the data. We can use these two values to calculate how much better the regression line (the line of best fit) is than just using the mean as a model (i.e. how much better is the best possible model than the worst model?). The improvement in prediction resulting from using the regression model rather than the mean is calculated by calculating the difference between SS_T and SS_R. This difference shows us the reduction in the inaccuracy of the model resulting from fitting the regression model to the data. This improvement is the **model sum of squares** (SS_M). Figure 7.4 shows each sum of squares graphically.

If the value of SS_M is large then the regression model is very different from using the mean to predict the outcome variable. This implies that the regression model has made a big improvement to how well the outcome variable can be predicted. However, if SS_M is small then using the regression model is little better than using the mean (i.e. the regression model is no better than taking our 'best guess'). A useful measure arising from these sums of squares is the proportion of improvement due to the model. This is easily calculated by dividing the sum of squares for the model by the total sum of squares. The resulting value is called R^2 and to express this value as a percentage you should multiply it by 100. R^2 represents the amount of variance in the outcome explained by the model (SS_M) relative to how much variation there was to explain in the first place (SS_T). Therefore, as a percentage, it represents the percentage of the variation in the outcome that can be explained by the model:

$$R^2 = \frac{SS_M}{SS_T} \tag{7.4}$$

This R^2 is the same as the one we met in Chapter 6 (section 6.5.2.3) and you might have noticed that it is interpreted in the same way. Therefore, in simple regression we can take the square root of this value to obtain Pearson's correlation coefficient. As such, the correlation coefficient provides us with a good estimate of the overall fit of the regression model, and R^2 provides us with a good gauge of the substantive size of the relationship.

A second use of the sums of squares in assessing the model is through the *F*-test. I mentioned way back in Chapter 2 that test statistics (like *F*) are usually the amount of systematic variance divided by the amount of unsystematic variance, or, put another way, the model compared against the error in the model. This is true here: *F* is based upon the ratio of the improvement due to the model (SS_M) and the difference between the model and the observed data (SS_R). Actually, because the sums of squares depend on the number

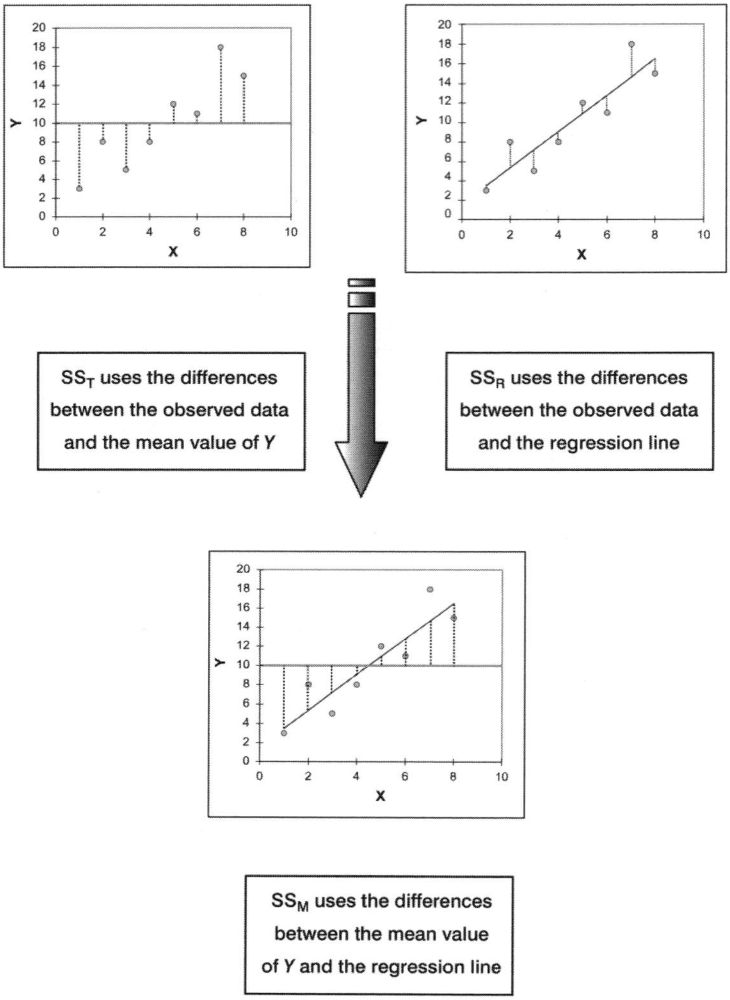

FIGURE 7.4 Diagram showing from where the regression sums of squares derive

of differences that we have added up, we use the average sums of squares (referred to as the **mean squares** or MS). To work out the mean sums of squares we divide by the degrees of freedom (this is comparable to calculating the variance from the sums of squares – see section 2.4.2). For SS_M the degrees of freedom are simply the number of variables in the model, and for SS_R they are the number of observations minus the number of parameters being estimated (i.e. the number of beta coefficients including the constant). The result is the mean squares for the model (MS_M) and the residual mean squares (MS_R). At this stage it isn't essential that you understand how the mean squares are derived (it is explained in Chapter 10). However, it is important that you understand that the **F-ratio** (equation (7.5)) is a measure of how much the model has improved the prediction of the outcome compared to the level of inaccuracy of the model:

$$F = \frac{MS_M}{MS_R} \tag{7.5}$$

If a model is good, then we expect the improvement in prediction due to the model to be large (so, MS_M will be large) and the difference between the model and the observed data to be small (so, MS_R will be small). In short, a good model should have a large *F*-ratio (greater than 1 at least) because the top of equation (7.5) will be bigger than the bottom. The exact magnitude of this *F*-ratio can be assessed using critical values for the corresponding degrees of freedom (as in the Appendix).

7.2.4. Assessing individual predictors ①

We've seen that the predictor in a regression model has a coefficient (b_1), which in simple regression represents the gradient of the regression line. The value of *b* represents the change in the outcome resulting from a unit change in the predictor. If the model was useless at predicting the outcome, then if the value of the predictor changes, what might we expect the change in the outcome to be? Well, if the model is very bad then we would expect the change in the outcome to be zero. Think back to Figure 7.4 (see the panel representing SS_T) in which we saw that using the mean was a very bad way of predicting the outcome. In fact, the line representing the mean is flat, which means that as the predictor variable changes, the value of the outcome does *not* change (because for each level of the predictor variable, we predict that the outcome will equal the mean value). The important point here is that a bad model (such as the mean) will have regression coefficients of 0 for the predictors. A regression coefficient of 0 means: (1) a unit change in the predictor variable results in no change in the predicted value of the outcome (the predicted value of the outcome does not change at all); and (2) the gradient of the regression line is 0, meaning that the regression line is flat. Hopefully, you'll see that it logically follows that if a variable significantly predicts an outcome, then it should have a *b*-value significantly different from zero. This hypothesis is tested using a *t*-test (see Chapter 9). The **t-statistic** tests the null hypothesis that the value of *b* is 0: therefore, if it is significant we gain confidence in the hypothesis that the *b*-value is significantly different from 0 and that the predictor variable contributes significantly to our ability to estimate values of the outcome.

Like *F*, the *t*-statistic is also based on the ratio of explained variance against unexplained variance or error. Well, actually, what we're interested in here is not so much variance but whether the *b* we have is big compared to the amount of error in that estimate. To estimate how much error we could expect to find in *b* we use the standard error. The standard error tells us something about how different *b*-values would be across different samples. We could take lots and lots of samples of data regarding record sales and advertising budgets and calculate the *b*-values for each sample. We could plot a frequency distribution of these samples to discover whether the *b*-values from all samples would be relatively similar, or whether they would be very different (think back to section 2.5.1). We can use the standard deviation of this distribution (known as the *standard error*) as a measure of the similarity of *b*-values across samples. If the standard error is very small, then it means that most samples are likely to have a *b*-value similar to the one in our sample (because there is little variation across samples). The *t*-test tells us whether the *b*-value is different from 0 relative to the variation in *b*-values across samples. When the standard error is small even a small deviation from zero can reflect a meaningful difference because *b* is representative of the majority of possible samples.

Equation (7.6) shows how the *t*-test is calculated and you'll find a general version of this equation in Chapter 9 (equation (9.1)). The b_{expected} is simply the value of *b* that we would expect to obtain if the null hypothesis were true. I mentioned earlier that the null hypothesis is that *b* is 0 and so this value can be replaced by 0. The equation simplifies to become the observed value of *b* divided by the standard error with which it is associated:

$$t = \frac{b_{\text{observed}} - b_{\text{expected}}}{\text{SE}_b} = \frac{b_{\text{observed}}}{\text{SE}_b} \quad (7.6)$$

The values of t have a special distribution that differs according to the degrees of freedom for the test. In regression, the degrees of freedom are $N - p - 1$, where N is the total sample size and p is the number of predictors. In simple regression when we have only one predictor, this reduces down to $N - 2$. Having established which t-distribution needs to be used, the observed value of t can then be compared to the values that we would expect to find if there was no effect (i.e. $b = 0$): if t is very large then it is unlikely to have occurred when there is no effect (these values can be found in the Appendix). SPSS provides the exact probability that the observed value or a larger value of t would occur if the value of b was, in fact, 0. As a general rule, if this observed significance is less than .05, then scientists assume that b is significantly different from 0; put another way, the predictor makes a significant contribution to predicting the outcome.

7.3. Doing simple regression on SPSS ①

So far, we have seen a little of the theory behind regression, albeit restricted to the situation in which there is only one predictor. To help clarify what we have learnt so far, we will go through an example of a simple regression on SPSS. Earlier on I asked you to imagine that I worked for a record company and that my boss was interested in predicting record sales from advertising. There are some data for this example in the file **Record1.sav**. This data file has 200 rows, each one representing a different record. There are also two columns, one representing the sales of each record in the week after release and the other representing the amount (in pounds) spent promoting the record before release. This is the format for entering regression data: the outcome variable and any predictors should be entered in different columns, and each row should represent independent values of those variables.

The pattern of the data is shown in Figure 7.5 and it should be clear that a positive relationship exists: so, the more money spent advertising the record, the more it is likely to sell. Of course there are some records that sell well regardless of advertising (top left of scatterplot), but there are none that sell badly when advertising levels are high (bottom right of scatterplot). The scatterplot also shows the line of best fit for these data: bearing in mind that the mean would be represented by a flat line at around the 200,000 sales mark, the regression line is noticeably different.

To find out the parameters that describe the regression line, and to see whether this line is a useful model, we need to run a regression analysis. To do the analysis you need to access the main dialog box by selecting Analyze Regression ▸Linear ▾. Figure 7.6 shows the resulting dialog box. There is a space labelled *Dependent* in which you should place the outcome variable (in this example **sales**). So, select **sales** from the list on the left-hand side, and transfer it by dragging it or clicking on ➔. There is another space labelled *Independent(s)* in which any predictor variable should be placed. In simple regression we use only one predictor (in this example, **adverts**) and so you should select **adverts** from the list and click on ➔ to transfer it to the list of predictors. There are a variety of options available, but these will be explored within the context of multiple regression. For the time being just click on OK to run the basic analysis.

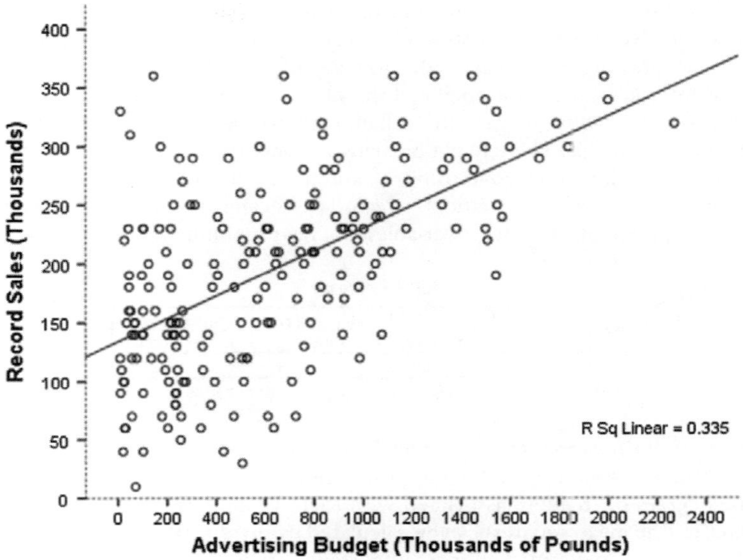

FIGURE 7.5 Scatterplot showing the relationship between record sales and the amount spent promoting the record

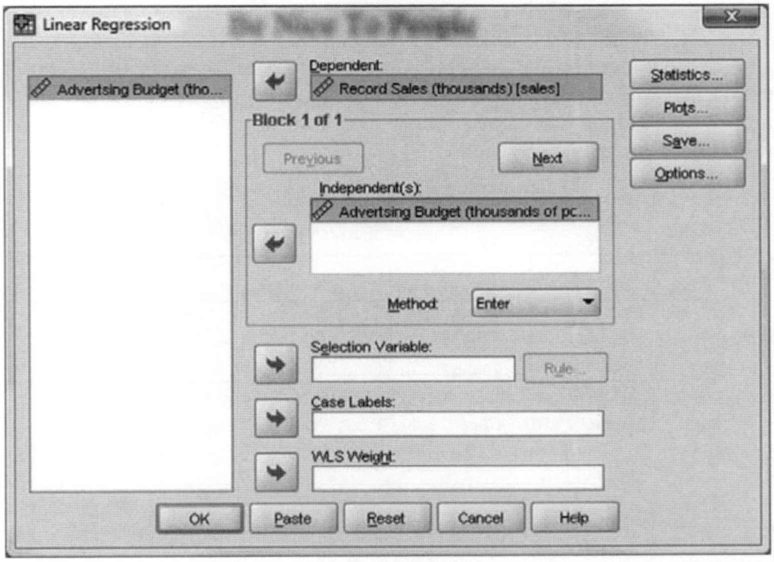

FIGURE 7.6 Main dialog box for regression

7.4. Interpreting a simple regression ①

7.4.1. Overall fit of the model ①

The first table provided by SPSS is a summary of the model (SPSS Output 7.1). This summary table provides the value of R and R^2 for the model that has been derived. For these data, R has a value of .578 and because there is only one predictor, this value represents the simple correlation between advertising and record sales (you can confirm this by running a correlation using what you were taught in Chapter 6). The value of R^2 is .335, which tells us that advertising expenditure can account for 33.5% of the variation in record sales. In other words, if we are trying to explain why some records sell more than others, we can look at the variation in sales of different records. There might be many factors that can explain this variation, but our model, which includes only advertising expenditure, can explain approximately 33% of it. This means that 66% of the variation in record sales cannot be explained by advertising alone. Therefore, there must be other variables that have an influence also.

SPSS OUTPUT 7.

Model Summary

Model	R	R Square	Adjusted R Square	Std. Error of the Estimate
1	.578[a]	.335	.331	65.991

a. Predictors: (Constant), Advertising Budget (thousands of pounds)

The next part of the output (SPSS Output 7.2) reports an analysis of variance (ANOVA – see Chapter 10). The summary table shows the various sums of squares described in Figure 7.4 and the degrees of freedom associated with each. From these two values, the average sums of squares (the mean squares) can be calculated by dividing the sums of squares by the associated degrees of freedom. The most important part of the table is the *F*-ratio, which is calculated using equation (7.5), and the associated significance value of that *F*-ratio. For these data, *F* is 99.59, which is significant at $p < .001$ (because the value in the column labelled *Sig.* is less than .001). This result tells us that there is less than a 0.1% chance that an *F*-ratio this large would happen if the null hypothesis were true. Therefore, we can conclude that our regression model results in significantly better prediction of record sales than if we used the mean value of record sales. In short, the regression model overall predicts record sales significantly well.

SPSS OUTPUT 7

ANOVA[b]

Model		Sum of Squares	df	Mean Square	F	Sig.
1	Regression	433687.833	1	433687.833	99.587	.000[a]
	Residual	862264.167	198	4354.870		
	Total	1295952.000	199			

a. Predictors: (Constant), Advertising Budget (thousands of pounds)

b. Dependent Variable: Record Sales (thousands)

SS_M SS_R SS_T MS_M MS_R

7.4.2. Model parameters ①

The ANOVA tells us whether the model, overall, results in a significantly good degree of prediction of the outcome variable. However, the ANOVA doesn't tell us about the individual contribution of variables in the model (although in this simple case there is only one variable in the model and so we can infer that this variable is a good predictor). The table in SPSS Output 7.3 provides details of the model parameters (the beta values) and the significance of these values. We saw in equation (7.2) that b_0 was the *Y* intercept and this value is the value *B* (in the SPSS output) for the constant. So, from the table, we can say that b_0 is 134.14, and this can be interpreted as meaning that when no money is spent on advertising (when $X = 0$), the model predicts that 134,140 records will be sold (remember that our unit of measurement was thousands of records). We can also read off the value of b_1 from the table and this value represents the gradient of the regression line. It is 0.096. Although this value is the slope of the regression line, it is more useful to think of this value as representing *the change in the outcome associated with a unit change in the predictor*. Therefore, if our predictor variable is increased by one unit (if the advertising budget is increased by 1), then our model predicts that 0.096 extra records will be sold. Our units of measurement were thousands of pounds and thousands of records sold, so we can say that for an increase in advertising of £1000 the model predicts 96 ($0.096 \times 1000 = 96$) extra record sales. As you might imagine, this investment is pretty bad for the record company: it invests £1000 and gets only 96 extra sales. Fortunately, as we already know, advertising accounts for only one-third of record sales.

SS OUTPUT 7.3

Coefficients[a]

Model		Unstandardized Coefficients		Standardized Coefficients		
		B	Std. Error	Beta	t	Sig.
1	(Constant)	134.140	7.537		17.799	.000
	Advertsing Budget (thousands of pounds)	.096	.010	.578	9.979	.000

a. Dependent Variable: Record Sales (thousands)

We saw earlier that, in general, values of the regression coefficient b represent the change in the outcome resulting from a unit change in the predictor and that if a predictor is having a significant impact on our ability to predict the outcome then this b should be different from 0 (and big relative to its standard error). We also saw that the t-test tells us whether the b-value is different from 0. SPSS provides the exact probability that the observed value of t would occur if the value of b in the population were 0. If this observed significance is less than .05, then scientists agree that the result reflects a genuine effect (see Chapter 2). For these two values, the probabilities are .000 (zero to 3 decimal places) and so we can say that the probability of these t-values or larger occurring if the values of b in the population were 0 is less than .001. Therefore, the bs are different from 0 and we can conclude that the advertising budget makes a significant contribution ($p < .001$) to predicting record sales.

SELF-TEST How is the *t* in SPSS Output 7.3 calculated? Use the values in the table to see if you can get the same value as SPSS.

7.4.3. Using the model ①

So far, we have discovered that we have a useful model, one that significantly improves our ability to predict record sales. However, the next stage is often to use that model to make some predictions. The first stage is to define the model by replacing the b-values in equation (7.2) with the values from SPSS Output 7.3. In addition, we can replace the X and Y with the variable names so that the model becomes:

$$\begin{aligned} \text{record sales}_i &= b_0 + b_1 \text{advertising budget}_i \\ &= 134.14 + (0.096 \times \text{advertising budget}_i) \end{aligned} \qquad (7.7)$$

It is now possible to make a prediction about record sales, by replacing the advertising budget with a value of interest. For example, imagine a record executive wanted to spend £100,000 on advertising a new record. Remembering that our units are already in thousands of pounds, we can simply replace the advertising budget with 100. He would discover that record sales should be around 144,000 for the first week of sales:

$$\begin{aligned} \text{record sales}_i &= 134.14 + (0.096 \times \text{advertising budget}_i) \\ &= 134.14 + (0.096 \times 100) \\ &= 143.74 \end{aligned} \tag{7.8}$$

SELF-TEST How many records would be sold if we spent £666,000 on advertising the latest CD by black metal band Abgott?

CRAMMING SAM'S TIPS **Simple regression**

- Simple regression is a way of predicting values of one variable from another.
- We do this by fitting a statistical model to the data in the form of a straight line.
- This line is the line that best summarizes the pattern of the data.
- We have to assess how well the line fits the data using:
  - R^2 which tells us how much variance is explained by the model compared to how much variance there is to explain in the first place. It is the proportion of variance in the outcome variable that is shared by the predictor variable.
  - *F*, which tells us how much variability the model can explain relative to how much it can't explain (i.e. it's the ratio of how good the model is compared to how bad it is).
- The *b*-value tells us the gradient of the regression line and the strength of the relationship between a predictor and the outcome variable. If it is significant (*Sig.* < .05 in the SPSS table) then the predictor variable significantly predicts the outcome variable.

7.5. Multiple regression: the basics ②

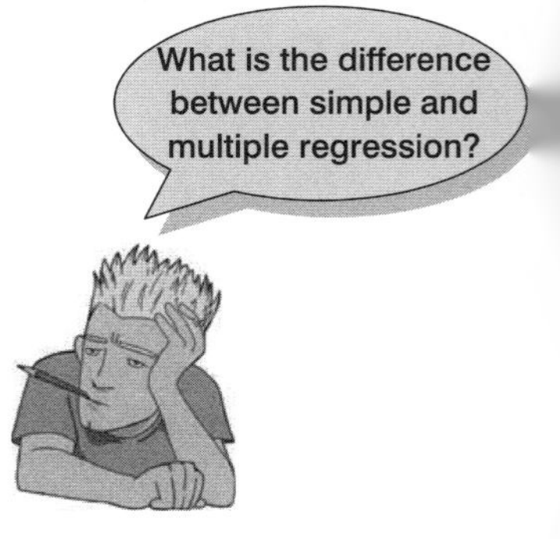

To summarize what we have learnt so far, in simple linear regression the outcome variable *Y* is predicted using the equation of a straight line (equation (7.2)). Given that we have collected several values of *Y* and *X*, the unknown parameters in the equation can be calculated. They are calculated by fitting a model to the data (in this case a straight line) for which the sum of the squared differences between the line and the actual data points is minimized. This method is called the method of least squares. Multiple regression is a logical extension of these principles to situations in which there are several predictors. Again, we still use our basic equation of:

$$\text{outcome}_i = (\text{model}) + \text{error}_i$$

but this time the model is slightly more complex. It is basically the same as for simple regression except that for every extra predictor you include, you have to add a coefficient; so, each predictor variable has its own coefficient, and the outcome variable is predicted from a combination of all the variables multiplied by their respective coefficients plus a residual term (see equation (7.9) – the brackets aren't necessary, they're just to make the connection to the general equation above):

$$Y_i = (b_0 + b_1X_{i1} + b_2X_{i2} + \ldots + b_nX_n) + \varepsilon_i \tag{7.9}$$

Y is the outcome variable, b_1 is the coefficient of the first predictor (X_1), b_2 is the coefficient of the second predictor (X_2), b_n is the coefficient of the nth predictor (X_n), and ε_i is the difference between the predicted and the observed value of Y for the ith participant. In this case, the model fitted is more complicated, but the basic principle is the same as simple regression. That is, we seek to find the linear combination of predictors that correlate maximally with the outcome variable. Therefore, when we refer to the regression model in multiple regression, we are talking about a model in the form of equation (7.9).

7.5.1. An example of a multiple regression model ②

Imagine that our record company executive was interested in extending his model of record sales to incorporate another variable. We know already that advertising accounts for 33% of variation in record sales, but a much larger 67% remains unexplained. The record executive could measure a new predictor in an attempt to explain some of the unexplained variation in record sales. He decides to measure the number of times the record is played on Radio 1 (the UK's biggest national radio station) during the week prior to release. The existing model that we derived using SPSS (see equation (7.7)) can now be extended to include this new variable (**airplay**):

$$\text{record sales}_i = b_0 + b_1\text{advertising budget}_i + b_2\textit{airplay}_i + \varepsilon_i \tag{7.10}$$

The new model is based on equation (7.9) and includes a b-value for both predictors (and, of course, the constant). If we calculate the b-values, we could make predictions about record sales based not only on the amount spent on advertising but also in terms of radio play. There are only two predictors in this model and so we could display this model graphically in three dimensions (Figure 7.7).

Equation (7.9) describes the tinted trapezium in the diagram (this is known as the regression *plane*) and the dots represent the observed data points. Like simple regression, the plane fitted to the data aims to best-predict the observed data. However, there are invariably some differences between the model and the real-life data (this fact is evident because some of the dots do not lie exactly on the tinted area of the graph). The b-value for advertising describes the slope of the left and right sides of the regression plane, whereas the b-value for airplay describes the slope of the top and bottom of the regression plane. Just like simple regression, knowledge of these two slopes tells us about the shape of the model (what it looks like) and the intercept locates the regression plane in space.

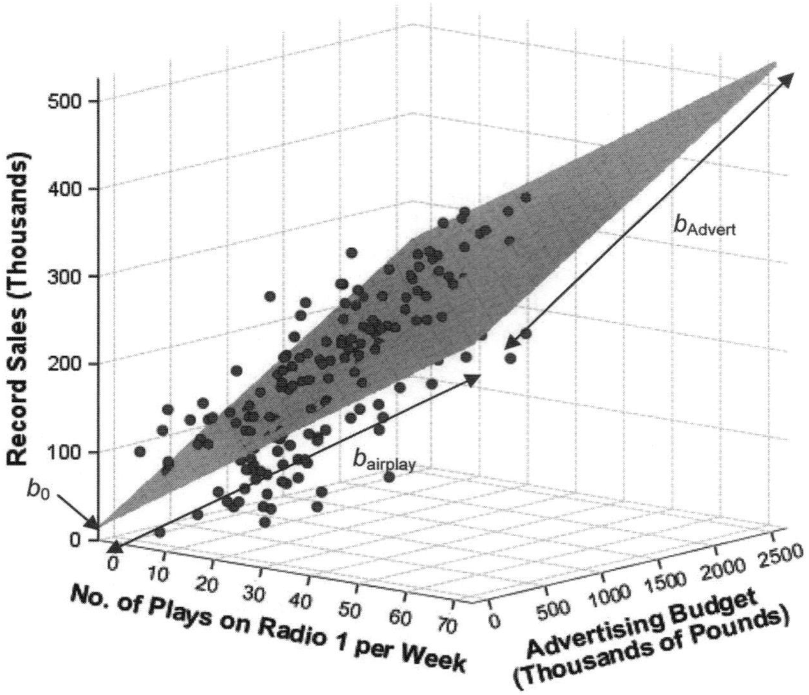

FIGURE 7.7
Scatterplot of the relationship between record sales, advertising budget and radio play

It is fairly easy to visualize a regression model with two predictors, because it is possible to plot the regression plane using a 3-D scatterplot. However, multiple regression can be used with three, four or even ten or more predictors. Although you can't immediately visualize what such complex models look like, or visualize what the *b*-values represent, you should be able to apply the principles of these basic models to more complex scenarios.

7.5.2. Sums of squares, *R* and R^2 ②

When we have several predictors, the partitioning of sums of squares is the same as in the single variable case except that the model we refer to takes the form of equation (7.9) rather than simply being a 2-D straight line. Therefore, SS_T can be calculated that represents the difference between the observed values and the mean value of the outcome variable. SS_R still represents the difference between the values of *Y* predicted by the model and the observed values. Finally, SS_M can still be calculated and represents the difference between the values of *Y* predicted by the model and the mean value. Although the computation of these values is much more complex than in simple regression, conceptually these values are the same.

When there are several predictors it does not make sense to look at the simple correlation coefficient and instead SPSS produces a multiple correlation coefficient (labelled **Multiple *R***). Multiple *R* is the correlation between the observed values of *Y* and the values of *Y* predicted by the multiple regression model. Therefore, large values of the multiple *R* represent a large correlation between the predicted and observed values of the outcome. A multiple *R* of 1 represents a situation in which the model perfectly predicts the observed data. As such, multiple R is a gauge of how well the model predicts the observed data. It follows that the resulting R^2 can be interpreted in the same way as simple regression: it is the amount of variation in the outcome variable that is accounted for by the model.

7.5.3. Methods of regression ②

If we are interested in constructing a complex model with several predictors, how do we decide which predictors to use? A great deal of care should be taken in selecting predictors for a model because the values of the regression coefficients depend upon the variables in the model. Therefore, the predictors included and the way in which they are entered into the model can have a great impact. In an ideal world, predictors should be selected based on past research.[5] If new predictors are being added to existing models then select these new variables based on the substantive *theoretical* importance of these variables. One thing *not* to do is select hundreds of random predictors, bung them all into a regression analysis and hope for the best. In addition to the problem of selecting predictors, there are several ways in which variables can be entered into a model. When predictors are all completely uncorrelated the order of variable entry has very little effect on the parameters calculated; however, we rarely have uncorrelated predictors and so the method of predictor selection is crucial.

7.5.3.1. Hierarchical (blockwise entry) ②

In **hierarchical regression** predictors are selected based on past work and the experimenter decides in which order to enter the predictors into the model. As a general rule, known predictors (from other research) should be entered into the model first in order of their importance in predicting the outcome. After known predictors have been entered, the experimenter can add any new predictors into the model. New predictors can be entered either all in one go, in a stepwise manner, or hierarchically (such that the new predictor suspected to be the most important is entered first).

7.5.3.2. Forced entry ②

Forced entry (or *Enter* as it is known in SPSS) is a method in which all predictors are forced into the model simultaneously. Like hierarchical, this method relies on good theoretical reasons for including the chosen predictors, but unlike hierarchical the experimenter makes no decision about the order in which variables are entered. Some researchers believe that this method is the only appropriate method for theory testing (Studenmund & Cassidy, 1987) because stepwise techniques are influenced by random variation in the data and so seldom give replicable results if the model is retested.

7.5.3.3. Stepwise methods ②

In **stepwise regressions** decisions about the order in which predictors are entered into the model are based on a purely mathematical criterion. In the *forward* method, an initial model is defined that contains only the constant (b_0). The computer then searches for the predictor (out of the ones available) that best predicts the outcome variable – it does this

[5] I might cynically qualify this suggestion by proposing that predictors be chosen based on past research that has utilized good methodology. If basing such decisions on regression analyses, select predictors based only on past research that has used regression appropriately and yielded reliable, generalizable models!

by selecting the predictor that has the highest simple correlation with the outcome. If this predictor significantly improves the ability of the model to predict the outcome, then this predictor is retained in the model and the computer searches for a second predictor. The criterion used for selecting this second predictor is that it is the variable that has the largest semi-partial correlation with the outcome. Let me explain this in plain English. Imagine that the first predictor can explain 40% of the variation in the outcome variable; then there is still 60% left unexplained. The computer searches for the predictor that can explain the biggest part of the remaining 60% (so, it is not interested in the 40% that is already explained). As such, this semi-partial correlation gives a measure of how much 'new variance' in the outcome can be explained by each remaining predictor (see section 6.6). The predictor that accounts for the most new variance is added to the model and, if it makes a significant contribution to the predictive power of the model, it is retained and another predictor is considered.

The *stepwise* method in SPSS is the same as the forward method, except that each time a predictor is added to the equation, a removal test is made of the least useful predictor. As such the regression equation is constantly being reassessed to see whether any redundant predictors can be removed. The *backward* method is the opposite of the forward method in that the computer begins by placing all predictors in the model and then calculating the contribution of each one by looking at the significance value of the *t*-test for each predictor. This significance value is compared against a removal criterion (which can be either an absolute value of the test statistic or a probability value for that test statistic). If a predictor meets the removal criterion (i.e. if it is not making a statistically significant contribution to how well the model predicts the outcome variable) it is removed from the model and the model is re-estimated for the remaining predictors. The contribution of the remaining predictors is then reassessed.

If you do decide to use a stepwise method then the backward method is preferable to the forward method. This is because of **suppressor effects**, which occur when a predictor has a significant effect but only when another variable is held constant. Forward selection is more likely than backward elimination to exclude predictors involved in suppressor effects. As such, the forward method runs a higher risk of making a Type II error (i.e. missing a predictor that does in fact predict the outcome).

7.5.3.4. Choosing a method ②

SPSS allows you to opt for any one of these methods and it is important to select an appropriate one. The forward, backward and stepwise methods all come under the general heading of *stepwise methods* because they all rely on the computer selecting variables based upon mathematical criteria. Many writers argue that this takes many important methodological decisions out of the hands of the researcher. What's more, the models derived by computer often take advantage of random sampling variation and so decisions about which variables should be included will be based upon slight differences in their semi-partial correlation. However, these slight statistical differences may contrast dramatically with the theoretical importance of a predictor to the model. There is also the danger of over-fitting (having too many variables in the model that essentially make little contribution to predicting the outcome) and under-fitting (leaving out important predictors) the model. For this reason stepwise methods are best avoided except for exploratory model building. If you must do a stepwise regression then it is advisable to **cross-validate** your model by splitting the data (see section 7.6.2.2).

When there is a sound theoretical literature available, then base your model upon what past research tells you. Include any meaningful variables in the model in their order of importance. After this initial analysis, repeat the regression but exclude any variables that were statistically redundant the first time around. There are important considerations in deciding which predictors should be included. First, it is important not to include too many predictors. As a general rule, the fewer predictors the better, and certainly include only predictors for which you have a good theoretical grounding (it is meaningless to measure hundreds of variables and then put them all into a regression model). So, be selective and remember that you should have a decent sample size – see section 7.6.2.3.

7.6. How accurate is my regression model? ②

When we have produced a model based on a sample of data there are two important questions to ask: (1) does the model fit the observed data well, or is it influenced by a small number of cases; and (2) can my model generalize to other samples? These questions are vital to ask because they affect how we use the model that has been constructed. These questions are also, in some sense, hierarchical because we wouldn't want to generalize a bad model. However, it is a mistake to think that because a model fits the observed data well we can draw conclusions beyond our sample. **Generalization** is a critical additional step and if we find that our model is not generalizable, then we must restrict any conclusions based on the model to the sample used. First, we will look at how we establish whether a model is an accurate representation of the actual data, and in section 7.6.2 we move on to look at how we assess whether a model can be used to make inferences beyond the sample of data that has been collected.

7.6.1. Assessing the regression model I: diagnostics ②

To answer the question of whether the model fits the observed data well, or if it is influenced by a small number of cases, we can look for outliers and influential cases (the difference is explained in Jane Superbrain Box 7.1). We will look at these in turn.

JANE SUPERBRAIN 7.1

The difference between residuals and influence statistics ③

In this section I've described two ways to look for cases that might bias the model: residual and influence statistics. To illustrate how these measures differ, imagine that the Mayor

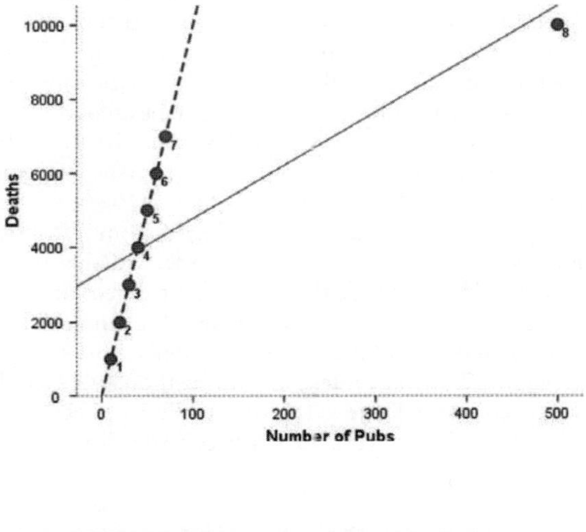

of London at the turn of the last century was interested in how drinking affected mortality. London is divided up into different regions called boroughs, and so he might measure the number of pubs and the number of deaths over a period of time in eight of his boroughs. The data are in a file called **pubs.sav**.

The scatterplot of these data reveals that without the last case there is a perfect linear relationship (the dashed straight line). However, the presence of the last case (case 8) changes the line of best fit dramatically (although this line is still a significant fit of the data – do the regression analysis and see for yourself).

What's interesting about these data is when we look at the residuals and influence statistics. The standardized residual for case 8 is the second *smallest*: this outlier produces a very small residual (most of the non-outliers have larger residuals) because it sits very close to the line that has been fitted to the data. How can this be? Look at the influence statistics below and you'll see that they're massive for case 8: it exerts a huge influence over the model.

Case Summaries[a]

	Standardized Residual	Mahalanobis Distance	Cook's Distance	Centered Leverage Value	DFFIT	DFBETA Intercept	DFBETA pubs
1	-1.33839	.28515	.21328	.04074	-495.72692	-509.65184	1.39249
2	-.87895	.22370	.08530	.03196	-305.09716	-321.12768	.80153
3	-.41950	.16969	.01814	.02424	-137.20167	-147.10661	.33016
4	.03995	.12314	.00015	.01759	12.38769	13.45081	-.02658
5	.49940	.08403	.02294	.01200	147.81622	161.44976	-.27267
6	.95885	.05237	.08092	.00748	273.00807	297.67748	-.41116
7	1.41830	.02817	.17107	.00402	391.72124	422.81664	-.44422
8	-.27966	6.03375	227.14286	.86196	-39478.58473	3351.95531	-85.66108
Total N	8	8	8	8	8	8	8

a. Limited to first 100 cases.

As always when you see a statistical oddity you should ask what was happening in the real world. The last data point represents the City of London, a tiny area of only 1 square mile in the centre of London where very few people lived but where thousands of commuters (even then) came to work and had lunch in the pubs. Hence the pubs didn't rely on the resident population for their business and the residents didn't consume all of their beer! Therefore, there was a massive number of pubs.

This illustrates that a case exerting a massive influence can produce a small residual – so look at both! (I'm very grateful to David Hitchin for this example, and he in turn got it from Dr Richard Roberts.)

7.6.1.1. Outliers and residuals ②

An outlier is a case that differs substantially from the main trend of the data (see Jane Superbrain Box 4.1). Figure 7.8 shows an example of such a case in regression. Outliers can cause your model to be biased because they affect the values of the estimated regression coefficients. For example, Figure 7.8 uses the same data as Figure 7.3 except that the score of one participant has been changed to be an outlier (in this case a person who was very calm in the presence of a very big spider). The change in this one point has had a dramatic effect on the regression model chosen to fit the data. With the outlier present, the regression model changes: its gradient is reduced (the line becomes flatter) and the intercept increases (the new line will cross the Y-axis at a higher point). It should be clear from this diagram that it is important to try to detect outliers to see whether the model is biased in this way.

How do you think that you might detect an outlier? Well, we know that an outlier, by its nature, is very different from all of the other scores. This being true, do you think that the model will predict that person's score very accurately? The answer is *no*: looking at Figure 7.8 it is evident that even though the outlier has biased the model, the model still predicts that one value very badly (the regression line is long way from the outlier). Therefore, if we were to work out the differences between the data values that were

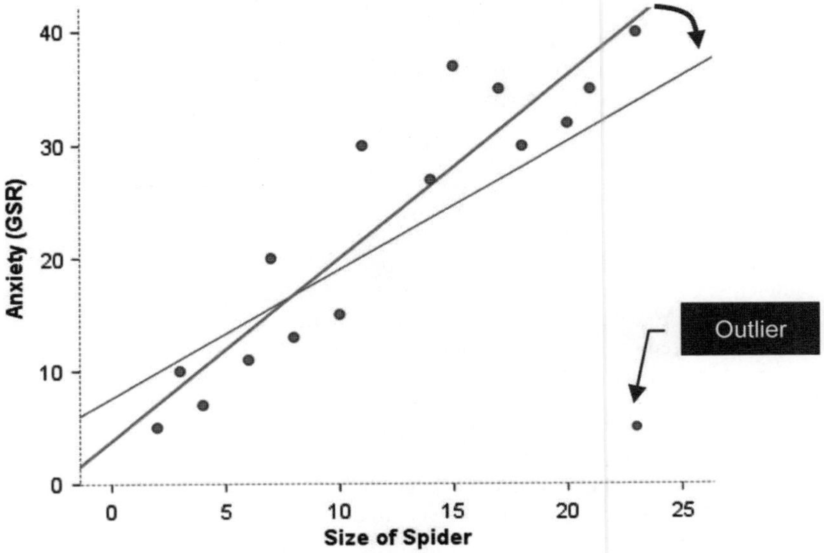

FIGURE 7.8 Graph demonstrating the effect of an outlier. The green line represents the original regression line for these data (see Figure 7.3), whereas the red line represents the regression line when an outlier is present

collected, and the values predicted by the model, we could detect an outlier by looking for large differences. This process is the same as looking for cases that the model predicts inaccurately. The differences between the values of the outcome predicted by the model and the values of the outcome observed in the sample are known as *residuals*. These residuals represent the error present in the model. If a model fits the sample data well then all residuals will be small (if the model was a perfect fit of the sample data – all data points fall on the regression line – then all residuals would be zero). If a model is a poor fit of the sample data then the residuals will be large. Also, if any cases stand out as having a large residual, then they could be outliers.

The *normal* or **unstandardized residuals** described above are measured in the same units as the outcome variable and so are difficult to interpret across different models. What we can do is to look for residuals that stand out as being particularly large. However, we cannot define a universal cut-off point for what constitutes a large residual. To overcome this problem, we use **standardized residuals**, which are the residuals divided by an estimate of their standard deviation. We came across standardization in section 6.3.2 as a means of converting variables into a standard unit of measurement (the standard deviation); we also came across *z*-scores (see section 1.7.4) in which variables are converted into standard deviation units (i.e. they're converted into scores that are distributed around a mean of 0 with a standard deviation of 1). By converting residuals into *z*-scores (standardized residuals) we can compare residuals from different models and use what we know about the properties of *z*-scores to devise universal guidelines for what constitutes an acceptable (or unacceptable) value. For example, we know from Chapter 1 that in a normally distributed sample, 95% of *z*-scores should lie between −1.96 and +1.96, 99% should lie between −2.58 and +2.58, and 99.9% (i.e. nearly all of them) should lie between −3.29 and +3.29. Some general rules for standardized residuals are derived from these facts: (1) standardized residuals with an absolute value greater than 3.29 (we can use 3 as an approximation) are cause for concern because in an average sample case a value this high is unlikely to happen by chance; (2) if more than 1% of our sample cases have standardized residuals with an absolute value greater than 2.58 (we usually just say 2.5) there is evidence that the level of error within our model is unacceptable (the model is a fairly poor fit of the sample data); and (3) if more than 5% of cases have standardized residuals with an absolute value greater than 1.96 (we can use 2 for convenience) then there is also evidence that the model is a poor representation of the actual data.

A third form of residual is the **Studentized residual**, which is the unstandardized residual divided by an estimate of its standard deviation that varies point by point. These residuals have the same properties as the standardized residuals but usually provide a more precise estimate of the error variance of a specific case.

7.6.1.2. Influential cases ③

As well as testing for outliers by looking at the error in the model, it is also possible to look at whether certain cases exert undue influence over the parameters of the model. So, if we were to delete a certain case, would we obtain different regression coefficients? This type of analysis can help to determine whether the regression model is stable across the sample, or whether it is biased by a few influential cases. Again, this process will unveil outliers.

There are several residual statistics that can be used to assess the influence of a particular case. One statistic is the **adjusted predicted value** for a case when that case is excluded from the analysis. In effect, the computer calculates a new model without a particular case and then uses this new model to predict the value of the outcome variable for the case that was excluded. If a case does not exert a large influence over the model then we would expect the adjusted predicted value to be very similar to the predicted value when the case is included. Put simply, if the model is stable then the predicted value of a case should be the same regardless of whether or not that case was used to calculate the model. The difference between the adjusted predicted value and the original predicted value is known as **DFFit** (see below). We can also look at the residual based on the adjusted predicted value: that is, the difference between the adjusted predicted value and the original observed value. This is the **deleted residual**. The deleted residual can be divided by the standard deviation to give a standardized value known as the **Studentized deleted residual**. This residual can be compared across different regression analyses because it is measured in standard units.

The deleted residuals are very useful to assess the influence of a case on the ability of the model to predict that case. However, they do not provide any information about how a case influences the model as a whole (i.e. the impact that a case has on the model's ability to predict *all* cases). One statistic that does consider the effect of a single case on the model as a whole is **Cook's distance**. Cook's distance is a measure of the overall influence of a case on the model and Cook and Weisberg (1982) have suggested that values greater than 1 may be cause for concern.

A second measure of influence is **leverage** (sometimes called **hat values**), which gauges the influence of the observed value of the outcome variable over the predicted values. The average leverage value is defined as $(k + 1)/n$ in which k is the number of predictors in the model and n is the number of participants.[6] The maximum value for leverage is $(N-1)/N$; however, SPSS calculates a version of the leverage that takes a maximum value of 1 (indicating that the case has complete influence over prediction). If no cases exert undue influence over the model then we would expect all of the leverage values to be close to the average value ($(k + 1)/n$). Hoaglin and Welsch (1978) recommend investigating cases with values greater than twice the average ($2(k + 1)/n$) and Stevens (2002) recommends using three times the average ($3(k + 1)/n$) as a cut-off point for identifying cases having undue influence. We will see how to use these cut-off points later. However, cases with large leverage values will not necessarily have a large influence on the regression coefficients because they are measured on the outcome variables rather than the predictors.

Related to the leverage values are the **Mahalanobis distances** (Figure 7.9), which measure the distance of cases from the mean(s) of the predictor variable(s). You need to look for the cases with the highest values. It is not easy to establish a cut-off point at which to worry,

[6] You may come across the average leverage denoted as p/n in which p is the number of parameters being estimated. In multiple regression, we estimate parameters for each predictor and also for a constant and so p is equivalent to the number of predictors plus one, $(k + 1)$.

FIGURE 7.9 Prasanta Chandra Mahalanobis staring into his distances

although Barnett and Lewis (1978) have produced a table of critical values dependent on the number of predictors and the sample size. From their work it is clear that even with large samples ($N = 500$) and 5 predictors, values above 25 are cause for concern. In smaller samples ($N = 100$) and with fewer predictors (namely 3) values greater than 15 are problematic, and in very small samples ($N = 30$) with only 2 predictors values greater than 11 should be examined. However, for more specific advice, refer to Barnett and Lewis's table.

It is possible to run the regression analysis with a case included and then rerun the analysis with that same case excluded. If we did this, undoubtedly there would be some difference between the *b* coefficients in the two regression equations. This difference would tell us how much influence a particular case has on the parameters of the regression model. To take a hypothetical example, imagine two variables that had a perfect negative relationship except for a single case (case 30). If a regression analysis was done on the 29 cases that were perfectly linearly related then we would get a model in which the predictor variable X perfectly predicts the outcome variable Y, and there are no errors. If we then ran the analysis but this time include the case that didn't conform (case 30), then the resulting model has different parameters. Some data are stored in the file **dfbeta.sav** which illustrate such a situation. Try running a simple regression first with all the cases included and then with case 30 deleted. The results are summarized in Table 7.1, which shows: (1) the parameters for the regression model when the extreme case is included or excluded; (2) the resulting regression equations; and (3) the value of *Y* predicted from participant 30's score on the *X* variable (which is obtained by replacing the *X* in the regression equation with participant 30's score for X, which was 1).

When case 30 is excluded, these data have a perfect negative relationship; hence the coefficient for the predictor (b_1) is –1 (remember that in simple regression this term is the same as Pearson's correlation coefficient), and the coefficient for the constant (the intercept, b_0) is 31. However, when case 30 is included, both parameters are reduced[7] and the difference between the parameters is also displayed. The difference between a parameter estimated using all cases and estimated when one case is excluded is known as the **DFBeta** in SPSS. DFBeta is calculated for every case and for each of the parameters in the model. So, in our hypothetical example, the DFBeta for the constant is –2, and the DFBeta for the predictor variable is 0.1. By looking at the values of DFBeta, it is possible to identify cases that have a large influence on the parameters of the regression model. Again, the units of measurement used will affect these values and so SPSS produces a **standardized DFBeta**. These standardized

[7] The value of b_1 is reduced because the data no longer have a perfect linear relationship and so there is now variance that the model cannot explain.

TABLE 7.1 The difference in the parameters of the regression model when one case is excluded

Parameter (*b*)	*Case 30 Included*	*Case 30 Excluded*	*Difference*
Constant (intercept)	29.00	31.00	−2.00
Predictor (gradient)	−0.90	−1.00	0.10
Model (regression line):	$Y = (-0.9)X + 29$	$Y = (-1)X + 31$	
Predicted *Y*	28.10	30.00	−1.90

values are easier to use because universal cut-off points can be applied. In this case absolute values above 1 indicate cases that substantially influence the model parameters (although Stevens, 2002, suggests looking at cases with absolute values greater than 2).

A related statistic is the **DFFit**, which is the difference between the predicted value for a case when the model is calculated including that case and when the model is calculated excluding that case: in this example the value is −1.90 (see Table 7.1). If a case is not influential then its DFFit should be zero – hence, we expect non-influential cases to have small DFFit values. However, we have the problem that this statistic depends on the units of measurement of the outcome and so a DFFit of 0.5 will be very small if the outcome ranges from 1 to 100, but very large if the outcome varies from 0 to 1. Therefore, SPSS also produces standardized versions of the DFFit values (**Standardized DFFit**). A final measure is that of the **covariance ratio (CVR)**, which is a measure of whether a case influences the variance of the regression parameters. A description of the computation of this statistic would leave most readers dazed and confused, so suffice to say that when this ratio is close to 1 the case is having very little influence on the variances of the model parameters. Belsey, Kuh and Welsch (1980) recommend the following:

EVERYBODY

- If $CVR_i > 1 + [3(k + 1)/n]$ then deleting the *i*th case will damage the precision of some of the model's parameters.
- If $CVR_i < 1 - [3(k + 1)/n]$ then deleting the *i*th case will improve the precision of some of the model's parameters.

In both equations, k is the number of predictors, CVR_i is the covariance ratio for the *i*th participant, and n is the sample size.

7.6.1.3. A final comment on diagnostic statistics ②

There are a lot of diagnostic statistics that should be examined after a regression analysis, and it is difficult to summarize this wealth of material into a concise conclusion. However, one thing I would like to stress is a point made by Belsey et al. (1980) who noted the dangers inherent in these procedures. The point is that diagnostics are tools that enable you to see how good or bad your model is in terms of fitting the sampled data. They are a way of assessing your model. They are *not*, however, a way of justifying the removal of data points to effect some desirable change in the regression parameters (e.g. deleting a case that changes a non-significant *b*-value into a significant one). Stevens (2002), as ever, offers excellent advice:

> If a point is a significant outlier on Y, but its Cook's distance is < 1, there is no real need to delete that point since it does not have a large effect on the regression analysis. However, one should still be interested in studying such points further to understand why they did not fit the model. (p. 135)

7.6.2. Assessing the regression model II: generalization ②

When a regression analysis is done, an equation can be produced that is correct for the sample of observed values. However, in the social sciences we are usually interested in generalizing our findings outside of the sample. So, although it can be useful to draw conclusions about a particular sample of people, it is usually more interesting if we can then assume that our conclusions are true for a wider population. For a regression model to generalize we must be sure that underlying assumptions have been met, and to test whether the model does generalize we can look at cross-validating it.

7.6.2.1. Checking assumptions ②

To draw conclusions about a population based on a regression analysis done on a sample, several assumptions must be true (see Berry, 1993):

- **Variable types**: All predictor variables must be quantitative or categorical (with two categories), and the outcome variable must be quantitative, continuous and unbounded. By quantitative I mean that they should be measured at the interval level and by unbounded I mean that there should be no constraints on the variability of the outcome. If the outcome is a measure ranging from 1 to 10 yet the data collected vary between 3 and 7, then these data are constrained.
- **Non-zero variance**: The predictors should have some variation in value (i.e. they do not have variances of 0).
- **No perfect multicollinearity**: There should be no perfect linear relationship between two or more of the predictors. So, the predictor variables should not correlate too highly (see section 7.6.2.4).
- **Predictors are uncorrelated with 'external variables'**: *External variables* are variables that haven't been included in the regression model which influence the outcome variable.[8] These variables can be thought of as similar to the 'third variable' that was discussed with reference to correlation. This assumption means that there should be no external variables that correlate with any of the variables included in the regression model. Obviously, if external variables do correlate with the predictors, then the conclusions we draw from the model become unreliable (because other variables exist that can predict the outcome just as well).
- **Homoscedasticity**: At each level of the predictor variable(s), the variance of the residual terms should be constant. This just means that the residuals at each level of the predictor(s) should have the same variance (homoscedasticity); when the variances are very unequal there is said to be heteroscedasticity (see section 5.6 as well).
- **Independent errors**: For any two observations the residual terms should be uncorrelated (or independent). This eventuality is sometimes described as a lack of autocorrelation. This assumption can be tested with the Durbin–Watson test, which tests for serial correlations between errors. Specifically, it tests whether adjacent residuals are correlated. The test statistic can vary between 0 and 4 with a value of 2 meaning that the residuals are uncorrelated. A value greater than 2 indicates a negative correlation between

[8] Some authors choose to refer to these external variables as part of an error term that includes any random factor in the way in which the outcome varies. However, to avoid confusion with the residual terms in the regression equations I have chosen the label 'external variables'. Although this term implicitly washes over any random factors, I acknowledge their presence here!

adjacent residuals, whereas a value below 2 indicates a positive correlation. The size of the Durbin–Watson statistic depends upon the number of predictors in the model and the number of observations. For accuracy, you should look up the exact acceptable values in Durbin and Watson's (1951) original paper. As a very conservative rule of thumb, values less than 1 or greater than 3 are definitely cause for concern; however, values closer to 2 may still be problematic depending on your sample and model.

- **Normally distributed errors**: It is assumed that the residuals in the model are random, normally distributed variables with a mean of 0. This assumption simply means that the differences between the model and the observed data are most frequently zero or very close to zero, and that differences much greater than zero happen only occasionally. Some people confuse this assumption with the idea that predictors have to be normally distributed. In fact, predictors do not need to be normally distributed (see section 7.11).
- **Independence**: It is assumed that all of the values of the outcome variable are independent (in other words, each value of the outcome variable comes from a separate entity).
- **Linearity**: The mean values of the outcome variable for each increment of the predictor(s) lie along a straight line. In plain English this means that it is assumed that the relationship we are modelling is a linear one. If we model a non-linear relationship using a linear model then this obviously limits the generalizability of the findings.

This list of assumptions probably seems pretty daunting but as we saw in Chapter 5, assumptions are important. When the assumptions of regression are met, the model that we get for a sample can be accurately applied to the population of interest (the coefficients and parameters of the regression equation are said to be *unbiased*). Some people assume that this means that when the assumptions are met the regression model from a sample is always identical to the model that would have been obtained had we been able to test the entire population. Unfortunately, this belief isn't true. What an unbiased model does tell us is that *on average* the regression model from the sample is the same as the population model. However, you should be clear that even when the assumptions are met, it is possible that a model obtained from a sample may not be the same as the population model – but the likelihood of them being the same is increased.

7.6.2.2. Cross-validation of the model ③

Even if we can't be confident that the model derived from our sample accurately represents the entire population, there are ways in which we can assess how well our model can predict the outcome in a different sample. Assessing the accuracy of a model across different samples is known as cross-validation. If a model can be generalized, then it must be capable of accurately predicting the same outcome variable from the same set of predictors in a different group of people. If the model is applied to a different sample and there is a severe drop in its predictive power, then the model clearly does *not* generalize. As a first rule of thumb, we should aim to collect enough data to obtain a reliable regression model (see the next section). Once we have a regression model there are two main methods of cross-validation:

- **Adjusted R^2**: In SPSS, not only are the values of R and R^2 calculated, but also an **adjusted R^2**. This adjusted value indicates the loss of predictive power or **shrinkage**. Whereas R^2 tells us how much of the variance in Y is accounted for by the regression model from our sample, the adjusted value tells us how much variance in Y would be accounted for if the model had been derived from the population from which the sample was taken. SPSS derives the adjusted R^2 using Wherry's equation. However, this equation has been criticized because it tells us nothing about how well the regression model would predict an entirely different set of data (how well can the model predict scores of a different sample of data from the same population?). One version of R^2 that does tell us how well the model cross-validates uses Stein's formula which is shown in equation (7.11) (see Stevens, 2002):

$$\text{adjusted } R^2 = 1 - \left[\left(\frac{n-1}{n-k-1}\right)\left(\frac{n-2}{n-k-2}\right)\left(\frac{n+1}{n}\right)\right](1-R^2) \tag{7.11}$$

In Stein's equation, R^2 is the unadjusted value, n is the number of participants and k is the number of predictors in the model. For the more mathematically minded of you, it is worth using this equation to cross-validate a regression model.

- **Data splitting:** This approach involves randomly splitting your data set, computing a regression equation on both halves of the data and then comparing the resulting models. When using stepwise methods, cross-validation is a good idea; you should run the stepwise regression on a random selection of about 80% of your cases. Then force this model on the remaining 20% of the data. By comparing the values of R^2 and b in the two samples you can tell how well the original model generalizes (see Tabachnick & Fidell, 2007, for more detail).

7.6.2.3. Sample size in regression ③

In the previous section I said that it's important to collect enough data to obtain a reliable regression model. Well, how much is enough? You'll find a lot of rules of thumb floating about, the two most common being that you should have 10 cases of data for each predictor in the model, or 15 cases of data per predictor. So, with five predictors, you'd need 50 or 75 cases respectively (depending on the rule you use). These rules are very pervasive (even I used the 15 cases per predictor rule in the first edition of this book) but they over simplify the issue considerably. In fact, the sample size required will depend on the size of effect that we're trying to detect (i.e. how strong the relationship is that we're trying to measure) and how much power we want to detect these effects. The simplest rule of thumb is that the bigger the sample size, the better! The reason is that the estimate of R that we get from regression is dependent on the number of predictors, k, and the sample size, N. In fact the expected R for random data is $k/(N-1)$ and so with small sample sizes random data can appear to show a strong effect: for example, with six predictors and 21 cases of data, $R = 6/(21-1) = .3$ (a medium effect size by Cohen's criteria described in section 6.3.2). Obviously for random data we'd want the expected R to be 0 (no effect) and for this to be true we need large samples (to take the previous example, if we had 100 cases not 21, then the expected R would be a more acceptable .06).

It's all very well knowing that larger is better, but researchers usually need some more concrete guidelines (much as we'd all love to collect 1000 cases of data it isn't always practical!). Green (1991) makes two rules of thumb for the *minimum* acceptable sample size, the first based on whether you want to test the overall fit of your regression model (i.e. test the R^2), and the second based on whether you want to test the individual predictors within the model (i.e. test b-values of the model). If you want to test the model overall, then he recommends a minimum sample size of $50 + 8k$, where k is the number of predictors. So, with five predictors, you'd need a sample size of $50 + 40 = 90$. If you want to test the individual predictors then he suggests a minimum sample size of $104 + k$, so again taking the example of 5 predictors you'd need a sample size of $104 + 5 = 109$. Of course, in most cases we're interested both in the overall fit and in the contribution of individual predictors, and in this situation Green recommends you calculate both of the minimum sample sizes I've just described, and use the one that has the largest value (so, in the five-predictor example, we'd use 109 because it is bigger than 90).

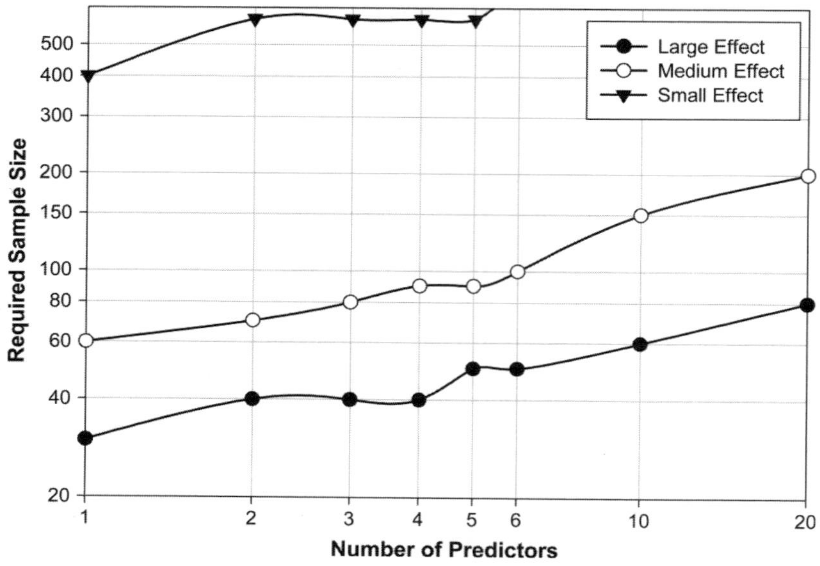

FIGURE 7.10 Graph to show the sample size required in regression depending on the number of predictors and the size of expected effect

Now, these guidelines are all right as a rough and ready guide, but they still oversimplify the problem. As I've mentioned, the sample size required actually depends on the size of the effect (i.e. how well our predictors predict the outcome) and how much statistical power we want to detect these effects. Miles and Shevlin (2001) produce some extremely useful graphs that illustrate the sample sizes needed to achieve different levels of power, for different effect sizes, as the number of predictors vary. For precise estimates of the sample size you should be using, I recommend using these graphs. I've summarized some of the general findings in Figure 7.10. This diagram shows the sample size required to achieve a high level of power (I've taken Cohen's, 1988, benchmark of .8) depending on the number of predictors and the size of expected effect. To summarize the graph very broadly: (1) if you expect to find a large effect then a sample size of 80 will always suffice (with up to 20 predictors) and if there are fewer predictors then you can afford to have a smaller sample; (2) if you're expecting a medium effect, then a sample size of 200 will always suffice (up to 20 predictors), you should always have a sample size above 60, and with six or fewer predictors you'll be fine with a sample of 100; and (3) if you're expecting a small effect size then just don't bother unless you have the time and resources to collect at least 600 cases of data (and many more if you have six or more predictors).

7.6.2.4. Multicollinearity ②

Multicollinearity exists when there is a strong correlation between two or more predictors in a regression model. Multicollinearity poses a problem only for multiple regression because (without wishing to state the obvious) simple regression requires only one predictor. **Perfect collinearity** exists when at least one predictor is a perfect linear combination of the others (the simplest example being two predictors that are perfectly correlated – they have a correlation coefficient of 1). If there is perfect collinearity between predictors it becomes impossible to obtain unique estimates of the regression coefficients because there are an infinite number of combinations of coefficients that would work equally well. Put simply, if we have two predictors that are perfectly correlated, then the values of b for each variable are interchangeable. The good news is that perfect collinearity is rare in real-life data. The bad news is that less than perfect collinearity is virtually unavoidable. Low levels of collinearity pose little threat to the models generated by SPSS, but as collinearity increases there are three problems that arise:

- **Untrustworthy *b*s**: As collinearity increases so do the standard errors of the *b* coefficients. If you think back to what the standard error represents, then big standard errors for *b* coefficients means that these *b*s are more variable across samples. Therefore, it means that the *b* coefficient in our sample is less likely to represent the population. Crudely put, multicollinearity means that the *b*-values are less trustworthy. Don't lend them money and don't let them go for dinner with your boy- or girlfriend. Of course if the *b*s are variable from sample to sample then the resulting predictor equations will be unstable across samples too.
- **It limits the size of *R***: Remember that *R* is a measure of the multiple correlation between the predictors and the outcome and that R^2 indicates the variance in the outcome for which the predictors account. Imagine a situation in which a single variable predicts the outcome variable fairly successfully (e.g. $R = .80$) and a second predictor variable is then added to the model. This second variable might account for a lot of the variance in the outcome (which is why it is included in the model), but the variance it accounts for is the same variance accounted for by the first variable. In other words, once the variance accounted for by the first predictor has been removed, the second predictor accounts for very little of the remaining variance (the second variable accounts for very little *unique variance*). Hence, the overall variance in the outcome accounted for by the two predictors is little more than when only one predictor is used (so *R* might increase from .80 to .82). This idea is connected to the notion of partial correlation that was explained in Chapter 6. If, however, the two predictors are completely uncorrelated, then the second predictor is likely to account for different variance in the outcome to that accounted for by the first predictor. So, although in itself the second predictor might account for only a little of the variance in the outcome, the variance it does account for is different to that of the other predictor (and so when both predictors are included, *R* is substantially larger, say .95). Therefore, having uncorrelated predictors is beneficial.
- **Importance of predictors**: Multicollinearity between predictors makes it difficult to assess the individual importance of a predictor. If the predictors are highly correlated, and each accounts for similar variance in the outcome, then how can we know which of the two variables is important? Quite simply we can't tell which variable is important – the model could include either one, interchangeably.

One way of identifying multicollinearity is to scan a correlation matrix of all of the predictor variables and see if any correlate very highly (by very highly I mean correlations of above .80 or .90). This is a good 'ball park' method but misses more subtle forms of multicollinearity. Luckily, SPSS produces various collinearity diagnostics, one of which is the **variance inflation factor (VIF)**. The VIF indicates whether a predictor has a strong linear relationship with the other predictor(s). Although there are no hard and fast rules about what value of the VIF should cause concern, Myers (1990) suggests that a value of 10 is a good value at which to worry. What's more, if the average VIF is greater than 1, then multicollinearity may be biasing the regression model (Bowerman & O'Connell, 1990). Related to the VIF is the **tolerance** statistic, which is its reciprocal (1/VIF). As such, values below 0.1 indicate serious problems although Menard (1995) suggests that values below 0.2 are worthy of concern.

Other measures that are useful in discovering whether predictors are dependent are the *eigenvalues of the scaled, uncentred cross-products matrix*, the *condition indexes* and the *variance proportions*. These statistics are extremely complex and will be covered as part of the interpretation of SPSS output (see section 7.8.5). If none of this has made any sense then have a look at Hutcheson and Sofroniou (1999: 78–85) who give a really clear explanation of multicollinearity.

7.7. How to do multiple regression using SPSS ②

7.7.1. Some things to think about before the analysis ②

A good strategy to adopt with regression is to measure predictor variables for which there are sound theoretical reasons for expecting them to predict the outcome. Run a regression analysis in which all predictors are entered into the model and examine the output to see which predictors contribute substantially to the model's ability to predict the outcome. Once you have established which variables are important, rerun the analysis including only the important predictors and use the resulting parameter estimates to define your regression model. If the initial analysis reveals that there are two or more significant predictors then you could consider running a forward stepwise analysis (rather than forced entry) to find out the individual contribution of each predictor.

I have spent a lot of time explaining the theory behind regression and some of the diagnostic tools necessary to gauge the accuracy of a regression model. It is important to remember that SPSS may appear to be very clever, but in fact it is not. Admittedly, it can do lots of complex calculations in a matter of seconds, but what it can't do is control the quality of the model that is generated – to do this requires a human brain (and preferably a trained one). SPSS will happily generate output based on any garbage you decide to feed into the data editor and SPSS will not judge the results or give any indication of whether the model can be generalized or if it is valid. However, SPSS provides the statistics necessary to judge these things, and at this point our brains must take over the job – which is slightly worrying (especially if your brain is as small as mine)!

7.7.2. Main options ②

Imagine that the record company executive was now interested in extending the model of record sales to incorporate other variables. He decides to measure two new variables: (1) the number of times the record is played on Radio 1 during the week prior to release (**airplay**); and (2) the attractiveness of the band (**attract**). Before a record is released, the executive notes the amount spent on advertising, the number of times the record is played on radio the week before release, and the attractiveness of the band. He does this for 200 different records (each made by a different band). Attractiveness was measured by asking a random sample of the target audience to rate the attractiveness of each band on a scale from 0 (hideous potato-heads) to 10 (gorgeous sex objects). The mode attractiveness given by the sample was used in the regression (because he was interested in what the majority of people thought, rather than the average of people's opinions).

These data are in the file **Record2.sav** and you should note that each variable has its own column (the same layout as for correlation) and each row represents a different record. So, the first record had £10,260 spent advertising it, sold 330,000 copies, received 43 plays on Radio 1 the week before release, and was made by a band that the majority of people rated as gorgeous sex objects (Figure 7.11).

The executive has past research indicating that advertising budget is a significant predictor of record sales, and so he should include this variable in the model first. His new variables (**airplay** and **attract**) should, therefore, be entered into the model *after* advertising budget. This method is hierarchical (the researcher decides in which order to enter variables into the model based on past research). To do a hierarchical regression in SPSS we have to enter the variables in blocks (each block representing one step in the hierarchy). To get to the main regression dialog box (Figure 7.12) select Analyze Regression ▸ Linear...; this dialog box is the same as when we encountered it for simple regression.

The main dialog box is fairly self-explanatory in that there is a space to specify the dependent variable (outcome) and a space to place one or more independent variables

FIGURE 7.11 Data layout for multiple regression

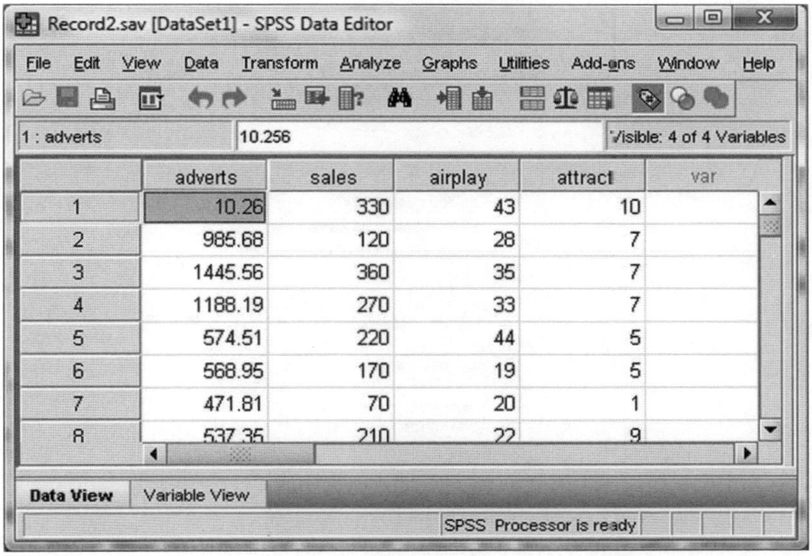

FIGURE 7.12 Main dialog box for block 1 of the multiple regression

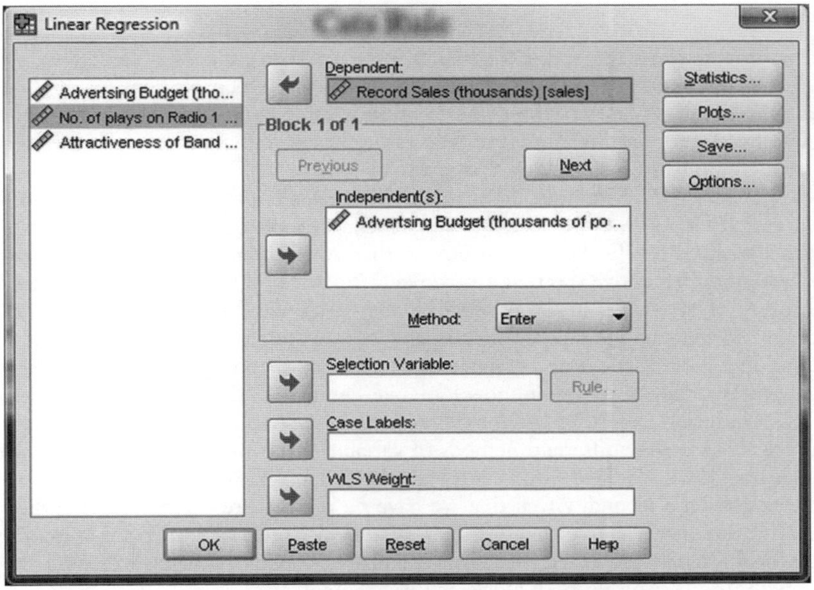

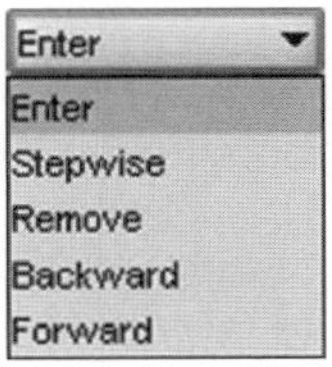

(predictor variables). As usual, the variables in the data editor are listed on the left-hand side of the box. Highlight the outcome variable (record sales) in this list by clicking on it and then drag it to the box labelled *Dependent* or click on ➧. We also need to specify the predictor variable for the first block. We decided that advertising budget should be entered into the model first (because past research indicates that it is an important predictor), so highlight this variable in the list and drag it to the box labelled *Independent(s)* or click on ➧. Underneath the *Independent(s)* box, there

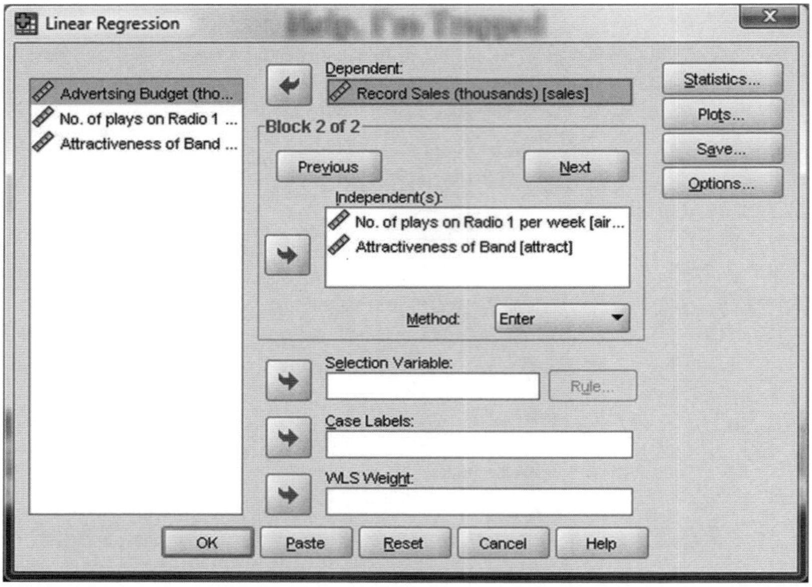

FIGURE 7.13 Main dialog box for block 2 of the multiple regression

is a drop-down menu for specifying the *Method* of regression (see section 7.5.3). You can select a different method of variable entry for each block by clicking on Enter, next to where it says *Method*. The default option is forced entry, and this is the option we want, but if you were carrying out more exploratory work, you might decide to use one of the stepwise methods (forward, backward, stepwise or remove).

Having specified the first block in the hierarchy, we need to move on to the second. To tell the computer that you want to specify a new block of predictors you must click on Next. This process clears the *Independent(s)* box so that you can enter the new predictors (you should also note that above this box it now reads *Block 2 of 2* indicating that you are in the second block of the two that you have so far specified). We decided that the second block would contain both of the new predictors and so you should click on **airplay** and **attract** (while holding down *Ctrl*) in the variables list and drag them to the *Independent(s)* box or click on ➡. The dialog box should now look like Figure 7.13. To move between blocks use the Previous and Next buttons (so, for example, to move back to block 1, click on Previous).

It is possible to select different methods of variable entry for different blocks in a hierarchy. So although we specified forced entry for the first block, we could now specify a stepwise method for the second. Given that we have no previous research regarding the effects of attractiveness and airplay on record sales, we might be justified in requesting a stepwise method for this block. However, because of the problems with stepwise methods, I am going to stick with forced entry for both blocks in this example.

7.7.3. Statistics ②

In the main regression dialog box click on Statistics... to open a dialog box for selecting various important options relating to the model (Figure 7.14). Most of these options relate to the parameters of the model; however, there are procedures available for checking the assumptions of no multicollinearity (collinearity diagnostics) and serial independence of errors

FIGURE 7.14 Statistics dialog box for regression analysis

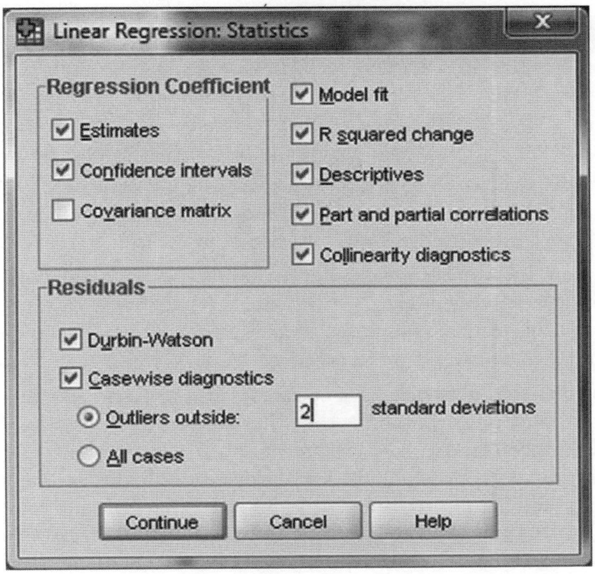

(Durbin–Watson). When you have selected the statistics you require (I recommend all but the covariance matrix as a general rule) click on Continue to return to the main dialog box:

- *Estimates*: This option is selected by default because it gives us the estimated coefficients of the regression model (i.e. the estimated *b*-values). Test statistics and their significance are produced for each regression coefficient: a *t*-test is used to see whether each *b* differs significantly from zero (see section 7.2.4).
- *Confidence intervals*: This option produces confidence intervals for each of the unstandardized regression coefficients. Confidence intervals can be a very useful tool in assessing the likely value of the regression coefficients in the population – I will describe their exact interpretation later.
- *Covariance matrix*: This option will display a matrix of the covariances, correlation coefficients and variances between the regression coefficients of each variable in the model. A variance–covariance matrix is produced with variances displayed along the diagonal and covariances displayed as off-diagonal elements. The correlations are produced in a separate matrix.
- *Model fit*: This option is vital and so is selected by default. It provides not only a statistical test of the model's ability to predict the outcome variable (the *F*-test, see section 7.2.3), but also the value of *R* (or multiple *R*), the corresponding R^2 and the adjusted R^2.
- *R squared change*: This option displays the change in R^2 resulting from the inclusion of a new predictor (or block of predictors). This measure is a useful way to assess the contribution of new predictors (or blocks) to explaining variance in the outcome.
- *Descriptives*: If selected, this option displays a table of the mean, standard deviation and number of observations of all of the variables included in the analysis. A correlation matrix is also displayed showing the correlation between all of the variables and the one-tailed probability for each correlation coefficient. This option is extremely useful because the correlation matrix can be used to assess whether predictors are interrelated (which can be used to establish whether there is multicollinearity).
- *Part and partial correlations*: This option produces the zero-order correlation (the Pearson correlation) between each predictor and the outcome variable. It also

produces the partial correlation between each predictor and the outcome, controlling for all other predictors in the model. Finally, it produces the part correlation (or semi-partial correlation) between each predictor and the outcome. This correlation represents the relationship between each predictor and the part of the outcome that is not explained by the other predictors in the model. As such, it measures the unique relationship between a predictor and the outcome (see section 6.6).

- *Collinearity diagnostics*: This option is for obtaining collinearity statistics such as the VIF, tolerance, eigenvalues of the scaled, uncentred cross-products matrix, condition indexes and variance proportions (see section 7.6.2.3).
- *Durbin-Watson*: This option produces the **Durbin–Watson test** statistic, which tests the assumption of independent errors. Unfortunately, SPSS does not provide the significance value of this test, so you must decide for yourself whether the value is different enough from 2 to be cause for concern (see section 7.6.2.1).
- *Casewise diagnostics*: This option, if selected, lists the observed value of the outcome, the predicted value of the outcome, the difference between these values (the residual) and this difference standardized. Furthermore, it will list these values either for all cases, or just for cases for which the standardized residual is greater than 3 (when the ± sign is ignored). This criterion value of 3 can be changed, and I recommend changing it to 2 for reasons that will become apparent. A summary table of residual statistics indicating the minimum, maximum, mean and standard deviation of both the values predicted by the model and the residuals (see section 7.7.5) is also produced.

7.7.4. Regression plots ②

Once you are back in the main dialog box, click on Plots... to activate the regression plots dialog box shown in Figure 7.15. This dialog box provides the means to specify several graphs, which can help to establish the validity of some regression assumptions. Most of these plots involve various *residual* values, which will be described in more detail in section 7.7.5.

On the left-hand side of the dialog box is a list of several variables.

- **DEPENDNT** (*the outcome variable*).
- ***ZPRED** (*the standardized predicted values* of the dependent variable based on the model). These values are standardized forms of the values predicted by the model.
- ***ZRESID** (*the standardized residuals*, or errors). These values are the standardized differences between the observed data and the values that the model predicts).
- ***DRESID** (*the deleted residuals*). See section 7.6.1.1 for details.
- ***ADJPRED** (*the adjusted predicted values*). See section 7.6.1.1 for details.
- ***SRESID** (*the Studentized residual*). See section 7.6.1.1 for details.
- ***SDRESID** (*the Studentized deleted residual*). This value is the deleted residual divided by its standard deviation.

The variables listed in this dialog box all come under the general heading of residuals, and were discussed in detail in section 7.6.1.1. For a basic analysis it is worth plotting *ZRESID (*Y*-axis) against *ZPRED (*X*-axis), because this plot is useful to determine whether the assumptions of random errors and homoscedasticity have been met. A plot of *SRESID (*y*-axis) against *ZPRED (*x*-axis) will show up any heteroscedasticity also. Although often these two plots are virtually identical, the latter is more sensitive on a case-by-case basis. To create these plots simply select a variable from the list, and transfer it to the space labelled

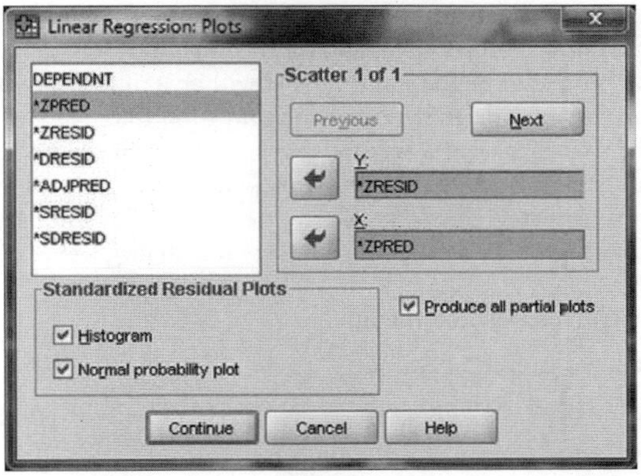

FIGURE 7.15 *Linear Regression: Plots* dialog box

either x or y (which refer to the axes) by clicking on ➡. When you have selected two variables for the first plot (as is the case in Figure 7.15) you can specify a new plot by clicking on Next. This process clears the spaces in which variables are specified. If you click on Next and would like to return to the plot that you last specified, then simply click on Previous. You can specify up to nine plots.

You can also select the tick-box labelled *Produce all partial plots* which will produce scatterplots of the residuals of the outcome variable and each of the predictors when both variables are regressed separately on the remaining predictors. Regardless of whether the previous sentence made any sense to you, these plots have several important characteristics that make them worth inspecting. First, the gradient of the regression line between the two residual variables is equivalent to the coefficient of the predictor in the regression equation. As such, any obvious outliers on a partial plot represent cases that might have undue influence on a predictor's regression coefficient. Second, non-linear relationships between a predictor and the outcome variable are much more detectable using these plots. Finally, they are a useful way of detecting collinearity. For these reasons, I recommend requesting them.

There are several options for plots of the standardized residuals. First, you can select a histogram of the standardized residuals (this is extremely useful for checking the assumption of normality of errors). Second, you can ask for a normal probability plot, which also provides information about whether the residuals in the model are normally distributed. When you have selected the options you require, click on Continue to take you back to the main regression dialog box.

7.7.5. Saving regression diagnostics ②

In section 7.6 we met two types of regression diagnostics: those that help us assess how well our model fits our sample and those that help us detect cases that have a large influence on the model generated. In SPSS we can choose to save these diagnostic variables in the data editor (so, SPSS will calculate them and then create new columns in the data editor in which the values are placed).

To save regression diagnostics you need to click on Save... in the main regression dialog box. This process activates the *save* new variables dialog box (see Figure 7.16). Once this dialog box is active, it is a simple matter to tick the boxes next to the required statistics. Most of the available options were explained in section 7.6 and Figure 7.16 shows, what I consider to be, a fairly basic set of diagnostic statistics. Standardized (and Studentized) versions of these diagnostics are generally easier to interpret and so I suggest selecting them in preference to the unstandardized versions. Once the regression has been run, SPSS creates a column in your data editor for each statistic requested and it has a standard set of variable names to describe each one. After the name, there will be a number that refers to the analysis that has been run. So, for the first regression run on a data set the variable names will be followed by a 1, if you carry out a second regression it will create a new set of variables with names followed by a 2, and so on. The names of the variables that will be created are below. When you have selected the diagnostics you require (by clicking in the appropriate boxes), click on Continue to return to the main regression dialog box:

- **pre_1**: unstandardized predicted value.
- **zpr_1**: standardized predicted value.
- **adj_1**: adjusted predicted value.
- **sep_1**: standard error of predicted value.
- **res_1**: unstandardized residual.
- **zre_1**: standardized residual.
- **sre_1**: Studentized residual.
- **dre_1**: deleted residual.
- **sdr_1**: Studentized deleted residual.
- **mah_1**: Mahalanobis distance.
- **coo_1**: Cook's distance.
- **lev_1**: centred leverage value.
- **sdb0_1**: standardized DFBETA (intercept).
- **sdb1_1**: standardized DFBETA (predictor 1).
- **sdb2_1**: standardized DFBETA (predictor 2).
- **sdf_1**: standardized DFFIT.
- **cov_1**: covariance ratio.

7.7.6. Further options ②

As a final step in the analysis, you can click on Options... to take you to the options dialog box (Figure 7.17). The first set of options allows you to change the criteria used for entering variables in a stepwise regression. If you insist on doing stepwise regression, then it's probably best that you leave the default criterion of .05 probability for entry alone. However, you can make this criterion more stringent (.01). There is also the option to build a model that doesn't include a constant (i.e. has no *Y* intercept). This option should also be left alone (almost always). Finally, you can select a method for dealing with missing data points (see SPSS Tip 6.1). By default, SPSS excludes cases listwise, which in regression means that if a person has a missing value for any variable, then they are excluded from the whole analysis. So, for example, if our record company executive didn't have an attractiveness score for one of his bands, their data would not be used in the regression model. Another option is to excluded cases on a pairwise basis, which means that if a participant has a score missing for a particular variable, then their data are excluded only from calculations involving the variable for which they have no score. So, data for the band for which there was no attractiveness rating would still be used to calculate the relationships between advertising budget, airplay and record sales. However, if you do this many of your variables may not make sense, and you can end up with absurdities such as R^2 either negative or greater than 1.0. So, it's not a good option.

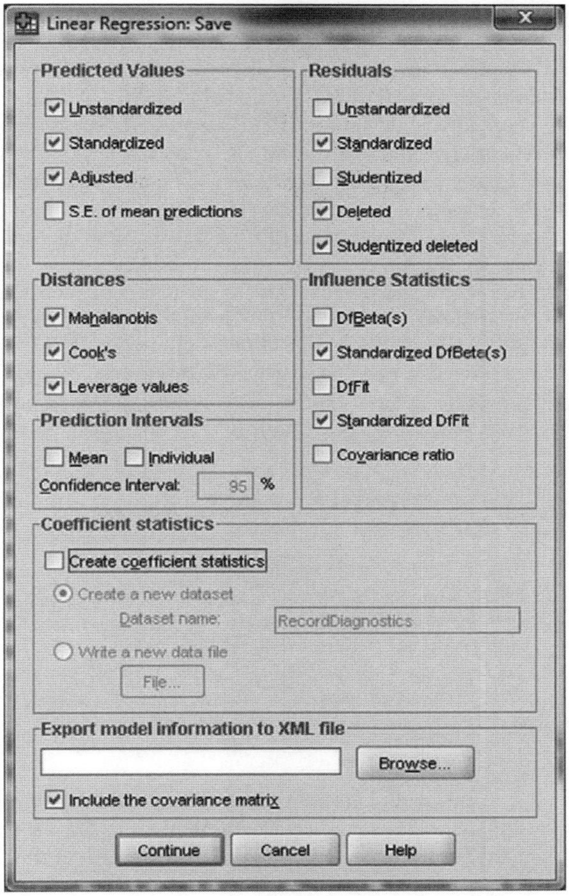

FIGURE 7.16 Dialog box for regression diagnostics

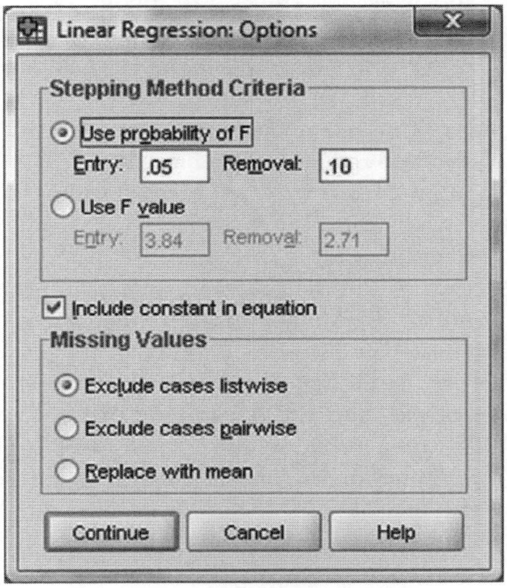

IGURE 7.17 ptions for linear egression

Another possibility is to replace the missing score with the average score for this variable and then include that case in the analysis (so, our example band would be given an attractiveness rating equal to the average attractiveness of all bands). The problem with this final choice is that it is likely to suppress the true value of the standard deviation (and more importantly the standard error). The standard deviation will be suppressed because for any replaced case there will be no difference between the mean and the score, whereas if data had been collected for that case there would, almost certainly, have been some difference between the score and the mean. Obviously, if the sample is large and the number of missing values small then this is not a serious consideration. However, if there are many missing values this choice is potentially dangerous because smaller standard errors are more likely to lead to significant results that are a product of the data replacement rather than a genuine effect. The final option is to use the Missing Value Analysis routine in SPSS. This is for experts. It makes use of the fact that if two or more variables are present and correlated for most cases in the file, and an occasional value is missing, you can replace the missing values with estimates far better than the mean (Tabachnick & Fidell, 2007: Chapter 4, describe some of these procedures).

7.8. Interpreting multiple regression ②

Having selected all of the relevant options and returned to the main dialog box, we need to click on OK to run the analysis. SPSS will spew out copious amounts of output in the viewer window, and we now turn to look at how to make sense of this information.

7.8.1. Descriptives ②

The output described in this section is produced using the options in the *Linear Regression: Statistics* dialog box (see Figure 7.14). To begin with, if you selected the *Descriptives* option, SPSS will produce the table seen in SPSS Output 7.4. This table tells us the mean and standard deviation of each variable in our data set, so we now know that the average number of record sales was 193,000. This table isn't necessary for interpreting the regression model, but it is a useful summary of the data. In addition to the descriptive statistics, selecting this option produces a correlation matrix too. This table shows three things. First, the table shows the value of Pearson's correlation coefficient between every pair of variables (e.g. we can see that the advertising budget had a large positive correlation with record sales, $r = .578$). Second, the one-tailed significance of each correlation is displayed (e.g. the correlation above is significant, $p < .001$). Finally, the number of cases contributing to each correlation ($N = 200$) is shown.

You might notice that along the diagonal of the matrix the values for the correlation coefficients are all 1.00 (i.e. a perfect positive correlation). The reason for this is that these values represent the correlation of each variable with itself, so obviously the resulting values are 1. The correlation matrix is extremely useful for getting a rough idea of the relationships between predictors and the outcome, and for a preliminary look for multicollinearity. If there is no multicollinearity in the data then there should be no substantial correlations ($r > .9$) between predictors.

If we look only at the predictors (ignore record sales) then the highest correlation is between the attractiveness of the band and the amount of airplay which is significant at a .01 level ($r = .182$, $p = .005$). Despite the significance of this correlation, the coefficient is small and so it looks as though our predictors are measuring different things (there is little collinearity). We can see also that of all of the predictors the number of plays on Radio 1 correlates best with the outcome ($r = .599$, $p < .001$) and so it is likely that this variable will best predict record sales.

CRAMMING SAM'S TIPS

Use the descriptive statistics to check the correlation matrix for multicollinearity; that is, predictors that correlate too highly with each other, $R > .9$.

SS OUTPUT 7.4
scriptive statistics
regression
lysis

Descriptive Statistics

	Mean	Std. Deviation	N
Record Sales (thousands)	193.2000	80.6990	200
Advertising Budget (thousands of pounds)	614.4123	485.6552	200
No. of plays on Radio 1 per week	27.5000	12.2696	200
Attractiveness of Band	6.7700	1.3953	200

Correlations

		Record Sales (thousands)	Advertising Budget (thousands of pounds)	No. of plays on Radio 1 per week	Attractiveness of Band
Pearson Correlation	Record Sales (thousands)	1.000	.578	.599	.326
	Advertising Budget (thousands of pounds)	.578	1.000	.102	.081
	No. of plays on Radio 1 per week	.599	.102	1.000	.182
	Attractiveness of Band	.326	.081	.182	1.000
Sig. (1-tailed)	Record Sales (thousands)	.	.000	.000	.000
	Advertising Budget (thousands of pounds)	.000	.	.076	.128
	No. of plays on Radio 1 per week	.000	.076	.	.005
	Attractiveness of Band	.000	.128	.005	.
N	Record Sales (thousands)	200	200	200	200
	Advertising Budget (thousands of pounds)	200	200	200	200
	No. of plays on Radio 1 per week	200	200	200	200
	Attractiveness of Band	200	200	200	200

7.8.2. Summary of model ②

The next section of output describes the overall model (so it tells us whether the model is successful in predicting record sales). Remember that we chose a hierarchical method and so each set of summary statistics is repeated for each stage in the hierarchy. In SPSS Output 7.5 you should note that there are two models. Model 1 refers to the first stage in the hierarchy when only advertising budget is used as a predictor. Model 2 refers to when all three predictors are used. SPSS Output 7.5 is the *model summary* and this table was produced using the *Model fit* option. This option is selected by default in SPSS because it provides us with some very important information about the model: the values of R, R^2 and the adjusted R^2. If the *R squared change* and *Durbin-Watson* options were selected, then these values are included also (if they weren't selected you'll find that you have a smaller table).

The model summary table is shown in SPSS Output 7.5 and you should notice that under this table SPSS tells us what the dependent variable (outcome) was and what the predictors were in each of the two models. In the column labelled R are the values of the multiple correlation coefficient between the predictors and the outcome. When only advertising budget is used as a predictor, this is the simple correlation between advertising and record sales (0.578). In fact all of the statistics for model 1 are the same as the simple regression model earlier (see section 7.4). The next column gives us a value of R^2, which we already know is a measure of how much of the variability in the outcome is accounted for by the predictors. For the first model its value is .335, which means that advertising budget accounts for 33.5% of the variation in record sales. However, when the other two predictors are included as well (model 2), this value increases to .665 or 66.5% of the variance in record sales. Therefore, if advertising accounts for 33.5%, we can tell that attractiveness and radio play account for an additional 33%.[9] So, the inclusion of the two new predictors has explained quite a large amount of the variation in record sales.

SPSS OUTPUT 7.5
Regression model summary

Model Summary[c]

					Change Statistics					
Model	R	R Square	Adjusted R Square	Std. Error of the Estimate	R Square Change	F Change	df1	df2	Sig. F Change	Durbin-Watson
1	.578[a]	.335	.331	65.9914	.335	99.587	1	198	.000	
2	.815[b]	.665	.660	47.0873	.330	96.447	2	196	.000	1.950

a. Predictors: (Constant), Advertising Budget (thousands of pounds)

b. Predictors: (Constant), Advertising Budget (thousands of pounds), Attractiveness of Band, No. of plays on Radio 1 per week

c. Dependent Variable: Record Sales (thousands)

The adjusted R^2 gives us some idea of how well our model generalizes and ideally we would like its value to be the same, or very close to, the value of R^2. In this example the difference for the final model is small (in fact the difference between the values is .665 − .660 = .005 (about 0.5%). This shrinkage means that if the model were derived from the population rather than a sample it would account for approximately 0.5% less variance in the outcome. Advanced students might like to apply Stein's formula to the R^2 to get some idea of its likely value in different samples. Stein's formula was given in equation (7.11) and can be applied by replacing n with the sample size (200) and k with the number of predictors (3):

$$
\begin{aligned}
\text{adjusted } R^2 &= 1 - \left[\left(\frac{200-1}{200-3-1}\right)\left(\frac{200-2}{200-3-2}\right)\left(\frac{200+1}{200}\right)\right](1-0.665) \\
&= 1 - [(1.015)(1.015)(1.005)](0.335) \\
&= 1 - 0.347 \\
&= 0.653
\end{aligned}
$$

This value is very similar to the observed value of R^2 (.665) indicating that the cross-validity of this model is very good.

The change statistics are provided only if requested and these tell us whether the change in R^2 is significant. The significance of R^2 can actually be tested using an F-ratio, and this F is calculated from the following equation (in which N is the number of cases or participants, and k is the number of predictors in the model):

$$F = \frac{(N-k-1)R^2}{k(1-R^2)}$$

[9] That is, 33% = 66.5% − 33.5% (this value is the *R Square Change* in the table).

In SPSS Output 7.5, the change in this F is reported for each block of the hierarchy. So, model 1 causes R^2 to change from 0 to .335, and this change in the amount of variance explained gives rise to an F-ratio of 99.587, which is significant with a probability less than .001. Bearing in mind for this first model that we have only one predictor (so $k = 1$) and 200 cases ($N = 200$), this F comes from the equation above:[10]

$$F_{Model1} = \frac{(200 - 1 - 1)0.334648}{1(1 - 0.334648)} = 99.587$$

The addition of the new predictors (model 2) causes R^2 to increase by .330 (see above). We can calculate the F-ratio for this change using the same equation, but because we're looking at the change in models we use the change in R^2, R^2_{Change}, and the R^2 in the new model (model 2 in this case so I've called it R_2^2) and we also use the change in the number of predictors, k_{Change} (model 1 had one predictor and model 2 had three predictors, so the change in the number of predictors is 3–1 = 2), and the number of predictors in the new model, k_2 (in this case because we're looking at model 2). Again, if we use a few more decimal places than in the SPSS table, we get approximately the same answer as SPSS:

$$\begin{aligned} F_{Change} &= \frac{(N - k_2 - 1)R^2_{Change}}{k_{Change}(1 - R_2^2)} \\ &= \frac{(200 - 3 - 1) \times 0.330}{2(1 - 0.664668)} \\ &= 96.44 \end{aligned}$$

As such, the change in the amount of variance that can be explained gives rise to an F-ratio of 96.44, which is again significant ($p < .001$). The change statistics therefore tell us about the difference made by adding new predictors to the model.

Finally, if you requested the Durbin–Watson statistic it will be found in the last column of the table in SPSS Output 7.5. This statistic informs us about whether the assumption of independent errors is tenable (see section 7.6.2.1). As a conservative rule I suggested that values less than 1 or greater than 3 should definitely raise alarm bells (although I urge you to look up precise values for the situation of interest). The closer to 2 that the value is, the better, and for these data the value is 1.950, which is so close to 2 that the assumption has almost certainly been met.

SPSS Output 7.6 shows the next part of the output, which contains an ANOVA that tests whether the model is significantly better at predicting the outcome than using the mean as a 'best guess'. Specifically, the F-ratio represents the ratio of the improvement in prediction that results from fitting the model, relative to the inaccuracy that still exists in the model (see section 7.2.3). This table is again split into two sections: one for each model. We are told the value of the sum of squares for the model (this value is SS_M in section 7.2.3 and represents the improvement in prediction resulting from fitting a regression line to the data rather than using the mean as an estimate of the outcome). We are also told the residual sum of squares (this value is SS_R in section 7.2.3 and represents the total difference between the model and the observed data). We are also told the degrees of freedom (df) for each term. In the case of the improvement due to the model, this value is equal to the number of predictors (1 for the first model and 3 for the second), and for SS_R it is the number of observations (200) minus the number of coefficients in the regression model. The first

[10] To get the same values as SPSS we have to use the exact value of R^2, which is 0.3346480676231 (if you don't believe me double-click on the table in the SPSS output that reports this value, then double-click on the cell of the table containing the value of R^2 and you'll see that .335 becomes the value that I've just typed!).

model has two coefficients (one for the predictor and one for the constant) whereas the second has four (one for each of the three predictors and one for the constant). Therefore, model 1 has 198 degrees of freedom whereas model 2 has 196. The average sum of squares (MS) is then calculated for each term by dividing the SS by the *df*. The *F*-ratio is calculated by dividing the average improvement in prediction by the model (MS_M) by the average difference between the model and the observed data (MS_R). If the improvement due to fitting the regression model is much greater than the inaccuracy within the model then the value of *F* will be greater than 1 and SPSS calculates the exact probability of obtaining the value of *F* by chance. For the initial model the *F*-ratio is 99.587, which is very unlikely to have happened by chance ($p < .001$). For the second model the value of *F* is even higher (129.498), which is also highly significant ($p < .001$). We can interpret these results as meaning that the initial model significantly improved our ability to predict the outcome variable, but that the new model (with the extra predictors) was even better (because the *F*-ratio is more significant).

SPSS OUTPUT 7

ANOVA[c]

Model		Sum of Squares	df	Mean Square	F	Sig.
1	Regression	433687.833	1	433687.833	99.587	.000[a]
	Residual	862264.167	198	4354.870		
	Total	1295952.0	199			
2	Regression	861377.418	3	287125.806	129.498	.000[b]
	Residual	434574.582	196	2217.217		
	Total	1295952.0	199			

a. Predictors: (Constant), Advertising Budget (thousands of pounds)

b. Predictors: (Constant), Advertising Budget (thousands of pounds), Attractiveness of Band, No. of Plays on Radio 1 per Week

c. Dependent Variable: Record Sales (thousands)

CRAMMING SAM'S TIPS

The fit of the regression model can be assessed using the **Model Summary** and **ANOVA** tables from SPSS. Look for the R^2 to tell you the proportion of variance explained by the model. If you have done a hierarchical regression then you can assess the improvement of the model at each stage of the analysis by looking at the change in R^2 and whether this change is significant (look for values less than .05 in the column labelled *Sig F Change.*). The ANOVA also tells us whether the model is a significant fit of the data overall (look for values less than .05 in the column labelled *Sig.*). Finally, there is an assumption that errors in regression are independent; this assumption is likely to be met if the Durbin–Watson statistic is close to 2 (and between 1 and 3).

7.8.3. Model parameters ②

So far we have looked at several summary statistics telling us whether or not the model has improved our ability to predict the outcome variable. The next part of the output is concerned with the parameters of the model. SPSS Output 7.7 shows the model parameters for both steps in the hierarchy. Now, the first step in our hierarchy was to include advertising budget (as we did for the simple regression earlier in this chapter) and so the parameters for the first model are identical to the parameters obtained in SPSS Output 7.3. Therefore, we will be concerned only with the parameters for the final model (in which all predictors were included). The format of the table of coefficients will depend on the options selected. The confidence interval for the *b*-values, collinearity diagnostics and the part and partial correlations will be present only if selected in the dialog box in Figure 7.14.

S OUTPUT 7.7
fficients of the
ession model[11]

Coefficients[a]

Model		Unstandardized Coefficients		Standardized Coefficients	t	Sig.	95% Confidence Interval for B	
		B	Std. Error	Beta			Lower Bound	Upper Bound
1	(Constant)	134.140	7.537		17.799	.000	119.278	149.002
	Advertising Budget (thousands of pounds)	.096	.010	.578	9.979	.000	.077	.115
2	(Constant)	-26.613	17.350		-1.534	.127	-60.830	7.604
	Advertising Budget (thousands of pounds)	.085	.007	.511	12.261	.000	.071	.099
	No. of plays on Radio 1 per week	3.367	.278	.512	12.123	.000	2.820	3.915
	Attractiveness of Band	11.086	2.438	.192	4.548	.000	6.279	15.894

a. Dependent Variable: Record Sales (thousands)

Coefficients[a]

Model		Correlations			Collinearity Statistics	
		Zero-order	Partial	Part	Tolerance	VIF
1	Advertising Budget (thousands of pounds)	.578	.578	.578	1.000	1.000
2	Advertising Budget (thousands of pounds)	.578	.659	.507	.986	1.015
	No. of plays on Radio 1 per week	.599	.655	.501	.959	1.043
	Attractiveness of Band	.326	.309	.188	.963	1.038

a. Dependent Variable: Record Sales (thousands)

Remember that in multiple regression the model takes the form of equation (7.9) and in that equation there are several unknown quantities (the *b*-values). The first part of the table gives us estimates for these *b*-values and these values indicate the individual contribution of each predictor to the model. If we replace the *b*-values in equation (7.9) we find that we can define the model as follows:

$$\begin{aligned} \text{sales}_i &= b_0 + b_1\text{advertising}_i + b_2\text{airplay}_i + b_3\text{attractiveness}_i \\ &= -26.61 + (0.08\text{advertising}_i) + (3.37\text{airplay}_i) \\ &\quad + (11.09\text{attractiveness}_i) \end{aligned} \tag{7.12}$$

The *b*-values tell us about the relationship between record sales and each predictor. If the value is positive we can tell that there is a positive relationship between the predictor and the outcome, whereas a negative coefficient represents a negative relationship. For these data all three predictors have positive *b*-values indicating positive relationships. So, as advertising budget increases, record sales increase; as plays on the radio increase, so do record sales; and finally more attractive bands will sell more records. The *b*-values tell us more than this, though. They tell us to what degree each predictor affects the outcome *if the effects of all other predictors are held constant*:

[11] To spare your eyesight I have split this part of the output into two tables; however, it should appear as one long table in the SPSS Viewer.

- **Advertising budget** (b = 0.085): This value indicates that as advertising budget increases by one unit, record sales increase by 0.085 units. Both variables were measured in thousands; therefore, for every £1000 more spent on advertising, an extra 0.085 thousand records (85 records) are sold. This interpretation is true only if the effects of attractiveness of the band and airplay are held constant.
- **Airplay** (b = 3.367): This value indicates that as the number of plays on radio in the week before release increases by one, record sales increase by 3.367 units. Therefore, every additional play of a song on radio (in the week before release) is associated with an extra 3.367 thousand records (3367 records) being sold. This interpretation is true only if the effects of attractiveness of the band and advertising are held constant.
- **Attractiveness** (b = 11.086): This value indicates that a band rated one unit higher on the attractiveness scale can expect additional record sales of 11.086 units. Therefore, every unit increase in the attractiveness of the band is associated with an extra 11.086 thousand records (11,086 records) being sold. This interpretation is true only if the effects of radio airplay and advertising are held constant.

Each of these beta values has an associated standard error indicating to what extent these values would vary across different samples, and these standard errors are used to determine whether or not the b-value differs significantly from zero. As we saw in section 7.4.2, a t-statistic can be derived that tests whether a b-value is significantly different from 0. In simple regression, a significant value of t indicates that the slope of the regression line is significantly different from horizontal, but in multiple regression, it is not so easy to visualize what the value tells us. Well, it is easiest to conceptualize the t-tests as measures of whether the predictor is making a significant contribution to the model. Therefore, if the t-test associated with a b-value is significant (if the value in the column labelled *Sig.* is less than .05) then the predictor is making a significant contribution to the model. The smaller the value of *Sig.* (and the larger the value of t), the greater the contribution of that predictor. For this model, the advertising budget ($t(196) = 12.26, p < .001$), the amount of radio play prior to release ($t(196) = 12.12, p < .001$) and attractiveness of the band ($t(196) = 4.55, p < .001$) are all significant predictors of record sales.[12] From the magnitude of the t-statistics we can see that the advertising budget and radio play had a similar impact, whereas the attractiveness of the band had less impact.

The b-values and their significance are important statistics to look at; however, the standardized versions of the b-values are in many ways easier to interpret (because they are not dependent on the units of measurement of the variables). The standardized beta values are provided by SPSS (labelled as Beta, β_1) and they tell us the number of standard deviations that the outcome will change as a result of one standard deviation change in the predictor. The standardized beta values are all measured in standard deviation units and so are directly comparable: therefore, they provide a better insight into the 'importance' of a predictor in the model. The standardized beta values for airplay and advertising budget are virtually identical (.512 and .511 respectively) indicating that both variables have a comparable degree of importance in the model (this concurs with what the magnitude of the t-statistics told us). To interpret these values literally, we need to know the standard deviations of all of the variables and these values can be found in SPSS Output 7.4.

[12] For all of these predictors I wrote $t(196)$. The number in brackets is the degrees of freedom. We saw in section 7.2.4 that in regression the degrees of freedom are $N - p - 1$, where N is the total sample size (in this case 200) and p is the number of predictors (in this case 3). For these data we get $200 - 3 - 1 = 196$.

- **Advertising budget** (*standardized* β = .511): This value indicates that as advertising budget increases by one standard deviation (£485,655), record sales increase by 0.511 standard deviations. The standard deviation for record sales is 80,699 and so this constitutes a change of 41,240 sales (0.511 × 80,699). Therefore, for every £485,655 more spent on advertising, an extra 41,240 records are sold. This interpretation is true only if the effects of attractiveness of the band and airplay are held constant.
- **Airplay** (*standardized* β = .512): This value indicates that as the number of plays on radio in the week before release increases by 1 standard deviation (12.27), record sales increase by 0.512 standard deviations. The standard deviation for record sales is 80,699 and so this constitutes a change of 41,320 sales (0.512 × 80,699). Therefore, if Radio 1 plays the song an extra 12.27 times in the week before release, 41,320 extra record sales can be expected. This interpretation is true only if the effects of attractiveness of the band and advertising are held constant.
- **Attractiveness** (*standardized* β = .192): This value indicates that a band rated one standard deviation (1.40 units) higher on the attractiveness scale can expect additional record sales of 0.192 standard deviations units. This constitutes a change of 15,490 sales (0.192 × 80,699). Therefore, a band with an attractiveness rating 1.40 higher than another band can expect 15,490 additional sales. This interpretation is true only if the effects of radio airplay and advertising are held constant.

SELF-TEST Think back to what the confidence interval of the mean represented (section 2.5.2). Can you guess what the confidence interval for *b* represents?

Imagine that we collected 100 samples of data measuring the same variables as our current model. For each sample we could create a regression model to represent the data. If the model is reliable then we hope to find very similar parameters in all samples. Therefore, each sample should produce approximately the same *b*-values. The confidence intervals of the unstandardized beta values are boundaries constructed such that in 95% of these samples these boundaries will contain the true value of *b* (see section 2.5.2). Therefore, if we'd collected 100 samples, and calculated the confidence intervals for *b*, we are saying that 95% of these confidence intervals would contain the true value of *b*. Therefore, we can be fairly confident that the confidence interval we have constructed for this sample will contain the true value of *b* in the population. This being so, a good model will have a small confidence interval, indicating that the value of *b* in this sample is close to the true value of *b* in the population. The sign (positive or negative) of the *b*-values tells us about the direction of the relationship between the predictor and the outcome. Therefore, we would expect a very bad model to have confidence intervals that cross zero, indicating that in some samples the predictor has a negative relationship to the outcome whereas in others it has a positive relationship. In this model, the two best predictors (advertising and airplay) have very tight confidence intervals indicating that the estimates for the current model are likely to be representative of the true population values. The interval for attractiveness is wider (but still does not cross zero) indicating that the parameter for this variable is less representative, but nevertheless significant.

If you asked for part and partial correlations, then they will appear in the output in separate columns of the table. The zero-order correlations are the simple Pearson's correlation coefficients (and so correspond to the values in SPSS Output 7.4). The partial correlations represent the relationships between each predictor and the outcome variable, controlling for the effects of the other two predictors. The part correlations represent the relationship between each predictor and the outcome, controlling for the effect that the other two variables have on the outcome. In effect, these part correlations represent the unique relationship that each predictor has with the outcome. If you opt to do a stepwise regression, you would find that variable entry is based initially on the variable with the largest zero-order correlation and then on the part correlations of the remaining variables. Therefore, airplay would be entered first (because it has the largest zero-order correlation), then advertising budget (because its part correlation is bigger than attractiveness) and then finally attractiveness. Try running a forward stepwise regression on these data to see if I'm right! Finally, we are given details of the collinearity statistics, but these will be discussed in section 7.8.5.

CRAMMING SAM'S TIPS

The individual contribution of variables to the regression model can be found in the **Coefficients** table from SPSS. If you have done a hierarchical regression then look at the values for the final model. For each predictor variable, you can see if it has made a significant contribution to predicting the outcome by looking at the column labelled *Sig.* (values less than .05 are significant). You should also look at the standardized beta values because these tell you the importance of each predictor (bigger absolute value = more important). The Tolerance and VIF values will also come in handy later on, so make a note of them!

7.8.4. Excluded variables ②

At each stage of a regression analysis SPSS provides a summary of any variables that have not yet been entered into the model. In a hierarchical model, this summary has details of the variables that have been specified to be entered in subsequent steps, and in stepwise regression this table contains summaries of the variables that SPSS is considering entering into the model. For this example, there is a summary of the excluded variables (SPSS Output 7.8) for the first stage of the hierarchy (there is no summary for the second stage because all predictors are in the model). The summary gives an estimate of each predictor's beta value if it was entered into the equation at this point and calculates a *t*-test for this value. In a stepwise regression, SPSS should enter the predictor with the highest *t*-statistic and will continue entering predictors until there are none left with *t*-statistics that have significance values less than .05. The partial correlation also provides some indication as to what contribution (if any) an excluded predictor would make if it were entered into the model.

SPSS OUTPUT

Excluded Variables[b]

Model		Beta In	t	Sig.	Partial Correlation	Collinearity Statistics		
						Tolerance	VIF	Minimum Tolerance
1	No. of plays on Radio 1 per week	.546[a]	12.513	.000	.665	.990	1.010	.990
	Attractiveness of Band	.281[a]	5.136	.000	.344	.993	1.007	.993

a. Predictors in the Model: (Constant), Advertising Budget (thousands of pounds)

b. Dependent Variable: Record Sales (thousands)

7.8.5. Assessing the assumption of no multicollinearity ②

SPSS Output 7.7 provided some measures of whether there is collinearity in the data. Specifically, it provides the VIF and tolerance statistics (with tolerance being 1 divided by the VIF). There are a few guidelines from section 7.6.2.3 that can be applied here:

- If the largest VIF is greater than 10 then there is cause for concern (Bowerman & O'Connell, 1990; Myers, 1990).
- If the average VIF is substantially greater than 1 then the regression may be biased (Bowerman & O'Connell, 1990).
- Tolerance below 0.1 indicates a serious problem.
- Tolerance below 0.2 indicates a potential problem (Menard, 1995).

For our current model the VIF values are all well below 10 and the tolerance statistics all well above 0.2; therefore, we can safely conclude that there is no collinearity within our data. To calculate the average VIF we simply add the VIF values for each predictor and divide by the number of predictors (k):

$$\overline{\text{VIF}} = \frac{\sum_{i=1}^{k} \text{VIF}_i}{k} = \frac{1.015 + 1.043 + 1.038}{3} = 1.032$$

The average VIF is very close to 1 and this confirms that collinearity is not a problem for this model. SPSS also produces a table of eigenvalues of the scaled, uncentred cross-products matrix, condition indexes and variance proportions (see Jane Superbrain Box 7.2). There is a lengthy discussion, and example, of collinearity in section 8.8.1 and how to detect it using variance proportions, so I will limit myself now to saying that we are looking for large variance proportions on the same *small* eigenvalues. Therefore, in SPSS Output 7.9 we look at the bottom few rows of the table (these are the small eigenvalues) and look for any variables that both have high variance proportions for that eigenvalue. The variance proportions vary between 0 and 1, and for each predictor should be distributed across different dimensions (or eigenvalues). For this model, you can see that each predictor has most of its variance loading onto a different dimension (advertising has 96% of variance on dimension 2, airplay has 93% of variance on dimension 3 and attractiveness has 92% of variance on dimension 4). These data represent a classic example of no multicollinearity. For an example of when collinearity exists in the data and some suggestions about what can be done, see Chapters 8 (section 8.8.1) and 17 (section 17.3.3.3).

SS OUTPUT 7.9

Collinearity Diagnostics[a]

Model	Dimension	Eigenvalue	Condition Index	Variance Proportions (Constant)	Advertising Budget (thousands of pounds)	No. of plays on Radio 1 per week	Attractiveness of Band
1	1	1.785	1.000	.11	.11		
	2	.215	2.883	.89	.89		
2	1	3.562	1.000	.00	.02	.01	.00
	2	.308	3.401	.01	**.96**	.05	.01
	3	.109	5.704	.05	.02	**.93**	.07
	4	2.039E-02	13.219	.94	.00	.00	**.92**

a. Dependent Variable: Record Sales (thousands)

CRAMMING SAM'S TIPS

To check the assumption of no multicollinearity, use the VIF values from the table **Labelled** coefficients in the SPSS output. If these values are less than 10 then that indicates there probably isn't cause for concern. If you take the average of VIF values, and this average is not substantially greater than 1, then that also indicates that there's no cause for concern.

JANE SUPERBRAIN 7.2

What are eigenvectors and eigenvalues? ④

The definitions and mathematics of eigenvalues and eigenvectors are very complicated and most of us need not worry about them (although they do crop up again in Chapters 16 and 17). However, although the mathematics of them is hard, they are quite easy to visualize! Imagine we have two variables: the salary a supermodel earns in a year, and how attractive she is. Also imagine these two variables are normally distributed and so can be considered together as a bivariate normal distribution. If these variables are correlated, then their scatterplot forms an ellipse. This is shown in the scatterplots below: if we draw a dashed line around the outer values of the scatterplot we get something oval shaped. Now, we can draw two lines to measure the length and height of this ellipse. These lines are the *eigenvectors* of the original correlation matrix for these two variables (a vector is just a set of numbers that tells us the location of a line in geometric space). Note that the two lines we've drawn (one for height and one for width of the oval) are perpendicular; that is, they are at 90 degrees, which means that they are independent of one another). So, with two variables, eigenvectors are just lines measuring the length and height of the ellipse that surrounds the scatterplot of data for those variables. If we add a third variable (e.g. experience of the supermodel) then all that happens is our scatterplot gets a third dimension, the ellipse turns into something shaped like a rugby ball (or American football), and because we now have a third dimension (height, width and depth) we get an extra eigenvector to measure this extra dimension. If we add a fourth variable, a similar logic applies (although it's harder to visualize): we get an extra dimension, and an eigenvector to measure that dimension. Now, each eigenvector has an *eigenvalue* that tells us its length (i.e. the distance from one end of the eigenvector to the other). So, by looking at all of the eigenvalues for a data set, we know the dimensions of the ellipse or rugby ball: put more generally, we know the dimensions of the data. Therefore, the eigenvalues show how evenly (or otherwise) the variances of the matrix are distributed.

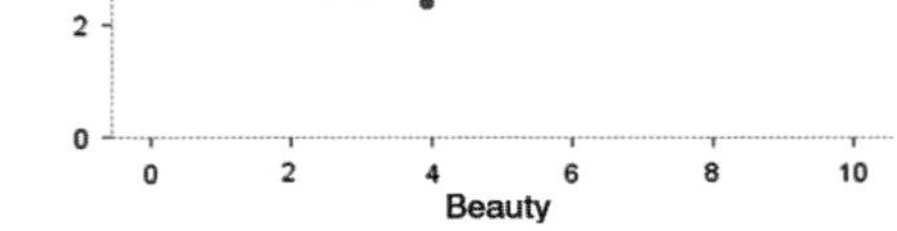

In the case of two variables, the *condition* of the data is related to the ratio of the larger eigenvalue to the smaller. Let's look at the two extremes: when there is no relationship at all between variables, and when there is a perfect relationship. When there is no relationship, the scatterplot will, more or less, be contained within a circle (or a sphere if we had three variables). If we again draw lines that measure the height and width of this circle we'll find that these lines are the same length. The eigenvalues measure the length, therefore the eigenvalues will also be the same. So, when we divide the largest eigenvalue by the smallest we'll get a value of 1 (because the eigenvalues are the same). When the variables are perfectly correlated (i.e. there is perfect collinearity) then the scatterplot forms a straight line and the ellipse surrounding it will also collapse to a straight line. Therefore, the height of the ellipse will be very small indeed (it will approach zero). Therefore, when we divide the largest eigenvalue by the smallest we'll get a value that tends to infinity (because the smallest eigenvalue is close to zero). Therefore, an infinite condition index is a sign of deep trouble.

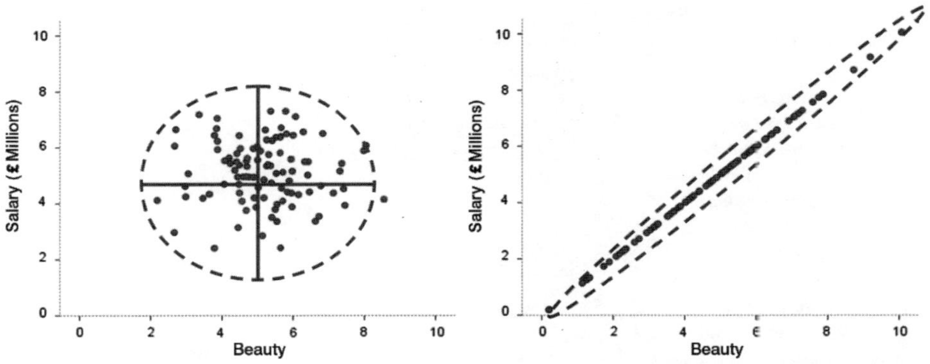

7.8.6. Casewise diagnostics ②

SPSS produces a summary table of the residual statistics and these should be examined for extreme cases. SPSS Output 7.10 shows any cases that have a standardized residual less than −2 or greater than 2 (remember that we changed the default criterion from 3 to 2 in Figure 7.14). I mentioned in section 7.6.1.1 that in an ordinary sample we would expect 95% of cases to have standardized residuals within about ±2. We have a sample of 200, therefore it is reasonable to expect about 10 cases (5%) to have standardized residuals outside of these limits. From SPSS Output 7.10 we can see that we have 12 cases (6%) that are outside of the limits: therefore, our sample is within 1% of what we would expect. In addition, 99% of cases should lie within ±2.5 and so we would expect only 1% of cases to lie outside of these limits. From the cases listed here, it is clear that two cases (1%) lie outside of the limits (cases 164 and 169). Therefore, our sample appears to conform to what we would expect for a fairly accurate model. These diagnostics give us no real cause for concern except that case 169 has a standardized residual greater than 3, which is probably large enough for us to investigate this case further.

S OUTPUT 7.10

Casewise Diagnostics[a]

Case Number	Std. Residual	Record Sales (thousands)	Predicted Value	Residual
1	2.125	330.00	229.9203	100.0797
2	-2.314	120.00	228.9490	-108.9490
10	2.114	300.00	200.4662	99.5338
47	-2.442	40.00	154.9698	-114.9698
52	2.069	190.00	92.5973	97.4027
55	-2.424	190.00	304.1231	-114.1231
61	2.098	300.00	201.1897	98.8103
68	-2.345	70.00	180.4156	-110.4156
100	2.066	250.00	152.7133	97.2867
164	-2.577	120.00	241.3240	-121.3240
169	3.061	360.00	215.8675	144.1325
200	-2.064	110.00	207.2061	-97.2061

a. Dependent Variable: Record Sales (thousands)

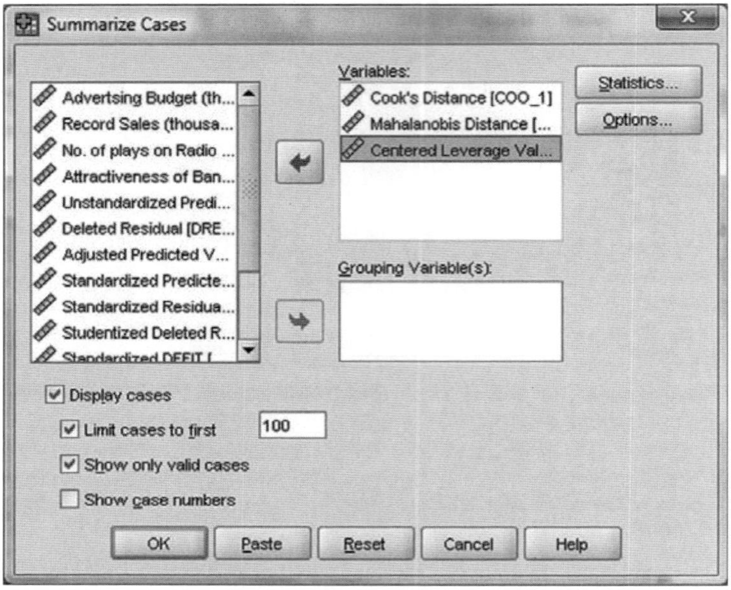

FIGURE 7.18 The summarize cases dialog box

You may remember that in section 7.7.5 we asked SPSS to save various diagnostic statistics. You should find that the data editor now contains columns for these variables. It is perfectly acceptable to check these values in the data editor, but you can also get SPSS to list the values in your viewer window too. To list variables you need to use the *Case Summaries* command, which can be found by selecting Analyze Reports ▸ Case Summaries.... Figure 7.18 shows the dialog box for this function. Simply select the variables that you want to list and transfer them to the box labelled *Variables* by clicking on ➡. By default, SPSS will limit the output to the first 100 cases, but if you want to list all of your cases then simply deselect this option. It is also very important to select the *Show case numbers* option because otherwise you might not be able to identify a problem case.

One useful strategy is to use the casewise diagnostics to identify cases that you want to investigate further. So, to save space, I created a coding variable (1 = include, 0 = exclude) so that I could specify the 12 cases listed in SPSS Output 7.11 in one group, and all other cases in the other. By using this coding variable and specifying it as a grouping variable in the *Summarize Cases* dialog box, I could look at those 12 cases together and discard all others.

SPSS Output 7.11 shows the influence statistics for the 12 cases that I selected. None of them have a Cook's distance greater than 1 (even case 169 is well below this criterion) and so none of the cases is having an undue influence on the model. The average leverage can be calculated as 0.02 ($k + 1/n = 4/200$) and so we are looking for values either twice as large as this (0.04) or three times as large (0.06) depending on which statistician you trust most (see section 7.6.1.2)! All cases are within the boundary of three times the average and only case 1 is close to two times the average. Finally, from our guidelines for the Mahalanobis distance we saw that with a sample of 100 and three predictors, values greater than 15 were problematic. We have three predictors and a larger sample size, so this value will be a conservative cut-off, yet none of our cases comes close to exceeding this criterion. The evidence suggests that there are no influential cases within our data (although all cases would need to be examined to confirm this fact).

We can look also at the DFBeta statistics to see whether any case would have a large influence on the regression parameters. An absolute value greater than 1 is a problem and

PSS OUTPUT 7.11

Case Summaries

		Case Number	Standardized DFBETA Intercept	Standardized DFBETA ADVERTS	Standardized DFBETA AIRPLAY	Standardized DFBETA ATTRACT	Standardized DFFIT	COVRATIO
1		1	-.31554	-.24235	.15774	.35329	.48929	.97127
2		2	.01259	-.12637	.00942	-.01868	-.21110	.92018
3		10	-.01256	-.15612	.16772	.00672	.26896	.94392
4		47	.06645	.19602	.04829	-.17857	-.31469	.91458
5		52	.35291	-.02881	-.13667	-.26965	.36742	.95995
6		55	.17427	-.32649	-.02307	-.12435	-.40736	.92486
7		61	.00082	-.01539	.02793	.02054	.15562	.93654
8		68	-.00281	.21146	-.14766	-.01760	-.30216	.92370
9		100	.06113	.14523	-.29984	.06766	.35732	.95888
10		164	.17983	.28988	-.40088	-.11706	-.54029	.92037
11		169	-.16819	-.25765	.25739	.16968	.46132	.85325
12		200	.16633	-.04639	.14213	-.25907	-.31985	.95435
Total	N		12	12	12	12	12	12

Case Summaries

		Case Number	Cook's Distance	Mahalanobis Distance	Centered Leverage Value
1		1	.05870	8.39591	.04219
2		2	.01089	.59830	.00301
3		10	.01776	2.07154	.01041
4		47	.02412	2.12475	.01068
5		52	.03316	4.81841	.02421
6		55	.04042	4.19960	.02110
7		61	.00595	.06880	.00035
8		68	.02229	2.13106	.01071
9		100	.03136	4.53310	.02278
10		164	.07077	6.83538	.03435
11		169	.05087	3.14841	.01582
12		200	.02513	3.49043	.01754
Total	N		12	12	12

in all cases the values lie within ±1, which shows that these cases have no undue influence over the regression parameters. There is also a column for the covariance ratio. We saw in section 7.6.1.2 that we need to use the following criteria:

- $CVR_i > 1 + [3(k + 1)/n] = 1 + [3(3 + 1)/200] = 1.06$.
- $CVR_i < 1 - [3(k + 1)/n] = 1 - [3(3 + 1)/200] = 0.94$.

Therefore, we are looking for any cases that deviate substantially from these boundaries. Most of our 12 potential outliers have CVR values within or just outside these boundaries. The only case that causes concern is case 169 (again!) whose CVR is some way below the bottom limit. However, given the Cook's distance for this case, there is probably little cause for alarm.

You would have requested other diagnostic statistics and from what you know from the earlier discussion of them you would be well advised to glance over them in case of any unusual cases in the data. However, from this minimal set of diagnostics we appear to have a fairly reliable model that has not been unduly influenced by any subset of cases.

CRAMMING SAM'S TIPS

You need to look for cases that might be influencing the regression model:

- Look at standardized residuals and check that no more than 5% of cases have absolute values above 2, and that no more than about 1% have absolute values above 2.5. Any case with the value above about 3, could be an outlier.
- Look in the data editor for the values of Cook's distance: any value above 1 indicates a case that might be influencing the model.
- Calculate the average leverage (the number of predictors plus 1, divided by the sample size) and then look for values greater than twice or three times this average value.
- For Mahalanobis distance, a crude check is to look for values above 25 in large samples (500) and values above 15 in smaller samples (100). However, Barnett and Lewis (1978) should be consulted for more detailed analysis.
- Look for absolute values of DFBeta greater than 1.
- Calculate the upper and lower limit of acceptable values for the covariance ratio, CVR. The upper limit is 1 plus three times the average leverage, whereas the lower limit is 1 minus three times the average leverage. Cases that have a CVR that fall outside of these limits may be problematic.

7.8.7. Checking assumptions ②

As a final stage in the analysis, you should check the assumptions of the model. We have already looked for collinearity within the data and used Durbin–Watson to check whether the residuals in the model are independent. In section 7.7.4 we asked for a plot of *ZRESID against *ZPRED and for a histogram and normal probability plot of the residuals. The graph of *ZRESID and *ZPRED should look like a random array of dots evenly dispersed around zero. If this graph funnels out, then the chances are that there is heteroscedasticity in the data. If there is any sort of curve in this graph then the chances are that the data have broken the assumption of linearity. Figure 7.19 shows several examples of the plot of standardized residuals against standardized predicted values. Panel (a) shows the graph for the data in our record sales example. Note how the points are randomly and evenly dispersed throughout the plot. This pattern is indicative of a situation in which the assumptions of linearity and homoscedasticity have been met. Panel (b) shows a similar plot for a data set that violates the assumption of homoscedasticity. Note that the points form the shape of a funnel so they become more spread out across the graph. This funnel shape is typical of heteroscedasticity and indicates increasing variance across the residuals. Panel (c) shows a plot of some data in which there is a non-linear relationship between the outcome and the predictor. This pattern is shown up by the residuals. A line illustrating the curvilinear relationship has been drawn over the top of the graph to illustrate the trend in the data. Finally, panel (d) represents a situation in which the data not only represent a non-linear relationship, but also show heteroscedasticity. Note first the curved trend in the data, and then also note that at one end of the plot the points are very close together whereas at the other end they are widely dispersed. When these assumptions have been violated you will not see these exact patterns, but hopefully these plots will help you to understand the types of anomalies you should look out for.

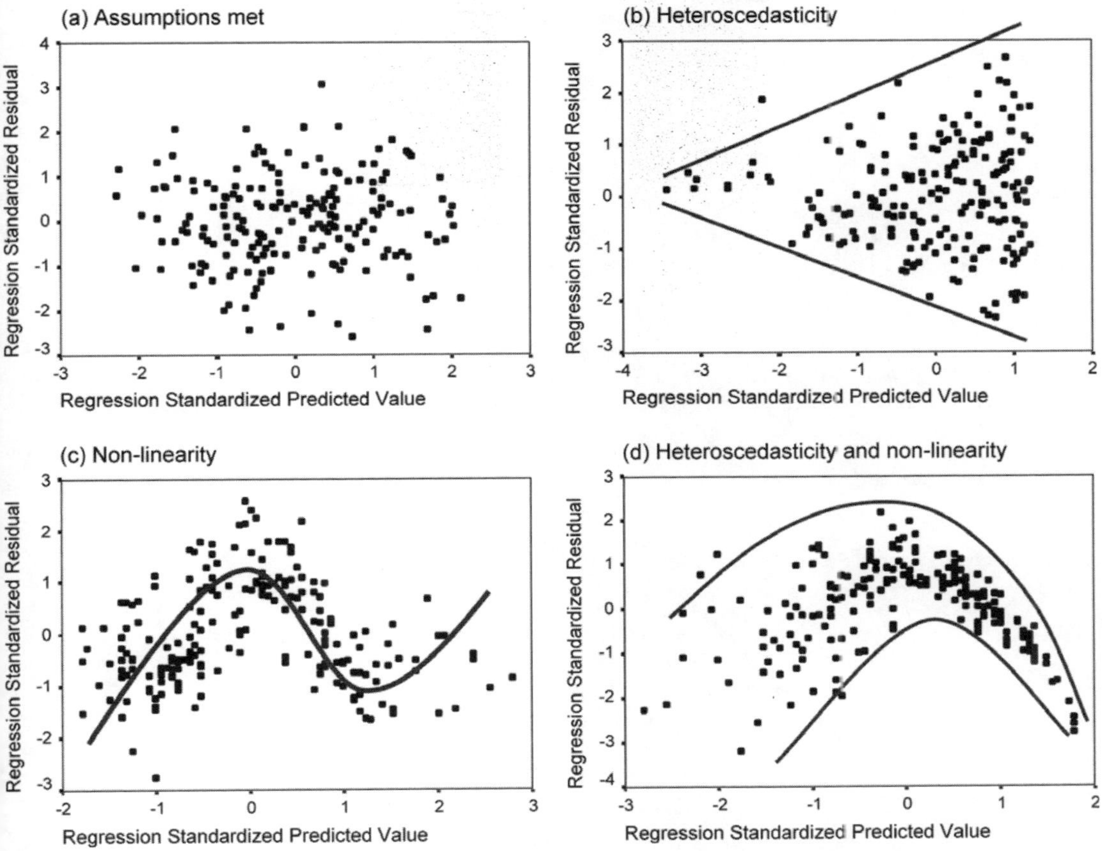

FIGURE 7.19 Plots of *ZRESID against *ZPRED

To test the normality of residuals, we must look at the histogram and normal probability plot selected in Figure 7.15. Figure 7.20 shows the histogram and normal probability plot of the data for the current example (left-hand side). The histogram should look like a normal distribution (a bell-shaped curve). SPSS draws a curve on the histogram to show the shape of the distribution. For the record company data, the distribution is roughly normal (although there is a slight deficiency of residuals exactly on zero). Compare this histogram to the extremely non-normal histogram next to it and it should be clear that the non-normal distribution is extremely skewed (unsymmetrical). So, you should look for a curve that has the same shape as the one for the record sales data: any deviation from this curve is a sign of non-normality and the greater the deviation, the more non-normally distributed the residuals. The normal probability plot also shows up deviations from normality (see Chapter 5). The straight line in this plot represents a normal distribution, and the points represent the observed residuals. Therefore, in a perfectly normally distributed data set, all points will lie on the line. This is pretty much what we see for the record sales data. However, next to the normal probability plot of the record sales data is an example of an extreme deviation from normality. In this plot, the dots

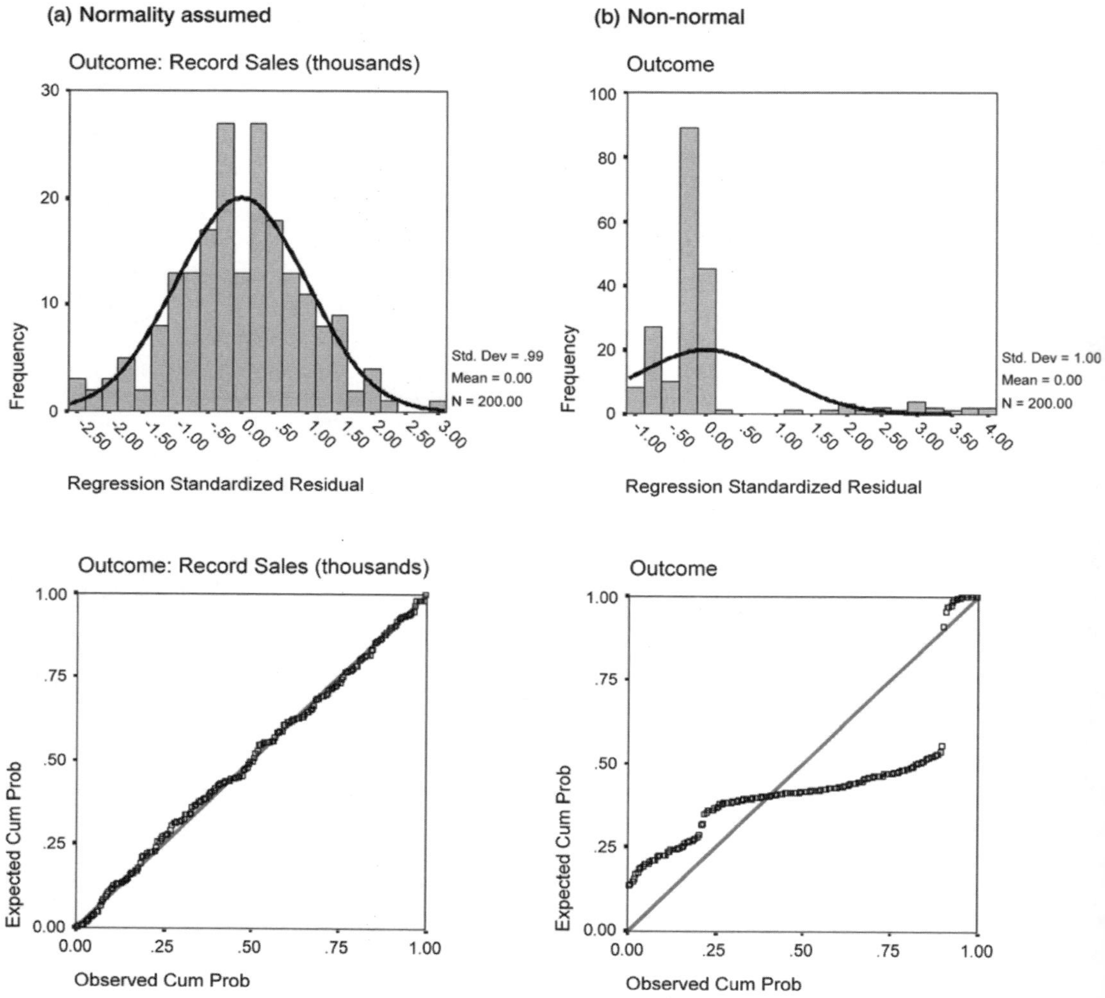

FIGURE 7.20 Histograms and normal P–P plots of normally distributed residuals (left-hand side) and non-normally distributed residuals (right-hand side)

are very distant from the line, which indicates a large deviation from normality. For both plots, the non-normal data are extreme cases and you should be aware that the deviations from normality are likely to be subtler. Of course, you can use what you learnt in Chapter 5 to do a K–S test on the standardized residuals to see whether they deviate significantly from normality.

A final set of plots specified in Figure 7.15 was the partial plots. These plots are scatterplots of the residuals of the outcome variable and each of the predictors when both variables are regressed separately on the remaining predictors. I mentioned earlier that obvious outliers on a partial plot represent cases that might have undue influence on a predictor's regression coefficient and that non-linear relationships and heteroscedasticity can be detected using these plots as well:

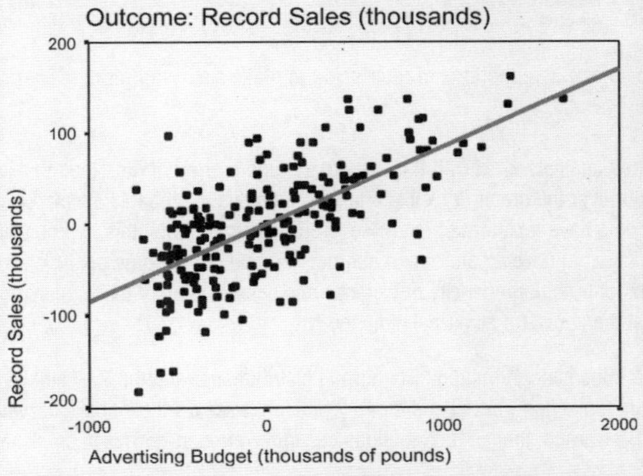

For advertising budget the partial plot shows the strong positive relationship to record sales. The gradient of the line is *b* for advertising in the model (this line does not appear by default). There are no obvious outliers on this plot, and the cloud of dots is evenly spaced out around the line, indicating homoscedasticity.

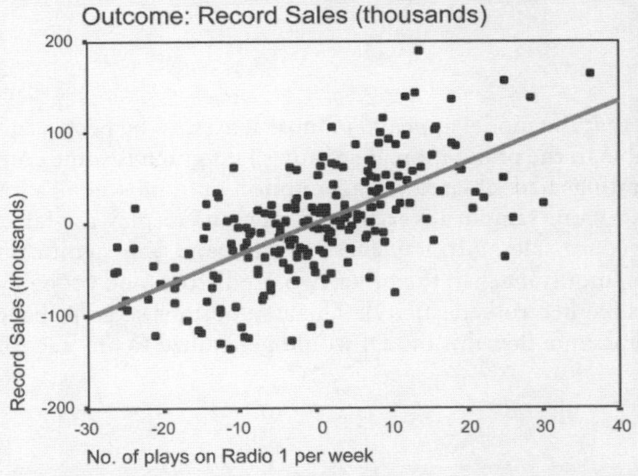

For airplay the partial plot shows a strong positive relationship to record sales. The gradient and pattern of the data are similar to advertising (which would be expected given the similarity of the standardized betas of these predictors). There are no obvious outliers on this plot, and the cloud of dots is evenly spaced around the line, indicating homoscedasticity.

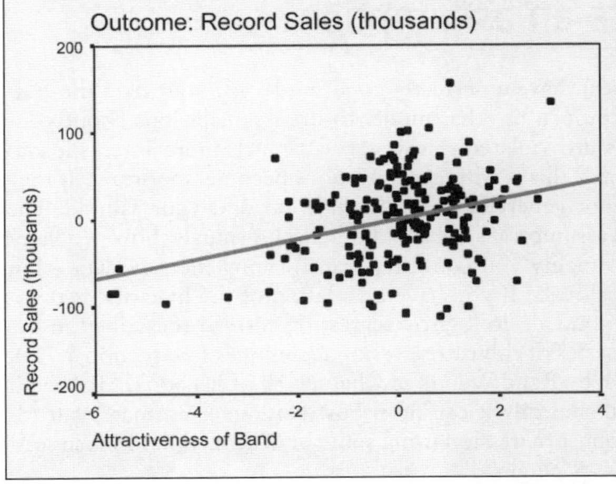

For attractiveness the partial plot shows a positive relationship to record sales. The relationship looks less linear than the other predictors do and the dots seem to funnel out, indicating greater variance at high levels of attractiveness. There are no obvious outliers on this plot, but the funnel-shaped cloud of dots might indicate a violation of the assumption of homoscedasticity. We would be well advised to collect some more data for unattractive bands to verify the current model.

CRAMMING SAM'S TIPS

You need to check some of the assumptions of regression to make sure your model generalizes beyond your sample:

- Look at the graph of* ZRESID plotted against* ZPRED. If it looks like a random array of dots then this is good. If the dots seem to get more or less spread out over the graph (look like a funnel) then this is probably a violation of the assumption of homogeneity of variance. If the dots have a pattern to them (i.e. a curved shape) then this is probably a violation of the assumption of linearity. If the dots seem to have a pattern and are more spread out at some points on the plot than others then this probably reflects violations of both homogeneity of variance *and* linearity. Any of these scenarios puts the validity of your model into question. Repeat the above for all partial plots too.
- Look at histograms and P–P plots. If the histograms look like normal distributions (and the P–P plot looks like a diagonal line), then all is well. If the histogram looks non-normal and the P–P plot looks like a wiggly snake curving around a diagonal line then things are less good! Be warned, though: distributions can look very non-normal in small samples even when they are!

We could summarize by saying that the model appears, in most senses, to be both accurate for the sample and generalizable to the population. The only slight glitch is some concern over whether attractiveness ratings had violated the assumption of homoscedasticity. Therefore, we could conclude that in our sample advertising budget and airplay are fairly equally important in predicting record sales. Attractiveness of the band is a significant predictor of record sales but is less important than the other two predictors (and probably needs verification because of possible heteroscedasticity). The assumptions seem to have been met and so we can probably assume that this model would generalize to any record being released.

7.9. What if I violate an assumption? ②

It's worth remembering that you can have a perfectly good model for your data (no outliers, influential cases, etc.) and you can use that model to draw conclusions about your sample, even if your assumptions are violated. However, it's much more interesting to generalize your regression model and this is where assumptions become important. If they have been violated then you cannot generalize your findings beyond your sample. The options for correcting for violated assumptions are a bit limited. If residuals show problems with heteroscedasticity or non-normality you could try transforming the raw data – but this won't necessarily affect the residuals! If you have a violation of the linearity assumption then you could see whether you can do logistic regression instead (described in the next chapter). Finally, there are a series of robust regression techniques (see section 5.7.4), which are described extremely well by Rand Wilcox in Chapter 10 of his book. SPSS can't do these methods directly (well, technically it can do robust parameter estimates but it's not easy), but you can attempt a robust regression using some of Wilcox's files for the software *R* (Wilcox, 2005) using SPSS's *R* plugin.

OLIVER TWISTED

Please, Sir, can I have some more ... robust regression?

'R you going to show us how to do robust regression?,' mumbles Oliver as he dribbles down his shirt 'I want to do one.' I've prepared a flash movie on the companion website that shows you how to use the *R* plugin to do robust regression. You have no excuses now for not using it.

7.10. How to report multiple regression ②

If you follow the American Psychological Association guidelines for reporting multiple regression then the implication seems to be that tabulated results are the way forward. The APA also seem in favour of reporting, as a bare minimum, the standardized betas, their significance value and some general statistics about the model (such as the R^2). If you do decide to do a table then the beta values and their standard errors are also very useful. Personally I'd like to see the constant as well because then readers of your work can construct the full regression model if they need to. Also, if you've done a hierarchical regression you should report these values at each stage of the hierarchy. So, basically, you want to reproduce the table labelled **Coefficients** from the SPSS output and omit some of the non-essential information. For the example in this chapter we might produce a table like that in Table 7.2.

See if you can look back through the SPSS output in this chapter and work out from where the values came. Things to note are: (1) I've rounded off to 2 decimal places throughout; (2) for the standardized betas there is no zero before the decimal point (because these values cannot exceed 1) but for all other values less than 1 the zero is present; (3) the significance of the variable is denoted by an asterisk with a footnote to indicate the significance level being used (if there's more than one level of significance being used you can denote this with multiple asterisks, such as $^*p < .05$, $^{**}p < .01$, and $^{***}p < .001$); and (4) the R^2 for the initial model and the change in R^2 (denoted as ΔR^2) for each subsequent step of the model are reported below the table.

TABLE 7.2 How to report multiple regression

	B	SE B	β
Step 1			
Constant	134.14	7.54	
Advertising Budget	0.10	0.01	.58*
Step 2			
Constant	−26.61	17.35	
Advertising Budget	0.09	0.01	.51*
Plays on BBC Radio 1	3.37	0.28	.51*
Attractiveness	11.09	2.44	.19*

Note: $R^2 = .34$ for Step 1, $\Delta R^2 = .33$ for Step 2 ($p < .001$). $^*p < .001$.

CHAMORRO-PREMUZIC, T., ET AL. (2008). *PERSONALITY AND INDIVIDUAL DIFFERENCES*, 44, 965–976.

LABCOAT LENI'S REAL RESEARCH 7.1

Why do you like your lecturers? ①

In the previous chapter we encountered a study by Chamorro-Premuzic et al. in which they measured students' personality characteristics and asked them to rate how much they wanted these same characteristics in their lecturers (see Labcoat Leni's Real Research 6.1 for a full description). In that chapter we correlated these scores; however, we could go a step further and see whether students' personality characteristics predict the characteristics that they would like to see in their lecturers.

The data from this study are in the file **Chamorro-Premuzic.sav**. Labcoat Leni wants you to carry out five multiple regression analyses: the outcome variable in each of the five analyses is the ratings of how much students want to see Neuroticism, Extroversion, Openness to experience, Agreeableness and Conscientiousness. For each of these outcomes, force Age and Gender into the analysis in the first step of the hierarchy, then in the second block force in the five student personality traits (Neuroticism, Extroversion, Openness to experience, Agreeableness and Conscientiousness). For each analysis create a table of the results.

Answers are in the additional material on the companion website (or look at Table 4 in the original article).

7.11. Categorical predictors and multiple regression ③

Often in regression analysis you'll collect data about groups of people (e.g. ethnic group, gender, socio-economic status, diagnostic category). You might want to include these groups as predictors in the regression model; however, we saw from our assumptions that variables need to be continuous or categorical with only two categories. We saw in section 6.5.5 that a point–biserial correlation is Pearson's r between two variables when one is continuous and the other has two categories coded as 0 and 1. We've also learnt that simple regression is based on Pearson's r, so it shouldn't take a great deal of imagination to see that, like the point–biserial correlation, we could construct a regression model with a predictor that has two categories (e.g. gender). Likewise, it shouldn't be too inconceivable that we could then extend this model to incorporate several predictors that had two categories. All that is important is that we code the two categories with the values of 0 and 1. Why is it important that there are only two categories and that they're coded 0 and 1? Actually, I don't want to get into this here because this chapter is already too long, the publishers are going to break my legs if it gets any longer, and I explain it anyway later in the book (sections 9.7 and 10.2.3) so, for the time being, just trust me!

7.11.1. Dummy coding ③

The obvious problem with wanting to use categorical variables as predictors is that often you'll have more than two categories. For example, if you'd measured religiosity you might have categories of Muslim, Jewish, Hindu, Catholic, Buddhist, Protestant, Jedi (for those of you not in the UK, we had a census here a few years back in which a significant portion of people put down Jedi as their religion). Clearly these groups cannot be distinguished using a single variable coded with zeros and ones. In these cases we have to use what's called **dummy variables**. Dummy coding is a way of representing groups of people using only zeros and ones. To do it, we have to create several variables; in fact, the number of variables we need is one less than the number of groups we're recoding. There are eight basic steps:

1 Count the number of groups you want to recode and subtract 1.
2 Create as many new variables as the value you calculated in step 1. These are your dummy variables.
3 Choose one of your groups as a baseline (i.e. a group against which all other groups should be compared). This should usually be a control group, or, if you don't have a specific hypothesis, it should be the group that represents the majority of people (because it might be interesting to compare other groups against the majority).
4 Having chosen a baseline group, assign that group values of 0 for all of your dummy variables.
5 For your first dummy variable, assign the value 1 to the first group that you want to compare against the baseline group. Assign all other groups 0 for this variable.
6 For the second dummy variable assign the value 1 to the second group that you want to compare against the baseline group. Assign all other groups 0 for this variable.
7 Repeat this until you run out of dummy variables.
8 Place all of your dummy variables into the regression analysis!

Let's try this out using an example. In Chapter 4 we came across an example in which a biologist was worried about the potential health effects of music festivals. She collected some data at the Download Festival, which is a music festival specializing in heavy metal. The biologist was worried that the findings that she had were a function of the fact that she had tested only one type of person: metal fans. Perhaps it's not the festival that makes people smelly, maybe it's only metal fans at festivals who get smellier (as a metal fan, I would at this point sacrifice the biologist to Satan for being so prejudiced). Anyway, to answer this question she went to another festival that had a more eclectic clientele. So, she went to the Glastonbury Music Festival which attracts all sorts of people because it has all styles of music there. Again, she measured the hygiene of concert-goers over the three days of the festival using a technique that results in a score ranging between 0 (you smell like you've bathed in sewage) and 5 (you smell of freshly baked bread). Now, in Chapters 4 and 5, we just looked at the distribution of scores for the three days of the festival, but now the biologist wanted to look at whether the type of music you like (your cultural group) predicts whether hygiene decreases over the festival. The data are in the file called

GlastonburyFestivalRegression.sav. This file contains the hygiene scores for each of three days of the festival, but it also contains a variable called **change** which is the change in hygiene over the three days of the festival (so it's the change from day 1 to day 3).[13] Finally, the biologist categorized people according to their musical affiliation: if they mainly liked alternative music she called them 'indie kid', if they mainly liked heavy metal she called them a 'metaller' and if they mainly liked sort of hippy/folky/ambient type of stuff then she labelled them a 'crusty'. Anyone not falling into these categories was labelled 'no musical affiliation'. In the data file she coded these groups 1, 2, 3 and 4 respectively.

The first thing we should do is calculate the number of dummy variables. We have four groups, so there will be three dummy variables (one less than the number of groups). Next we need to choose a baseline group. We're interested in comparing those that have different musical affiliations against those that don't, so our baseline category will be 'no musical

[13] Not everyone could be measured on day 3, so there is a change score only for a subset of the original sample.

TABLE 7.3 Dummy coding for the Glastonbury Festival data

	Dummy Variable 1	Dummy Variable 2	Dummy Variable 3
No Affiliation	0	0	0
Indie Kid	0	0	1
Metaller	0	1	0
Crusty	1	0	0

affiliation'. We give this group a code of 0 for all of our dummy variables. For our first dummy variable, we could look at the 'crusty' group, and to do this we give anyone that was a crusty a code of 1, and everyone else a code of 0. For our second dummy variable, we could look at the 'metaller' group, and to do this we give anyone that was a metaller a code of 1, and everyone else a code of 0. We have one dummy variable left and this will have to look at our final category: 'indie kid'. To do this we give anyone that was an indie kid a code of 1, and everyone else a code of 0. The resulting coding scheme is shown in Table 7.3. The thing to note is that each group has a code of 1 on only one of the dummy variables (except the base category that is always coded as 0).

As I said, we'll look at why dummy coding works in sections 9.7 and 10.2.3, but for the time being let's look at how to recode our grouping variable into these dummy variables using SPSS. To recode variables you need to use the *Recode* function. Select Transform → x-y Recode into Different Variables... to access the dialog box in Figure 7.21.

The recode dialog box lists all of the variables in the data editor, and you need to select the one you want to recode (in this case **music**) and transfer it to the box labelled *Numeric Variable → Output Variable* by clicking on ➡. You then need to name the new variable (the output variable as SPSS calls it), so go to the part that says *Output Variable* and in the box below where it says *Name* write a name for your first dummy variable (you might call it **Crusty**). You can also give this variable a more descriptive name by typing something in the box labelled *Label* (for this first dummy variable I've called it No Affiliation vs. Crusty). When you've done this click on Change to transfer this new variable to the box labelled *Numeric Variable → Output Variable* (this box should now say *music → Crusty*).

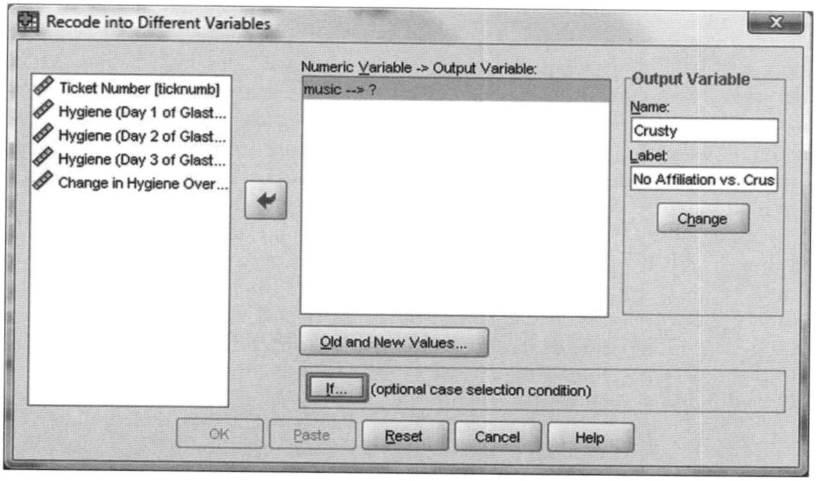

FIGURE 7.21 The recode dialog box

OLIVER TWISTED

Please, Sir, can I have some more … recode?

'Our data set has missing values,' worries Oliver. 'What do we do if we only want to recode cases for which we have data?' Well, we can set some other options at this point, that's what we can do. This is getting a little bit more involved so if you want to know more, the additional material for this chapter on the companion website will tell you. Stop worrying Oliver, everything will be OK.

Having defined the first dummy variable, we need to tell SPSS how to recode the values of the variable **music** into the values that we want for the new variable, **music1**. To do this click on Old and New Values... to access the dialog box in Figure 7.22. This dialog box is used to change values of the original variable into different values for the new variable. For our first dummy variable, we want anyone who was a crusty to get a code of 1 and everyone else to get a code of 0. Now, crusty was coded with the value 3 in the original variable, so you need to type the value 3 in the section labelled *Old Value* in the box labelled *Value*. The new value we want is 1, so we need to type the value 1 in the section labelled *New Value* in the box labelled *Value*. When you've done this, click on Add to add this change to the list of changes (the list is displayed in the box labelled *Old* → *New*, which should now say *3* → *1* as in the diagram). The next thing we need to do is to change the remaining groups to have a value of 0 for the first dummy variable. To do this just select All other values and type the value 0 in the section labelled *New Value* in the box labelled *Value*.[14] When you've done this, click on Add to add this change to the list of changes (this list will now also say *ELSE* → *0*). When you've done this click on Continue to return to the main dialog box, and then click on OK to create the first dummy variable. This variable will appear as a new column in the data editor, and you should notice that it will have a value of 1 for anyone originally classified as a crusty and a value of 0 for everyone else.

SELF-TEST Try creating the remaining two dummy variables (call them **Metaller** and **Indie_Kid**) using the same principles.

7.11.2. SPSS output for dummy variables ③

Let's assume you've created the three dummy coding variables (if you're stuck there is a data file called **GlastonburyDummy.sav** (the 'Dummy' refers to the fact it has dummy variables in it – I'm not implying that if you need to use this file you're a dummy)). With dummy variables, you have to enter all related dummy variables in the same block (so use the *Enter* method).

[14] Using this All other values option is fine when you don't have missing values in the data, but just note that when you do (as is the case here) cases with both system-defined and user-defined missing values will be included in the recode. One way around this is to recode only cases for which there is a value (see Oliver Twisted Box). The alternative is specifically to recode missing values using the Range: option. It is also a good idea to use the *frequencies* or *crosstabs* commands after a recode and check that you have caught all of these missing values.

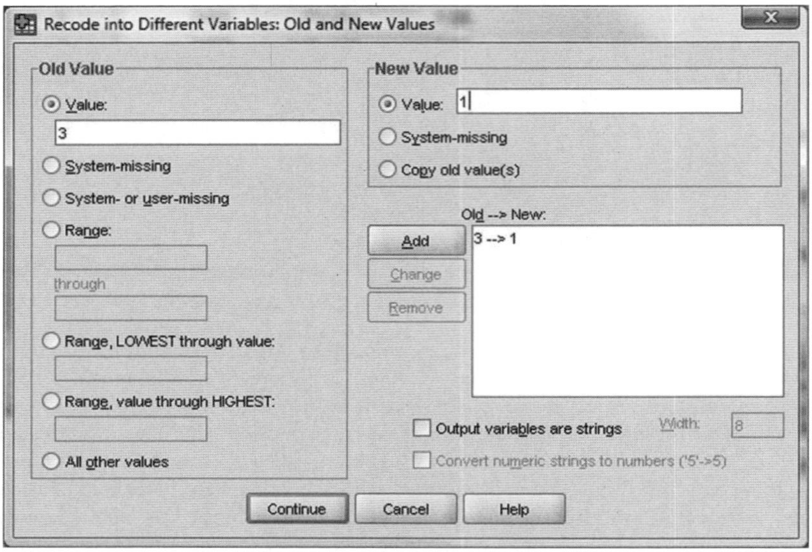

FIGURE 7.22 Dialog boxes for the *Recode* function (see also SPSS Tip 7.1)

SPSS TIP 7.1 Using syntax to recode ③

If you're doing a lot of recoding it soon becomes pretty tedious using the dialog boxes all of the time. I've written the syntax file, **RecodeGlastonburyData.sps**, to create all of the dummy variables we've discussed. Load this file and run the syntax, or open a syntax window (see Section 3.7) and type the following:

```
DO IF (1-MISSING(change)).
RECODE music (3=1)(ELSE = 0) INTO Crusty.
RECODE music (2=1)(ELSE = 0) INTO Metaller.
RECODE music (1=1)(ELSE = 0) INTO Indie_Kid.
END IF.
VARIABLE LABELS Crusty 'No Affiliation vs. Crusty'.
VARIABLE LABELS Metaller 'No Affiliation vs. Metaller'.
VARIABLE LABELS Indie_Kid 'No Affiliation vs. Indie Kid'.
VARIABLE LEVEL Crusty Metaller Indie_Kid (Nominal).
FORMATS Crusty Metaller Indie_Kid (F1.0).
EXECUTE.
```

Each RECODE command is doing the equivalent of what you'd do using the compute dialog box in Figure 7.22. So, the three lines beginning RECODE ask SPSS to create three new variables (**Crusty, Metaller** and **Indie_Kid**), which are based on the original variable **music**. For the first variable, if **music** is 3 then it becomes 1, and every other value becomes 0. For the second, if **music** is 2 then it becomes 1, and every other value becomes

(Continued)

(Continued)

0, and so on for the third dummy variable. Note that all of these RECODE commands are within an IF statement (beginning DO IF and ending with END IF). This tells SPSS to carry out the RECODE commands only if a certain condition is met. The condition we have set is (1- MISSING(change)). MISSING is a built-in command that returns 'true' (i.e. the value 1) for a case that has a system- or user-defined missing value for the specified variable; it returns 'false' (i.e. the value 0) if a case has a value. Hence, MISSING(change) returns a value of 1 for cases that have a missing value for the variable 'change' and 0 for cases that do have values. We want to recode the cases that *do* have a value for the variable change, therefore I have specified '1- MISSING(change)'. This command reverses MISSING(change) so that it returns 1 (true) for cases that have a value for the variable **change** and 0 (false) for system- or user-defined missing values. To sum up, the DO IF (1- MISSING(change)) tells SPSS 'Do the following RECODE commands if the case has a value for the variable **change**.'

The lines beginning VARIABLE LABELS just tells SPSS to assign the text in the quotations as labels for the variables **Crusty**, **Metaller** and **Indie_Kid** respectively. The line beginning VARIABLE LEVEL then sets these three variables to be 'nominal', and the line beginning FORMATS changes the three variables to have a width of 1 and 0 decimal places (hence the 1.0) – in other words, it changes the format to be a binary number.

The final line has the command EXECUTE without which none of the commands beforehand will be executed! Note also that every line ends with a full stop.

So, in this case we have to enter our dummy variables in the same block; however, if we'd had another variable (e.g. socio-economic status) that had been transformed into dummy variables, we could enter these dummy variables in a different block (so, it's only dummy variables that have recoded the same variable that need to be entered in the same block).

SELF-TEST Use what you've learnt in this chapter to run a multiple regression using the change scores as the outcome, and the three dummy variables (entered in the same block) as predictors.

Let's have a look at the output.

OUTPUT 7.12

Model Summary[b]

					Change Statistics					
Model	R	R Square	Adjusted R Square	Std. Error of the Estimate	R Square Change	F Change	df1	df2	Sig. F Change	Durbin-Watson
1	.276[a]	.076	.053	.68818	.076	3.270	3	119	.024	1.893

a. Predictors: (Constant), No Affiliation vs. Indie Kid, No Affiliation vs. Crusty, No Affiliation vs. Metaller

b. Dependent Variable: Change in Hygiene Over The Festival

ANOVA[b]

Model		Sum of Squares	df	Mean Square	F	Sig.
1	Regression	4.646	3	1.549	3.270	.024[a]
	Residual	56.358	119	.474		
	Total	61.004	122			

a. Predictors: (Constant), No Affiliation vs. Indie Kid, No Affiliation vs. Crusty, No Affiliation vs. Metaller

b. Dependent Variable: Change in Hygiene Over The Festival

SPSS Output 7.12 shows the model statistics. This shows that by entering the three dummy variables we can explain 7.6% of the variance in the change in hygiene scores (the R^2-value × 100). In other words, 7.6% of the variance in the change in hygiene can be explained by the musical affiliation of the person. The ANOVA (which shows the same thing as the R^2 change statistic because there is only one step in this regression) tells us that the model is significantly better at predicting the change in hygiene scores than having no model (or, put another way, the 7.6% of variance that can be explained is a significant amount). Most of this should be clear from what you've read in this chapter already; what's more interesting is how we interpret the individual dummy variables.

SPSS OUTPUT

Coefficients[a]

Model		Unstandardized Coefficients		Standardized Coefficients	t	Sig.
		B	Std. Error	Beta		
1	(Constant)	-.554	.090		-6.134	.000
	No Affiliation vs. Crusty	-.412	.167	-.232	-2.464	.015
	No Affiliation vs. Metaller	.028	.160	.017	.177	.860
	No Affiliation vs. Indie Kid	-.410	.205	-.185	-2.001	.048

a. Dependent Variable: Change in Hygiene Over The Festival

SPSS Output 7.13 shows a basic **Coefficients** table for the dummy variables (I've excluded the confidence intervals and collinearity diagnostics). The first thing to notice is that each dummy variable appears in the table with a useful label (such as No Affiliation vs. Crusty). This has happened because when we recoded our variables we gave each variable a label; if we hadn't done this then the table would contain the rather less helpful variable names (crusty, metaller and Indie_Kid). The labels that I suggested giving to each variable give us a hint about what each dummy variable represents. The first dummy variable (No Affiliation vs. Crusty) shows the difference between the change in hygiene scores for the no affiliation group and the crusty group. Remember that the beta value tells us the change in the outcome due to a unit change in the predictor. In this case, a unit change in the predictor is the change from 0 to 1. As such it shows the shift in the change in hygiene scores that results from the dummy variable changing from 0 to 1 (Crusty). By including all three dummy variables at the same time, our baseline category is always zero, so this actually represents the difference in the change in hygiene scores if a person has no musical affiliation, compared to someone who is a crusty. This difference is the difference between the two group means.

To illustrate this fact, I've produced a table (SPSS Output 7.14) of the group means for each of the four groups and also the difference between the means for each group and the no affiliation group. These means represent the average change in hygiene scores for the three groups (i.e. the mean of each group on our outcome variable). If we calculate the difference in these means for the No Affiliation group and the crusty group we get, Crusty – no affiliation = (–0.966) – (–0.554) = –0.412. In other words, the change in hygiene scores is greater for the crusty group than it is for the no affiliation group (crusties' hygiene decreases more over the festival than those with no musical affiliation). This value is the same as the *unstandardized* beta value in SPSS Output 7.13! So, the beta values tell us the relative difference between each group and the group that we chose as a baseline category. This beta value is converted to a t-statistic and the significance of this t reported. This t-statistic is testing, as we've seen before, whether the beta value is 0 and when we have two categories coded with 0 and 1, that means it's testing whether the difference between group means is 0. If it is significant then it means that the group coded with 1 is significantly different from the baseline category – so, it's testing the difference between two means, which is the context in which students are most familiar with the *t*-statistic (see Chapter 9). For our first dummy variable, the *t*-test is significant, and the beta value has a negative value so we could say that the change in hygiene scores goes down as a person changes from having no affiliation to being a crusty. Bear in mind that a decrease in hygiene scores represents more change (you're becoming smellier) so what this actually means is that hygiene decreased significantly more in crusties compared to those with no musical affiliation!

S OUTPUT 7.14

OLAP Cubes

Variables=Change in Hygiene Over The Festival

Musical Affiliation	Mean	Std. Deviation	N
Indie Kid	-0.964	0.670	14
Metaller	-0.526	0.576	27
Crusty	-0.966	0.760	24
No Musical Affiliation	-0.554	0.708	58
Crusty - No Musical Affiliation	-0.412	0.052	-34
Metaller - No Musical Affiliation	0.028	-0.133	-31
Indie Kid - No Musical Affiliation	-0.410	-0.038	-44
Total	-0.675	0.707	123

Moving on to our next dummy variable, this compares metallers to those that have no musical affiliation. The beta value again represents the shift in the change in hygiene scores if a person has no musical affiliation, compared to someone who is a metaller. If we calculate the difference in the group means for the no affiliation group and the metaller group we get, metaller – no affiliation = (–0.526) – (–0.554) = 0.028. This value is again the same as the unstandardized beta value in SPSS Output 7.13! For this second dummy variable, the *t*-test is not significant, so we could say that the change in hygiene scores is the same if a person changes from having no affiliation to being a metaller. In other words, the change in hygiene scores is not predicted by whether someone is a metaller compared to if they have no musical affiliation.

For the final dummy variable, we're comparing indie kids to those that have no musical affiliation. The beta value again represents the shift in the change in hygiene scores if a person has no musical affiliation, compared to someone who is an indie kid. If we calculate the difference in the group means for the no affiliation group and the indie kid group we get, indie kid – no affiliation = (–0.964) – (–0.554) = –0.410. It should be no surprise to you by now that this is the unstandardized beta value in SPSS Output 7.13! The *t*-test is significant, and the beta value has a negative value so, as with the first dummy variable, we could say that the change in hygiene scores goes down as a person changes from having no affiliation to being an indie kid. Bear in mind that a decrease in hygiene scores represents more change (you're becoming smellier) so what this actually means is that hygiene decreased significantly more in indie kids compared to those with no musical affiliation!

EVERYBODY

So, overall this analysis has shown that compared to having no musical affiliation, crusties and indie kids get significantly smellier across the three days of the festival, but metallers don't. This section has introduced some really complex ideas that I expand upon in Chapters 9 and 10. It might all be a bit much to take in, and so if you're confused or want to know more about why dummy coding works in this way I suggest reading sections 9.7 and 10.2.3 and then coming back here. Alternatively, read Hardy's (1993) excellent monograph!

What have I discovered about statistics? ①

This chapter is possibly the longest book chapter ever written, and if you feel like you aged several years while reading it then, well, you probably have (look around, there are cobwebs in the room, you have a long beard, and when you go outside you'll discover a second ice age has been and gone leaving only you and a few woolly mammoths to populate the planet). However, on the plus side, you now know more or less everything you ever need to know about statistics. Really, it's true; you'll discover in the coming chapters that everything else we discuss is basically a variation on the theme of regression. So, although you may be near death having spent your life reading this chapter (and I'm certainly near death having written it) you are a stats genius – it's official!

We started the chapter by discovering that at 8 years old I could have really done with regression analysis to tell me which variables are important in predicting talent competition success. Unfortunately I didn't have regression, but fortunately I had my dad instead (and he's better than regression). We then looked at how we could use statistical models to make similar predictions by looking at the case of when you have one predictor and one outcome. This allowed us to look at some basic principles such as the equation of a straight line, the method of least squares, and how to assess how well our model fits the data using some important quantities that you'll come across in future chapters: the model sum of squares, SS_M, the residual sum of squares, SS_R, and the total sum of squares, SS_T. We used these values to calculate several important statistics such as R^2 and the F-ratio. We also learnt how to do a regression on SPSS, and how we can plug the resulting beta values into the equation of a straight line to make predictions about our outcome.

Next, we saw that the question of a straight line can be extended to include several predictors and looked at different methods of placing these predictors in the model (hierarchical, forced entry, stepwise). Next, we looked at factors that can affect the accuracy of a model (outliers and influential cases) and ways to identify these factors. We then moved on to look at the assumptions necessary to generalize our model beyond the sample of data we've collected before discovering how to do the analysis on SPSS, and how to interpret the output, create our multiple regression model and test its reliability and generalizability. I finished the chapter by looking at how we can use categorical predictors in regression (and in passing we discovered the *recode* function). In general, multiple regression is a long process and should be done with care and attention to detail. There are a lot of important things to consider and you should approach the analysis in a systematic fashion. I hope this chapter helps you to do that!

So, I was starting to get a taste for the rock-idol lifestyle: I had friends, a fortune (well, two gold-plated winner's medals), fast cars (a bike) and dodgy-looking 8 year olds were giving me suitcases full of lemon sherbet to lick off mirrors. However, my parents and teachers were about to impress reality upon my young mind …

Key terms that I've discovered

Adjusted predicted value
Adjusted R^2
Autocorrelation
b_i

β_i
Cook's distance
Covariance ratio (CVR)
Cross-validation
Deleted residual
DFBeta
DFFit
Dummy variables
Durbin–Watson test
F-ratio
Generalization
Goodness of fit
Hat values
Heteroscedasticity
Hierarchical regression
Homoscedasticity
Independent errors
Leverage
Mahalanobis distances
Mean squares
Model sum of squares
Multicollinearity
Multiple R
Multiple regression
Outcome variable
Perfect collinearity
Predictor variable
Residual
Residual sum of squares
Shrinkage
Simple regression
Standardized DFBeta
Standardized DFFit
Standardized residuals
Stepwise regression
Studentized deleted residuals
Studentized residuals
Suppressor effects
t-statistic
Tolerance
Total sum of squares
Unstandardized residuals
Variance inflation factor (VIF)

Smart Alex's tasks

- **Task 1**: A fashion student was interested in factors that predicted the salaries of catwalk models. She collected data from 231 models. For each model she asked them their salary per day on days when they were working (**salary**), their age (**age**), how many years they had worked as a model (**years**), and then got a panel of experts from modelling agencies to rate the attractiveness of each model as a percentage with 100% being perfectly attractive (**beauty**). The data are in the file **Supermodel.sav**. Unfortunately, this fashion student bought some substandard statistics text and so doesn't know how to analyse her data.☺ Can you help her out by conducting a multiple regression to see which variables predict a model's salary? How valid is the regression model? ②
- **Task 2**: Using the Glastonbury data from this chapter (with the dummy coding in **GlastonburyDummy.sav**), which you should've already analysed, comment on whether you think the model is reliable and generalizable. ③
- **Task 3**: A study was carried out to explore the relationship between **Aggression** and several potential predicting factors in 666 children that had an older sibling. Variables measured were **Parenting_Style** (high score = bad parenting practices), **Computer_Games** (high score = more time spent playing computer games), **Television** (high score = more time spent watching television), **Diet** (high score = the child has a good diet low in E-numbers), and **Sibling_Aggression** (high score = more aggression seen in their older sibling). Past research indicated that parenting style and sibling aggression were good predictors of the level of aggression in the younger child. All other variables were treated in an exploratory fashion. The data are in the file **Child Aggression.sav**. Analyse them with multiple regression. ②

Answers can be found on the companion website.

Further reading

Bowerman, B. L., & O'Connell, R. T. (1990). *Linear statistical models: An applied approach* (2nd ed.). Belmont, CA: Duxbury. (This text is only for the mathematically minded or postgraduate students but provides an extremely thorough exposition of regression analysis.)

Hardy, M. A. (1993). *Regression with dummy variables.* Sage university paper series on quantitative applications in the social sciences, 07–093. Newbury Park, CA: Sage.

Howell, D. C. (2006). *Statistical methods for psychology* (6th ed.). Belmont, CA: Duxbury. (Or you might prefer his *Fundamental Statistics for the Behavioral Sciences,* also in its 6th edition, 2007. Both are excellent introductions to the mathematics behind regression analysis.)

Miles, J. N. V., & Shevlin, M. (2001). *Applying regression and correlation: a guide for students and researchers.* London: Sage. (This is an extremely readable text that covers regression in loads of detail but with minimum pain – highly recommended.)

Stevens, J. (2002). *Applied multivariate statistics for the social sciences* (4th ed.). Hillsdale, NJ: Erlbaum. Chapter 3.

Online tutorial

The companion website contains the following Flash movie tutorials to accompany this chapter:

- Regression using SPSS
- Robust Regression

Interesting real research

Chamorro-Premuzic, T., Furnham, A., Christopher, A. N., Garwood, J., & Martin, N. (2008). Birds of a feather: Students' preferences for lecturers' personalities as predicted by their own personality and learning approaches. *Personality and Individual Differences*, *44*, 965–976.

24 Introduction: The Research Process

MICHAEL CROTTY

... Many arrows, loosèd several ways,
Fly to one mark...

Willam Shakespeare, Henry V

They call it 'scaffolded learning'. It is an approach to teaching and learning that, while careful to provide an initial framework, leaves it to the learner to establish longer term structures.

What is presented here is offered in this spirit. It is to be seen as in no way a definitive construction of the social research process but merely a framework for the guidance of those wishing to explore the world of research.

Research students and fledgling researchers—and, yes, even more seasoned campaigners—often express bewilderment at the array of methodologies and methods laid out before their gaze. These methodologies and methods are not usually laid out in a highly organised fashion and may appear more as a maze than as pathways to orderly research. There is much talk of their philosophical underpinnings, but how the methodologies and methods relate to more theoretical elements is often left unclear. To add to the confusion, the terminology is far from consistent in research literature and social science texts. One frequently finds the same term used in a number of different, sometimes even contradictory, ways.

In response to this predicament, here is one reasonably clear-cut way of using terms and grasping what is involved in the process of social research. It is obviously not the only way in which these terms are used, nor is it being suggested that it is the only defensible way to use them. Equally, it is not the only way of analysing and understanding the research process. This is scaffolding, not an edifice. Its aim is to provide researchers with a sense of stability and direction as they go on to do their own building; that is, as they move towards understanding and expounding the research process after their own fashion in forms that suit their particular research purposes.

FOUR ELEMENTS

As a starting point, it can be suggested that, in developing a research proposal, we need to put considerable effort into answering two questions in particular. First, what methodologies and methods will we be employing in the research we propose to do? Second, how do we justify this choice and use of methodologies and methods?

The answer to the second question lies with the purposes of our research—in other words, with the research question that our piece of inquiry is seeking to answer. It is obvious enough that we need a process capable of fulfilling those purposes and answering that question.

There is more to it than that, however. Justification of our choice and particular use of methodology and methods is something that reaches into the assumptions about reality that we bring to our work. To ask about these assumptions is to ask about our theoretical perspective.

It also reaches into the understanding you and I have of what human knowledge is, what it entails, and what status can be ascribed to it. What kind of knowledge do we believe will be attained by our research? What characteristics do we believe that knowledge to have? Here we are touching upon a pivotal issue. How should observers of our research—for example, readers of our thesis or research report—regard the outcomes we lay out before them? And why should our readers take these outcomes seriously? These are epistemological questions.

Already our two initial questions have expanded. We find ourselves with four questions now:

- What *methods* do we propose to use?
- What *methodology* governs our choice and use of methods?
- What *theoretical perspective* lies behind the methodology in question?
- What *epistemology* informs this theoretical perspective?

At issue in these four questions are basic elements of any research process, and we need to spell out carefully what we mean by each of them.

- *Methods*: the techniques or procedures used to gather and analyse data related to some research question or hypothesis.
- *Methodology*: the strategy, plan of action, process or design lying behind the choice and use of particular methods and linking the choice and use of methods to the desired outcomes.
- *Theoretical perspective*: the philosophical stance informing the methodology and thus providing a context for the process and grounding its logic and criteria.
- *Epistemology*: the theory of knowledge embedded in the theoretical perspective and thereby in the methodology.

In social research texts, the bulk of discussion and much of the terminology relate in one way or another to these four elements. What one often finds, however, is that forms of these different process elements are thrown together in grab-bag style as if they were all comparable terms. It is not uncommon to find, say, symbolic interactionism, ethnography and constructionism simply set side by side as 'methodologies', 'approaches', 'perspectives', or something similar. Yet they are not truly comparable. Lumping them together without distinction is a bit like talking about putting tomato sauce, condiments and groceries in one basket. One feels compelled to say, 'Hang on a moment! Tomato sauce is one of many forms of condiment. And all condiments are groceries. Let's do some sorting out here'. Similarly, one may feel urged to do some sorting out when confronted by items like symbolic interactionism, ethnography and constructionism all slung together.

Ethnography, after all, is a *methodology*. It is one of many particular research designs that guide a researcher in choosing methods and shape the use of the methods chosen. Symbolic interactionism, for its part, is a *theoretical perspective* that informs a range of methodologies, including some forms of ethnography. As a theoretical perspective, it is an approach to understanding and explaining society and the human world, and grounds a set of assumptions that symbolic interactionist researchers typically bring to their methodology of choice.

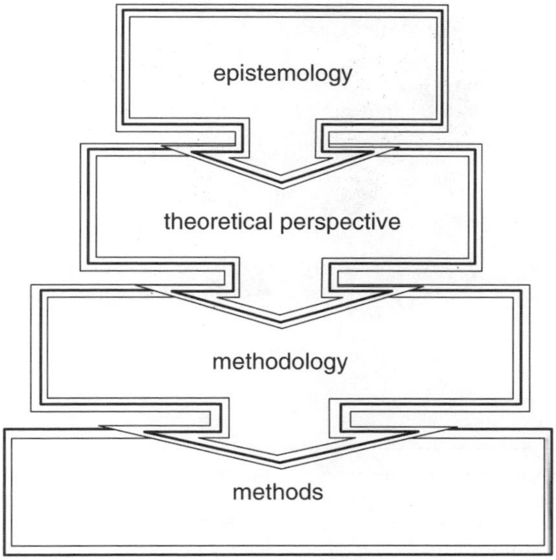

Figure 1

Constructionism[1] is an *epistemology* embodied in many theoretical perspectives, including symbolic interactionism as this is generally understood. An epistemology, we have already seen, is a way of understanding and explaining how we know what we know. What all this suggests is that symbolic interactionism, ethnography and constructionism need to be *related* to one another rather than merely set side by side as comparable, perhaps even competing, approaches or perpectives.

So there are epistemologies, theoretical perspectives and methodologies. If we add in *methods*, we have four elements that inform one another, as depicted in Figure 1.

One or other form of constructionism is the epistemology found, or at least claimed, in most perspectives other than those representing positivist and post-positivist paradigms. As we have just noted, the epistemology generally found embedded in symbolic interactionism is thoroughly constructionist in character. So, if we were to write down the four items we are talking about, we would be justified in drawing an arrow from constructionism to symbolic interactionism to indicate this relationship. Ethnography, a methodology that sprang in the first instance from anthropology and anthropological theory, has been adopted by symbolic interactionism and adapted to its own purposes. For that reason, our next arrow may go from symbolic interactionism to ethnography. Ethnography, in turn, has its methods of preference. Participant observation has traditionally been accorded pride of place. So, out with the pen for yet another arrow. Here, then, we have a specific example of an epistemology, a theoretical perspective, a methodology and a method, each informing the next as suggested in Figure 2.

The textbooks describe several epistemological positions, quite a number of theoretical stances, many methodologies, and almost countless methods. An attempt to list a representative sampling of each category might result in something like Table 1. (But note the several 'etceteras' occurring in this table. It is not an exhaustive listing.)

To denote another typical string, an arrow could start with 'objectivism'. Objectivism is the epistemological view that things exist as *meaningful* entities independently of consciousness and experience, that they have truth and meaning residing in them as objects ('objective' truth and

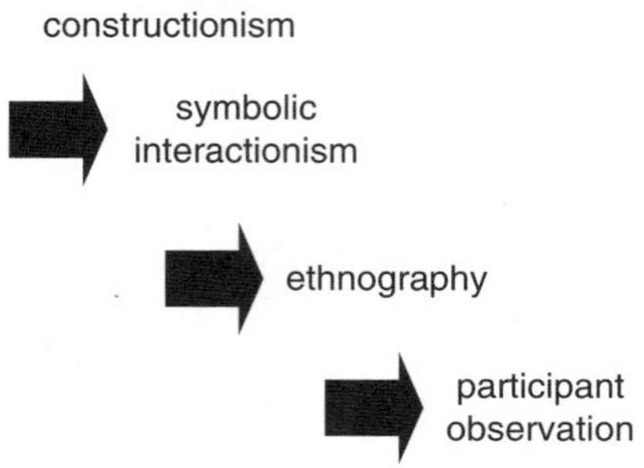

Figure 2

Table 1

Epistemology	Theoretical perspective	Methodology	Methods
Objectivism Constructionism Subjectivism (*and their variants*)	Postivism (and post-postivism) Interpretivism • Symbolic interactionism • Phenomenology • Hermeneutics Critical inquiry Feminism Postmodernism *etc.*	Experimental research Survey research Ethnography Phenomenological research Grounded theory Heuristic inquiry Action research Discourse analysis Feminist standpoint research *etc.*	Sampling Measurement and scaling Questionnaire Observation • participant • non-participant Interview Focus group Case study Life history Narrative Visual ethnographic methods Statistical analysis Data reduction Theme identification Comparative analysis Cognitive mapping Interpretative methods Document analysis Content analysis Conversation analysis *etc.*

meaning, therefore), and that careful (scientific?) research can attain that objective truth and meaning. This is the epistemology underpinning the positivist stance. Research done in positivist spirit might select to engage in survey research and employ the quantitative method of statistical analysis (see Figure 3). Once again the arrows go across the columns from first to last.

What purpose can these four elements serve?

For one thing, they can help to ensure the soundness of our research and make its outcomes convincing. Earlier we recognised the need to justify the methodologies and methods employed in our research. Setting forth our research process in terms of these four elements enables us to do this, for it constitutes a penetrating analysis of the process and points up the theoretical assumptions that underpin it and determine the status of its findings.

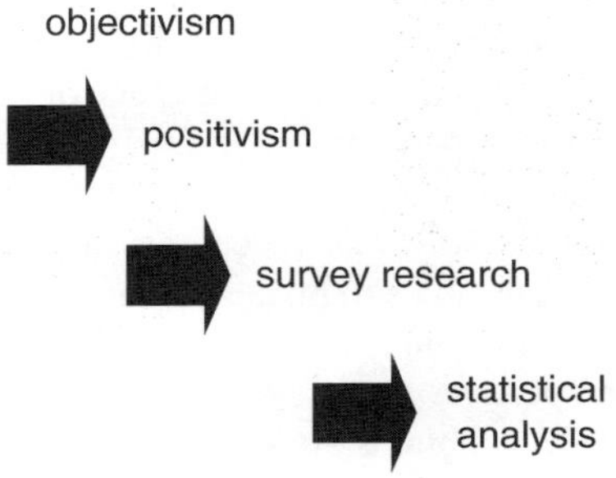

Figure 3

How might we outline our research proposal in these terms?

RESEARCH METHODS

First, we describe the concrete techniques or procedures we plan to use. There will be certain activities we engage in so as to gather and analyse our data. These activities are our research methods.

Given our goal of identifying and justifying the research process, it is important that we describe these methods as specifically as possible. To this end, we will not just talk about 'carrying out interviews' but will indicate in very detailed fashion what kind of interviews they are, what interviewing techniques are employed, and in what sort of setting the interviews are conducted. We will not just talk about 'participant observation' but will describe what kind of observation takes place and what degree of participation is involved. We will not just talk about 'identifying themes in the data' but will show what we mean by themes, how the themes emerge, how they are identified, and what is done with them when they do.

RESEARCH METHODOLOGY

We now describe our strategy or plan of action. This is the research design that shapes our choice and use of particular methods and links them to the desired outcomes.

What is called for here is not only a description of the methodology but also an account of the rationale it provides for the choice of methods and the particular forms in which the methods are employed. Take ethnographic inquiry, for instance. Ethnographic inquiry in the spirit of symbolic interactionism seeks to uncover meanings and perceptions on the part of the people participating in the research, viewing these understandings against the backdrop of the people's overall worldview or 'culture'. In line with this approach, the researcher strives to see things from the perspective of the participants. It is this that makes sense of the researcher's stated intention to carry out *unstructured* interviews and to use a *non-directive* form of questioning within them.

THEORETICAL PERSPECTIVE

Next we describe the philosophical stance that lies behind our chosen methodology. We attempt to explain how it provides a context for the process and grounds its logic and criteria.

Inevitably, we bring a number of assumptions to our chosen methodology. We need, as best we can, to state what these assumptions are. This is precisely what we do when we elaborate our theoretical perspective. Such an elaboration is a statement of the assumptions brought to the research task and reflected in the methodology as we understand and employ it. If, for example, we engage in an ethnographic form of inquiry and gather data via participant observation, what assumptions are embedded in this way of proceeding? By the very nature of participant observation, some of the assumptions relate to matters of language and issues of intersubjectivity and communication. How, then, do we take account of these assumptions and justify them? By expounding our theoretical perspective, that is, our view of the human world and social life within that world, wherein such assumptions are grounded.

Symbolic interactionism is a theoretical perspective that grounds these assumptions in most explicit fashion. It deals directly with issues such as language, communication, interrelationships and community. As we shall see in more detail in Chapter 4, symbolic interactionism is all about those basic social interactions whereby we enter into the perceptions, attitudes and values of a community, becoming persons in the process. At its heart is the notion of being able to put ourselves in the place of others—the very notion we have already expressed in detailing our methodology and have catered for in the choice and shaping of our methods.

EPISTEMOLOGY

Finally, we need to describe the epistemelogy inherent in the theoretical perspective and therefore in the methodology we have chosen.

The theoretical perspective we have described is a way of looking at the world and making sense of it. It involves knowledge, therefore, and embodies a certain understanding of what is entailed in knowing, that is, *how we know what we know*. Epistemology deals with 'the nature of knowledge, its possibility, scope and general basis' (Hamlyn 1995, p. 242). Maynard (1994, p. 10) explains the relevance of epistemology to what we are about here: 'Epistemology is concerned with providing a philosophical grounding for deciding what kinds of knowledge are possible and how we can ensure that they are both adequate and legitimate'. Hence our need to identify, explain and justify the epistemological stance we have adopted.

There are, of course, quite a range of epistemologies. For a start, there is objectivism. Objectivist epistemology holds that meaning, and therefore meaningful reality, exists as such apart from the operation of any consciousness. That tree in the forest is a tree, regardless of whether anyone is aware of its existence or not. As an object of that kind ('objectively', therefore), it carries the intrinsic meaning of 'tree-ness'. When human beings recognise it as a tree, they are simply discovering a meaning that has been lying there in wait for them all along. We might approach our piece of ethnographic research in that spirit. Much of the early ethnography was certainly carried out in that spirit. In this objectivist view of 'what it means to know', understandings and values are considered to be objectified in the people we are studying and, if we go about it in the right way, we can discover the objective truth.

Another epistemology—constructionism—rejects this view of human knowledge. There is no objective truth waiting for us to discover it. Truth, or meaning, comes into existence in and out of our engagement with the realities in our world. There is no meaning without a mind. Meaning is not discovered, but constructed. In this understanding of knowledge, it is clear that different people may construct meaning in different ways, even in relation to the same phenomenon. Isn't this precisely what we find when we move from one era to another or from one culture to another? In this view of things, subject and object[2] emerge as partners in the generation of meaning.

We will be discussing objectivism in the context of positivism and post-positivism. We will deal with constructionism at some length (Chapter 3) since it is the epistemology that qualitative researchers tend to invoke. A third epistemological stance, subjectivism, comes to the fore in structuralist, post-structuralist and postmodernist forms of thought (and, in addition, often appears to be what people are actually describing when they claim to be talking about constructionism). In subjectivism, meaning does not come out of an interplay between subject and object but is imposed on the object by the subject. Here the object as such makes no contribution to the generation of meaning. It is tempting to say that in constructionism meaning is constructed out of something (the object), whereas in subjectivism meaning is created out of nothing. We humans are not that creative, however. Even in subjectivism we make meaning out of something. We import meaning from somewhere else. The meaning we ascribe to the object may come from our dreams, or from primordial archetypes we locate within our collective unconscious, or from the conjunction and aspects of the planets, or from religious beliefs, or from … That is to say, meaning comes from anything *but* an interaction between the subject and the object to which it is ascribed.

Much more can be said about possible epistemological stances, and the three we have referred to are not to be seen as watertight compartments. Hopefully, enough has been said here for us to recognise that epistemology bears mightily on the way we go about our research. Is there objective truth that we need to identify, and can identify, with precision and certitude? Or are there just humanly fashioned ways of seeing things whose processes we need to explore and which we can only come to understand through a similar process of meaning making? And is this making of meaning a subjective act essentially independent of the object, or do both subject and object contribute to the construction of meaning? Embedded in these questions is a range of epistemological stances, each of which implies a profound difference in how we do our researching and how we present our research outcomes.

WHAT ABOUT ONTOLOGY?

In the research literature there is frequent mention of ontology and you might be wondering why ontology does not figure in the schema developed to this point.

Ontology is the study of being. It is concerned with 'what is', with the nature of existence, with the structure of reality as such. Were we to introduce it into our framework, it would sit alongside epistemology informing the theoretical perspective, for each theoretical perspective embodies a certain way of understanding *what is* (ontology) as well as a certain way of understanding *what is means to know* (epistemology).

Ontological issues and epistemological issues tend to emerge together. As our terminology has already indicated, to talk of the construction of meaning is to talk of the construction of meaningful reality. Because of this confluence, writers in the research literature have trouble keeping ontology and epistemology apart conceptually. Realism (an ontological notion asserting that realities exist outside the mind) is often taken to imply objectivism (an epistemological notion asserting that meaning exists in objects independently of any consciousness). In some cases we even find realism identified with objectivism. Guba and Lincoln (1994, p. 108) certainly posit a necessary link between the two when they claim that 'if, for example, a "real" reality is assumed, the posture of the knower must be one of objective detachment or value freedom in order to be able to discover "how things really are" and "how things really work"'. In the chapters that follow, you and I will be listening to a large number of scholars who disagree with this position. Heidegger and Merleau-Ponty, for instance, frequently invoke a 'world always already there', but they are far from being objectivists.

True enough, the world is there regardless of whether human beings are conscious of it. As Macquarrie tells us (1973, p.57): 'If there were no human beings, there might still be galaxies, trees, rocks, and so on—and doubtless there were, in those long stretches of time before the evolution of *Homo sapiens* or any other human species that may have existed on earth'. But what kind of a world is there before conscious beings engage with it? Not an intelligible world, many would want to say. Not a world of meaning. It becomes a world of meaning only when meaning-making beings make sense of it.

From this point of view, accepting a world, and things in the world, existing independently of our consciousness of them does not imply that meanings exist independently of consciousness, as Guba and Lincoln seem to be saying. The existence of a world without a mind is conceivable. Meaning without a mind is not. Realism in ontology and constructionism in epistemology turn out to be quite compatible. This is itself an example of how ontological issues and epistemological issues arise together. Given that state of affairs, it would seem that we can deal with the ontological issues as they emerge without expanding our schema to include ontology.

This is borne out when we look at literature that plays up the importance of the ontological dimension in research. In many instances the authors are not talking about ontology at all. Blaikie (1993, p. 6), for example, acknowledges that the 'root definition of *ontology* is the "science or study of being"'. However, 'for the purposes of the present discussion', he takes ontology to mean 'the claims or assumptions that a particular approach to social enquiry makes about the nature of social reality' (p. 6). This, in itself, is unexceptionable. We need to recognise, however, that this is no longer ontology in its philosophical sense. Blaikie's use of the term roughly corresponds to what you and I are calling 'theoretical perspective'. It refers to how one views the world. Blaikie tells us that positivism 'entails an *ontology* of an ordered universe made up of atomistic, discrete and observable events' (p. 94). He tells us that, in the ontology of critical rationalism (the approach launched by Karl Popper), nature and social life 'are regarded as consisting of essential uniformities' (p.95). He tells us that interpretivism 'entails an *ontology* in which social reality is regarded as the product of processes by which social actors together negotiate the meanings for actions and situations' (p. 96). This is stretching the meaning of ontology well and truly beyond its boundaries.

It would seem preferable to retain the usage of 'theoretical perspective' and reserve the term 'ontology' for those occasions when we do need to talk about 'being'. This is something you and I cannot avoid doing when we come to grapple with, say, the philosophy of Martin Heidegger, for that is a radical ontology and needs to be dealt with in strictly ontological terms. Happy days ahead!

In the Middle Ages, the great ontological debate was between realists and nominalists and concerned the extramental reality, or irreality, of 'universals'. Are there, for example, just individual human beings or does 'humankind' have real existence too? Does humankind as such denote a reality in the world or is it just something that exists only in the mind? In more recent centuries, the major ontological debate has been between realists and idealists and concerns the extramental reality, or irreality, of anything whatsoever. While neither debate is without relevance to an analysis of the research process, it still seems the case that ontological issues can be dealt with adequately without complicating our four-column schema further by expressly introducing ontology.

IN ALL DIRECTIONS

Back we go to our arrows. We have been drawing arrows from left to right—from one item in one column to another item in the next column to the right. We should feel very free to do this.

First of all, there are few restrictions on where these left-to-right arrows may go. Any limitations that exist would seem to relate to the first two columns. We need to rule out drawing an arrow from constructionism or subjectivism to positivism (or, therefore, post-postivism), since positivism is objectivist by definition. Without a thoroughly objectivist epistemology, positivism would not be positivism as we understand it today. Nor would we want to draw an arrow from objectivism or subjectivism to phenomenology. Constructionism and phenomenology are so interwined that one could hardly be phenomenological while espousing either an objectivist or a subjectivist epistemology. And postmodernism well and truly jettisons any vestiges of an objectivist view of knowledge and meaning. Other than that, as we draw our arrows from column to column, it would seem that 'the sky's the limit'. Certainly, if it suits their purposes, any of the theoretical perspectives could make use of any of the methods. There are typical strings, to be sure, and we have noted two of them in Figure 2 and Figure 3, but 'typical' does not mean 'mandatory'.

Secondly, we can draw arrows from a particular item to more than one item in the column to the right. Historically, objectivism, constructionism and subjectivism have each informed quite a number of different perspectives. Similarly, one theoretical perspective often comes to be embodied in a number of methodologies. Symbolic interactionism is a case in point. It has informed both ethnography and grounded theory and we might well draw arrows from that theoretical perspective to each of those methodologies. Again, while critical inquiry will certainly be linked to action research, we can also draw an arrow from critical inquiry to ethnography. Yes, the critical form of inquiry has come to be embodied in ethnography too, transforming it in the process. Now it is no longer a characteristically uncritical form of research that merely seeks to understand a culture. It is critical ethnography, a methodology that strives to unmask hegemony and address oppressive forces. In the same way, there can be a feminist ethnography or a postmodernist ethnography.

Still, we should not be so carried away with our sense of freedom in drawing arrows from left to right that we forget to draw arrows in other directions as well. Our arrows can fly from right to left too. In terms of what informs what, going from left to right would seem a logical progression. At the same time, in describing our piece of research, we found our starting point in methods and methodology. This suggests that, to mark the chronological succession of events in our research, the arrows may need to be drawn from right to left as well.

Certainly, they may. Not too many of us embark on a piece of social research with epistemology as our starting point. 'I am a constructionist. Therefore, I will investigate …' Hardly. We typically start with a real-life issue that needs to be addressed, a problem that needs to be solved, a question that needs to be answered. We plan our research in terms of that issue or problem or question. What, we go on to ask, are the further issues, problems or questions implicit in the one we start with? What, then, is the aim and what are the objectives of our research? What strategy seems likely to provide what we are looking for? What does that strategy direct us to do to achieve our aims and objectives? In this way our research question, incorporating the purposes of our research, leads us to methodology and methods.

We need, of course, to justify our chosen methodology and methods. In the end, we want outcomes that merit respect. We want the observers of our research to recognise it as sound research. Our conclusions need to stand up. On some understandings of research (and of truth), this will mean that we are after objective, valid and generalisable conclusions as the outcome of our research. On other understandings, this is never realisable. Human knowledge is not like that. At best, our outcomes will be suggestive rather than conclusive. They will be plausible, perhaps even convincing, ways of seeing things—and, to be sure, helpful ways of seeing things—but certainly not any 'one true way' of seeing things. We may be positivists or non-positivists, therefore. Either way, we need to be concerned about the process we have engaged in; we need to lay that process out for the scrutiny of the observer; we need to defend that process as a form of human inquiry that should be taken seriously. It is this that sends us to our theoretical perspective and epistemology and calls upon us to expound them incisively. From methods and methodology to theoretical perspective and epistemology, then. Now our arrows are travelling from right to left.

Speaking in this vein sounds as if we create a methodology for ourselves—as if the focus of our research leads us to devise our own ways of proceeding that allow us to achieve our purposes. That, as it happens, is precisely the case. In a very real sense, every piece of research is unique and calls for a unique methodology. We, as the researcher, have to develop it.

If that is the case, why are we bothering with the plethora of methodologies and methods set forth for us so profusely that they seem like William James's 'blooming, buzzing confusion'? Why don't we just sit down and work out for ourselves how we are to go about it?

In the end, that is precisely what we have to do. Yet a study of how other people have gone about the task of human inquiry serves us well and is surely indispensable. Attending to recognised research designs and their various theoretical underpinnings exercises a formative influence upon us. It awakens us to ways of research we would never otherwise have conceived of. It makes us much more aware of what is *possible* in research. Even so, it is by no means a matter of plucking a methodology off the shelf. We acquaint ourselves with the various methodologies. We evaluate their presuppositions. We weigh their strengths and weaknesses. Having done all that and more besides, we still have to forge a methodology that will meet *our* particular purposes in *this* research. One of the established methodologies may suit the task that confronts us. Or perhaps none of them do and we find ourselves drawing on several methodologies, moulding them into a way of proceeding that achieves the outcomes we look to. Perhaps we need to be more inventive still and create a methodology that in many respects is quite new. Even if we tread this track of innovation and invention, our engagement with the various methodologies in use will have played a crucial educative role.

Arrows right to left as well as left to right. What about arrows up and down? Yes, that too. Renowned critical theorist Jürgen Habermas carried on a debate with hermeneuticist Hans-Georg Gadamer over many years and out of that interplay there developed for Habermas a 'critical hermeneutics'. Here we have critical theory coming to inform hermeneutics. In our four-column model, the arrow would rise up the same column ('theoretical perspective') from critical inquiry to hermeneutics. Similarly, we can talk of critical feminism or feminist critical inquiry, of postmodernist feminism or postmodernist critical inquiry. There is plenty of scope for arrows up and down.

THE GREAT DIVIDE

In the model we are following here, you will notice that the distinction between qualitative research and quantitative research occurs at the level of methods. It does not occur at the level of epistemology or theoretical perspective. What does occur back there at those exalted levels is a distinction between objectivist/positivist research, on the one hand, and constructionist or subjectivist research, on the other. Yet, in most research textbooks, it is qualitative research and quantitative research that are set against each other as polar opposites. Just as the student of Latin is taught very early on via the opening lines of *Casesar's Gallic Wars* that 'All Gaul is divided into three parts', so every beginning researcher learns at once that all research is divided into two parts—and these are 'qualitative' and 'quantitative', respectively.

Our model suggests that this divide—objectivist research associated with quantitative methods over against constructionist or subjectivist research associated with qualitative methods—is far from justified. Most methodologies known today as forms of 'qualitative research' have in the past been carried out in an utterly empiricist, positivist manner. This is true, as we have already noted, of the early history of ethnography. On the other hand, quantification is by no means ruled out within non-positivist research. We may consider ourselves utterly devoted to qualitative research methods. Yet, when we think about investigations carried out in the normal course of our daily lives, how often measuring and counting turn out to be essential to our purposes. The ability to measure and count is a precious human achievement and it behoves us not to be dismissive of it. We should accept that, whatever research we engage in, it is possible for either qualitative methods or quantitative methods, or both, to serve our purposes. Our research can be qualitative or quantitative, or both qualitative and quantitative, without this being in any way problematic.

What would seem to be problematic is any attempt to be at once objectivist and constructionist (or subjectivist). On the face of it, to say that there is objective meaning and, in the same breath, to say that there is no objective meaning certainly does appear contradictory. To be sure, the postmodernist world that has grown up around us calls all our cherished antinomies into question, and we are invited today to embrace 'fuzzy logic' rather than the logic we have known in the past with its principle of contradiction. Nevertheless, even at the threshold of the 21st century, not too many of us are comfortable with such ostensibly blatant contradiction in what we claim.

To avoid such discomfort, we will need to be consistently objectivist or consistently constructionist (or subjectivist).

If we seek to be consistently objectivist, we will distinguish scientifically established objective meanings from subjective meanings that people hold in everyday fashion and that at best 'reflect' or 'mirror' or 'approximate' objective meanings. We will accept, of course, that these subjective meanings are important in people's lives and we may adopt qualitative methods of ascertaining what those meanings are. This is epistemologically consistent. It has a downside, all the same. It makes people's everyday understandings inferior, epistemologically, to more scientific understandings. In this way of viewing things, one cannot predicate of people's everyday understandings the truth claims one makes for what is scientifically established.

If we seek to be consistently constructionist, we will put all understandings, scientific and non-scientific alike, on the very same footing. They are all constructions. None is objective or absolute or truly generalisable. Scientific knowledge is just a particular form of constructed knowledge designed to serve particular purposes—and, yes, it serves them well. Constructionists may indeed make use of quantitative methods but their constructionism makes a difference. We need to ask ourselves, in fact, what a piece of quantitative research looks like when it is informed by a constructionist epistemology. What difference does that make to it? Well, for a start, it makes a big difference to the truth claims proffered on its behalf, all the more so as one moves towards subjectivism rather than constructionism. No longer is there talk of objectivity, or validity, or generalisability. For all that, there is ample recognition that, after its own fashion, quantitative research has valuable contributions to make, even to a study of the farthest reaches of human being.

Is this scaffolding proving helpful? If so, let us go on to examine the items in some of its columns. We will confine ourselves to the first two columns. We will look at epistemological issues and issues relating to theoretical perspectives.

As already foreshadowed, the epistemological stance of objectivism will be considered in the context of positivism, with which it is so closely allied. Constructionism, as the epistemology claimed in most qualitative approaches today, deserves extended treatment. Our discussion of the constructionist theorising of knowledge will set it against the subjectivism only too often articulated under the rubric of constructionism and found self-professedly in much structuralist, post-structuralist and postmodernist thought.

After our discussion of positivism, the theoretical perspectives we go on to study are interpretivism, critical inquiry, feminism and postmodernism. Thinking about postmodernism will make it necessary for us to delve also into structuralism and post-structurealism.

As we discuss these perspectives and stances, we should remind ourselves many times over that we are not exploring them for merely speculative purposes. You and I will allow ourselves to be led at times into very theoretical material indeed. Nevertheless, we will refuse to wear the charge of being abstract intellectualisers, divorced from experience and action. It is our very inquiry into human experience and action that sends us this far afield. The long journey we are embarking upon arises out of an awareness on our part that, at every point in our research—in our observing, our interpreting, our reporting, and everything else we do as researchers—we inject a host of assumptions. These are assumptions about human knowledge and assumptions about realities encountered in our human world. Such assumptions shape for us the meaning of research questions, the purposiveness of research methodologies, and the interpretability of research findings. Without unpacking these assumptions and clarifying them, no one (including ourselves!) can really divine what our research has been or what it is now saying.

Performing this task of explication and explanation is precisely what we are about here. Far from being a theorising that takes researchers from their research, it is a theorising embedded in the research act itself. Without it, research is not research.

25

The Emergence of the Social Sciences

MARC J. SMITH

1 Introduction

As you saw in Chapters 1 and 2, the creation of objective knowledge has been a central goal of science for quite a while. This chapter explores attempts by social scientists to create 'objective knowledge' about the social world. A special emphasis is placed upon the way in which our assumptions about the construction of knowledge have implications for the collection and interpretation of empirical evidence. There are seven sections in this chapter. The first two examine the ideas associated with positivism, particularly the six general assumptions which underpin this approach. We see how positivism played an important role in generating claims about objective knowledge in the social sciences. Most significantly, the positivist approach draws a great deal from the Enlightenment thinkers outlined in Chapter 2, especially in the way in which they placed a stress upon the search for certainty and universal explanations. Section 3 focuses upon how the construction of objective knowledge or 'hard science' has been, and can be, misleading. Two case studies, on scientific racism and positivist criminology, are used to demonstrate how the values and prejudices of social scientists can masquerade as social facts in scientific accounts of social differences and in the relationship between normal and abnormal behaviour.

In sections 4 and 5 we see how important it is to distinguish positivism from the broader approach of empiricism, by focusing upon the differences between the positivist approaches in the twentieth century and the falsificationist method developed by Karl Popper. Section 6 explores one social science discipline, economics, in order to demonstrate how the empiricist approaches identified in this chapter appear within a particular field of human knowledge. Economics is a good example; first, because of its associations with objective accounts of social relations and, second, because of the clearly identifiable positions which exist within economic methodology. Finally, in section 7 we return briefly to the six general assumptions of positivism to highlight the differences between empiricism and positivism.

Positivism develops ideas established during the Enlightenment, but ...

In Chapter 2 we looked at the origins of scientific thinking and the ways in which these ideas were applied to the study of social phenomena during the Enlightenment. In this chapter we consider the legacy of the Enlightenment in explaining and understanding social life. The most significant feature of social science in the last two centuries has been the rise to dominance and the subsequent fall of the positivist tradition. Positivism has been increasingly questioned since the middle of the twentieth century. Even if positivism is something that many social researchers would like to forget, it is hard to imagine any social scientific approach which does not, even now, draw from or develop its ideas in opposition to the positivist approach. The label of positivism has been applied to a wide variety of approaches in the social sciences, all of which claimed to offer a 'scientific' or **objective** picture of the social world and its constituent parts. As a result, the term 'positivism' has become very ambiguous and often contains different assumptions for different people. To make matters worse, 'positivism' is often used as a synonymous term for 'empiricism', but it is important to recognize that empiricism is a broad church and that it is possible to be empiricist without being positivist.

... take care, positivism means different things to different social scientists.

9

	Definition	Implication
Naturalism	Positivists are committed to naturalism, the idea that it is possible to transfer the assumptions and methods of natural sciences to the study of social objects, often referred to as the 'unification of method'.	This means that you would study behaviour, institutions and society in much the same way as studying, for example, chemical processes, hydraulic systems, geological structures. The closed system of a scientific experiment is often taken as a model for knowledge production in the social sciences.
Phenomenalism	Phenomenalism is the assumption that only knowledge gained through observed experience can be taken seriously. If something cannot be directly experienced it is said to be **metaphysical** – beyond our physical senses.	If we cannot touch it, see it, hear it, taste it or smell it, then an object cannot be said to exist except in so far as it is an idea of something. For example, 'happiness' is something which exists only in people's minds and cannot be directly physically experienced.
Nominalism	Nominalism shares with phenomenalism the argument that concepts must be based upon experience, but it also asserts that concepts have no use other than as names. Words are seen as pure reflections of things. It is, of course, very difficult to do this because the words we use are usually far more than simple descriptions.	All concepts or ideas which are not directly experienced through the senses are meaningless. In a strict sense, concepts such as the 'unconscious' and 'capitalism' are all names for things which we can't directly experience through our senses. Therefore, by this criteria, such concepts are meaningless.
Atomism	Atomism is a particular approach to the definition of objects. Atomism states that the objects of scientific study are discrete, that is, the objects cannot be broken down into any smaller parts. These objects act as the foundations of a scientific study. Collective objects are thus the sum total of their smaller atomic components.	When approaching any field of study, atomists look for the smallest observable units which cannot be broken down any further. When studying a society the most discrete unit is often taken as the individual. Atomistic explanations of society would start with the individual and regard society as no more than a collection of individuals.
Scientific Laws	The purpose of science is to develop laws. To develop a scientific law you start from the observation of a particular set of objects and look for regularities. The regular appearance of two or more things together, or in some kind of sequence, can be called an **empirical regularity.** This is sometimes described as a constant conjunction of events. You then explore whether the same regularities occur in other similar circumstances. A scientific law is a general statement which describes and explains empirical regularities which occur in different places and at different times.	The search for scientific laws involves finding empirical regularities, such as the well known example of smoking tobacco and developing lung cancer. Social scientists adopting this assumption would look for empirical regularities between, say, • poverty and crime, • the money supply and price inflation, • school class sizes and literacy levels, • gender and earnings, and so on. In practice, one is usually taken as the cause of the other. For instance, high levels of poverty are seen as a causal factor in crime levels.
Facts/Values	Facts and values are seen as distinct. Only facts can be regarded as scientific. Facts can be empirically verified, that is, observed, measured and explained by reference to observational evidence. Values involve subjective assessments and claims about what ought to be. Thus values cannot be observed, measured or explained.	Social scientists accepting these assumptions would distinguish scientific statements, which describe what is the case, from unscientific value-laden statements. For example, a measure of the number of homeless is often viewed as a fact whereas the statement that homelessness is a social evil is a value statement.

assumptions of positivism

naturalism
phenomenalism
nominalism
atomism
scientific laws
facts/values

When this box appears, the shaded portions will indicate which assumptions are at work.

Figure 3.1 The six general assumptions of positivism.
The terms in bold are also defined in the glossary.

As a result, the potential for conceptual confusion is very large, so this chapter offers a guide to the issues raised by the positivist and empiricist approaches within the social sciences.

1.1 Defining positivism

In Chapter 2 you discovered that the idea of science is closely associated with authoritative knowledge. Positivism is, perhaps, the most important attempt to generate authoritative knowledge about the social world. Actually, it is possible to define 'positivism' in many different ways. Nevertheless, it can be argued that there are three generations of positivists within the social sciences, as the social theorist William Outhwaite has usefully suggested:

See sections 2 and 3.

- the positivist traditions established in the nineteenth century (Auguste Comte, Herbert Spencer and some interpretations of Émile Durkheim);

See section 4.

- the logical positivism of the Vienna Circle (A.J. Ayer and Rudolf Carnap) in the early twentieth century;
- the 'standard positivist account', developed in the post-war period in the West, (associated with Carl Hempel) which emphasized the importance of value freedom, hard facts and prediction as a basis for offering policy proposals for governments, businesses and other private institutions.

(adapted from Outhwaite, 1987, pp.5–8)

Although there are three generations of positivist thinkers, it is important to establish what they hold in common. Norman Blaikie in *Approaches to Social Enquiry* (1993) suggests that certain shared assumptions can be identified without overlooking the significant differences between them. These six general assumptions, presented in Figure 3.1, are not solely associated with positivism but only positivism puts them together in this unique way. In particular, positivist science has a preference for empirical data which can be observed and measured so that the various component parts can be compared for their relative frequency. On the basis of such quantitative evidence, it is possible to generate law-like regularities which may then be generalized to other situations. Each of the six assumptions is explored in the sections that follow by reference to different forms of positivism.

Summary

Positivist approaches to the social sciences claim the label scientific, for they assume things can be studied as hard facts and the relationships between these facts established as scientific laws. For positivists, such laws have the status of truth and social objects can be studied in much the same way as natural objects.

2 Positivism and the foundations of the social sciences

As you will be aware from Chapter 2, the Enlightenment introduced new ways of thinking about the natural and social worlds, and that, after the Enlightenment, the world could no longer be explained as a manifestation of some divine plan in which the Church provided an authoritative account of both the natural and the social worlds in the name of God. Human beings were seen increasingly as the originators of knowledge. This means that instead of simply describing and clarifying what God had created, knowledge was seen as human-made and constantly open to question. Critical inquiry came to be seen as essential to human progress. The social transformations of the seventeenth and eighteenth centuries also produced a whole series of new objects of analysis, including 'society', the 'economy', the 'mind', the 'modern state', the 'individual' and the 'realm of ideas', and these objects have become the focus of analysis for the social sciences.

Post-Enlightenment knowledge is increasingly seen as human-made, rather than divine in origin.

The commitment to science as a means of promoting human progress is evident in the writings of Antoine Destutt de Tracy, a French rationalist philosopher working in the midst of the French Revolution. De Tracy proposed the foundation of the discipline of 'ideology' as the 'scientific study of ideas' as early as 1797. In this way, it was argued, science could reveal how society worked and, with this in mind, a rational social order could be sketched out, planned and implemented. Science, defined as the pursuit of truth, offered a means of social engineering so that social evils, such as conflict and war, could be eliminated and human progress achieved. Thus the choice of progress or catastrophe was seen as resting in human hands. In the context of the maelstrom of changes accompanying the emergence of the modern world, it was not altogether surprising that the certainties of religious faith were replaced by the belief in the certainties of science.

Rational scientific knowledge of human societies raises the possibility of improving the human condition.

This section highlights three approaches from the nineteenth century (Outhwaite's first generation of positivists) which have had an impact on contemporary social science. The positivism of Auguste Comte, the evolutionary utilitarianism of Herbert Spencer and the study of the social facts advocated by Émile Durkheim, each in their different ways, linked science to progress. You should bear in mind that each of these earlier positivist approaches illustrates some, but not all, of the six general assumptions of positivism identified in Figure 3.1.

↓ Missing from 2nd Edition.

2.1 Comte and the positivist philosophy

The most influential early positivist was Auguste Comte (1798–1857). Comte was a 'man with a mission', for he believed it was possible to reconstruct human knowledge in order to build a better society. He brought together the search for truth (from modern science) with the faith in progress which has been a key feature of Western thinking since the Enlightenment. For Comte, the Enlightenment was the last step in clearing away the mistaken assumptions of premodern knowledge systems. In so doing, human beings were placed at the centre of knowledge production.

Comte
naturalism
phenomenalism
nominalism
atomism
scientific laws
facts/values

However, Comte believed that one task remained. the construction of a new system of knowledge which could offer new certainties and new truths. Although Comte seems to have been associated more often with sociology, his work was also a crucial step in the development of both economics and political science.

Scientific knowledge was seen as a way of identifying new foundations and new certainties in modern societies.

Comte is adopting the assumption of naturalism.

For Comte, knowledge was characterized by change and development. He argued that earlier fictitious or religious forms of knowledge, based upon superstitions, were in decay. In fact, they had already given way to philosophical criticisms which were to stimulate the Enlightenment. Comte defined this critical stage as the period of metaphysics, but he argued that it was destructive rather than constructive, for although the Enlightenment had usefully challenged the prevailing way of thinking, it did not provide a suitable alternative to religion in a way which secured the stability of the social order. He proposed his own brand of scientific certainty to fill the vacuum left by the collapse of traditional and religious ideas. In order to find a replacement for 'divine truths', Comte looked to the natural sciences to establish a new foundation for objective knowledge. To emphasize this, he called his approach to the study of society 'social physics' and believed that it was possible to discover the scientific laws that governed social life in just the same way as laws had been identified in Newtonian physics, such as the physical laws of motion and light.

See Chapter 2, section 2.1 on Newton's view of science.

Comte sees science as a way of addressing human needs.

Through the use of the scientific method, as he defined it, Comte sought to restore order to his own society, and heal the wounds of the war, destruction and disorder which had characterized Europe since the French Revolution of 1789. When so much was uncertain, science seemed to provide a new way of establishing fixed and solid knowledge which could act as a means of reassurance. By looking at Comte's scientific vision we can see that the emergence of the social sciences was closely tied to his beliefs about what constituted a civilized society. Indeed, Comte envisaged that *social physics* could fill the gap left by the decline of faith and provide a new force for social cohesion or 'civic morality'. Figure 3.2 demonstrates how Comte saw each stage in the development of knowledge as grounded in a particular social order.

	I	II	III
Stage of knowledge	fictitious knowledge	metaphysical knowledge	scientific knowledge
Foundation of beliefs	faith and custom	philosophy	rational logic
Social base	family	state	humanity

Figure 3.2 Comte's three stages of scientific development and the corresponding bases of the social order.

With the passing of the social orders based upon the authority of the household and the authority of the state, the time was ripe for a new social order which could deliver the needs and desires of humanity as a whole. In the same way, fictitious and metaphysical knowledge would give way to science (Bryant, 1985). Positivism has now all but disappeared, but the link

certainty not available – Hume.

between scientific knowledge and meeting the needs and wants of human beings is its most tangible legacy.

Comte sought to build upon the established disciplines of the natural sciences constructing a hierarchy of disciplines which reflected the degree to which the forms of knowledge in question had succeeded in overcoming pre-scientific stages of development (stages I to II in Figure 3.2). He argued that astronomy, physics, chemistry and physiology had already moved through these stages. For example, in astronomy the fictitious stage can be seen in the belief that the Earth was the centre of the universe, the metaphysical stage endowed the planets with emotional qualities, and scientific astronomy marked a definite break by providing objective scientific laws which explain the solar system. Comte believed that his own project of social physics represented the beginning of just such a movement in social science taking it from the second to the third stage. In this way, he believed that the processes at work in society could be understood and explained with the same clarity as the scientific theories of planetary orbits around the Sun. For Comte, social science should attempt to emulate the progress of the natural sciences and develop scientific laws.

Comte is assuming that scientific laws are the goal of intellectual inquiry, and that science involves moving beyond metaphysics.

Activity 3.1

Turn now to Reading A, 'The positive philosophy and scientific laws', which is an extract from Auguste Comte's *The Positive Philosophy* (1853/1871). Make notes on Comte's account of the emergence of the positive science and try to answer the following questions:

- How does Comte see 'progress' in relation to scientific knowledge?
- What is the role played by statics and dynamics in the study of social facts?

You may find it useful to glance back at the circuit of knowledge in Chapter 2 (Figure 2.5) and look for the connections which Comte emphasizes as important when studying society.

Social scientists often distinguish between the analysis of social structure and the analysis of social change and, in Comte's work, we can see how this came about. Comte's positive science sought to identify the laws of *social statics* and of *social dynamics*. Once we identify these laws, he argued, social engineering was a real possibility. The *laws of social statics* were an attempt to draw upon the closest natural science to human existence, the study of human anatomy. The comparison of society to a living body served as a powerful analogy during the early development of social science. In doing this, Comte provided a way of identifying the internal operation of an existing set of social institutions and the conditions which generated co-operation. The *laws of social dynamics* offered a means of accounting for evolutionary change and the complex processes at work in the development of European societies.

See Figure 2.7 'The anatomy class' in Chapter 2.

Positivism established the tendency to view scientific laws of change as separate from scientific laws of social relations.

The most important conceptual legacy of Comte is this distinction between *statics* and *dynamics*: social, political and economic structures and relations at a given time are different from the processes which impact upon these structures. Fitting these two dimensions together is still a problem for contemporary social scientists. For instance, the models of economics are often static models which do not recognize process and change except as a series of time-slices (a sequence of static states). This can be seen in the case of the concept of equilibrium in a market (where supply and demand for a specific commodity are balanced at a given price). This model of the market is limited because it assumes that the values of given products (i.e. prices) do not change over time, making the model unrealistic and raising questions about its usefulness as a representation of the economy. Any approach which attempts to explain the working of the real economy (or any other object in social science) is subject to severe limitations unless it succeeds in integrating both of these dimensions. Similarly, in psychology, the treatment of the personality as having fixed characteristics which do not evolve in response to experiences and social interaction is likely to prove inadequate when applied to the study of human beings throughout their lifespan. It is not just in the so-called 'hard' social sciences that we find this issue. In the field of cultural studies a great deal of emphasis is placed upon the study of language. The key foundational work in the study of language is Ferdinand de Saussure's *Course in General Linguistics* (1916/1959). This emphasizes the distinction between synchrony (the structure of language at a moment in history) and diachrony (the processes through which meaningful language systems change) – a direct application of the static/dynamic distinction to the form and development of language systems.

You will come back to this when you read Chapter 6, section 2 on the relationship between structure and language.

So far we have concentrated upon the legacy of Comte's positivist approach for contemporary social science. Nevertheless, it is also interesting and useful to look at how Comte analysed his own society. By situating Comte, that is, by locating Comte's work historically and socially, we can see how he was responding to a particular set of problems and issues, namely the 'disorder' of European societies in the late eighteenth and early nineteenth centuries. While this does not invalidate the uses of Comte's ideas, it should raise questions about why we find elements of his works within the social sciences today. We can gain a better insight into the implications of this approach by looking at the way in which he characterizes the laws of statics and dynamics in European societies. Comte concentrates upon the role of military conquest and the annexation of territory in accounting for the laws of *social dynamics*. In addition, when defining his object of analysis in the laws of *social statics*, he treats humanity as if it is solely constituted by the 'white race'. Such arguments are a reflection of Comte's own cultural values and the broader cultural assumptions of European societies in the nineteenth century. The focus upon conquest and annexation between nations was central to this period in a similar way to the way in which concern about globalization affects social scientific research today.

The exclusive focus on the 'white race' was also a common feature of early social science, although this was often left as an implicit assumption. Since the standard of living in European societies in Comte's lifetime was grounded in colonial conquest, it should not be surprising that the knowledge constructed, in many subtle ways, not only justified but actually celebrated the dominance of European societies over other societies. This

Eurocentric orientation, and the exclusion of non-European peoples from explicit consideration, reveals the historically and socially specific content of Comte's work. We address this issue in more detail in section 3 when we consider scientific racism. The impact of Comte's positivism can be seen in the assertion that it was possible to study facts independently of values, even though he clearly undermines his own claim to have achieved this in his own work. Nevertheless, the distinction between facts and values was to have a profound effect on the development of social scientific disciplines, regardless of whether Comte's adoption of the organic analogy (treating society as if it worked like a body) offered a feasible working model. While Comte made an explicit link between knowledge and human progress, he left one question unresolved: how was it possible to measure human progress? This is the concern of the next section. L Addressed by J. Bentham.

In positivism, values were often portrayed as facts even though this approach claimed to eliminate values, prejudice and common sense from scientific knowledge.

2.2 Positivism, utilitarianism and human happiness

Spencer

naturalism
phenomenalism
nominalism
atomism
scientific laws
facts/values

In the later nineteenth century, the organic analogy was more systematically developed by Herbert Spencer (1820–1903). Spencer was a Victorian liberal who drew upon both the ideas of utilitarian liberalism and Charles Darwin's evolutionary theory to provide a scientific explanation of the industrial and trading success of Britain during one of the most sustained periods of high growth in Western history. Spencer's legacy can be seen in the association of positivism with justifications of inequality. Spencer based his approach upon the utilitarian ideas of Jeremy Bentham (1748–1832), who had constructed a way of measuring human progress. So, to understand Spencer we must first explore the ideas of utilitarianism in a little more detail.

Bentham devised a means of calculating the consequences of various courses of action in terms of utility – that is, the satisfaction of our preferences. The assumptions underlying this model are revealing. Bentham characterized human beings as essentially pleasure seeking or pain avoiding. He also endowed them with the capacity to make rational choices which would maximize pleasure and minimize pain (which he referred to as the 'felicific calculus'). This is the foundation of the framework which social scientists now call cost–benefit analysis and which established the guiding principles of contemporary economics, political science and some branches of psychology. In addition, Bentham provided a powerful and compelling basis for relating social science to policy making.

Human progress is understood here as the consequence of changes which overall produce more benefits than costs.

Using Bentham's felicific calculus, it was then possible, once the likely consequences of a policy were established, to advise politicians on which policy would promote 'the greatest good for the greatest number'. By securing the goals of human happiness and collective welfare, this approach also offers a way of delivering human progress. Because of its focus upon effects rather than causes, utilitarianism is often described as consequentialism. In addition, this approach treated collective bodies as if they were simply the aggregate (the sum total effect) of the observable actors involved. The economy is thus an aggregate of individuals, firms and households; the political process is the aggregate of voters in elections, and parties and pressure groups (which are aggregates of their members) in between elections; and so on.

The utilitarian approach places special emphasis upon the assumption of atomism. Spencer adopts the general assumptions of positivism, except for nominalism.

Activity 3.2

Turn to Reading B, drawn from 'Of the principle of utility' from Jeremy Bentham's *An Introduction to the Principles of Morals and Legislation* (1824/1987).

- Identify the first seven principles of Bentham's calculus for ensuring that the common welfare is maximized. You may also wish to consider how accurately this approach describes human decision making.

This reading is something of a manifesto for establishing how to go about the activity of social inquiry as well as how human knowledge fits into the needs of policy makers. Remember that social science has always existed with the purpose of making social conditions better. The question you should ask yourself is whether this is the best way of doing so. (Whatever your response, also ask yourself why you made this judgement.)

Further uses of utilitarianism are developed in Chapter 4.

There are many ways of applying this approach; for the moment we concentrate on Spencer's use of utilitarianism. Spencer portrayed the market system, through which individuals made their pleasure-seeking and pain-avoiding choices, as an evolutionary mechanism operating along the lines of Darwin's principle of natural selection. So, Spencer argued that the organization of society can only be analysed in terms of the consequences of human actions, and that the flow of benefits and costs in society reflected the 'survival of the fittest'. We can trace the consequences of these assumptions in Spencer's approach to social inequalities. The hierarchical organization of society becomes the logical consequence of competitive processes in the market economy, implying that those at the top are the fittest and those at the bottom are the least fit. It was also common in this period of imperialist expansion to categorize social groups in racial terms, both externally in the colonies and internally when considering the lower classes, the peasantry or marginalized ethnic groups. Thus, in the same way as Comte, Spencer's work can be seen as a rationalization of the eugenicist concerns with racial degeneration rather than with the objective study of facts. When we situate social scientists and philosophers of social science, we can then begin to see how the cultural values of the time and place flow into academic writing.

Durkheim
naturalism
phenomenalism
nominalism
atomism
scientific laws
facts/values

2.3 Durkheim and the positivist science

Now we return to an old favourite. The social scientist most often given the label of positivist is Émile Durkheim (1858–1917), although it is far from clear that his approach can be categorized so easily. For the time being, let's treat him as a positivist to keep things straightforward. Above all, Durkheim argued that each discipline had its own distinctive (set of) object(s) of analysis and that these objects could be studied in the same way as the natural sciences, as 'social facts'. In particular, Durkheim pioneered the careful and systematic study of empirical evidence, which we tend to attribute to scientific approaches in the study of society. In *The Rules of Sociological Method* (1895/1982), Durkheim recognized that the way in which the object of analysis in each discipline was defined had an important effect on the way the discipline was constructed, and how this limited the scope of inquiry, that psychologists should stick to the mind, economists to the economy, and so on. In the case of sociology, with society as the object, he argued that the complexity of social relations demanded greater care in the treatment of empirical evidence than was common in his day. He attempted to establish relations of cause and effect between variables which tend to occur in the same place and time (empirical regularities). In *Suicide* (1897/1952), Durkheim employed the comparative-historical method: suicide rates were compared for different countries and regions and across different social groups, as well as over time. This enabled him to establish the correlations or **empirical regularities** which could be taken seriously in a scientific account of suicide.

Durkheim developed a strong case for the identification of empirical regularities as the basis for establishing scientific laws in the social sciences.

9

There are considerable problems in trying to establish relations of cause and effect between things which tend to correspond in a regular way. How we draw connections depends upon whether we find an explanation convincing or plausible. Durkheim argued that the study of suicide offered a way of clarifying this problem. Suicide rates are relatively consistent over time in different locations and different groups. Since, in each year, suicides involve different people, Durkheim argued that it was safe to assume that an explanation could be found by looking for an external cause which tended to coincide with the suicide rates. Conventional wisdom at the time placed the causes of suicide (defined as an irrational act) within the constitution of the individuals concerned. Unlike crime, where the same people can commit the same action again over time and with the same motives, in the case of suicide the same people cannot take their own lives twice. As a result, suicide has been described as the ultimate dependent variable, for once the effect (suicide) is established then there is only the task of specifying definite causes which explain its occurrence. Thus the study of suicide provided a useful means of demonstrating the potential for Durkheim's scientific approach. In addition, this allowed Durkheim to challenge the prevailing moralistic and religious approaches – which attributed suicide to sin, madness, personal defects and abnormalities – as speculative and lacking empirical substantiation. He accepted that psychology could explain the motives of a specific individual but not provide a general explanation of suicide as a 'social fact'.

Durkheim saw suicide as a clear-cut 'effect' of some other cause – by looking for empirical regularities he hoped to isolate the causes.

Durkheim's chosen sources of empirical data also helped in the identification of relevant and plausible independent variables. The statistics were derived from death certificates which also contained relatively accurate evidence of religious affiliation, location and family dependency. From this evidence, Durkheim identified and eliminated variables, such as climate and mental illness, which had featured heavily in accounts of suicide at the time. For instance, he identified that while members of the Jewish faith had a high recorded rate of mental illness, they nevertheless had low levels of suicide – disproving the link between mental health and suicide. He concluded that three variables should be taken seriously: membership of religious groupings such as Catholic, Jewish or Protestant faiths; the location of members of society in towns and in the countryside; and whether there were dependants who would suffer from such an event. Durkheim was careful to limit his claims to the examination of the propensities of groups to contribute 'definite quotas of voluntary deaths', rather than suggesting that such relationships were automatically evident in individual cases (or there would be, for example, no unmarried Protestants left alive in towns).

Social facts were categorized as either normal or abnormal (pathological).

Durkheim also used the medical and organic metaphors in describing social facts as manifestations of normal or pathological conditions, a common feature of positivist approaches in this period. In the next section, we consider two examples of how social scientists contributed towards the definition of subordinate groups in society as abnormal and pathological. As you saw in Chapter 2, the use of analogies and metaphors is a consistent feature of scientific knowledge. However, this raises immediate difficulties in accepting such scientific approaches as free of cultural values. You also need to consider what science means and to whom is it meaningful whenever you explore an approach in social science.

Summary

Positivism was, in part, a response to the disorder and chaos witnessed within European societies in the early nineteenth century. It also offered a confident vision for the production of objective knowledge as a basis for reconstructing social life. The optimism expressed by such approaches made positivist science a plausible framework for social science as western Europe prospered in the later nineteenth century.

The study of social facts and scientific laws became the common feature of social scientific practice; values remained unacknowledged, rather than absent, from social science.

Early positivism represented more of an attitude to social life than one agreed method. This allowed it to be combined with other approaches (such as utilitarianism) and to become an adaptable set of tools for policy making.

3 The normal and the pathological: positivism in practice

So that you can see how science conveys powerful meanings and associations, this section explores two case studies which demonstrate the implications of early positivism when applied to social objects – the emergence of scientific racism and positivist criminology. The study of the abnormal in order to establish the normal operation of social and cognitive processes is a common technique in social scientific investigation. For economists and political scientists, crises in the running of a society provide an opportunity for reflection upon basic principles and often reveal new features which had previously been overlooked. In psychology, it has been argued, the study of unusual and 'dysfunctional' cases can reveal processes in cognition and the development of personalities which had previously been

Summary

Rather than ignore 'racist' values, they 'transmuted' them into Facts.

The case studies of scientific racism and positivist criminology demonstrate the ways in which human beings can be constructed as objective categories. In both cases the prejudices of social scientists were portrayed as social facts and were received as such by the academic audience. For positivists, facts are clearly separate from values.

The central problem in establishing how the values of a particular culture come to be translated into social scientific facts is whether this is simply a matter of the scientific method becoming contaminated, that it needs cleaning up, or that the assumption of the separation of facts and values is itself untenable.

The individuals who were categorized as having abnormal or pathological features were treated along medical lines and the role of social scientists was to establish a cure. The voices which remained unheard in these studies were those of the objectified individuals, who were reduced to a position of powerlessness.

4 Positivism, language and science

***Carnap/Ayer* logical positivism**

- naturalism
- phenomenalism
- nominalism
- atomism
- scientific laws
- facts/values

Logical positivists endorse all six assumptions and seek to remove all traces of metaphysics from scientific knowledge.

9

In this section we examine probably the most influential form of positivism in the twentieth century, logical positivism. This approach drew upon the techniques of formal logic in order to create an objective account of human knowledge; to achieve objectivity, every sentence and every statement had to be the direct expression of observable things and all speculative ideas removed. We also explore how, in the post-war period, some positivists developed a more practically oriented approach, which came to be known as standard positivism. These approaches dominated empirical social science in the 1950s and 1960s. This was because they appeared to be able to generate objective or 'authoritative' knowledge which could be relied upon to identify the 'facts of a given situation' and thus could be used for social planning.

4.1 The logical positivist approach

Logical positivism places an exceptional emphasis upon sensory perception and the role of observation in research as the foundation of knowledge. For this reason, logical positivism is often seen as an 'extreme' version of the positivist approaches for it attempts to eradicate **metaphysics** completely from the production of scientific knowledge. Scientific statements are seen as pictures or snapshots of the things they refer to, like reflections in a mirror. The two case studies you encountered in the previous section demonstrate the extent to which values interfered with the claims of positivism to eliminate speculation and subjective viewpoints. The stated aim of the logical positivist approach is to cleanse scientific knowledge of speculative thinking, for it is not tied in a direct and demonstrable way to experience.

'Noumenal' world of Kant.

Picture theory.

The origins of this approach can be identified in Bertrand Russell's and Alfred Whitehead's *Principia Mathematica* (1910–13/1935) and the work of the young Ludwig Wittgenstein, *Tractatus Logico-Philosophicus* (1921/1961). The logical positivist approach was promoted by the Vienna Circle, a group of philosophers, intellectuals and scientists who clarified the logical positivist approach and sought to develop these anti-metaphysical ideas in the 1920s. Although, in common with the earlier nineteenth-century positivists, they sought to eradicate speculative metaphysics from science, they were well aware of the way in which speculative assumptions had actually prevented earlier positivists from achieving this goal. In other words, the earlier positivist approaches had simply not managed to live up to the standards of science. Logical positivism advocated an approach to the generation of new knowledge and human progress whereby sense experiences were taken as the starting-point for all ideas.

Logical positivists adopt the position of atomism – see Figure 3.1.

Following Wittgenstein, the logical positivists accepted that statements should reflect the atomic facts of the world and for them the world is made up of such separate irreducible atomic objects and their configurations. To each object, they argued, corresponds a definite statement which provides an accurate picture of that object. In this **mimetic** approach words should be a simple mirror reflection of things. This approach was popularized by Rudolf Carnap in *The Unity of Science* (1932/1995) and A.J. Ayer in *Language, Truth and Logic* (1936/1990). Such texts had a profound effect on the practices of social scientists in the mid twentieth century, until Karl Popper published his alternative approach to scientific method in English in the late 1950s. For Rudolf Carnap (1891–1970), a member of the Vienna Circle who was to have an enormous effect on the interpretation of the natural sciences in post-war America, this approach can be best described as **physicalism**. It was believed that, since there was only one set of physical things to study, a common language could be developed to encompass all human experiences. Carnap saw the physical language as the universal descriptive language which could be applied to the study of all things. The various specialized vocabularies of the sciences, he argued, could all be related back to the same set of 'physical determinations'. Therefore it was possible to unify the sciences into one common body of knowledge, although he added that this was simply physics.

For positivists, scientific statements should be simple pictures of the observable world.

From the opening sections of this chapter you will recall how early positivism was extremely ambitious in its claims about establishing objective knowledge. However, unlike the earlier positivist efforts of Comte, logical positivists were concerned to be much more cautious about what it was possible to claim before a statement acquired the status of truth. In order to achieve this, they took the form of language used in the construction of scientific knowledge as a much more serious issue. The logical positivists developed their approach in an attempt to ensure that human values and metaphysical speculation did not interfere with the acquisition and accumulation of objective knowledge. In particular, they drew upon the use of the linguistic distinction between **analytic** and **synthetic** statements in order to demonstrate how an empiricist science could be developed. This distinction was a key element of empiricism before and after the Enlightenment. The use of this distinction led many to refer to this new approach as the 'linguistic turn' in the philosophy of the social sciences. Analytic statements are seen as true by definition, such as the classic example of 'All bachelors are unmarried'. Synthetic statements, on the other hand, are based upon observation and, as such, can be seen to be contributing new knowledge, such as 'London contains more bachelors than any other part of Britain'.

Logical positivists use the distinction between analytic and synthetic statements to clarify the idea of objective scientific knowledge – you may find it useful to look back at the emergence of empiricism (see Chapter 2, section 3.3).

The aim of the logical positivist movement was to eliminate all the so-called analytic statements in science which were speculative synthetic statements. If it had been held to be true that all single men tend to drink too much, we could construct a statement such as 'All bachelors are drunkards'. Of course, this statement is inaccurate in synthetic terms, for observation would reveal the existence of unmarried teetotal males, and we would have to replace it with something like 'Some bachelors are drunkards on Friday nights'. It is not an analytic statement because being a bachelor simply means being an unmarried male, it does not by definition alone mean that the person in question drinks too much alcohol. Consequently, the claim in the statement 'All bachelors are drunkards' involves a speculative rather than a true claim about the behaviour of all unmarried males, and implies certain things about the behaviour of married males. A synthetic claim which conforms to the criteria established by the logical positivists could be 'On average, males consume more alcohol than females in a given year even taking into account differential body weight'. However, such a claim would not be true by definition, only in terms of its accuracy as a picture of observed experience. In other words, the truth of such statements can only be established by reference to observable evidence and if behaviour changes then the statement would have to change.

Statements which violate the distinction between analytic and synthetic are seen as meaningless.

The social sciences are packed full of claims which purport to be true, but which in fact violate the distinction between analytic and synthetic statements. For instance, the claim that 'All men are instrumental and all women are expressive' acts as an important foundational assumption – sometimes explicitly stated – in many areas of work on the family or in studies of working patterns. Nevertheless, in terms of the criteria established by the logical positivists, this conflates the analytic statement 'All men are human beings of the male sex' with the synthetic statement 'In the situation x, males tend to behave in ways which are instrumental'. The extent to which men and women are instrumental and expressive is a matter for empirical assessment; it would have to be demonstrated through observational evidence that the statement was an accurate one. If the central aim of logical positivism is to eliminate statements which conflate the analytic with the synthetic then, following this process of elimination, we would be left only with those analytic statements which were 'true by definition' and synthetic statements which were 'true by reference to empirical evidence'. In this way, through the careful application of the scientific method, logical positivists would hope to accumulate more accurate knowledge of social behaviour.

9

The logical positivist approach uses the method of **induction** which involves collecting observational data and building theories to explain the observations. It is assumed that we experience our perceptions and impressions without any prior sets of theories to organize them. In short, we soak up sensations in the way that sponges absorb water. Supporters of induction also assume that, through repeated experiences of the same phenomena within particular instances, the phenomena will operate in much the same way in other such instances of which we have no experience. This then has the status of a general law. Thus the method of inducof the same sense-data. Inductive approaches tend to treat the act of observation as if the observer plays no constructive role in the act and simply absorbs information, and so treat the mind as a passive receiver of sense-data, soaking up information, to which it responds in a predictable way. These are unrealistic assumptions which we examine again when we look at Popper in section 5.

See section 5.

Hempel standard positivism

naturalism
phenomenalism
nominalism
atomism
scientific laws
facts/values

4.3 The standard positivist approach

In response to these problems some positivist philosophers, such as Carl Hempel (1905–1997), place a greater stress on the deductive process to explain the steps involved in theory construction. Hempel's work modifies the arguments of the logical positivists to take account of the way in which scientists usually start with a set of general laws and theories before directly engaging in empirical research. His emphasis upon deduction came to be regarded as the model for the post-war standard positivist account of the scientific method. **Deduction** refers to the mental process through which valid conclusions can be logically deduced from valid premises, that is, a generalization or universal law. Deduction is used to establish a series of logical steps in the process of forming a theoretical statement about the world. Usually, a general claim is made and this is applied to a particular case or instance with a definite set of conditions. Finally, a conclusion is posed and the scientist engages in research to establish whether the predicted outcome is indeed the case. The truth value of the premise acts as a guarantor of the truth value of the conclusions, for the conclusions do not go beyond what is already contained within the premises. Let's look at two examples of deductive reasoning to illustrate the relationship between premises and conclusions.

Example A

1 Heavy people leave deep footprints.

2 This person makes deep footprints.

3 This person is heavy.

Example B

1 All children are cruel.

2 This person is a child.

3 This person is cruel.

The starting-point in deductive reasoning is theoretical (although the theory may have been established through induction at some point) and then observation serves as a basis for testing statements (regardless of how the statements are derived). In this general sense, deductive reasoning is compatible with all kinds of approaches to **knowledge construction** and does not of itself stand or fall as a logical technique, even if the initial premises are false, as Example B demonstrates, for not all children are cruel. In this case, logical consistency (alongside predictive success) is an important feature of a scientific explanation. It is important to recognize, as did Hempel, that the strict limits placed upon the scientific method developed by the Vienna Circle were too restrictive for science to be an innovative process.

The logical positivists had argued that a statement is either cognitively significant (in describing the world as it is) or it is simply meaningless. However, Hempel recognized that the empirical content of a theoretical statement could only be considered to be meaningful when the theory is placed within its 'interpretive system'. As with the logical positivist approach, Hempel is concerned to identify the empirical regularities which are significant in definite situations. Empirical regularities are not only seen as necessary for establishing a causal law, they are sufficient; that is, all you need for a law statement is 'if A then B'.

So, within the standard positivist approach, scientific explanations involve a particular way of developing a logical argument. We can see this when we look at how deduction was viewed as a process through which valid conclusions are deduced from valid premises in order to ensure logical consistency, as in Examples A and B above. In this model of scientific inquiry, one proceeds from general law statements (within specific conditions) to explain and predict particular cases. The combination of the laws and specified conditions (the premises) are often defined as the explanans statement and the conclusion is described as the explanandum statement (Hempel, 1965; but for a quick introduction see: Keat and Urry, 1982, pp.12–13; Hacking, 1983, pp.2–6). With this approach, providing that it is possible to identify the operating laws at work and the conditions within which these laws operate, then it should be feasible to predict the outcome accurately. The emphasis on the role of prediction implies that there should be complete symmetry between predicting something and explaining it. Successful prediction in this model is the same as providing a satisfactory explanation. So, in practice, if a scientific theory appears to predict an outcome accurately, then it must be true.

Standard positivists put a special emphasis on the symmetrical relationship between explanation and prediction.

An example of this way of thinking can be seen in the study of human behaviour, developed by the psychologists B.F. Skinner and J.B. Watson, in the development of the concept of 'operant conditioning'. This approach, which became known as **behaviourism**, focuses upon the ways in which individuals respond to various stimuli and/or conditions in ways that maximize rewards and minimize punishments. One of the theoretical premises of this approach is the assumption that human beings are passive recipients of external pushes or pulls and that they modify their behaviour accordingly. The behaviourist approach also rests upon the assumption that it is misleading to speculate about the inner states or human creativity in explaining social life. In this way, it is plausible to construct a scientific statement, starting from a series of principles or laws (for example, operant conditioning) which are accepted as the motivation for certain forms of human behaviour, and examine an activity which demonstrates these laws in specific conditions, such as obedience or disobedience in schools. By establishing the conditions in which obedience is reinforced and/or disobedience deterred, it is possible to explain the level of order or disorder in certain schools. The success of this explanation would be measured in terms of its ability to produce the predicted results in the conditions of an experiment (to remove the possible influence of other variables in the empirical evidence); that is, a **closed system**. Of course, this whole approach rests upon the implicit assumption that the organization of school life can only be studied through the observation of the actual behaviour of the individuals involved – teachers, head, pupils, governors and so on.

Similar to 9 Utilitarian view –

Behaviourism is covered in more detail in Chapter 5.

9

5.1 Situating Popper

Popper empiricism

- naturalism
- phenomenalism
- nominalism
- atomism
- scientific laws
- facts/values

Values are part of the research process, but they must be strictly controlled through reference to empirical evidence.

Many of the familiar ideas we hold about natural and social scientific method were initially developed within one or other tradition in Vienna in the early twentieth century. You have already encountered one of these approaches, logical positivism, in the previous section. Vienna was a cosmopolitan crossroads through which the peoples of Europe flowed. They brought with them a wide range of ideas, adding these to the mix of German philosophical traditions which were already well established (we examine the impact of these traditions on the social sciences in the next chapter). The events in Europe in the 1930s (the rise of the Nazi regime and the spread of anti-semitism) were to lead to an intellectual diaspora. Whole scientific communities fled from Nazi persecution either for 'political crimes' or because they were Jewish. Many of the most influential natural and social scientists in the twentieth century took refuge in the USA and, as a consequence, the philosophical sensitivities of central Europe came into direct contact with the empirical techniques of American social science. This was to produce an explosion in theorizing about the assumptions and methods of the social sciences from the 1950s onwards. One particular approach, that of Karl Popper, was to have a profound impact on social scientific method in the West after World War II.

Popper (1902–1992) wanted to rescue the idea of the scientific method from the emerging criticisms of positivism and believed that there was a better way of resolving the problems involved. He concentrated on examining induction, which, as you will recall, emphasizes the importance of starting with observations of particular instances and then moving towards constructing theories and laws which explain what is happening in more than one of these particular instances. For Popper, the inductive method simply cannot sustain the explanatory weight placed upon it. He raises two problems with induction, the 'psychological problem' and the 'logical problem'.

- The 'psychological problem' involves finding an answer to the question of why 'reasonable people' expect new situations to operate in the same way as ones they know from experience. For Hume, the psychological problem is resolved through 'custom' or habit, which enables us to function in our everyday lives. *Hume: We have to live, make progress.*
- The 'logical problem' involves the question of whether we are justified in leaping from statements about situations we have experienced to statements about situations we have not experienced. You saw in the previous sections how central to the positivist approaches was the shift from particular instance to general law. *Hume: Problem of Induction.*

Popper starts from the assumption that we can never be certain that an explanatory statement about one set of conditions will work just as well elsewhere.

For Popper, science should not operate by the rules of everyday common sense whereby we simply assume that a new situation will be the same as the situations we already know and understand. Popper asks us to focus upon the logical problem of not knowing what is going to happen in a new situation and accept this condition as something we scientists simply have to live with. Rather than expecting our knowledge to be confirmed, he developed a methodology around the possibility of refutating our existing theories. He argued that we cannot expect statements about situations we have not experienced to be true (Popper, 1972, pp.1–31). This also led him to rethink the concept of 'truth', not as an absolute (that a statement is simply true or false), but rather as a matter of degree (he defined truth as 'verisimilitude'). Actually, there is a deeper foundational problem with induction, most clearly identified by P.F. Strawson (1952). Many scientists adopted induction on the grounds that it worked, that it was possible simply to observe, measure and explain, and that, over time, the principle of induction had, through observation, become accepted. However, in logical terms, the principle of induction is exactly that – a theoretical principle established prior to experience. Hence at the heart of the induction approach there is a contradiction, in that the operating principle violates its own rules.

Induction violates its own rules, for it is still a theoretical principle prior to experience itself.

Popper's view was that, if we believe a particular approach can be confirmed and gather evidence accordingly, we are left in a position where we are unlikely to make 'scientific discoveries'. This would mean that we simply reinforce what we already know rather than finding new ways of stating and solving problems (Popper, 1959, pp.269–76). Popper attributed this insight, in part, to Albert Einstein's self-critical attitude towards his theory of relativity. Rather than treating his work as the establishment of a new set of truths to replace the Newtonian truths which had been established for more than two centuries, Einstein regarded his own theories of physics as tentative steps on the road to a general theory. He also attempted to specify the conditions in which his account could be disproven (rather than indicating ways in which his arguments could be confirmed). For Popper, it was precisely this undogmatic 'attitude' towards science which came as a revelation, and not Einstein's theories of physics. In this critical attempt to apply the powers of reason, controlled through empirical tests, he was to make the claim that science could deliver progress even without truth. Thus we can never be conclusively certain of any of our statements about the world, for there is always the possibility of a 'disconfirming instance'.

Popper proposes that all explanations should be subject to empirical tests and that a healthy sense of doubt was crucial for the progress of knowledge.

5.2 Conjectures and refutations: Popper's falsificationist solution

It is important to distinguish Popper's approach from that of the logical positivists of the Vienna Circle. On the crucial question of the **demarcation criteria** between science and non-science, the logical positivists saw this simply in terms of whether a statement described the world as it was observed, or whether that statement was a metaphysical one and hence meaningless. For Popper, a statement is never meaningless, even if it is unscientific. In the development of his 'hypothetico-deductive model', Popper challenged the logical positivist demarcation criteria. The falsificationist method rests upon the assumption that the demarcation criteria between what is science and what is pseudo-science rests upon whether the statement involved is testable or not, rather than whether it is true or false. A pseudo-scientific statement is one which is tautologous, in that the conclusion is already implied in the premises and, as such, there is no possibility of falsification.

Popper adopts naturalism, but changes the criteria for demarcating scientific from non-scientific knowledge.

The origin of the hypothesis is unimportant for Popper, whether it is from a dream or a fanciful wish it remains useful so long as it can be submitted to an empirical test. Science is no longer the search for truth but, he argued, the careful and systematic use of the scientific method, that is, constructing statements about the world and testing them against the evidence. Thus Popper retained his commitment to the use of empirical evidence, but without the traps of positivism, such as the tendency to collect evidence which simply justified our existing beliefs and theories. This, he sugggested, would lead to stagnation in the accumulation of knowledge rather than progress (Popper, 1959, 1963). If you cannot disprove existing knowledge, then it will never change. Popper claimed to have solved the problem of induction. He argued that there is no way of arriving at a theory simply from experiment and/or observation. Without an original conjecture, one would not know where to start or which knowledge to seek in the first place.

Scientific hypotheses should be bold conjectures which could be tested against empirical evidence.

For Popper, **falsification** rather than **verification** becomes the criterion of science; in other words, scientists should find ways of disproving their working hypotheses and theories. The focus on refutation rather than confirmation prompts scientists to think harder about what they are doing and to innovate when the things they take for granted are questioned. Science becomes not the search for universal or objective truth, but a method, a set of logical procedures for the construction or testing of hypotheses, a process of 'trial and error'. Popper's approach specifies the means through which scientists can create progress rather than identifying the ends of knowledge. This approach is the only one compatible with Popper's liberal assumptions about what should constitute an 'open society', whereby each possible explanation of events is scrutinized in an open-minded and sensible way within an atmosphere of tolerance. For him, conjectures or hypotheses which survive attempts at refutation are seen as 'corroborated' but not confirmed (Popper, 1959, 1963). Popper asks us to be intentionally critical, to test ideas against the evidence to the limit and to avoid being dogmatic in research. Falsificationism, therefore, is as much an attitude to research as a set of methodological procedures.

Falsification is a set of procedures for scrutinizing existing knowledge claims and embodies the sceptical attitude proposed by Popper.

Activity 3.5

Now turn to Reading F, 'The professional stranger', by Eileen Barker, (1988) in which she discusses some of the problems encountered in her research into the Unification Church.

- Make notes on the steps involved in her research investigation and the choice of research techniques.
- Try to identify the working hypotheses of this investigation into a religious movement.

This is a fairly amibitious research project using quite a range of ways to gather evidence, yet it is all driven by a particular purpose. When you read social scientific research papers, you may find that the intention of the researcher is not immediately apparent – sometimes you have to read between the lines to identify what is going on. Don't worry if you find the second task quite difficult; if you read on you will find the answer.

For someone studying examples of social research in their chosen research field, there is a problem in trying to relate existing research sources to their own research practice. In particular, it is often difficult to disentangle the key working hypothesis from the broad set of issues examined in any individual study. Few studies clearly pinpoint one key idea or conjecture. In the case of Eileen Barker's research into the motivations which lead people to join a new religious movement, a whole range of issues immediately present themselves. Barker's research explores what it means to join the Unification Church – what motivates new recruits, how the sect introduces new members to the rituals and beliefs of the movement, what new members get out of the experience – as well as exploring how the Unification Church is viewed by people in the UK. However, there is an underlying hypothesis in this study which is a response to contemporary debates about new religious movements. Barker is responding specifically to newspaper accounts of the indoctrination and 'brainwashing' of new members in this and other religious sects. Therefore her key conjecture is:

> The Unification Church 'brainwashes' its members.

During the course of her study, Barker actually discovered that most members left the movement after a short period of time, usually 'burned out' from excessively intense involvement (Barker, 1984). This meant that the key conjecture had been falsified, for brainwashed members simply would not leave. Consequently, she was able to move on from the widely held simplistic hypothesis and investigate more effectively the complex motivations involved. As a result, we now know a great deal more about what it means to join a religious sect, which reinforces Popper's argument that refutation leads to the accumulation of knowledge.

The falsificationist version of the 'hypothetico-deductive method' developed by Popper is the most widely respected and influential version of the deductive model. However, we should also note that Popper's approach is an idealized reconstruction of the process through which scientists construct their theories and weigh up their hypotheses against the empirical evidence (modelled upon physics). For Popper, scientific advance can only come through the testing and attempted falsification of hypotheses replacing them, if necessary, by modified or new ones. Scientific progress thus involves a continual process of conjecture and refutation.

For Popper, statements which cannot be empirically tested are pseudo-scientific, but they are not meaningless.

(unlike the logical positivists).

Statements which cannot be empirically tested are simply non-scientific or tautological, and theories composed of such statements are dismissed as 'pseudo-sciences'. Popper specifically identifies psychoanalysis, astrology and Marxism as such approaches, so that the claims made by Freud, 'Mystic Meg' and Marx all suffer from the same flaws. For instance, Popper suggests that Marx made categorical rather than conditional claims about the nature of capitalism. A categorical claim contains the assumption that the statement must be true in all circumstances where it is relevant. For example, Marx made the categorical claim that, within the capitalist system, the interests of capital always overcome the interests of the workers. For Popper, the evidence that workers' interests can overcome the interests of capitalists suggests that this depends upon precise empirical conditions. In addition, he argues, Marx made a series of predictions which have not been borne out by experience, regarding the laws of motion of capitalism and the historical inevitability of revolution in advanced capitalist societies. By Popper's account of the **demarcation criteria**, Marxism falls far short of a scientific theory because it ignores refuting evidence.

The testing of hypotheses in the social sciences (or the treatment of established theories as conjectures) is a common feature of post-war sociological research. In the research on *The Symmetrical Family* (1973), the work of Michael Young and Peter Willmott can be seen as an attempt to test the 'march of progress thesis' against empirical evidence in the early 1970s. This thesis was developed within functionalist sociology in the 1940s and 1950s and portrays the normal family as nuclear in form and increasingly democratic in its internal relations between marital partners and between parents and children. One critic referred to this as a picture of 'sympathetic spouses and well adjusted children'. In their sample of homes in the south east of England, Young and Willmott demonstrate the corroboration of this thesis in both middle-class and working-class households. Interestingly, the research of Ann Oakley in *The Sociology of Housework* (1974), using **qualitative** data (in-depth interviews with forty housewives), can be taken as a falsification of these results, since she reveals women's profound dissatisfaction with housework and persistent inequalities between husbands and wives.

Falsification can be achieved through a variety of research methods. It is not solely connected to survey evidence.

An example of falsification of a hypothesis can be seen in the research of John Goldthorpe et al. in *The Affluent Worker Studies* (1968–9) which attempts to test the 'embourgeoisement thesis' (the conjecture that the working class were becoming middle class), a theme of sociology since the late nineteenth century. They discovered in their examination of the personal lives, working lives and political attitudes of workers who moved to the 'new town' of Luton following World War II that, while the working class is not becoming middle class, but is certainly experiencing a period of change. The traditional class-conscious working class, it is argued, is being transformed into instrumental self-interested affluent workers. In this case, an alternative hypothesis was generated – which had previously not been considered, so creating new knowledge. On a more critical note, this whole venture rests upon the assumption that the working class was actually a homogenous, class-conscious and organized proletariat in the first place, which historical research has since thrown into doubt. The identification of complex divisions in the organization of the working class over the last century, in terms of skill differentials, forms of association and cultural values, raises fundamental problems with the view that a largely homogenous working class is becoming more divided and fractured.

Both the 'march of progress thesis' and the 'embourgeoisement thesis' can be taken as examples of a common tendency in the social sciences to form hypotheses that assume that progress has indeed taken place, that human relations are becoming fairer and more just, more democratic and egalitarian, and that generally the lives of all members of society are getting better and better. Conversely, you may also encounter hypotheses based upon the assumption that human relations are worsening, that the social fabric is collapsing and that a 'golden age' of order, tranquillity and stability has vanished. These assumptions reflect an alternative underlying value position that 'progress' means decadence and degeneration. This attitude was

Falsification highlights the danger in believing that progress or social decline automatically occur over time. For Popper, progress is knowledge achieved by demonstrating that something is untrue.

epitomized by the political rhetoric of Sir John Stokes when he claimed that 'The twentieth century is a grotesque mistake.' Many hypotheses developed in social research in relation to the decline of religious participation, the 'rising tide' of crime, the increase in divorce and single parenthood are often based upon this underlying assumption. Such blanket claims about progress and moral decline should be regarded with a great deal of care, if not suspicion.

The success of the supporters of positivism in establishing this approach as the model of scientific inquiry to take seriously has helped create a storyline which often treats the Vienna Circle as the 'only game in town' in the 1920s. Many versions of the story of science go on to trace the success of Popper, a fellow Austrian, in developing the cutting edge of scientific inquiry in the post-war period. Popper became so highly regarded that some saw him as the 'Kant of the twentieth century'. In addition, his presence at the London School of Economics in the 1950s gave him a pivotal position in influencing social scientific practice. Until the 1960s, half of all the UK's graduates in the social sciences passed through the LSE and many went on to take up the new social science lectureships created by the expansion of higher education in the 1960s and 1970s. This academic generation placed Popper's approach firmly on the agenda of most undergraduate programmes. In fact, a whole range of alternatives existed in the early twentieth century which have had, and continue to have, an impact on social scientific practice, and many of these had their roots in Vienna. These idealist approaches, which put a greater emphasis on the role of ideas in the organization of empirical experience, are explored in greater detail in Chapter 4. Even social scientists in the post-war period who used the falsificationist approach did so in a variety of ways. It is also fair to say that social scientists have often paid lip-service to Popper's falsificationism although in practice they have behaved as if they were verificationists. This means that we need to be careful when examining how existing research is constructed. You will have the opportunity to explore the relationship between formal, perhaps idealized, accounts of scientific method and the actual practices of scientists in Chapter 5.

As you have seen in the previous sections on the history of science, approaches to the scientific method come and go, and each 'true view' has been replaced by another. For Popper, then, truth was a matter of degree rather than an absolute, because there was no way of being certain that the theories and assumptions we presently hold are true for all time. Instead, Popper turned critical inquiry and scepticism into a virtue by linking progress in knowledge to the refutation of existing laws and theories. Popper saw the development of scientific knowledge as an endless journey in which we have to discard worn-out truths in order to move on.

Summary

The method of induction, while popular as a conventional tool among natural and social scientists, became increasingly associated with confirming established opinions in the twentieth century. In addition, Popper and others argued that induction was not only untenable but self-contradictory. For Popper, the demarcation between science and non-science was whether or not a conjecture was testable.

Falsificationism was developed as an alternative approach, to allow for the use of the scientists' faculties for critical reasoning in the context of strict guidelines on the need for empirical testing at all stages of inquiry. In particular, truth was sacrificed to ensure progress in knowledge. This approach was empiricist but also managed to avoid some of the problems associated with positivism.

6 Positivist and empiricist approaches on the economy

In economics, positivism is associated with descriptive approaches to the economy, demonstrating how it works through the use of empirical evidence.

If we look at one social science discipline, in this case economics, we have the opportunity to explore the implications of each of the approaches discussed in this chapter so far. In particular, we focus on the positivist and falsificationist approaches in this field of knowledge. 'Positive economics' is an explicitly acknowledged label which many economists have taken to indicate the factual and scientific character of their work. The term 'positive' is taken to refer to the acceptance of a clear separation of facts from values, and hence positive economics is often defined in opposition to normative economics. Defined in this way, positive economics is descriptive economics, concerned with what 'is', whereas normative economics is value driven, concerned with what 'ought to be'. Positive economics has its roots in the advocacy of **induction** and **phenomenalism** by John Stuart Mill in *A System of Logic* (1843/1879) and the dominance of his *Principles of Political Economy* (1848/1970) in the teaching of economics in Britain in the nineteenth century. This did not go unchallenged, and deductivism was soon proposed as an alternative within economics. For much of the history of economics, the methodological pendulum has swung between these two positions. A useful example of the positivist attitude towards research can be found in Richard Lipsey's *Introduction to Positive Economics* (1963/1979), a standard textbook from the 1960s to the 1980s:

> Very roughly speaking, the scientific approach consists in relating questions to evidence. When presented with a controversial issue, the scientist will ask what is the evidence on both sides. He [*sic*] may then take a stand on the issue with more or less conviction depending on the weight of the evidence. If there is little or no evidence, the scientist will say that, at present, it is impossible to take a stand. He will then set about searching for relevant evidence. If he finds that the issue is framed in terms of questions about which it is impossible to gather evidence, he will try to recast the questions so that they can be answered by an appeal to evidence. This approach to a problem is what sets scientific inquiries off from other kinds of inquiries. ... Experimental science such as chemistry and some branches of psychology, have an advantage because it is possible to produce relevant evidence through controlled laboratory

> experiments. Other sciences ... must wait for time to throw up observations that may be used to test hypotheses.
>
> (Lipsey, 1979, pp.7–8)

The effect of textbook statements such as these should not be underestimated, for in any discipline we start to learn and become familiar with the material in a particular subject through standard disciplinary textbooks. This extract contains an uncritical approach towards the relationship between facts and values and does not even glance at the contentious issues surrounding the choice of topic and methods. Moral questions are treated as if they are of no concern to social researchers, in a way which is common in research within the natural sciences. This attitude expresses the view that science is the detached exercise of certain specified methods, regardless of the qualities of the objects in question. Human behaviour is seen as predictable in its responses to various stimuli; for instance, seasonal consumption patterns in the market place are quite predictable (we buy more toys just before Christmas, and tennis balls in June and July). Consequently, positive economics tends to treat explanations as useful only in so far as they make reliable predictions, preferably about large groups of individuals. In this context, a reliable prediction is one which is supported by repeated tests against empirical evidence.

Positive economics usually assumes that good explanations must be predictively successful.

As you saw in the quotation above from Lipsey, the importance of prediction is very closely tied to the desire to achieve some means of closure. Since it is not plausible to replicate the experimental situation when studying economic processes, positive economics has attempted to achieve this theoretically. This can be demonstrated by examining the theory of perfect competition, a set of assumptions about the operation of exchange relationships in markets. The acts of exchange in this model take place between firms and/or households. In the hypothetical state of perfect competition it is assumed that, at a particular price, the demand for goods or services will be balanced with the available supply of the same goods or services. The price in this condition is described as the equilibrium price. When we examine the assumptions about the actors involved, it becomes clearer how much this condition is an abstraction from real economic processes. The firms in this model are seen as 'price takers'; that is, they can respond to changes in prices by immediately altering their production rates. In addition, it is assumed that firms can enter and exit from different markets without difficulty. The consumers (or households) are assumed to have perfect knowledge of the goods and services and can alter their purchasing behaviour quickly and simply according to the principles of cost–benefit analysis. The behaviour of all the actors in this model is in terms of opportunity cost, that as individuals make choices to do things they prevent themselves from doing other things, as much as in terms of the satisfaction of their preferences through the action chosen. On the basis of this simple model then, complications are gradually introduced (such as the existence of monopolies, the presence of trade unions and restrictions introduced by the state) in an attempt to replicate the actual conditions of markets.

See Chapter 2, section 2.2 on experimental and theoretical closure in science.

Ultimately, the assumptions which underlie the rational behaviour of actors in the model are the weak point of the whole exercise, for human intentions, desires and interpretations are difficult to predict with the precision of a calculus. Much depends upon whether such theoretical devices are seen as heuristic devices for attempting to explain and understand complex social objects or as an accurate portrayal of real processes and events. While Lipsey raises the importance of refutations in generating scientific explanations and the impossibility of absolute proof, his account of theory construction and the collection of empirical evidence in economics is drawn from the 'covering law model' developed by Hempel which you explored in sections 4.3 and 4.4, as Figure 3.7 demonstrates. I must hasten to add that many contemporary economists would question the usefulness of this approach. I include it here simply as a useful example of the practical implications of constructing a positivist social science.

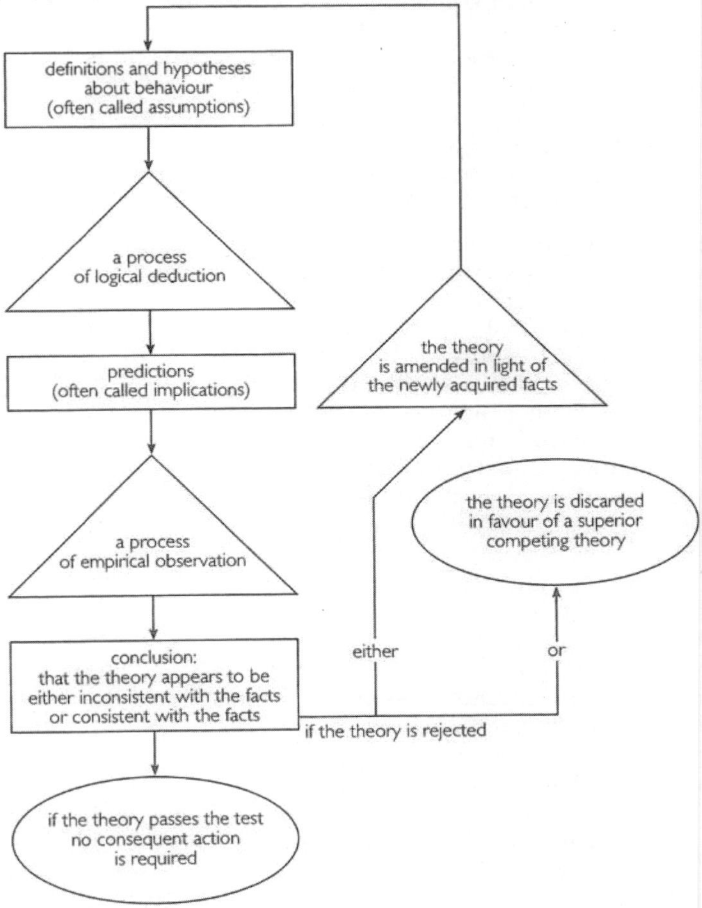

Figure 3.7 Richard Lipsey's version of the covering law model.

An interesting alternative approach, which still seeks to produce objective knowledge, can be seen in Milton Friedman's article 'The Methodology of Positive Economics' (Friedman, 1953). This approach has had a significant impact upon working economists as a guide to action in the processing of empirical data sets. Friedman argues strongly in favour of economics as an objective science. However, in some respects, his *methodological instrumentalist* approach differs from the covering law approach of Hempel. Unlike standard positivism, Friedman questions whether prediction should be the key criterion for establishing the authenticity of a theory. For

The instrumentalist approach in positive economics places less emphasis on prediction and sees all statements as guides to understanding.

Friedman, economic theories are instruments which cannot be seen in any way as true or false, and predictions hold no explanatory uses. Bruce Caldwell, an economist and historian of economic thought, suggests that these differences are instructive across the social sciences: 'Economists should not fall into the trap of believing that they have explained things when all they have done is predict accurately' (Caldwell, 1994, p.186).

Social scientists have often fallen into such traps by assuming that good predictors provide an explanation. Statistical correlations, where two variables reveal a common or similar frequency, are often used to good effect in identifying potential relationships. However, it is possible to achieve high correlations between variables where causal explanations are as yet undiscovered or are unlikely to be discovered. Some evidence exists of correlations between sunspot activity and particular weather systems. In contrast, the discovery of a high correlation between the growth of the stork population in western Europe and the human birth-rate can be seen as less plausible except for social scientists who believe in fairy stories.

With its emphasis upon prediction, economics is packed full of examples of statistical correlations which have been taken too seriously and transformed, inappropriately, into causal explanations. Economic policy makers in the early 1980s accepted Friedman's emphasis on the close relationship between the growth in the money supply in the economy and the inflation rate. Evidence suggested that when there was more money in circulation, following a time lag, prices increased, an argument supported by periods of hyperinflation such as in Germany in the early 1920s or in the first years of the Yeltsin administration in Russia in the early 1990s. However, this theory was applied in reverse under Thatcher's first administration of 1979–82, with the government limiting the money supply in order to deflate the economy and control inflation. In this situation, the predictive power of the theory was undermined. In the early 1980s the various indicators of the money supply suggested an increase in the supply, exceeding the targets suggested by economists, yet inflation declined. By 1985 the Bank of England expressed serious doubts about the money supply as a predictor and went on to question Friedman's analysis of the money–price relationship. In a more whimsical intervention, a Keynesian economist demonstrated that Scottish dysentery rates were a better predictor of inflation trends than the money supply. Others suggested that this was a good illustration of Goodhart's Law, which states that a theory works until it is applied as economic policy and affects the behaviour of those who are the object of the study. In this case, the change of government policy changed the processes at work in the economy and hence undermined the accuracy of the theory.

Economics contains evidence of significant progress through the falsificationist method to scientific knowledge.

Mark Blaug, whose work is largely responsible for the rebirth of interest in economic methodology since the late 1970s, suggests that the falsificationist approach developed by Popper offers a good description of what many economists do as well as a method which the remainder should adopt (Blaug, 1992). Blaug rests his case on the evidence of innovation and progress (both theoretical and empirical progress) in economics in the twentieth century, which he suggests emerged from the refutation of earlier approaches and the bold conjectures of economists which have survived attempts at refutation. Among his examples are the welfare economics of Antoine Pigou and Kenneth Arrow, the game theory of John von Neumann and Oskar Morgenstern, and econometrics (economic forecasting) by Paul Samuelson and others (Blaug, 1994, pp.109–36).

What is common to all the approaches you have encountered in this chapter, whether they are positivist or falsificationist, is their commitment to empiricism and the belief of their supporters that their method is applicable in all circumstances. Tony Lawson provides us with useful warning against attempting to impose a particular method regardless of the object in question:

> Imagine a situation in which an instrument of some sort has been found to be useful for a specific task. Let us suppose that a big stick is used successfully to beat and thereby to clean a dusty old mat. Imagine also that the inference is automatically made that if such an instrument is found to be useful for one job it must also be useful for any related jobs. Specifically, let us suppose that it is inferred from the success of the big stick in helping to clean the dusty old mat that it must also be of use in cleaning a dusty glass window – and that the window is duly beaten. No doubt many will find such an inference and act preposterous. But why? Presumably because we know enough of the nature of glass windows and big sticks to infer that (a) beating the window with a stick is unlikely to prove to be a successful way of cleaning it (to say the least); while (b) alternative more promising ways of cleaning the window can easily be devised. Imagine, furthermore, that the 'stick-cleans-windows' theory is put to the test and consequent upon the repeated instances of broken glass the inference repeatedly drawn is that it is necessary to 'try that little bit harder' – perhaps on the grounds that it is the wrong windows so far that have been beaten, and/or it is simply imagined that success is (always) around the corner. No doubt the perpetrator of the theory would be dismissed as a rather unreflective dogmatist. Certainly, he or she is unlikely to be retained for long as a window cleaner.
>
> (Lawson, 1994, p.258)

Lawson, a contemporary **realist** economist, believes that the things we study as social scientists have complex internal structures. This matters, he suggests, when we construct concepts and select methods to study our chosen objects. If this is the case – that one size does not fit all – then we need to be more flexible and innovative in our models of scientific inquiry.

Don't worry about realism yet, it's in Chapter 7.

7 Conclusion: the common foundations of empiricism

For much of this chapter we have explored a range of the key approaches which have all claimed to be able to generate objective scientific knowledge and the different ways in which they justify this claim. However, despite such wide differences regarding the relationship between theory and observation, the verificationist and falsificationist programmes have a great deal in common, especially their understanding of causality. For all these approaches an 'empirical regularity' is both necessary and sufficient for

9

establishing a **causal law**. This means that all empiricist approaches view closed systems as the means through which scientific explanations can be attained.

The battlefield between these competing approaches, rather than being strewn with dead bodies and mortally wounded scientists and philosophers, is more reminiscent of a ritual mock battle by the English Civil War Society – a great deal of smoke but very little real conflict. Ian Hacking, a philosopher of natural science, provides a neat summation of the differences between the positivist and verificationist assumptions of Carnap on the one hand and the falsificationism of Popper on the other. The differences between them can be seen as superficial when you consider the common foundations of each approach:

> Carnap thought that 'meanings' and a theory of 'language' matter to the philosophy of science. Popper despised them as scholastic. Carnap tried to explicate good reason in terms of a theory of 'confirmation'. Popper held that rationality consists in 'method'. Carnap believed in 'induction'; Popper held that there is no logic except 'deduction' ... whenever we find two philosophers who line up exactly opposite on a series of half a dozen points we know that in fact they agree about almost everything. They share an image of science.
>
> (Hacking, 1983, pp.4–5)

Despite the differences between the uses of induction and deduction, verification and falsification, there are common foundations.

Ultimately, in terms of what scientists actually do, there is not a great deal of difference between 'corroboration' and 'confirmation' except in terms of which formal logic such scientists adopt as their background frame of reference and mode of presentation. Even so, they agree upon the 'pretty sharp distinction between observation and theory', that 'scientific terminology is or ought to be precise', and that there should be a 'unity of science', that all sciences should utilize the same logic and methods (Hacking, 1983, p.5). On the big issues of the foundations of scientific knowledge and its role in generating human progress, it is impossible to slip a cigarette paper between them.

Activity 3.6

Now briefly return to the introduction at the start of this chapter and reread the six epistemological principles of positivism (Figure 3.1). Once you have completed this, make a list of the differences between the positivist approach and the more general empiricist position (as expressed by Popper, for instance).

So far, you have encountered a range of approaches which have been identified as positivist in some way or, more broadly, empiricist. Empiricism is often used as a synonymous label for positivism, but it also includes positions which can be described as post-positivist. Since Popper remains committed to empiricism and describes his approach as post-positivist, positivism can be categorized as a sub-branch of empiricism. Earlier, you saw how logical positivism subscribes to all of the six general assumptions of positivism. Empiricism involves the collection of observable empirical evidence of discrete variables or objects in order to test a hypothesis in a new situation as a way of generating new knowledge. Out of the six assumptions, **empiricism** unreservedly accepts the assumptions of **phenomenalism, atomism** and the possibility of general **scientific laws**.

Once we take Popper's falsificationist approach into account, we can also see it is possible to remain an empiricist without holding to the other three assumptions in the same way. In falsificationism it is possible to test value-laden statements which have no relationship to previous experience but which nevertheless remain open to (preferably simple) empirical test conditions. Thus in empiricism it is also possible to reject the principle of **nominalism,** for ideas are more than names for things we can experience. Post-positivist empiricism accepts that meaningful interpretations can play a legitimate part in science, which can cause problems in clearly distinguishing **facts** from **values**. However, this means that all statements, if they are to be regarded as objective in any sense, must be tied down by reference to strict empirical tests. Finally, falsificationism also qualifies our acceptance of **naturalism**, by accommodating different criteria for demarcating science from non-science. For some empiricists, science, it seems, is a set of methodological procedures rather than the identification of a true account of reality.

Popper empiricism

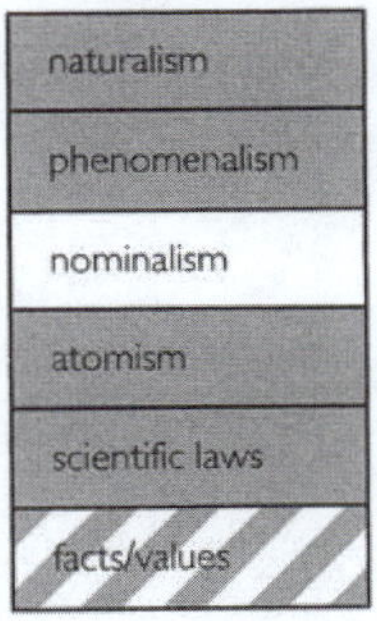

Values are part of the research process, but they must be strictly controlled through reference to empirical evidence.

The differences between positivist and falsificationist approaches can be identified in terms of the origin and role of theories in the activity of empirical research. For Popper, there remains a need to control values and subjective assumptions in research, but to rule these out would be to eliminate valuable intuitions and insights which have been shown to work. It would seem that Popper has some sense of what scientists actually do. Certainly, while Popper rejects metaphysics in science, he, like the logical positivists, does not accept that this problem can be eliminated by restructuring the formal language system of science, nor does he see metaphysical statements as meaningless. Despite the assumptions held in common among empiricists, there are substantial differences in their accounts of the imagination involved in theory construction. For logical positivists, ideas should be a simple reflection of our impressions and perceptions, and that the words on a page should mean the same thing to whoever reads them. Popper accepts that ideas do not always emerge from observation, but also from hunches, guesswork, even those 'eureka' moments when we receive a flash of inspiration. However, if the ideas are not able to be independently tested against experiences they cannot be trusted. For Popper, theories are still separate from observations, so the way we imagine the world is still separate from our sensations, perceptions and impressions of it. It is to the role of the human imagination in constructing social scientific knowledge that we now turn in the next chapter.

26

Imagination and Complexity in the Social Sciences

MARC J. SMITH

1 Introduction

In the earlier chapters we focused upon empiricist approaches in social research and considered how they applied natural scientific methods to the study of social objects. All of these accounts were primarily geared towards providing scientific explanations of distinct social objects rather than attempting to understand the meaning of social relationships and processes. As you will recall from Chapter 3, in the empiricist approach, theory and observation are treated as distinct things. Chapter 4 now challenges this assumption by arguing that it is not possible to separate theory and observation in this way and by examining the important role played by the human mind in the organization and interpretation of these observational experiences. While you will find that the approaches to social research covered here disagree about the precise role of imaginative interpretation of experience, they all agree that it is impossible to separate observation from the mental constructs we use to organize and understand our perceptions. Without such constructs in place, it is suggested, we simply cannot make sense of the complex world around us. For the sake of convenience, and to distinguish them clearly from empiricism, from this point onwards these approaches are labelled 'idealism'. There are many definitions of idealism, but in this chapter we are using the label to identify approaches which see knowledge as the use of ideas to organize experience.

Let's explore how different idealist approaches are from those of empiricism. For a start, they suggest that we should pay closer attention to the concepts and constructions which we invent and use as social scientists and recognize that we only come into contact with the 'real world' through these constructions. Moreover, as idealists reject the idea that observation is theory free, the clear separation of facts and values, which characterized empiricist social science, no longer holds so much weight as a key assumption of social science. Idealist approaches attempt to find a way of resolving the relationship between the development of scientific explanations and the role of interpretative understanding and cultural values. It is these very issues and problems that led empiricists to reject the formative role of values in scientific research in the first place. So, while empiricism tried to sidestep the issue, idealism takes this bull by the horns.

g

You may want to have a glance back at both Figure 3.1 and section 6 in Chapter 3.

We know from Chapter 3 that all empiricists are committed to **phenomenalism**. This assumes that the validity of a statement derives from the way it refers to empirical evidence. In short, empiricists assert that observations are the raw material from which we fashion theory. Positivist and empiricist approaches to the scientific method treat the role of interpretations, constructs, models and the human imagination as secondary factors in, if not irrelevant to, the study of empirical evidence. For instance, in logical positivism theoretical statements about observable evidence are treated as pictures of a definite state of affairs or, if they attempt to do more than this, they are seen as flawed by metaphysical assumptions. For empiricists, interpretative skills are seen, at best, as a necessary evil which must be constantly constrained by reference to empirical evidence. In Popper's case, scientific guesswork and hunches are constrained through repeated attempts at falsification. In the pursuit of **objective knowledge**, whereby facts and values are seen to be distinct, any attempt to bring subjective

g

assessment into scientific research is regarded as a suspicious and potentially dangerous practice which tends to give rise to bias, distortion and prejudice.

In this chapter we also examine the problems involved in understanding the relationship between explanations and predictions. Idealist approaches enable us to account for **complexity** in social scientific research, as well as the simpler relationships established within the experimental setting. This means we will be considering accounts of social life which attempt to generate explanations which do not depend upon a **closed system** of variables that can be clearly observed and measured. If it is recognized that social life is too complex to reproduce through experimental, theoretical and statistical closure, then we should consider the role of the imagination of social scientists in putting together meaningful and plausible accounts of social relations and processes. In the following sections we look at four ways in which the role of imaginative thinking within natural and social scientific research is taken much more seriously.

See Chapter 2, section 2.2.

Each section addresses one of the four approaches (see Figure 4.1) which attempt to integrate the human imagination with scientific research, but reach different conclusions on how this should be done. In section 2, on the conceptual organization of experience, we briefly revisit the contribution of the Enlightenment thinker Immanuel Kant. In particular, we trace the role of interpretation and imagination in the organization of impressions and perceptions in both the natural and social sciences. Understanding Kant's position will enable you to gain a better sense of the three approaches in contemporary social science which are considered in the subsequent sections.

Idealism questions the assumption that only closed systems offer a basis for scientific laws and raises the possibility of social science using open systems – see Chapter 2, section 2.2.

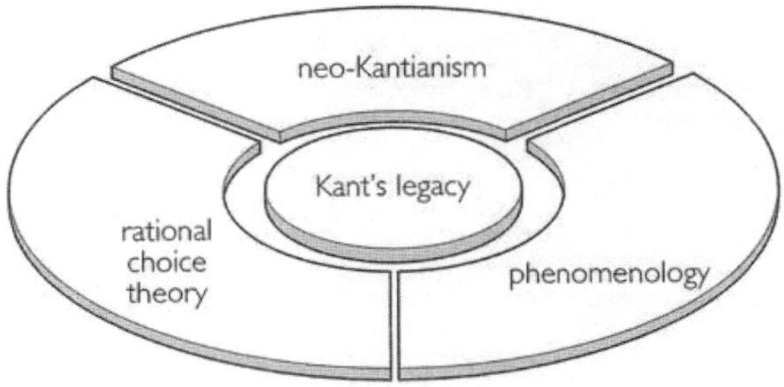

Figure 4.1 Imaginative approaches in the social sciences: the chapter structure.

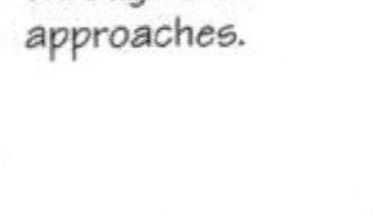

As in Chapter 1, this sign helps you to keep track of your progress through the approaches.

In section 3 we explore the neo-Kantian approaches which have had a significant role in defining the problems familiar to the disciplines of the social sciences today. Here, we look at the use of 'ideal types' as a way of simplifying complex evidence. Ideal types are concepts which exaggerate aspects of social life in order to demonstrate the mechanisms through which social existence is produced. For instance, Max Weber developed three ideal types to characterize the dynamic patterns of behaviour in any interaction situation – habitual action, emotional action and rational action. None of these types actually exists in a pure state, but they serve as useful devices for organizing evidence and building a useful account of empirical reality. At this point, you will find the first of two sections on geographical models. Geographical Models 1 demonstrates how the neo-Kantian approach has been developed in one social scientific discipline.

Section 4 examines rational choice theory, a standpoint which differs, in some respects, from the other approaches considered in this chapter. Rational choice theory regards human beings as purposive rational actors and explores the ways in which the treatment of individuals as purely rational and self-interested can generate insights into human behaviour. This rational calculating individual is often characterized as a 'minimaxing' actor (for making decisions which minimize costs and maximize benefits). In addition, this approach is often portrayed as one which offers the possibility of general laws. You will be expected to consider whether this characterization of human action is an accurate one and to identify some of the problems in making unrealistic assumptions about human actors and the organization of social relations.

See Chapter 3, section 2.2, on Bentham.

Finally, in section 5 we return to some of the themes raised briefly in Chapter 1 by considering the meaningful construction of social life. This section explores approaches developed by phenomenological or interpretive accounts of natural and social science. As you saw in Chapter 1 in Schütz's story of the person on the street, the cartographer and the stranger, this approach attempts to bridge the gap between subjective everyday experiences and objective explanations in social science. At the close of section 5, you will find the second part of the disciplinary case study. Geographical Models 2 explores how these phenomenological approaches can be applied in a particular social science. At any point in this chapter, to help you build a picture of the range of contemporary approaches in social research considered here, you may find it useful to refer to Table 4.1, which

See Chapter 1, section 4.1.

Table 4.1 A quick guide to idealist approaches to knowledge construction.

	Varieties of Idealism			
	Neo-Kantian Idealism	**Rational Choice Theory**	**Hermeneutics and Phenomenology**	**Empiricism**
Theory and Observation	The complex empirical world is 'organized' through the use of mental constructs for comparing and contrasting evidence.	Theoretical work involves the reconstruction of rational decisions within definite constraints on the basis of calculations of costs and benefits of various courses of action.	The problem facing social science is the gulf between the everyday experiences of social actors and the detached accounts of social life produced by social scientists.	The scientific method involves a clear separation of theory and observation.
Facts and Values	The social sciences should be relevant to the problems of a particular society in question at a specific time.	Facts can only be identified through the subjective values and the intentional choices of individuals.	Scientific facts are the commonsense assumptions of the social scientists, for values remain unacknowledged in concept formation.	Facts and values are treated as separate to eliminate from scientific knowledge the researchers' subjective biases.
Explanation and Prediction	An empirical regularity beween variables is necessary but not sufficient for establishing a causal law. The complexity of causal factors in any empirical situation makes it difficult to make accurate predictions. Rational choice theory applies the same formal model across different situations.		Social settings only exist through the intersubjective relations of the actors involved as the product of meaningful communication.	For empiricists, successful predictions are effective explanations. Empirical regularities have the status of scientific laws.

provides a quick guide to the key assumptions, similarities and differences between idealist approaches, as well as a comparison with empiricism. A more detailed version of this table can be found in the conclusion to this chapter, once you have become more familiar with these approaches and what they mean in practice.

Before we look at these approaches more closely, we should consider what it is they attempt to address. All of these approaches consider the problems of thinking about experience and argue that the human imagination is a powerful tool which enables us to sift and sort the mass of sensory perceptions, impressions and experiences we constantly encounter. This enables us to establish patterns and formulate guidelines for our own choices and actions. In the study of natural objects, the role of the human imagination can be seen in the tendency to read social qualities or human sentiments into natural processes, that is, **anthropomorphism**. For instance, it is common to read what Western societies conventionally regard as feminine qualities into the forces of nature. Weather systems can be described as tempestuous and unpredictable, the product of mysterious forces. Within Western culture, this involves an implicit contrast to scientific attempts to observe, measure, dismantle and tame nature. For feminist interpretations of science, this is another reflection of the androcentric (male-centred) assumptions of the dominant culture of Western societies. g

Let's explore the way in which the human imagination can lead us astray by taking a clear-cut example, that of media representations of animal behaviour. You may have noticed in natural history programmes that studies of primates reveal strongly subjective currents by identifying human qualities in the behaviour of various species of apes and monkeys. The popular science of Desmond Morris in *The Naked Ape* (1969) and *The Human Zoo* (1970) provides a good example of the problems of thinking about instinctive drives in human behaviour. Morris uses social qualities (such as 'male promiscuity') to define animal behaviour. Then, when explaining human courtship and sexual behaviour, the human male role is portrayed as a product of natural tendencies demonstrated by primates. For Morris, these natural tendencies always resurface in human behaviour when moral norms do not keep such 'animal passions' under control. In short, Morris has attributed social characteristics to animals, only to read them back into human behaviour as instinctual, in the process implying that male promiscuity is natural.

Even when describing natural things we need to take care – the words we use are always packed full of meaning.

You may have also noticed how such representations ignore the way that concepts such as 'promiscuity' can only be understood within a cultural setting. In this case, 'promiscuity' makes sense where there are moral and legal limitations on the number of sexual partners – something which cannot be identified in animal behaviour. Such imaginings, far from being neutral pictures of the world, are loaded with culturally specific values which involve complex sets of assumptions about permissible and impermissible behaviour. If such problems arise in the exploration of the relationship of society and nature, it should not be surprising that similar issues exist in the study of social objects. The remainder of this chapter provides you with some tools for unpacking the kinds of problem associated with thinking through the relationship between interpretation and observation, as well as continuing to explore the role of cultural values in social scientific practice.

2 The conceptual organization of experience: Kant's legacy

This section considers imaginative thinking in scientific knowledge. In Chapter 2 we saw how Immanuel Kant characterized the Enlightenment as a process containing the ethos of the critical spirit, that we should question all assumptions. To achieve this, he established a compromise position between **rationalism** (reason will lead us to the truth) and **empiricism** (observation and experimentation will lead us to the truth). Kant's approach emerged as a response to the inadequacies of both of these positions, although each approach had strengths as well as weaknesses (see Caygill, 1995). Empiricism, you will remember, had a solid foundation in sensory experience; however, it oversimplifies the relationship between theory and observation, for it treats the mind as a blank slate as if it is empty before receiving physical sensations. Rationalism, on the other hand, emphasized the important role of human reason in developing theories about the empirical world, but it also tended to neglect the role of observational evidence as a way of testing the validity of theoretical statements. Kant's compromise between these two positions sought to emphasize the strengths of each. For Kant, it is only through a 'synthesis' of both rational thinking and observable experiences that we can comprehend the world. In short, without reason we cannot make sense of our experiences and without observation we have nothing on which to employ our capacity for rational thought. It should be stressed that this is a synthesis, not a way of fitting the evidence conveniently within one's own theoretical model. This compromise became the basis of the range of approaches which attempted to place human imagination more clearly at the centre of social scientific inquiry.

Kant found a compromise between reason and observation by claiming that it is impossible to have one without the other – they should be seen as a synthesis.

It is useful to reconsider empiricism in a little more detail to gain a better sense of what Kant had in mind. This will help us to understand how he challenged the distinction between **analytic** and **synthetic** statements which came to be so central for the logical positivists. For the positivists, only analytic statements (that is, those that are true by definition) can be known through reason alone rather than through human experience. Such analytic statements are logically true by virtue of the meanings of the words they contain. Consider the statement 'Roses are flowers'. If we already understand what roses are, then this statement has the same logical status as 'A short man is a man'. It does not tell us anything new, for we already know this to be true by definition. The truth of all other statements rests upon observation, such as 'These roses are yellow and fragrant'. Statements like this are synthetic, for they express in ideas the textures, colours, sounds, odours, tastes and motions of the objects of our experiences. Kant was inspired by the clear thinking and conceptual tools developed by empiricists like David Hume, but he argued that empiricists were not asking the most appropriate questions.

It is often said that before we can recognize the right answers we have to ask the right questions. Empiricism asks us to consider the question, 'What objects do we experience?' – and consequently finds answers to human problems in the observable relations of human life. Let's think through what it means in practice to ask the empiricist question. If you ask yourself,

Empiricists ask the question: *what can we experience?*

'What did I experience yesterday?', then you are likely to respond with a fairly descriptive survey of your own perceptions, feelings, sensations and impressions in relation to specific events for a given amount of time. Kant's critical philosophy seeks an answer to a very different question, a *transcendental* question about *what can be known?* A transcendental question, therefore, involves asking, 'What are the conditions of possibility of (something)?' – in this case, identifying what must be in place for our knowledge of observable things to be possible. Let's apply this to your experiences of yesterday. A transcendental question here would involve something like, 'What prior concepts do we need to make sense of and organize our experiences yesterday?' For the sake of illustration, let's assume that you went to work and you had a 'horrible' time. Your boss or line manager was inconsiderate, rude and, at times, even abusive. So the question is, 'How do I make sense of and organize these experiences of working yesterday?' We do this through mental constructs which exist prior to these observed experiences. In this highly specific example, we can draw upon our prior conceptions of 'considerateness' and 'horridness' in human behaviour, and this may serve as a useful way of making sense of the events and for making a judgement such as 'My boss shouted at me at work and behaved badly. I hate my boss!' However, in such situations there will also be a range of alternative prior concepts that are relevant. Ideas of 'consideration' tend to be culturally specific. So, to make a comparison across cultures, we could draw upon prior concepts such as 'self-orientation' and 'collective-orientation'. For instance, you may judge that the 'boss' was only behaving in this way to serve the interests of the organization in question (treating the business as the collective) rather than having purely self-interested motives. Your account of the situation might then take the form of the statement 'He was only doing his job. In any case, all bosses are b******s!' Even here, such ideas may apply only to a limited range of societies which clearly distinguish the self from the collective order, so broader categories could be used. While Kant had categories in mind that were much more abstract, such as quality and quantity, examples like this reveal how difficult it is to separate perception and imagination.

Kantians ask the question: *what do we need to make sense of experience? Answer: mental constructs.*

Hofstede.

Now, let's look at an example which draws from everyday experiences but is also relevant to social scientific explanations of the relationship between the built environment and the rural environment. For instance, you might decide to take a walk one day in the countryside and record your feelings about the environment and natural objects and then, on the following day, record a walk within a declining inner-city environment. According to an empiricist, the different accounts generated would be simply a picture of senses and impressions for the two walks. However, for a Kantian, we can only make sense of these experiences in terms of the mental frameworks and assumptions we already have in place about the nature of urban and rural environments. So we could describe our country walk in terms of open spaces, clean air, relaxed pace of life, friendly relationships and our closer affinity with nature, while the urban environment we might describe as more hemmed in, polluted, hectic, involving anonymous human relations and feeling somewhat divorced from the natural setting of the previous day. These oppositions are themselves part of our historical and cultural tendencies to contrast the countryside with the town in ways which oppose the values of 'community' (involving long-held

Empiricism: Observation - Kantian :- Preconceptions affect observation

Mental constructs are the conditions of possibility of observed experiences, for if they were not in place prior to experiences, we could not make sense of our impressions and perceptions.

particularistic relations between individuals) to the more instrumental, impersonal relations involved in 'association' (see Figures 4.2 and 4.3). Of course, there are many other ways of thinking about urban and rural environments. Nevertheless, for a Kantian, such perceptions and impressions can only make sense within mental frameworks, however defined, and the concepts, categories and judgements they involve. Such conceptualizations can surface in all sorts of ways and may emerge within social scientific explanations of a range of issues. For instance, the urban environment is often described as being more prone to criminality than the rural environment, either without question or through the uncritical use of crime statistics.

Figure 4.2 Urban life representation.

Figure 4.3 Rural life representation.

When Kant's basic standpoint was introduced above, you saw how the 'phenomenal world' of appearances is the product of our experiences of the objects of analysis and the mental constructs which give shape and a logical form to these experiences. The objects are seen as 'things-in-themselves' or 'noumena', existing beyond our cognitive faculties. The concept of 'noumena' does not tell us anything substantive about the objects or things. It only indicates that the world of things is so complex and difficult to understand that we cannot simply reproduce it in our thoughts in the manner of a picture. All we can do is develop constructs, concepts and models which make experience intelligible. Thus perceptions and sensory impressions are arranged in 'space' and 'time' in a way which allows us to 'compare' and 'contrast' and consider one piece of data as the 'cause' of another (Russell, 1912/1959, Chapter 8). At this point, you should just note that, in order to make sense of your perceptions, you already engage in the use of whole sets of taken-for-granted assumptions and you have quite a range of mental constructs to choose from.

Idealist approaches identify simple ways of organizing, interpreting and explaining complex empirical evidence.

Whether we are reflecting upon yesterday's experiences or are engaged in social research, we always depend upon a variety of prior concepts to make sense of our experiences. This recognizes the mind as a creative agent in the production of knowledge, whereas empiricism tends to treat the mind as passive in relation to perceptions and sensory impressions. Nevertheless, this approach does not seek to go beyond the boundaries of our senses.

Let's look at an example, this time from contemporary social scientific research, such as the study of the causes and consequences of crime. At first sight, the study of crime appears to offer a clear-cut example of a field of research where **analytic** and **synthetic** statements can be clearly identified. Among the typical analytic statements in this area (that is, statements which are true by definition) would be:

Statement A Criminal actions involve behaviour which breaks the law.

A synthetic statement (generating new knowledge from empirical evidence), an empiricist would argue, would involve statements such as:

Statement B In regions within the UK which have experienced an above average rise in unemployment, a corresponding increase in the crime rate can be identified.

Traditional criminological research (within the disciplines of both psychology and sociology) tends to assume that the objects in question (in this case, the crime rate and the unemployment rate) can be clearly identified. This also assumes that a useful comparison can be made between the two variables. Actually, crime is typically related to a wide range of measurable variables based on age, class, gender, ethnicity, location and so on. However, this still ignores a range of significant issues about the definition of crime rates and the complex institutional processes within the criminal justice system through which criminal statistics are produced. The range of possible factors in accounting for crime is huge and each variable identified is difficult to disentangle from the available evidence. Definitions of crime are located within the institutional environments of law-enforcement agencies such as the courts and police force, and shaped by a series of authoritative decisions made by individuals who occupy significant positions within these criminal justice agencies. Crime statistics focus upon reported crime, criminal charges and criminal convictions and can be taken as indicative of different stages or snapshots of a process. For an action to become criminal, it has to be recognized as a breach of the law and taken seriously by the police. Subsequently, this action may be investigated and sufficient evidence collected to sustain a case so that an individual can be charged, and only in the case of criminal conviction is the final statistic realized. All of these factors involved in the production of crime statistics point to the complexity of the social processes involved. Any attempt to develop a social scientific account of the causes and consequences of crime is inevitably shaped by the debates and concerns of the criminal justice system and the moral climate on crime and punishment. Consequently, the relationship between theory and observation is a problematic one in so far as the empirical evidence is shaped through both the complex interpretations of the actors involved in the criminal justice system and the interpretations and values of the social researchers themselves. Just as social researchers use ideas to organize evidence, so too do the people being studied.

As you can see from the examples in Figure 4.4, experience can only be conceived in spatial, temporal and causal terms, and knowledge cannot

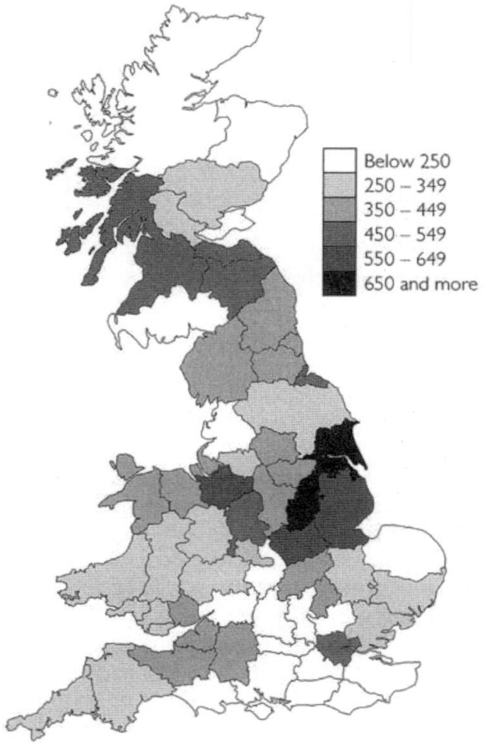

(a) Crimes of violence against the person per 100,000 population in each area in 1989.

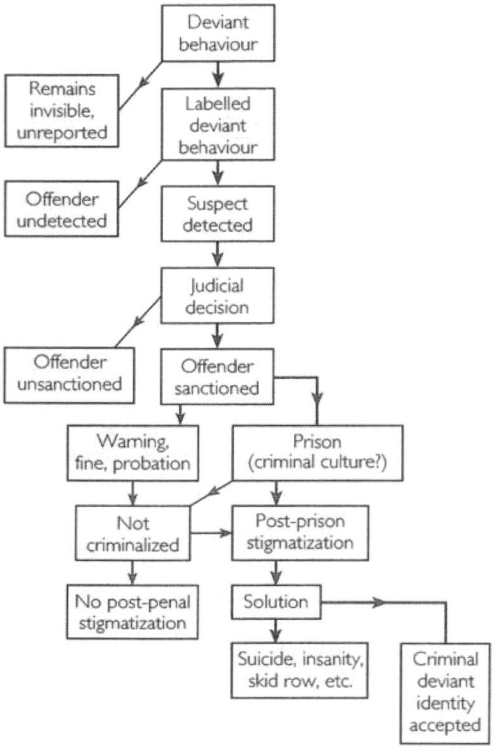

(b) Simplified flow chart of: → major stages in becoming deviant; → routes out of deviance.

Criminal damage >£2000	16.5 : 1
Offences under the Public Order Act 1986	17.0 : 1
Offence by prostitute	0.01 : 1
Drunkenness	16.5 : 1
Common assault	7.0 : 1
Assault on constable	5.5 : 1
TV licence evasion	0.5 : 1
Taking and driving away	33.0 : 1
Other	9.5 : 1

(c) Ratio of male to female offenders found guilty of non-motoring summary offences: England and Wales, 1993.

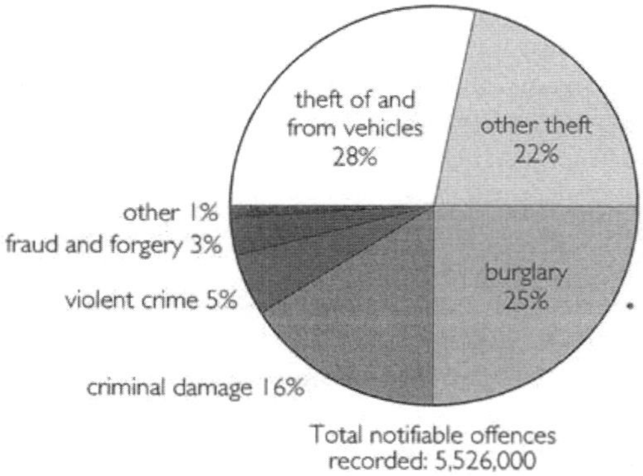

(d) Notifiable offences recorded by the police by offence type: England and Wales, 1993.

Figure 4.4 Interpreting crime.

be constructed without the concepts that allow us to think about our experiences. Hence, it is possible to think of statements – such as the examples above – which are both synthetic and contain concepts which were known prior to experience.

Let's revisit the synthetic statement on crime above. The statement as it stands identifies an empirical regularity between unemployment and criminal behaviour: a rise in unemployment is associated with an increase in the recorded incidence of criminal actions (along the lines of: if A, then B). But how do we make sense of such a statement? In order to understand this statement, we must also possess a set of assumptions and preconceptions of what motivates human conduct, whether this is material greed and acquisitiveness, social pressures, the denial of opportunities for self-improvement, or more generally a culture based upon materialism. Kant described any statement with these qualities as a **synthetic a priori statement** in a clear attempt to distinguish his approach from the empiricist distinction between analytic and synthetic statements. It is this conception of the human subject as a creative and purposive agent in the construction of knowledge which marks Kant's legacy to social science. When we recognize that there is no unmediated contact with the real world, that sense experiences are not reflected in an automatic fashion in our ideas and concepts, then we are forced to confront questions about the relationship between theory and observation, which empiricism avoids. In particular, we need to be aware of the way in which constructs can be uncritically imposed upon empirical evidence to create the patterns which we take for granted (as you saw in the case of scientific racism in Chapter 3). Kant's concern to explore the conditions of possibility and the limits to human knowledge has been a source of inspiration to a variety of approaches. It is these approaches which we consider in the following sections of this chapter.

Preconceptions, 'Assumptions', 'apriori' Existing before the fact.

9

Kant provides a way of dealing with the inter-relationships between rational thought and empirical evidence.

Before we focus upon the role of the human imagination in the social sciences in any more detail, we should briefly consider what happens when we apply these insights to the conceptual organization of our experiences of objects in the natural sciences. The problems of interpretation can be illustrated by drawing upon Norwood Hanson's work on the conceptual foundations of science in *Patterns of Discovery* (1958). Hanson, a philosopher of natural science, attempts to raise questions about the nature of perception as conventionally understood by philosophers of science in the 1950s. Hanson draws upon Wittgenstein's later work, *Philosophical Investigations* (1953/1967).

You may recall that Wittgenstein's early work influenced the logical positivists by seeing statements as pictures of the world. In his later work, Wittgenstein viewed language as a series of games, each with its own rules. In effect, he undermined any distinction between the real world and language. Wittgenstein argues that problems of philosophy arise not from the world but from language, with our concepts defining our experiences. Rather than seeing the world as something which we can approach through language, he saw the world as existing only within language. For Hanson, scientists may observe the same visual data but this is not the same as *seeing*, for 'People, not their eyes, see' (Hanson, 1958, p.6). Hanson demonstrates that biologists may see different things from the same observation by comparing two interpretations of observing an amoeba under a micro-

See Chapter 3, section 4.1.

scope. For one biologist, the amoeba is a '*single-celled* animal' (analogous to other forms of cells with a wall, cytoplasm and a nucleus) whereas for the other, it is a 'non-celled *animal*' (analogous to other whole animals which ingest and digest food). In either case, 'these data are moulded by different theories or interpretation or intellectual constructions' (Hanson, 1958, p.5).

Activity 4.1

Turn to Reading A, 'There is more to seeing than meets the eye', from Norwood Hanson's *Perception and Discovery* (1969).

- What are the different ways of 'seeing' and 'observing' in the argument developed by Hanson?

In this extract, the objects observed are either geometric or sketches of physical objects. When we apply Hanson's ideas to the study of social life, further complications arise. Think of any recent event you have experienced with someone with whom you have regular contact. Make notes on the event and then contact the person and discuss it with them – you might be surprised at how much your interpretations differ. You should ask yourself why these interpretations are different.

Identical evidence can be interpreted in very different ways, depending upon the assumptions in each approach.

In a more striking example from the history of the natural sciences, Hanson contrasts the different interpretations placed upon the observation of the morning Sun rising in the east by two early astronomers, Johannes Kepler and Tycho Brahe. Both astronomers observed the same physical stimuli, a yellow disc emerging from behind a green land surface against a blue sky, yet they saw very different things. For Kepler, the Sun was stationary and the Earth moved, whereas for Brahe, the Earth was stationary and the other planetary objects moved around the Earth. The question here is not only the accuracy of each account, but the extent to which we can interpret the same observations in a variety of ways. This example is useful in demonstrating the difficulties of interpretation. However, when we look at the problem encountered in the social sciences where the observer is not distinct from the object but is actually part of it, then the difficulties multiply.

As you work through this chapter, you will see that the approaches developed assume that the models used in social research are simplifications of a more complex (and, some would argue, incomprehensible) reality. For experience to be intelligible, we have to simplify. These approaches also raise important issues about the relationship between subject (researcher) and objects of analysis within the social sciences. The scientific approaches you encountered in Chapters 2 and 3 assumed that it was possible to deploy the same method in the study of human life as had been used in the study of natural objects. In the natural sciences, it is plausible to treat objects of analysis as distinct from the researcher. In the social sciences, however, the researcher is part of the object under investigation. There is a clear difference between studying physical matter or biological species and studying thinking, creative, interacting, unpredictable human beings. As

Social relation. 'Society'.

social researchers draw upon the stock of knowledge and the language system of their own societies, this also means that the concepts and models developed are inevitably part of the object as well. Thus, in the study of social life there is no easy separation of subject and object.

Any attempt to impose the methods and assumptions of the natural sciences upon the study of social life, according to Peter Winch in *The Idea of a Social Science* (1958), is a mistake because the understanding of natural objects is completely different from understanding social objects. Winch recommends that the study of social objects should involve the recognition that all human behaviour is meaningful and involves both rule-governed and rule-following behaviour. In the social sciences, it is harder to establish whether human beings do observe the same things in the same way. In addition, as we saw earlier in the example of studying crime, the objects under observation are themselves much more difficult to define. Certainly, they are not as clear-cut as defining an amoeba or the sunrise. In the social sciences, we are in fact observing and contemplating ourselves as complex creatures living in conditions of uncertainty. So, as social scientists, we face the most difficult task of any scientific activity. It is to the issue of understanding complexity that we turn in the next section.

The application of the assumptions and methods of natural science within social research tends to ignore the important differences between studying things and studying people.

Summary

Perception and sense impressions are organized in meaningful ways only through the mental frameworks and associations which are taken for granted. These mental frameworks act as a means of sifting and sorting the mass of sensory experiences into some recognizable shape and order.

There are different ways of 'seeing' and this accounts for the ways in which human beings can interpret the same evidence in very different – and sometimes opposed – ways when they attempt to imagine social life.

to 2nd Ed.

3 Understanding complexity

Empiricists tend to see the observation of variables as the basis for establishing causal explanations. For idealists, the empiricist starting-point is deficient in two respects. First, the social world is much more complex than the use of **closed systems** can allow for. Second, observations only make sense through the use of prior concepts. In this section we explore the relationship between causal explanations and interpretative understanding. Explanations are more often associated with the natural sciences, while understanding is usually seen as characteristic of the arts and humanities. The natural sciences are said to be able to generate universal law statements which apply across space and time, while the arts and humanities only represent unique events in a particular time and place. The social sciences carved out their own space between these two traditions and have had to straddle these two modes of inquiry. Over the last century and a half, an intellectual and scientific movement has emerged which explicitly attempted to use Kant's ideas in order to study social relations and historical change. This approach came to be labelled neo-Kantianism. Although there remained considerable variation within this movement, there has always been a common concern to resolve the dilemmas raised by attempting to reconcile the tensions between hard facts and cultural values, between theoretical constructs and empirical observations and between explanation and understanding. Neo-Kantian debates about what would be the most appropriate methods for social science originated in economics, but they also had important implications for the subsequent development of sociology, psychology, geography and political studies. These approaches are so influential that they often remain unacknowledged. They have become such an integral part of social scientific inquiry that few feel the need to acknowledge them. They are simply part of the conceptual landscape of social science.

3.1 The emergence of neo-Kantianism

The neo-Kantian approach attempts to do two things. First, it attempts to resolve the dilemmas posed by accommodating both objective truth and subjective values in the same approach. Second, it attempts to find a way of addressing the thorny question of cultural values and their relationship to the generation of cultural and historical knowledge. Two key figures in this school, Wilhelm Windelband and Heinrich Rickert, both criticized positivism in the study of social life. Windelband's work provided us with a way of thinking about our methodological options, while Rickert (considered in more detail in section 3.2) raised interesting issues about the relationship between facts and values. In this section we focus upon Wilhelm Windelband, whose *History and Natural Science* (1894) regarded both the natural sciences and the human sciences as the study of empirical reality. Nevertheless, he distinguished between studying natural things and studying people and their institutions. For Windelband, there was a methodological difference between two forms of scientific thought:

Elsewhere this sign **g** *will direct you to the glossary, but revisit this section if you need to.*

- **nomothetic** – involving the construction of generalizing models and the identification of general laws;
- **idiographic** – the individualizing method of the cultural sciences concerned with the detailed depiction of particular circumstances.

This made it possible to distinguish between the study of natural objects in establishing objective knowledge and the important role played by the values and interests of the researcher in the study of social life. In the social sciences the objects are other subjects – thinking, creative and communicative beings. Scientists have different interests in their objects of analysis and define them in different ways. In the natural sciences, Windelband argued, the objects (physical matter) remain constant, allowing for the development of a 'science of laws', whereas in the social sciences the objects involved are 'unique configurations of events'. He argued that history and the humanities involve the use of individualizing or 'idiographic' method, while the natural sciences aim to produce general laws, the 'nomothetic' method. Within the nomothetic framework, values are seen as the product of an evaluative procedure and as such are subjective and cannot serve as the objective basis for establishing general laws. The social sciences are thus caught between two approaches to the study of social life, with one approach emphasizing the importance of scientific general laws and the other treating each set of social circumstances as unique. This helps to explain the competing options faced by social scientists.

For neo-Kantians, social scientific explanations offer a choice between developing general laws and attempts to understand unique events.

In the remainder of this section we explore how this innovative distinction had an impact on the emergence of economics and psychology. The relationship between nomothetic and idiographic positions can be illustrated by briefly considering the *Methodenstreit* (the debate over method), which originated in Germany in the late nineteenth century. This was primarily focused upon which key organizing principles should act as a foundation for economic research and for social research in general. It had become widely accepted that it was appropriate to study the economy idiographically, understanding the complexities of each economic system rather than in terms of discovering general universal laws. By focusing upon actual economic conditions, it was hoped that the social scientific knowledge produced would deliver human progress and the social improvement of the condition of the working classes through the actions of the state. This established the idea that state policy and social scientific research could work hand in hand. One of these early economists, Carl Menger, was concerned that this focus on social problem solving would lead to 'economics without thinking'. So, in *Problems of Economics and Sociology* (1883/1981), Menger developed a nomothetic account of the general relations of economic phenomena rather than describing economic processes in a particular time and place. He suggested that it was possible to

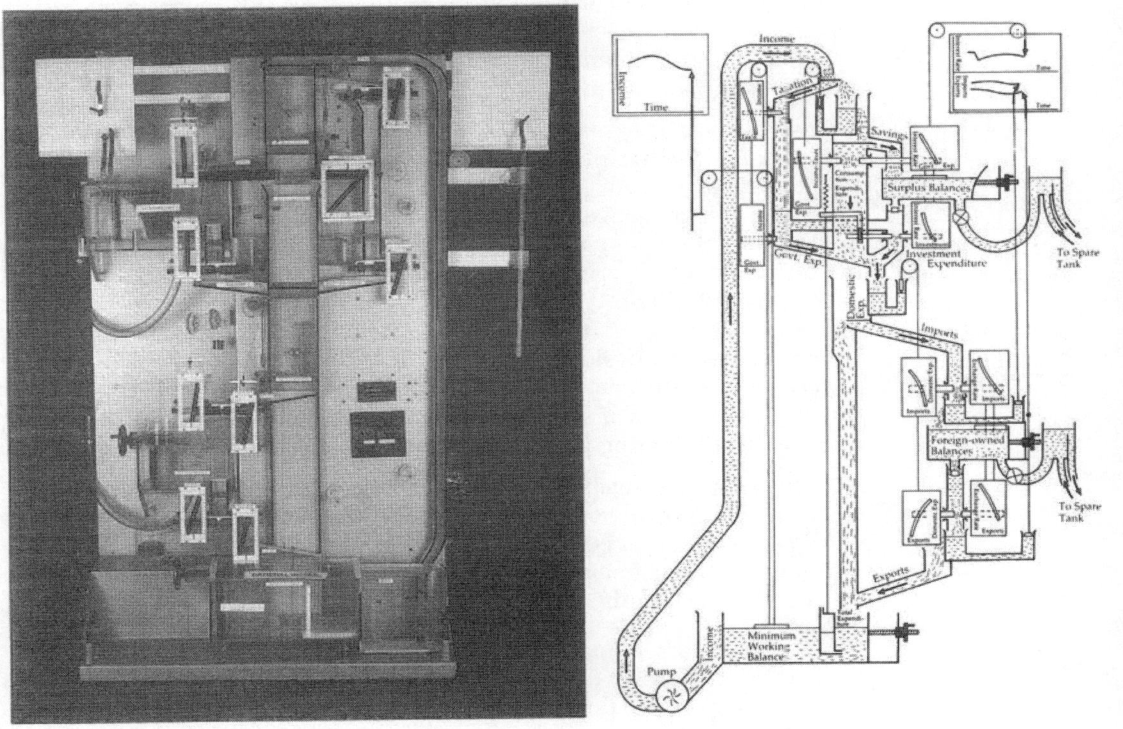

Figure 4.5 Representation of macroeconomics – the economy as a machine.

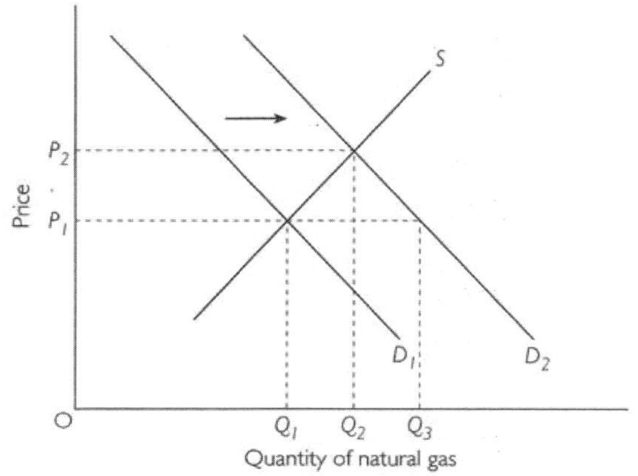

Figure 4.6 Representation of microeconomics. Alterations in the price of a particular commodity, in this case natural gas, relate to the quantity consumed. This is a fairly typical example of the way economists see the relationship in a market between price and the level of supply and demand for goods and services.

view the branches of economics (economic history, economic theory, economic policy and public finance) as each having its own distinctive forms of theory and method.

This was to have a profound effect on twentieth-century economics. For Menger, the appropriate method for economic theory involved two steps: first, break down phenomena into their smallest elements and, second, use these to deduce the development of more complex social phenomena. Thus a 'market' was no more than the sum total of consumer choices and the relations between them operating as a function of the individual actions which produced them. This approach to studying social life was to become known as **methodological individualism**. Menger was to establish a line of argument which rejected the aggregate concepts of macroeconomics in favour of microeconomics, which focused upon individuals, households and firms as decision makers (see examples in Figures 4.5 and 4.6).

g

In many social sciences, the difference between nomethetic and idiographic approaches came to be institutionalized in the branches of disciplines, such as the difference between theory and applied research work.

There was clear disagreement about which scientific method (nomothetic or idiographic) the discipline of economics should follow. In psychology, we find examples of both idiographic and nomothetic approaches living side by side. The emergence of experimental psychology enabled psychologists to develop a clearly nomothetic approach to scientific method. In particular, the technique of experimental closure was developed by the physiological psychologist Wilhelm Wundt, who established the first psychological laboratory in Leipzig in 1879 in order to demonstrate the interrelationships between sensory physiology and the 'mind'. Wundt, like all neo-Kantians, rejected the empiricist treatment of the mind (as a blank page for impressions) in favour of an active consciousness which could be selective in making discriminating judgements about our experiences. For Wundt:

> scientific investigation has three problems to be solved. ... The first is the analysis of composite processes; the second is the demonstration of combinations into which the elements discovered in the analysis enter; the third is the investigation of the laws that are operative in the formation of such combinations.
>
> (Wundt, 1897, p.25, cited in Manicas, 1987, p.183)

In this way, by clearly defining an object of analysis, psychologists began to carve out a space for their discipline, although the way in which the object of analysis, the mind, was defined in psychology was to change again with the emerging dominance of positivism. In particular, by focusing upon closed systems in the positivist way, the discipline of psychology was to lose its sense of the empirical complexity of social relations. However, in both psychology and economics the neo-Kantian framework came to be widely accepted. One of the legacies of this approach is the establishment of the distinction between theoretical and applied study in economics, psychology, geography, sociology and social policy.

Summary

The debate on method centred on what form social scientific inquiry should take – idiographic approaches study concrete social processes in a particular time and place, whereas nomothetic approaches attempt to construct accounts of general laws in some branches of the social sciences along the lines of the assumptions and methods of the natural sciences (especially physics).

Differences remained unresolved among the various alternative models emerging in the social science disciplines. Nevertheless, the debate triggered an increased awareness of the distinctive problems of social science posed by the role of cultural values in social research.

3.2 Facts, values and relevance in social science

The relationship between facts and values has generated a huge amount of heated discussion in the social sciences. As you saw in Chapter 3, taking their cue from logical positivism, many social scientists have been concerned to keep values out of scientific research. The contribution by the German philosopher Heinrich Rickert on the relationship between values and social science is the key starting-point for all the debates since. Rickert distinguished between the logical methods of the natural and the social sciences but also raised the possibility of differences between them because of the way in which the objects of analysis in each science are related to the values of those engaged in research. In the natural sciences, physics is formally nomothetic for it attempts to identify general laws and the objects concerned (atoms, neutrons, etc.) are not related to values. However, Rickert argued that some forms of natural science were formally idiographic (that is, concerned with unique situations), rather than nomothetic. For instance, in some areas of biology attempts have been made to establish the unique characteristics of earth-bound species, even though biologists have the same relationship to their objects as physicists.

In the social sciences, the objects of analysis are defined as value laden and culturally meaningful. Nevertheless, economics still concentrates upon developing general laws from the identification of recurrent patterns of events (as do many branches of sociology, psychology and political science). Rickert suggested that other approaches in the social sciences, influenced by history, are concerned much more with unique events and particular conditions. This helps to explain the variety of approaches in the social sciences.

Nomothetic and idiographic approaches coexist in both the natural sciences and the social sciences.

Sociology has often been described as containing two traditions, with one attempting to generate causal explanations in general terms and the other concerned with interpreting and understanding social life. These differences have also been developed into the methodological criteria of reliability and validity. **Reliable knowledge** can be defined as evidence which is supported through repeated testing under the same conditions, while **valid knowledge** (if difficult to replicate) is often defined as being true to life in a particular place and time. Nevertheless, in each case there is a clear attempt to represent reality even if there is considerable disagreement about what should be done. Both criteria claim to produce authentic knowledge, although they do so in different ways.

Values are always involved in social research – this should be acknowledged so that social scientific knowledge is related to specific social and historical conditions.

Identifying the values and purposes of social scientists raised problems which were to become known as the value judgement debate. Neither the nomothetic method nor the idiographic method provide us with clear criteria for deciding *what* we should actually study. Rickert suggested that it is possible to define objects and form concepts about them by following the criteria of **value relevance**. This means that, for a social scientist, the objects of analysis would be defined in such a way that they would already connect with the cultural values of the society in question and hold some meaning for the members of that culture. Therefore, it was argued, we should treat all social scientific concepts as expressions of the values of a given community and the conventional standards of morality considered to be universal within that community. The principle of value relevance means that concepts should be relevant to the problems of a particular society at a particular time. This also means that value judgements are the concern of philosophers in that time and place and cannot be established for all time.

Earlier in this chapter, we explored some of the problems involved in studying crime. In terms of the issues raised by value relevance, it is possible to identify important shifts in the study of criminality over the last forty years. The study of crime can be said to have moved through three stages:

- an attempt to establish the objective cause of criminality;
- a period concerned with processes through which crime was viewed as constructed by the criminal justice system itself;
- more recently, greater attention focused on the consequences of crime in terms of the experiences of victims and the development of crime prevention strategies.

Each phase of empirical research and theorizing can be related to the prevailing social issues at the time that the research took place. In the first phase, crime was attributed to definite causes, with some types of individuals identified as having criminal dispositions. This is often referred to as the positivist approach to crime. In the second phase, it was seen as a product of decisions by people in the criminal justice system. This phase emerged in the 1960s and 1970s when many social scientists were concerned with the ways that the police and courts constructed criminality. In the last phase, crime has been understood as something all rational individuals are capable of doing unless there is the possibility of being caught. This phase has been influential since the 1980s, with a move to more crime prevention measures. Each phase connects to a different set of concerns within Western societies.

3.3 Using ideal types

We noted previously, in the introduction, the use of ideal types in social science. This technique was popularized in social scientific research by Max Weber, who adopted an explicitly interdisciplinary approach using sources from economics, sociology, psychology, political studies and history. He was not concerned to demarcate the different forms of scientific method but, instead, wanted to bring them together in a coherent and unified approach. For Weber, this would provide a bridge between the interpretative understanding of human action and the scientific explanation of the causes and consequences of a particular relationship. To do this, Weber used the ideal type, a device which had been developed by Menger's economic theory. An **ideal type** is a theoretical device for generalizing beyond a particular situation, but one which accepts the complexity of social relations. It does not have the status that empiricists attribute to general laws for, in idealist approaches, it is assumed that closed systems are inappropriate for studying people. Ideal types are simplistic and exaggerated categories providing a yardstick against which it is possible to compare and contrast empirical evidence.

An important pair of ideal types in economics is the 'command economy' and the 'free market'. In terms of these 'ideal types', free markets are largely self-regulating systems for distributing goods and services, with a minimal state involvement ensuring that grievances are resolved and trust is maintained. Command economies have extensive state involvement in both producing and distributing goods and services as well as in fixing prices. They are portrayed as polar opposites in terms of the level of competition and degree of free choice displayed by the actors involved. In the free market these actors are assumed to be completely rational creatures operating according to opportunity cost (that we make purchasing decisions in markets fully aware that our choices always mean that we have to deny ourselves something else). In fact, although each ideal type is often used to describe empirical reality, neither can be said to actually exist. In practice there is no such thing as a perfectly free economy or a command economy for, as Figure 4.7 indicates, all actual economies can be located in between these types. In some cases, we can use these ideal types to identify how economies change, as in the transformation in post-communist Russia. For these reasons, Weber saw ideal types above all as useful devices for simplifying and identifying patterns in a concrete and complex empirical reality.

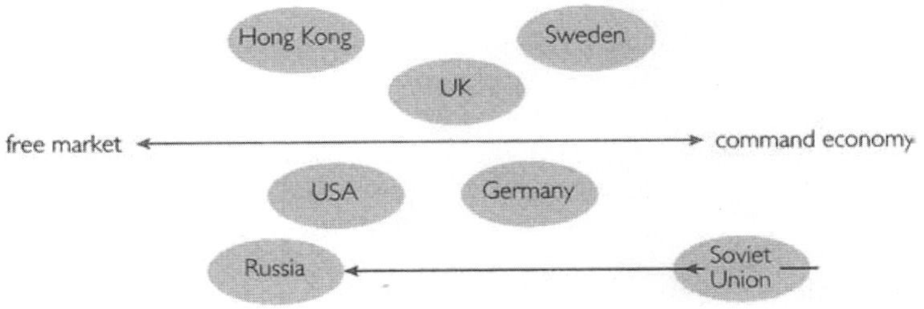

Figure 4.7 A use of ideal types in economics.

So, we can use the ideal type as an organizing device through which it is possible to establish the patterns of activity involved across social and economic institutions. By focusing upon patterns, these devices offer no final answers but allow for the development of useful models of human activity. Weber used them throughout his own research; for example, the

Ideal types simplify and allow for the identification of patterns of social relations within complex empirical evidence.

ideal types of traditional authority, charismatic authority and rational-legal authority. Authority relations are defined as ways of making power relations legitimate. Each of these, in turn, derives from Weber's more abstract ideal types of human action (that is, idealized in three ways: habitual, emotional and/or rational).

In order to understand the usefulness of this approach, imagine that Weber was alive in the 1980s in the UK and was faced with the social and political phenomenon of 'Thatcherism'. Using Weber's authority types, it is possible to develop a coherent and suggestive, if incomplete, picture of the Thatcher administrations in the UK which serves as a useful foundation for further research. The Conservative administrations in the 1980s consistently drew upon and reinvented 'traditional national' values as well as engaging in debates about the decline of moral values. Thatcher, as a 'charismatic' political figure, cultivated a populist appeal whereby she was able to draw upon the support of individuals within groups, such as trade unionists, whose interests are often seen as opposed to the Conservative agenda. The programmes for privatization, for taxation reforms and for the reform of the Civil Service can be seen as a return to a conception of bureaucratic administration that could be regarded as closer to the ideal type of 'bureaucracy as an efficient and rational machine for getting things done' which Weber would have seen as most suitable for a liberal democracy. In this way, the use of such ideal types provides a means of organizing the mass of empirical evidence about politics in the 1980s. This enables us to make sense of a more complex reality and even to deal with the evidence that appears to be contradictory. For instance, Thatcherism involved a 'strong state' (less freedom) in many areas of moral concern such as law and order, but also a considerable increase in personal freedom in the economy. By considering the 'strong state' as a strategy for maintaining traditional authority and the 'free market' (minimal state) policy as a means of generating popular support (through tax cuts and council house sales), we can see both as attempts to legitimate power in the way that Weber suggests. Of course, such an account only provides a partial picture of one brief period in British history. Nevertheless, it is a useful demonstration of neo-Kantian research practice.

4.0 in 2nd Edition.

4.1 Game theory

The rational principles of the praxeological method were developed for more general use in the social sciences by Oscar Morgenstern (a student of Mises) and John von Neumann, in *The Theory of Games and Economic Behaviour* (1944). This approach has only become popular as a research approach across the social sciences since the 1960s. Game theory provides a means of describing and explaining social relationships in contexts where actors make rational choices in rule-governed situations. It is assumed that all participants in a 'game' understand the possible choices or 'moves' open to all players and their likely outcomes. Applications of this analogy have been very wide ranging – from decisions on family planning, criminal behaviour, voting behaviour and electoral campaigning, to the Cuban missile crisis and the environmental impact of overgrazing on commonly owned land. The actors in this approach are assumed to have certain characteristics; in particular, they are considered to be 'minimaxers' in their behaviour (a label for describing the tendencies of rational actors to minimize their perceived costs and maximize their perceived benefits).

Game theory enables social scientists to identify rule-governed patterns of behaviour within which all choices are made by purely rational and self-interested players.

This can be illustrated by focusing upon two of the well known games applied to non-economic situations. In the game of 'chicken' (an American teenage dare game with cars), two actors race their cars towards each other in the certain knowledge that, unless one of them moves out of the way, both may be seriously injured or worse. The object of the game is to test the nerve of participants and the likely outcome is that one of the vehicles will veer away, leaving both unscathed but one of the actors shamed in the process. Allison (1971) has applied this game to the superpower confrontation in 1962 between Khrushchev and Kennedy following the deployment of Soviet nuclear missiles in Cuba within easy range of the American mainland. As the confrontation intensified, Kennedy called the bluff of the Soviet leadership by threatening nuclear confrontation, and as a result the Russian navy withdrew. Allison argues that these events can be explained as a complex game of chicken involving very high stakes, with the ultimate victors being the Americans, especially because of the increase in prestige for Kennedy, and the recognition by the Soviet leadership that they had severely underestimated the resolve of the American leadership.

In a more complex game, prisoners' dilemma, the capacity of actors to make rational choices which generate unanticipated consequences is addressed. This game is most often illustrated through an imaginary sketch in which two partners in crime have been taken for questioning by the police. The police inspector is well aware that there is very little substantive evidence with which to take the case to court and that a successful prosecution depends upon the statements of the two suspects to provide the necessary evidence of wrongdoing. The suspects are faced with a choice of either telling the truth about the crime, in the anticipation of receiving a lenient penalty, or keeping quiet, without knowing whether the partner will do the same and not confess. Since the two suspects are separated from each other, this game is based upon each one's trust in the other partner and their perceptions of which choice would serve their self-interest. In terms of the consequences of their actions, if both refuse to confess they are unlikely to receive a harsh punishment and may avoid any penalty. If one confesses and the other does not, then the suspect who remains silent is likely to receive a harsh punishment and the confessor a suspended sentence for cooperating with the authorities. If both confess, then both are likely to receive a moderate to harsh punishment. The scores involved in such choices are represented in Figure 4.13.

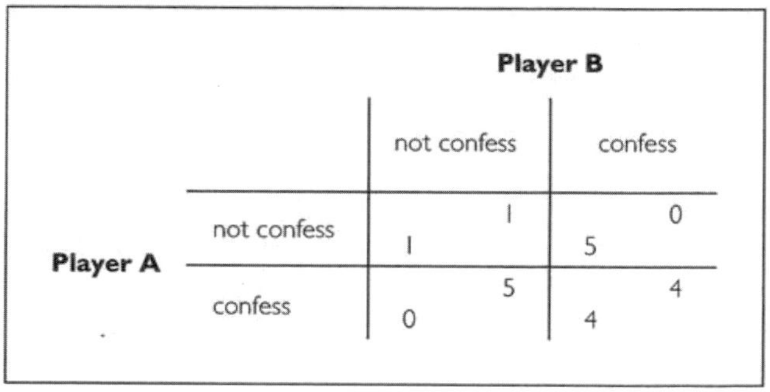

Figure 4.13 One variation of the prisoners' dilemma game. The lowest score produces the best outcome; the highest score produces the worst outcome.

When we examine the aggregate consequences of these choices in numerical terms, it is clear that the combined choices of both not to confess would produce the best outcome, a score of 2. The worst outcome of 8 follows from both confessing. A minimaxing individual in this situation would resolve to choose the outcome which minimized the risk of a harsh punishment and which took into account the lack of trust in the other partner. From the point of view of each individual the minimax decision would be to confess in the hope that the other partner did not, and so escape harsh punishment. However, if both actors in this situation applied this rational decision to their situation and opted to confess, the aggregate outcome would be the worst outcome. In this way, game theorists argue, it is possible for rational individuals to act in ways which appear to be the best in the light of the circumstances and yet the unintended consequence of their individual actions is to produce the worst outcome for all involved.

In prisoners' dilemma, the rational decisions of the actors produce the worst possible outcomes for all the players involved.

This rational choice framework has been adapted for the study of electoral politics by James Buchanan and others in developing public choice theory (see Buchanan et al., 1978; Buchanan and Tullock, 1981; Green, 1987). The focus on public or political choices as rational decisions has led to it being labelled the 'economics of politics'. Buchanan's approach is interesting in its attempts to examine the interrelationship between the rational choices of voters and of political leaders, and how their combined decisions had effects on public policy (Buchanan et al., 1978). For Buchanan, the electorate is composed of individuals who behave like consumers in the marketplace and the votes they cast in elections are the same as purchases. Consequently, voters are seen to vote for the party which offers them the most in terms of their perceived self-interest. This approach to voters in the 1960s and 1970s seemed to provide a means of explaining the decline of voting according to party loyalty and class background and the rise of issue-based voting alongside the increase in electoral volatility more generally. It is assumed that voters overall would prefer to have lower taxes at the same time as greater public spending on services such as health, education and social services. For political leaders who, as rational actors, attempt to bid for votes in order to win power, these apparently contradictory demands by the electorate lead them into a situation where they can only keep themselves in power by increasing state intervention without passing on the costs to the taxpayer.

The consequence of such a policy, according to Buchanan, is increased public debt and the undermining of wealth creation sectors (private business) by state regulation and higher corporate taxation. Buchanan was associated with New Right or neo-liberal demands for 'rolling back the frontier of the state' under Thatcher in the UK and Reagan in the USA. He adds that the rational choices of members of the bureaucracy also lead to an expansion of the state, supposedly in the interests of the citizen, but really to serve the self-interest of the administrators in expanding their own power and rewards. In this case, as in prisoners' dilemma, the rational self-interested choices of those involved lead to a situation where everyone suffers in the long term. Buchanan argues that the expansion of the state undermines the economic growth upon which the social programmes depend because the tax base shrinks.

Activity 4.4

Now turn to Reading C, an extract from Garrett Hardin's *The Tragedy of the Commons* (1968), and Reading D, 'When rationality fails' (1989), by Jon Elster.

- Identify how Hardin follows the game of prisoners' dilemma identified above.
- Make a list of what you consider to be the strengths and weaknesses of Hardin's extract.
- Identify the main themes of Elster's account of the limits of rational choice explanations.

As you read through the extract by Hardin you may be struck by the way that certain premises and assumptions can lead you to certain conclusions. As you read through Elster, you should think about whether Hardin's assumptions about people are really true.

4.2 Problems in rational choice theory

The assumptions of game theory are open to criticism on a number of grounds, which all hinge on the extent to which the models used are realistic. In particular, a great deal of doubt can be cast upon the definition of the concept of rationality in rational choice theory; this has, in turn, raised questions about when the model can usefully be applied and when it would be inappropriate. To address these problems it is worthwhile to consider what it means for behaviour to be rational or irrational.

Rational choice theory works well when life is reasonably certain and predictable and the issues are kept simple – however, most situations are uncertain, unpredictable and complex.

The relationship between our choices and desires is often less clear-cut than the advocates of rational choice theory suggest for, in some situations, human beings act against their desires or experience conflicting desires. Since all decisions in the market involve these sorts of choices, it may not be accurate to characterize economic choices as rational calculations of costs and benefits. The characterization of rationality also depends upon the situation in which it takes place. What appears to be rational behaviour in one context may seem irrational in another situation, so that a universal principle of rational choice is unlikely to be established. Our personal attachments, traditional beliefs and even wishful thinking also play an important part in the formation of choices. The rational choice model assumes that, even if human beings are rational 'minimaxers', they make choices with full and perfect knowledge of the possible end consequences of their decisions and of the various means for achieving the same results. It can be argued that all of these assumptions are unrealistic. For instance, the behaviour of stockbrokers during a crash in the investment markets does conform to the rational model in that they sell stocks and shares in order to avoid further loss of value. However, in conditions of normal trading this profession operates by rules of thumb, intuition and hunches even though their occupational description would suggest the purely rational pursuit of profit taking.

The philosopher and economist Friedrich Hayek began to address some of these difficulties and became deeply critical of attempts to develop purely rational accounts of social life. In particular, he argued that the social scientific method should take proper account of the complexity of social phenomena within open systems. For Hayek the problem is **scientism**, which involves any claim to know the most appropriate way of investigating a social phenomenon before considering it (Hayek, 1952). Hayek warns against obstacles to the further advance of modern science, such as:

- the belief that ideas of things, such as 'laws', 'causes' and 'social order', possess some reality (that by analysing ideas we learn about the attributes of reality);
- the tendency of human actors to interpret external events after their own images;
- the attribution of a designing mind to the objects in question.

He was particularly concerned to counter the belief that it was possible to reconstruct the real world in social scientific theories and use this knowledge rationally to reconstruct actual societies (which he associated with the social engineering of fascism and communism). Hayek suggests that it is impossible to comprehend collective entities such as 'capitalism', 'society' and the 'economy', for:

> The concrete knowledge which guides the action of any group of people never exists as a consistent and coherent body. It only exists in the dispersed, incomplete and inconsistent form in which it appears in many individual minds, and the dispersion and imperfection of all knowledge are two of the basic facts from which the social sciences have to start.
>
> (Hayek, 1952, pp.49–50)

Hayek also starts from a position of **methodological individualism**. However, unlike in rational choice theory, people are not treated as discrete atoms but are seen as engaged in mutual discovery through relationships. The examples Hayek has in mind include the long-term evolution of a system of language or the emergence of a system of monetary exchange. These evolving systems are seen as the unintended and unanticipated consequences of all the shared experiences of exchange.

Methodological individualism breaks things down into their smallest components and uses this to reconstruct more complex relations.

> The way in which footpaths are formed in a wild broken country is just such an instance. At first everyone will seek for himself what seems to him the best path. But the fact that such a path has been used once is likely to make it easier to traverse and therefore more likely to be used again; and thus gradually more and more clearly defined tracks arise and come to be used to the exclusion of other possible ways. Human movements through the region come to conform to a definite pattern which, although the result of deliberate decisions of many people, has yet not been consciously designed by anyone.
>
> (Hayek, 1952, pp.70–1)

While the nomothetic method which identifies 'recurrent events of a particular kind' (Hayek, 1952, p.118) predominates in natural science in relation to social science, Hayek sees idiographic explanations of particular or unique situations as playing as important a role as that of generalization. He suggests that the role of theory is to constitute the wholes through recognizing the importance of the related parts and comprehending the intentions, shared experiences and tacit knowledge of subjective individuals. In the next section we turn to those approaches which focus upon the roles of tacit and subjective knowledge in social science.

Summary

Rational choice approaches resolve the problems of cultural values by focusing upon the 'subjective preferences' of rational individuals. In praxeology and game theory, the rationality of individuals is established at an abstract theoretical level prior to empirical research and typically adopts a 'minimaxing' approach to decision making.

The imaginative use of games to identify the process of decisions made by individuals in complex and unpredictable situations provides social scientists with a means of identifying the similarities in decision making in very different contexts, highlighting the rule-governed nature of social life.

The assumption of rationality in these approaches provides a useful indication of the problems created by wishful thinking in social scientific research. In such cases, social scientists imagine an object (such as society, the economy, the mind, or the polity), treat it as a thing in itself and neglect the very processes by which such objects are constructed in the first place.

5 Meaning and subjectivity

For neo-Kantian idealists, general explanations have a useful role in social science even if they are only part of the whole picture; rational choice theories raise the prospect of a purely rational or 'minimaxing' approach to human decision making. However, the third group of idealist approaches, which we examine now, embraces the subjective dimension of social life wholeheartedly. They regard the existence of objects of analysis that we think of as real, as the product of our interpretations. In addition, individuals are not viewed as atoms bouncing off each other, but as having a sense of the shared existence through which identities are constructed. This does not mean that such 'objective things' have no effect – if we believe something to be real, it is real enough in its consequences for we behave as if it does exist. This section is concerned with a variety of approaches which have come to be known as forms of hermeneutics or phenomenology and which contain some useful insights into the problems of social science. We focus upon the interpretive approaches and their exploration of the self, interaction and meanings. The aim of hermeneutics is to make the obscure clear and plain, by identifying the processes and context of all approaches which attempt to understand society and culture. To do this, we should place ourselves inside the mind of the author or the social actor under consideration. The concept of **subjectivity** used in this approach is not the calculating machine of rational choice theory but, instead, it involves the meaningful interpretation of unpredictable relationships in everyday life.

Hermeneutics and phenomenology seek to understand the subjective and meaningful construction of the complex social world.

The emergence of contemporary hermeneutics, defined as the theory of the interpretation of meaning, can be traced to Wilhelm Dilthey's *Introduction to the Human Sciences* (1883; for brief extracts see Rickman, 1976). Dilthey's main concern was to identify a distinctly 'human science' which did not treat the study of society and history as the automatic play of objective forms and processes. For Dilthey, the natural sciences presented an inappropriate analogue for social science because natural objects cannot meaningfully interpret and construct their own cultural environment, whereas human beings can. Therefore, the study of society and history involved very different ground rules from those of natural scientific research because all human values, ideas, concepts, purposes and desires are seen as an inescapable part of understanding social life. This means that while human beings acted *upon* the natural environment, they also acted *within* the social environment. So the social and cultural forms taken as the objects of the social sciences were the expressions of the mind rather than external to the mind. The 'lived experiences' of individuals are thus the source of understanding. To deal with this, Dilthey argued, we have to recognize the problem of the *hermeneutic circle*: 'The whole of a work must be understood from individual words and their combination but full understanding of an individual part presupposes understanding of the whole' (Dilthey, 1896, cited in Bryant, 1985, pp.66–7). A common metaphor for explaining this idea is the sentence analogue, whereby the meaning of a word is identified by reference to its place in a sentence and the meaning of the sentence is established through the meaning of the individual words. Thus all mental constructions are historically and socially specific and hence prone to change as part of the web of cultural forms. There is, therefore, a crucial

Hermeneutics focuses upon the lived experience of human beings in their social and historical context.

difference between the approaches here and all the other approaches considered so far in this chapter. Here, there is no 'knowing subject' above and beyond the experiences of those being studied. In the following sections we look at ways in which this approach has been developed in the social sciences, particularly psychology, sociology and geography.

5.1 The self-concept and social interaction

The approaches considered in this section start from the assumption that the 'real world' is actively constructed by human beings, even though social scientists tend to behave as if it is independent of our knowledge. The first grouping we should consider, interactionism, draws from the philosophy of **pragmatism**. This is concerned with the way in which meanings and interpretations are the product of the 'pragmatic concerns' of practical problems and purposes of social life. The mind is treated as a tool for solving problems encountered in everyday life. This problem-solving approach has had a profound impact upon the interactionist approach in psychology (sometimes labelled humanistic psychology or sociological social psychology) and in sociology.

Pragmatic approaches treat social inquiry as a form of problem solving closely related to the concerns of everyday life.

Interactionism treats social actors and their small face-to-face interactions as the basis of all social life, so that the meaning of any concept or idea (personal, political, philosophical or scientific) can only be located in the experiential consequences which it produces. On the basis of this, the pragmatist William James distinguished 'knowledge about' from 'knowledge of' (James, 1890). 'Knowledge about' – that which is acquired through textbooks – is conveyed in abstract general principles which can be learned and memorized. However, 'knowledge of' – practical knowledge acquired through experience in everyday life – is established through trial and error and can take an unconscious or tacit form. This treats the concept of the mind as a 'thinking process' always in development, rather than as a fixed thing. In this way, individuals can define objects and their context, identify sensible courses of action or modes of conduct, imagine the consequences of these choices and, finally, select an appropriate course of action.

Practically adequate knowledge is derived through a process of trial and error.

Other forms of interactionist thinking, like that of psychologist and sociologist George Herbert Mead, focused more upon the social context in the shaping of choices. For Mead, in *Mind, Self and Society* (1934), meaning can be identified in the actual behaviour of the actors and the development of the mind as an unfolding process can be seen in the activities of children. In the *play stage* children play out roles and characters in order to be someone else, such as cowboys and Indians, doctors and nurses, etc. In the more advanced *game stage* the child learns to develop an inner conversation with the 'generalized other', which enables the child to predict the behaviour of others. The prediction of the routine habitual practices of others and responding in similarly predictable ways enables the everyday social interaction of human beings to take place while avoiding conflict. In Mead's own words:

For Mead, the concept of self is not fixed but the changing product of an ongoing process of interaction.

> in a game where a number of individuals are involved, then the child taking one role must be ready to take the role of everyone else ... [and] must have the responses of each position involved in his [*sic*] own position. He must know what everyone

> else is going to do in order to carry out his own play. He has to take all of these roles. They do not all have to be present in consciousness at the same time, but at some moments he has to have three or four individuals present in his own attitude, such as the one who is going to throw the ball, the one who is going to catch it and so on.
>
> (Mead 1934, p.151)

Often the things we know about can help us understand situations of which we have little or no experience.

This can be demonstrated through the example of the metaphor of the *looking glass self*, whereby other people act like mirrors for an individual's imagination. This is based upon three steps: the individual imagining how he or she looks to others; the imagination of how others judge the individual; and the emotional reaction of the individual to the imagined judgement. In this way, we constantly monitor ourselves at the level of our own imagination and, consequently, an adequate social science should attempt to address the existence of these processes (Cooley, 1902). Social interaction can be seen as an ongoing process, rather like the changing patterns of a kaleidoscope, instead of following a definite fixed plan. The search for patterns can be seen in the identification of 'career' patterns in different situations. It is possible to identify similar patterns in occupational careers, criminal careers (Becker, 1963) and the moral career of a mental patient (Goffman, 1987, pp.117–56). In criminal and non-criminal career patterns we would expect the rewards and respect to fit their place in the career ladder; Goffman reminds us that careers can be brilliant but also disappointing. A career in this approach is defined by the relationship between the internal processes through which we define our concept of self and the external processes through which we understand our social positions, lifestyles and institutional locations. It also helps us to see that labelling someone as criminal, or as mentally ill, matters. Goffman suggests that these moral aspects of careers can help us understand the relationship between the self and social institutions in the treatment careers of 'mentally ill' patients. Nevertheless, this approach is limited to considering what we can empirically observe rather than attempting to identify the assumptions upon which these actions and interactions are based.

Activity 4.5

If we consider identities to be social locations, it is worthwhile thinking through what it means to ask yourself the question 'Who am I?' before engaging in social research. Various dimensions of your identity should come to mind, such as your age, gender, ethnicity, social class, marital status and so on. You will consider some of these to be more important than others.

- Make a list of the relevant dimensions for your own identity.
- Organize this list in terms of their importance.
- Which of these dimensions has changed in importance and why?
- Quickly list the areas of social science which really interest you. Are these related to the dimensions of your identity? If so, in what ways?

5.2 Phenomenology and intersubjective meaning

Phenomenology asks us to dig deeper than in previous approaches, in order to explore the taken-for-granted assumptions of social research. The German philosopher who established contemporary phenomenology, Edmund Husserl, asks us to reconsider the idea of the 'objective world', and the way that some approaches treat subjectivity as a pale reflection of some deeper or more authentic state of affairs. As you saw in Chapter 2, Descartes started with 'I think therefore I exist' as a foundational principle. However, for Husserl, the starting-point always involved an intention, 'I think something'. This means that the act of describing experience actually creates the object of analysis. Therefore, the distinction between 'surface appearances' and some 'underlying reality' is no more than a convenient fiction for positivist scientists. To get around this problem, Husserl argued, we have to 'bracket' the objective. This means that we should suspend our belief in the existence of the objective world and abstain from making judgements about whether the world does or does not exist. This process has been characterized as the peeling away of the layers of ideas to identify the pre-scientific forms of experience of the *Lebenswelt* (life-world), rather like peeling away the layers of an onion.

Phenomenology treats the distinction between surface appearances and reality as the product of the conscious mind.

Schütz developed this in a more practical way. In *The Phenomenology of the Social World* (1932/1967), he argued that it is through the condition of **intersubjectivity** that the individual actors involved are able to grasp each other's consciousness and construct their life-world. By sharing time and space, the two or more individual actors involved in communication could engage in a process of understanding which involves the discovery of what is going on in the other person's mind (Schütz, 1932/1967, pp.112–13). Although Weber had developed the use of ideal types as a theoretical tool against which empirical evidence could be compared, this still treated the evidence as factual even though it was open to various interpretations. Instead, Schütz argued that there were no hard facts, only interpretations – that facts are intersubjectively constructed. As you saw in Chapter 1, Schütz sought to establish connections between the second-order constructs of social science and the first-order constructs of everyday life (Schütz, 1953). At the heart of Schütz's approach is the sociological formulation often described as 'cookery-book' or 'recipe' knowledge, the notion that we do not need to understand the origins of a particular set of practices in order to select the ingredients, bake the cake and 'eat and enjoy it' (Schütz, 1943, p. 137).

9

Phenomenology sees consciousness as the product of the intersubjective relations between actors engaged in communication.

Schütz suggests that we need to identify the recipe knowledge of social scientists as well as everyday life.

Two points should be highlighted here. First, the social world is constructed by actors who possess free will and who can and will behave in spontaneous ways not anticipated by the 'fictitious consciousness' of the scientific model. Second, scientists employ the same procedures of typification as actors in everyday life. For Schütz, in the natural sciences it is plausible to collect 'facts and regularities', but, when faced with the problem of understanding social existence, we need to account for the motives, the means and ends, the shared relationships and the plans and expectations of human actors. In the next two sections we explore some of the ways in which this approach has been applied.

Social scientific practice should find ways to connect the 'first-order' constructs of everyday life and the 'second-order' constructs of social scientific knowledge.

5.3 Ethnomethodology and tacit knowledge

While phenomenology offers a useful philosophical critique of social scientific knowledge, the sociologist Harold Garfinkel developed this into a viable research programme which attempted to reconstruct the 'taken-for-granted' commonsense assumptions (tacit knowledge) of people in their everyday lives. This became known as ethnomethodology (literally, 'people-method'), combining Schütz's insights with the empirical research strategies of symbolic interactionists (Garfinkel, 1967). The interactionists used ethnographic research techniques, such as in-depth interviews and participant observation, to attempt to reconstruct social life in a way that was as true to life as possible. However, they limited their evidence to the relationships they could observe, even if they didn't see observation in quite the same way as empiricists did.

Ethnomethodology seeks to find ways of locating and reconstructing the taken-for-granted commonsense assumptions of social practices.

Garfinkel wanted to delve deeper into the lives of his subjects and aimed to reconstruct the tacit knowledge that they could not even express (which Schütz had labelled 'cookery-book' or recipe knowledge). For Garfinkel, human actors continually create and transform their social existence, so that the supposedly objective contexts in which we live are fragile and transitory. Garfinkel suggests that actors are constantly attempting to make sense of the mass of sensations they experience. To do this, actors draw upon their stock of stories and meaningful interpretations. The moment that the evidence seems to suggest the application of a particular story, the sensory evidence is transformed into a support for the story. Garfinkel labels this technique the 'documentary method', involving a constant reciprocal process of interaction between the story-lines and evidence. Consequently, the stock of stories itself undergoes renegotiation and transformation as identities are reinvented.

Ethnomethodologists demonstrate that the rules of social life are more flexible and fragile than is often assumed.

Some of Garfinkel's research strategies bordered on the unethical, for they deliberately disturbed 'normal' relationships to see what would happen. For example, he engaged in the disruption of conversations to identify how much the respondents would adapt. He would play chess in seminars with new students and, after a period of following the rules, would then violate minor rules to see how far his students would adapt. Taken by surprise in this way, the students would accommodate the rule changes in the game and play accordingly. More controversially, he trained a number of his students to pretend to be lodgers in their own homes when they left the university for the vacation. These students simply behaved politely at home as they would have done when visiting a distant relative, yet the minor changes in behaviour provoked considerable familial conflict and disorientation. In these ways, Garfinkel was able to identify the tacit assumptions of games, conversations and family life, and reconstruct the complex processes by which the 'objective world' only appears as such because we construct it in that way. Similar investigations have been carried out by Aaron Cicourel in *The Social Organisation of Juvenile Justice* (1976), which examined the taken-for-granted assumptions of the police and courts in defining and processing 'juvenile delinquents' in two comparable Californian cities. The differences in delinquency rates, Cicourel argued, were the product of the different judicial cultures in each city. In another example, Robert Bellah drew upon this strategy in his investigation of new religious movements. Bellah used a range of qualitative research techniques to identify the commonsense assumptions of religious people in their everyday lives to establish the intensity of belief and the extent of their commitment to religious values (Bellah, 1976). These different studies have different objects and are responding to very different debates; nevertheless, they all have a common concern to establish the taken-for-granted commonsense assumptions (or recipe knowledge) of the people involved.

Activity 4.6

Turn to Reading E from Roger Jeffery's 'Normal rubbish: deviant patients in casualty departments' (1979).

- Make notes on the forms of taken-for-granted typifications used in the treatment of patients in the casualty department and how they are used to place a value on the patients.
- Consider in which other ways you would engage in the study of casualty wards. In what ways would you say that Jeffery's approach has limits?

In this reading you should note the strengths and weaknesses of this kind of social scientific practice. Does Jeffery identify things that other social scientists overlook?

Summary

A common theme in hermeneutic and phenomenological accounts of social life is the identification of the meanings, intentions and context of the author of a text or the social actor in his or her natural setting. The focus of analysis is the social and historical conditions in which a specific set of ideas or actions is located.

Interactionist and ethnomethodological approaches sought to draw upon these insights in developing an active research programme into the self-concepts and/or tacit assumptions of everyday social life.

Schütz made a distinctive contribution to social scientific method by attempting to overcome the tendency towards detachment associated with the application of natural science methods to social objects. In order to prevent social scientists imposing their own typifications upon objects in social research, an adequate approach should seek to ensure that the concepts used are also intelligible in everyday life.

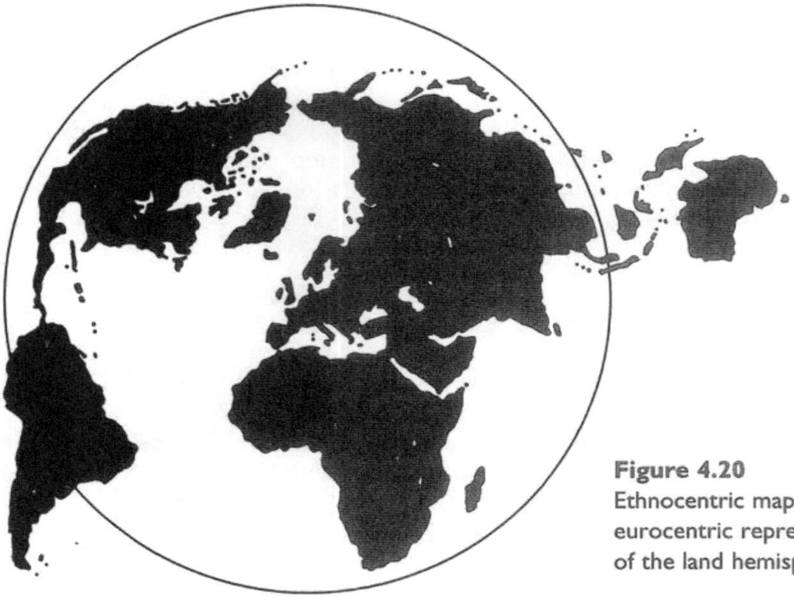

Figure 4.20
Ethnocentric mapping III: eurocentric representation of the land hemisphere.

6 Conclusion: taking imagination seriously

Let's briefly summarize the idealist approaches considered in this chapter. They fall into three broad categories.

- Various forms of neo-Kantianism which, in different ways, attempt to explain or understand, or both explain and understand social life. They can be differentiated in terms of how they see social science – as nomothetic or idiographic, voluntarist or determinist.
- Approaches which place a special emphasis on rationality as a basis for human decision making, such as praxeology and rational choice theory. These tend to emphasize explanations of social behaviour but at the expense of understanding. As a result, there is a danger of making the evidence fit the model.
- Hermeneutic and phenomenological accounts of the meaningful construction of the social world which seek to understand how individuals interact and make sense of the world.

Earlier in this chapter you considered the quick guide to idealist approaches to knowledge construction (Table 4.1) which offered a bold initial comparison of these approaches and how they differed from the empiricist approach to knowledge construction in Chapter 2. In particular, you were asked to think about how the various idealisms can be compared and contrasted in the ways that they understood the relationships between theory and observation, facts and values and explanation and prediction. Now in Table 4.2 you have the chance to go through these steps again, but in a little more detail, taking into account the key ideas developed throughout this chapter.

Table 4.2 Varieties of idealism.

<table>
<tr><th></th><th colspan="3">Varieties of Idealism</th><th></th></tr>
<tr><th></th><th>Neo-Kantian Idealism</th><th>Rational Choice Theory</th><th>Hermeneutics and Phenomenology</th><th>Empiricism</th></tr>
<tr><td>Theory and Observation</td><td>Theoretical statements identify relationships between variables.
Complex empirical evidence is 'organized' by ideal types (exaggerated characteristics of social life) as devices for comparing and contrasting.
Ideal types provide a bridge between understanding human action and explaining social relations.</td><td>Theoretical work involves the rational reconstruction of principles and concepts which explain empirical relations.
Theory reflects the capacity of individual actors to make rational decisions within definite constraints (such as the supply of resources like information).
The key assumption is the 'minimaxing' individual making choices on the basis of calculations of costs and benefits of various courses of action.</td><td>The problem facing social science is the gulf between the everyday experiences of social actors (first-order constructs) and the detached accounts of social life produced by social scientists (second-order constructs).
Scientific detachment results in social scientists imposing their conception of the way social processes operate upon the object in question.
Detached science tells us more about the scientist than the object.
Understanding is just as, if not more, important than explaining.</td><td>The scientific method involves a clear separation of theory and observation (although empiricists disagree about the relationship between the two).

All theoretical statements must derive from (or are subject to repeated tests against) empirical evidence.

Theoretical statements apply to all circumstances where the objects in question exist.</td></tr>
<tr><td>Facts and Values</td><td>Value relevance – concept formation in the social sciences should be relevant to the problems of a particular society in question at a specific time.
Value judgements are the concern of the philosophers in that time and place and the values of the social researcher should be clearly stated.</td><td>Social scientific facts can only be identified through the subjective values and the intentional choices of individuals.
Rational choice theories focus upon exchange relationships in a range of social settings.
There is some question as to whether this approach is actually deeply value-laden in its advocacy of individualism.</td><td>Social science is deeply value laden, for the social scientists define their own identities through common stock of knowledge of the society they study.
Scientific facts are the commonsense assumptions of the social scientists (values remain unacknowledged in concept formation).
Social scientists need to be much more critically aware of their own taken-for-granted assumptions and make these clear to their audiences.</td><td>Facts and values are treated as separate things.

It is important to ensure that the subjective biases of the researcher do not interfere with the account of empirical evidence.

It is feasible and desirable to have a value-free social science. Some empiricists accept that there are problems in keeping values out of scientific knowledge.</td></tr>
<tr><td>Explanation and Prediction</td><td colspan="2">An empirical regularity between variables (constant conjunction of events) is necessary but not sufficient for establishing a causal law. This acknowledges the complexity of causal factors in any empirical situation but raises problems in terms of making accurate predictions (intelligibilty determinism).
It is possible to develop either nomethetic or idiographic accounts of social life. Nomothetic explanations identify general relations sustained over time. Idiographic explanations focus upon individual circumstances as unique and acknowledge the importance of interpretations in generating knowledge. Rational choice theory adopts a nomothetic account of explanation which applies the same formal model across different situations.
Theories are useful and suggestive simplifications of more complex processes rather than perfectly accurate depictions of real life. Thus prediction in social science involves the identification of patterns rather than specific outcomes.</td><td>Social settings only exist through the intersubjective relations of the actors involved.
Knowledge can only be understood in the historical and social situation in which it was produced.
Social life is the product of the complex processes through which individuals and groups (re)negotiate their way through social life.
The complexity of social life and the distribution of (often tacit) knowledge means that nomothetic approaches fail to account for events as unique concrete circumstances.</td><td>Empiricism assumes that there is a symmetry of explanation and prediction.

Any explanation must be predictively accurate to be sustained.

A constant conjunction of events is both necessary and sufficient to generate a causal law of social life (regularity determinism).</td></tr>
</table>

As you can see, there are considerable differences between these idealist approaches. In particular, they disagree about the precise ways in which social scientific practice should proceed. On the one hand, the rational choice theorists believe that an all-purpose theoretical framework can be devised to *explain* human decision making and behaviour. On the other hand, the phenomenologists argue that the choices we face are specific to each location, so the best we can do is to try to *understand* these situations. Neo-Kantians, however, try to juggle both preferences. They are divided over the choice of whether to develop general theoretical explanations of all situations (the nomothetic approach) *or* limit themselves to understanding all situations as unique (the idiographic approach) *or*, like Weber, try to find a way of generalizing in a looser way so that they don't have to explain the conditions of all situations in much detail.

Despite all of these differences, they are all critical of the empiricist account of what makes a causal relationship. While empiricists assume that an empirical regularity between variables sustained over time is in itself enough to justify the claim that a causal relationship is at work, for idealists these regularities have a much more tentative status. An idealist approach sees them as useful for indicating the patterns we should attempt to explain and understand, so that they become 'intelligible' to the people who study them. For this reason, a successful prediction like 'if *x* one day then *y* the next', is not enough to construct a causal law; it must also make sense within the existing body of conceptual knowledge through which we interpret our perceptions and experiences. In addition to this, idealists still hold in common certain distinctive features which can be highlighted as follows.

- The transfer of the assumptions and methods of the natural sciences (in conditions of closure) to the study of social objects in complex open systems is an inappropriate way to proceed.
- Any attempt to generate general laws should take into account the role of human interpretations and the lack of a clear separation between the subject and object in social science.

These approaches can be labelled idealist in the broadest sense. Idealism, as you will have noticed, is something of an umbrella label. However, it is possible to link all of these approaches by noting their emphasis upon the role of ideas and human imagination in organizing experience and constructing knowledge about the social world. Idealists tend to be anti-naturalist in considering empiricist accounts of the scientific method for studying social objects, believing that it is inappropriate to apply those assumptions and methods to studying people. Idealists emphasize the creative and interpretative characteristics of human beings and the impossibility of social researchers ever fully removing their values from the study of social relations and processes. Even Weber adopts the position of 'value relevance', that social research should be relevant to the problems of the day. Some idealists, by treating knowledge as a social product, reject both the separation of facts and values and the separation of theory and observation. So the key thing to remember is idealist approaches highlight the way in which observation is not as simple an activity as empiricists would have us believe.

READING A
There is more to seeing than meets the eye

Norwood Hanson

There was a young man of East Bosham
Who took out his eyeballs to wash 'em,
His mother said: 'Jack,
If you don't put 'em back,
I'll jump on the beggars and squash 'em.'

The word 'observe' has many uses. Two of these must be kept distinct. ... 'Observe' sometimes serves in just the ways that 'look' and 'listen' serve, and it sometimes serves as 'see' and 'hear' serve. Thus we may speak of a man as a careful, systematic, industrious observer, or of his careful, systematic, and industrious observations. We may also, however, refer to his observations as his findings, his discoveries, what he has been successful in seeing. The word 'observe', then, is sometimes used to indicate what a person is doing, and sometimes used to signal the success of what he is doing. ... We know from common experience that the world does not go dark when we shut our eyes, nor do flowers lose their scent when we catch cold. So apparently we require ways of talking about what does go dark when I shut my eyes. ... We might talk about sensations ... by talking about *looks, appearances, glimpses, scents, flavors, sounds*, and so on. We say we see the sun. But all we really have to go on is the look of a brilliant yellow-white disc. We say we see a round penny, but the cash value of that in terms of sensation is just the appearance in our visual field of a copper-brown oval patch. We think we hear the telephone. But all we really hear is ding-a-ling. ...

The major mistake [is the] assimilation of the concept of *sensation* to the concept of *observation*. ... Visual sensations likewise are not *seeings*, though any case of seeing entails our having had at least one visual sensation. A visual sensation of a brilliant yellow-white disc is not itself a seeing of the sun, though any case of seeing the sun entails our having had at least one visual sensation of a brilliant yellow-white disc. ... In the strictest sense of 'see' what I see are two dimensional color patches; not the sun, the hills, and the trees, but only the looks or visual appearance of the sun, hills, and trees. The squinter may not see two candles, but he sees two bright somethings; these somethings are the candle-looks, the sense-data. The theory is not inventing fictitious entities; it is only drawing attention to our immediate object of sense, objects which we ordinarily ignore in favor of talking about common physical objects like candles, hills, trees, and the sun. ...

The conceptual organization of one's visual field is the all-important factor here. It is not something visually apprehended in the way that lines and shapes and colors are visually apprehended. ... It is rather the *way* in which lines, shapes, and colors are visually apprehended. I have been inviting you to consider a given constellation of lines and shapes (what psychologists call 'a stimulus pattern') and to consider further the different ways in which this given constellation of pattern can be apprehended visually, the different sorts of conceptual organization that can be accorded to that constellation. ... So while scientists are right in saying that they see physical objects ... we cannot leave things at that. For this would lead to some very uncomplicated ... views as to the nature of laboratory science, views to the effect that *seeing* is just an opening of one's eyes and looking; that *observing* is simply being in a position to watch when a phenomenon takes place, and the *facts* are just the things and situations in the world that we see when our eyes are open, the things we trip over when our eyes are closed. ... Wittgenstein said that 'we find certain things about seeing puzzling because we do not find the whole business of seeing puzzling enough.' ...

What follows is intended to show that the theories about seeing we have so far considered are too simple by far to be adequate. Consider first this well-known figure [Figure 1]. ...

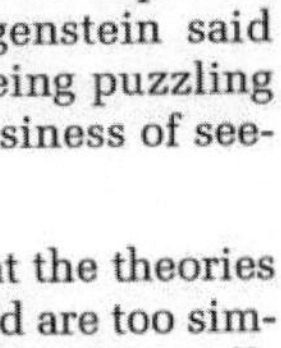

Figure 1

We do not begin with the visual sensation and only then turn our theories and interpretations loose on it. In a most important way our theories and interpretations are in the *seeing* from the outset. *Figure 1* is seen as a box from underneath or from above, or as an octagon, or as a flat, flat-line drawing, or first one of these then another – but not all of them at once. ... Other figures to which all these remarks apply are these [Figure 2].

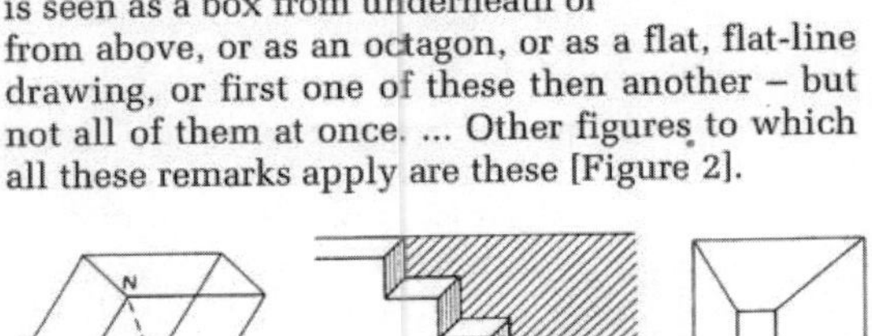

Figure 2

With each of these there are at least three possibilities open to us. We can see these figures in either a convex aspect or a concave aspect or as a flat-line drawing; or first one, then another – but not any two simultaneously. ...

Let us conclude with two well-known figures from experimental psychology [Figures 3(a) and 3(b)]. For those of you who see 3(a) as a duck, let me point out Bugs Bunny; and for those of you who see only a rabbit, let me point out Donald Duck. *Figure 3(b)* is complex in the same sort of way. Some of you will see an old, rather hag-like individual here; others will see a very young, stylish woman looking away. ...

Figure 3a

Figure 3b

Some people can *only* see these figures one way or the other; much as when we have at last solved the child's puzzle, having found the face in the branches of the tree, we can never see the tree any other way thereafter. The fact is always present in the tree. ...

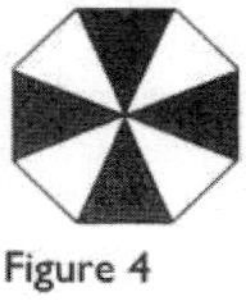

Figure 4

Some will see [Figure 4] as a white cross on a black ground. Others will see this as a black cross on a white ground. ... If I drew for you exactly what I saw when I reported 'white cross on black ground,' how would it differ from your drawing of what you see when you report 'black cross on white ground'? So too with Koehler's goblet [Figure 5].

Figure 5

Again, our retinas may react normally to this. But while I see a Venetian goblet, you may see two men staring at each other. Have we seen different things? Of course we have. And yet if I draw my cup for you, you may say, 'By Jove, that is exactly what I saw, two men in a staring contest.' ...

Look back at Figure 3a, and then consider Figure 6. The context clearly gives us the clue regarding which aspect of the duck–rabbit is appropriate.

Figure 6

Source: Hanson, 1969, pp.61–97, 104.

READING B
Race relations in the city

John Rex and Robert Moore

The problem of race relations which confronted and perplexed the people of Birmingham in the early 1960s was one of immense practical political importance. ... It is important, therefore, that sociologists studying it should report their findings not merely to an academic audience, but to the widest possible audience of citizens. ... A sociological study of race relations must, in the first place, be distinguished from one which is purely historical and one which is psychological in its approach. This is not by any means to suggest that the historian and the psychologist do not have a considerable contribution to make to the study of race relations. It is to suggest, however, that neglect of the sociological dimensions of the problem could be disastrously misleading.

The inadequacy of historical explanation taken by itself rests upon the historian's inability to make explicit the general process which his explanation assumes. Very few historians, of course, confine themselves to reporting unique historical sequences of events. In their use of conjunctions like 'because', 'so', and 'therefore', they refer implicitly to general psychological and sociological laws. ... The prime virtue of the historian lies in the techniques which he has at his disposal for assessing the evidence as to what actually occurred. The explanatory laws to which he refers are for him a secondary matter. In the study of race relations his contribution will lie in his ability to record precisely what occurred in the situation of race contact. The interpretation of these occurrences is a task which falls to the generalizing, theoretical human sciences, above all to psychology and sociology. But psychology alone cannot explain the kind of problem with which we are concerned. If, for example, we are concerned to explain prejudice and discriminatory behaviour, the psychologist could only hope to show either that there was some universal human tendency towards behaving in these ways or that there was a deviant minority who were prejudiced because of their disturbed personalities. ...

It is also the case that a great deal of it was sufficiently explained, once we knew something of Birmingham's social structure and conflicts, and the constellation of interests and roles which was built into Birmingham society. At the very least it must be said that the universal factors and those having their roots in the individual personality could only be known if the factors arising from the social, economic, and cultural system were first sorted out. This point was emphasized for us by the feeling which we and many Birmingham people had about the race relations situation. This was the feeling that individuals were often acting in contradiction of their own ideals and sometimes of their own interests. They adopted discriminatory policies reluctantly, regretfully, and sometimes guiltily because they felt compelled to do so by circumstances beyond their control. Sometimes we felt that they acted as men possessed by some evil demon. But it is the task of sociologists to substitute casual explanation for demonology and what we have tried to do is to show that that which possessed them was not a demon, but the social system of which they were part. ...

False beliefs about an ethnic outgroup may serve to ensure that both an adherence to an ideal of social justice and a strong competitive position for one's group can be maintained. What we have to do is not merely to classify behaviour as prejudiced but to understand the part which customs, beliefs, norms, and expectations play in a larger social structure, be it the structure of an ethnic minority group or that of the overall urban society, marked as it is by diverse intergroup conflicts. Once we understand urban society as a structure of social interaction and conflict, prejudiced behaviour may be shown to fit naturally into or even to be required by that structure. Prejudice may be a social as well as a psychological phenomenon. ... Once we have grasped the idea of urban society as a number of overlapping and sometimes contradictory systems of social relations it soon becomes clear that the commonly used vocabulary of race relations which includes such words as 'assimilation', 'integration', and 'accommodation' is inadequate. Such vocabularies assume a 'host–immigrant' framework in which the culture and values of the host society are taken to be non-contradictory and static and in which the immigrant is seen as altering his own patterns of behaviour until they finally conform to those of the host society. ...

Several processes seem to operate. Firstly, class conflicts which are inherent in the situation because of shortage of facilities may cross-cut ethnic conflicts. Thus a tenant may come to see himself primarily as a tenant rather than as an Irishman or a West Indian. Or a landlord may come to put his economic interest as a landlord before his ethnic loyalty. Secondly, the children of a particular ethnic group may, through their school contacts, move into a different social world and so too may some adults. And, thirdly, since the available means of association (for instance, churches and political parties) are not historically geared to the existing conflict situation, membership of these organizations may serve to blur the lines of conflict. ...

There are a great many different situations which might easily be confused under the too-restricted terminology of the sociology of race relations. We would wish to distinguish at least two variables: (1) the degree of the involvement in the legal, social, and moral norms of the host society on the part of the immigrants; and (2) the degree of conflict between the various ethnic groups. These are the variables which apply to the different groups. If we try a little artificially to put them in tabular form, our table might look something like this:

Degree of Involvement	Degree of Intergroup Conflict
(1) Anomie, lack of social orientation	(1) A free market situation between individuals competing for facilities
(2) 'Living in the colony'	(2) Mobilization of monopoly power by ethnic groups in a market situation
(3) 'Living in the colony' but accepting formal rights in the host society	(3) Use of violence and/or mobilization of political power
(4) Acceptance of some social norms governing relations with strangers, apart from legal norms	(4) Collective bargaining and temporary contractual agreement
(5) Abandonment of the colony except for reasons of retrospective sentiment	

What we have done ... is to employ some of the concepts which have been outlined ... in order to analyse the social system of an urban ward when immigrant lodging-houses have emerged and are thought to constitute a social problem. We show the various social pressures which have operated to produce this situation and the kind of social interaction which has been produced on a community level. But we do this not because we wish to say that this outcome is inevitable in an expanding urban society. Rather, we hope that by drawing attention to some of the determinants of the situation we may make its rational control possible.

Source: Rex and Moore, 1967, pp.1–3, 13–14, 17–18.

READING C
The tragedy of the commons

Garrett Hardin

Consider the problem 'How can I win the game of tick-tack-toe?' It is well known that I cannot, if I assume ... that my opponent understands the game perfectly. Put another way, there is no 'technical solution' to the problem. I can win only by giving a radical meaning to the word 'win.' I can hit my opponent over the head; or I can drug him; or I can falsify the records. Every way in which I 'win' involves, in some sense, an abandonment of the game, as we intuitively understand it. ... It is fair to say that most people who anguish over the population problem are trying to find a way to avoid the evils of overpopulation without relinquishing any of the privileges they now enjoy. They think that farming the seas or developing new strains of wheat will solve the problem – technologically. ... The population problem cannot be solved in a technical way, any more than can the problem of winning the game of tick-tack-toe. ...

Population ... naturally tends to grow ... exponentially. In a finite world this means that the per capita share of the world's goods must steadily decrease. ... It is clear that we will greatly increase human misery if we do not, during the immediate future, assume that the world available to the terrestrial human population is finite. 'Space' is no escape. ... We may well call it 'the tragedy of the commons,' using the word 'tragedy' as the philosopher Whitehead used it: 'The essence of dramatic tragedy is not unhappiness. It resides in the solemnity of the remorseless working of things.' ... The tragedy of the commons develops in this way. Picture a pasture open to all. It is to be expected that each herdsman will try to keep as many cattle as possible on the commons. Such an arrangement may work reasonably satisfactorily for centuries because tribal wars, poaching, and disease keep the numbers of both man and beast well below the carrying capacity of the land. Finally, ... the inherent logic of the commons remorselessly generates tragedy. As a rational being, each herdsman seeks to maximize his gain. ... The rational herdsman concludes that the only sensible course for him to pursue is to add another animal to his herd. And another; and another [and so on]. But this is the conclusion reached by each and every rational herdsman sharing a commons. Therein is the tragedy. Each man is locked into a system that compels him to increase his herd without limit – in a world that is limited. Ruin is the destination toward which all men rush, each pursuing his own best interest in a society that believes in the freedom of the commons. Freedom in a commons brings ruin to all. ...

In a reverse way, the tragedy of the commons reappears in problems of pollution. Here it is not a question of taking something out of the commons, but of putting something in – sewage, or chemical, radioactive, and heat wastes into water; noxious and dangerous fumes into the air; and distracting and unpleasant advertising signs into the light of sight. ... The rational man finds that his share of the cost of the wastes he discharges into the commons is less than the cost of purifying his wastes before releasing them. Since this is true for everyone, we are locked into a system of 'fouling our own nest,' so long as we behave only as independent, rational, free enterprisers. ...

The tragedy of the commons is involved in population problems in another way. In a world governed solely by the principle of 'dog eat dog', ... parents who bred too exuberantly would leave fewer descendants, not more, because they would be unable to care adequately for their children. ... If each human family were dependent only on its resources; if the children of improvident parents starved to death; *if*, thus, overbreeding brought its own 'punishment', ... *then* there would be no public interest in controlling the breeding of families. But our society is deeply committed to the welfare state, and hence is confronted with another aspect of the tragedy of the commons. ... To couple the concept of freedom to breed with the belief that everyone born has an equal right to the commons is to lock the world into a tragic course of action. ... We must now recognize ... the necessity of abandoning the commons in breeding. No technical solution can rescue us from the misery of overpopulation. Freedom to breed will bring ruin to all.

Source: Hardin, 1968, pp. 1243–8.

READING D
When rationality fails

Jon Elster

Rational-choice theory aims at explaining human behaviour. To achieve this, it must, in any given case, proceed in two steps. The first step is to determine what a rational person would do in the circumstances. The second step is to ascertain whether this is what the person actually did. If the person did what the theory predicted he would do, it can add the case to its credit side. Similarly, the theory can fail at each of the two steps. First, it can fail to yield determinate predictions. Second, people can fail to conform to its predictions – they can behave irrationally. ...

An action, to be rational, must be the final result of three optimal decisions. First, it must be the best means of realizing a person's desire, given his beliefs. Next, these beliefs must themselves be optimal, given the evidence available to him. Finally, the person must collect an optimal amount of evidence – neither too much nor too little. That amount depends both on his desires – on the importance he attaches to the decision – and on his beliefs about the costs and benefits of gathering more information. The whole process, then, can be visualized as depicted in Fig. 1. ...

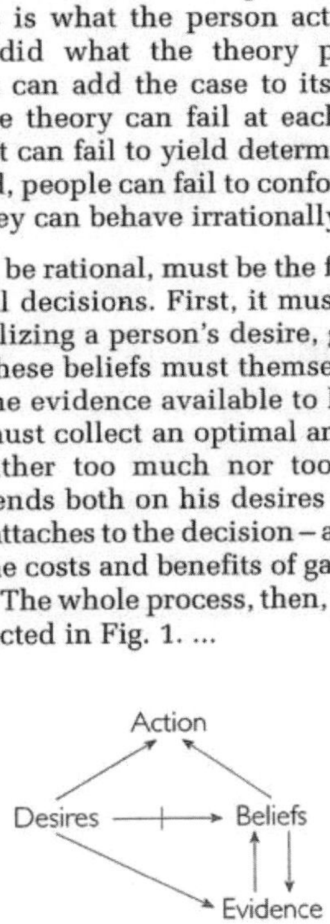

Figure 1

I shall explain how rational-choice theory can fail. ... Consider first indeterminacy of action. ... I am trivially indifferent between two identical cans of Campbell's soup in the supermarket. I want one of them, but it doesn't matter which. Less trivially, a manager might maximize profits in two different ways: by a low volume of sales with high profits per sale or a high volume with low profits per sale. What he does might be very important for the workers who will be laid off if he chooses the low-volume option, but if profit is all he cares about we will not be able to explain why he chooses one rather than the other option. ... Important decisions often involve incommensurable options. The choice, say, between going to law school or to a school of forestry, assuming that both attract me strongly, is a choice of career and life style. If I had tried both for a lifetime, I might be able to make an informed choice between them. As it is, I know too little about them to make a rational decision. What often happens in such cases is that peripheral considerations move to the center. ... Perhaps I opt for law school because that will make it easier for me to visit my parents on weekends. This way of deciding is as good as any – but it is not one that can be underwritten by rational-choice theory as superior to, say, simply tossing a coin.

Beliefs are indeterminate when the evidence is insufficient to justify a judgement about the likelihood of the various outcomes of action. ... Consider a firm's decision about how much to invest in research and development. To decide rationally, the firm must estimate the probable outcome of the investment – how likely it is that its innovative activities will lead to a profitable innovation – as well as the investments made by other firms and the probable outcome of those investments. Now the outcome of innovative activities is inherently uncertain. The firm cannot foresee with any precision whether it will hit the jackpot or come out with empty hands. Against the background of a constantly changing technology, past records are not good predictors of future success. ... Under winner-take-all conditions, this is crucial. The more a firm invests in research and development, the greater are its chances of getting there first. If other firms invest a large amount, our firm has a poor chance of winning. The rational decision might well be not to invest at all. Other firms, however, are presumably going through the same calculations. If they all decide to invest little, our firm should invest heavily. But once again, this reasoning applies equally to the other firms, and if they all invest heavily, our firm should drop out. ...

Deciding how much evidence to collect can be tricky. If the situation is highly stereotyped, as a medical diagnosis is, we know pretty well the costs and benefits of additional information. In situations that are unique, novel and urgent, like fighting a battle or helping the victim of a car accident, both costs and benefits are highly uncertain. There is a risk of acting too soon, on too little information – and a risk of delaying until it is too late. ... Thus we just have to act, more or less arbitrarily. In between these two extremes fall most choice situations of everyday life. ... When rational choice is indeterminate, some other mechanism must take up the slack. That could be the principle of 'satisficing,' of choosing something that is good enough.

Source: Elster, 1989, pp.30–5.

27

Paradigms, Conventions and Relativism

MARC J. SMITH

I Introduction

In the earlier chapters we focused upon whether it is possible and desirable to apply the assumptions and methods of the natural sciences to study social objects of analysis. So far, these approaches have lined up either for or against **naturalism**. The positivist and empiricist answer to this issue is that we should adopt a naturalist position, while many idealists question whether we should study people in this way. Nevertheless, most of the idealist approaches considered in Chapter 4 tend to accept the positivist view of scientific method as an accurate description of natural science; they just do not see it as appropriate for studying social life. In contrast, many of the approaches considered in this chapter see natural scientific knowledge itself as situated in definite historical and social locations – as social products or conventions. For this reason, we use the label **conventionalism** to designate all of these views. These conventionalist approaches shook the foundations of natural scientific thinking, sometimes provoking considerable hostility. However, in addition to telling us more about natural science and natural scientists, they also opened up new possibilities for reinterpreting the history and the philosophy of the social sciences.

In the last chapter we saw how the same observations can be interpreted in various ways, whether we are observing natural or social things. So far you have worked through the debates on the relationship between interpretation and observation. These debates prepared the way for thinking through a new relationship between natural and social science. Rather than the social sciences trying to copy natural scientific methods, both have attempted to share their ideas about how knowledge works. The relationship is now two-way rather than one-way. Conventionalism raises important and difficult issues about the nature of the natural sciences themselves as well as the ways in which positivist or empiricist methods are applied to the study of social objects such as 'society', 'the economy', 'the state', 'the environment' and 'the mind'. These issues can be expressed in a series of closely related questions all of which are addressed in the following sections of this chapter.

- What is the relationship between approaches in the philosophy of science and the actual practices of both natural and social science? How realistic are these approaches in describing the scientific process of discovery?
- To what extent is scientific knowledge a social product or convention and what are the implications of this for the status of science? What is the role of the communities and institutions which produce scientific knowledge?
- Do accounts which portray the growth of scientific knowledge as a slow process of testing and accumulating evidence take adequate account of the role of hunches, guesswork and flashes of inspiration?
- If scientific knowledge changes periodically as scientific communities change, such that the status of science is *relative* to the cultures which produce it, is it possible to remain committed to the idea of progress in human knowledge?
- What are the implications of adopting either a relativist or a rationalist position in the social sciences?

- How are conventionalist accounts of scientific knowledge interpreted within the disciplines of the social sciences?

So, while in Chapter 3 we saw how there was already an increased resistance to the application of natural science methods to the social sciences, the studies raised in this chapter will actually challenge your understanding about what makes a natural science 'scientific'; that is, what makes it a true account of reality.

Before we address these questions, let's consider the structure of the present chapter (shown in Figure 5.1). In section 2 we focus upon the approaches which have generated an increased sense of doubt about empiricist accounts of knowledge. For empiricists, one of the key ways in which science is demarcated from non-science is whether it can be tested and falsified. However, we will explore how scientists build escape clauses into their theoretical constructs to avoid refutation. In section 3 we examine the arguments and evidence developed by Thomas Kuhn and others who, in their different ways, contributed to this crisis in the construction of knowledge. Kuhn was a historian of scientific thought and practice who initially set out to write about the unification of scientific method. In the course of his research, he became increasingly convinced that a universal and rational scientific method could not be established. In section 4 we return to the falsificationists to consider how they have responded to these arguments, focusing on the ideas of Imre Lakatos and how they have been applied. The empiricists suggested that conventionalism had given up on progress and offered no basis for making authoritative judgements about the world. Finally, section 5 explores the debate between empiricists and conventionalists in a little more detail by reassessing the relationship between rationality and relativism.

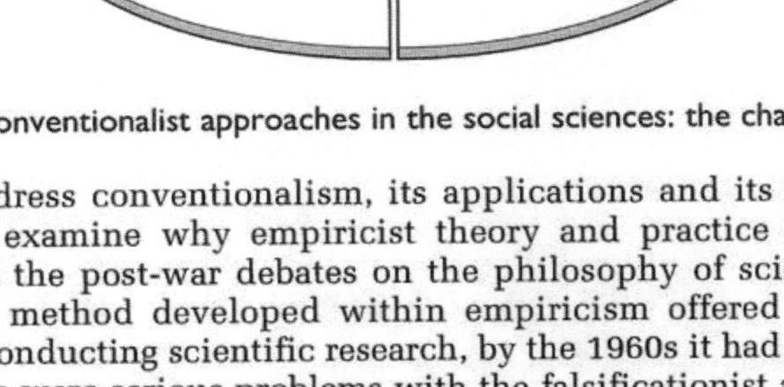

Figure 5.1 Conventionalist approaches in the social sciences: the chapter structure.

This sign will help you chart your way through the approaches in the chapter.

Before we address conventionalism, its applications and its critics, it is important to examine why empiricist theory and practice came to be questioned in the post-war debates on the philosophy of science. While the scientific method developed within empiricism offered a powerful rationale for conducting scientific research, by the 1960s it had become evident that there were serious problems with the falsificationist approach. In the social sciences, one of the main problems which emerged was the difficulty in disproving a proposition within the body of work from which it had been generated. In effect, it was possible in both the natural and the social sciences to build escape clauses from falsification into any scientific statement so that the critical edge of the approach was blunted.

2 Falsificationist escape clauses

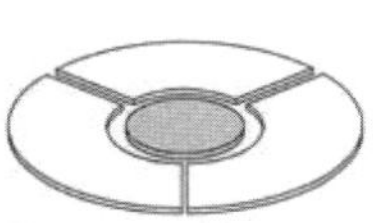

We start off with Popper, but come back to falsificationism again in section 4.

One of the most important problems in empiricist accounts of the scientific method is that of identifying a set of circumstances in which a scientific statement can be falsified through the acquisition of new empirical evidence. Statements and propositions attempting to explain the workings of the 'real world' do not exist in isolation but within complex theoretical systems. To begin, it is useful to distinguish between two types of theoretical statement.

Elsewhere this sign **g** will direct you to the glossary, but revisit this section if you need to.

- **Bedrock assumptions** specify the underlying assumptions within a particular scientific approach. These can be formally defined but can also be tacit, taken-for-granted rules and procedures which are rarely questioned. In short, they act as the 'bedrock' for building contextual hypotheses.
- **Contextual hypotheses** are generated when these bedrock assumptions are used within a definite context, producing statements which take into account the complex conditions of the objects in question. Contextual hypotheses also convey the combined operation of established laws working together within these conditions.

Scientists are often so busy testing statements about definite situations that they rarely consider their bedrock assumptions.

It has become increasingly apparent in the history of the scientific method that theories, hypotheses and propositions can continue to exist for some time despite the existence of conclusive evidence for their refutation. A good example of bedrock assumptions in the natural sciences can be seen in Newton's 'laws of motion'. In a similar way, the assumption that human beings are 'rational calculating individuals' is adopted in some branches of the social sciences. If it can be demonstrated that scientists evade falsification by introducing qualifications or by restricting empirical tests to contextual hypotheses rather than their bedrock assumptions, then how viable are the approaches? It is these issues which we consider in section 2.1. A Popperian response might be to describe this as bad science – a violation of the spirit if not the letter of falsificationism. However, Popper's approach applies to the testing of singular conjectures or hypotheses. In practice, empirical tests are conducted in the context of complex configurations of principles, laws, theories and previous empirical tests. This means that the conclusive refutation of a specific hypothesis can take place only within a reassessment of the whole body of theory concerned. But scientists become attached to specific bodies of theory, so are empiricist accounts idealized reconstructions of scientific method rather than an accurate and useful account of actual practice? This important question will be addressed throughout the chapter.

2.1 Interpretation and observation in the natural sciences

While the following sections explore the attachments and practices of natural and social scientists engaged in organized communities, here we consider the relationship between testing hypotheses and the theoretical systems in which hypotheses make sense, particularly what has become known as the Duhem-Quine thesis. In *The Aim and Structure of Physical Theory* (1914/1962), Pierre Duhem, a French philosopher and historian of

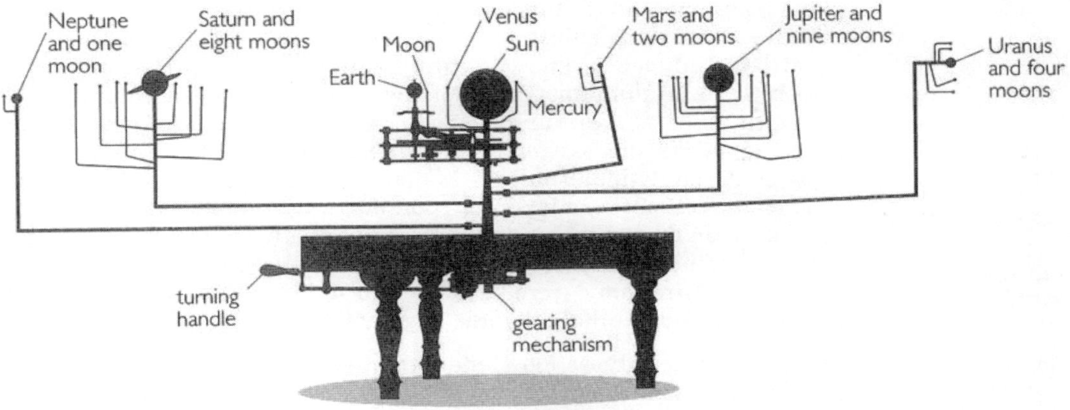

Figure 5.2 The orbital movements of the solar system: a clockwork model.

science, reassessed the history of physics from Newton onwards. He was concerned with the way scientific statements exist, not in isolation, but as part of complex hierarchies of theories and with reference to accumulated empirical evidence. So Duhem explored examples of situations where the available empirical evidence did not match the existing theories.

Astronomy provides a useful illustration of these problems. Until 1781 it had been assumed that the solar system consisted of six planets – Mercury, Venus, Earth, Mars, Jupiter and Saturn, ordered in terms of their distance from the Sun (see Figure 5.2). The discovery in that year of the planet Uranus, beyond Jupiter, created a new problem for astronomers. Using Newton's laws of motion and his law of gravity (as bedrock assumptions) in conjunction with a range of additional contextual hypotheses about the conditions within which the object existed (such as the various effects of other known planetary objects and taking into account their proximity and relative mass), astronomical scientists were able to plot a theoretical orbit for Uranus. For this example, it is important to note that planets exert gravitational pulls of varying strengths upon neighbouring planets. If we can estimate the gravitational effects of known planetary objects, then we should be able to plot their respective orbits around the Sun. However, the observational evidence of Uranus did not match the theoretical orbit established by the astronomers. This raised questions about the existing assumptions involved in the contemporary theories of astronomy. Two options exist in such a situation: either to question the bedrock assumptions and initiate a root-and-branch reassessment of the body of theory concerned, *or* to develop better contextual hypotheses but still founded upon existing bedrock assumptions.

New discoveries in scientific research often require a reappraisal of existing scientific theories.

In this example from natural science, the calculations of astronomers John Couch Adams and Urbain Leverrier (working independently in the mid 1840s) raised doubts about the contextual hypotheses developed on the orbit of Uranus; they raised the possibility of an additional planet orbiting beyond Uranus and exerting a gravitational effect on its orbit. The discrepancies between the theory and empirical evidence were, in this case, accurately explained in terms of their description of the mass and orbit of another planet (which was identified by telescope soon afterwards as the planet Neptune). So, in this example, by sticking to their bedrock assumptions and by making adjustments to the contextual hypotheses, Adams and Leverrier produced useful scientific knowledge. However, being loyal to your bedrock assumptions does not always work out so successfully. When attempting to explain unexpected features in the orbit of Mercury, Leverrier posed the existence of a planet closer to the Sun which was exerting a gravitational pull on Mercury. He labelled this planet Vulcan. This modification to contextual hypotheses was not to be so successful, for no such planet exists. This left an anomaly between theory and evidence which remained unresolved until the bedrock assumptions of Newtonian physics in astronomy were thrown into doubt eighty years later, when Einstein questioned these theories of gravitation.

Explaining new discoveries generates a choice between modifying existing theories or reassessing the foundations.

Examples such as these led Duhem to question the standards of scientific theorizing. Francis Bacon had argued that 'true science' should involve the identification of all possible contending theories in the explanation of a specific phenomenon and the use of experimental tests to identify the inaccuracies and flaws in each theory until all but one of the contending theories had been eliminated and absolute certainty could be established. For Duhem, no such definitive test of a single hypothesis could be devised and applied. He suggested that it was possible only to examine **theoretical systems** against the available empirical evidence. When faced with a situation in which observations do not fit the existing theoretical framework, scientists must make a choice between the modification of bedrock assumptions and revision of contextual hypotheses. Whereas Duhem had related testing statements to theoretical systems, more recently Willard von Quine's essay 'Two Dogmas of Empiricism' (1953/1965) argued that such tests could throw whole **knowledge systems** into doubt. Rather than seeing scientific knowledge as just bundles of individual theories focused upon the same object of analysis and/or set of problems, Quine saw them as a 'sort of man-made fabric' woven together in complex ways. This means that when you start to unpick certain patterns in knowledge, the whole fabric can unravel. Therefore, empirical tests can also throw our view of reality into doubt. In Quine's account, it is the whole field of inquiry of human knowledge which is disturbed by the emergence of anomalies between empirical evidence and established theories, in much the same way as a stone can cause ripples on the surface of a pond. We see the full implications of this in section 4.

To revisit Bacon, see Chapter 2, section 3.1.

The Duhem thesis – an empirical test can never falsify an isolated hypothesis, it challenges the whole theoretical system of which it is a part.

The Quine thesis – an empirical test can never falsify an isolated hypothesis, it challenges the whole knowledge system of which it is a part.

Quine's intervention is also important for highlighting the way in which scientists actually seek to avoid falsification by building escape clauses into their theories and explanations. They do this either by reformulating the contextual hypotheses or by making adjustments in the theoretical system in order to protect the bedrock assumptions from refutation (Quine, 1953/1965; Gillies, 1993). Such difficulties are not only a feature of natural science, they emerge in the social sciences as well. They exist regardless of the differences between the objects of analysis within the natural and the social sciences. In all areas where there is a fairly structured and extensive body of thought in a particular social science, we can witness a reluctance to question bedrock assumptions. In the next section we explore how these problems exist in the social sciences through two case studies, one drawn from political studies and the other from sociology.

Summary

The falsificationist method focuses upon the testing of single hypotheses. This runs into difficulty when put into practice in the natural sciences. Knowledge systems comprise different forms of theoretical statements which are defined in relationship to each other as well as in relation to empirical evidence.

Rather than reassessing the bedrock assumptions, scientists frequently test the contextual hypotheses generated from these bedrock assumptions. When these are found to be inadequate, then further contextual hypotheses are developed in the conduct of research without raising doubts about the underlying assumptions.

2.2 Escaping refutation in the social sciences

Now that you have explored some of the problems involved in falsification in natural science, let's look at how this affects social scientific practices. In the following two examples you will find that social scientists too have avoided falsification by introducing 'escape clauses' into their theoretical frameworks. In the cases of both pluralist political science and functionalist sociology, elaborate safeguards were developed to ensure that falsifying evidence did not undermine the bedrock assumptions. First, we consider the discipline of political science, which until the 1970s sought to explain the dynamic process of political choices and the exercise of power with the supposed precision of a natural science. Political scientists such as Robert Dahl and Nelson Polsby explicitly adopted the empiricist approach towards social research when constructing the pluralist model of the state and politics. Dahl presents a useful definition of his pluralist method: 'Based upon the study of individuals in political situations, this approach calls for the examination of the political relationships of men [*sic*] ... with the object of formulating and testing hypotheses concerning uniformities of behaviour' (Dahl, 1961, p.764).

Pluralists contend that a stable political system involves periodic elections and competition among pressure groups between elections. The concept of power is treated as an empirical regularity, whereby the behaviour of one agent causes uncharacteristic behaviour in another. Dahl characterized this as: 'A has the power over B to the extent that he can get B to do something that B would not otherwise do' (Dahl, 1957, pp.203–4). Individuals are taken as the basic unit of analysis, from which Dahl goes on to examine the personalities, groups, roles, offices, governments, nation-states and other aggregates of human individuals. This approach limits research on power to actual decision-making behaviour within situations where observable conflict of interests exists. The interests of the individuals or groups are defined as 'expressed policy preferences' (such as demand for change or support for the status quo), which are, in turn, revealed through political participation. This means that we should take what political actors say and what they do as a direct expression of their interests. By focusing upon the specific outcomes of observable behaviour, the pluralist approach is able to gather 'reliable evidence' (which has been subjected to further tests and which produced the same or similar results). This usually takes the form of quantitative data in order to facilitate correlations between variables (statistical comparisons). Pluralists used statistical controls to simulate a **closed system** involving a limited number of simple variables (see Blalock, 1964).

9

If we consider Dahl's own use of this method, we can acquire a better view of what this means in practice. In *Who Governs?* (1960), Dahl examined observable concrete decision making in New Haven (USA), where he lived and worked. This involved studying the expression of policy preferences, the initiation of proposals and the casting of votes for, or against, formally sanctioned decisions. The key policy issues identified as objects of analysis in this study were urban development, public education and nominations for political office. Dahl concluded, on the basis of the empirical evidence collected in this way, that no one group dominated in all policy areas, all of the time. This evidence enabled him to argue that New Haven, while not an ideal democracy, was considerably more polyarchic (involving rule by the many) than oligarchic (involving rule by the few). In addition, Dahl concluded that the resources which contributed to the exercise of power were so dispersed and fragmented that direct political influence was limited (with most citizens having an indirect influence through use of the vote). According to Dahl, polyarchy was sustained between elections by the participation of pressure groups in the political process. The pluralist approach assumes that all individuals are willing and able to form and maintain a group when their own interests are affected, that all have equal access to an impartial decision-making process and that they will be mobilized to act on their own behalf. As demonstrated in Figure 5.3, the pluralist argument suggests that pressure-group politics involves a shifting balance of power among contending pressure groups engaged in political negotiations, with policy decisions achieved through compromise. With such assumptions built into the theoretical framework, the pluralists were likely to find the evidence they needed to reinforce their theories.

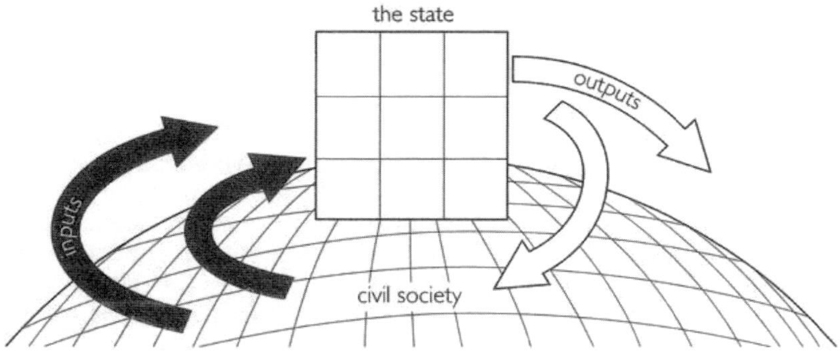

Figure 5.3 The pluralist model of state and society: a systems model.

In trying to establish the preconditions of political stability in New Haven, Dahl challenged the conventional explanations of what makes a political system democratic. Rather than just considering the basic rights, duties and procedures that serve to distinguish democratic from non-democratic systems, he placed a greater emphasis upon the importance of moral customs, laws and the physical, social and economic condition of the people. In other words, for Dahl, the relations of civil society are just as important as formal political constitutions. The conclusions of this study have been subject to intense criticism and evaluation, particularly on methodological grounds. The focus upon observed decision making inhibits the identification of other factors and is unrealistic in view of the fact that political decisions may be made behind the scenes in advance of the formal decision-making process in the political executive (in the UK, the Cabinet) or the parliamentary chamber. The pluralist approach ignored the way that decision making is based on an agenda, the processes involved in excluding some issues from the agenda, and the problems of equating the interests of a particular group with the public statements of those groups (their 'express policy preferences'). Pluralists have increasingly accepted that such problems have to be addressed in their research, although this has often been limited to the reformulation of the contextual hypotheses about the capacity of democratic political systems to contain undemocratic tendencies. They have not questioned the bedrock assumptions of this approach concerning political institutions or the empiricist research strategy which focuses on the collection of observed data from concrete decisions.

Social scientists also face the choice of modifying contextual hypotheses or reassessing their bedrock assumptions.

According to Jordan and Richardson (1987), recent work has clearly recognized the problems in the pluralist approach. The following contextual hypotheses have been challenged:

- the neutrality of the state;
- the separation of the state from civil society;
- the tendency for groups to balance each other;
- the view that policy making is the product of negotiation and compromise between contending interests.

Pluralists now accept that the institutions of the state can behave like interest groups, that groups may not have equal power even in the long run, that some significant groups remain disorganized (and hence are disenfranchized in pressure-group politics) and that some groups may colonize key departments of state to secure their interests and exclude the concerns of competing groups. Pluralists have accepted the importance of the formation of agendas in which decisions are made. They have also recognized that some issues can be excluded from the agenda. Nevertheless, they have not questioned the bedrock assumption that objects can be identified only through empirical evidence of actual observable decisions. This still means that pluralists use the express preferences of the various groups as an index of their interests. While this modified pluralist approach clearly recognizes the imperfections of democratic political systems, it does not lead pluralists to reassess the bedrock assumptions of their research programme itself.

Pluralists have developed elaborate safeguards to ensure that falsifying evidence does not undermine their bedrock assumptions.

For the second example of the use of falsificationist escape clauses in the social sciences, we turn to sociology. In the 1940s and 1950s a fairly well established body of theories in the basic principles of sociology came to be accepted. The theories were grouped together under the umbrella label of 'functionalism' and were most associated with the American sociologist Talcott Parsons. The effect of this distinct body of theory on the development of sociology was enormous for both supporters and critics. The underlying metaphors of the functionalist approach were derived from the **organic analogy**, in that society was compared to a human body with all the institutional parts functioning to ensure the health (or, in some cases, sickness) of the whole society which, in turn, was treated as more than the sum of its parts. The smooth operation of the social system, according to Parsons, depends upon the functional operation of the economy, the polity, cultural institutions and the kinship subsystem (Parsons, 1951). In addition, this theoretical system is founded upon the implicit normative assumption that the existence of social order and consensus is the normal state of affairs.

This theoretical assumption of social consensus as a normal condition, even in the relatively optimistic and prosperous conditions of post-war Western societies, was clearly at odds with empirical evidence on social conflict and became even more so by the 1960s and 1970s. Nevertheless, the response within the functionalist approach was to limit the damage of such evidence by constructing elaborate contextual hypotheses around the theme of 'strain' in the social system – leaving the bedrock assumptions of functionalism unchallenged. When addressing the effects of strains on individual behaviour, Robert Merton had argued (Merton, 1938) that dysfunctional criminal and deviant behaviour could be understood in terms of the relationship between individual choices and the value system (in this case, the key American value was material success). Merton distinguished between the legitimate and illegitimate means through which individuals could choose to attain the ends of material success and the degree of attachment that those individuals had towards the accepted goals of the American social system. This allowed Merton to identify the following five types of human response to the constraints of the norms and values of American culture.

- *Conformity* – positive commitment to the legitimate means and ends (the ideal citizen – this is quite hard to live up to).
- *Innovation* – negative on the means but a positive commitment to success (rule-bending to achieve status and wealth).
- *Ritualism* – positive on the means but negative on the ends, when people behave in an acceptable way without any commitment to, or hope of, achieving personal success (what most of us do most of the time).
- *Retreatism* – negative on both means and ends, whereby individuals seek to 'drop out' of society (but not create an alternative).
- *Rebellion* – a rejection of the established means and ends in favour of an alternative social order with its own ends and the identification of the means of achieving this (religious conversion or revolutionary activity).

Escapes from falsification can be achieved by constructing a theoretical framework whereby all types of evidence are taken to be a confirmation of the theories.

In this way, the existence of deviance and crime cannot be taken as a refutation of the bedrock assumptions of functionalist theory of what makes a healthy society, because such behaviour is explained as the consequence of a failure of integration into the established norms and values of the social system in question as well as a source of innovation and change. Thus cases of conformity and deviance are both covered by the theory through the use of different contextual hypotheses to explain different forms of behaviour and, in each case, the bedrock assumptions remain unchallenged. By building in these kinds of escape clauses, functionalism can have it both ways, for all evidence supports the framework in one way or another. Later versions of the functionalist account drew more explicitly upon cost–benefit approaches to establish the positive and negative aspects of forms of behaviour which go against the values of the social system. If the positive consequences of such cases outweigh the negative consequences, even 'maladjusted behaviour' can be seen as achieving a 'net positive functionality'. Evidence which appears, at first sight, to be a refutation of the functionalist view can be interpreted in a way which supports (instead of undermining) the framework. Rather than assuming that all relations are functional in a positive way, they can be seen as contributing to the social order as long as they have more benefits than costs.

Activity 5.1

Turn to Reading A, from Ezra F. Vogel and Norman W. Bell's 'The emotionally disturbed child as the family scapegoat' (1968).

- Identify the positive and negative functions of family relations in Vogel and Bell's account.
- Try to identify how Vogel and Bell evade falsification.

As you read this provocative extract, bear in mind the context in which it was written and how it relates to the cultural values in that location.

In the functionalist account of social systems, one of the most important institutions for constructing the moral fabric of society is the family unit. The family is portrayed as the key source of values, expressiveness and personal identity in an otherwise increasingly instrumental society. In the 1960s the structure of family life began to alter as the 'strains' of contemporary Western societies began to place increased pressure on the nuclear family unit. Both the changing structure of the family and the evidence of 'emotional disturbance' in otherwise 'functional family units' raised questions about the theoretical statements in the functionalist approach. When faced with the problem of questioning their basic principles or their contextual hypotheses, functionalists chose the latter. As in the case of Vogel and Bell, the consequences of the strains (here, increased divorce rates and single parent households) were seen by Parsons as bearable within the social system as long as the costs in personal lives did not undermine the role that such a flexible household unit played in other subsystems. In this specific example, the negative consequences for the children concerned were more than outweighed by the positive consequences in other areas of the social system. Clearly, few scientists would question their bedrock assumptions immediately and some exploration of new contextual hypotheses should be expected. However, in both of these cases from political studies and sociology, the substantive falsification of explanatory statements did not produce a critical reassessment of bedrock assumptions and the anomalies endured. We reconsider what we question and what we don't in social scientific practice when we explore the ideas of Lakatos later in the chapter.

Summary

In the cases of both pluralism in political science and functionalism in sociology, social scientists came to accept theoretical approaches based upon specific bedrock assumptions in explaining social life.

In both cases, when faced with empirical evidence which went against their expectations, the contextual hypotheses were modified in order to protect the bedrock assumptions involved. In short, falsification was limited to contextual hypotheses.

3 Paradigms and conventions: the end of progress?

In the middle sections of this chapter we explore approaches which consider scientific knowledge to be defined as a social product – as a convention which scientists and others hold to be true. As you saw in section 1, **conventionalism** has been used as a broad label to describe these approaches. To some extent, Popper's account of verisimilitude (that truth was a matter of degree, not an absolute) had prepared the way for this line of argument. However, with the conventionalists, this questioning of the foundations of knowledge was taken further to undermine the faith in 'rationality' and 'progress' as well. In *The Structure of Scientific Revolutions* (1962/1970), Kuhn developed an argument that is often identified as the cause of a 'crisis of rationality' in Western scientific thinking. He concluded that scientific knowledge does not produce an independently true account of the external world but reflects the organized activities of scientific communities. Kuhn was not the first conventionalist in the study of natural science, but his importance here is due to the role which his concept of **paradigm** has played in the social sciences since the 1960s. Now, before we consider how the idea of paradigm has been understood and applied in the social sciences, let's look at Kuhn's historical account of scientific change in a little more detail.

If you want to revisit Popper, see Chapter 3, section 5.1.

3.1 Kuhn's account of scientific change

The idea of paradigmatic change was a direct challenge to the idea of progress through the accumulation of knowledge.

Empiricist accounts of scientific knowledge had been committed to the idea of progress through the gradual accumulation of knowledge. Even though Popper had given up on the search for truth, the whole point of falsification was to build on existing knowledge in a cumulative way (rather like walking up a never-ending staircase). Kuhn's approach, however, suggested that it was not even possible to identify a progression in knowledge. Through a careful study of the ways in which natural science has developed and changed, Kuhn suggested that scientific knowledge went through long periods of stability interrupted by short periods of sudden transformation. In addition, instead of establishing a universal standard against which it was possible to compare all statements about the world, Kuhn argued that knowledge was a social product and, as such, changed as society changes. He described each phase of stability in the history of science as a period of **normal science**. This occurs when the rules of scientific method are well established and the role of scientists is limited to solving problems and puzzles without questioning the rules within which they work. These rules involve widely accepted **demarcation criteria** through which we can distinguish which forms of knowledge which are scientific and which are not. In the case of logical positivism, the demarcation criteria between science and non-science were such that if something could not be reduced to a simple observation statement and the theories could not be empirically verified, then it contained metaphysical components and was thus meaningless. These rules become part of the institutional life in which scientists work and their work is judged according to how closely they operate by the accepted principles of their disciplinary fields.

Kuhn developed the concept of 'paradigm' to characterize changes in the 'standards governing permissible problems, concepts and explanations' (Kuhn, 1970, p.106) within the context of a historical and sociological approach. The concept of paradigm is a matter of much dispute (which we come back to in section 3.2). However, the idea of paradigm in this context can be taken to mean the 'universally recognized scientific achievements that ... provide model problems and solutions to a community of practitioners' (Kuhn, 1970, p.viii) and therefore forms the implicit taken-for-granted commonsense assumptions of a scientific community. In this way, paradigms are more than sets of theories, they are scientific communities through which knowledge is produced and understood.

Each paradigm has its own demarcation criteria between which ideas and forms of evidence should or should not be taken seriously as scientific knowledge.

This historical account of scientific knowledge starts with a **pre-paradigmatic stage** in which a range of approaches compete for dominance although none is able to achieve it. Kuhn argued that the social sciences remain in this state, for they have not as yet achieved the maturity of one dominant set of rules. The natural sciences, he argued, have achieved this. For instance, the development of Newton's physics marked the emergence of a paradigm in physics, closely followed by paradigms in chemistry, biology and physiology. Kuhn described the dominance of normal science within which the activities of scientists can be characterized as puzzle solving within an established set of principles and methodological procedures. Newton's mechanics provided physics with just such a workable set of principles (rules of experimental inquiry and scientific laws of motion) for the development of further scientific laws and the identification of facts. However, by the middle of the ninenteenth century a series of problems or anomalies emerged in the application of Newton's laws to astronomical objects which could not be adequately explained. By the 1890s these anomalies had accumulated to the point that physics was in a state of crisis and, with the emergence of an alternative set of principles, physics experienced a scientific revolution as a new paradigm emerged to replace the old one (see Figure 5.4).

This view of the history of science involving long periods of stability marked by sudden breaks draws from common narrative structure of historical story-telling.

Kuhn argues that a scientific revolution like the one from Newton's to Einstein's physics involves a 'gestalt shift'. This means that the scientists involved would have to go through a 'conversion experience' in order to move from the old paradigm to the new one. In the case of physics, Newton's mechanistic laws were replaced by Einstein's theory of relativity. However, many scientists were left behind in this process, unable to cope with the trauma of such a transformation. Kuhn agrees with Planck's view: 'a new scientific truth does not triumph by convincing its opponents and making them see the light, but rather because its opponents eventually die and a new generation grows up that is familiar with it' (Planck cited in Kuhn, 1970, p.151).

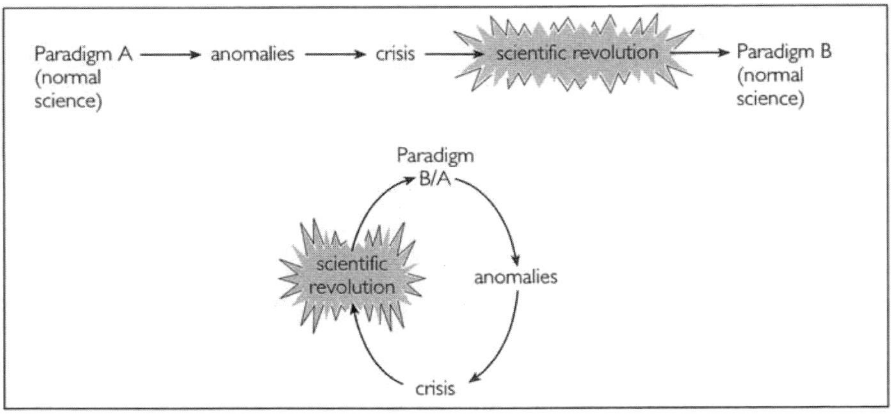

Figure 5.4 Kuhn's theory of scientific revolution.
The figure shows two ways of representing Kuhn's account of the transformations involved in a scientific revolution. Each representation tells a different story. In the linear one, the shift of paradigms implies a kind of progress (perhaps that Einstein's physics improves on Newton's). In the cyclical version, a paradigm shift sends us full circle – it implies that science changes but does not progress.

Paradigm shifts are intergenerational transformations in the bedrock assumptions of knowledge held to be true by scientific communities.

In practice, the shift takes place over a generation or even longer, for few of those who have worked their way up the academic career ladder are likely to question the theories upon which their research and careers are based. Each of these paradigms is mutually exclusive and the members of the scientific communities which construct each paradigm interpret their experiences so differently that they can be said to occupy 'different worlds'. In Chapter 3 you saw how experience could be interpreted in different ways, but nevertheless it was generally assumed that the interpreters had enough in common to communicate their interpretations effectively to each other. In Kuhn's account of paradigmatic differences, this would not be feasible. This can be seen when we look at examples of paradigm shifts. For instance, by the middle of the twentieth century, Einstein's theories provided the underlying rules for physics in the new normal science in much the same way as Newton's had in the previous paradigm. A physicist viewing the physical universe with the assumptions developed by Einstein would see a different universe from that of Newton. It is possible to see this as yet another addition to scientific knowledge, but the questions which Einstein raised struck right at the heart of the assumptions that had dominated physics for centuries.

g

Paradigms are incommensurable – the ideas generated by one paradigm cannot be used to judge the truth value of the ideas of another paradigm.

To suggest that members of different paradigms experience different worlds has further implications. Kuhn argued that each paradigm has its own way of demarcating science from non-science. Consequently, paradigms are **incommensurable**; in other words, it is impossible to use the criteria of one paradigm to judge the truthfulness of the theories of another. In effect, this means that there is no such thing as universally true knowledge, but it also means that paradigms do not progress, they merely change. Kuhn argued that because the standards of assessment are internal to each paradigm, then scientific revolutions involve a shift in the standards governing which explanations we can consider to be legitimate. Paradigms are seen as incommensurable, in that they involve mutually exclusive foundational assumptions. This is expressed in the different vocabularies of each paradigm.

During the tranquillity of periods of 'normal science', the scientific assumptions go unquestioned, with problems subject to the procedure of puzzle solving, whereby established theories are modified to maintain consistency with the evidence. Gradually, anomalies within a paradigm build up to the point of generating a crisis which precipitates a scientific revolution or paradigm shift, allowing a new paradigm to emerge through a form of conversion experience of gestalt shift (analogous to a religious conversion) rather than by a series of rational logical steps (see Figure 5.4).

Ian Hacking has written a useful summary of the key features of Kuhn's approach which helps us to differentiate the conventionalist position from the common foundations of empiricist approaches, and which relates closely to the conclusion of Chapter 3. You may recall that, for empiricists, theory and observation are distinct, science has a tight deductive structure, concepts should be precise, the sciences should be unified, the **context of discovery** is distinct from the **context of justification** and scientific knowledge provides, or should aspire to provide, universal explanations of things. Hacking highlights the way in which conventionalism provides a very different account of scientific knowledge because it disagrees with all the standpoints and assumptions on which empiricists are agreed. For Hacking:

You may find it useful to revisit section 7 of Chapter 3 where you met Hacking before.

g

> There is no sharp distinction between observation and theory.
> Science is not cumulative.
> A live science does not have a tight deductive structure.
> Living scientific concepts are not particularly precise.
> Methodological unity of science is false; there are lots of disconnected tools used for various forms of inquiry.
> The sciences themselves are disunified. They are composed of a large number of only loosely overlapping little disciplines many of which in the course of time cannot comprehend each other ...
> The context of justification cannot be separated from the context of discovery.
> Science is in time and is essentially historical.
>
> (Hacking, 1983, p.6)

However, this does not mean that Kuhn offered no basis for considering knowledge as good or bad. He became concerned that many portrayals of his ideas assumed that his account provided no basis for making judgements about knowledge. Consequently, he later identified five characteristics of good scientific theory, as a way of making these judgements:

Accuracy that a theory should be accurate within its domain of inquiry

Consistency that a theory should be internally consistent as well as consistent with other theories

Broad scope that a theory should explain more than it set out to explain

Simplicity that a theory provides a clear and simple account of complex objects

Fruitfulness that a theory should identify new phenomena or previously unnoticed relationships between such phenomena

(adapted from Kuhn, 1977, pp.320–9)

The meaning of the concept of paradigm is open to question on two grounds. First, Kuhn himself was very imprecise as to how a paradigm

The imprecise definition of the idea of 'paradigm' has produced many and varied uses in the natural and social sciences.

could be defined. Margaret Masterman identified twenty-one different uses of the concept of paradigm in Kuhn's landmark text alone (Masterman, 1970). Kuhn responded in the second edition of his book with a sharper definition of paradigm as a 'disciplinary matrix' consisting of a strong network of commitments, theoretical, instrumental and methodological (Kuhn, 1970). Second, this conceptual confusion has led to different uses of the concept of paradigm between different disciplines and even different uses within each social science discipline. In the next section, we find it is often used loosely to mean a 'model' of the social world or to identify a school of thought, a tradition or a perspective. However, it is the many and varied uses of Kuhn's work which has made his approach so influential.

If we look at Kuhn's use of the term in his historical account of natural sciences, paradigms would have to dominate exclusively in a field of knowledge for a significant period of time. We can see something approaching this in sociology in the 1950s, when functionalism (considered in section 2.2) came close to exercising a dominance along these lines. Nevertheless, alternative approaches continued to coexist with functionalism in sociology and soon re-emerged in the 1960s. Actually, Kuhn only expected a paradigm to emerge in economics, so in terms of Kuhn's own use of the concept of paradigm the social sciences remain **pre-paradigmatic** (by which he understood them to occupy a pre-scientific phase of development). Kuhn's approach views scientific knowledge as a social product and the rules by which we judge knowledge to be scientific as merely conventions. Critics of Kuhn's approach, such as Karl Popper and Imre Lakatos, have argued that conventionalist approaches offer little hope for humanity. A defender of falsificationism, Lakatos suggested that, by giving up on the possibility of progress and by attributing scientific knowledge to the internal workings of communities of scientists, Kuhn's account was in fact the 'mob psychology' of scientific knowledge (Lakatos, 1970).

Summary

Thomas Kuhn situates scientific knowledge in the context of the historical and social practices which define natural science in a particular time and place. Consequently, the truth of a scientific statement is only relevant to those who share the belief system upon which such 'truths' are based.

Kuhn argues that each paradigm possesses its own demarcation criteria on what constitutes science and non-science. Paradigms replace one another through scientific revolutions and they are incommensurable. If one paradigm can never be used to judge another and the occupants of each paradigm are in 'different worlds', then progress is no longer a relevant term in the description of scientific knowledge.

If the way we think shapes the way we interpret evidence, we face substantial problems in distinguishing theories from observations and facts from values. This directly challenges the foundations of empiricist accounts of scientific knowledge.

3.2 Paradigms in the social sciences

How have these arguments been used to understand changes in the social sciences? Earlier it was argued that Kuhn's significance was a consequence of the widespread uses to which the concept of paradigm had been put in the social sciences. To make these changes comprehensible, these uses can be identified as falling into three broad categories.

- **Paradigm 1** – the strict sense identified by Kuhn in his account of the natural sciences, when a single dominant framework, disciplinary matrix or normal science exists and one demarcation criterion operates between science and non-science operates. In this case, paradigms are incommensurable and they are assumed to succeed one another rather than compete, although competition between alternatives may occur in the relatively short-lived periods of crisis and evolution.
- **Paradigm 2** – where the intellectual foundations of the community are such that to move from this paradigm to another would require reorientation of the type identified by Kuhn as a gestalt shift. In this case, we can identify a distinct scientific community with its own institutional foundation and academic career ladder existing within a particular field of knowledge. This use acknowledges the presence of competing paradigms in the same field of knowledge but requires them to be incommensurable.
- **Paradigm 3** – used to designate a school of thought, theoretical perspective or set of problems. This is the loosest but most common use, in which the term paradigm is seen as synonymous with a 'model' of a particular aspect of social life. This use does not require incommensurability between different paradigms nor does it require a reasonably coherent scientific community with an institutional foundation in research and educational settings (although these features may be present and are usually necessary for the long-term survival of the approach).

Elsewhere this sign **g** *will direct you to the glossary, but revisit this section if you need to.*

We can explore the use of each of these conceptions of paradigm through two case studies, one from psychology and the other from economics. Within the social sciences, there are no perfect applications of Kuhn's original sense of **Paradigm 1**, where clearly identified foundational principles have replaced each other in quick succession, but we'll consider some examples which come pretty close. One of the nearest illustrations can be seen in psychology with the emergence of the behaviourist approach. Even here, the absolute dominance of one approach (of one world-view) implied by Kuhn is not apparent, for other approaches exist on the fringes of the discipline. However, behaviourism was influential in establishing psychology as a scientific discipline and, despite a great deal of self-criticism within the discipline, psychology is often identified as the closest of the social sciences to the natural sciences. This association of behaviourism with the dominant scientific method was also reinforced by the adoption of behaviourist approaches in sociology and 'political science' (including pluralism, identified earlier in section 2.2). The behaviourist approach focuses upon observable behaviour and specifically excludes any reference to inner states or intrinsic qualities which, by their character, cannot be observed.

Behaviourism is largely concerned with the relationship between individual human beings and their social and physical environment. This is partly a product of the origins of the behaviourist programme in the animal experimentation of John B. Watson. In his early studies of rat behaviour, Watson developed a theoretical framework which argued that consciousness was irrelevant to psychology and that, as a result, the introspective approach of Wundt, the dominant approach until the early twentieth century, was an inappropriate basis for establishing an objective science of behaviour (Watson, 1928). The rats in Watson's experiments were subjected to different environments within experimental conditions and to a range of rewards and punishments for their responses to various problems, such as finding food in a maze. (Figures 5.5 and 5.6 illustrate similar experimental work.)

See Chapter 4, section 3.1.

Figure 5.5 Scientists monitoring the behaviour of rats in a maze experiment.

Figure 5.6 Diagram of the maze used in a behaviourist experiment.

The results of this experimentation established that rats could learn to respond to their environment and to various sanctions so establishing that their behaviour was not static but could be modified. Watson was at the forefront of arguing that the techniques developed in the objective study of animal behaviour could also be used within human psychology. This involved refocusing psychology towards the study of behaviour so that it could become a 'purely objective experimental branch of natural science'. Behaviourism required a move away from the study of the conscious mind, mental stages and images as subjectively defined. This challenged the existing approach of introspection which took subjective states as its starting-point. It is this difference in approach which marks off behaviourism from introspection and other earlier forms of experimental psychology, as a **Paradigm 1**. Since each approach operated through different demarcation criteria between science and non-science, there is no common basis for establishing objective knowledge or for judging between them. So introspection and behaviourism can be characterized as incommensurable.

In psychology, the shift from introspection to behaviourism is often seen as a paradigmatic shift.

It is worthwhile exploring this approach in a little more detail in order to highlight the ways in which psychologists have responded to behaviourism more recently. The central principle of behaviourist psychology is the explanation of the process of learning as one of **operant conditioning**. This assumes that behavioural modifications of individuals are a response to the consequences of their behaviour. The environment is assumed to react towards the individual in three ways – negative, neutral and positive – and that this reaction can act as a reinforcer (a reward) or as a punishment for the behaviour concerned. Of course, rewards and punishments can have a neutral effect, in that they may not alter behaviour. Nevertheless, there are four possible ways in which the modification of individual behaviour can take place.

Positive reinforcement – takes place when a particular form of behaviour produces pleasurable consequences for the individuals concerned and encourages similar behaviour in the future.	*Negative reinforcement* – takes place when an inhibiting or an aversive feature is removed, enabling the individual to carry out a particular form of behaviour and encouraging similar behaviour in the same circumstances.
Positive punishment – introducing (or the threat of introducing) an aversive stimulus in order to support or discourage particular forms of behaviour in the future.	*Negative punishment* – removing (or the threat of removing) a reward of entitlement which would otherwise provide pleasurable consequences in order to suppress or discourage particular forms of behaviour in the future.

Behaviourist psychologists have used this system of reinforcers and punishments to examine the processes of childhood socialization and to recommend therapeutic uses of behaviour modification where the behaviour of children was considered to be inappropriate or 'abnormal'. Similarly, in the treatment of criminality, solutions were sought in the modification of behavioural traits, rather than assuming that criminals would be deterred in future through the application of a particular standard form of punishment. If it were assumed that consciousness was not relevant to the study of behaviour then, when conducting research, it could be assumed that human beings are no different from non-human animals. All behaviour could be studied in experimental conditions, or through careful observation, in order to establish patterns of modification in learning behaviour. These studies could be replicated and the data verified to establish their authenticity, creating objective scientific accounts of human behaviour. The work of Watson became an important reference point for the generational shift from introspection to behaviourism in psychology. However, alternatives remained in existence, such as Gestalt psychology and psychoanalysis, although they remained marginalized in the discipline until the debates of the 1950s and 1960s which saw the reintroduction of the concept of the self as an intentional and purposeful social actor.

Introspection works from the subjective mental states of individuals, while behaviourism regards them as irrelevant for generating scientific knowledge.

In the behaviourist approach, a great deal of stress is placed upon the role of the stimulus–response relationship, whereby the behaviour of the individual is seen as an effect of external stimuli, with responses taking one of the four forms identified above. However, the same evidence can also be interpreted as an example of purposeful behaviour (or, if we are talking about animals, behaviour that appears to have a purpose) rather than as a conditioned reflex to a particular stimulus. The cognitive psychologist Edward C. Tolman (Tolman et al., 1946) argued that an alternative model of the learning process, whereby knowledge of past experiences is stored in a cognitive map of the environment, provided an account which could explain the variation of responses to the same stimuli in human and animal behaviour (in addition to the evidence explained by the behaviourist approach). Cognitive psychology assumes that the acquisition of information allows for 'rule-governed behaviour' but that these rules are flexible and adaptive in the light of subsequent experiences. There is some dispute as to whether cognitive psychology replaced the behaviourist approach in psychology as the most influential theory. In addition, Tolman's approach co-exists with that of the later behaviourists, such as Burrhus F. Skinner, in a different disciplinary context where a range of new alternatives was also emerging. Human cultures are defined by Skinner as the composite of behaviours of the individuals who form a particular community. Skinner sought to purge any conception of individual autonomy and creativity. Like Watson, he was particularly concerned to challenge the conception of the 'autonomous man' within voluntarist approaches to social life (Skinner, 1953, 1971). For Skinner, it is not ideas, wants, values or desires which determine behaviour, for these can only be identified through the study of those aspects of social relationships and personal choices which, in a causal explanation, would be conventionally defined as effects (the dependent variables). In the field of social psychology, the emergence of a range of new approaches placed a greater emphasis upon the meaningful, personal and social aspects of the lived experience of social actors. Such humanistic and critical social psychologies focused on subjective experience as a foundation for knowledge and the role of social actors in actively constructing the social world, and moved beyond the experimental setting to draw upon a wider range of empirical research strategies.

Activity 5.2

Reading B includes three short extracts from *Theory and Social Psychology* (Sapsford *et al.*, eds, 1998): 'Experimental social psychology' by Patrick McGhee, 'Humanistic and experiential social psychology' by Richard Stevens and 'Critical social psychology' by Margaret Wetherell. Read these extracts now.

- Identify the differences between each approach and consider which of the three senses of paradigms adequately describes this area of social scientific knowledge.

You may also find it useful to think about how these different kinds of psychology lead to different approaches to research methods: defining the object of analysis differently may mean having to gather evidence in ways which match.

Psychology has now fragmented into those areas where one approach dominates in a paradigmatic way and those areas where contesting approaches coexist.

Cognitive psychology has, in time, become a scientific community in its own right with an institutional basis in research and teaching organizations separate from other approaches; in this context, it appears to exist in a paradigmatic way (in the sense of **Paradigm 2**) as a methodological framework in most of the areas of psychology, with the exception of social psychology. In social psychology, the influence of the cognitive framework is more limited. Here it has become known as psychological social psychology competing with a range of approaches from sociological social psychology. So, in the case of social psychology, the use of **Paradigm 3** would be more appropriate as a descriptive label for cognitive psychology (that is, psychological social psychology). The problems of applying the concept of paradigm to other social sciences are just as complex. In the case of economics, even Kuhn himself held out some hope of a singular mature science developing in the sense of **Paradigm 1**, although it should be added that his own perspective was coloured by the apparent success and widespread acceptance of Keynesian economic management strategies in the Western post-war boom from the 1950s to the early 1960s.

Activity 5.3

Turn to Reading C, 'Economic paradigms', on the Keynesian and monetarist approaches to the economy, from Vane and Thompson's *An Introduction to Macroeconomic Policy* (1982), and 'Economic crisis: the Marxist view' from Hunt and Sherman's *Economics: An Introduction to Traditional and Radical Views* (1981).

- Identify the key assumptions in each of the three approaches and consider whether these approaches are incommensurable.
- Identify which concept of paradigm best describes the differences between them.

As in the examples from psychology in Activity 5.2, you should look for clues as to the similarities and differences between these approaches.

Keynesianism and monetarism are often described as different paradigms in economics.

In economics the contrast between Keynesian and monetarist approaches to the study of the economy has often been couched in Kuhnian terms. These economic theories represent opposing philosophies about the role of the state in the organization of production, distribution and exchange which are reflected in completely irreconcilable positions in policy terms. In substantive terms, Keynesianism presumes that the state can intervene in the free market in various ways with positive consequences in terms of employment, prices and growth. In this approach, the state ensures that the level of total aggregate demand is such that the economy does not fall into recession nor does it become overheated, causing inflationary pressure. This precarious state of affairs, where the state moderates the tendencies of the business cycle through fiscal and monetary fine-tuning, is achieved through the intervention of a benevolent state, which seeks to maximize the common good. This approach, then, assumes that the economy can be planned, or at least guided, towards certain common goals and that when the market fails (such as in the decline of an industrial sector) the state can intervene directly and take control of key sectors in the public interest.

Monetarism, on the other hand, rejects the role of the state as a benevolent actor and assumes that an economy functions most efficiently when left to its own devices. The activity of the state is interpreted as a form of interference which damages exchange relations and diverts valuable and scarce resources from profitable uses (through taxation) by maintaining declining sectors of industry (through subsidies or state ownership). From the monetarist standpoint, the intervention of the state (by increasing the money supply) is the cause of both inflationary pressure and the perpetuation of inefficient sectors of the economy. In addition, the growth of state intervention creates a greater tax burden which further undermines incentives for wealth production more generally, as well as 'crowding out' private sector capital from the limited opportunities for investment.

With such well rehearsed arguments and the existence of institutional groupings of Keynesian economists (for instance, at Cambridge University) and monetarist economists (for instance, at Liverpool University), it is easy to see how these two opposed approaches could be interpreted as different worlds. However, on closer examination the relationship between the two approaches is not so simple. The ideas of the economist John Maynard Keynes are often contrasted with the neo-classical economics which preceded them. Neo-classical economics assumed that the market would inevitably resolve any imbalances (slumps and booms) through the adjustments of the 'invisible hand' of the price mechanism whereby, according to Say's Law, the supply of goods will always find its own demand at a given price. The 'Keynesian revolution' was a revolution in the sense that it became possible to envisage the state adopting a proactive rather than a reactive relationship to the problems of the market. However, this is not the same thing as a scientific revolution, because the conceptual landscape remained much the same as before. Moreover, the object of analysis in both Keynesian and monetarist approaches remained the market, for it was defined as a set of exchange relations between firms, households and individuals. In addition, the values of commodities are identified in terms of exchange value. As to how they define their field of analysis, both approaches remain committed to identifying the same objects in the same way. Where these approaches disagree, then, is over the legitimate role of the state in the market as well as over the normative issue of whether it is possible and desirable to create an egalitarian society.

Compared with the 'Marxist paradigm', Keynesian and monetarist economics have common foundations.

If, however, we contrast both of these approaches with Marxist economics, a different set of issues arises. For the Marxist economist, the object of analysis is not simply the exchange relations which characterize capitalist markets but also the productive relations and the productive forces which together make up the economy. Exchange relations are treated as operating upon the level of surface appearances and present an 'ideological' obstacle to understanding the underlying real workings of the economy (preventing us from seeing the world as it really is). In the Marxist approach, the relations between capitalist and working classes are characterized by irreconcilable conflicts of interest which, at any given time, may or may not manifest themselves in visible social and political conflict. In addition, periodic economic crises are treated as the symptoms of underlying productive processes in a class-divided society. For Keynesians and monetarists, however, 'capitalism' in the sense identified by Marxists cannot be observed and as such cannot be said to exist. Similarly, we can observe workers but not the proletariat, and individual businesses and firms but not capitalism. Clearly, different demarcation criteria are at work.

9

Now, let's see how these differences relate to the three senses of paradigm identified earlier. While the difference between Keynesianism and monetarism appears to illustrate **Paradigm 3**, the difference between both of these approaches and the Marxist theory of the capitalist economy seems closer to the meaning of **Paradigm 2**. The move from seeing the economy as a set of exchange relations to seeing the economy as constituted by definite productive relations could be seen as a movement between different worlds. Economics does not offer an example of **Paradigm 1**, and from this study we can see that a crisis in theorizing within a particular discipline does not constitute a revolution unless an alternative paradigm is emerging which is itself incommensurable with the paradigm it is replacing (Katouzian, 1987, pp.100–6).

The previous sections illustrated the ways in which definite approaches seem to emerge in the social sciences and can dominate in a particular discipline. However, the frequency of the turnover of theories and methods in the social sciences seems to ensure that such dominance is short-lived. One possible answer to the question of why this occurs could lie in the social conditions in which these dominant approaches in Western societies emerged during the 1950s (which produced behaviourist psychology, Keynesian economics, functionalist sociology, pluralist political science and quantitative geography). If scientific knowledge is a social product, it is interesting that periods of consensus within disciplines occurred simultaneously with greater social solidarity in the societies which produced this knowledge. This period witnessed a sustained period of economic growth, political stability and greater opportunities for wider sections of Western societies. Similarly, perhaps the social scientific discord which has occurred since is related to the decline of social cohesion in Western societies since the 1960s. If we take seriously the argument that knowledge is a social product, then it is possible to see Kuhn's work itself as a product of social conditions in the same way. In the following sections we focus upon the other main contributors to conventionalist interpretations from this period. These approaches raise important questions about Kuhn's description of the history of the scientific method.

Dominant paradigms in the social sciences tend to coincide with periods of greater social stability and consensus in the lives of the scientific communities involved.

Summary

The application of Kuhn's concept of paradigm to the social sciences is common but inconsistent. Anything close to the strict use identified by Kuhn (**Paradigm 1**) has only been witnessed for brief periods where a particular approach has influenced a social scientific discipline (as in the case of behaviourism in psychology and functionalism in sociology).

The treatment of paradigms as incommensurable but not necessarily dominant (**Paradigm 2**) is particularly useful in identifying the bedrock assumptions of different theoretical systems in social science. This is often confused with the 'loose use' of paradigm as a particular 'model' or 'school of thought' in open competition with other models or schools (**Paradigm 3**).

3.3 Conventionalism beyond Kuhn I: question everything!

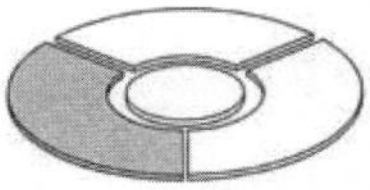

An approach associated with conventionalism is methodological pluralism.

So far, we have concentrated upon one example of conventionalism, Thomas Kuhn's historical account of science. Other conventionalists, such as Paul Feyerabend, place less emphasis upon fairly well defined periods of stability and change in the history of scientific knowledge. Feyerabend, perhaps more than anyone else, has challenged the tendency to look for order in knowledge. In *Against Method* (1975), he argued that the most important characteristic of scientific knowledge is its messy, accidental and discontinuous nature. This was directed as much against Kuhn's concept of paradigm as a period of normal science as it was against positivism. Feyerabend developed a standpoint which suggested that science was not rational, that no knowledge rules had operated effectively in any case, and that scientific knowledge could be oppressive rather than an instrument of progress. Further than this, he argued that rival theories themselves (rather than paradigms) are incommensurable, so that it was impossible to identify a basis for defining one form of knowledge as superior to another form at any point in time. For Feyerabend, to treat science as a rational and objective enterprise was a myth (that is, folklore for scientists). In addition, he portrayed the pursuit of rational scientific explanations (running from the positivists through to Popper) as undesirable because it substituted the accumulation of knowledge for the goal of emancipating human beings.

'Anything goes' – Feyerabend's view that the only defensible position is the idea that all ideas are equally valid.

Feyerabend was concerned that no ideas should be rejected just because they did not conform to a particular standard of useful or true knowledge. This principle of 'anything goes' earned him the label of 'epistemological anarchist'. The anarchistic vision he held was a positive one (in the sense that it referred to the positive condition of freedom from authority rather than a condition of chaos). Here, though, it was applied to knowledge systems rather than political systems. He never saw himself as a political anarchist, but more of a Dadaist who questioned our expectations. Kuhn and Feyerabend seem to offer different ways of thinking about the limits of truth, progress and reason. Feyerabend's conception of knowledge is relativist; he holds that all views are equally privileged, true and valid (Harré and Krausz, 1996). He hoped that it would be possible to live in a situation where all views could be taken seriously, that no ideas should be disregarded in case they become useful in another time and place. Feyerabend questioned the key principles of science just when it was reeling from the impact of Kuhn's work. Instead, he advocated the **principle of proliferation** as the alternative strategy to the imposition of one dominant view. The challenge that Feyerabend's approach presents can be seen in his comparison of scientific textbooks from the 1950s and the handbook for the Witchfinder General dating from the fifteenth century.

> In 1484, the Roman Catholic Church published the *Malleus Maleficarum*, the outstanding textbook on Witchcraft. ... It has four parts: phenomena, aetiology, legal aspects, theological aspects of Witchcraft. ... The aetiology is pluralistic, there is not just the official explanation, there are other explanations as well, purely materialistic explanations included. Of course, in the end only one of the offered explanations is accepted, but the alternatives are discussed and so one can judge the arguments that lead to their elimination. This feature makes the *Malleus* superior to almost every physics, biology, chemistry textbook of today. Even the theology is pluralistic, heretical views are not passed over in silence, nor are they ridiculed; they are described, examined and removed by argument. The authors know the subject, they know ... the positions of their opponents, they argue against these positions and they use the best knowledge available at the time in their arguments.
>
> (Feyerabend, 1978, p.92)

Feyerabend explicitly ties this critical questioning of established conceptions of authoritative knowledge to the desire to maximize the freedom and realize the untapped potential of individual human beings. In terms of the circuit of knowledge established through modern scientific thinking (considered in Chapter 2), Feyerabend questions science, reason, truth and progress in order to emancipate humanity, breaking the circuit in the process (see Figure 5.7). The existence of a single orthodox account of what constitutes authoritative knowledge is portrayed as a form of oppression and he raises the ways in which science can involve an increasingly diverse range of theories with equal standing.

Feyerabend questions the circuit of modern scientific knowledge established in an integrated way since the Enlightenment.

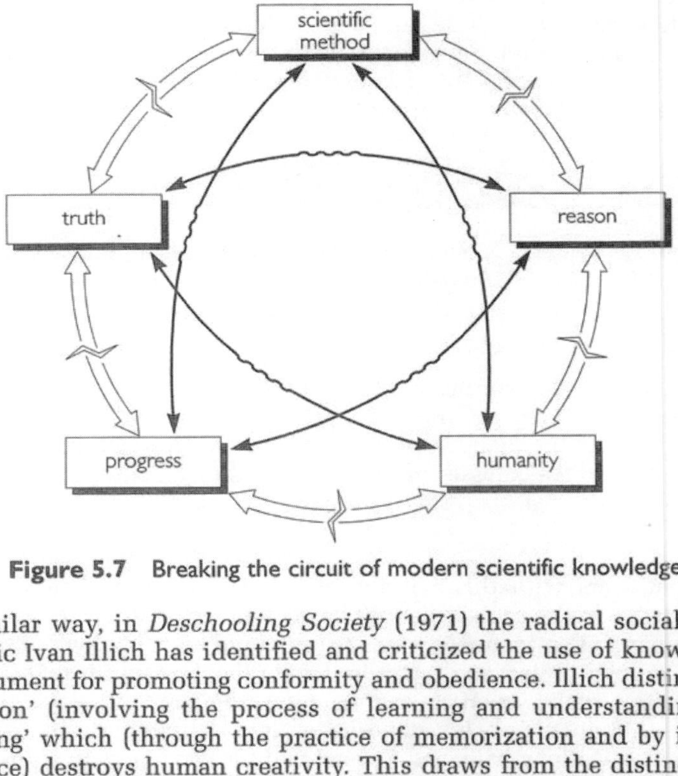

Figure 5.7 Breaking the circuit of modern scientific knowledge.

In a similar way, in *Deschooling Society* (1971) the radical social theorist and critic Ivan Illich has identified and criticized the use of knowledge as an instrument for promoting conformity and obedience. Illich distinguished 'education' (involving the process of learning and understanding) from 'schooling' which (through the practice of memorization and by instilling obedience) destroys human creativity. This draws from the distinction between 'knowledge about' and 'knowledge of' developed by William James. Illich suggested that the damaging effects of schooling on the realization of the full potential of individuals could be identified within all educational and academic institutions, ranging from the infant school to the university; such institutions were designed to reward those pupils and students who memorized and reproduced the authoritative knowledge rather than to encourage creative and free thinking. Illich's answer was to identify how a plurality of ways of thinking could be fostered and monolithic knowledge dislodged from its pre-eminence in the education system. This was to be achieved through learning webs, where tutors and students could come together around common interests and define their own curriculum, and through skill exchanges, which would enable the practitioners in a particular field to pass on their skills and experience through practical applied study.

See Chapter 4, section 5.1.

Science should help make human beings free and not enslave them within a dogmatic set of methodological rules.

Feyerabend and others, in the late 1960s and early 1970s, offered a radical way of challenging established conventions about scientific knowledge. In particular, they challenged the assumption that this form of knowledge, by virtue of its ability to distinguish truth and falsehood, could lay claim to a superior status over other forms of knowledge. In the place of one way of seeing the world, they advocated **methodological pluralism**. This approach is based upon the philosophical position of **relativism**, the view that no form of knowledge is more valid than any other. However, two examples of inconsistency have been identified in Feyerabend's work. First, while he does not believe that reason can lead us to the truth (he adopts an anti-rationalist stance), he still argues for the use of 'rules of thumb' in research which does not exclude the use of 'rational standards' in explaining phenomena. Second, Feyerabend continues to accept the possibility of progress in the development of knowledge which the rejection of a universal rational standard would appear to preclude.

Activity 5.4

Turn to Reading D, 'Methodological pluralism', from Bruce Caldwell's *Beyond Positivism* (1994).

- Briefly identify the steps in establishing methodological pluralism raised by Caldwell.

This is a practical manifesto for raising questions about the way a discipline is organized. Think about any discipline with which you are familiar and try to identify the broad approaches within it. Now think about the strengths and weaknesses of these approaches.

Sympathizers with this critique of the claims associated with scientific knowledge in the social sciences have embraced the idea of methodological pluralism, whereas critics, such as the social anthropologist Ernest Gellner, have warned against the relativism that this view implies. For Gellner, this means that social scientists cannot support or condemn any theoretical position – they are merely left standing on the sidelines of serious discussion. In particular, Gellner criticized Feyerabend for leaving us in a position where, for example, it is impossible to condemn events such as the Holocaust. In effect, Gellner was asking what is the point of social science if it does not have an impact on the organization of social life. Feyerabend responded by arguing that his approach was not relativistic in that sense. Gellner is addressing the issue of moral relativism, whereas Feyerabend is concerned with **epistemological** questions. At this point it is important to separate questions of truth (addressed by Feyerabend) from questions of 'the good' (raised by Gellner). Actually, in *Science in a Free Society* (1978) Feyerabend advocated that all knowledge should contribute to human freedom and not oppression, so it is clear that his values did motivate his approach to knowledge construction – even Feyerabend, then, links questions of truth to questions about 'the good'. The problem of the relationship between rationality and relativism is addressed in more detail in the final section of this chapter, but first we shall consider the role of explanations which adopt the position of social constructionism in the study of natural science.

3.4 Conventionalism beyond Kuhn 2: the sociology of knowledge and science

In this section you have the opportunity to go back to the issue of scientific practice by exploring approaches which consider the practical experiences of scientists. A common strand throughout all conventionalist approaches is the emphasis placed upon the institutional and cultural context of knowledge production. In the field of the sociology of knowledge and science, Barry Barnes in *Interests and the Growth of Knowledge* (1977) and David Bloor in *Knowledge and Social Imagery* (1976) have developed what they call the 'strong programme' to explain how the social context of research affects the development of knowledge in both the natural and the social sciences. Barnes and Bloor point to the variation in knowledge between groups, the variations in different individual interpretations of the same experience, and the role of the interests of scientists and researchers in maintaining deference to their expertise and their own personal advancement. In particular, they identify the disjunction between the tentative character of the evidence upon which scientific knowledge is based and the strong degree of certainty which the use of the label 'scientific' presumes. In this approach, all knowledge is mediated through a culture and language which scientists themselves inhabit. The label of 'strong programme' reflects an attempt to adopt the relativist position more explicitly compared with the weaker versions in Kuhn's and Feyerabend's approaches. Barnes's and Bloor's research identified that scientific knowledge is the product of a range of social factors within the academic, professional and industrial contexts in which the knowledge was generated. This approach, sometimes loosely called 'social constructionism', draws upon the insights of hermeneutics, phenomenology, ethnomethodology and cultural anthropology, because of the way in which all these approaches focus upon the situatedness of human knowledge.

See Chapter 4, section 5 and Geographical Models 2.

Such studies ask whether the social sciences should follow the formal procedures of scientific method when natural scientists do not do so themselves. The history of science is littered with useful accidents, such as the discovery of penicillin, or with informed guesswork, such as the discovery of DNA. In such cases, progress in the accumulation of knowledge was not delivered by the careful and rigid application of a particular scientific method. Kaplan's work had already prepared the way for this by pointing to the difference between the 'reconstructed logics' favoured by philosophers of science (that all philosophies are idealized stories of what should be done) and the 'logics in use' in the everyday practices of scientists where hunches, guesswork, leaps of intuition and accidents play an important part in the construction of knowledge. Kaplan is, in effect, distinguishing between what scientists do and what they say they do (Kaplan, 1964). Textbooks from the philosophy of science tend to present a highly formal account of the scientific method and tend to avoid the complex settings in which research takes place. In particular, they often focus upon the most successful examples of research rather than the ambiguous evidence of the work of scientists in general.

The sociology of science considers what scientists do, not just what they say they do.

In 1994, at the British Association for the Advancement of Science, Harry Collins (Professor of Sociology of Science at the University of Bath)

Science is a social product – it conveys the authoritative knowledge of the social and historical context in which it was produced.

presented a case for questioning the status of science as a superior form of knowledge. He raised the extent to which a scientific community depends upon trust. In particular, Collins focused upon the ways in which the results of scientific investigations are more ambiguous, the scientific theories are more flexible and that progress is more uncertain than most theoretical accounts of science suggest. In his view, what is regarded as 'science' is the end product of a complex process of legitimation in the identification of authoritative knowledge and is dependent upon the social context in which such knowledge is produced. Collins argued that the designation of particular forms of knowledge as scientific is dependent upon the plausibility of this knowledge for the scientific community involved. (See Figure 5.8.) He went further to say that, in the light of this, knowledge should not be subject to any universal standard. Collins concluded that scientific knowledge is a social construct and that science is tied to definite social and historical conditions, so that when conditions change so too does knowledge (Collins, 1994).

Figure 5.8 The mechanics of celebrity can be seen in the academic performance. Scientific knowledge is produced and communicated in organized communities ... some large, some small. Jacques Derrida addresses the assembled academic congregation at the University of Sussex (1 December 1997).

The identification of variations in the forms of knowledge as if they were matters of cultural difference was derived from interpretative sociology and anthropology. This involved the careful empirical study of communities of scientists through in-depth interviews and participant observation in order to identify the taken-for-granted assumptions of scientists and to reconstruct the processes through which scientific knowledge was made. The distinctive contribution of anthropological insights to a discussion of natural and social scientific method can be seen in the short story 'The Philosopher, the Scientist and the Anthropologist', related in Zygmunt Bauman's *Hermeneutics and Social Science* (1978):

> On one occasion Sir Karl Popper told his audience a story which had obviously shaken him. It concerned an anthropologist invited to join some other first-class brains in discussing an important matter in the methodology of science. At the end of long and heated arguments, to which the anthropologist listened in silence, he was asked to express his view. Much to the dismay of everybody present, the anthropologist replied that he paid little attention to the actual content of the dispute. The content was, he thought, the least interesting of what he saw and heard. Of incomparably greater interest were other things: how the debate was launched, how it developed, how one intervention triggered off another and how they fell into sequences, how the contributors determined whether they were in disagreement etc. Our anthropologist, presumably viewed the topic which aroused so much passion as just one of those 'native beliefs' whose truth or falsity is largely irrelevant for a scholarly study. This was why he was not particularly interested in the topic. Instead, he recorded with genuine interest the interaction in which the learned experts engaged. ... Sir Karl was, of course, indignant. For him statements are about something and are to be judged, in this way or another, by being tested against this something. ... He would try to extract from the sentence the message it contained, and then attempt to put the truth of the message to the test.
>
> (Bauman, 1978, p.172)

One way to try to understand what scientists (or even philosophers!) do is to observe them directly in their own environments, in the way that social scientists observe other small groups of people involved in communication and interaction.

Activity 5.5

Turn to Reading E, 'Two sociological perspectives on science', from Michael Mulkay's *Sociology of Science* (1991). Then consider the two journalistic extracts in Reading F: John Turney's 'Faking it to make it' (1989) and Stuart Sutherland's 'What if teacher is a cheat?' (1989).

- Identify which of the two approaches considered by Michael Mulkay is relevant for understanding the accounts of the practices of science given by Turney and Sutherland.

In this activity you should notice that each of the perspectives on science identified by Mulkay could be applied to the two journalistic accounts. However, you should also have noticed that the perspective adopted can lead you to look at them in very different ways and reach different conclusions. You may find it useful to to look back at Activity 3.3 in Chapter 3; again here the question is whether the research is evidence of 'bad science' or whether the way we see science itself needs to be rethought.

The scientific ethnographic studies of scientists, notably by Bruno Latour and Steve Woolgar (1979), Michael Mulkay (1972, 1991) and Karin Knorr-Cetina (1981), emphasize the differences between the informal and accidental dimensions of the research activity itself and the formal style of presenting results in scientific journals (Figure 5.9) and within the media as though a logical procedure had been followed from beginning to end of the research process. For sociologists of science, scientific communities are characterized by networks and forms of social interaction – like any other form of community. The interactions which take place are seen as governed by the same criteria of trust and credibility that obtain in other acts of exchange. In this case, the acts of exchange involve data, ideas and other forms of knowledge, whether the exchange is portrayed as an act of gift giving (Hagstrom, 1965) or as an investment in the collective body of knowledge which can be converted later into status, power and perhaps wealth by the investors (Bourdieu, 1975).

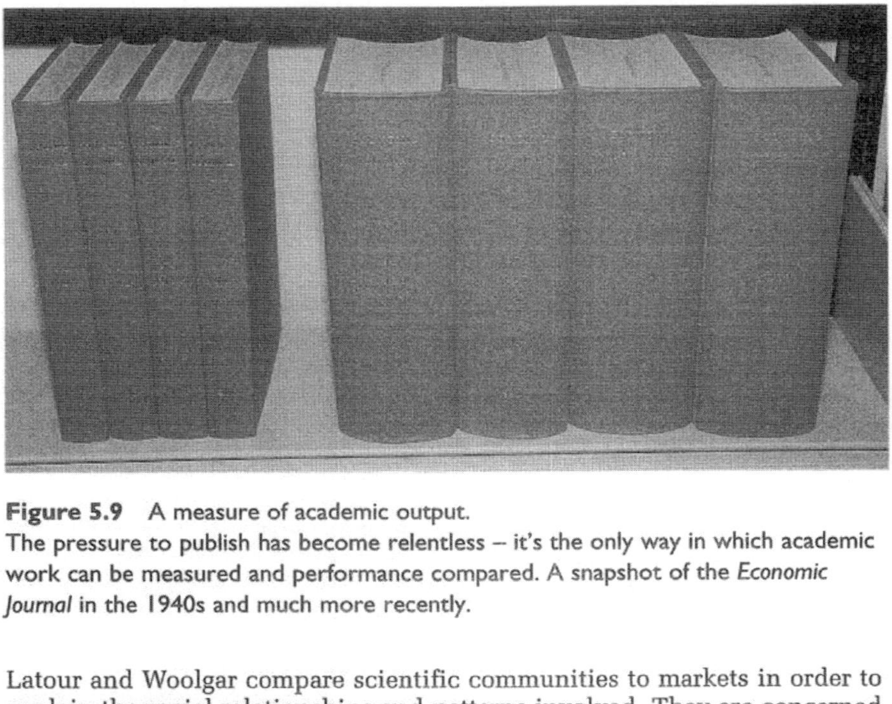

Figure 5.9 A measure of academic output.
The pressure to publish has become relentless – it's the only way in which academic work can be measured and performance compared. A snapshot of the *Economic Journal* in the 1940s and much more recently.

Scientific knowledge is the product of the complex social practices of scientific communities.

Latour and Woolgar compare scientific communities to markets in order to explain the social relationships and patterns involved. They are concerned to avoid general debates on whether science is a social construct and prefer to explore the process of research itself. They focus upon areas which they describe as 'hot' research, the cutting edge of research activity where scientists are more likely to meet unexpected problems and have to innovate to generate useful new knowledge. The research conducted by sociologists of science provides useful insights into the actual practices of scientists and the development of scientific communities. Such studies also focus upon the relations of communication and power which operate in scientific communities and the role of patronage and sponsorship (see Figure 5.10).

Figure 5.10 The master–disciple relationship in scientific work.
The recruitment process for joining an academic community is long, arduous and intensive (a doctoral student submits his research for scrutiny from his supervisor).

In a similar way, in the social sciences the success of a particular research approach is largely governed by social conditions such as:

- the compatibility of a research approach with existing evidence and research, or the extent to which the conclusions generated offer an 'acceptable' way of resolving an established problem;
- the support of academic colleagues who, through the process of peer review, can affect the reception of a particular piece of research (Figures 5.11 and 5.12);
- the relevance or usefulness of the social research in question for both the scientific community and wider society, particularly for the justification or questioning of policy making in a specific field of government;
- the contribution of the research to a currently exciting area of academic work rather than to a field of inquiry which is considered to be dormant or exhausted.

These four considerations have been portrayed in a favourable light. A critical interpretation would consider the success of a particular piece of research in the extent to which it does not challenge the orthodox interpretations of the field, and in the ways in which it attracts the patronage of established academics who sponsor or dismiss the work in question. Also important is the degree to which it serves the interests of those who control politics (and thus the financial basis for future research) and the extent to

Figure 5.11 Learning to use the tools of the trade.
A student tries to remember Kant's advice 'have courage in your own understanding' when presenting a paper in a seminar conducted by Professor William Outhwaite.

which the choice of research topic and method reflects fashion and fad rather than some other criteria for establishing the relevance and usefulness of research. This approach highlights the dangers involved when social research remains unquestioned, because it confirms the existing body of opinion in a particular field and simply reinforces what is already taken for granted.

Figure 5.12 Peer review: the exchange of ideas in an academic setting.
Contributing in a constructive way means that you stick your neck out and make your views heard. But you should also expect your colleagues to be critical as well as supportive.

Summary

Feyerabend presents a case for the acceptance of a proliferating diversity of competing scientific theories as a positive state for scientific and socially useful knowledge. This encourages greater tolerance and explicitly links the generation of knowledge to the development of human potential.

Sociologists of science identify the organization of knowledge in communities, the mechanics of celebrity and intellectual patronage and the relationship between knowledge and the interests of academic institutions as crucial factors in understanding the social construction of knowledge.

4 Rationality and relativism: keeping progress

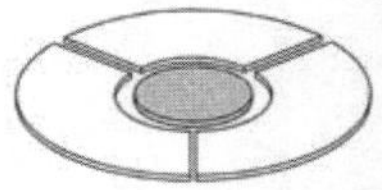

Through the work of Lakatos falsificationism learned something from its critics.

The studies of scientific knowledge by Kuhn, Feyerabend and the sociologists of science provoked a crisis of rationality in the philosophy of science (particularly undermining the more positivistically inclined approaches). The sceptical treatment of truth by Popper and Lakatos ensured that supporters of **naturalism** and rational scientific methods in the social sciences could still draw upon a versatile approach. Lakatos usefully qualifies the Popperian approach and tries to draw some lessons from the work of the conventionalists. He draws upon the historical evidence produced by Kuhn on the ways in which knowledge is organized in communities of scientists and how academic and scientific organizations are as important as the methodologies adopted. However, his approach is committed to the principle that the gradual accumulation of knowledge should deliver progress. Popper and Lakatos are more often described as critical rationalists because they challenge empiricist assumptions about the role of ideas and theories. However, for both of them experience acts as the arbiter for testing scientific theories.

Defenders of falsificationism seek to draw upon the insights of conventionalism without losing the accumulation of knowledge as a source of 'progress'.

Lakatos, in his 1970 article 'Falsification and the Methodology of Scientific Research Programmes', argued that philosophers of science were faced with three alternatives: induction, conventionalism and falsificationism. He ruled out induction on the grounds that theories were not a direct reflection of experience. He rejected conventionalism for giving up on the accumulation of knowledge as a means of delivering progress, for this is the point of being a scientist in the first place. Regarding the last approach, he argued that it was important to distinguish various forms of falsificationist approaches. He gave the label **dogmatic falsificationism** to the scientists who interpreted Popper in too simplistic a way and immediately discarded any hypotheses which had been refuted. This position was to be distinguished from Popper's falsificationist approach, which accepted that a hypothesis, even if empirically refuted, may still be useful as a predictive statement in a different context. Such statements, Popper argued, should simply be shelved for the time being unless they had been comprehensively falsified. This was in part a recognition of the problems in conclusively falsifying scientific statements, which we explored when considering the Duhem-Quine thesis. However, because Popper's position remained focused upon individual laws, theories and evidence on a particular problem, Lakatos labelled Popper's approach **naive methodological falsificationism.** Actually, it was Popper's focus upon individual theories and the importance of protecting individual freedom that prompted Lakatos to argue that Popper and Feyerabend had, in fact, a great deal in common.

In recognizing that theories do not exist in isolation, Lakatos addressed Kuhn's contributions on the way in which knowledge was culturally and historically located. However, unlike Kuhn, he argued that a viable methodology had to be both descriptively accurate and prescriptively useful (that is, it indicates what we 'should' do in scientific research). In developing **sophisticated methodological falsificationism,** Lakatos felt that he could account for the institutional life of scientists and offer a guide for further scientific research. Lakatos distinguished between the 'hard core' which held the key foundational assumptions of a scientific research programme, and the 'protective belt' of auxiliary hypotheses which could be tested and falsified at any point in time. This is very much the same distinction between bedrock assumptions and contextual hypotheses which we considered earlier in section 2.

Negative heuristic – all theoretical systems contain assumptions about what it is not possible to study.

Lakatos suggested that a scientific research programme (his alternative to the concept of paradigm) is governed by two sets of methodological rules. First, the *negative heuristic* dictates which research pathways cannot be studied. This protects the hard core from criticism: anyone who does this is often treated as a heretic or dangerous to the programme. For instance, behaviourist approaches which focus upon human actions as a series of effects resulting from various stimuli (such as pluralism in political science and political sociology) could not accept the existence of human beings as creative and reflective beings. You may recall that behaviourists reject the existence of inner selves as speculative and hold that such considerations are not the concern of science.

Positive heuristic – all theoretical systems contain assumptions about which pathways of research are feasible and which are likely to be fruitful.

Now that we have established the grounds for excluding things from an inquiry, let's focus upon the second set of methodological rules, the *positive heuristic*. This indicates the research pathways which are legitimate and worthwhile. For instance, in the case of pluralism in political studies (considered earlier in the chapter) it is concrete decision-making situations which could be observed, measured and explained that are considered to be legitimate and worthwhile objects of analysis. For Lakatos, even if a set of theories and core assumptions has been falsified, as long as they continue to offer useful predictions, then it is worth keeping them. In addition, in the absence of a more adequate alternative, Lakatos suggests that it is better to hang on to a bad theory than to have no theory at all. He also makes a plea for tolerance with the emergence of budding research programmes. Overall, scientific research programmes, even if inadequate, can be identified as progressive or degenerating in the long term. This is a considerable way from Popper's falsificationism, yet it retains his commitment towards progress and the accumulation of knowledge. For instance, many sociological perspectives would fit this description. For instance, both functionalism and Marxism have encountered severe problems in explaining social life and have for a time appeared to degenerate. Nevertheless, with a reworking of their protective belt, both have bounced back at different times as neo-functionalism and neo-Marxism, taking into account some of the criticisms launched against them. In each case, the bedrock assumptions of both the old and new versions remain consistent. Neo-Marxism, for instance, retains its commitment towards defining the economy in terms of class structure and gives the economy a determinate role, in the long term, in explaining the development of capitalist societies.

In the social sciences, this defence of the idea of 'progress' developed by Lakatos continues to offer an attractive alternative to the relativistic assumptions of conventionalism. However, one of the difficulties in applying this approach is the problem of clearly identifying the hard core of bedrock assumptions which are taken for granted by the participants in a research programme. Another problem emerges when we attempt to find a means of distinguishing a progressive from a degenerating research programme. For Lakatos, a progressive problem shift takes place when the newly emergent theory accounts for the successes of the previous theory, contains a greater empirical content than the existing approaches, and has been subject to attempts at falsification and has been corroborated.

Scientists are usually considering the protective belt of the research programme, not the hard core of bedrock assumptions.

Activity 5.6

Now read the extract 'The schizophrenia research programme' by Mary Boyle (Reading G).

- Identify the hard core and the protective belt in this example of social scientific research. What is the evidence that the research programme is either progressing or degenerating?

Think about the issues which you explored in section 2 when you considered the differences between assumptions and contextual hypotheses. You should remember the ways in which scientists and social scientists, when they find their assumptions are challenged, dodge difficult questions simply by modifying the contextual hypotheses. Is the distinction between the hard core and the protective belt any different? In particular, ask yourself whether Boyle's evidence on the schizophrenia research programme leads you to question this as a particular example of a 'failed' programme. The survival of the schizophrenia research programme and its search for a biological explanation started in the early part of the twentieth century – perhaps even Lakatos is too optimistic about the capacities of scientists to discard ideas which have been repeatedly found wanting.

The Methodology of Scientific Research Programmes (MSRP) is particularly important in social scientific disciplines which retain a commitment to falsificationism and the application of the assumptions and methods of the natural sciences to social objects. While Lakatos draws upon Kuhn's account of the collective dimension of research, he does not reject the possibility of progress through the accumulation of knowledge in particular disciplines. He argues that it is rational to use some criterion to demarcate scientific knowledge from other forms of knowledge. However, the distinction between the hard core and the protective belt allows for the existence of unfalsifiable (that is, metaphysical) claims at the heart of the research programme. So, in some respects, his approach is at odds with empiricism as it is generally understood. Nevertheless, Lakatos found a way of maintaining a commitment to the accumulation of knowledge and progress while addressing the concerns originally identified by Duhem and Quine.

See section 2.1 of this chapter.

Summary

Lakatos establishes a compromise between the goals of progress that lie at the heart of the rational scientific method and the actual practices of scientists. This approach acknowledges the importance of studies of scientific communities, but also argues that the relativism and the treatment of scientific knowledge as a social product offer an inadequate foundation for identifying useful knowledge and for making progress.

5 Reassessing rationality and relativism: towards a conclusion

There is a tendency for critical rationalists (such as Popper and Lakatos) to be presented in complete opposition to relativists (such as Kuhn, Feyerabend and Collins). However, as we discussed in the last section, this oversimplifies the differences and similarities between their approaches to science. Consider Figure 5.13. All of the philosophers represented below disagree with each other about what science involves and what knowledge

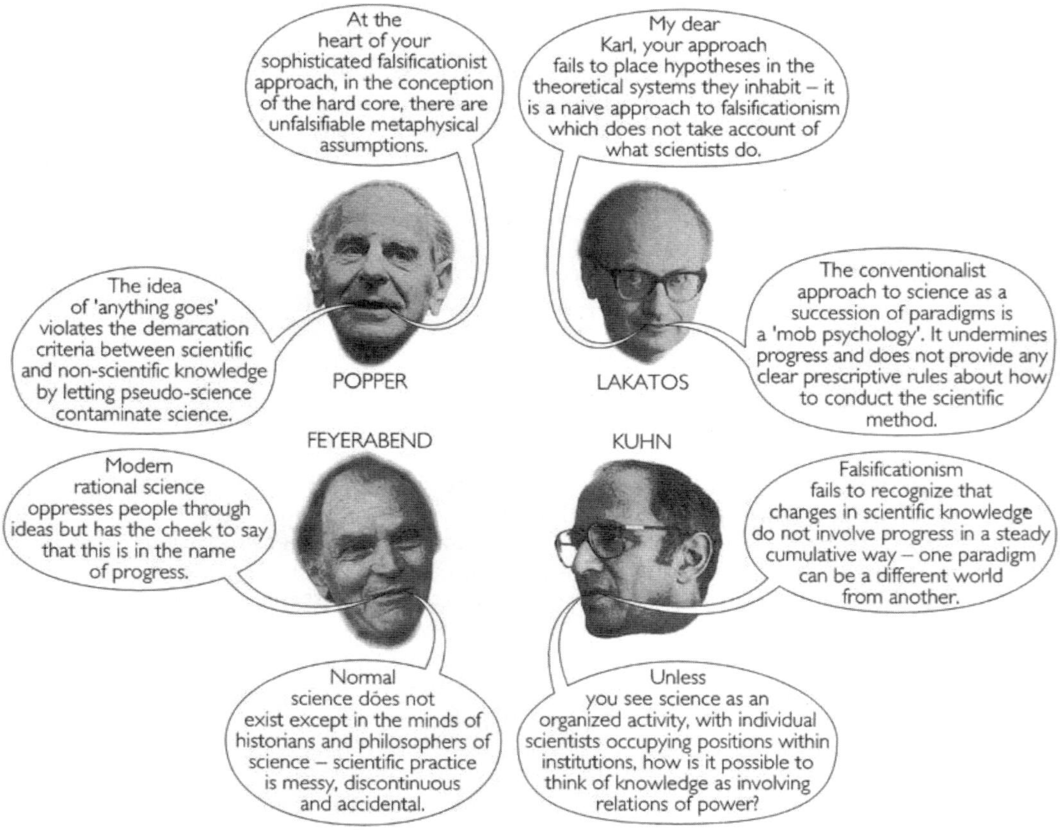

Figure 5.13 Philosophers like to argue a great deal ...

should be about. They disagree, in particular, on the role of falsification, whether progress is possible, the relationship between theory and observation, the role of scientific communities, and the relationship between science and freedom. Now consider Figure 5.14 on the connections between these positions. Actually, the disagreements only make sense when we consider the common terrain on which they stand (in other words, they agree on a great deal). Perhaps we need to reconsider the tendency to think of simple oppositional debates between rational science and relativism.

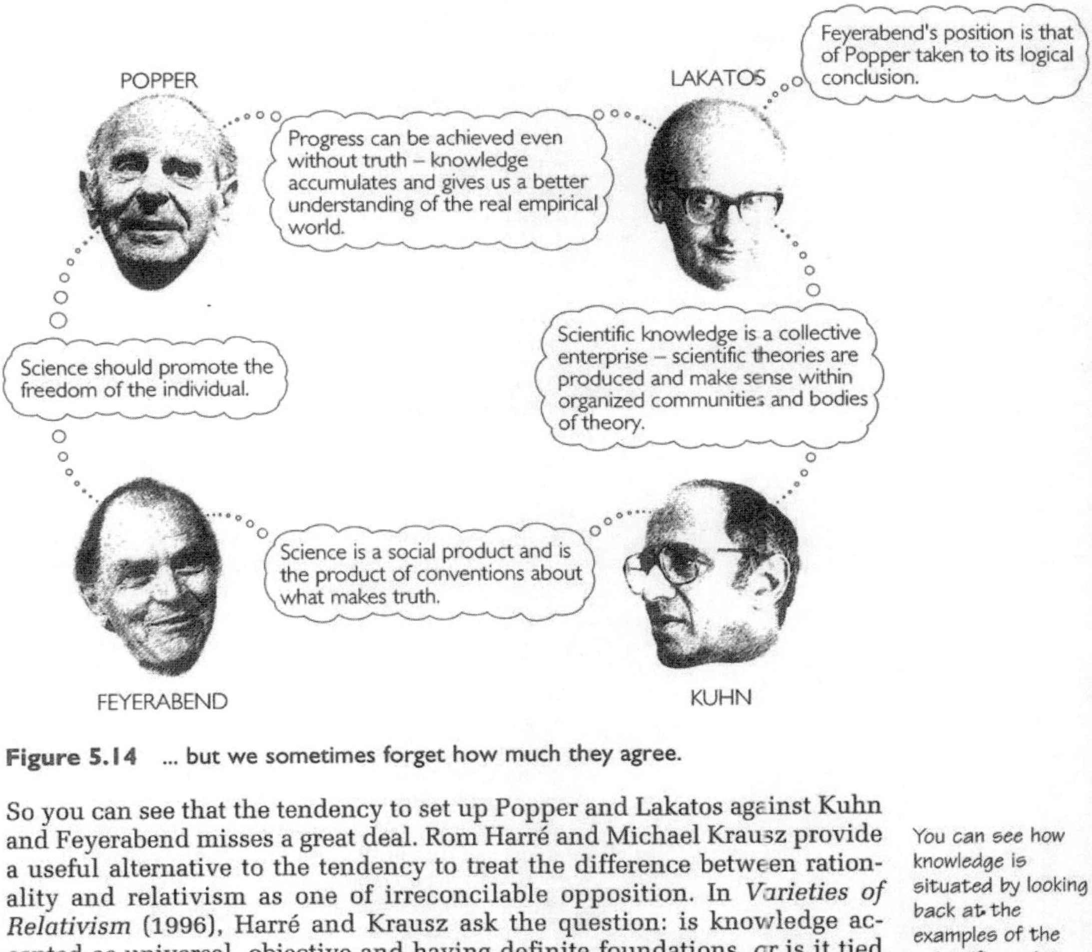

Figure 5.14 ... but we sometimes forget how much they agree.

So you can see that the tendency to set up Popper and Lakatos against Kuhn and Feyerabend misses a great deal. Rom Harré and Michael Krausz provide a useful alternative to the tendency to treat the difference between rationality and relativism as one of irreconcilable opposition. In *Varieties of Relativism* (1996), Harré and Krausz ask the question: is knowledge accepted as universal, objective and having definite foundations, *or* is it tied to particular social contexts, subjectively constructed and without firm foundations? For our purposes, let's accept the claim that there are no firm foundations to knowledge and that science is constructed within definite historically located cultures. Let's also accept the bold relativist view that this is a universal claim which applies to all forms of knowledge. We are still making a bold universal claim about science (the opposition doesn't work!). Once we have suspended our belief in the high status of scientific knowledge in Western culture, this leads us to question what social scientists have attempted to do. In particular, if natural scientists fail to live up to the standards of science, then why should social scientists try to copy them?

You can see how knowledge is situated by looking back at the examples of the scientific racist approach and positivist criminology in Chapter 3.

READING C
Theorizing the economy

Economic paradigms

Howard R. Vane and John L. Thompson

In the 1930s the central problem facing economists was the need to provide an explanation of, and remedy for, the severe unemployment which prevailed at that time. ... Keynes put forward the view that unemployment reflected a state of deficient aggregate demand [total spending]. Since government expenditure is an important component of aggregate demand Keynesians believed that an increase in government expenditure would have a strong and direct effect in reducing the level of unemployment. ...

The revival of the belief in the potency of monetary policy that has occurred since the 1960s has largely been associated with ... (i) the importance of controlling the money supply and (ii) the need to follow a monetary rule in the conduct of monetary policy in order to avoid economic instability. During the 1950s through to the mid-1960s, instability in Western capitalist economies was largely reflected in the problem of inflation ... whereas in contrast many economies have experienced not only high rates of inflation but also high levels of unemployment since the end of the 1960s. ... Monetarists have argued that the inflation of the post-war years was stimulated by the widespread adoption of cheap-money policies and resulted from excessive money creation. Monetarists believe that most of the disturbances which affect the economy are monetary in origin. ... From this belief arises the first of two policy prescriptions central to monetarist analysis, namely that the authorities should seek to control the money supply. The second ... is that the authorities should follow a monetary rule rather than pursue discretionary monetary policy. ...

Although monetarism implies non-intervention in macroeconomic policies involving the management of aggregate demand, intervention especially on a micro basis is quite compatible with monetarist analysis of how the economy works. [For monetarists] the natural rate of unemployment is determined by the structure of ... the economy and by the institutional framework of the labour market. Monetarists argue that if governments wish to reduce the natural rate (i.e. achieve higher employment levels) they should pursue microeconomic policies towards improving the structure of the labour market in order to increase (i) the efficiency of labour markets and (ii) the occupational and geographical mobility of labour. ...

Keynesians argue [however] that the economy is inherently unstable and subject to fluctuations between long periods of unemployment and stagnation and periods of rapid expansion and inflation. [They] argue that (i) in the case of a disturbance the economy may take too long to return to the neighbourhood of equilibrium, and (ii) consequently discretionary demand-management policies are necessary to maintain the economy at a high and stable level of employment. ... The major issue dividing monetarists and Keynesians today concerns the role of macroeconomic stabilization policy whereas monetarists argue that the economy is inherently stable (unless disturbed by erratic monetary growth) and that policy should be carried out according to rules.

Source: Vane and Thompson, 1982, pp.307–12.

Economic crisis: the Marxist view

E.K. Hunt and Howard J. Sherman

It was this ceaseless drive to accumulate more capital that created many of the contradictions to capitalist development. The capitalist would begin with the acquisition of more machines and tools of the types that were currently being used. This would require a proportional increase in the number of workers employed in order to operate the new equipment. But the capitalist had been able to keep the wage rate at the subsistence level only because there existed what Marx called an 'industrial reserve army' of unemployed labor, which was living below the subsistence level and striving to take jobs that would pay a mere subsistence wage. Therefore, capitalists usually had no problem in keeping wage rates down. As the industrial expansion took place, however, the increasing demand for labor soon depleted the ranks of the reserve. When this happened, the capitalist began to find that he had to pay higher wages to get enough labor. ...

The most profitable course of action seemed to be changing the techniques of production by introducing new labor-saving machinery so that each laborer would then be working with more capital, and output per laborer would be increased. This labor-saving investment would enable the capitalist to expand output with the same or an even smaller work force [and] the reserve army was replenished by workers displaced by the new productive techniques. [The] concentration of wealth and economic power in the hands of fewer and fewer capitalists was another important consequence of capital accumulation. ... Competition between capitalists tended to create a situation in which the strong either crushed or absorbed the weak [and] to remain competitive, a firm would constantly have to increase the productivity of its laborers. ...

Business cycles or crises would occur regularly and with increasing severity as the capitalist economy developed. There would be a long-run tendency for the rate of profit to fall, and this would exacerbate the other problems of capitalism. Industrial power would become increasingly concentrated in fewer and fewer giant monopolistic and oligopolistic firms, and wealth would become concentrated in the hands of fewer and fewer capitalists. The plight of the laborer would steadily deteriorate. Given these increasingly bad conditions, the system could not be perpetuated. Eventually, life under capitalism would become so intolerable that workers would revolt, overthrow the whole system, and create a more rational socialist economy.

Source: Hunt and Sherman, 1981, pp.90–4.

READING D
Methodological pluralism

Bruce Caldwell

The approach to economic methodology advocated here is labelled 'methodological pluralism' because it takes as a starting assumption that no universally applicable, logically compelling method of theory appraisal exists. (Or, more correctly, even if it exists, we can never be sure that we have found it, even if we have.) ...

- The starting point of methodological analysis is the rational reconstruction of the methodological content both of the writings of economic methodologists and of the various research programs within the discipline.
- The next step is the critical assessment of the methodological content [to] highlight the strengths (if any) and limitations of the particular approach under examination. ...

A practitioner of normal science working in a well-established research tradition can safely assert that the choice problem is solved. Using the techniques he learned in graduate school, he busies himself doing substantive work in economics, applying those methods to various problems, solving puzzles in a good Kuhnian style. For such a scientist, explicit discussions of methodology seem utterly inane. When pushed to discuss methodological matters, however, the same scientist often responds that methodological debate is useless because the questions asked are unanswerable. 'No one ever agrees on methodological questions, so why waste time studying them?' he is apt to counter, 'And besides, only people working in fringe areas, like Institutionalists or Marxists, ever talk about methodology, and those people shouldn't even be considered scientists!'

When the research tradition in which this normal scientist works breaks down in a revolutionary period, he may briefly turn to methodology or to history to see what went wrong. What he wants to find is some definitive answer about the 'correct' method. What he discovers instead is a plurality of answers, each with its own weaknesses and strengths. This reinforces his prior autagonistic attitude toward methodological discussion, but luckily for him, it is not necessary to ruminate over the idiocy of methodology for too long. A new paradigm emerges, with its own accepted methods and procedures, he can happily busy himself with substantive work once more. This caricature of the normal scientist with anti-methodological biases is harshly drawn, but sadly enough, the general attitude attributed to him is not all that hard to find.

- [We should engage in] the critical discussion of the strengths (if any) and limitations of the rationally reconstructed methodological positions under examination.
- There are a number of research programs within economics whose epistemological and methodological foundations differ radically from those of mainstream theory. ... This approach ensures that novelty is promoted, that criticism is not dogmatic, and that a dialogue takes place among members of alternative research programs.

Answers to some possible objections

1 The initial assumption is wrong; methodologists should research for a universally applicable method of choice. A variation of this objection reads, 'Thus-and-so methodology (falsificationism, a priorism, instrumentalism, and so on) is the best methodology for economic science to follow.'

The response of the methodological pluralist must be – convince me.

2 Methodological pluralism, if taken seriously, undermines all substantive work in economic science. How can a working economist try to make a contribution in his chosen field if he is always aware that the methodology he uses is open to criticism?

The response of the methodological pluralists is that substantive work in economics need not halt; neither angst nor inaction are necessary byproducts of methodological pluralism. ...

3 Methodological pluralism, if taken seriously, leads to methodological anarchism, under which any particular methodological view could claim legitimacy.

There are safeguards against this outcome. Simply put, methodological discussion is as much a form of persuasion as it is a means of ensuring that problems are viewed from different perspectives.

Source: Caldwell, 1994, pp.245–51.